# Advanced C+

## Master the technique of confidently writing robust C++ code

Gazihan Alankus

Olena Lizina

Rakesh Mane

Vivek Nagarajan

Brian Price

# Advanced C++

Authors: Gazihan Alankus, Olena Lizina, Rakesh Mane, Vivek Nagarajan, and Brian Price

Technical Reviewers: Anil Achary and Deepak Selvakumar

Managing Editor: Bhavesh Bangera

Acquisitions Editors: Kunal Sawant, Koushik Sen, and Sneha Shinde

Production Editor: Samita Warang

Editorial Board: Shubhopriya Banerjee, Bharat Botle, Ewan Buckingham, Mahesh Dhyani, Manasa Kumar, Alex Mazonowicz, Bridget Neale, Dominic Pereira, Shiny Poojary, Abhisekh Rane, Erol Staveley, Ankita Thakur, Nitesh Thakur, and Jonathan Wray.

First Published: October 2019

Production Reference: 1311019

ISBN: 978-1-83882-113-5

Published by Packt Publishing Ltd.

Livery Place, 35 Livery Street

Birmingham B3 2PB, UK

# Table of Contents

## Chapter 2A: No Ducks Allowed – Types and Deduction    71

# Chapter 2B: No Ducks Allowed – Templates and Deduction 139

## Chapter 4: Separation of Concerns - Software Architecture, Functions, and Variadic Templates          273

# Chapter 5: The Philosophers' Dinner – Threads and Concurrency    321

# Chapter 6: Streams and I/O      391

## Chapter 7: Everybody Falls, It's How You Get Back Up – Testing and Debugging    477

# Chapter 8: Need for Speed – Performance and Optimization     535

# Preface

## About

This section briefly introduces the authors, the coverage of this book, the technical skills you'll need to get started, and the hardware and software requirements required to complete all of the included activities and exercises.

## About the Book

C++ is one of the most widely used programming languages and is applied in a variety of domains, right from gaming to **graphical user interface** (**GUI**) programming and even operating systems. If you're looking to expand your career opportunities, mastering the advanced features of C++ is key.

The book begins with advanced C++ concepts by helping you decipher the sophisticated C++ type system and understand how various stages of compilation convert source code to object code. You'll then learn how to recognize the tools that need to be used in order to control the flow of execution, capture data, and pass data around. By creating small models, you'll even discover how to use advanced lambdas and captures and express common API design patterns in C++. As you cover later chapters, you'll explore ways to optimize your code by learning about memory alignment, cache access, and the time a program takes to run. The concluding chapter will help you to maximize performance by understanding modern CPU branch prediction and how to make your code cache-friendly.

By the end of this book, you'll have developed programming skills that will set you apart from other C++ programmers.

## About the Authors

**Gazihan Alankus** holds a PhD in computer science from Washington University in St. Louis. Currently, he is an assistant professor at the Izmir University of Economics in Turkey. He teaches and conducts research on game development, mobile application development, and human-computer interaction. He is a Google developer expert in Dart and develops Flutter applications with his students in his company Gbot, which he founded in 2019.

**Olena Lizina** is a software developer with 5 years experience in C++. She has practical knowledge of developing systems for monitoring and managing remote computers with a lot of users for an international product company. For the last 4 years, she has been working for international outsourcing companies on automotive projects for well-known automotive concerns. She has been participating in the development of complex and highly performant applications on different projects, such as **HMI (Human Machine Interface)**, navigation, and applications for work with sensors.

**Rakesh Mane** has over 18 years experience in the software industry. He has worked with proficient programmers from a variety of regions: India, the US, and Singapore. He has mostly worked in C++, Python, shell scripting, and database. In his spare time, he likes to listen to music and travel. Also, he likes to play with, experiment with, and break things using software tools and code.

**Vivek Nagarajan** is a self-taught programmer who started out in the 1980s on 8-bit systems. He has worked on a large number of software projects and has 14 years of professional experience with C++. Aside from this, he has worked on a wide variety of languages and frameworks across the years. He is an amateur powerlifter, DIY enthusiast, and motorcycle racer. He currently works as an independent software consultant.

**Brian Price** has over 30 years experience working in a variety of languages, projects, and industries, including over 20 years experience in C++. He was worked on power station simulators, SCADA systems, and medical devices. He is currently crafting software in C++, CMake, and Python for a next-generation medical device. He enjoys solving puzzles and the Euler project in a variety of languages.

## Learning Objectives

By the end of this book, you will be able to:

- Delve into the anatomy and workflow of C++
- Study the pros and cons of different approaches to coding in C++
- Test, run, and debug your programs
- Link object files as a dynamic library
- Use templates, SFINAE, constexpr if expressions and variadic templates
- Apply best practice to resource management

## Audience

If you have worked in C++ but want to learn how to make the most of this language, especially for large projects, this book is for you. A general understanding of programming and knowledge of using an editor to produce code files in project directories is a must. Some experience with strongly typed languages, such as C and C++, is also recommended.

## Approach

This fast-paced book is designed to teach you concepts quickly through descriptive graphics and challenging exercises. The book will have "call-outs," with key take away points and the most common pitfalls to keep you interested, while breaking up the topics into manageable sections.

## Hardware Requirements

For the optimal student experience, we recommend the following hardware configuration:

- Any entry-level PC/Mac with Windows, Linux, or macOS will suffice
- Processor: Dual core or equivalent
- Memory: 4 GB RAM (8 GB preferred)
- Storage: 35 GB of available space

## Software Requirements

You'll also need the following software installed in advance:

- Operating system: Windows 7 SP1 32/64-bit, Windows 8.1 32/64-bit, or Windows 10 32/64-bit, Ubuntu 14.04 or later, or macOS Sierra or later
- Browser: Google Chrome or Mozilla Firefox

## Installation and Setup

Before you embark on this book, you will need to install the following libraries used in this book. You will find the steps to install these here.

### Installing CMake

We will use CMake version 3.12.1 or later. We have two options for installation.

Option 1:

If you are using Ubuntu 18.10, you can install CMake globally using the following command:

```
sudo apt install cmake
```

When you run the following command:

```
cmake -version
```

You should see the following output:

```
cmake version 3.12.1

CMake suite maintained and supported by Kitware (kitware.com/cmake).
```

If the version you see here is lower than 3.12.1 (for example, 3.10), you should install CMake locally using the following instructions.

Option 2:

If you are using an older Linux version, you may get a CMake version that is lower than 3.12.1. Then, you need to install it locally. Use the following commands:

```
wget \
https://github.com/Kitware/CMake/releases/download/v3.15.1/cmake-3.15.1-
Linux-x86_64.sh


sh cmake-3.15.1-Linux-x86_64.sh
```

When you see the software license, type *y* and press *Enter*. When asked about the installation location, type *y* and press Enter again. This should install it to a new folder in your system.

Now, we will add that folder to our path. Type the following. Note that the first line is a bit too long and the line breaks in this document. You should write it as a single line, as follows:

```
echo "export PATH=\"$HOME/cmake-3.15.1-Linux-x86_64/bin:$PATH\"" >> .bash_
profile


source .profile
```

Now, when you type the following:

```
cmake -version
```

You should see the following output:

```
cmake version 3.15.1

CMake suite maintained and supported by Kitware (kitware.com/cmake).
```

3.15.1 is the current latest release at the time of writing this document. Since it is newer than 3.12.1, this will suffice for our purposes.

**Installing Git**

Test the current installation by typing the following:

```
git --version
```

You should see a line such as the following:

```
git version 2.17.1
```

If you see the following line instead, you need to install **git**:

```
command 'git' not found
```

Here is how you can install **git** in Ubuntu:

```
sudo apt install git
```

## Installing g++

Test the current installation by typing the following:

```
g++ --version
```

You should see an output such as the following:

```
g++ (Ubuntu 7.4.0-1ubuntu1~18.04) 7.4.0

Copyright (C) 2017 Free Software Foundation, Inc.

This is free software; see the source for copying conditions. There is NO

warranty; not even for MERCHANTABILITY or FITNESS FOR A PARTICULAR PURPOSE.
```

If it is not installed, type the following code to install it:

```
sudo apt install g++
```

## Installing Ninja

Test the current installation by typing the following:

```
ninja --version
```

You should see an output such as the following:

```
1.8.2
```

If it is not installed, type the following code to install it:

```
sudo apt install ninja-build
```

## Installing Eclipse CDT and cmake4eclipse

There are multiple ways of installing Eclipse CDT. To get the latest stable version, we will use the official installer. Go to this website and download the Linux installer: https://www.eclipse.org/downloads/packages/installer.

Follow the instructions there and install **Eclipse IDE for C/C++ Developers**. Once you have installed it, run the Eclipse executable. If you did not change the default configuration, typing the following command in the terminal will run it:

```
~/eclipse/cpp-2019-03/eclipse/eclipse
```

You will choose a workspace folder and then you will be greeted with a **Welcome** tab in the main Eclipse window.

Now, we will install **cmake4eclipse**. An easy way to do this is to go to this website and drag the **Install** icon to the Eclipse window: https://github.com/15knots/cmake4eclipse#installation. It will ask you to restart Eclipse, after which you are ready to modify the CMake project to work with Eclipse.

**Installing GoogleTest**

We will install **GoogleTest** in our system, which will also install other packages that are dependent on it. Write the following command:

```
sudo apt install libgtest-dev google-mock
```

This command installs the include files and source files for **GoogleTest**. Now, we need to build the source files that we installed to create the **GoogleTest** library. Run the following commands to do this:

```
cd /usr/src/gtest
sudo cmake CMakeLists.txt
sudo make
sudo cp *.a /usr/lib
```

## Installing the Code Bundle

Copy the code bundle for the class to the **C:/Code** folder.

## Additional Resources

The code bundle for this book is also hosted on GitHub at https://github.com/TrainingByPackt/Advanced-CPlusPlus.

We also have other code bundles from our rich catalog of books and videos available at https://github.com/PacktPublishing/. Check them out!

# 1

# Anatomy of Portable C++ Software

**Learning Objectives**

By the end of this chapter, you will be able to:

- Establish the code-build-test process

- Describe the various stages of compilation

- Decipher complicated C++ type systems

- Configure projects with unit tests

- Convert source code to object code

- Write readable code and debug it

In this chapter, we will learn to establish the code-build-test model that will be used throughout the book, write beautiful code, and perform unit tests.

# Introduction

C++ is one of the oldest and most popular languages that you can use to write efficient code. It is both "close to the metal," like C, and has advanced object-oriented features, like Java. Being an efficient low-level language makes C++ the language of choice for domains in which efficiency is paramount, such as games, simulations, and embedded systems. At the same time, being an object-oriented language with advanced features such as generics, references, and countless others makes it suitable for large projects that are developed and maintained by multiple people.

Almost any programming experience involves organizing your code base and using libraries written by others. C++ is no different. Unless your program is simple, you will distribute your code into multiple files that you need to organize, and you will use various libraries that fulfill tasks, usually in a much more efficient and robust way than your code would. C++ projects that do not use any third-party libraries are edge cases that do not represent the majority of projects, which use many libraries. These projects and their libraries are expected to work in different hardware architectures and operating systems. Therefore, it is important to spend time on project setup and understand the tools used to manage dependencies if you are going to develop anything meaningful with C++.

Most modern and popular high-level languages have standard tools to maintain projects, build them, and handle their library dependencies. Many of these have repositories that host libraries and tools that automatically download and use libraries from those repositories. For example, Python has **pip**, which takes care of downloading and using appropriate versions of libraries that the programmer wants to use. Similarly, JavaScript has **npm**, Java has **maven**, Dart has **pub**, and C# has **NuGet**. In most of these languages, you list the name of the library and the version that you would like to use, and the tool automatically downloads and uses the compatible version of the library. These languages benefit from the fact that the programs are built and run in a controlled environment in which a certain level of hardware and software requirements are satisfied. C++, on the other hand, is expected to work in a variety of contexts with different architectures, including very primitive hardware. Hence, C++ programmers are less pampered when it comes to building programs and performing dependency management.

# Managing C++ Projects

In the world of C++, we have several tools that help in managing project sources and their dependencies. For example, `pkg-config`, `Autotools`, `make`, and `CMake` are the most notable ones in the community. Compared to the tools of the other high-level languages, these are much more complicated to use. `CMake` has arisen among these as the de facto standard for managing C++ projects and their dependencies. It is more opinionated compared to `make`, and it is accepted as the direct project format for most IDEs (Integrated Development Environments).

While `CMake` helps with managing projects and their dependencies, the experience is still far from higher-level languages in which you list the libraries and their versions that you want to use and everything else is taken care of for you. With CMake, you still are responsible for installing libraries properly in your development environment, and you are expected to use compatible versions for each library. In popular Linux distributions with extensive package managers, you can easily install binary versions of most popular libraries. However, sometimes, you may have to compile and install the libraries yourself. This is a part of the whole C++ developer experience, which you will gather by learning more about the development platform of your choice. Here, we will focus more on how to properly set up our CMake projects, including understanding and resolving issues related to libraries.

## The Code-Build-Test-Run Loop

In order to base our discussion on a solid foundation, we will immediately start with a practical example. We will start with a C++ code base template that you can use as a starting point for your own projects. We will see how we can build and compile it using CMake on the command line. We will also set up the Eclipse IDE for C/C++ developers and import our CMake project. The use of an IDE will provide us with facilities that ease the creation of source code and enable us to debug our programs line by line to view what exactly happens during the execution of our program and correct our mistakes in an informed fashion rather than trial and error and superstition.

## Building a CMake Project

The de facto standard for C++ projects is to use CMake to organize and build the project. Here, we will use a basic template project as a starting point. The following is the folder structure of a sample template:

```
README.md
CMakeLists.txt
include/CxxTemplatePublic.h
src/CxxTemplate.cpp
src/CxxTemplate.h
.gitignore
LICENSE
cmake/modules/DumpVariables.cmake
cmake/modules/DumpProps.cmake
```

Figure 1.1: Folder structure of a sample template

In the preceding figure, the **.gitignore** file lists the file patterns that should not be added to the **git** version control system. Such ignored files include the outputs of the build process, which are created locally and should not be shared among computers.

The files in the **include** and **src** folders are the actual C++ source files, and the **CMakeLists.txt** file is the CMake script file that glues the project together by handling the **source compilation rules**, **library dependencies**, and other project settings. CMake rules are high-level platform-independent rules. CMake uses them to create various types of **make** files for different platforms.

Building a project with CMake is a two-step process. First, we get CMake to generate platform-dependent configuration files for a native build system that will compile and build the project. Then, we will use the generated files to build the project. The platform-dependent build systems that CMake can generate configuration files for include **UNIX Makefiles**, **Ninja build files**, **NMake Makefiles**, and **MinGW Makefiles**. The choice here depends on the platform in use, the availability of these tools, and personal preference. **UNIX Makefiles** are a de facto standard for **Unix** and **Linux**, whereas **NMake** is its **Windows** and **Visual Studio** counterpart. **MinGW**, on the other hand, is a **Unix**-like environment in **Windows** in which **Makefiles** are also in use. **Ninja** is a modern build system that provides exceptional speed compared to other build systems coupled with multi-platform support, which we choose to use here. Furthermore, in addition to these command-line build systems, we can also generate IDE projects for **Visual Studio**, **XCode**, **Eclipse CDT**, and many others, and build our projects inside the IDE. Therefore, **CMake** is a meta tool that will create the configuration files for another system that will actually build the project. In the next section, we will solve an exercise, wherein we will generate **Ninja build files** using **CMake**.

## Exercise 1: Using CMake to Generate Ninja Build Files

In this exercise, we will use **CMake** to generate **Ninja build files**, which are used to build C++ projects. We will first download our source code from a **git** repository and will use CMake and Ninja to build it. The aim of this exercise is to use CMake to generate Ninja build files, build the project, and then run them.

> **Note**
>
> The link to the GitHub repository can be found here: https://github.com/TrainingByPackt/Advanced-CPlusPlus/tree/master/Lesson1/Exercise01/project.

Perform the following steps to complete the exercise:

1.  In a terminal window, type the following command to download the **CxxTemplate** repository from GitHub onto your local system:

    ```
    git clone https://github.com/TrainingByPackt/Advanced-CPlusPlus/tree/
    master/Lesson1/Exercise01/project
    ```

    The output of the previous command is similar to the following:

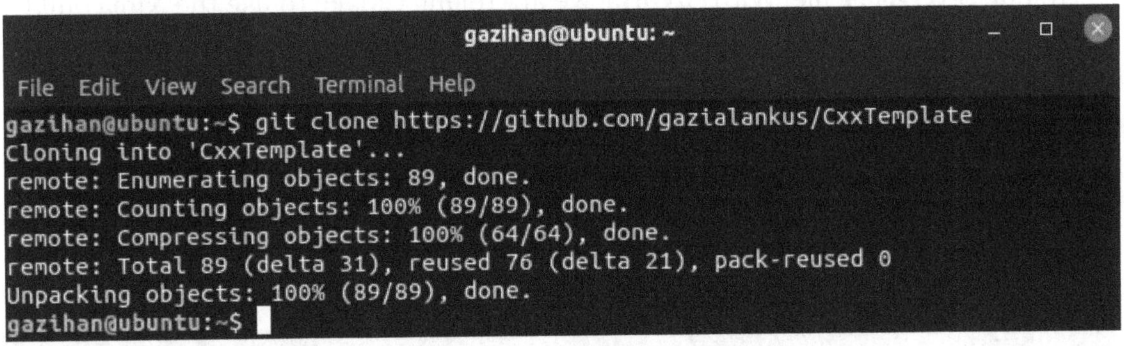

Figure 1.2: Checking out the sample project from GitHub

    Now you have the source code in the **CxxTemplate** folder.

2.  Navigate into the **CxxTemplate** folder by typing the following command in the terminal:

    ```
    cd CxxTemplate
    ```

3.  Now you can list all the files in the project by typing the following command:

    ```
    find .
    ```

4. Generate our Ninja build file using the **cmake** command in the **CxxTemplate** folder. To do that, write the following command:

```
cmake -Bbuild -H. -GNinja
```

The output of the preceding command is as follows:

```
-- The C compiler identification is GNU 7.4.0
-- The CXX compiler identification is GNU 7.4.0
-- Check for working C compiler: /usr/bin/cc
-- Check for working C compiler: /usr/bin/cc -- works
... (more lines)
-- Configuring done
-- Generating done
-- Build files have been written to:
/home/username/code/CxxTemplate/build
```

Figure 1.3: Generating the Ninja build file

Let's explain parts of the preceding command. With **-Bbuild**, we are telling CMake to use the **build** folder to generate build artifacts. Since this folder does not exist, CMake will create it. With **-H.**, we are telling CMake to use the current folder as the source. By using a separate **build** folder, we will keep our source files clean and all the build artifacts will live in the **build** folder, which is ignored by Git thanks to our **.gitignore** file. With **-GNinja**, we are telling CMake to use the Ninja build system.

5. Run the following commands to list the project files and to check the files that were created inside the **build** folder:

```
ls
ls build
```

The preceding command will show the following output in the terminal:

```
-- Build files have been written to: /home/gazihan/CxxTemplate/build
gazihan@ubuntu:~/CxxTemplate$ ls
build  cmake  CMakeLists.txt  include  LICENSE  README.md  src
gazihan@ubuntu:~/CxxTemplate$ ls build
build.ninja  CMakeCache.txt  CMakeFiles  cmake_install.cmake  rules.ninja
gazihan@ubuntu:~/CxxTemplate$
```

Figure 1.4: Files in the build folder

It's clear that the preceding files will be present inside the build folder. **build.ninja** and **rules.ninja** in the preceding output are the Ninja build files that can actually build our project in this platform.

> **Note**
>
> By using CMake, we did not have to write the Ninja build files and avoided committing to the Unix platform. Instead, we have a meta-build system that can generate low-level build files for other platforms such as UNIX/Linux, MinGW, and Nmake.

6.  Now, go into the **build** folder and build our project by typing the following commands in the terminal:

```
cd build
ninja
```

You should see a final output like the following:

```
gazihan@ubuntu:~/CxxTemplate$ cd build
gazihan@ubuntu:~/CxxTemplate/build$ ninja
[2/2] Linking CXX executable CxxTemplate
gazihan@ubuntu:~/CxxTemplate/build$
```

Figure 1.5: Building with ninja

7.  Type **ls** in the **build** folder and check whether we have generated the CxxTemplate executable or not:

```
ls
```

The previous command yields the following output in the terminal:

```
gazihan@ubuntu:~/CxxTemplate/build$ ls
build.ninja       CMakeFiles          CxxTemplate
CMakeCache.txt    cmake_install.cmake rules.ninja
gazihan@ubuntu:~/CxxTemplate/build$
```

Figure 1.6: Files in the build folder after running ninja

In the preceding figure, you can see that the CxxTemplate executable is generated.

8. In the terminal, type the following command to run the **CxxTemplate** executable:

```
./CxxTemplate
```

The previous command in the terminal will provide the following output:

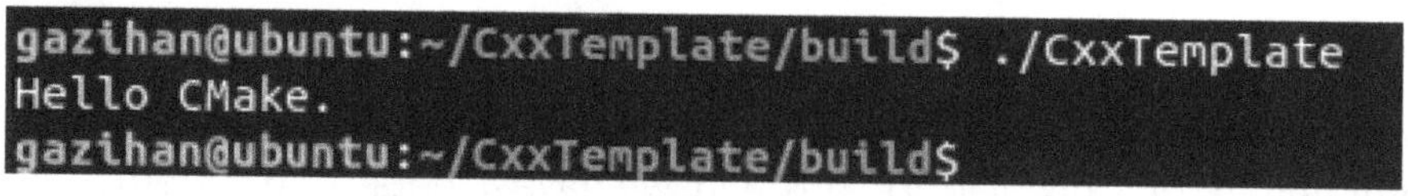

```
gazihan@ubuntu:~/CxxTemplate/build$ ./CxxTemplate
Hello CMake.
gazihan@ubuntu:~/CxxTemplate/build$
```

Figure 1.7: Running the executable

The following line from the **src/CxxTemplate.cpp** file is responsible for writing the previous output:

```
std::cout << "Hello CMake." << std::endl;
```

Now you have successfully built a CMake project in Linux. Ninja and CMake work quite well together. You have to run CMake only once and Ninja will detect whether CMake should be called again and will call it for you. For example, even if you add new source files to your **CMakeLists.txt** file, you only need to type the **ninja** command in the terminal, and it will run CMake automatically for you to update the Ninja build files. Now that you have learned about building a CMake project in Linux, in the next section, we will look at how to import a CMake project into Eclipse CDT.

## Importing a CMake Project into Eclipse CDT

A Ninja build file is useful for building our project in Linux. However, a CMake project is portable and can be used with other build systems and IDEs as well. Many IDEs accept CMake as their configuration file and provide a seamless experience as you modify and build your project. In this section, we will discuss how to import a CMake project into Eclipse CDT, which is a popular cross-platform C/C++ IDE.

There are multiple ways of using Eclipse CDT with CMake. The default one that CMake provides is the one-way generation of the IDE project. Here, you create the IDE project once, and any modifications you make to your IDE project will not change back the original CMake project. This is useful if you manage your project as a CMake project and do one-time builds with Eclipse CDT. However, it's not ideal if you want to do your development in Eclipse CDT.

Another way of using CMake with Eclipse CDT is to use the custom **cmake4eclipse** plugin. When using this plugin, you do not abandon your **CMakeLists.txt** file and make a one-way switch to Eclipse CDT's own project manager. Instead, you keep managing your project through the **CMakeLists.txt** file, which continues to be the main configuration file of your project. Eclipse CDT actively works with your **CMakeLists.txt** file to build your project. You can add or remove source files and make other changes in your **CMakeLists.txt**, and the **cmake4eclipse** plugin applies those changes to the Eclipse CDT project at every build. You will have a nice IDE experience while keeping your CMake project current. The benefit of this approach is that you can always quit using Eclipse CDT and use your **CMakeLists.txt** file to switch to another build system (such as Ninja) later. We will use this second approach in the following exercise.

## Exercise 2: Importing the CMake File into Eclipse CDT

In the last exercise, you developed a CMake project and you would like to start using Eclipse CDT IDE to edit and build that project. In this exercise, we will import our CMake project into the Eclipse CDT IDE using the **cmake4eclipse** plugin. Perform the following steps to complete the exercise:

1. Open Eclipse CDT.

2. Create a new C++ project in the location of our current project (the folder that contains the **CMakeLists.txt** file and the **src** folder). Go to **File | New | Project**. A **New Project** dialog box appears like the one in the following screenshot:

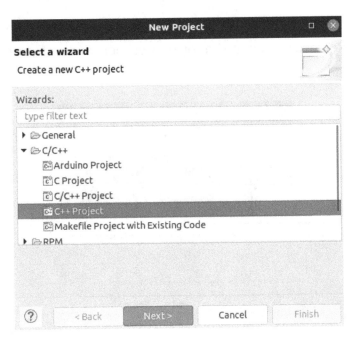

Figure 1.8: New Project dialog box

3. Select the **C++ Project** option and click on the **Next** button. A **C++ Project** dialog box appears like the one in the following screenshot:

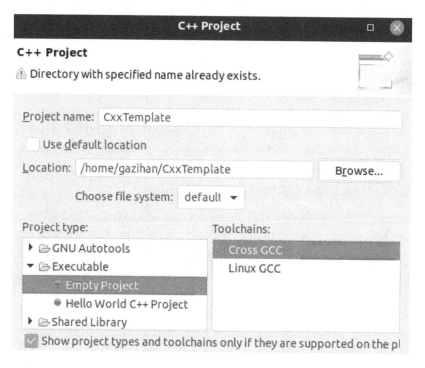

Figure 1.9: C++ Project dialog box

4. Accept everything, including switching to the C/C++ perspective, and click **Finish**.

5. Click on the **Restore** button at the top-left corner to view the newly created project:

Figure 1.10: The Restore button

6. Click on the **CxxTemplate** project. Go to **Project | Properties**, then select **Tool Chain Editor** under **C/C++ Build** from the left pane and set **Current builder** to **CMake Builder (portable)**. Then, click on the **Apply and Close** button:

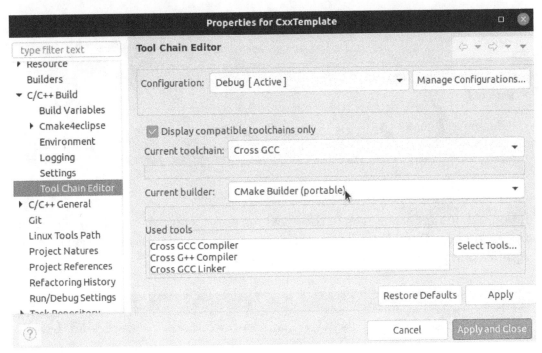

Figure 1.11: Project properties

7. Then, choose the **Project | Build All** menu item to build the project:

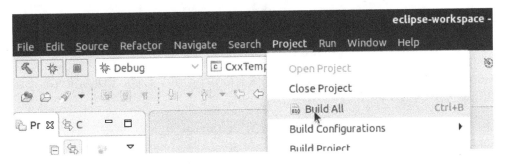

Figure 1.12: Building the project

8. In the following **Console** pane, you will see the output of CMake as if you called it from the command line, followed by a call to `make all` that actually builds our project:

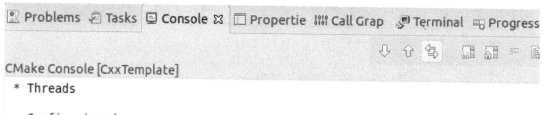

**Figure 1.13: The build output**

9. If you did not get any errors in the previous steps, you can run the project using the menu item **Run | Run**. If you are given some options, choose **Local C/C++ Application** and **CxxTemplate** as the executable:

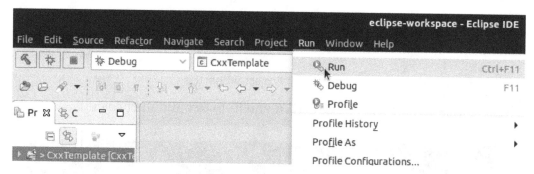

**Figure 1.14: Running a project**

10. When it runs, you will see the output of the program in the **Console** pane as follows:

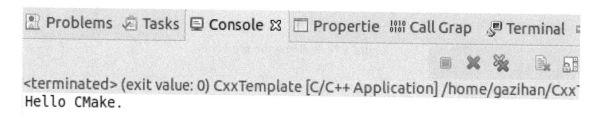

**Figure 1.15: Output of the project**

You have successfully built and run a CMake project using Eclipse CDT. In the next exercise, we will introduce a frequent change to our projects by adding new source files with new classes.

## Exercise 3: Adding New Source Files to CMake and Eclipse CDT

As you develop significantly bigger C++ projects, you will tend to add new source files to it as the project grows to meet the set expectations. In this exercise, we will add a new .cpp and .h file pair to our project and see how CMake and Eclipse CDT work together with these changes. We will add these files inside the project using the new class wizard, but you can also create them with any other text editor. Perform the following steps to add new source files to CMake and Eclipse CDT:

1. First, open the project that we have been using until now. In the **Project Explorer** pane on the left, expand the root entry, **CxxTemplate**, and you will see the files and folders of our project. Right-click the **src** folder and select **New | Class** from the pop-up menu:

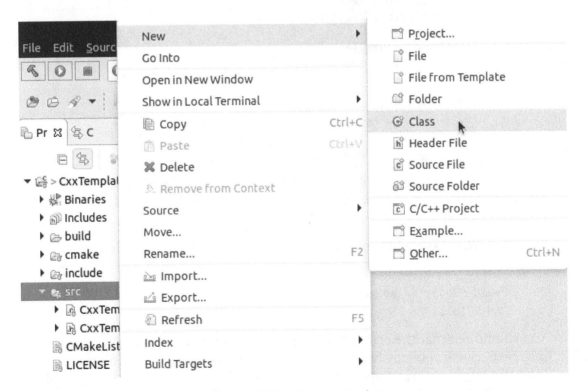

Figure 1.16: Creating a new class

2. In the dialog box that opened, type **ANewClass** for the class name. When you click on the **Finish** button, you will see the **ANewClass.cpp** and **ANewClass.h** files generated under the **src** folder.

3.  Now, let's write some code into the **ANewClass** class and access it from the
    **CxxTemplate** class that we already had. Open **ANewClass.cpp** and change the
    beginning of the file to match the following, and then save the file:

    ```
    #include "ANewClass.h"
    #include <iostream>

    void ANewClass::run() {
        std::cout << "Hello from ANewClass." << std::endl;
    }
    ```

    You will see that Eclipse warns us with a **Member declaration not found** message:

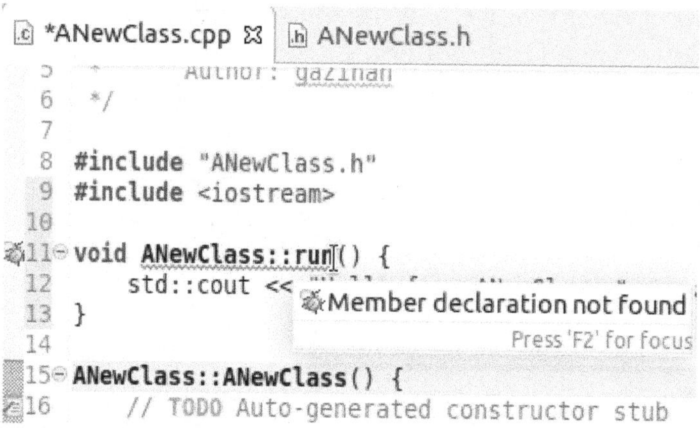

    **Figure 1.17: Analyzer warning**

    This error is generated since we need to add this to our **ANewClass.h** file as well.
    Such warnings are made possible by analyzers in IDEs and are quite useful as they
    help you fix your code as you are typing, without running the compiler.

4.  Open the **ANewClass.h** file, add the following code, and save the file:

    ```
    public:
        void run(); // we added this line
        ANewClass();
    ```

You should see that the error in the **.cpp** file went away. If it did not go away, it
may be because you may have forgotten to save one of the files. You should make
it a habit to press *Ctrl* + *S* to save the current file, or *Shift* + *Ctrl* + *S* to save all the
files that you edited.

5. Now, let's use this class from our other class, **CxxTemplate.cpp**. Open that file, perform the following modifications, and save the file. Here, we are first importing header files and in the constructor of **CxxApplication**, we are printing text to the console. Then, we are creating a new instance of **ANewClass** and calling its **run** method:

```
#include "CxxTemplate.h"
#include "ANewClass.h"

#include <string>

...

CxxApplication::CxxApplication( int argc, char *argv[] ) {
  std::cout << "Hello CMake." << std::endl;
  ::ANewClass anew;
  anew.run();
}
```

**Note**

The complete code of this file can be found here: https://github.com/
TrainingByPackt/Advanced-CPlusPlus/blob/master/Lesson1/Exercise03/src/
CxxTemplate.cpp.

6. Try to build the project by clicking on the **Project | Build All** menu options. You will get some undefined reference errors in two lines. This is because our project is built with CMake's rules and we did not let CMake know about this new file. Open the **CMakeLists.txt** file, make the following modification, and save the file:

```
add_executable(CxxTemplate
  src/CxxTemplate.cpp
  src/ANewClass.cpp
)
```

Try to build the project again. This time you should not see any errors.

7.  Run the project using the **Run | Run** menu option. You should see the following output in the terminal:

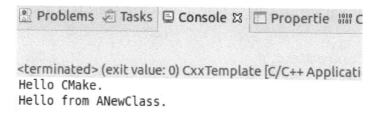

Figure 1.18: Program output

You modified a CMake project, added new files to it, and ran it fine. Note that we created the files in the **src** folder and let the **CMakeLists.txt** file know about the CPP file. If you do not use Eclipse, you can simply continue with the usual CMake build commands and your program will run successfully. So far, we have checked out the sample code from GitHub and built it both with plain CMake and with the Eclipse IDE. We also added a new class to the CMake project and rebuilt it in Eclipse IDE. Now you know how to build and modify CMake projects. In the next section, we will perform an activity of adding a new source-header file pair to the project.

## Activity 1: Adding a New Source-Header File Pair to the Project

As you develop C++ projects, you add new source files to it as the project grows. You may want to add new source files for various reasons. For example, let's say you are developing an accounting application in which you calculate interest rates in many places of your project, and you want to create a function in a separate file so that you can reuse it throughout your project. To keep things simple, here we will create a simple summation function instead. In this activity, we will add a new source-header file pair to the project. Perform the following steps to complete the activity:

1.  Open the project that we created in the earlier exercise in the Eclipse IDE.

2.  Add the **SumFunc.cpp** and **SumFunc.h** file pair to the project.

3.  Create a simple function named **sum** that returns the sum of two integers.

4.  Call the function from the **CxxTemplate** class constructor.

5.  Build and run the project in Eclipse.

The expected output should be similar to the following:

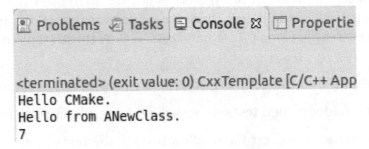

**Figure 1.19: Final output**

> **Note**
>
> The solution for this activity can be found on page 620.

In the following section, we will talk about how to write unit tests for our projects. It is common to divide projects into many classes and functions that work together to achieve the desired goal. You must manage the behavior of these classes and functions with unit tests to ensure that they behave in expected ways.

## Unit Testing

Unit tests are an important part of programming in general. Basically, unit tests are little programs that use our classes in various scenarios with expected results, live in a parallel file hierarchy in our project, and do not end up in the actual executable but are executed separately by us during development to ensure that our code is behaving in expected ways. We should write unit tests for our C++ programs to ensure that they behave as they are supposed to after each change.

### Preparing for the Unit Tests

There are several C++ test frameworks that we can use with CMake. We will use **Google Test**, which has several benefits over other options. In the next exercise, we will prepare our project for unit testing with Google Test.

## Exercise 4: Preparing Our Project for Unit Testing

We have installed Google Test but our project is not set up to use Google Test for unit testing. In addition to the installation, there are settings that need to be carried out in our CMake project to have Google Test unit tests. Follow these steps to implement this exercise:

1. Open Eclipse CDT and select the CxxTemplate project that we have been using.

2. Create a new folder named **tests** as we will perform all our tests there.

3. Edit our base **CMakeLists.txt** file to allow tests in the **tests** folder. Note that we already had code to find the **GTest** package that brings **GoogleTest** capability to CMake. We will add our new lines just after that:

```
find_package(GTest)
if(GTEST_FOUND)
set(Gtest_FOUND TRUE)
endif()
if(GTest_FOUND)
include(GoogleTest)
endif()
# add these two lines below
enable_testing()
add_subdirectory(tests)
```

This is all we need to add to our main **CMakeLists.txt** file.

4. Create another **CMakeLists.txt** file inside our **tests** folder. This will be used because of the **add_subdirectory(tests)** line that we had in our main **CMakeLists.txt** file. This **tests/CMakeLists.txt** file will manage the test sources.

5. Add the following code in the **tests/CMakeLists.txt** file:

```
include(GoogleTest)
add_executable(tests CanTest.cpp)
target_link_libraries(tests GTest::GTest)
gtest_discover_tests(tests)
```

Let's dissect this code line by line. The first line brings in the Google Test capability. The second line creates the **tests** executable, which will include all our test source files. In this case, we only have one **CanTest.cpp** file, which will just verify that the testing works. After that, we link the **GTest** library to the **tests** executable. The last line identifies all individual tests in the **tests** executable and adds them to **CMake** as a test. This way, various test tools will be able to tell us which individual tests failed and which ones passed.

6. Create a **tests/CanTest.cpp** file. Add this code to simply verify that tests are running, without actually testing anything in our actual project:

```
#include "gtest/gtest.h"

namespace {

class CanTest: public ::testing::Test {};

TEST_F(CanTest, CanReallyTest) {
  EXPECT_EQ(0, 0);
}

}

int main(int argc, char **argv) {
  ::testing::InitGoogleTest(&argc, argv);
  return RUN_ALL_TESTS();
}
```

The **TEST_F** line is an individual test. Now, **EXPECT_EQ(0, 0)** is testing whether zero is equal to zero, which will always succeed if we can actually run the test. We will later add the results of our own classes here to be tested against various values. Now we have the necessary setup for Google Test in our project. Next, we will build and run these tests.

## Building, Running, and Writing Unit Tests

Now, we will discuss how to build, run, and write unit tests. The example that we have so far is a simple dummy test that is ready to be built and run. Later, we will add tests that make more sense and view the output of passing and failing tests. In the following exercise, we will build, run, and write unit tests for the project that we created in the previous exercise.

## Exercise 5: Building and Running Tests

So far, you have created a project with **GoogleTest** set up, but you did not build or run the tests we created. In this exercise, we will build and run the tests that we created. Since we added our **tests** folder using **add_subdirectory**, building the project will automatically build the tests. Running the tests will require some more effort. Perform the following steps to complete the exercise:

1. Open our CMake project in Eclipse CDT.

2. To build the tests, simply build the project just like you did before. Here is the output of building the project one more time from Eclipse after a full build using **Project | Build All**:

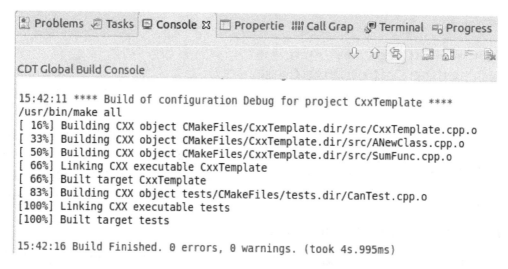

Figure 1.20: Build operation and its output

3. If you do not see this output, your console may be in the wrong view. You can correct it as shown in the following figures:

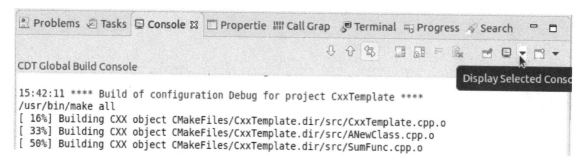

Figure 1.21: Viewing the correct console output

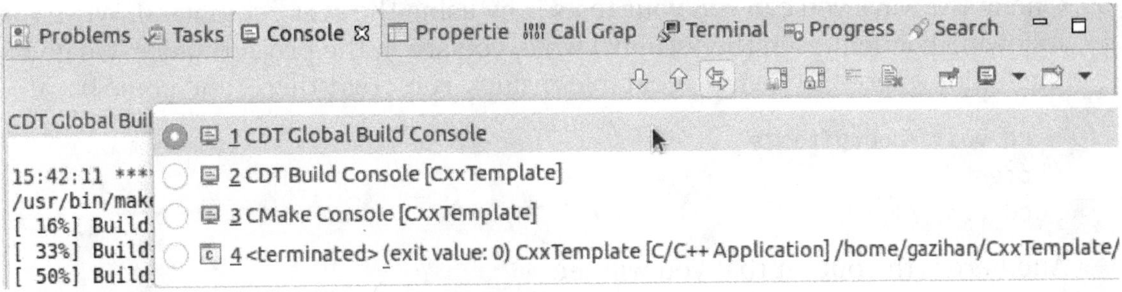

Figure 1.22: Viewing the correct console output

As you can see, our project now has two executable targets. They both live in the **build** folder, as with any other build artifact. Their locations are **build/Debug/ CxxTemplate** and **build/Debug/tests/tests**. Since they are executables, we can simply run them.

4. We ran **CxxTemplate** before and will not see any extra output now. Run the other executable by typing the following command in the terminal while we are in our project folder:

```
./build/Debug/tests/tests
```

The preceding code generates the following output in the terminal:

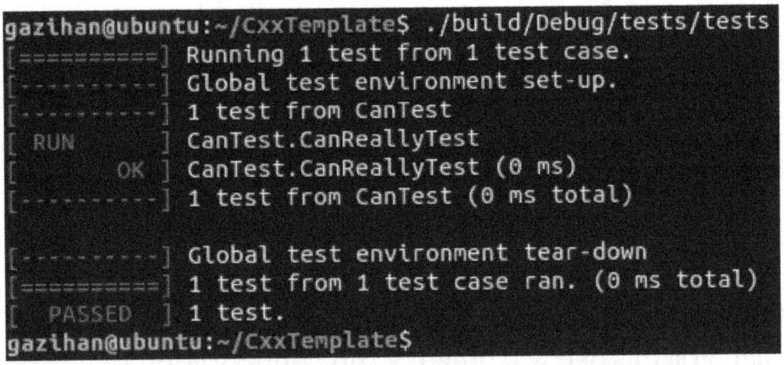

Figure 1.23: Running the tests executable

This is the simple output of our **tests** executable. If you want to see whether the tests have passed, you can simply run this. However, testing is so much more than that.

5.  One of the ways you can run your tests is by using the **ctest** command. Write the following commands in the terminal while you are in the project folder. We go to the folder where the **tests** executable resides, run **ctest** there, and come back:

```
cd build/Debug/tests
ctest
cd ../../..
```

And here is the output that you will see:

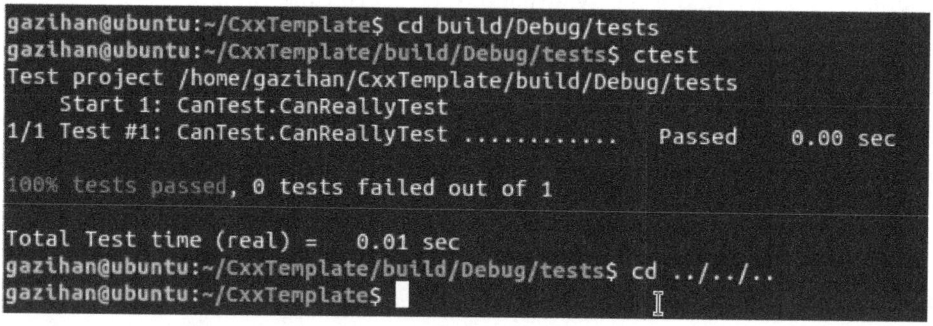

```
gazihan@ubuntu:~/CxxTemplate$ cd build/Debug/tests
gazihan@ubuntu:~/CxxTemplate/build/Debug/tests$ ctest
Test project /home/gazihan/CxxTemplate/build/Debug/tests
    Start 1: CanTest.CanReallyTest
1/1 Test #1: CanTest.CanReallyTest ............   Passed    0.00 sec

100% tests passed, 0 tests failed out of 1

Total Test time (real) =   0.01 sec
gazihan@ubuntu:~/CxxTemplate/build/Debug/tests$ cd ../../..
gazihan@ubuntu:~/CxxTemplate$
```

Figure 1.24: Running ctest

> **Note**
>
> The **ctest** command can run your **tests** executable with a number of options, including the ability to submit test results automatically to online dashboards. Here, we will simply run the **ctest** command; its further features are left as an exercise for the interested reader. You can type **ctest --help** or visit the online documentation to discover **ctest** further at https://cmake.org/cmake/help/latest/manual/ctest.1.html#.

6.  Another way to run the tests is to run them inside Eclipse, in a nice graphical report format. For this, we will create a run configuration that is test-aware. In Eclipse, click on **Run | Run Configurations...**, right-click **C/C++ Unit** on the left, and select **New Configuration**.

7. Change the name from **CxxTemplate Debug** to **CxxTemplate Tests** as follows:

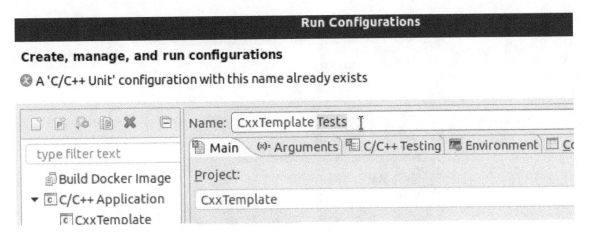

Figure 1.25: Changing the name of the run configuration

8. Under **C/C++ Application**, select the **Search Project** option:

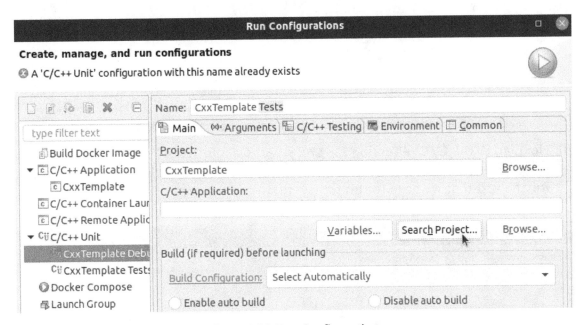

Figure 1.26: Run Configurations

9. Choose **tests** in the new dialog:

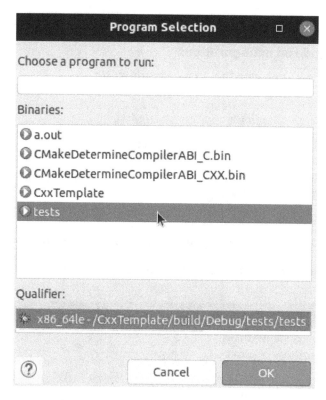

Figure 1.27: Creating the test run configuration and selecting the tests executable

10. Next, go to the **C/C++ Testing** tab and select **Google Tests Runner** in the dropdown. Click on **Apply** at the bottom of the dialog and click on the **Run** option for the test that we have to run for the first time:

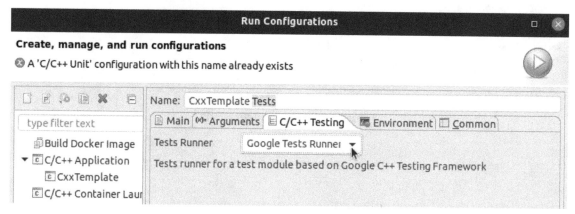

Figure 1.28: Run Configurations

11. In the upcoming runs, you can either click the dropdown next to the play button in the toolbar, or choose **Run | Run History** to choose **CxxTemplate Tests**:

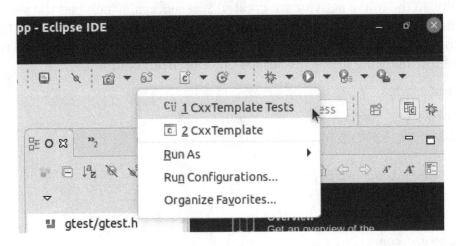

Figure 1.29: Finalizing the run configuration settings and selecting a configuration to run

The result will be similar to the following screenshot:

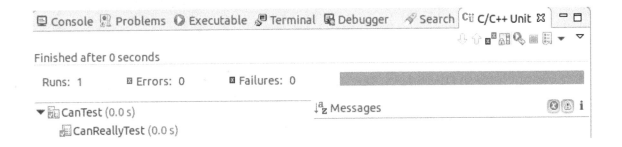

Figure 1.30: Run results of the unit test

This is a nice report that contains entries for all tests–only one for now. You may prefer this if you do not want to leave the IDE. Furthermore, when you have many tests, this interface can help you filter them effectively. Now you have built and run tests that were written using Google Test. You ran them in a couple of different ways, including directly executing the test, using **ctest**, and using Eclipse CDT. In the next section, we will solve an exercise wherein we will actually test the functionality of our code.

## Exercise 6: Testing the Functionality of Code

You have run simple tests but now you want to write meaningful tests that are testing functionality. In the initial activity, we created **SumFunc.cpp**, which had the **sum** function. Now, in this exercise, we will write a test for that file. In this test, we will use the **sum** function to add two numbers and verify that the result is correct. Let's recall the contents of the following files with the **sum** function from before:

- **src/SumFunc.h**:

```
#ifndef SRC_SUMFUNC_H_
#define SRC_SUMFUNC_H_

int sum(int a, int b);

#endif /* SRC_SUMFUNC_H_ */
```

- **src/SumFunc.cpp**:

```
#include "SumFunc.h"
#include <iostream>

int sum(int a, int b) {
   return a + b;
}
```

- Relevant lines of **CMakeLists.txt**:

```
add_executable(CxxTemplate
   src/CxxTemplate.cpp
   src/ANewClass.cpp
   src/SumFunc.cpp
)
```

Also, let's recall our **CantTest.cpp** file, which has the **main()** function of our unit tests:

```
#include "gtest/gtest.h"

namespace {

class CanTest: public ::testing::Test {};

TEST_F(CanTest, CanReallyTest) {
   EXPECT_EQ(0, 0);
}
```

```
  }

  int main(int argc, char **argv) {
    ::testing::InitGoogleTest(&argc, argv);
    return RUN_ALL_TESTS();
  }
```

Perform the following steps to complete the exercise:

1.  Open our CMake project in Eclipse CDT.

2.  Add a new test source file (**tests/SumFuncTest.cpp**) with the following content:

    ```cpp
    #include "gtest/gtest.h"
    #include "../src/SumFunc.h"

    namespace {

      class SumFuncTest: public ::testing::Test {};

      TEST_F(SumFuncTest, CanSumCorrectly) {
        EXPECT_EQ(7, sum(3, 4));
      }
    }
    ```

    Note that this does not have a **main()** function since **CanTest.cpp** has one and these will be linked together. Secondly, note that this includes **SumFunc.h**, which is in the **src** folder of the project and uses it as **sum(3, 4)** inside the test. This is how we use our project code in tests.

3.  Make the following change in the **tests/CMakeLists.txt** file to build the test:

    ```cmake
    include(GoogleTest)
    add_executable(tests CanTest.cpp SumFuncTest.cpp ../src/SumFunc.cpp) #
    added files here
    target_link_libraries(tests GTest::GTest)
    gtest_discover_tests(tests)
    ```

    Note that we added both the test (**SumFuncTest.cpp**) and the code that it tests (**../src/SumFunc.cpp**) to the executable, as our test code is using the code from the actual project.

4. Build the project and run the test as before. You should see the following report:

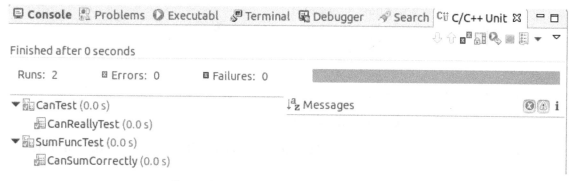

Figure 1.31: Output after running the test

We can add such tests to our project and all of them will appear on the screen as shown in the preceeding screenshot.

5. Now, let's add one more test that will actually fail. In the **tests/SumFuncTest.cpp** file, make the following change:

```
TEST_F(SumFuncTest, CanSumCorrectly) {
  EXPECT_EQ(7, sum(3, 4));
}

// add this test
TEST_F(SumFuncTest, CanSumAbsoluteValues) {
  EXPECT_EQ(6, sum(3, -3));
}
```

Note that this test assumes that the absolute values of the inputs are summed up, which is incorrect. The result of this call is **0** but is expected to be **6** in this example. This is the only change that we have to make in our project to add this test.

6. Now, build the project and run the test. You should see this report:

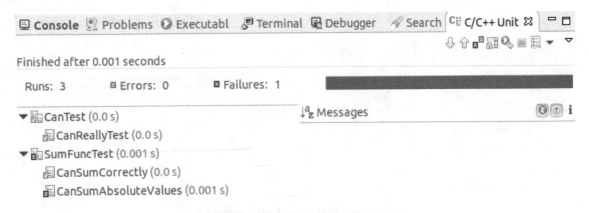

Figure 1.32: The build report

As you can see in the preceding figure, the first two tests passed and the last test failed. When we see this output, there are two options: either our project code is wrong, or the test is wrong. In this case, our test is wrong. This is because our **CanSumAbsoluteValues** test case expects that **6** is equal to **sum(3, -3)**. This is because we assumed that our function sums up the absolute values of the integers provided. However, this is not the case. Our function simply adds the given numbers, whether they are positive or negative. Therefore, this test had a faulty assumption and failed.

7. Let's change the test and fix it. Change the test so that we expect the sum of **-3** and **3** to be **0**. Rename the test to reflect what this test actually does:

```
TEST_F(SumFuncTest, CanSumCorrectly) {
  EXPECT_EQ(7, sum(3, 4));
}

// change this part
TEST_F(SumFuncTest, CanUseNegativeValues) {
  EXPECT_EQ(0, sum(3, -3));
}
```

8. Run it now and observe in the report that all the tests pass:

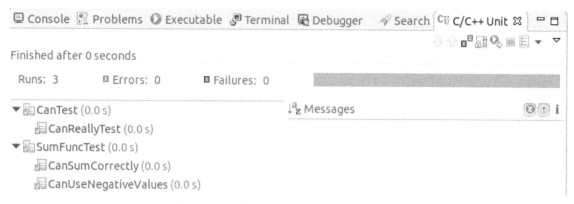

Figure 1.33: Test execution is successful

Finally, we have set up Google Test with CMake both in our system and project. We also wrote, built, and ran unit tests with Google Test, both in the terminal and in Eclipse. Ideally, you should write unit tests for every class and cover every possible usage. You should also run the tests after each major change and make sure you do not break existing code. In the next section, we will perform an activity of adding a new class and its test.

## Activity 2: Adding a New Class and Its Test

As you develop a C++ project, you add new source files to it as the project grows. You also write tests for them to ensure that they are working properly. In this activity, we will add a new class that simulates **1D** linear motion. The class will have double fields for **position** and **velocity**. It will also have a **advanceTimeBy()** method, which receives a double **dt** parameter, which modifies **position** based on the value of **velocity**. Use **EXPECT_DOUBLE_EQ** instead of **EXPECT_EQ** for double values. In this activity, we will add a new class and its test to the project. Follow these steps to perform this activity:

1. Open the project that we have created in the Eclipse IDE.

2. Add the **LinearMotion1D.cpp** and **LinearMotion1D.h** file pair to the project that contains the **LinearMotion1D** class. In this class, create two double fields: **position** and **velocity**. Also, create an **advanceTimeBy(double dt)** function that modifies **position**.

3. Write tests for this in the **tests/LinearMotion1DTest.cpp** file. Write two tests that represent motion in two different directions.

4. Build and run it in the Eclipse IDE.

5. Verify that the tests have passed.

The final test results should look similar to the following:

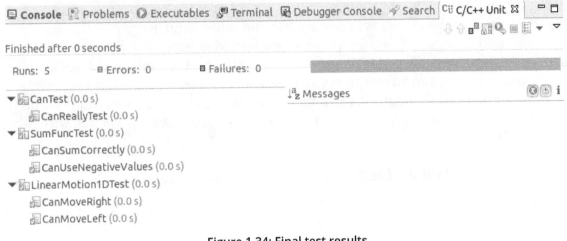

Figure 1.34: Final test results

> **Note**
>
> The solution for this activity can be found on page 622.

Adding new classes and their tests is a very common task in C++ development. We create classes for various reasons. Sometimes, we have a nice software design plan and we create the classes that it calls for. Other times, when a class becomes too large and monolithic, we separate some of its responsibility to another class in a meaningful way. Having this task be practical is important to prevent dragging your feet and ending up with huge monolithic classes. In the following section, we discuss what happens during the compilation and linking stages. This will give us a better perspective of what is happening under the hood of C++ programs.

# Understanding Compilation, Linking, and Object File Contents

One of the main reasons for using C++ is efficiency. C++ gives us control over memory management, which is why understanding how objects are laid out in memory is important. Furthermore, C++ source files and libraries are compiled to object files for the target hardware and linked together. Often, C++ programmers have to deal with linker problems, which is why understanding the steps of the compilation and being able to investigate object files is important. On the other hand, large projects are developed and maintained by teams over a long period of time, which is why creating clean and understandable code is important. As with any other software, bugs arise in C++ projects and need to be identified, analyzed, and resolved carefully by observing the program behavior. Therefore, learning how to debug C++ code is also important. In the next section, we will learn how to create code that is efficient, plays well with other code, and is maintainable.

## Compilation and Linking Steps

A C++ project is created as a set of source code files and project configuration files that organize the sources and library dependencies. In the compilation step, these sources are first converted to object files. In the linking step, these object files are linked together to form the executable that is the ultimate output of the project. The libraries that the project uses are also linked at this step.

In the upcoming exercises, we will use our existing project to observe the compilation and linking stages. Then, we will manually recreate them to view the process in more detail.

## Exercise 7: Identifying Build Steps

You have been building your projects without investigating the details of the build actions. In this exercise, we will investigate the details of our project's build steps. Perform the following to complete the exercise:

1. Open the terminal.

2. Navigate to the **build** folder wherein our **Makefile** file resides by typing the following command:

```
cd build/Debug
```

3.  Clean the project and run the build in **VERBOSE** mode using the following command:

    ```
    make clean
    make VERBOSE=1 all
    ```

    You will get a detailed output of the build process in the terminal, which may look a bit crowded:

```
gazihan@ubuntu:~/CxxTemplate$ cd build/Debug
gazihan@ubuntu:~/CxxTemplate/build/Debug$ make clean
gazihan@ubuntu:~/CxxTemplate/build/Debug$ make VERBOSE=1 all
/home/gazihan/cmake-3.15.1-Linux-x86_64/bin/cmake -S/home/gazihan/CxxTemplate -B
/home/gazihan/CxxTemplate/build/Debug --check-build-system CMakeFiles/Makefile.c
make 0
/home/gazihan/cmake-3.15.1-Linux-x86_64/bin/cmake -E cmake_progress_start /home/
gazihan/CxxTemplate/build/Debug/CMakeFiles /home/gazihan/CxxTemplate/build/Debug
/CMakeFiles/progress.marks
make -f CMakeFiles/Makefile2 all
make[1]: Entering directory '/home/gazihan/CxxTemplate/build/Debug'
make -f CMakeFiles/CxxTemplate.dir/build.make CMakeFiles/CxxTemplate.dir/depend
make[2]: Entering directory '/home/gazihan/CxxTemplate/build/Debug'
cd /home/gazihan/CxxTemplate/build/Debug && /home/gazihan/cmake-3.15.1-Linux-x86
_64/bin/cmake -E cmake_depends "Unix Makefiles" /home/gazihan/CxxTemplate /home/
gazihan/CxxTemplate /home/gazihan/CxxTemplate/build/Debug /home/gazihan/CxxTempl
ate/build/Debug /home/gazihan/CxxTemplate/build/Debug/CMakeFiles/CxxTemplate.dir
/DependInfo.cmake --color=
make[2]: Leaving directory '/home/gazihan/CxxTemplate/build/Debug'
make -f CMakeFiles/CxxTemplate.dir/build.make CMakeFiles/CxxTemplate.dir/build
make[2]: Entering directory '/home/gazihan/CxxTemplate/build/Debug'
[  9%] Building CXX object CMakeFiles/CxxTemplate.dir/src/CxxTemplate.cpp.o
/usr/bin/c++    -g    -std=gnu++17 -o CMakeFiles/CxxTemplate.dir/src/CxxTemplate.
cpp.o -c /home/gazihan/CxxTemplate/src/CxxTemplate.cpp
[ 18%] Building CXX object CMakeFiles/CxxTemplate.dir/src/ANewClass.cpp.o
/usr/bin/c++    -g    -std=gnu++17 -o CMakeFiles/CxxTemplate.dir/src/ANewClass.cp
p.o -c /home/gazihan/CxxTemplate/src/ANewClass.cpp
[ 27%] Building CXX object CMakeFiles/CxxTemplate.dir/src/SumFunc.cpp.o
/usr/bin/c++    -g    -std=gnu++17 -o CMakeFiles/CxxTemplate.dir/src/SumFunc.cpp.
o -c /home/gazihan/CxxTemplate/src/SumFunc.cpp
[ 36%] Building CXX object CMakeFiles/CxxTemplate.dir/src/LinearMotion1D.cpp.o
/usr/bin/c++    -g    -std=gnu++17 -o CMakeFiles/CxxTemplate.dir/src/LinearMotion
1D.cpp.o -c /home/gazihan/CxxTemplate/src/LinearMotion1D.cpp
[ 45%] Linking CXX executable CxxTemplate
/home/gazihan/cmake-3.15.1-Linux-x86_64/bin/cmake -E cmake_link_script CMakeFile
```

Figure 1.35: The build process part 1

```
s/CxxTemplate.dir/link.txt --verbose=1
/usr/bin/c++  -g   CMakeFiles/CxxTemplate.dir/src/CxxTemplate.cpp.o CMakeFiles/C
xxTemplate.dir/src/ANewClass.cpp.o CMakeFiles/CxxTemplate.dir/src/SumFunc.cpp.o
CMakeFiles/CxxTemplate.dir/src/LinearMotion1D.cpp.o  -o CxxTemplate -lpthread
make[2]: Leaving directory '/home/gazihan/CxxTemplate/build/Debug'
[ 45%] Built target CxxTemplate
make -f tests/CMakeFiles/tests.dir/build.make tests/CMakeFiles/tests.dir/depend
make[2]: Entering directory '/home/gazihan/CxxTemplate/build/Debug'
cd /home/gazihan/CxxTemplate/build/Debug && /home/gazihan/cmake-3.15.1-Linux-x86
_64/bin/cmake -E cmake_depends "Unix Makefiles" /home/gazihan/CxxTemplate /home/
gazihan/CxxTemplate/tests /home/gazihan/CxxTemplate/build/Debug /home/gazihan/Cx
xTemplate/build/Debug/tests /home/gazihan/CxxTemplate/build/Debug/tests/CMakeFil
es/tests.dir/DependInfo.cmake --color=
make[2]: Leaving directory '/home/gazihan/CxxTemplate/build/Debug'
make -f tests/CMakeFiles/tests.dir/build.make tests/CMakeFiles/tests.dir/build
make[2]: Entering directory '/home/gazihan/CxxTemplate/build/Debug'
[ 54%] Building CXX object tests/CMakeFiles/tests.dir/CanTest.cpp.o
cd /home/gazihan/CxxTemplate/build/Debug/tests && /usr/bin/c++    -g   -std=gnu+
+17 -o CMakeFiles/tests.dir/CanTest.cpp.o -c /home/gazihan/CxxTemplate/tests/Can
Test.cpp
[ 63%] Building CXX object tests/CMakeFiles/tests.dir/SumFuncTest.cpp.o
cd /home/gazihan/CxxTemplate/build/Debug/tests && /usr/bin/c++    -g   -std=gnu+
+17 -o CMakeFiles/tests.dir/SumFuncTest.cpp.o -c /home/gazihan/CxxTemplate/tests
/SumFuncTest.cpp
[ 72%] Building CXX object tests/CMakeFiles/tests.dir/__/src/SumFunc.cpp.o
cd /home/gazihan/CxxTemplate/build/Debug/tests && /usr/bin/c++    -g   -std=gnu+
+17 -o CMakeFiles/tests.dir/__/src/SumFunc.cpp.o -c /home/gazihan/CxxTemplate/sr
c/SumFunc.cpp
[ 81%] Building CXX object tests/CMakeFiles/tests.dir/LinearMotion1DTest.cpp.o
cd /home/gazihan/CxxTemplate/build/Debug/tests && /usr/bin/c++    -g   -std=gnu+
+17 -o CMakeFiles/tests.dir/LinearMotion1DTest.cpp.o -c /home/gazihan/CxxTemplat
e/tests/LinearMotion1DTest.cpp
[ 90%] Building CXX object tests/CMakeFiles/tests.dir/__/src/LinearMotion1D.cpp.
o
cd /home/gazihan/CxxTemplate/build/Debug/tests && /usr/bin/c++    -g   -std=gnu+
```

Figure 1.36: The build process part 2

```
+17 -o CMakeFiles/tests.dir/__/src/LinearMotion1D.cpp.o -c /home/gazihan/CxxTemp
late/src/LinearMotion1D.cpp
[100%] Linking CXX executable tests
cd /home/gazihan/CxxTemplate/build/Debug/tests && /home/gazihan/cmake-3.15.1-Lin
ux-x86_64/bin/cmake -E cmake_link_script CMakeFiles/tests.dir/link.txt --verbose
=1
/usr/bin/c++   -g   CMakeFiles/tests.dir/CanTest.cpp.o CMakeFiles/tests.dir/SumFu
ncTest.cpp.o CMakeFiles/tests.dir/__/src/SumFunc.cpp.o CMakeFiles/tests.dir/Line
arMotion1DTest.cpp.o CMakeFiles/tests.dir/__/src/LinearMotion1D.cpp.o  -o tests
/usr/lib/x86_64-linux-gnu/libgtest.a -lpthread
cd /home/gazihan/CxxTemplate/build/Debug/tests && /home/gazihan/cmake-3.15.1-Lin
ux-x86_64/bin/cmake -D TEST_TARGET=tests -D TEST_EXECUTABLE=/home/gazihan/CxxTem
plate/build/Debug/tests/tests -D TEST_EXECUTOR= -D TEST_WORKING_DIR=/home/gaziha
n/CxxTemplate/build/Debug/tests -D TEST_EXTRA_ARGS= -D TEST_PROPERTIES= -D TEST_
PREFIX= -D TEST_SUFFIX= -D NO_PRETTY_TYPES=FALSE -D NO_PRETTY_VALUES=FALSE -D TE
ST_LIST=tests_TESTS -D CTEST_FILE=/home/gazihan/CxxTemplate/build/Debug/tests/te
sts[1]_tests.cmake -D TEST_DISCOVERY_TIMEOUT=5 -P /home/gazihan/cmake-3.15.1-Lin
ux-x86_64/share/cmake-3.15/Modules/GoogleTestAddTests.cmake
make[2]: Leaving directory '/home/gazihan/CxxTemplate/build/Debug'
[100%] Built target tests
make[1]: Leaving directory '/home/gazihan/CxxTemplate/build/Debug'
/home/gazihan/cmake-3.15.1-Linux-x86_64/bin/cmake -E cmake_progress_start /home/
gazihan/CxxTemplate/build/Debug/CMakeFiles 0
gazihan@ubuntu:~/CxxTemplate/build/Debug$
```

Figure 1.37: The full build output

Here are some of the lines from this output. The following lines are the important ones related to the compilation and linkage of the main executable:

```
/usr/bin/c++    -g   -pthread -std=gnu++1z -o CMakeFiles/CxxTemplate.dir/
src/CxxTemplate.cpp.o -c /home/username/Packt/Cpp2019/CxxTemplate/src/
CxxTemplate.cpp
```

```
/usr/bin/c++    -g   -pthread -std=gnu++1z -o CMakeFiles/CxxTemplate.
dir/src/ANewClass.cpp.o -c /home/username/Packt/Cpp2019/CxxTemplate/src/
ANewClass.cpp
```

```
/usr/bin/c++    -g   -pthread -std=gnu++1z -o CMakeFiles/CxxTemplate.dir/
src/SumFunc.cpp.o -c /home/username/Packt/Cpp2019/CxxTemplate/src/SumFunc.
cpp
```

```
/usr/bin/c++    -g   -pthread -std=gnu++1z -o CMakeFiles/CxxTemplate.dir/
src/LinearMotion1D.cpp.o -c /home/username/Packt/Cpp2019/CxxTemplate/src/
LinearMotion1D.cpp

/usr/bin/c++   -g   CMakeFiles/CxxTemplate.dir/src/CxxTemplate.cpp.o
CMakeFiles/CxxTemplate.dir/src/ANewClass.cpp.o CMakeFiles/CxxTemplate.dir/
src/SumFunc.cpp.o CMakeFiles/CxxTemplate.dir/src/LinearMotion1D.cpp.o  -o
CxxTemplate -pthread
```

4.  The **c++** command here is just a symbolic link to the **g++** compiler. To see that it's actually a chain of symbolic links, type the following command:

    ```
    namei /usr/bin/c++
    ```

You will see the following output:

```
gazihan@ubuntu:~/CxxTemplate/build/Debug$ namei /usr/bin/c++
f: /usr/bin/c++
 d /
 d usr
 d bin
 l c++ -> /etc/alternatives/c++
   d /
   d etc
   d alternatives
   l c++ -> /usr/bin/g++
     d /
     d usr
     d bin
     l g++ -> g++-8
       l g++-8 -> x86_64-linux-gnu-g++-8
         - x86_64-linux-gnu-g++-8
gazihan@ubuntu:~/CxxTemplate/build/Debug$ 
```

Figure 1.38: The chain of symbolic links for /usr/bin/c++

Therefore, we will use **c++** and **g++** interchangeably throughout our discussion. In the build output that we quoted earlier, the first four lines are compiling each **.cpp** source file and creating the corresponding **.o** object file. The last line is linking together these object files to create the **CxxTemplate** executable. The following figure visually presents this process:

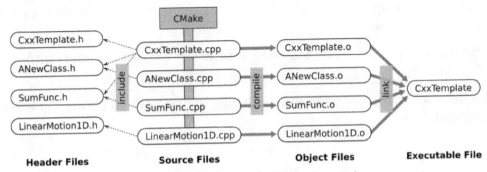

Figure 1.39: Execution stages of a C++ project

As the previous figure shows, the CPP files that are added to CMake as a part of a target, along with the header files that they included, are compiled to object files, which are later linked together to create the target executable.

5. To understand this process even further, let's carry out the compilation steps ourselves. In the terminal, go to the project folder and create a new folder named **mybuild** using the following commands:

```
cd ~/CxxTemplate
mkdir mybuild
```

6. Then, run the following commands to compile the CPP source files to object files:

```
/usr/bin/c++ src/CxxTemplate.cpp -o mybuild/CxxTemplate.o -c
/usr/bin/c++ src/ANewClass.cpp -o mybuild/ANewClass.o -c
/usr/bin/c++ src/SumFunc.cpp -o mybuild/SumFunc.o -c
/usr/bin/c++ src/LinearMotion1D.cpp -o mybuild/LinearMotion1D.o -c
```

7. Go into the **mybuild** directory and see what's there using the following command:

```
cd mybuild
ls
```

We see the following output as expected. These are our object files:

```
gazihan@ubuntu:~/CxxTemplate/build/Debug$ cd ~/CxxTemplate
gazihan@ubuntu:~/CxxTemplate$ mkdir mybuild
gazihan@ubuntu:~/CxxTemplate$ /usr/bin/c++ src/CxxTemplate.cpp -o mybuild/CxxTem
plate.o -c
gazihan@ubuntu:~/CxxTemplate$ /usr/bin/c++ src/ANewClass.cpp -o mybuild/ANewClas
s.o -c
gazihan@ubuntu:~/CxxTemplate$ /usr/bin/c++ src/SumFunc.cpp -o mybuild/SumFunc.o
-c
gazihan@ubuntu:~/CxxTemplate$ /usr/bin/c++ src/LinearMotion1D.cpp -o mybuild/Lin
earMotion1D.o -c
gazihan@ubuntu:~/CxxTemplate$ cd mybuild
gazihan@ubuntu:~/CxxTemplate/mybuild$ ls
ANewClass.o  CxxTemplate.o  LinearMotion1D.o  SumFunc.o
gazihan@ubuntu:~/CxxTemplate/mybuild$
```

Figure 1.40: Compiled object files

8.  In the next step, link the object files together to form our executable. Type the following command:

    ```
    /usr/bin/c++  CxxTemplate.o ANewClass.o SumFunc.o LinearMotion1D.o  -o
    CxxTemplate
    ```

9.  Now, let's see our executable among the list of files here by typing the following command:

    ```
    ls
    ```

    This shows the new **CxxTemplate** file in the following figure:

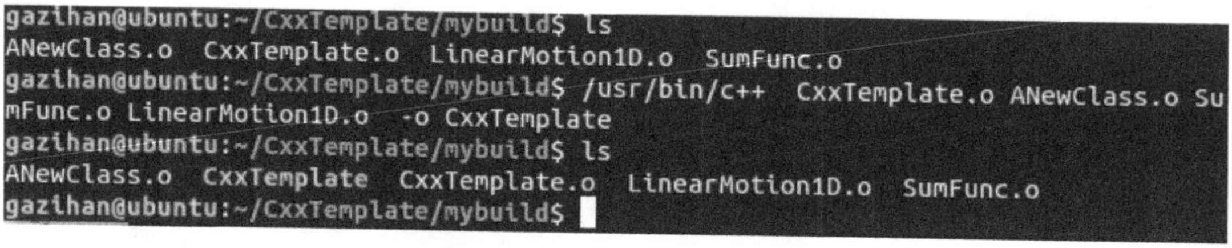

Figure 1.41: Linked executable file

10. Now, run our executable by typing the following command:

    ```
    ./CxxTemplate
    ```

    And see the output that we had before:

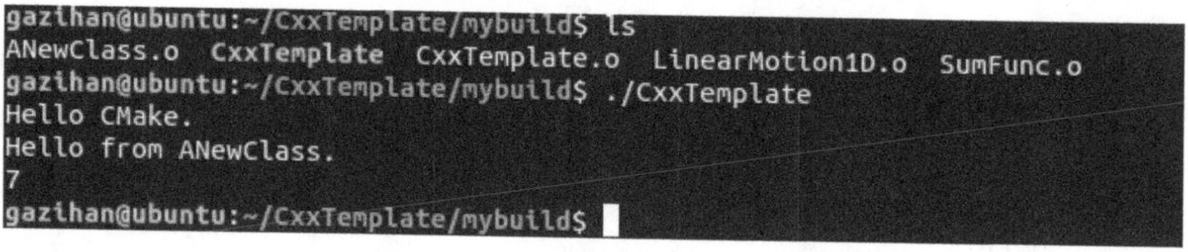

Figure 1.42: Executable file output

Now that you have examined the details of the build process and have recreated them yourself, in the next section, let's explore the linking process.

## The Linking Step

In this section, let's look at a connection between two source files and how they end up in the same executable. Look at the **sum** function in the following figure:

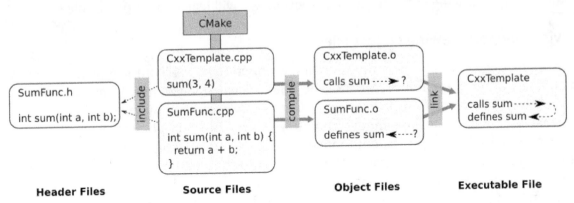

Figure 1.43: The linking process

The **sum** function's body is defined in **SumFunc.cpp**. It has a forward declaration in **SumFunc.h**. This way, the source files that want to use the **sum** function can know about its signature. Once they know its signature, they can call it and trust that the actual function definition will be there during runtime, without actually having any interaction with **SumFunc.cpp** where the function is defined.

After compilation, **CxxTemplate.cpp**, which calls the **sum** function, carries that call into its object file. Still, it does not know where the function definition is. The object file of **SumFunc.cpp** has that definition, but it has nothing to do with **CxxTemplate.o**, yet.

During the linking step, the linker matches the call in **CxxTemplate.o** with the definition in **SumFunc.o**. The call works fine in the executable as a result. Had the linker not found the definition of the **sum** function, it would have given a linker error.

The linker finds the **sum** function by its name and parameters. This is called **resolving a symbol**. The classes, functions, and variables defined in object files are placed in a symbol table and each reference to a symbol is resolved via a lookup at this table. When the symbol is not there, you receive a `symbol could not be resolved` error.

This took us through the two stages of the build process: **compilation** and **linking**. Notice that we used rather simpler commands compared to that of CMake, when we compiled our sources manually. Feel free to type **man g++** to see all the options there. Later, we discussed linking and how symbols are resolved. We also talked about possible issues with the linking step. In the next section, we will learn about object files.

## Diving Deeper: Viewing Object Files

For the linking step to work without errors, we need to have all our symbol references match our symbol definitions. Most of the time, we can analyze how things will be resolved just by looking at the source files. Sometimes, in complex situations, we may have a difficult time understanding why a symbol is not being resolved. In such situations, looking at the contents of object files to investigate references and definitions can be useful to resolve the problem. Besides linker errors, understanding object file contents and how linking works in general is useful for a C++ programmer. Knowing what is happening under the hood may help programmers understand the whole process in a better way.

When our source code is compiled to object files, our statements and expressions are converted to assembly code, which is the low-level language that the CPU understands. Each instruction in assembly contains an operation, followed by operators, which are registers of the CPU. There are instructions to load data to and from registers and operate on values in registers. The **objdump** command in Linux helps us view the contents of these object files.

> **Note**
>
> We will utilize Compiler Explorer, a nice online tool that is easier to use, where you can write code on the window to the left, and on the right, you can see the compiled assembly code. Here is the link to the Compiler Explorer: https://godbolt. org.

## Exercise 8: Exploring Compiled Code

In this exercise, we will use Compiler Explorer to compile some simple C++ code in which we define and call a function. We will investigate the compiled assembly code to understand how exactly names are resolved and calls are made. This will give us a better understanding of what happens under the hood and how our code works in the executable format. Perform the following steps to complete the exercise:

1. Add the following code in **Compiler Explorer**:

```
int sum(int a, int b) {
    return a + b;
}

int callSum() {
    return sum(4, 5);
}
```

We have two functions; one is calling the other. Here is the compiled output:

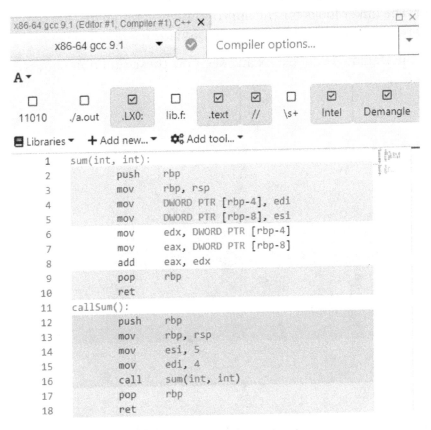

Figure 1.44: The compiled code

While it's not very clear, you can more or less make out what it is doing. We are not going to dive into the details of assembly code, but we will focus on how symbols are resolved during the linker stage. Let's focus on the following lines for now:

```
sum(int, int):

    ...

callSum():

    ...

        call  sum(int, int)

    ...
```

The `call sum(int, int)` line does what you expect: it calls the preceding `sum` function and places the arguments in some registers. The important point here is that the functions are identified by their names and the types of their parameters in order. The linker looks for the appropriate function with this signature. Note that the return value is not a part of the signature.

2.  Disable the **Demangle** checkbox and see how these function names are actually stored:

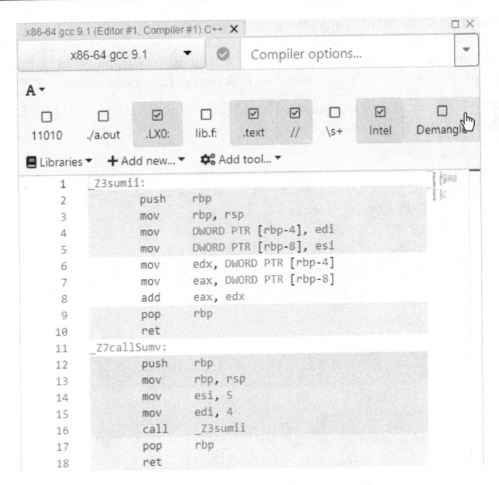

Figure 1.45: Compiled code without demangling

Here, our lines became this:

```
_Z3sumii:

...

_Z7callSumv:

...
        call    _Z3sumii

...
```

The preceding are the mangled names of these functions. After _Z, the number tells us how long the function name is, so that the following letters are correctly interpreted. After the function name, we have v for no parameters and i for an **int** parameter. You can change these function signatures to view other possible types.

3. Now, let's look at how classes are compiled. Add the following code into **Compiler Explorer** under the existing code:

```
class MyClass {
private:
    int a = 5;
    int myPrivateFunc(int i) {
        a = 4;
        return i + a;
    }
public:
    int b = 6;
    int myFunc(){
        return sum(1, myPrivateFunc(b));
    }
};

MyClass myObject;

int main() {
    myObject.myFunc();
}
```

Here is the compiled version of these added lines:

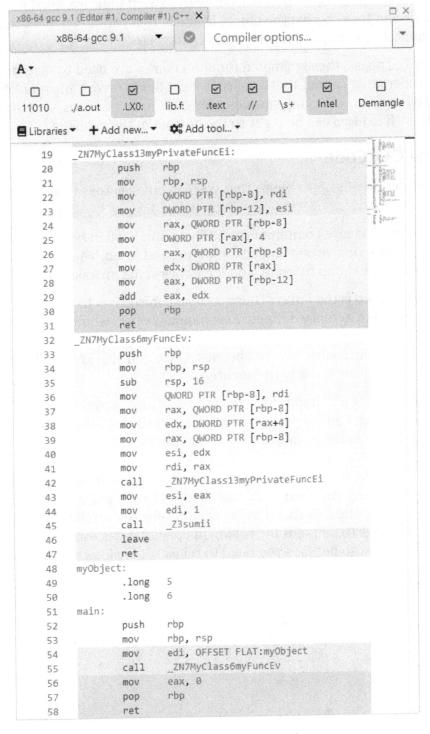

Figure 1.46: The compiled version

You may be surprised that there is no class definition in the compiled code. The methods are similar to global functions, but with a twist: their mangled names contain the class name and they receive the object instance as a parameter. Creating an instance simply allocates space for the fields of the class.

During the linker phase, these mangled function names are used to match callers with callees. For callers that cannot find a callee, we get linker errors. Most linker errors can be resolved by carefully checking sources. However, in some cases, viewing the object file contents with **objdump** can help get to the bottom of the problem.

## Debugging C++ Code

There are different levels of problems that you can come across while developing a C++ project:

- First, you may receive compiler errors. These can happen because of a mistake you made in syntax, or a wrong choice for a type, and so on. The compiler is the first hoop you have to jump through, and it catches some mistakes you may have made.

- The second hoop is the linker. There, a typical mistake is to use something that is declared, but not actually defined. This happens often when you use the wrong header file for a library—the header file advertises a certain signature that does not exist in any of the source files or libraries. Once you also jump through the linker hoop, your program is ready to execute.

- Now, the next hoop to jump through is to avoid any runtime errors. Your code may have compiled and linked properly, but it may be doing things that do not work, such as dereferencing a null pointer or dividing by zero.

To find and fix runtime errors, you have to interact with and monitor the running application in some way. An often-used technique is to add **print** statements to the code and monitor the logs that it generates, hoping to correlate the application behavior with the logs to pinpoint the region in code that has the problem. While this works for some cases, sometimes you need to take a closer look at the execution.

A debugger is a better tool to fight runtime errors. A debugger can let you run code line by line, continue running and pause on the lines that you want, investigate the values of memory, and pause on errors, among other things. This lets you watch what exactly is going on with memory as your program is running and identify the line of code that results in the unwanted behavior.

**gdb** is the canonical command-line debugger that can debug C++ programs. However, it may be difficult to use as debugging is inherently a visual task—you want to be able to look at lines of code, values of variables, and the output of the program at the same time. Luckily, Eclipse CDT includes a visual debugger that is easy to use.

## Exercise 9: Debugging with Eclipse CDT

You have been simply running your projects and viewing the output. Now you want to learn how to debug your code in detail. In this exercise, we will explore Eclipse CDT's debugging capabilities. Perform the following steps to complete the exercise:

1. Open the CMake project in Eclipse CDT.

2. To ensure that we have an existing run configuration, click **Run | Run Configurations**. There, you should see a **CxxTemplate** entry under **C/C++ Application**.

> **Note**
>
> Since we ran our project before, it should be there. If not, please go back and create it again.

3. Close the dialog box to continue.

4.  To start the debugger, find the toolbar entry that looks like an insect (bug) and click on the dropdown next to it. Select **CxxTemplate** to debug the main application. If it asks you to switch to the debug perspective, accept. Now, this is what Eclipse will look like:

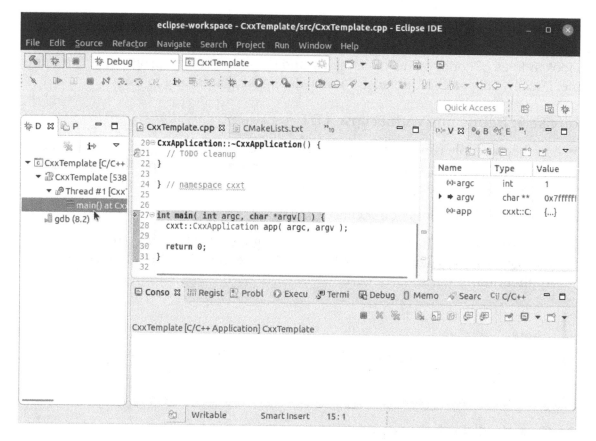

Figure 1.47: Eclipse debug screen

At the moment, our code froze at the very first line of our **main()** function, which is shown with the green highlight and the arrow in the center code view. On the left, we see the running threads, of which there is only one. On the right, we see the variables that are accessible in this context. On the bottom, we see the **gdb** output that Eclipse uses behind the scenes to actually debug the executable. Now, there is not much to be debugged with our main function.

5.  Click **Step Over** either under the **Run** menu or in the toolbar a couple of times and see that the application will terminate soon. In the end, you will see the **libc-start.c** library, which is the caller of the **main** function. You can close it and switch to your source files when done. When you do not see the red stop button anymore, you know that the program execution is over.

6. Edit our **main** function by adding the following code:

```
int i = 1, t = 0;
do {
  t += i++;
} while (i <= 3);
std::cout << t << std::endl;
```

The post-increment operator mixed with the occasional **do-while** loop can be a head-scratcher for some. This is because we try to execute the algorithm in our heads. However, our debugger is perfectly able to run it step by step and show us what exactly happens during execution.

7. Start debugging after adding the preceding code. Click on the dropdown next to the **Debug** button in the toolbar and select **CxxTemplate**. Press F6 a couple of times to step over in the code. It will show us how the variables change as well as the line of code that will be executed next:

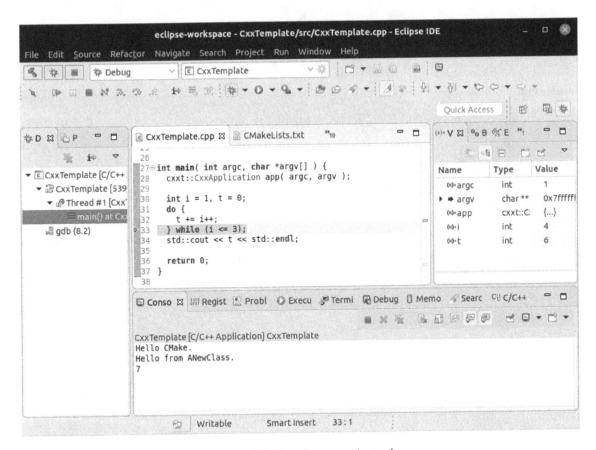

Figure 1.48: Stepping over the code

8. Seeing the variables change after the execution of each line of code makes the algorithm much clearer to understand. As you press F6, note that the following are the values after each execution of the t += i++; line:

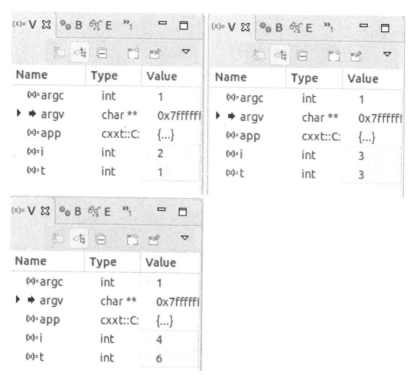

Figure 1.49: Variable states through time

The preceding output clearly explains how the values are changing and why **6** is printed at the end.

9. Explore other features of the debugger. While the variable view is useful, you can also hover over any variable and browse its value:

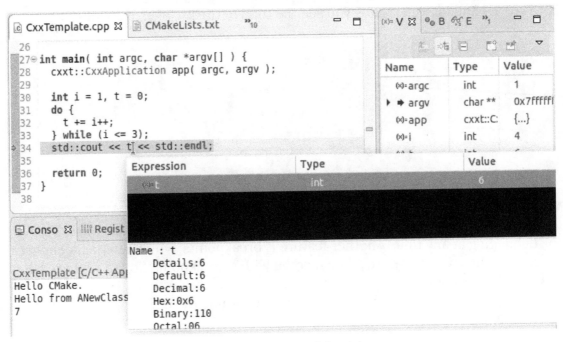

Figure 1.50: View option of the debugger

Furthermore, the **Expression** view helps you calculate things that are otherwise not clear from the values that you browse.

10. Click on **Expression** on the right-hand side and click on the **Add** button:

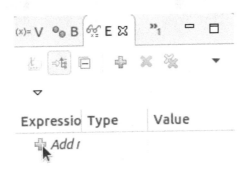

Figure 1.51: Adding an expression

11. Type **t+i** and hit *Enter*. Now you see the total in the list of expressions:

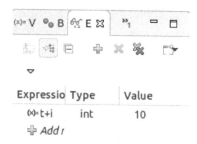

Figure 1.52: Expression view with a new expression

You can press the red square in the toolbar or select **Run | Terminate** to stop debugging at any time. Another feature is breakpoints, which tell the debugger to pause whenever it goes to a line marked with a breakpoint. So far, we have been stepping through our code line by line, which may be very time-consuming in a large project. Instead, you usually want to continue the execution until it arrives at the code that you are interested in.

12. Now, instead of going line by line, add a breakpoint in the line that does the printing. For this, double-click on the area to the left of the line number of this line. In the following figure, the dot represents a breakpoint:

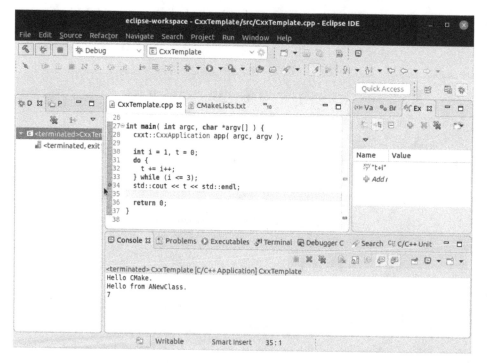

Figure 1.53: Workin with breakpoints

13. Now start the debugger. As usual, it will start paused. Now select **Run | Resume** or click on the toolbar button. It will run the three executions of the loop and pause at our breakpoint. This way, we saved time by stepping through code that we are not investigating:

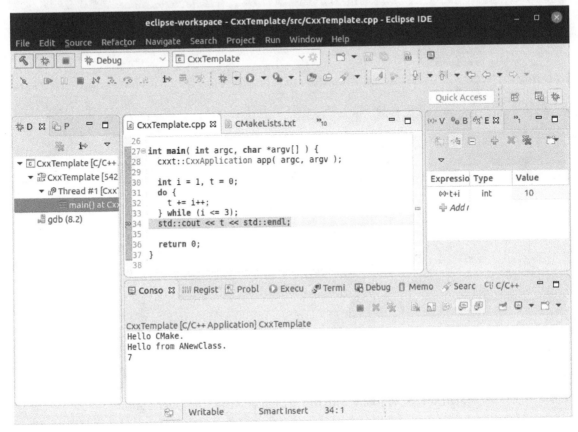

**Figure 1.54: Working with the debugger**

14. While we have been dealing with the loop that we added, we ignored the line that creates an **app** object. The **Step Over** command was skipping this line. However, we also have the option to go into the constructor call that is in this line. For that, we will use **Run | Step Into** or the corresponding toolbar button.

15. Stop the debugger and start it again. Click on **Step Over** to go to the line where the application is created:

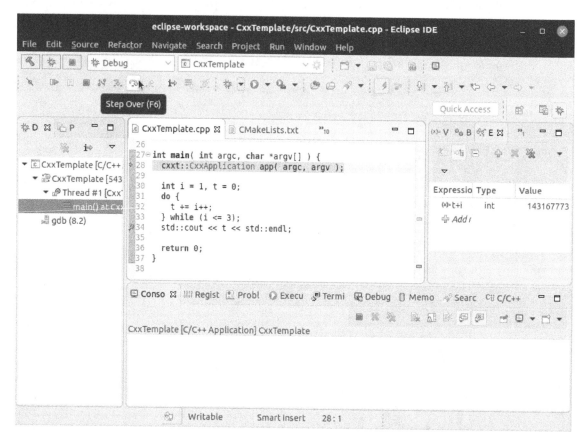

Figure 1.55: Working with the debugger – the Step Over option

16. The highlighted is the next line that would be executed if we step over again. Instead, press the Step Into button. This will take us into the constructor call:

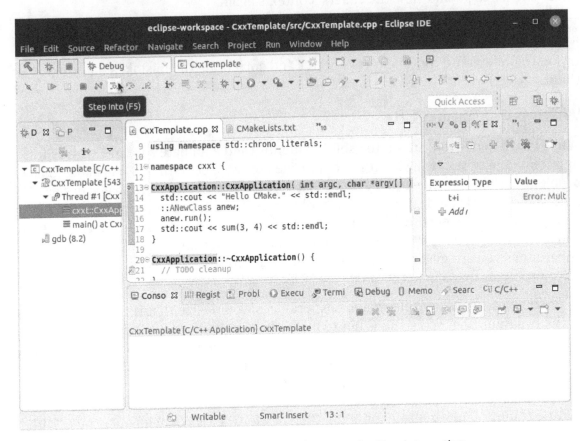

Figure 1.56: Working with the debugger – the Step Into option

This is a handy feature for diving deeper into the function instead of simply stepping over it. Also, notice the call stack in the left debug view. You can always click on the lower entries to go and view the callers' contexts again.

This was a brief introduction to the Eclipse CDT debugger, which uses GDB under the hood to give you a visual debugging experience. You may find debugging useful when trying to understand runtime errors better and correcting the mistakes that caused them.

# Writing Readable Code

While visual debuggers are quite useful to identify and eliminate runtime errors or unintended program behavior, it is a better idea to write code that is less likely to have problems to begin with. One way to do that is to strive to write code that is easier to read and to understand. Then, finding problems in code becomes more like identifying contradictions between English sentences and less like solving cryptic puzzles. When you are writing code in a way that is understandable, your mistakes will often be apparent as you are making them and will be easier to spot when you come back to solve problems that slipped through.

After some unenjoyable maintenance experiences, you realize that the primary purpose of the programs that you write is not to make the computer do what you want to, but to tell the reader what the computer will do when the program runs. This usually means that you need to do more typing, which IDEs can help with. This may also mean that you sometimes write code that is not the most optimal in terms of execution time or memory used. If this goes against what you have learned, consider that you may be trading a minuscule amount of efficiency for the risk of being incorrect. With the vast processing power and memory at our disposal, you may be making your code unnecessarily cryptic and possibly buggy in the vain quest for efficiency. In the next sections, we will list some rules of thumb that may help you write code that is more readable.

## Indentation and Formatting

C++ code, as in many other programming languages, is composed of program blocks. A function has a set of statements that form its body as a block. A loop's block statements will execute in iterations. An **if** statement's block executes if the given condition is true and the corresponding **else** statement's block executes otherwise.

Curly braces, or lack thereof for single-statement blocks, inform the computer, whereas indentation in the form of white space informs the human reader about the block structure. The lack of indentation, or misleading indentation, can make it very difficult for the reader to understand the structure of the code. Therefore, we should strive to keep our code well-indented. Consider the following two code blocks:

```
// Block 1
if (result == 2)
firstFunction();
secondFunction();
```

```
// Block 2
if (result == 2)
   firstFunction();
secondFunction();
```

While they are identical in terms of execution, it is much clearer in the second one that `firstFunction()` is executed only if `result` is **2**. Now consider the following code:

```
if (result == 2)
   firstFunction();
   secondFunction();
```

This is simply misleading. If the reader is not careful, they might easily assume that `secondFunction()` is executed only if `result` is **2**. However, this code is identical to the two previous examples in terms of execution.

If you feel like correcting indentation is slowing you down, you can use your editor's formatting facilities to help you. In Eclipse, you can select a block of code and use **Source | Correct Indentation** to fix the indentation of that selection, or use **Source | Format** to also fix other formatting issues with code.

Beyond indentation, other formatting rules such as placing the curly brace at the correct line, inserting spaces around binary operators, and inserting a space after each comma are also very important formatting rules that you should abide by to keep your code well-formatted and easy to read.

In Eclipse, you can set formatting rules per-workspace in **Window** | **Preferences** | **C/ C++** | **Code Style** | **Formatter** or per-project in **Project** | **Properties** | **C/C++ General** | **Formatter**. You can either select one of the industry-standard styles such as K&R or GNU, or you can modify them and create your own. This becomes especially important when you use **Source** | **Format** to format your code. For example, if you choose to use spaces for indentation but Eclipse's formatting rules are set to tabs, your code would become a mixture of tabs and spaces.

## Use Meaningful Names as Identifiers

In our code, we use identifiers to name many items—variables, functions, class names, types, and so on. For the computer, these identifiers are merely a sequence of characters to distinguish them from one another. However, for the reader, they're much more. The identifier should completely and unambiguously describe the item that it represents. At the same time, it should not be overly long. Furthermore, it should abide by the style standards that are in use.

Consider the following code:

```cpp
studentsFile File = runFileCheck("students.dat");


bool flag = File.check();


if (flag) {
    int Count_Names = 0;

    while (File.CheckNextElement() == true) {
        Count_Names += 1;
    }


    std::cout << Count_Names << std::endl;
}
```

While this is a perfectly valid piece of C++ code, it is quite difficult to read. Let's list the problems with it. First of all, let's look at the style problems of the identifiers. The **studentsFile** class name starts with a lowercase letter, which should have been uppercase instead. The **File** variable should have started with a lowercase letter. The **Count_Names** variable should have started with a lowercase letter and should not have had an underscore in it. The **CheckNextElement** method should have started with a lowercase letter. While these may seem arbitrary rules, being consistent in naming carries extra information about the name—when you see a word that starts with an uppercase letter, you immediately understand that it must be a class name. Furthermore, it is simply a distraction to have names that do not obey the standard in use.

Now, let's look beyond the style and inspect the names themselves. The first problematic name is the **runFileCheck** function. A method is an action that returns a value: its name should both clearly explain what it does as well as what it returns. "Check" is an overused word that is too vague for most situations. Yes, we checked it, it's there—what should we do with it then? In this case, it seems we actually read the file and create a **File** object. In that case, **runFileCheck** should have been **readFile** instead. This clearly explains the action being taken, and the return value is what you would expect. If you wanted to be more specific about the return value, **readAsFile** could be another alternative. Similarly, the **check** method is vague and should be **exists** instead. The **CheckNextElement** method is also vague and should be **nextElementExists** instead.

Another overused vague word is **flag**, which is often used for Boolean variables. The name suggests an on/off situation but gives no clue as to what its value would mean. In this case, its **true** value means that the file exists, and the **false** value means that the file does not exist. The trick for naming Boolean variables is to devise a question or statement that is correct when the value of the variable is **true**. In this example, **fileExists** and **doesFileExist** are two good choices.

Our next misnamed variable is **Count_Names**, or **countNames** with its correct capitalization. This is a bad name for an integer because the name does not suggest a number—it suggests an action that results in a number. Instead, an identifier such as **numNames** or **nameCount** would clearly communicate what the number inside means.

## Keeping Algorithms Clear and Simple

When we read code, the steps that are taken and the flow should make sense. Things that are done indirectly–byproducts of functions, multiple actions being done together in the name of efficiency, and so on–are things that make it difficult to understand your code for the reader. For example, let's look at the following code:

```cpp
int *input = getInputArray();
int length = getInputArrayLength();


int sum = 0;
int minVal = 0;
for (int i = 0; i < length; ++i) {
  sum += input[i];


  if (i == 0 || minVal > input[i]) {
    minVal = input[i];
  }


  if (input[i] < 0) {
    input[i] *= -1;
  }
}
```

Here, we have an array that we are processing in a loop. At first glance, it is not very clear what exactly the loop is doing. The variable names are helping us understand what is going on, but we must run the algorithm in our heads to be sure that what's being advertised by those names is really happening here. There are three different operations that are taking place in this loop. Firstly, we are finding the sum of all the elements. Secondly, we are finding the minimum element in the array. Thirdly, we are taking the absolute value of each element after these operations.

Now consider this alternative version:

```cpp
int *input = getInputArray();
int length = getInputArrayLength();


int sum = 0;
for (int i = 0; i < length; ++i) {
```

```
    sum += input[i];
}

int minVal = 0;
for (int i = 0; i < length; ++i) {
  if (i == 0 || minVal > input[i]) {
    minVal = input[i];
  }
}

for (int i = 0; i < length; ++i) {
  if (input[i] < 0) {
    input[i] *= -1;
  }
}
```

Now everything is much clearer. The first loop finds the sum of the inputs, the second loop finds the minimum element, and the third loop finds the absolute value of each element. Although it's much clearer and more understandable, you may feel like you are doing three loops, and therefore wasting CPU resources. The drive to create more efficient code may compel you to merge these loops. Note that the efficiency gains you have here would be minuscule; your program's time complexity would still be $O(n)$.

While creating code, readability and efficiency are two constraints that can often be in competition. If you want to develop readable and maintainable code, you should always prioritize readability. Then, you should strive to develop code that is also efficient. Otherwise, code that has low readability risks being difficult to maintain, or worse, risks having bugs that are difficult to identify and fix. Your program's high efficiency would be irrelevant when it is producing incorrect results or when the cost of adding new features to it becomes too high.

## Exercise 10: Making Code Readable

There are style and indentation problems in the following code. Spaces are used inconsistently, and the indentation is incorrect. Also, the decision on single-statement **if** blocks having curly braces or not is inconsistent. The following piece of code has problems in terms of indentation, formatting, naming, and clarity:

```cpp
//a is the input array and Len is its length
        void arrayPlay(int *a, int Len) {


            int S = 0;
            int M = 0;
            int Lim_value = 100;
            bool flag = true;
            for (int i = 0; i < Len; ++i) {
            S += a[i];

                if (i == 0 || M > a[i]) {
                M = a[i];
                }

                if (a[i] >= Lim_value) {
                    flag = true;
                }

                if (a[i] < 0) {
                a[i] *= 2;
                }
            }
        }
```

Let's fix these problems and make it compatible with a common C++ code style. Perform the following steps to complete this exercise:

1. Open Eclipse CDT.

2. Create a new **ArrayPlay.cpp** file in the **src** folder and paste the preceding code. Make sure you do not have any text selected. Then, go to **Source | Format** from the top menu and accept the dialog to format the entire file. This makes our code look like the following:

```cpp
//a is the input array and Len is its length
    void arrayPlay(int *a, int Len) {

        int S = 0;
```

```
        int M = 0;
        int Lim_value = 100;
        bool flag = true;
        for (int i = 0; i < Len; ++i) {
            S += a[i];

            if (i == 0 || M > a[i]) {
                M = a[i];
            }

            if (a[i] >= Lim_value) {
                flag = true;
            }

            if (a[i] < 0) {
                a[i] *= 2;
            }
        }
    }
```

Now that the code is a bit easier to follow, let's try to understand what it does. Thanks to the comments, we understand that we have an input array, **a**, whose length is **Len**. Better names for these would be **input** and **inputLength**.

3. Let's make that first change and rename **a** to **input**. If you are using Eclipse, you can select **Refactor | Rename** to rename one occurrence and all others will be renamed as well. Do the same for **Len** and rename it to **inputLength**.

4. The updated code will look like the following. Note that we do not need the comment anymore since parameter names are self-explanatory:

```
    void arrayPlay(int *input, int inputLength) {

        int S = 0;
        int M = 0;
        int Lim_value = 100;
        bool flag = true;
        for (int i = 0; i < inputLength; ++i) {
            S += input[i];

            if (i == 0 || M > input[i]) {
                M = input[i];
            }
```

```
            if (input[i] >= Lim_value) {
                flag = true;
            }

            if (input[i] < 0) {
                input[i] *= 2;
            }
        }
    }
```

5.  We have a couple of other variables defined before the loop. Let's try to understand them. It seems all it does with S is to add each element to it. Therefore, S must be **sum**. M, on the other hand, seems to be the minimum element—let's name it **smallest**.

6.  **Lim_value** seems to be a threshold, where we simply want to know whether it has been crossed. Let's rename it **topThreshold**. The **flag** variable is set to true if this threshold is crossed. Let's rename it to **isTopThresholdCrossed**. Here is the state of the code after these changes with **Refactor | Rename**:

```
void arrayPlay(int *input, int inputLength) {

        int sum = 0;
        int smallest = 0;
        int topThreshold = 100;
        bool isTopThresholdCrossed = true;
        for (int i = 0; i < inputLength; ++i) {
            sum += input[i];

            if (i == 0 || smallest > input[i]) {
                smallest = input[i];
            }

            if (input[i] >= topThreshold) {
                isTopThresholdCrossed = true;
            }

            if (input[i] < 0) {
                input[i] *= 2;
            }
        }
    }
```

Now, let's see how we can make this code simpler and easier to understand. The preceding code is doing these things: calculating the sum of the input elements, finding the smallest one, determining whether the top threshold was crossed, and multiplying each element by two.

7. Since all of these are done in the same loop, the algorithm is not very clear now. Fix that and have four separate loops:

```
void arrayPlay(int *input, int inputLength) {

    // find the sum of the input
    int sum = 0;
    for (int i = 0; i < inputLength; ++i) {
        sum += input[i];
    }

    // find the smallest element
    int smallest = 0;
    for (int i = 0; i < inputLength; ++i) {
        if (i == 0 || smallest > input[i]) {
            smallest = input[i];
        }
    }

    // determine whether top threshold is crossed
    int topThreshold = 100;
    bool isTopThresholdCrossed = true;
    for (int i = 0; i < inputLength; ++i) {
        if (input[i] >= topThreshold) {
            isTopThresholdCrossed = true;
        }
    }

    // multiply each element by 2
    for (int i = 0; i < inputLength; ++i) {
        if (input[i] < 0) {
            input[i] *= 2;
        }
    }
}
```

Now the code is much clearer. While it's very easy to understand what each block is doing, we also added comments to make it even more clear. In this section, we gained a better understanding of how our code is converted to executables. Then, we discussed ways of identifying and resolving possible errors with our code. We finalized this with a discussion about how to write readable code that is less likely to have problems. In the next section, we will solve an activity wherein we will be making code more readable.

## Activity 3: Making Code More Readable

You may have code that is unreadable and contains bugs, either because you wrote it in a hurry, or you received it from someone else. You want to change the code to eliminate its bugs and to make it more readable. We have a piece of code that needs to be improved. Improve it step by step and resolve the issues using a debugger. Perform the following steps to implement this activity:

1. Below you will find the source for **SpeedCalculator.cpp** and **SpeedCalculator.h**. They contain the `SpeedCalculator` class. Add these two files to your project.

2. Create an instance of this class in your `main()` function and call its `run()` method.

3. Fix the style and naming problems in the code.

4. Simplify the code to make it more understandable.

5. Run the code and observe the problem at runtime.

6. Use the debugger to fix the problem.

Here's the code for **SpeedCalculator.cpp** and **SpeedCalculator.h** that you will add to your project. You will modify them as a part of this activity:

```
// SpeedCalculator.h
#ifndef SRC_SPEEDCALCULATOR_H_
#define SRC_SPEEDCALCULATOR_H_

class SpeedCalculator {
private:
    int numEntries;
    double *positions;
    double *timesInSeconds;
    double *speeds;
public:
    void initializeData(int numEntries);
    void calculateAndPrintSpeedData();
};
```

```cpp
#endif /* SRC_SPEEDCALCULATOR_H_ */



//SpeedCalculator.cpp
#include "SpeedCalculator.h"
#include <cstdlib>
#include <ctime>
#include <iostream>
#include <cassert>

void SpeedCalculator::initializeData(int numEntries) {
    this->numEntries = numEntries;
    positions = new double[numEntries];
    timesInSeconds = new double[numEntries];
    srand(time(NULL));
    timesInSeconds[0] = 0.0;
    positions[0] = 0.0;
    for (int i = 0; i < numEntries; ++i) {
    positions[i] = positions[i-1] + (rand()%500);
    timesInSeconds[i] = timesInSeconds[i-1] + ((rand()%10) + 1);
    }
}

void SpeedCalculator::calculateAndPrintSpeedData() {
    double maxSpeed = 0;
    double minSpeed = 0;
    double speedLimit = 100;
    double limitCrossDuration = 0;

    for (int i = 0; i < numEntries; ++i) {
        double dt = timesInSeconds[i+1] - timesInSeconds[i];
        assert (dt > 0);
        double speed = (positions[i+1] - positions[i]) / dt;
            if (maxSpeed < speed) {
                maxSpeed = speed;
            }
            if (minSpeed > speed) {
                minSpeed = speed;
            }
        if (speed > speedLimit) {
            limitCrossDuration += dt;
        }
```

```
        speeds[i] = speed;
    }

    std::cout << "Max speed: " << maxSpeed << std::endl;
        std::cout << "Min speed: " << minSpeed << std::endl;
        std::cout << "Total duration: " <<
    timesInSeconds[numEntries - 1] - timesInSeconds[0] << " seconds" <<
    std::endl;
        std::cout << "Crossed the speed limit for " << limitCrossDuration << "
    seconds"<< std::endl;
        delete[] speeds;
    }
```

**Note**

The solution for this activity can be found on page 626.

## Summary

In this chapter, we learned how to create C++ projects that are portable and maintainable. We first learned how to create CMake projects and how to import them to Eclipse CDT, giving us the choice to use the command line or an IDE. The rest of the chapter focused on eliminating various problems in our projects. First, we learned how to add unit tests to a project and how to use them to ensure that our code works as intended. We continued this with a discussion about the compilation and linking steps that our code goes through and observed the contents of object files to gain a better understanding of executable files. Then, we learned how to debug our code visually in the IDE to eliminate runtime errors. We finished this discussion with a number of rules of thumb that help create readable, understandable, and maintainable code. These methods will come in handy on your C++ journey. In the next chapter, we will learn more about C++'s type system and templates.

# No Ducks Allowed – Types and Deduction

## Learning Objectives

By the end of this chapter, you will be able to:

- Implement your own classes that behave like built-in types

- Implement classes that control which functions the compiler creates (Rule of Zero/Rule of Five)

- Develop functions using auto variables, like you always have

- Implement classes and functions by making use of strong typing to write safer code

This chapter will give you a good grounding in the C++ type system and allow you to write your own types that work in that system.

# Introduction

C++ is a strongly typed, statically typed language. The compiler uses type information related to the variables that are used and the context in which they are used to detect and prevent certain classes of programming errors. This means that every object has a type and that type does not change, ever. In contrast, dynamically typed languages such as Python and PHP defer this type checking until runtime (also known as late binding), and the type of a variable may change during the execution of the application. These languages use the duck test instead of the variables type – that is, "if it walks and talks like a duck, then it must be a duck." Statically typed languages such as C++ rely on the type to determine whether a variable can be used for a given purpose, while dynamically typed languages rely on the presence of certain methods and properties to determine its suitability.

C++ was originally described as "C with classes". What does this mean? Basically, C provided a set of built-in fundamental types – int, float, char, and so on – along with pointers and arrays of these items. You aggregate these into data structures of related items using a struct. C++ extends this to classes so that you can define your own types completely with the operators that can be used to manipulate them, thereby making them first-class citizens in the language. Since its humble beginnings, C++ has evolved to be way more than just "C with classes", as it can now express the object-oriented paradigm (encapsulation, polymorphism, abstraction, and inheritance), the functional paradigm, and generic programming (templates).

In this book, we will focus on what it means for C++ to support the object-oriented paradigm. As your experience as a developer grows and you are exposed to languages such as Clojure, Haskell, Lisp, and other functional languages, they will help you to write robust C++ code. Dynamically typed languages such as Python, PHP, and Ruby have already influenced the way we write C++ code. With the arrival of C++17 came the introduction of the `std::variant` class – a class that holds whatever type that we choose (at compile time) and acts a lot like variables in dynamic languages.

In the previous chapter, we learned how to create C++ projects that are portable and maintainable using CMake. We learned how to incorporate unit tests in our projects to help write correct code and how to debug problems when they arise. We learned how the toolchain takes our code and runs it through a pipeline of programs to produce the executable files. We finished with some rules of thumb that help us to create readable, understandable, and maintainable code.

In this chapter, we will go on a whirlwind tour of the C++ type system, declaring and using our own types as we go.

# C++ Types

As a strongly and, statically typed language, C++ provides several fundamental types and the ability to define their own types with as much or as little functionality as needed to solve the problem at hand. This section will start by introducing the fundamental types, initializing them, declaring a variable, and associating a type with it. We will then explore how to declare and define a new type.

## C++ Fundamental Types

C++ includes several *fundamental types*, or *built-in types*. The C++ standard defines the minimum size in memory for each type and their relative sizes. The compiler recognizes these fundamental types and has built-in rules that define what operations can and cannot be performed on them. There are also rules for implicit conversions between types; for example, conversion from an int type to a float type.

> **Note**
>
> See the **Fundamental Types** section at https://en.cppreference.com/w/cpp/language/types for a brief description of all the built-in types.

## C++ Literals

C++ literals are used to tell the compiler the values that you wish to associate with a variable either when you declare it or when you assign to it. Each of the built-in types in the previous section has a form of literal associated with it.

> **Note**
>
> See the **Literals** section at https://en.cppreference.com/w/cpp/language/expressions for a brief description of the literals for each type.

## Specifying Types – Variables

As C++ is a statically typed language, it is necessary to specify the type of a variable when it is declared. When you declare a function, it is necessary to specify the return type and the types of arguments that are being passed to it. There are two choices for specifying the type to a variable when you declare it:

- **Explicitly**: You, as the programmer, are dictating exactly what the type is.

- **Implicitly** (using auto): You are telling the compiler to look at the value that was used to initialize the variable and determine its type. This is known as (auto) **type deduction**.

The general form of declaration for a scalar variable is one of the following:

```
type-specifier var;                 // 1. Default-initialized variable

type-specifier var = init-value;    // 2. Assignment initialized
variable

type-specifier var{init-value};     // 3. Brace-initialize variable
```

**type-specifier** indicates what type (fundamental or user-defined) you wish to associate with the **var** variable. All three forms result in the compiler allocating some storage to hold the value in, and all future references to **var** will refer to that location. **init-value** is used to initialize the storage location. Default initialization does nothing for built-in types and will call the constructor of a user-defined type according to the function overloading resolution to initialize the storage.

The compiler must know how much memory to allocate and provides an operator to determine how large a type or variable is – **sizeof**.

Based on our declarations, the compiler will set aside space in the computer's memory to store the data item that the variable refers to. Consider the following declarations:

```
int value = 42;        // declare value to be an integer and initialize to 42

short a_value{64};     // declare a_value to be a short integer and initialize
                       //    to 64

int bad_idea;          // declare bad_idea to be an integer and DO NOT
                       // initialize it. Use of this variable before setting
                       // it is UNDEFINED BEHAVIOUR.

float pi = 3.1415F;    // declare pi to be a single precision floating point
                       // number and initialize it to pi.
```

```
double e{2.71828};   // declare e to be a double precision floating point
                     // number and initialize it to natural number e.
auto title = "Sir Robin of Loxley"; // Let the compiler determine the type
```

If these are declared within the scope of a function, then the compiler allocates the memory for them from what is known as the stack. The memory layout for this may look something like the following:

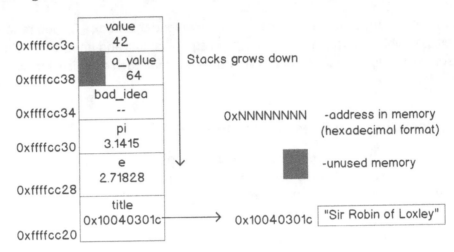

Figure 2A.1: Memory layout of variables

The compiler will allocate the memory in the order we declare the variables. The unused memory occurs because the compiler allocates the memory so that the fundamental types are generally accessed atomically and are aligned to the appropriate memory boundaries for efficiency. Note that **title** is of the **const char \*** type, which is a **pointer** that we'll discuss next, along with **const**. The **"Sir Robin of Loxley"** string will be stored in a different part of memory that is initialized when the program is loaded. We will discuss program memory later.

A slight modification of the scalar declaration syntax gives us the syntax for declaring arrays of values:

```
type-specifier ary[count];                          // 1. Default-initialized

type-specifier ary[count] = {comma-separated list}; // 2. Assignment
initialized

type-specifier ary[count]{comma-separated list};    // 3. Brace-initialized
```

This can be done for multi-dimensional arrays like so:

```
type-specifier ary2d[countX][countY];

type-specifier ary3d[countX][countY][countZ];

// etc...
```

Note that **count**, **countX**, and other items in the preceding declarations must be evaluated to a constant during compile time, otherwise this will result in an error. Additionally, the number of items in the comma-separated initializer list must be less than or equal to **count** or, again, there will be a compilation error. In the next section, we'll apply the concepts we've learned so far in an exercise.

> **Note**
>
> Before solving any practical in this chapter, download this book's GitHub repository (https://github.com/TrainingByPackt/Advanced-CPlusPlus) and import the folder of Lesson 2A in Eclipse so that you can view the codes for each exercise and activity.

## Exercise 1: Declaring Variables and Exploring Sizes

This exercise will set up all the exercises for this chapter and then get you familiar with declaring and initializing variables that are of a built-in type. You will also be introduced to the **auto declaration**, **arrays**, and **sizeof**. Let's get started:

1. Open Eclipse (used in *Chapter 1, Anatomy of Portable C++ Software*) and if the Launcher window appears, click on Launch.

2. Go to **File**, select **Project...** under **New ▶**, and go to Select C++ Project (not the C/ C++ Project).

3. Click **Next >**, clear the **Use default location** checkbox, and enter **Lesson2A** as the **Project name**.

4. Select **Empty Project** for the **Project Type**. Then, click on **Browse...** and navigate to the folder containing the Lesson2A examples.

5. Click on **Open** to select the folder and close the dialog.

6. Click **Next >**, **Next >**, and then **Finish**.

7. To help you with the exercises, we will configure the workspace to automatically save the files before builds. Go to **Window** and select **Preferences**. Under **General**, open **Workspace** and select **Build**.

8. Check the **Save automatically before build** box and then click **Apply and Close**.

9. Just like *Chapter 1, Anatomy of Portable C++ Software*, this is a CMake-based project, so we need to change the current builder. Click on **Lesson2A** in the **Project Explorer** and then on **Properties** under the **Project** menu. Select Tool Chain Editor under C/C++ Build from the left pane and set Current builder to Cmake Build (portable).

10. Click **Apply and Close**. Then, choose the **Project | Build All** menu item to build all the exercises. By default, the console at the bottom of the screen will display the **CMake Console [Lesson2A]**:

```
Problems  Tasks  Console    Properties  Call Graph  C/C++ Unit  Search  Debug
CMake Console [Lesson2A]
-- Check for working CXX compiler: /usr/bin/c++
-- Check for working CXX compiler: /usr/bin/c++ -- works
-- Detecting CXX compiler ABI info
-- Detecting CXX compiler ABI info - done
-- Detecting CXX compile features
-- Detecting CXX compile features - done
-- Found GTest: /usr/lib/libgtest.a
-- Configuring done
-- Generating done
-- Build files have been written to: /home/brian/Documents/advanced/Lesson2A/build/Debug
22:58:09 Buildscript generation finished (took 4155 ms)
```

Figure 2A.2: CMake console output

11. In the top-right corner of the console, click on the **Display Selected Console** button and then select **CDT Global Build Console** from the list:

Figure 2A.3: Selecting a different console

This will show the outcome of the build – it should show 0 errors and 3 warnings:

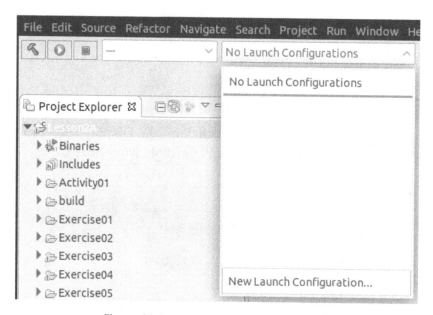

Figure 2A.4: Build process console output

12. As the build was successful, we want to run Exercise1. At the top of the window, click on the drop-down list where it says **No Launch Configurations**:

Figure 2A.5: Launch Configuration menu

13. Click on **New Launch Configuration....** Leave the defaults as is and click **Next >**.

14. Change **Name** to **Exercise1** and then click **Search Project**:

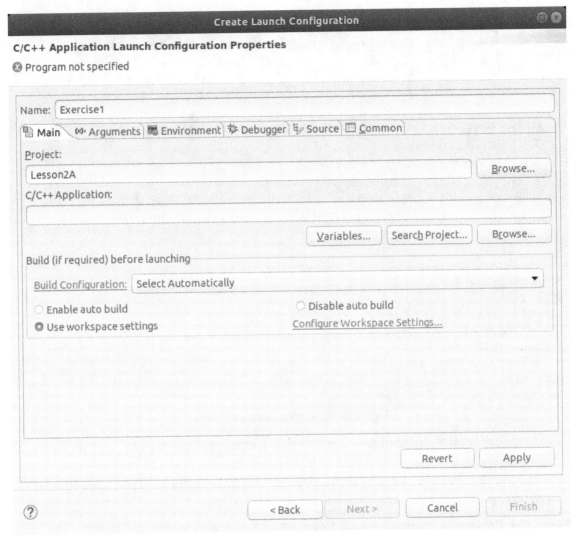

Figure 2A.6: Exercise1 Launch Configuration

15. From the list of programs displayed in the Binaries window, click on **Exercise1** and click **OK**.

16. Click **Finish**. This will result in exercise1 being displayed in the Launch Configuration drop-down box:

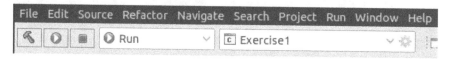

Figure 2A.7: Change to Launch Configuration

17. To run **Exercise1**, click on the **Run** button. Exercise1 will execute and display its output in the console:

```
Problems  Tasks  Console ⌧  Properties  Call Graph  C/C++ Unit
<terminated> (exit value: 0) exercise1 [C/C++ Application] /home/brian/Documents/advanc

------ Exercise 1 ------
sizeof(int) = 4
sizeof(short) = 2
sizeof(float) = 4
sizeof(double) = 8
sizeof(title) = 8
sizeof(ary) = 60 = 15 * 4
Complete.
```

Figure 2A.8: Output from exercise1

The program does nothing of worth – it just outputs the sizes of various types on your system. But this shows that the program is valid and can be compiled. Note that the numbers for your system may be different (especially the sizeof(title) value).

18. In the **Project Explorer**, expand **Lesson2A**, then **Exercise01**, and double-click on **Exercise1.cpp** to open the file for this exercise in the editor:

```
int main(int argc, char**argv)
{
    std::cout << "\n\n------ Exercise 1 ------\n";

    int value = 42;        // declare value to be an integer & initialize to
42
    short a_value{64};     // declare a_value to be a short integer &
                           // initialize to 64
    int bad_idea;          // declare bad_idea to be an integer and DO NOT
                           // initialize it. Use of this variable before
```

```
                            // setting it is UNDEFINED BEHAVIOUR.

        float pi = 3.1415F; // declare pi to be a single precision floating
                            // point number and initialize it to pi.

        double e{2.71828};  // declare e to be a double precision floating
point
                            // number and initialize it to natural number e.

        auto title = "Sir Robin of Loxley";
                            // Let the compiler determine the type
        int ary[15]{};      // array of 15 integers - zero initialized

        // double pi = 3.14159;  // step 24 - remove comment at front
        // auto speed;           // step 25 - remove comment at front
        // value = "Hello world";// step 26 - remove comment at front
        // title = 123456789;    // step 27 - remove comment at front
        // short sh_int{32768};  // step 28 - remove comment at front

        std::cout << "sizeof(int) = " << sizeof(int) << "\n";
        std::cout << "sizeof(short) = " << sizeof(short) << "\n";
        std::cout << "sizeof(float) = " << sizeof(float) << "\n";
        std::cout << "sizeof(double) = " << sizeof(double) << "\n";
        std::cout << "sizeof(title) = " << sizeof(title) << "\n";
        std::cout << "sizeof(ary) = " << sizeof(ary)
                  << " = " << sizeof(ary)/sizeof(ary[0])
                  << " * " << sizeof(ary[0]) << "\n";
        std::cout << "Complete.\n";
        return 0;
    }
```

One thing to note about the preceding program is that the first statement of the main function is actually an executable statement and not a declaration. C++ allows you to declare a variable just about anywhere. Its predecessor, C, originally required that all variables must be declared before any executable statements.

**Best Practice**

Declare a variable as close as possible to where it will be used and initialize it.

19. In the editor, uncomment the line marked as **step 24** by removing the delimiters (**//**) at the beginning of the line:

```
double pi = 3.14159;  // step 24 - remove comment at front
// auto speed;            // step 25 - remove comment at front
// value = "Hello world";// step 26 - remove comment at front
// title = 123456789;     // step 27 - remove comment at front
// short sh_int{32768};   // step 28 - remove comment at front
```

20. Click on the **Run** button again. This will cause the program to be built again. This time, the build will fail with an error:

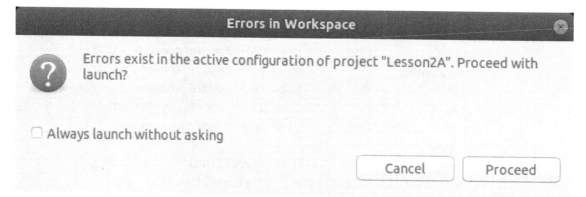

**Figure 2A.9: Errors in Workspace dialog**

21. Click on **Cancel** to close the dialog. If **CDT Build Console [Lesson2A]** is not displayed, then select it as the active console:

```
 Problems  Tasks  Console ⋈  Properties  Call Graph  C/C++ Unit  Search  Debug
CDT Build Console [Lesson2A]
[ 44%] Building CXX object CMakeFiles/Exercise1.dir/Exercise01/Exercise1.cpp.o
/home/brian/Documents/advanced/Lesson2A/Exercise01/Exercise1.cpp: In function 'int main(int, char**)':
/home/brian/Documents/advanced/Lesson2A/Exercise01/Exercise1.cpp:32:12: error: conflicting declaration 'double pi'
    double pi = 3.14159;  // step 24 - remove comment at front
            ^~
/home/brian/Documents/advanced/Lesson2A/Exercise01/Exercise1.cpp:22:11: note: previous declaration as 'float pi'
    float pi = 3.1415F; // declare pi to be a single precision floating
          ^~
make[2]: *** [CMakeFiles/Exercise1.dir/Exercise01/Exercise1.cpp.o] Error 1
CMakeFiles/Exercise1.dir/build.make:62: recipe for target 'CMakeFiles/Exercise1.dir/Exercise01/Exercise1.cpp.o' failed
make[1]: *** [CMakeFiles/Exercise1.dir/all] Error 2
make: *** [all] Error 2
CMakeFiles/Makefile2:183: recipe for target 'CMakeFiles/Exercise1.dir/all' failed
Makefile:94: recipe for target 'all' failed
"/usr/bin/make all" terminated with exit code 2. Build might be incomplete.

23:19:13 Build Failed. 4 errors, 0 warnings. (took 3s.220ms)
```

**Figure 2A.10: Duplicate declaration error**

This time, the build fails because we have tried to redefine the type of the variable, that is, pi. The compiler gives helpful information about where we need to look to fix it.

22. Restore the comment delimiter to the start of the line. In the editor, uncomment the line marked as **step 25** by removing the delimiters (//) at the beginning of the line:

```
// double pi = 3.14159;   // step 24 - remove comment at front
auto speed;               // step 25 - remove comment at front
// value = "Hello world";// step 26 - remove comment at front
// title = 123456789;     // step 27 - remove comment at front
// short sh_int{32768};   // step 28 - remove comment at front
```

23. Click on the **Run** button again. When the Errors in Workspace dialog appears, click **Cancel**:

```
Problems   Tasks   Console ⋈   Properties   Call Graph   C/C++ Unit   Search   Debug
CDT Build Console [Lesson2A]
[ 38%] Built target Exercise7
Scanning dependencies of target Exercise1
[ 44%] Building CXX object CMakeFiles/Exercise1.dir/Exercise01/Exercise1.cpp.o
/home/brian/Documents/advanced/Lesson2A/Exercise01/Exercise1.cpp: In function 'int main(int, char**)':
/home/brian/Documents/advanced/Lesson2A/Exercise01/Exercise1.cpp:33:5: error: declaration of 'auto speed' has no initializer
      auto speed;           // step 25 - remove comment at front
      ^~~~
make[2]: *** [CMakeFiles/Exercise1.dir/Exercise01/Exercise1.cpp.o] Error 1
make[1]: *** [CMakeFiles/Exercise1.dir/all] Error 2
make: *** [all] Error 2
CMakeFiles/Exercise1.dir/build.make:62: recipe for target 'CMakeFiles/Exercise1.dir/Exercise01/Exercise1.cpp.o' failed
CMakeFiles/Makefile2:183: recipe for target 'CMakeFiles/Exercise1.dir/all' failed
Makefile:94: recipe for target 'all' failed
"/usr/bin/make all" terminated with exit code 2. Build might be incomplete.

23:21:44 Build Failed. 4 errors, 0 warnings. (took 4s.477ms)
```

Figure 2A.11: Auto declaration error – no initialization

Again, the build fails, but this time, we did not give the compiler enough information to deduce the type of speed – auto typed variables MUST be initialized.

24. Restore the comment delimiter to the start of the line. In the editor, uncomment the line marked as **step 26** by removing the comment starting delimiter (//) at the beginning of the line:

```
// double pi = 3.14159;   // step 24 - remove comment at front
// auto speed;            // step 25 - remove comment at front
value = "Hello world";// step 26 - remove comment at front
// title = 123456789;     // step 27 - remove comment at front
// short sh_int{32768};   // step 28 - remove comment at front
```

25. Click on the **Run** button again. When the Errors in Workspace dialog appears, click **Cancel**:

```
CDT Build Console [Lesson2A]
[ 38%] Built target Exercise7
Scanning dependencies of target Exercise1
[ 44%] Building CXX object CMakeFiles/Exercise1.dir/Exercise01/Exercise1.cpp.o
/home/brian/Documents/advanced/Lesson2A/Exercise01/Exercise1.cpp: In function 'int main(int, char**)':
/home/brian/Documents/advanced/Lesson2A/Exercise01/Exercise1.cpp:34:13: error: invalid conversion from 'const char*' to 'int' [-fpermissive]
     value = "Hello world";// step 26 - remove comment at front
             ^~~~~~~~~~~~~
make[2]: *** [CMakeFiles/Exercise1.dir/Exercise01/Exercise1.cpp.o] Error 1
CMakeFiles/Exercise1.dir/build.make:62: recipe for target 'CMakeFiles/Exercise1.dir/Exercise01/Exercise1.cpp.o' failed
CMakeFiles/Makefile2:183: recipe for target 'CMakeFiles/Exercise1.dir/all' failed
make[1]: *** [CMakeFiles/Exercise1.dir/all] Error 2
make: *** [all] Error 2
Makefile:94: recipe for target 'all' failed
"/usr/bin/make all" terminated with exit code 2. Build might be incomplete.

23:22:58 Build Failed. 4 errors, 0 warnings. (took 1s.651ms)
```

Figure 2A.12: Assignment of an incorrect value type to a variable

This time, the build fails because we have tried to assign the wrong type of data, that is, "Hello world", which is a const char*, to a variable of type int, that is, **value**.

26. Restore the comment delimiter to the start of the line. In the editor, uncomment the line marked as **step 27** by removing the delimiters (//) at the beginning of the line:

```
// double pi = 3.14159;   // step 24 - remove comment at front
// auto speed;            // step 25 - remove comment at front
// value = "Hello world";// step 26 - remove comment at front
title = 123456789;    // step 27 - remove comment at front
// short sh_int{32768};   // step 28 - remove comment at front
```

27. Click on the **Run** button again. When the Errors in Workspace dialog appears, click **Cancel**:

```
🗎 Problems  ⚙ Tasks  ▣ Console ✕  ▭ Properties  ▦ Call Graph  ᴄᵘ C/C++ Unit  ⌕ Search  ⚙ Debug
CDT Build Console [Lesson2A]
[ 38%] Built target Exercise7
Scanning dependencies of target Exercise1
[ 44%] Building CXX object CMakeFiles/Exercise1.dir/Exercise01/Exercise1.cpp.o
/home/brian/Documents/advanced/Lesson2A/Exercise01/Exercise1.cpp: In function 'int main(int, char**)':
/home/brian/Documents/advanced/Lesson2A/Exercise01/Exercise1.cpp:35:13: error: invalid conversion from 'int' to 'const char*'
     title = 123456789;     // step 27 - remove comment at front
             ^~~~~~~~~
make[2]: *** [CMakeFiles/Exercise1.dir/Exercise01/Exercise1.cpp.o] Error 1
CMakeFiles/Exercise1.dir/build.make:62: recipe for target 'CMakeFiles/Exercise1.dir/Exercise01/Exercise1.cpp.o' failed
CMakeFiles/Makefile2:183: recipe for target 'CMakeFiles/Exercise1.dir/all' failed
make[1]: *** [CMakeFiles/Exercise1.dir/all] Error 2
make: *** [all] Error 2
Makefile:94: recipe for target 'all' failed
"/usr/bin/make all" terminated with exit code 2. Build might be incomplete.

23:24:09 Build Failed. 4 errors, 0 warnings. (took 2s.379ms)
```

Figure 2A.13: Assignment of an incorrect value type to an auto variable

Again, the build fails because we have tried to assign the wrong type of data, that is, 123456789 of type **int**, to title, which is a **const char\***. A very useful thing to note here is that **title** was declared with the **auto** type. The error message that was generated by the compiler tells us that title was deduced to be of the **const char\*** type.

28. Restore the comment delimiter to the start of the line. In the editor, uncomment the line marked as **step 28** by removing the delimiters (//) at the beginning of the line:

```
// double pi = 3.14159;   // step 24 - remove comment at front
// auto speed;             // step 25 - remove comment at front
// value = "Hello world";// step 26 - remove comment at front
// title = 123456789;      // step 27 - remove comment at front
short sh_int{32768};   // step 28 - remove comment at front
```

29. Click on the **Run** button again. When the Errors in Workspace dialog appears, click **Cancel**:

```
Problems  Tasks  Console ⊠  Properties  Call Graph  C/C++ Unit  Search  Debug
CDT Build Console [Lesson2A]
[ 38%] Built target Exercise7
Scanning dependencies of target Exercise1
[ 44%] Building CXX object CMakeFiles/Exercise1.dir/Exercise01/Exercise1.cpp.o
/home/brian/Documents/advanced/Lesson2A/Exercise01/Exercise1.cpp: In function 'int main(int, char**)':
/home/brian/Documents/advanced/Lesson2A/Exercise01/Exercise1.cpp:36:23: error: narrowing conversion of '32768' from 'int' to 'short int'
    short sh_int{32768};  // step 28 - remove comment at front
                 ^
make[2]: *** [CMakeFiles/Exercise1.dir/Exercise01/Exercise1.cpp.o] Error 1
CMakeFiles/Exercise1.dir/build.make:62: recipe for target 'CMakeFiles/Exercise1.dir/Exercise01/Exercise1.cpp.o' failed
CMakeFiles/Makefile2:183: recipe for target 'CMakeFiles/Exercise1.dir/all' failed
make[1]: *** [CMakeFiles/Exercise1.dir/all] Error 2
make: *** [all] Error 2
Makefile:94: recipe for target 'all' failed
"/usr/bin/make all" terminated with exit code 2. Build might be incomplete.

23:25:20 Build Failed. 4 errors, 0 warnings. (took 3s.21ms)
```

Figure 2A.14: Assignment of a value that's too large to fit in the variable

Again, the build fails, but this time because the value that we tried to initialize **sh_int** with (**32768**) does not fit in the memory allocated to the **short** type. A short occupies two bytes of memory and is considered a signed quantity of 16 bits. This means that the range of values that can be stored in a short is $-2^{(16-1)}$ to $2^{(16-1)}-1$, or **-32768** to **32767**.

30. Change the value from **32768** to **32767** and click on the **Run** button. This time, the program compiles and runs because the value can be represented by a **short**.

31. Change the value from **32767** to **-32768** and click on the **Run** button. Again, the program compiles and runs because the value can be represented by a **short**.

32. Restore the comment delimiter to the start of the line. In the editor, make any change you can think of to explore variable declaration using any of the fundamental types and their associated literals and then click on the **Run** button as often as necessary. Examine the output in the Build Console for any error messages because it might help you find the error.

In this exercise, we learned how to set up the Eclipse development, implement variable declaration, and troubleshoot problems with declarations.

## Specifying Types – Functions

Now that we can declare a variable to be of a certain type, we need to do something with those variables. In C++, we do things by calling a function. A function is a sequence of statements that deliver an outcome. That outcome could be a mathematical calculation (for example, an exponent) that is then sent to a file or written to a Terminal.

Functions allow us to break our solution into sequences of statements that are easier to manage and understand. As we write these packaged statements, we can reuse them where it makes sense. If we need it to operate differently based on the context, then we pass in an argument. If it returns a result, then the function needs a return type.

As C++ is a strongly typed language, we need to specify the types related to the functions that we implement – the type of value returned by the function (including no return) and the type of argument(s) that are passed to it, if any.

The following is a typical hello world program:

```
#include <iostream>


void hello_world()
{
    std::cout << "Hello world\n";
}


int main(int argc, char** argv)
{
```

```
    std::cout << "Starting program\n";

    hello_world();

    std::cout << "Exiting program\n";

    return 0;

}
```

Two functions have been declared in the preceding example – `hello_world()` and `main()`. The `main()` function is the entry point to every C++ program ever written and it returns an `int` value that is passed into the host system. It is known as the exit code.

Everything from the declaration of the return type up to the opening brace ({}) is known as the **function prototype**. It defines three things, namely the return type, the name of the function, and the number and types of an argument.

For the first function, the return type is `void` – that is, it returns no value; it has a name of `hello_world` and takes no arguments:

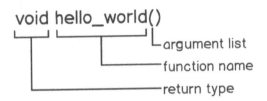

Figure 2A.15: Declaration of a function that takes no arguments and returns nothing

The second function returns an `int` value, has the name of `main`, and takes two arguments. These arguments are `argc` and `argv` and have the `int` and *pointer to a pointer of* `char` types, respectively:

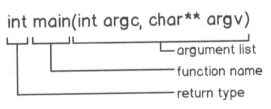

Figure 2A.16: Declaration of a function that takes two arguments and returns an int

Everything after the function prototype is known as the **function body**. The function body contains variable declarations and the statements to execute.

A function must be declared before it is used – that is, the compiler needs to know its arguments and its return type. If the function is defined in the file that it is to be used in after the call to it, then you can solve this problem by providing a forward declaration of the function before it is used.

A forward declaration is made by placing the function prototype that was terminated by a semicolon in the file before it is called. For **hello_world()**, this would be done as follows:

```
void hello_world();
```

For the main function, this would be done as follows:

```
int main(int, char**);
```

A function prototype does not need the names of the arguments, only the types. However, to help the users of the function, it is a good idea to keep them.

In C++, the definition of the function can be in one file and needs to be called from a different file. So, how does the second file know the prototype of the function it wishes to call? This is achieved by placing the forward declarations into a separate file known as a header file and including it in the second file.

## Exercise 2: Declaring Functions

In this exercise, we will test what the compiler needs to know when it encounters a function call and implements a forward declaration to resolve an unknown function. Let's get started.

1. Open the **Lesson2A** project in Eclipse, and then, in the **Project Explorer**, expand **Lesson2A**, then **Exercise02** and double-click on **Exercise2.cpp** to open the file for this exercise into the editor.

2. Click on the **Launch Configuration** drop-down menu and select **New Launch Configuration....**

3. Configure **Exercise2** to run with the name **Exercise2**. When that is complete, it will be the currently selected Launch Configuration.

4.  Click on the **Run** button. Exercise 2 will run and produce the following output:

```
Problems    Tasks   Console    Properties    Call Graph   C/C++ Unit
<terminated> (exit value: 0) exercise2 [C/C++ Application] /home/brian/Documents/advan


------ Exercise 2 ------
The greatest common divisor of 44 and 121 is 11
Complete.
```

Figure 2A.17: Output from the exercise2 program

5.  Go into the editor and change the code by moving the **gcd** function so that it's after **main**. It should look as follows:

```cpp
int main(int argc, char**argv)
{
    std::cout << "\n\n------ Exercise 2 ------\n";
    std::cout << "The greatest common divisor of 44 and 121 is " <<
gcd(44, 121) << "\n";
    std::cout << "Complete.\n";
    return 0;
}

int gcd(int x, int y)
{
    while(y!=0)
    {
        auto c{x%y};
        x = y;
        y = c;
    }
    return x;
}
```

6. Click on the **Run** button again. When the Errors in Workspace dialog appears, click **Cancel**. In the **CDT Build Console [Lesson2A]**, we will see the reason for the failure:

```
 Problems  Tasks  Console   Properties  Call Graph  C/C++ Unit  Search  Debug
CDT Build Console [Lesson2A]
/home/brian/Documents/advanced/Lesson2A/Exercise02/Exercise2.cpp:15:69: error: 'gcd' was not declared in this scope
        std::cout << "The greatest common divisor of 44 and 121 is " << gcd(44, 121) << "\n";
                                                                         ^~~
/home/brian/Documents/advanced/Lesson2A/Exercise02/Exercise2.cpp:15:69: note: suggested alternative: 'gcvt'
        std::cout << "The greatest common divisor of 44 and 121 is " << gcd(44, 121) << "\n";
                                                                         ^~~
                                                                         gcvt
make[2]: *** [CMakeFiles/Exercise2.dir/Exercise02/Exercise2.cpp.o] Error 1
CMakeFiles/Exercise2.dir/build.make:62: recipe for target 'CMakeFiles/Exercise2.dir/Exercise02/Exercise2.cpp.o' failed
make[1]: *** [CMakeFiles/Exercise2.dir/all] Error 2
make: *** [all] Error 2
CMakeFiles/Makefile2:72: recipe for target 'CMakeFiles/Exercise2.dir/all' failed
Makefile:94: recipe for target 'all' failed
"/usr/bin/make all" terminated with exit code 2. Build might be incomplete.

23:28:50 Build Failed. 4 errors, 0 warnings. (took 2s.201ms)
```

Figure 2A.18: Build failure due to undefined function

This time, the compiler does not know what to do with the call to the **gcd()** function. It has no knowledge of the function at the point it needs to call it, even though it is defined in the same file but after the call.

7. In the editor, place the forward declaration before the definition of the main function. Also add a semicolon (;) at the end:

```
int gcd(int x, int y);
```

8. Click on the **Run** button again. This time, the program compiles and the original output is restored.

In this exercise, we learned how to forward declare functions and troubleshoot compiler errors that occur when a function is not declared before it is used.

In the early versions of C compilers, this was acceptable. The program would assume that the function existed and returned an int. The functions' arguments could be inferred from the call. However, this is not true in the case of modern C++ as you must declare a function, class, variable, and so on before using it. In the next section, we'll learn about pointer types.

## Pointer Types

Because of its origins in the C language, that is, writing optimally efficient systems and having direct access to hardware, C++ allows you to declare a variable as a pointer type. It is of the following format:

```
type-specifier* pvar = &var;
```

This is the same as before, except for two things:

- Use of the special declarator asterisk (∗) to indicate that the variable named pvar points to a location or address in memory.

- It is initialized using the special operator ampersand (&), which in this context tells the compiler to return the address of the **var** variable.

As C is a high-level language, but with low-level access, pointers allow users to access memory directly, which is helpful when we wish to provide input/output to hardware and thus control it. Another use of pointers is to allow functions to be provided with access to common data items and remove the need to copy large amounts of data when calling functions as it defaults to passing by value. To access the value that's being pointed to by the pointer, the special operator asterisk (∗) is used to **dereference** the location:

```
int five = 5;              // declare five and initialize it
int *pvalue = &five;       // declare pvalue as pointer to int and have it
                           // point to the location of five

*pvalue = 6;               // Assign 6 into the location five.
```

The following diagram shows how the compiler allocates the memory. **pvalue** requires memory to store the pointer, while **five** needs memory to store the integer value of 5:

Figure 2A.19: Memory layout for pointer variables

When accessing a user-defined type via a pointer, there is a second special operator (->) that is also used for dereferencing member variables and functions. In modern C++, these pointers are referred to as **raw pointers** and the way in which they are used has changed significantly. Working with pointers in C and C++ has always proved challenging for programmers, and their incorrect use is the source of many problems, the most common being resource leaks. A resource leak is a scenario where a program has grabbed a resource (a memory, a file handle, or other system resource) for its use and fails to let it go when it's finished with it. These resource leaks can lead to performance issues, program failures, and even system crashes. The use of raw pointers in modern C++ to manage the ownership of a resource is now deprecated since smart pointers arrived in C++11. Smart pointers (implemented as classes in the STL) now do the housekeeping required to be a good citizen in your host system. More about this will be covered in *Chapter 3, The Distance Between Can and Should – Objects, Pointers, and Inheritance.*

In the preceding code, when **pvalue** is declared, the compiler allocates memory to store only the address of the memory it will be referring to. Like other variables, you should always ensure that a pointer is initialized before it is used as dereferencing an uninitialized pointer results in an undefined behavior. Exactly how much memory is allocated to store a pointer is dependent upon the system that the compiler is designed for and how many bits the processor supports. But all pointers will be of the same size, regardless of what type they point to.

A pointer can also be passed to a function. This allows the function to access the data being pointed to and possibly modify it. Consider the following implementation of swap:

```
void swap(int* data1, int* data2)

{

    int temp{*data1};        // Initialize temp from value pointed to by
    data1

        *data1 = *data2;     // Copy data pointed to by data2 into location

                             // pointed to by data1

        *data2 = temp;       // Store the temporarily cached value from
    temp

                             // into the location pointed to by data2

}
```

This shows how to declare pointers as arguments to a function, how to get the value from the pointer by using the dereferencing operator *, as well as how to set a value through the dereference operator.

The following example allocates memory from the host system using the new operator and releases it back to the host system using the delete operator:

```
char* name = new char[20];    // Allocate 20 chars worth of memory and
assign it

                              // to name.

    Do something with name


delete [] name;
```

In the preceding code, the first line creates an array of 20 characters using the array allocation form of the new operator. It makes a call to the host system to allocate 20 * sizeof(char) bytes of memory for our use. Exactly how much memory is allocated is up to the host system, but it is guaranteed to be at least 20 * sizeof(char) bytes. If it fails to allocate the required memory, then one of two things will happen:

- It will throw an exception

- It will return **nullptr**. This is a special literal that was introduced in C++11. Earlier, C++ used 0 or NULL to indicate a non-valid pointer. C++11 made this a strongly typed value as well.

On most systems, the first outcome will be the result, and you will need to deal with the exception. The second outcome is possible from two scenarios – calling the nothrow variant of new, that is, **new(std::nothrow) int [250]**, or on embedded systems where the overhead of exception processing is not sufficiently deterministic.

Finally, note that the call to delete uses the array form of the delete operator, that is, with square brackets, []. It is important to ensure that the same form is used with the new and delete operators. When new is used on a user-defined type (which will be discussed in the next section), it does more than just allocate memory:

```
MyClass* object = new MyClass;
```

In the preceding code, the call to new allocates sufficient memory to store MyClass and, if successful, it then proceeds to call the constructor to initialize the data:

```
MyClass* objects = new MyClass[12];
```

In the preceding code, the call to new allocates sufficient memory to store 12 copies of MyClass and, if successful, it then proceeds to call the constructor 12 times to initialize the data for each object.

Note that **object** and **objects**, which were declared in the preceding snippets of code, have the **same type**. Strictly speaking, **objects** should be a pointer to an array of MyClass, but it is actually a pointer to an instance of MyClass. **objects** points to the first instance in the array of MyClass.

Consider the following excerpt of code:

```
void printMyClasses(MyClass* objects, size_t number)
{
  for( auto i{0U} ; i<number ; i++ ) {
    std::cout << objects[i] << "\n";
  }
}
```

```
}


void process()

{

    MyClass objects[12];


    // Do something with objects
    printMyClasses(objects, sizeof(objects)/sizeof(MyClass));

}
```

In the process() function, **objects** is of the "array of 12 MyClass items" type, but when it is passed to **printMyClasses()**, it is converted (by the compiler) into the "a pointer to MyClass" type. This is by design (inherited from C) and is known as **array decay** and can be the cause of errors by new programmers. We could attempt to declare **printMyClasses()** as follows:

```
void printMyClasses(MyClass objects[12], size_t number)
```

This would still suffer from array decay as the compiler changes the argument object to MyClass*; it does not keep the dimension information in this case. Array decay is the reason that we need to pass number to the **printMyClasses()** function: so that we know how many items are in the array. C++ provides two mechanisms for dealing with array decay:

- Use of iterators to pass a range into the method. STL containers (see the C++ *Pre-Packaged Templates* section in *Chapter 2B, No Ducks Allowed – Templates and Deduction*) offer the **begin()** and **end()** methods so that we can obtain iterators that allow algorithms to traverse an array or part thereof.

> **Note**
>
> For C++20, the ISO standard committee is considering the inclusion of a concept known as Ranges that will allow both the begin and end iterators to be captured in one object.

- Use of templates (see the *Non-Type Template Arguments* section in *Chapter 2B, No Ducks Allowed – Templates and Deduction*).

## Exercise 3: Declaring and Using Pointers

In this exercise, we will implement functions that take pointers and arrays as arguments and compare their behavior while considering array decay. Let's get started:

1. Open the **Lesson2A** project in Eclipse, and then in the Project Explorer, expand **Lesson2A**, then **Exercise03**, and double-click on **Exercise3.cpp** to open the file for this exercise into the editor.

2. Click on the **Launch Configuration** drop-down menu and select **New Launch Configuration....** Configure **Exercise3** to run with the name **Exercise3**. When that is complete, it will be the currently selected Launch Configuration.

3. Click on the **Run** button. Exercise 3 will run and produce the following output:

```
 Problems   Tasks   Console ⊠  Properties  1010
                                             0101
<terminated> (exit value: 0) exercise3 [C/C++ Application]


------ Exercise 3 ------
value = 42
Setting value via pvalue
value = 96

sizeof(ary) = 40
elements in (ary) = 10
---print_array_size---
sizeof(ary) = 8
elements in (ary) = 2
---print_array_size2---
sizeof(ary) = 8
elements in (ary) = 2

buffer = 'Hello, World'
buffer = 'Hallo, World' - after *(p+1) = 'a';

Complete.
```

Figure 2A.20: Exercise 3 output

4. In the editor, insert a blank line somewhere and click on the **Run** button. (By changing the file, it will force the build system to recompile **Exercise3.cpp**.)

5.  If we now look at the **CDT Global Build Console**, we will see two warnings from the compiler:

```
 Problems  Tasks  Console ▨  Properties  Call Graph  C/C++ Unit  Search  Debug
CDT Global Build Console
Scanning dependencies of target Exercise3
[ 55%] Building CXX object CMakeFiles/Exercise3.dir/Exercise03/Exercise3.cpp.o
/home/brian/Documents/advanced/Lesson2A/Exercise03/Exercise3.cpp: In function 'void print_array_size2(int*)':
/home/brian/Documents/advanced/Lesson2A/Exercise03/Exercise3.cpp:22:48: warning: 'sizeof' on array function parameter 'ary'
    std::cout << "sizeof(ary) = " << sizeof(ary) << "\n";
                                            ^
/home/brian/Documents/advanced/Lesson2A/Exercise03/Exercise3.cpp:19:34: note: declared here
 void print_array_size2(int ary[10])
                            ^
/home/brian/Documents/advanced/Lesson2A/Exercise03/Exercise3.cpp:23:54: warning: 'sizeof' on array function parameter 'ary'
    std::cout << "elements in (ary) = " << sizeof(ary)/sizeof(ary[0]) << "\n";
                                                   ^
/home/brian/Documents/advanced/Lesson2A/Exercise03/Exercise3.cpp:19:34: note: declared here
 void print_array_size2(int ary[10])
                            ^
[ 61%] Linking CXX executable Exercise3
[ 61%] Built target Exercise3
[ 72%] Built target Exercise4
[ 83%] Built target Exercise5
[100%] Built target tests
```

Figure 2A.21: Exercise 3 compiler warnings

The preceding screenshot does not show the full warning message. For the gcc compiler being used here, the full warning is as follows:

```
exercise3.cpp:22:45: warning: 'sizeof' on array function parameter 'ary'
will return size of 'int*' [-Wsizeof-array-argument].
```

The warning gives us more information about the declaration that causes the issue. It traces back to the following function:

```
void print_array_size2(int ary[10])
{
    std::cout << "---print_array_size2---\n";
    std::cout << "sizeof(ary) = " << sizeof(ary) << "\n";
    std::cout << "elements in (ary) = " << sizeof(ary)/sizeof(ary[0]) <<
"\n";
}
```

Here, we can see an example of array decay – actually, **unexpected array decay**. Since the days of C, arrays and pointers are (almost) interchangeable. So, as far as the compiler is concerned, the argument that's passed to **print_array_size2()** is of the **int\*** type and is borne out by the warning stating that sizeof **will return size of 'int\*'**:

```
Problems  Tasks  Console ⌗  Properties  ▤
<terminated> (exit value: 0) exercise3 [C/C++ Application]

------ Exercise 3 ------
value = 42
Setting value via pvalue
value = 96

sizeof(ary) = 40
elements in (ary) = 10
---print_array_size---
sizeof(ary) = 8
elements in (ary) = 2
---print_array_size2---
sizeof(ary) = 8
elements in (ary) = 2

buffer = 'Hello, World'
buffer = 'Hallo, World' - after *(p+1) = 'a';

Complete.
```

Figure 2A.22: Exercise 3 partial output

The `sizeof(ary)/sizeof(arg[0])` calculation should return the number of elements in an array. The first `elements in (ary) = 10` is generated from the main function and ary was declared as `ary[10]`, so it is correct. The `elements in (ary) = 2` under the ---print_array_size2--- banner shows the problem with array decay and why the compiler generated a warning. Why the value of 2? On a test PC, a pointer occupies 8 bytes (64 bits), while an int only occupies 4 bytes, so we get 8/4 = 2.

6.  In the editor, locate the line in main() where ary is declared and change it to the following:

    ```
    int ary[15]{};
    ```

7.  Click on the **Run** button. If you examine the **CDT Global Build Console**, you will see that the number of errors is still the same. This is another symptom of array decay. Let's say we're given the following function prototype:

    ```
    void print_array_size2(int ary[10])
    ```

You may expect that trying to pass **int ary[15]** would cause an error or at least a warning since the argument prototypes do not match. As we stated previously, the compiler treats the argument as **int\* ary**, so the function may as well have been declared as follows:

```
void print_array_size2(int* ary)
```

8. In the editor, change the name of **print_array_size2** to **print_array_size** all through the file. Click on the **Run** button. When the Errors in Workspace dialog appears, click **Cancel**. Open the **CDT Global Build Console** and examine the error message:

```
Problems  Tasks  Console ⌗  Properties  Call Graph  C/C++ Unit  Search  Debug
CDT Build Console [Lesson2A]
[ 38%] Built target Exercise7
[ 50%] Built target Exercise1
Scanning dependencies of target Exercise3
[ 55%] Building CXX object CMakeFiles/Exercise3.dir/Exercise03/Exercise3.cpp.o
/home/brian/Documents/advanced/Lesson2A/Exercise03/Exercise3.cpp: In function 'void print_array_size(int*)':
/home/brian/Documents/advanced/Lesson2A/Exercise03/Exercise3.cpp:19:6: error: redefinition of 'void print_array_size(int*)'
 void print_array_size(int ary[10])
      ^~~~~~~~~~~~~~~~
/home/brian/Documents/advanced/Lesson2A/Exercise03/Exercise3.cpp:12:6: note: 'void print_array_size(int*)' previously defined
 void print_array_size(int* ary)
      ^~~~~~~~~~~~~~~~
```

Figure 2A.23: Redefinition error

This time, the compiler generates a redefinition error pointing to the two print_array_size methods that appear to have different argument types – **int\* ary** and **int ary[10]**. This is the confirmation that, when used as an argument to a function, **int ary[10]** generates the same as if **int\*** ary was declared.

9. Restore the file to its original state.

10. In the **main()** function, locate the line with **Step 11** in a comment and remove the comment at the beginning of the line. Click on the **Run** button. When the Errors in Workspace dialog appears, click **Cancel**. Open the **CDT Global Build Console** and examine the error message:

```
Problems  Tasks  Console ⌗  Properties  Call Graph  C/C++ Unit  Search  Debug
CDT Build Console [Lesson2A]

/home/brian/Documents/advanced/Lesson2A/Exercise03/Exercise3.cpp:19:34: note: declared here
 void print_array_size2(int ary[10])
                            ^
/home/brian/Documents/advanced/Lesson2A/Exercise03/Exercise3.cpp: In function 'int main(int, char**)':
/home/brian/Documents/advanced/Lesson2A/Exercise03/Exercise3.cpp:53:10: error: invalid conversion from 'const char*' to 'ch
       p = title;            // Step 11 - remove comment
           ^~~~~
make[2]: *** [CMakeFiles/Exercise3.dir/Exercise03/Exercise3.cpp.o] Error 1
make[1]: *** [CMakeFiles/Exercise3.dir/all] Error 2
make: *** [all] Error 2
```

Figure 2A.24: Redefinition error

The full error message is as follows:

```
exercise3.cpp:53:9: error: invalid conversion from 'const char*' to
'char*' [-fpermissive]
```

This occurs because the compiler determined the type of **title** to be **const char\***
and p of type **char\***. The const-ness is important. The p pointer allows us to
change the value of whatever it points at.

11. Take a look at the following line:

```
p = title;
```

Change it to the following:

```
title = p;
```

12. Click on the **Run** button. This time, it builds and runs properly. It is OK to assign a
non-const pointer to a const pointer.

In this exercise, we learned that arrays need to treated carefully when passing them
into functions as critical information (the size of the array) will be lost in the call.

## Creating User Types

The great thing about C++ is that you can create your own types using **struct**, **class**,
**enum**, or **union** and the compiler will treat it as a fundamental type throughout the
code. In this section, we will explore creating our own type and the methods that we
need to write to manipulate it, as well as some methods that the compiler will create for
us.

### Enumerations

The simplest user-defined type is the enumeration. Enumerations got an overhaul
in C++11 to make them even more type-safe, so we have to consider two different
declaration syntaxes. Before we look at how to declare them, let's figure out why we
need them. Consider the following code:

```
int check_file(const char* name)
{
  FILE* fptr{fopen(name,"r")};
  if ( fptr == nullptr)
     return -1;
  char buffer[120];
  auto numberRead = fread(buffer, 1, 30, fptr);
  fclose(fptr);
  if (numberRead != 30)
     return -2;
```

```
    if(is_valid(buffer))
        return -3;
    return 0;
}
```

This is typical of many C library functions where a status code is returned and you need the main page to know what they mean. In the preceding code, **-1, -2, -3,** and **0** are known as **magic numbers**. You need to read the code to understand what each number means. Now, consider the following version of the code:

```
FileCheckStatus check_file(const char* name)
{
    FILE* fptr{fopen(name,"r")};
    if ( fptr == nullptr)
        return FileCheckStatus::NotFound;
    char buffer[30];
    auto numberRead = fread(buffer, 1, 30, fptr);
    fclose(fptr);
    if (numberRead != 30)
        return FileCheckStatus::IncorrectSize;
    if(is_valid(buffer))
        return FileCheckStatus::InvalidContents;
    return FileCheckStatus::Good;
}
```

This uses an enumeration class to communicate the result and attach the meaning to the name of the values. A user of the function can now use the enumerations as the code is easier to understand and use. So, the magic numbers (related to the status) have been replaced with an enumerated value that has a descriptive title. Let's learn about the declaration of **FileCheckStatus** by referring to the following pieces of code:

```
enum FileCheckStatus          // Old-style enum declaration
{
    Good,                     // = 0 - Value defaults to 0
    NotFound,                 // = 1 - Value set to one more than previous
```

```
    IncorrectSize,              // = 2 - Value set to one more than previous

    InvalidContents,            // = 3 - Value set to one more than previous
};
```

If we want to use the values from the magic numbers, then we would declare them like so:

```
enum FileCheckStatus            // Old-style enum declaration
{
    Good = 0,

    NotFound = -1,

    IncorrectSize = -2,

    InvalidContents = -3,
};
```

Alternatively, by turning the order around, we can set the first value and the compiler will do the rest:

```
enum FileCheckStatus            // Old-style enum declaration
{
    InvalidContents = -3,       // Force to -3

    IncorrectSize,              // set to -2(=-3+1)

    NotFound,                   // Set to -1(=-2+1)

    Good,                       // Set to  0(=-1+1)
};
```

The preceding function can also be written as follows:

```
FileCheckStatus check_file(const char* name)
{
    FILE* fptr{fopen(name,"r")};
    if ( fptr == nullptr)
        return NotFound;
    char buffer[30];
    auto numberRead = fread(buffer, 1, 30, fptr);
    fclose(fptr);
```

```
   if (numberRead != 30)
      return IncorrectSize;
   if(is_valid(buffer))
      return InvalidContents;
   return Good;
}
```

Note that the scoping directive, **FileCheckStatus::**, is missing from the code, but it will still compile and work. This raises the issue of scope, which we will discuss in detail later in the *Visibility, Lifetime, and Access* section of *Chapter 2B, No Ducks Allowed – Templates and Deduction*. For now, know that every type and variable has a scope and the problem with old-style enumerations is that their enumerators are added into the same scope as the enumeration. Let's say we have two enumerations defined as follows:

```
enum Result
{
    Pass,
    Fail,
    Unknown,
};


enum Option
{
    Keep,
    Discard,
    Pass,
    Play
};
```

We now have a problem in which the **Pass** enumerator is defined twice and has two different values. Old-style enumerations also allow us to write a valid compiler but apparently nonsensical code, such as the following:

```
Option option{Keep};
Result result{Unknown};


if (option == result)
```

```
{
    // Do something
}
```

As we are trying to develop code that is clear in intent and easy to understand, comparing a result to an option has no meaning. The problem is that the compiler would implicitly convert the value into an integer and thus be able to compare it.

C++11 introduced a new concept that is referred to as an **enum class** or **scoped enumeration**. The scoped enumeration definition of the preceding code looks as follows:

```
enum class Result
{
    Pass,
    Fail,
    Unknown,
};

enum class Option
{
    Keep,
    Discard,
    Pass,
    Play
};
```

This means that the preceding code will no longer compile:

```
Option option{Keep};        // error: must use scope specifier Option::Keep
Result result{Unknown};     // error: must use scope specifier
Result::Unknown

if (option == result)       // error: can no longer compare the different
types
{
    // Do something
}
```

As the name implies, **scoped enumeration** places the enumerators inside the scope of the enumeration name. In addition, a scoped enumeration will no longer be implicitly converted into an integer (hence the if statement will fail to compile). You can still convert the enumerator into an integer, but you will need to cast it:

```
int value = static_cast<int>(Option::Play);
```

## Exercise 4: Enumerations – Old and New School

In this exercise, we will implement a program that uses enumerations to represent predefined values and determine the consequential changes required when they are changed to a scoped enum. Let's get started:

1.  Open the **Lesson2A** project in Eclipse, and then in the **Project Explorer**, expand **Lesson2A**, then **Exercise04**, and double-click on **Exercise4.cpp** to open the file for this exercise in the editor.

2.  Click on the **Launch Configuration** drop-down menu and select **New Launch Configuration....** Configure **Exercise4** to run with the name **Exercise4**.

3.  When that is complete, it will be the currently selected Launch Configuration.

4.  Click on the **Run** button. Exercise 4 will run and produce the following output:

```
🔲 Problems  🗐 Tasks  🖳 Console ⊠  🔳 Properties  ᛄᚸᛃ Call Graph  Cᵘ C/C++ Unit
<terminated> (exit value: 0) exercise4 [C/C++ Application] /home/brian/Documents/advanc

------ Exercise 4 ------
apple = 0
orange = 2
apple = 2
apple == orange
printOrange => 1
printOrange => 2
Complete.
```

Figure 2A.25: Exercise 4 output

5.  Examine the code in the editor. Currently, we can compare apples and oranges. At the definition of **printOrange()**, change the argument to be **Orange**:

```
void printOrange(Orange orange)
```

6. Click on the **Run** button. When the Errors in Workspace dialog appears, click **Cancel**:

```
  Problems   Tasks   Console ⊠   Properties   Call Graph   C/C++ Unit   Search   Debug
CDT Build Console [Lesson2A]
[ 66%] Building CXX object CMakeFiles/Exercise4.dir/Exercise04/Exercise4.cpp.o
/home/brian/Documents/advanced/Lesson2A/Exercise04/Exercise4.cpp: In function 'int main(int, char**)':
/home/brian/Documents/advanced/Lesson2A/Exercise04/Exercise4.cpp:45:18: warning: comparison between 'enum Apple' and 'en
     if (apple == orange)
         ^~~~~
/home/brian/Documents/advanced/Lesson2A/Exercise04/Exercise4.cpp:56:22: error: cannot convert 'Apple' to 'Orange' for ar
     printOrange(apple);
                 ^
```

Figure 2A.26: Cannot convert error

By changing the argument type, we forced the compiler to enforce the type of the value that was passed to the function.

7. Call the **printOrange()** function twice by passing the **orange enum** variable in the initial call and the **apple** variable in the second call, respectively:

```
printOrange(orange);
printOrange(apple);
```

This shows that the compiler is implicitly converting the orange and apple into an **int** so that it can call the function. Also, note the warning about comparing **Apple** and **Orange**.

8. Restore the **printOrange()** function by taking an int argument and changing the definition of the **orange enum** to the following:

```
enum class Orange;
```

9. Click on the **Run** button. When the Errors in Workspace dialog appears, click **Cancel**:

```
  Problems   Tasks   Console ⊠   Properties   Call Graph   C/C++ Unit   Search   Debug
CDT Build Console [Lesson2A]
         orange = Valencia;
                  ^~~~~~~
/home/brian/Documents/advanced/Lesson2A/Exercise04/Exercise4.cpp:48:18: note: suggested alternative: 'alloca'
         orange = Valencia;
                  ^~~~~~~
                  alloca
/home/brian/Documents/advanced/Lesson2A/Exercise04/Exercise4.cpp:55:23: error: cannot convert 'Orange' to 'int' for argun
     printOrange(orange);
                 ^
make[2]: *** [CMakeFiles/Exercise4.dir/Exercise04/Exercise4.cpp.o] Error 1
make[1]: *** [CMakeFiles/Exercise4.dir/all] Error 2
make: *** [all] Error 2
"/usr/bin/make all" terminated with exit code 2. Build might be incomplete.

23:43:31 Build Failed. 9 errors, 0 warnings. (took 3s.362ms)
```

Figure 2A.27: Multiple errors for scoped enum changes

10. Locate the first error listed for this build:

```
Problems  Tasks  Console ⊠  Properties  Call Graph  C/C++ Unit  Search  Debug
CDT Build Console [Lesson2A]
23:45:22 **** Incremental Build of configuration Debug for project Lesson2A ****
/usr/bin/make all
[ 11%] Built target Exercise2
[ 22%] Built target Exercise6
[ 38%] Built target Exercise7
[ 50%] Built target Exercise1
[ 61%] Built target Exercise3
[ 66%] Building CXX object CMakeFiles/Exercise4.dir/Exercise04/Exercise4.cpp.o
/home/brian/Documents/advanced/Lesson2A/Exercise04/Exercise4.cpp: In function 'int main(int, char**)':
/home/brian/Documents/advanced/Lesson2A/Exercise04/Exercise4.cpp:37:19: error: 'Hamlin' was not declared in this scope
     Orange orange{Hamlin};
                   ^~~~~~
```

**Figure 2A.28: First scoped enum error**

11. The first thing to note about scoped enums is that when you reference the enumerators, they must have a scope specifier. Therefore, in the editor, go and change this line to the following:

```
Orange orange{Orange::Hamlin};
```

12. Click on the **Run** button. When the Errors in Workspace dialog appears, click **Cancel**. Good news – the error count dropped to 8 from 9. Check the errors in the console and locate the first one:

```
Problems  Tasks  Console ⊠  Properties  Call Graph  C/C++ Unit  Search  Debug
CDT Build Console [Lesson2A]
[ 50%] Built target Exercise1
[ 61%] Built target Exercise3
Scanning dependencies of target Exercise4
[ 66%] Building CXX object CMakeFiles/Exercise4.dir/Exercise04/Exercise4.cpp.o
/home/brian/Documents/advanced/Lesson2A/Exercise04/Exercise4.cpp: In function 'int main(int, char**)':
/home/brian/Documents/advanced/Lesson2A/Exercise04/Exercise4.cpp:40:30: error: no match for 'operator<<' (operand types are
     std::cout << "orange = " << orange << "\n";
     ~~~~~~~~~~~~~~~~~~~~~~~~~^~~~~~~~~
In file included from /usr/include/c++/7/iostream:39:0,
                 from /home/brian/Documents/advanced/Lesson2A/Exercise04/Exercise4.cpp:9:
/usr/include/c++/7/ostream:108:7: note: candidate: std::basic_ostream<_CharT, _Traits>::__ostream_type& std::basic_ostream<
     operator<<(__ostream_type& (*__pf)(__ostream_type&))
     ^~~~~~~~~
```

**Figure 2A.29: Second scoped enum error**

This error reports that it is not able to find an insertion operator (<<) for an ostream that knows how to handle the **Orange** type. Because this involves a template-based class (which we'll talk about later), the error messages become very long-winded. Take a minute to look at all the messages that appear from this error to the next (red lines). It shows you what the compiler was trying to do to be able to compile that line.

13. Change the indicated line to read the following:

```
std::cout << "orange = " << static_cast<int>(orange) << "\n";
```

14. Click on the **Run** button. When the Errors in Workspace dialog appears, click **Cancel**. Good news – the error count dropped to 6 from 8. Check the errors in the console and locate the first one:

```
 Problems  Tasks  Console ⊠  Properties  Call Graph  C/C++ Unit  Search  Debug
CDT Build Console [Lesson2A]
23:48:55 **** Incremental Build of configuration Debug for project Lesson2A ****
/usr/bin/make all
[ 11%] Built target Exercise2
[ 22%] Built target Exercise6
[ 38%] Built target Exercise7
[ 50%] Built target Exercise1
[ 61%] Built target Exercise3
Scanning dependencies of target Exercise4
[ 66%] Building CXX object CMakeFiles/Exercise4.dir/Exercise04/Exercise4.cpp.o
/home/brian/Documents/advanced/Lesson2A/Exercise04/Exercise4.cpp: In function 'int main(int, char**)':
/home/brian/Documents/advanced/Lesson2A/Exercise04/Exercise4.cpp:45:15: error: no match for 'operator==' (operand types are
        if (apple == orange)
            ~~~~~~^~~~~~~~~
```

Figure 2A.30: Third scoped enum error

This error reports (finally) that you cannot compare apples and oranges. At this point, we decide that the program is attempting to do something that makes no sense and there is no point in attempting to fix the rest. We could fix this error by casting it to an int again, but we would need to cast for the next error as well. The final error would then be that Valencia is missing the **Orange::** scope specifier.

15. It is left as an exercise for you to get the file to compile again with **orange** as a scope enumeration.

In this exercise, we found that scope enums improve the strong type checking of C++ and if we wish to use them as an integral value, then we need to cast them, unlike non-scope enums, which are implicitly converted.

### Troubleshooting Compiler Errors

As seen from the preceding exercise, the compiler can generate a very large amount of error and warning messages from one error. This is why it is recommended to find the first error and fix it first. Development in IDEs or using build systems that color-code errors can make this easier.

## Structures and Classes

Enumerations are the first of the user-defined types, but they do not really extend the language so that we can express the solutions to our problems at the appropriate level of abstraction. Structs and classes, however, allow us to capture and group the data and then associate methods to manipulate that data in a consistent and meaningful manner.

If we consider the multiplication of two matrices, A (*m x n*) and B (*n x p*), which results in matrix C (*m x p*), then the equation for the ith row and jth column of C is as follows:

$$c_{ij} = \sum_{k=1}^{n} a_{ik} b_{kj}$$

Figure 2A.31: Equation of ith row and jth column

If we had to write it every time we wished to multiply two matrices, we would end up with many nested for loops. But if we could abstract a matrix into a class, then we could express it as simple as we express the multiplication of two integers or two floating-point numbers:

```
Matrix a;

Matrix b;

// Code to initialize the matrices


auto c = a * b;
```

This is the beauty of object-oriented design – data encapsulation and the abstraction of concepts are explained at such a level that we can easily understand what the program is trying to achieve without getting buried in the details. Once we have established that the matrix multiplication is correctly implemented, then we are free to focus on solving our problem at a higher level.

The discussion that follows refers to classes, but it applies equally to structs and, mostly, to unions. We will outline the differences between classes, structs, and unions after we learn how to define and use a class.

## Fraction Class

To show you how to define and use a class, we will work on developing the **Fraction** class to implement rational numbers. When defined, we can use **Fraction** like any other built-in type (add, subtract, multiply, divide) without worrying about the details – this is abstraction. We can now just think and reason about a fraction at a higher level, that is, an abstract level.

The **Fraction** class will do the following:

- Contain two integer member variables, **m_numerator** and **m_denominator**
- Provide methods to copy itself, assign to it, multiply, divide, add, and subtract
- Provide a method to write to an output stream

To attain the preceding objective, we have the following definitions:

| Addition | $\dfrac{a}{b} + \dfrac{c}{d} = \dfrac{a.d + b.c}{b.d}$ | Multiplication | $\dfrac{a}{b} \times \dfrac{c}{d} = \dfrac{a.c}{b.d}$ |
|---|---|---|---|
| Subtraction | $\dfrac{a}{b} - \dfrac{c}{d} = \dfrac{a.d - b.c}{b.d}$ | Division | $\dfrac{a}{b} \div \dfrac{c}{d} = \dfrac{a}{b} \times \dfrac{d}{c} = \dfrac{a.d}{b.c}$ |

**Figure 2A.32: Definitions of operations**

In addition, the operations that we perform will need to normalize the fraction by reducing it to the lowest terms. To do this, the numerator and the denominator are both divided by their greatest common divisor (GCD).

## Constructors, Initialization, and Destructors

A class definition, as expressed in C++ code, is the pattern that's used for creating objects in memory and manipulating objects through their methods. The first thing that we need to do is tell the compiler that we wish to declare a new type – a class. To declare the **Fraction** class, we start with the following:

```
class Fraction

{

};
```

We place this in a header file, **Fraction.h**, as we wish to reuse this class specification in other areas of our code.

The next thing we need to do is introduce the data to be stored in the class, which in this case are **m_numerator** and **m_denominator**. These are both of the int type:

```
class Fraction

{

    int m_numerator;

    int m_denominator;

};
```

We have now declared the data to be stored and given them names that anyone familiar with mathematics would understand regarding what each member variable stores:

$$fraction = \frac{numerator}{denominator}$$

**Figure 2A.33: Formula of fraction**

As this is a class, by default, any item that's declared is assumed to be **private**. This means that no external entity can access these variables. It is this feature of hiding (making data private, and for that matter, some methods) that enables encapsulation in C++. C++ has three class access modifiers:

- **public**: This means that the member (variable or function) is accessible from anywhere outside of the class.

- **private**: This means that the member (variable or function) cannot be accessed from outside the class. In fact, it cannot even be viewed. Private variables and functions can only be accessed from within the class or by a friend method or class. The private members (variables and functions) are used by the public functions to achieve the desired functionality.

- **protected**: This is a cross between private and public. From outside the class, the variable or function is private. However, for any class that is derived from the class that declares the protected members, they are treated as public.

At this point in our definition of the class, this is not very useful. Let's change the declaration to the following:

```
class Fraction
{
public:
    int m_numerator;
    int m_denominator;
};
```

By doing this, we can access the internal variables. The `Fraction number;` variable declaration will cause the compiler to do two things:

- Allocate enough memory to hold both the data items (depending on the types, this may or may not involve padding, that is, the inclusion or addition of unused memory to align members for the most efficient access). The `sizeof` operator can tell us how much memory is allocated for our class.

- Initialize the data items by calling the **default constructor**.

These steps are the same that the compiler does for built-in types, that is, step 2 does nothing, leading to uninitialized variables. But what is this default constructor? And what does it do?

Firstly, the default constructor is a special member function. It is one of the many possible constructors, three of which are deemed special member functions. Constructors can be declared with zero, one, or more arguments, just like any other function, but they do NOT specify a return type. Constructors serve the special purpose of initializing all the member variables to place the object into a well-defined state. If the member variables are themselves a class, then it may not be necessary to specify how to initialize the variable. It the member variable is of a built-in type, then we will need to provide the initial values for them.

## Class Special Member Functions

When we define a new type (struct or class), the compiler will create up to six (6) special member functions for us:

- **Default Constructor** (`Fraction::Fraction()`): This is called when no arguments are provided (such as in the preceding section). This can be achieved by either having no argument list for the constructor or by defining a default value for all the arguments, such as `Fraction(int numerator=0, denominator=1)`. The compiler provides an **implicit inline** default constructor that performs the default initialization of member variables – for built-in types, this means do nothing.

- **Destructor** (`Fraction::~Fraction()`): This is a special member function that is called when the object's lifetime ends. Its purpose is to release any resources that were allocated and kept by the object during its lifetime. The compiler provides a **public inline** member function that calls the destructors of the member variables.

- **Copy Constructor** (`Fraction::Fraction(const Fraction&)`): This is another constructor where the first parameter is a form of **Fraction&** and there are no other arguments, or the remainder of the arguments have default values. The form of the first argument is one of **Fraction&, const Fraction&, volatile Fraction&**, or **const volatile Fraction&**. We will deal with **const** later but not with **volatile** in this book. The compiler provides a **non-explicit public inline** member function, usually with the form of **Fraction::Fraction(const Fraction&)**, that copies each of the member variables in the order of initialization.

- **Copy Assignment** (`Fraction& Fraction::operator=(Fraction&)`): This is a member function with the name **operator=** and the first argument is either a value or any of the reference types of the class, in this case, **Fraction, Fraction&, const Fraction&, volatile Fraction&**, or **const volatile Fraction&**. The compiler provides a **public inline** member function, usually with the form of **Fraction::Fraction(const Fraction&)**, that copies each of the member variables in the order of initialization.

- **Move Constructor** (`Fraction::Fraction(Fraction&&)`): This is a new type of constructor that was introduced in C++11 where the first parameter is a form of `Fraction&&` and there are no other arguments, or the remainder of the arguments have default values. The form of the first argument is one of `Fraction&&, const Fraction&&, volatile Fraction&&`, or `const volatile Fraction&&`. The compiler provides a **non-explicit public inline** member function, usually with the form of `Fraction::Fraction(Fraction&&)`, that moves each of the member variables in the order of initialization.

- **Move Assignment** (`Fraction& Fraction::operator=(Fraction&&)`): This is a new type of assignment operator that was introduced in C++11 and is a member function with the name **operator=**, and the first argument is any of the forms that are allowed for the move constructor. The compiler provides a **public inline** member function, usually with the form of `Fraction::Fraction(Fraction&&)`, that copies each of the member variables in the order of initialization.

Except for the default constructor, these functions deal with managing the resources owned by this class – that is, how to copy/move them and how to dispose of them. On the other hand, the default constructor is more like any other constructor that takes values – it only initializes the resources.

We can declare any of these special functions, force them to be defaulted (that is, have the compiler generate the default version), or force them to not be created. There are also rules about when these are automatically generated in the presence of the other special functions. The first four functions are relatively straightforward conceptually, but the two "move" special member functions take some additional explanation. We will deal with what is known as move semantics in detail in *Chapter 3, The Distance Between Can and Should – Objects, Pointers, and Inheritance*, but for now it is essentially what it indicates – it moves something from one object to the other.

## Implicit Versus Explicit Constructors

The preceding description talks about the compiler generating implicit or non-explicit constructors. If a constructor exists that can be called with one argument, for example, a Copy Constructor, or a Move Constructor, by default, the compiler is allowed to invoke it if necessary so that it can convert it from one type to another type, allowing an expression, function call, or assignment to be encoded. This is not always a desired behavior, and we may wish to prevent the implicit conversion and ensure that if the user of our class really wants that conversion, then they have to write it out in the program. To achieve this, we prefix the declaration of the constructor with the **explicit** keyword, like so:

```
explicit Fraction(int numerator, int denominator = 1);
```

The explicit keyword can be applied to other operators as well, where the compiler may use it for type conversion.

## Class Special Member Functions – Compiler Generation Rules

Firstly, the **Default Constructor** will not be generated if we declare any other form of constructor – default, copy, move, or user-defined. None of the other special member functions affect its generation.

Secondly, a **Destructor** will not be generated if a destructor is declared. None of the other special member functions affect its generation.

The generation of the other four special functions is dependent on the presence of the declaration of the destructor or one of the other special functions, as shown in the following table:

| If the user declares | Then the compiler generates | | | |
| --- | --- | --- | --- | --- |
| | Copy Constructor | Copy assignment | Move Constructor | Move assignment |
| Copy Constructor | No - user defined | Yes | No | No |
| Copy assignment | Yes | No - user defined | No | No |
| Move Constructor | Deleted | Deleted | No - user defined | No |
| Move assignment | Deleted | Deleted | No | No - user defined |
| Destructor | Yes | Yes | No | No |

Figure 2A.34: Special Member Function Generation Rules

## Defaulting and Deleting Special Member Functions

Prior to C++11, if we wanted to prevent the use of a copy constructor or copy assignment member function, then we had to declare the function as private and not provide a definition of the function:

```
class Fraction
{
public:
  Fraction();


private:
  Fraction(const Fraction&);
```

```
Fraction& operator=(const Fraction&);
```

```
};
```

In this manner, we ensured that if anyone tried to access the copy constructor or copy assignment from outside the class, then the compiler would generate an error stating that the function is not accessible. This still declares the functions, and they are accessible from within the class. It is an effective means, but not perfect, to remove these special member functions from use.

But we can do better since C++11 introduced two new declaration forms that allow us to override the default behavior of the compiler, as defined in the preceding rules.

Firstly, we can force the compiler to not generate the method by declaring it with the = **delete** suffix, like so:

```
Fraction(const Fraction&) = delete;
```

> **Note**
>
> We can omit the name of the parameter if it is not used. This is true for any function or member function. In fact, depending on the warning level that's been set for the compiler, it may even generate a warning that the argument is not being used.

Alternatively, we can force the compiler to generate its default implementation of a special member function by using the = **default** suffix, like so:

```
Fraction(const Fraction&) = default;
```

If this is only the declaration of the function, then we can also omit the name of the argument. Although, good practice dictates that we should name the argument to indicate its use. That way, the users of our classes do not need to look at the implementation of calling the function.

> **Note**
>
> Declaring a special member function using the default suffix is deemed to be a user-defined member function for the purpose of the aforementioned rules.

## Rule of Three/Five and Rule of Zero

As we discussed previously, with the exception of the default constructor, the special member functions deal with the semantics of managing the resources owned by this class – that is, how to copy/move them and how to dispose of them. This leads to two "rules" within the C++ community about dealing with the special functions.

Prior to C++11, there was the **Rule of Three**, which dealt with the copy constructor, copy assignment operator, and the destructor. It basically states that we need to implement one of these methods since the management of the encapsulated resource is non-trivial.

With the introduction of the move constructor and move assignment operator in C++11, this rule was expanded to the **Rule of Five**. No changes were made to the essence of the rule. Simply, the number of special member functions increased to five. Remembering the rules for compiler generation, there is an additional reason for ensuring all five special methods are implemented (or forced via = default), and that is, if the compiler does not have access to a move-semantic function, it will attempt to use a copy-semantic function, and this may not be what is desired.

> **Note**
>
> For more details, see the C.ctor: Constructors, assignments, and destructors section of the C++ Core Guidelines, which can be found here: http://isocpp.github.io/CppCoreGuidelines/CppCoreGuidelines.

## Constructors – Initializing the Object

The main task of a constructor is to put the object into a stable state so that any operations performed on or by the object through its member functions result in a consistent defined behavior. While the previous statement is true of the copy and move constructors, they achieve this by different semantics (copying or moving from another object).

There are four different mechanisms available for us to control the initial state of an object. C++ has a lot of rules for which initialization is used in such a case. We will not go into the details of the C++ standard's default initialization, zero initialization, value initialization, constant initialization, and so on. Just know that the best approach is to be explicit about the initialization of your variables.

The **first** and least preferred initialization mechanism is to assign values to the member variables in the body of the constructor, like so:

```
Fraction::Fraction()
{
    this->m_numerator = 0;
    this->m_denominator = 1;
}
```

```
Fraction::Fraction(int numerator, int denominator)
{
    m_numerator = numerator;
    m_denominator = denominator;
}
```

It is clear what values are used to initialize the variables. Strictly speaking, this is not the initialization of the class – according to the standard, initialization is complete when the body of the constructor is called. This is simple to maintain, particularly in this class. For larger classes that have multiple constructors and many member variables, it can be a maintenance problem. If you change one constructor, you will need to change them all. It also has the problem that if the member variable is of a reference type (which we'll talk about later), then it cannot be done in the body of the constructor.

The default constructor uses the **this** pointer. Every member function, including constructors and destructors, are called with one implicit argument (even though it is never declared) – the **this** pointer. **this** points to the current instance of the object. The -> operator is another dereference operator and is shorthand in this case, that is, *(this).m_numerator. The use of **this->** is optional and can be omitted. Other languages, such as Python, require the implicit pointer/reference to be declared and used (the convention in Python is to call *self*).

The **second** mechanism is the use of a member initialization list, which has a caveat in its use. For our Fraction class, we have the following:

```
Fraction::Fraction() : m_numerator(0), m_denominator(1)
{
}
```

```
Fraction::Fraction(int numerator, int denominator) :
```

```
        m_numerator(numerator), m_denominator(denominator)

    {

    }
```

The sections of code after the colon, :, and before the opening brace, {, in (`m_numerator(0)`, `m_denominator(1)` and `m_numerator(numerator)`, `m_denominator(denominator)` are the member initialization lists. We can initialize a reference type in the member initialization list.

> **Member Initialization List Order**
>
> Regardless of the order in which you place the members in the member initialization list, the compiler will initialize the members in the order that they are declared in the class.

The **third** and **recommended** initialization is the default member initialization that was introduced in C++11. We define default initial values when the variable is declared either using assignment or the brace initializer:

```
class Fraction

{

public:

    int m_numerator = 0;      // equals initializer

    int m_denominator{1};     // brace initializer

};
```

If the constructor does not define the initial value of the member variable, then this default value will be used to initialize the variable. This has the advantage of ensuring that all the constructors produce the same initialization unless they have been explicitly modified in the definition of the constructor.

C++11 also introduced a fourth style of initialization, known as constructor delegation. It is a modification of the Member Initialization List where, instead of listing the member variables and their initial values, another constructor is called. The following example is contrived, and you would not write a class this way, but it shows the syntax for the constructor delegation:

```
Fraction::Fraction(int numerator) : m_numerator(numerator), m_denominator(1)

{

}
```

```cpp
Fraction::Fraction(int numerator, int denominator) : Fraction(numerator)
{
    auto factor = std::gcd(numerator, denominator);
    m_numerator /= factor;
    m_denominator = denominator / factor;
}
```

You call the single argument constructor from the constructor with two arguments.

## Exercise 5: Declaring and Initializing Fractions

In this exercise, we will implement class member initialization using the different techniques available to us, including constructor delegation. Let's get started:

1. Open the **Lesson2A** project in Eclipse, and then in the **Project Explorer**, expand **Lesson2A**, then **Exercise05**, and double-click on **Exercise5.cpp** to open the file for this exercise in the editor.

2. Click on the **Launch Configuration** drop-down menu and select **New Launch Configuration....** Configure **Exercise5** to run with the name Exercise5.

3. When that is complete, it will be the currently selected Launch Configuration.

4. Click on the **Run** button. **Exercise 5** will run and produce something similar to the following output:

```
Problems  Tasks  Console ⊠  Properties  Call Graph  C/C++
<terminated> (exit value: 0) exercise5 [C/C++ Application] /home/brian/Docum


------ Exercise 5 ------
fraction = -1116194048/22036
sizeof(Fraction) = 8 bytes
sizeof(Fraction.m_numerator)   = 4 bytes
sizeof(Fraction.m_denominator) = 4 bytes
Complete.
```

Figure 2A.35: Exercise 5 typical output

The values that were reported for the fraction come from not initializing the member variables in any way. If you run it again, you will most likely get a different fraction.

5. Click on the **Run** button a few times. You will see that the fraction changes.

6.  In the editor, change the constructor to read as follows:

```
Fraction() : m_numerator{0}, m_denominator{1}
{
}
```

7.  Click on the **Run** button and observe the output:

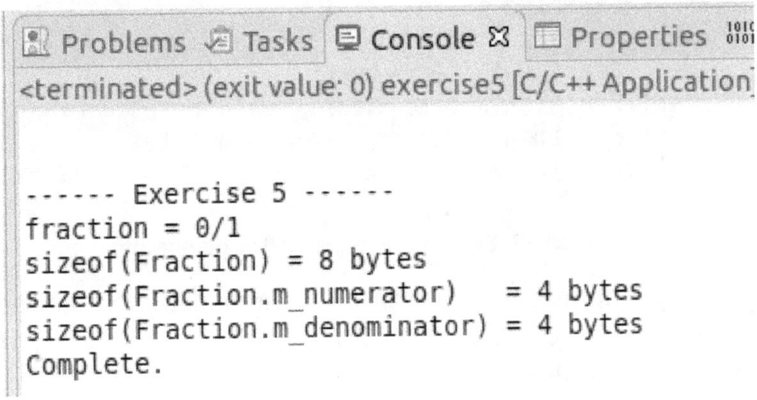

```
Problems  Tasks  Console ⊠  Properties
<terminated> (exit value: 0) exercise5 [C/C++ Application


------ Exercise 5 ------
fraction = 0/1
sizeof(Fraction) = 8 bytes
sizeof(Fraction.m_numerator)   = 4 bytes
sizeof(Fraction.m_denominator) = 4 bytes
Complete.
```

Figure 2A.36: Modified Exercise 5 output

This time, the fraction value is defined by the values we specified in the member initialization list.

8.  In the editor, add the following two **constructors**:

```
Fraction(int numerator) : m_numerator(numerator), m_denominator(1)
{
}

Fraction(int numerator, int denominator) : Fraction(numerator)
{
    auto factor = std::gcd(numerator, denominator);
    m_numerator /= factor;
    m_denominator = denominator / factor;
}
```

9.  In the main function, change the declaration of **fraction** to include initialization:

```
Fraction fraction{3,2};
```

10. Click on the **Run** button and observe the output:

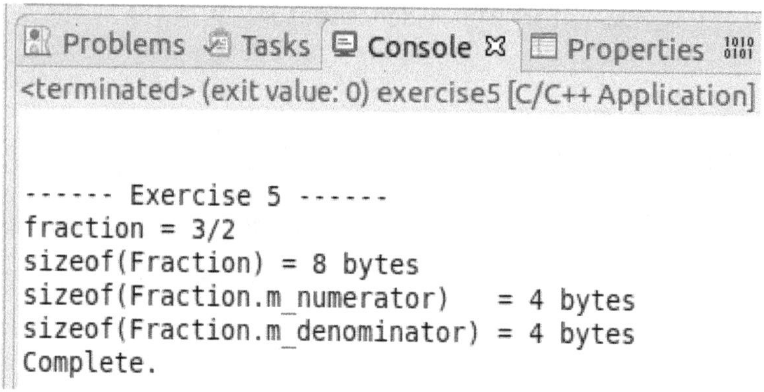

```
  Problems    Tasks   Console    Properties   1010
                                              0101
<terminated> (exit value: 0) exercise5 [C/C++ Application]


------ Exercise 5 ------
fraction = 3/2
sizeof(Fraction) = 8 bytes
sizeof(Fraction.m_numerator)   = 4 bytes
sizeof(Fraction.m_denominator) = 4 bytes
Complete.
```

Figure 2A.37: Example of constructor delegation

In this exercise, we implemented member variable initialization using the member initialization list and constructor delegation. We *will return to fractions in Exercise 7, Adding Operators to the Fraction Class.*

## Values Versus References and Const

So far, we have only dealt with value types, that is, the variable holds the value of the object. A pointer holds a value (which is the address of the object) that we are interested in (or nullptr). But this can lead to inefficiencies and problems with managing resources. We will talk about addressing the inefficiencies here but deal with the resource management problem in *Chapter 3, The Distance Between Can and Should – Objects, Pointers, and Inheritance.*

Consider the following problem..We have a 10×10 matrix of double types that we wish to write an inversion function for. The class is declared as follows:

```
class Matrix10x10
{
private:
  double m_data[10][10];
};
```

If we were to take **sizeof(Matrix10x10)**, we would get **sizeof(double)** x 10 x 10 = 800 bytes. Now, if we were to implement an inversion matrix function for this, its signature might look like this:

```
Matrix10x10 invert(Matrix10x10 lhs);
```

```
Matrix10x10 mat;
// set up mat
Matrix10x10 inv = invert(mat);
```

Firstly, this means that the compiler would need to pass the value held by **mat** to the **invert()** function and copy the 800 bytes onto the stack. The function then does whatever it needs to do to invert the matrix (an L-U decomposition, calculation of the determinant – whatever approach the implementer chooses) and then copy the 800-byte result back to the **inv** variable. Passing large values on the stack is never a good idea, for two reasons:

- The stack is a finite resource that's given to our program by the host operating system.
- Copying large values around the system is inefficient.

This approach is known as pass-by-value. That is, the value of an item we wish to process is copied to the function.

In C (and C++), this limitation is addressed by the use of pointers. The preceding code may become the following:

```
void invert(Matrix10x10* src, Matrix10x10* inv);
```

```
Matrix10x10 mat;
Matrix10x10 inv;
// set up mat
invert(&mat, &inv);
```

Here, we just pass the address of the src and target for the inverse result as two pointers (which is a small number of bytes). Unfortunately, this results in code inside the function that has to use the dereference operator (*) every time we use **src** or **inv**, making the code more difficult to read. In addition, the use of pointers has led to many problems.

C++ introduced a better approach – the variable alias or reference. A reference type is declared with the ampersand (**&**) operator. So, we can declare the invert method as follows:

```
void invert(Matrix10x10& src, Matrix10x10& inv);
```

```
Matrix10x10 mat;

Matrix10x10 inv;

// set up mat

invert(mat, inv);
```

Note that calling the method requires no special operator to pass the reference. From the compiler's viewpoint, a reference is still a pointer with one limitation – it cannot hold a nullptr. From the programmer's viewpoint, a reference allows us to reason about our code without having to worry about having the right dereference operator in the right place. This is known as **pass-by-reference**.

We saw references being passed to the copy constructor and the copy assignment method. The types of references, when used for their move equivalents, are known as **rvalue reference operators** and will be explained in *Chapter 3, The Distance Between Can and Should – Objects, Pointers, and Inheritance*.

One advantage of **pass-by-value** was that we cannot inadvertently modify the value of the variable that's passed into a method. Now, if we pass-by-reference, we can no longer guarantee that the method we are calling will not modify the original variable. To address this, we can change the signature of the invert method to read as follows:

```
void invert(const Matrix10x10& src, Matrix10x10& inv);
```

The const keyword tells the compiler that, when it is processing the definition of the **invert()** function, it is illegal to assign a new value to any part of the value referenced by **src**. If the method does attempt to modify src, the compiler will generate an error.

In the Specifying Types – Variables section, we found that the declaration of **auto title** resulted in **title** being of the **const char \*** type. Now, we can explain the **const** part.

The **title** variable is **a pointer to a char that is constant**. In other words, we cannot change the value of the data stored in the memory that we are pointing to. Therefore, we cannot do the following:

```
*title = 's';
```

This is because the compiler will generate an error related to changing a constant value. We can, however, change the value stored in the pointer. We are allowed to do the following:

```
title = "Maid Marian";
```

We have now been introduced to references for use as argument types to functions, but they can also be used as member variables instead of pointers. There are differences between references and pointers:

A reference must refer to an actual object (no equivalent of nullptr). A reference cannot be changed once it has been initialized (this has the consequence that a reference must either be default member initialized or appear in the member initialization list).The object must exist for as long as the reference to it exists (if the object can be destroyed before the reference is destroyed, then there is the potential for undefined behavior if an attempt is made to access the object).

## Exercise 6: Declaring and Using Reference Types

In this exercise, we will declare and use reference types to make the code efficient and easier to read. Let's get started:

1. Open the **Lesson2A** project in Eclipse, and then in the **Project Explorer**, expand **Lesson2A**, then **Exercise06**, and double-click on **Exercise6.cpp** to open the file for this exercise in the editor.

2. Click on the **Launch Configuration** drop-down menu and select **New Launch Configuration....** Configure **Exercise6** to run with the name Exercise6.

3. When that is complete, it will be the currently selected Launch Configuration.

4. Click on the **Run** button. Exercise 6 will run and produce something similar to the following output:

```
Problems  Tasks  Console ⊠  Properties  Call Graph  C/C-
<terminated> (exit value: 0) exercise6 [C/C++ Application] /home/brian/Docu
------ Exercise 6 ------
value = 42
Setting value via rvalue
value = 96

Swapping 123 and 456
Swapped 456 and 123
value = 96; rvalue = 96; a = 456
Setting rvalue to a and then assigning 32 to rvalue
value = 32; rvalue = 32; a = 456
Complete.
```

Figure 2A.38: Exercise 6 output

By examining the code and comparing it with the output, we will find that the **rvalue** variable allows us to manipulate (read from and write to) the data stored in the **value** variable. We have a reference, **rvalue**, to the **value** variable. We can also see that the values stored in the **a** and **b** variables were exchanged by the **swap()** function.

5. In the editor, change the function definition of swap:

```
void swap(const int& lhs, const int& rhs)
```

6. Click on the **Run** button. When the Errors in Workspace dialog appears, click **Cancel**. The first error that's reported by the compiler is shown here:

```
 Problems  Tasks  Console   Properties  Call Graph  C/C++ Unit  Search  Debug
CDT Build Console [Lesson2A]
23:52:13 **** Incremental Build of configuration Debug for project Lesson2A ****
/usr/bin/make all
[ 11%] Built target Exercise2
Scanning dependencies of target Exercise6
[ 16%] Building CXX object CMakeFiles/Exercise6.dir/Exercise06/Exercise6.cpp.o
/home/brian/Documents/advanced/Lesson2A/Exercise06/Exercise6.cpp: In function 'void swap(const int&, const int&)':
/home/brian/Documents/advanced/Lesson2A/Exercise06/Exercise6.cpp:15:11: error: assignment of read-only reference 'lhs'
     lhs = rhs;
           ^~~

/home/brian/Documents/advanced/Lesson2A/Exercise06/Exercise6.cpp:16:11: error: assignment of read-only reference 'rhs'
     rhs = tmp;
           ^~~

make[2]: *** [CMakeFiles/Exercise6.dir/Exercise06/Exercise6.cpp.o] Error 1
CMakeFiles/Exercise6.dir/build.make:62: recipe for target 'CMakeFiles/Exercise6.dir/Exercise06/Exercise6.cpp.o' failed
CMakeFiles/Makefile2:109: recipe for target 'CMakeFiles/Exercise6.dir/all' failed
Makefile:94: recipe for target 'all' failed
make[1]: *** [CMakeFiles/Exercise6.dir/all] Error 2
```

Figure 2A.39: Read-only error on assignment

By changing the arguments from **int& lhs** to **const int& lhs**, we've told the compiler that the arguments should not be changed inside this function. And because we assign to lhs in the function, the compiler generates the error about lhs being read-only and terminates.

## Implementing Standard Operators

To use fractions like a built-in class, we need them to work with the standard mathematical operators (+, -, *, /) and their assignment counterparts (+=, -=, *=, /=). If you are unfamiliar with assignment operators, then consider the following two expressions – they produce the same output:

```
a = a + b;
a += b;
```

The syntax for declaring these two operators for Fraction is as follows:

```
// member function declarations

Fraction& operator+=(const Fraction& rhs);

Fraction operator+(const Fraction& rhs) const;


// normal function declaration of operator+

Fraction operator+(const Fraction& lhs, const Fraction& rhs);
```

Because the **operator+=** method modifies the contents of the left-hand variable (adds a to b and then stores it again in a), it is recommended that it is implemented as a member variable. In this case, as we have not created a new value, we can just return a reference to the existing lhs.

The operator+ method, on the other hand, should not modify lhs nor rhs and return a new object. The implementer is free to implement it as a member function or as a free function. Both are shown in the preceding code, but only one should exist. The interesting thing to note about the member function's implementation is the const keyword at the end of the declaration. This tells the compiler that when this member function is called, it will not modify the internal state of the object. While both approaches are valid, if possible, **operator+** should be implemented as a normal function, outside of the class.

The same approach can be used for the other operators - **(subtract)**, **\* (multiply)**, and **/ (divide)**. The preceding methods implement the semantics for the standard mathematical operators and make our type act like the built-in types.

## Implementing the Output Stream Operator (<<)

C++ abstracts Input/Output (I/O) into the stream class hierarchy in the standard library (which we will talk about in *Chapter 2B, No Ducks Allowed – Templates and Deduction*). In *Exercise 5, Declaring and Initializing Fractions*, we saw that we could insert the fraction into an output stream as follows:

```
std::cout << "fraction = " << fraction.getNumerator() << "/"
                          << fraction.getDenominator() << "\n";
```

So far, for our Fraction class, we have written out the numerator and denominator values by accessing the data values from outside using the `getNumerator()` and `getDenominator()` methods, but there is a better way to do this. As part of making our classes first-class citizens in C++, where it makes sense, we should overload the I/O operators. In this chapter, we will only look at the output operator, <<, also known as the insertion operator. That way, we can replace the previous code with a much cleaner version:

```
std::cout << "fraction = " << fraction << "\n";
```

We can overload the operator as either a friend function or a normal function (if the class provides getter functions of the data that we need to insert). For our purpose, we define it as a normal function:

```
inline std::ostream& operator<< (std::ostream &out, const Fraction &rhs)
{
    out << rhs.getNumerator() << " / " << rhs.getDenominator();
    return out;
}
```

## Structuring Our Code

Before we delve into the exercise where we implement the operators and turn our Fraction into a full-blown type in the C++ world, we need to have a brief discussion about where we put the bits and pieces of our class – the declaration and the definition. The declaration is the blueprint for our class that indicates what data storage it requires and the methods that it will implement. The definition is the actual implementation details of each of the methods.

In languages such as Java and C#, the declaration and the definition are one and the same and they must exist in one file (Java) or across multiple files (C# partial classes). In C++, depending on the class and how much you wish to expose to other classes, the declaration MUST appear in a header file (which can be **#included** in other files for use) and the definition can appear in one of three places – inline in the definition, **inline** in the same file as the definition, or in a separate implementation file.

The header file is usually named with the .hpp extension, while the implementation file is typically one of *.**cpp** or *.**cxx**. The implementation file is also known as a **translation unit**. By defining a function as inline, we allow the compiler to optimize the code in a way that the function may not even exist in the final program – it has substituted the steps we put into the function into the locations that we call the function from.

## Exercise 7: Adding Operators to the Fraction Class

In this exercise, we aim to implement operators in our Fraction class using unit tests to develop the functionality. This makes our Fraction class a real type. Let's get started:

1. Open the **Lesson2A** project in Eclipse, and then in the **Project Explorer**, expand **Lesson2A**, then **Exercise07**, and double-click on **Exercise7.cpp** to open the file for this exercise in the editor.

2. Click on the **Launch Configuration** drop-down menu and select **New Launch Configuration...**. Configure Exercise7 to run with the name Exercise7.

3. When that is complete, it will be the currently selected Launch Configuration.

4. We also need to configure a unit test. In Eclipse, click on the menu item called **Run | Run Configurations...**, right-click **C/C++ Unit** on the left-hand side, and select **New Configuration**.

5. Change the name from `Lesson2A Debug` to `Exercise7 Tests`.

6. Under **C/C++ Application**, select the **Search Project** option and choose **tests** in the new dialog.

7. Next, go to the **C/C++ Testing** tab and select **Google Tests Runner** in the dropdown. Click on **Apply** at the bottom of the dialog and click on the **Run** option for the test, which we have to run for the first time:

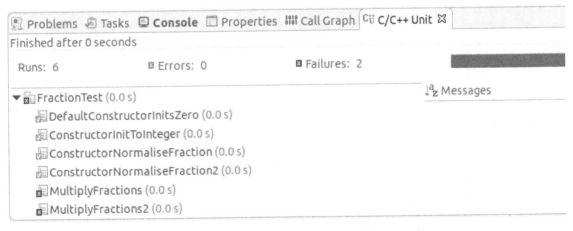

Figure 2A.40: Failing tests – multiplication

8. Open the **Fraction.cpp** file in the editor and locate the **operator*=** function. Update it with the following code:

```
Fraction& Fraction::operator*=(const Fraction& rhs)
{
    Fraction tmp(m_numerator*rhs.m_numerator, m_denominator*rhs.m_
denominator);
    *this = tmp;
    return *this;
}
```

9. Click on the **Run** button to rerun the tests. This time, all the tests pass:

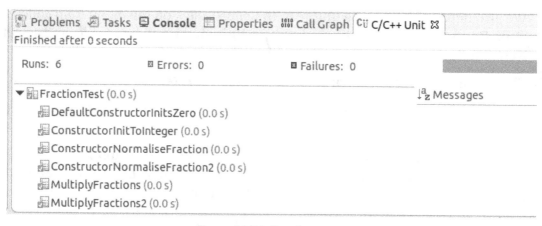

**Figure 2A.41: Passing tests**

10. In your IDE, open the **tests/FractionTests.cpp** file and find the two tests that were failing. One tested **operator*=()**, while the other tested **operator*()**. How did fixing **operator*=()** fix **operator*()**? If you open Fraction.hpp in the editor, you will find that the **operator*()** function was implemented for you by making a call to **operator*=()**, that is, it is marked inline and is a normal function and not a member function. In general, this is the approach to take when overloading these operators – the one that modifies the object that is calling it is a member function, whereas the one that has to generate a new value is a normal function that calls the member function.

11. Open **Fraction.hpp** in the editor and change the line near the top of the file so that it reads like so:

```
#define EXERCISE7_STEP   11
```

12. Click on the **Run** button to rerun the tests – this time, we have added two more tests that fail – `AddFractions` and `AddFractions2`:

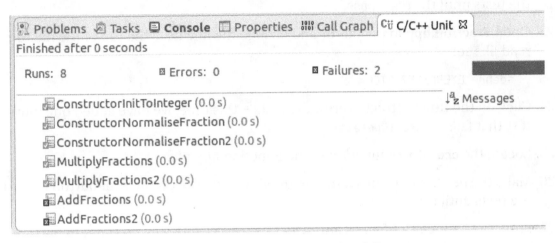

Figure 2A.42: Additional tests to fail

13. Locate the `operator+=` function in the **Function.cpp** file.

14. Make the necessary changes to the function and click on the **Run** button to rerun the tests until the tests pass. Look at the equations that define its operation given earlier and see how `operator*=()` was implemented.

15. Open **Fraction.hpp** in the editor and change the line near the top of the file to read like so:

    ```
    #define EXERCISE7_STEP   15
    ```

16. Click on the **Run** button to rerun the tests – his time, we have added two more tests that fail – `SubtractFractions` and `SubtractFractions2`.

17. Locate the `operator-=` function in the Function.cpp file.

18. Make the necessary changes to the function and click on the **Run** button to rerun the tests until the tests pass.

19. Open **Fraction.hpp** in the editor and change the line near the top of the file to read like so:

    ```
    #define EXERCISE7_STEP   19
    ```

20. Click on the **Run** button to rerun the tests – this time, we have added two more tests that fail – **DivideFractions** and **DivideFractions2**.

21. Locate the **operator/=** function in the **Function.cpp** file.

22. Make the necessary changes to the function and click on the **Run** button to rerun the tests until the tests pass.

23. Open **Fraction.hpp** in the editor and change the line near the top of the file to read like so:

```
#define EXERCISE7_STEP  23
```

24. Click on the **Run** button to rerun the tests – this time, we have added one more test that fails – **InsertOperator**.

25. Locate the **operator<<** function in the Function.hpp file.

26. Make the necessary changes to the function and click on the **Run** button to rerun the tests until the tests pass.

27. From the **Launch Configuration**, select **Exercise7** and click on the **Run** button. This will produce the following output:

```
 Problems  Tasks  Console   Properties   Call Graph  C/C++ Unit
<terminated> (exit value: 0) exercise7 [C/C++ Application] /home/brian/Documents/advanced/Less

------ Exercise 7 ------
5 / 1
1 / 24 * 3 / 5 = 1 / 40
1 / 24 + 3 / 5 = 77 / 120
1 / 24 - 3 / 5 = -67 / 120
1 / 24 / 3 / 5 = 5 / 72
sizeof(Fraction) = 8 bytes
sizeof(Fraction.m_numerator)   = 4 bytes
sizeof(Fraction.m_denominator) = 4 bytes
Complete.
```

Figure 2A.43: Functional Fraction class

This completes our implementation of the **Fraction** class for now. We will return to it again when we consider exceptions in *Chapter 3, The Distance Between Can and Should – Objects, Pointers, and Inheritance*, so that we can deal with illegal values in our fractions (denominators of 0).

## Function Overloading

C++ supports a feature known as function overloading, which is where two or more functions have the same name, but their argument list is different. The number of arguments can be the same, but at least one of the argument types has to be different. Alternatively, they may have a different number of arguments. So, the function prototype for the multiple functions are different. However, two functions cannot have the same function name, the same argument types, and a different return type. The following is an example of overloading:

```cpp
std::ostream& print(std::ostream& os, int value) {
    os << value << " is an int\n";
    return os;
}


std::ostream& print(std::ostream& os, float value) {
    os << value << " is a single precision float\n";
    return os;
}


std::ostream& print(std::ostream& os, double value) {
    os << value << " is a double precision float \n";
    return os;
}


// The next function causes the compiler to generate an error
// as it only differs by return type.
void print(std::ostream& os, double value) {
    os << value << " is a double precision float!\n";
}
```

So far, the multiple constructors on **Fraction** and the overloaded arithmetic operators are all examples of overloaded functions that the compiler has to refer to when it meets one of these functions. Consider the following code:

```
int main(int argc, char** argv) {
    print(42);
}
```

When the compiler meets the line **print(42)**, it needs to work out which of the previously defined functions to call, so it performs the following process (grossly simplified):

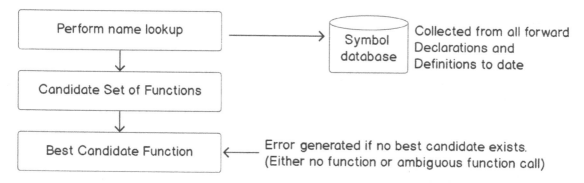

Figure 2A.44: Function overload resolution (simplified)

The C++ standard defines rules for how the compiler determines the best candidate function based on how it has to manipulate (that is, convert) the arguments to get a match. If no conversions are required, then that function is the best match.

## Classes, Structs, and Unions

When you define a class and do not specify an access modifier (public, protected, private), all the members will be private by default:

```
class Fraction
{
    Fraction() {};          // All of these are private
    int m_numerator;
    int m_denominator;
};
```

When you define a struct and do not specify an access modifier (public, protected, private), all the members will be public by default:

```
struct Fraction
{
    Fraction() {};              // All of these are public
    int m_numerator;
    int m_denominator;
};
```

There is one other difference, which we will look at after we explain inheritance and polymorphism. A union is a different type of data construct from a struct and a class but is the same. A union is a special type of struct declaration where all the members occupy the same memory and only one member is valid at a given time. An example of a **union** declaration is as follows:

```
union variant
{
    int m_ivalue;
    float m_fvalue;
    double m_dvalue;
};
```

When you define a union and do not specify an access modifier (public, protected, private), all the members will be public by default.

The main problem with a union is that there is no intrinsic way to know which of the values is valid at any given time. This is resolved by defining what is known as a *tagged union* – that is, a struct that holds the union and an enum that identifies whether it is the valid value. There are also other restrictions on what can and cannot be included in a union (for example, only one member can have a default member initializer). We will not be exploring unions in depth in this book.

## Activity 1: Graphics Processing

In a modern computing environment, matrices are used everywhere to solve various problems – to solve simultaneous equations, to analyze electricity power grids or electric circuits, to perform manipulations on objects for graphics rendering, and to deliver implementations of machine learning. In the world of graphics, whether two-dimensional (2D) or three-dimensional (3D), all the operations that you would want to perform on your objects can be done with the help of matrix multiplication. Your team has been tasked with developing a representation of points, transformation matrices, and the operations that you might want to perform on them. Follow these steps to achieve this:

1. Load the prepared project from the **Lesson2A/Activity01** folder.

2. Create a class called **Point3d** that can be constructed by default to be the origin, or using an initializer list of three or four values (data is stored directly in the class).

3. Create a class called **Matrix3d** that can be constructed by default to an identity matrix, or using a nested initializer list to provide all the values (data is stored directly in the class).

4. On **Point3d**, overload `operator()` so that it takes the (`index`) argument in order to return the value at `x(0)`, `y(1)`, `z(2)`, and `w(3)`.

5. On **Matrix3d**, overload `operator()` to take (`row, col`) arguments so that it returns the value.

6. Add the unit tests to verify all of the aforementioned features.

7. Add `operator*=(const Matrix3d&)` and `operator==(const Matrix3d&)` to the **Matrix3d** class, as well as the unit tests for them.

8. Add free functions for multiplying two **Matrix3d** objects and a **Matrix3d** object by a **Point3d** object with unit tests.

9. Add standalone methods for creating a matrix to translate, scale, and rotate (around the x, y, z axes) and their unit tests.

After implementing the preceding steps, the expected output is as follows:

```
------ Activity 1 ------
The point [ 1, 1, 1, 1 ]
...rotated around X by 90 degrees
...rotated around Y by 90 degrees
...rotated around Z by 90 degrees
moves to [ 1, 1, -1, 1 ]
...scaled by x=2, y = 3, z = 4
moves to [ 2, 3, -4, 1 ]
...translated by dx=-2, dy = 1, dz = -3
moves to [ 0, 4, -7, 1 ]

Complete.
```

Figure 2A.45: Successfully running the activity program

For the purpose of this activity, we will not be worrying about the possibility of out of range on indices. We will talk about this in *Chapter 3, The Distance Between Can and Should – Objects, Pointers, and Inheritance*. An identity matrix is a square matrix (4 x 4, in our case) where all the values on the diagonal are set to one (1) and all the other values are zero (0).

When working with 3D graphics, we use an augmented matrix for the points (vertices) and for the transformations so that all the transformations (translation, scaling, rotation) can be achieved by using multiplication.

An **n** x **m** matrix is an array of n rows of m numbers. For example, a **2** x **3** matrix could look like this:

$$\begin{bmatrix} 1 & 5 & 7 \\ 2 & 6 & 8 \end{bmatrix}$$

Figure 2A.46: Matrix of 2x3

A vertex in three dimensions can be represented as a **three-tuple (x,y,z)**. However, we augment it with another ordinate, **w (=1 for a vertex, =0 for a direction)**, making it a **four-tuple (x, y, z, 1)**. Rather than using a tuple, we place it in a **4 x 1** matrix, as follows:

$$\begin{bmatrix} x \\ y \\ z \\ 1 \end{bmatrix}$$

Figure 2A.47: 4x1 Matrix

If we multiply the **4 x 1** matrix (point) by a **4 x 4** matrix (transformation), we can manipulate the point. If **Ti** represents a transformation, then we can multiply the transformations together to achieve some manipulation of the point:

$$T_1 \times T_2 \times T_3 \times \cdots \times T_n = T_t$$

Figure 2A.48: Multiplying transformations

To multiply a transformation matrix, **A x P = B**, we do the following:

$$\begin{bmatrix} a_{11} & a_{12} & a_{13} & a_{14} \\ a_{21} & a_{22} & a_{23} & a_{24} \\ a_{31} & a_{32} & a_{33} & a_{34} \\ a_{41} & a_{42} & a_{43} & a_{44} \end{bmatrix} \times \begin{bmatrix} x \\ y \\ z \\ 1 \end{bmatrix} = \begin{bmatrix} a_{11}x + a_{12}y + a_{13}z + a_{14} \\ a_{21}x + a_{22}y + a_{23}z + a_{24} \\ a_{31}x + a_{32}y + a_{33}z + a_{34} \\ a_{41}x + a_{42}y + a_{43}z + a_{44} \end{bmatrix}$$

Figure 2A.49: Multiplying transformation matrix

We can also express it like so:

$$b_i = \sum_{j=1}^{4} a_{ij} p_j$$

Figure 2A.50: Expression of multiplying transformations

Likewise, the same can be done for two **4 x 4** matrices, multiplied together, **AxB=C**:

$$c_{ij} = \sum_{k=1}^{4} a_{ik} b_{kj} \qquad \qquad \text{For i = 1 to 4, j = 1 to 4}$$

$$c_{ij} = \sum_{k=1}^{4} a_{ik} b_{kj}$$

Figure 2A.51 Expression of 4x4 matrix multiplication:

The matrices for the transformations are as follows:

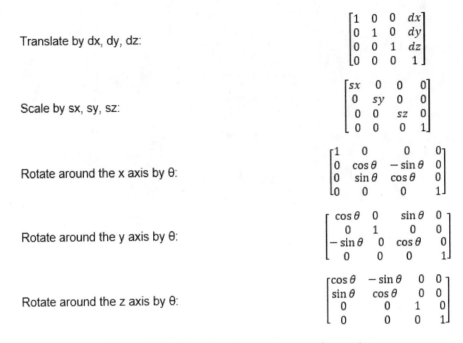

Translate by dx, dy, dz:

$$\begin{bmatrix} 1 & 0 & 0 & dx \\ 0 & 1 & 0 & dy \\ 0 & 0 & 1 & dz \\ 0 & 0 & 0 & 1 \end{bmatrix}$$

Scale by sx, sy, sz:

$$\begin{bmatrix} sx & 0 & 0 & 0 \\ 0 & sy & 0 & 0 \\ 0 & 0 & sz & 0 \\ 0 & 0 & 0 & 1 \end{bmatrix}$$

Rotate around the x axis by θ:

$$\begin{bmatrix} 1 & 0 & 0 & 0 \\ 0 & \cos\theta & -\sin\theta & 0 \\ 0 & \sin\theta & \cos\theta & 0 \\ 0 & 0 & 0 & 1 \end{bmatrix}$$

Rotate around the y axis by θ:

$$\begin{bmatrix} \cos\theta & 0 & \sin\theta & 0 \\ 0 & 1 & 0 & 0 \\ -\sin\theta & 0 & \cos\theta & 0 \\ 0 & 0 & 0 & 1 \end{bmatrix}$$

Rotate around the z axis by θ:

$$\begin{bmatrix} \cos\theta & -\sin\theta & 0 & 0 \\ \sin\theta & \cos\theta & 0 & 0 \\ 0 & 0 & 1 & 0 \\ 0 & 0 & 0 & 1 \end{bmatrix}$$

Figure 2A.52: List of matrices for transformation

> **Note**
>
> The solution for this activity can be found on page 635.

## Summary

In this chapter, we learned about types in C++. Firstly, we touched on the built-in types and then learned how to create our own types that behave like the built-in types. We learned how to declare and initialize variables, got a glimpse of what the compiler generates from the source, where it puts variables, how the linker puts it together, and then what that looks like in the computer's memory. We learned some of the C++ tribal wisdom around the Rule of Zero and the Rule of Five. These form the building blocks of C++. In the next chapter, we will look at creating functions and classes with C++ templates and explore further type deduction as it applies to templates.

# 2B

# No Ducks Allowed – Templates and Deduction

**Learning Objectives**

By the end of this chapter, you will be able to:

- Develop your own classes to an even greater effect using inheritance and polymorphism

- Implement an alias to make your code easier to read

- Develop templates using SFINAE and constexpr to simplify your code

- Implement your own solutions using the STL to leverage generic programming

- Describe the context and basic rules for type deduction

This chapter will show you how to define and extend your types through inheritance, polymorphism, and templates.

## Introduction

In the previous chapter, we learned how to develop our own types (classes) with the help of unit tests and made them behave like built-in types. We were introduced to function overloading, Rule of Three/Five, and Rule of Zero.

In this chapter, we will learn how to extend the type system even further. We'll learn how to create functions and classes using templates and revisit function overloading since it's impacted by the use of templates. We'll be introduced to a new technology, **SFINAE**, and use it to control the parts of our templates that are included in the generated code.

## Inheritance, Polymorphism, and Interfaces

So far in our journey of object-oriented design and C++, we have focused on abstraction and data encapsulation. We will now turn our attention to **inheritance** and **polymorphism**. What is inheritance? What is polymorphism? Why do we need it? Consider the following three objects:

**Figure 2B.1: Vehicle objects**

In the preceding diagram, we can see that there are three very different objects. They have some things in common. They all have wheels (a different number), an engine (different size, power, or configuration), start engine, drive, apply brakes, stop engine, and so on, using which we can do something.

So, we can abstract them into something called a vehicle that demonstrates these attributes and general behaviors. If we express this as a C++ class, it might look like the following:

```
class Vehicle
{
public:
  Vehicle() = default;
  Vehicle(int numberWheels, int engineSize) :
        m_numberOfWheels{numberWheels}, m_engineSizeCC{engineSize}
  {
  }
```

```cpp
  bool StartEngine()
  {
    std::cout << "Vehicle::StartEngine " << m_engineSizeCC << " CC\n";
    return true;
  };
  void Drive()
  {
    std::cout << "Vehicle::Drive\n";
  };
  void ApplyBrakes()
  {
    std::cout << "Vehicle::ApplyBrakes to " << m_numberOfWheels << "
wheels\n";
  };
  bool StopEngine()
  {
    std::cout << "Vehicle::StopEngine\n";
    return true;
  };


private:
  int m_numberOfWheels {4};
  int m_engineSizeCC{1000};
};
```

The **Vehicle** class is a more generalized (or abstract) expression of **Motorcycle**, **Car**, and **Truck**. We can now create more specialized types by reusing what is already available in the Vehicle class. We are going to reuse Vehicle's properties and methods by using inheritance. The syntax for inheritance is as follows:

```cpp
class DerivedClassName : access_modifier BaseClassName
{
  // Body of DerivedClass
};
```

We have come across access modifiers such as **public, protected** and **private** before. They control how we have access to the base classes' members. The Motorcycle class will be derived as follows:

```
class Motorcycle : public Vehicle
{
public:
    Motorcycle(int engineSize) : Vehicle(2, engineSize) {};
};
```

In this case, the Vehicle class is referred to as the **base class** or the **super class**, while the Motorcycle class is referred to as the **derived class** or **subclass**. Graphically, we can represent this as follows, where the arrows point from the derived class to the base class:

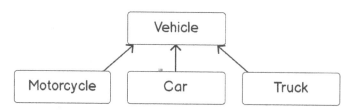

**Figure 2B.2: Vehicle class hierarchy**

But a motorcycle drives differently from a generic vehicle. So, we need to modify the **Motorcycle** class so that it behaves differently. The updated code will be as follows:

```
class Motorcycle : public Vehicle
{
public:
    Motorcycle(int engineSize) : Vehicle(2, engineSize) {};

    void Drive()
    {
        std::cout << "Motorcycle::Drive\n";
    };
};
```

If we think about object-oriented design, this is about modeling a problem space in terms of objects that collaborate. These objects communicate with each other through messages. Now, we have two classes that respond to the same message (the **Drive()** method) in different ways. The sender of the message has no knowledge of what will happen and doesn't really care, and this is the essence of polymorphism.

> **Note**
>
> Polymorphism comes from the Greek words poly and morph, where **poly** means many and **morph** means form. So, polymorphism means **having many forms**.

We can now use these classes to try out polymorphism:

```cpp
#include <iostream>

int main()
{
  Vehicle vehicle;
  Motorcycle cycle{1500};
  Vehicle* myVehicle{&vehicle};

  myVehicle->StartEngine();
  myVehicle->Drive();
  myVehicle->ApplyBrakes();
  myVehicle->StopEngine();

  myVehicle = &cycle;
  myVehicle->StartEngine();
  myVehicle->Drive();
  myVehicle->ApplyBrakes();
  myVehicle->StopEngine();

  return 0;
}
```

If we compile and run this program, we get the following output:

```
$ ./vehicle.exe
Vehicle::StartEngine 1000 CC
Vehicle::Drive
Vehicle::ApplyBrakes to 4 wheels
Vehicle::StopEngine
Vehicle::StartEngine 1500 CC
Vehicle::Drive
Vehicle::ApplyBrakes to 2 wheels
Vehicle::StopEngine
```

Figure 2B.3: Vehicle program output

In the preceding screenshot, the lines after the line **Vehicle::StartEngine 1500 cc** are all related to the **Motorcycle**. But the Drive line still shows **Vehicle::Drive** and not the expected **Motorcycle::Drive**. What's going on? The problem is that we have not told the compiler that the **Drive** method in the **Vehicle** class can be modified (or overridden) by a derived class. We need to make one change in our code:

```
virtual void Drive()
{
  std::cout << "Vehicle::Drive\n";
};
```

By adding the **virtual** keyword before the member function declaration, we are telling the compiler that a derived class can (but doesn't have to) override or replace the function. If we make this change and then compile and run the program, we get the following output:

```
$ ./vehicle.exe
Vehicle::StartEngine 1000 CC
Vehicle::Drive
Vehicle::ApplyBrakes to 4 wheels
Vehicle::StopEngine
Vehicle::StartEngine 1500 CC
Motorcycle::Drive
Vehicle::ApplyBrakes to 2 wheels
Vehicle::StopEngine
```

Figure 2B.4: Vehicle program output with virtual methods

Now, we have learned about inheritance and polymorphism. We used a pointer to a **Vehicle** class to control the **Motorcycle** class. Another change to the code should be made as a matter of best practice. We should also change the declaration of the **Drive** function in the **Motorcyle** as follows:

```
void Drive() override
{
    std::cout << "Motorcycle::Drive\n";
};
```

C++11 introduced the **override** keyword as a hint to the compiler, stating that a particular method should have the same function prototype as a method somewhere in its parent tree. If it cannot find one, then the compiler will report an error. This is a very useful feature and can save you from hours of debugging. If there is some way for the compiler to report an error, use it. The earlier a defect is detected, the easier it is to fix. One final change is that whenever we add a virtual function to a class, we must declare its destructor **virtual**:

```
class Vehicle
{
public:
    // Constructors - hidden
    virtual ~Vehicle() = default;  // Virtual Destructor


    // Other methods and data -- hidden
};
```

We saw this with the **Drive()** function before it was made virtual. When the destructor is called through the pointer to a Vehicle, it needs to know which destructor to call. Thus, making it virtual enables this. If you fail to do so, then you can end up with resource leaks or spliced objects.

## Inheritance and Access Specifiers

As we mentioned previously, the general form of inheriting one subclass from a super class is as follows:

```
class DerivedClassName : access_modifier BaseClassName
```

When we derived Motorcycle class from Vehicle class, we use the following code:

```
class Motorcycle : public Vehicle
```

The access modifier is optional and is one of the ones that we have met before: **public**, **protected**, and **private**. In the following table, you can see the accessibility of the base classes' members. If access_modifier is omitted, then the compiler assumes private was specified.

| Access specifier In Base Class | Effective Access specifier in Derived Class when | | |
|---|---|---|---|
| | public Base class | protected Base class | private Base class |
| public | public | protected | private |
| protected | protected | protected | private |
| private | inaccessible | inaccessible | inaccessible |

Figure 2B.5: Accessibility of base class members in derived classes

## Abstract Classes and Interfaces

All the classes that we have talked about up until now are **concrete class** – they can be instantiated as a type for a variable. There is another type of class – an **abstract class**– that contains at least one **pure virtual member function**. A pure virtual function is a virtual function that has no definition (or implementation) in the class. And because it has no implementation, the class is malformed (or abstract) and cannot be instantiated. If you attempt to create a variable of an abstract type, then the compiler will generate an error.

To declare a pure virtual member function, end the function prototype declaration with = 0. To make Drive() a pure virtual function in the Vehicle class, we would declare it as follows:

```
virtual void Drive() = 0;
```

Now, to be able to use a derived class as a variable type (for example, the **Motorcycle** class), it must define an implementation of the **Drive()** function.

You can, however, declare a variable to be either a pointer to the abstract class or a reference to the abstract class. In either case, it must point to, or reference, some non-abstract class derived from the abstract class.

In Java, there is a keyword interface that allows you to define a class that is all pure virtual functions. The same is achieved in C++ by declaring a class that only declares public pure virtual functions (and a virtual destructor). In this way, we define an interface.

> **Note**
>
> Before solving any practical in this chapter, download this book's GitHub repository (https://github.com/TrainingByPackt/Advanced-CPlusPlus) and import the folder for Lesson 2B in Eclipse so that you can view the code for each exercise and activity.

## Exercise 1: Implementing Game Characters with Polymorphism

In this exercise, we will demonstrate inheritance, interfaces, and polymorphism. We will start with an ad hoc implementation of a role-playing game and evolve it to be more generic and expandable. Let's get started:

1.  Open Eclipse and create a new project named **Lesson2B** using the files found in the **Lesson2B** examples folder.

2.  As this is a **CMake-based project**, change the current builder to **Cmake Build (portable)**.

3.  Go to the **Project | Build All** menu to build all exercises. By default, the console at the bottom of the screen will display the **CMake console [Lesson2B]**.

4.  Configure a **New Launch Configuration** named L2BExercise1 that runs the **Exercise1** binary and click on **Run** to build and run **Exercise 1**. You will receive the following output:

```
------ Exercise 1 ------
Gandalf: Abracadabara
Glenda: Chill people
Ben Grimm: Clobbering time
Gandalf: Casts spell
Glenda: Applies soothing balm
Ben Grimm: Hits the nearest bad guy
Complete.
Destroying Warrior: Ben Grimm
Destroying Healer: Glenda
Destroying Wizard: Gandalf
```

**Figure 2B.6: Exercise 1 default output**

5. Open **Exercise1.cpp** in the editor and examine the existing code. You will notice that the three characters are implemented as separate classes and that they are each instantiated and manipulated separately by calling **speak()** and **act()** directly. This is fine for a small program. But as the game grew to tens or hundreds of characters, it would become unmanageable. So, we need to abstract all the characters. Add the following Interface declaration to the top of the file:

```
class ICharacter
{
public:
    ~ICharacter() {
        std::cout << "Destroying Character\n";
    }
    virtual void speak() = 0;
    virtual void act() = 0;
};
```

Normally, the destructor would be empty, but here, it has logging to show the behavior.

6. Derive the **Wizard**, **Healer**, and **Warrior** classes from this interface class and add the **override** keyword to the end of the declarations of the **speak()** and **act()** functions for each class:

```
class Wizard : public Icharacter { ...
```

7. Click the **Run** button to rebuild and run the exercise. We will now see that the base class destructor is also called after the destructor of the derived class:

```
------ Exercise 1 ------
Gandalf: Abracadabara
Glenda: Chill people
Ben Grimm: Clobbering time
Gandalf: Casts spell
Glenda: Applies soothing balm
Ben Grimm: Hits the nearest bad guy
Complete.
Destroying Warrior: Ben Grimm
Destroying Character
Destroying Healer: Glenda
Destroying Character
Destroying Wizard: Gandalf
Destroying Character
```

Figure 2B.7: Output of the modified program

8. Create the characters and manage them in a container such as a **vector**. Create the following two methods in the file, before the **main()** function:

```cpp
void createCharacters(std::vector<ICharacter*>& cast)
{
    cast.push_back(new Wizard("Gandalf"));
    cast.push_back(new Healer("Glenda"));
    cast.push_back(new Warrior("Ben Grimm"));
}

void freeCharacters(std::vector<ICharacter*>& cast)
{
    for(auto* character : cast)
    {
        delete character;
    }
    cast.clear();
}
```

9. Replace the content of **main()** with the following code:

```cpp
int main(int argc, char**argv)
{
    std::cout << "\n------ Exercise 1 ------\n";

    std::vector<ICharacter*> cast;

    createCharacters(cast);
    for(auto* character : cast)
    {
        character->speak();
    }
    for(auto* character : cast)
    {
        character->act();
    }
    freeCharacters(cast);

    std::cout << "Complete.\n";
    return 0;
}
```

10. Click the **Run** button to rebuild and run the exercise. Here is the output that is generated:

```
------ Exercise 1 ------
Gandalf: Abracadabara
Glenda: Chill people
Ben Grimm: Clobbering time
Gandalf: Casts spell
Glenda: Applies soothing balm
Ben Grimm: Hits the nearest bad guy
Destroying Character
Destroying Character
Destroying Character
Complete.
```

Figure 2B.8: Output of the polymorphic version

As you can see from the preceding screenshot, the logging for **Destroying Wizard** and so on has disappeared. The problem is that the container holds the pointers to the base class and that it doesn't know how to call the full destructor in each case.

11. To fix this, simply declare the destructor for **ICharacter** as virtual:

```
virtual ~ICharacter() {
```

12. Click the **Run** button to rebuild and run the exercise. The output now reads as follows:

```
------ Exercise 1 ------
Gandalf: Abracadabara
Glenda: Chill people
Ben Grimm: Clobbering time
Gandalf: Casts spell
Glenda: Applies soothing balm
Ben Grimm: Hits the nearest bad guy
Destroying Wizard: Gandalf
Destroying Character
Destroying Healer: Glenda
Destroying Character
Destroying Warrior: Ben Grimm
Destroying Character
Complete.
```

Figure 2B.9: Output from the full polymorphic version

We have now implemented an interface to our **ICharacter** characters and used them polymorphically by simply calling the **speak()** and **act()** methods through a base class pointer stored in a container.

## Classes, Structs, and Unions Revisited

Previously, we discussed that the difference between a class and a struct was the default access modifier – private for class and public for struct. This difference goes one step further – it applies to the base class if it does not specify anything:

```
class DerivedC : Base   // inherits as if "class DerivedC : private Base" was
used

{
};


struct DerivedS : Base // inherits as if "struct DerivedS : public Base" was
used

{
};
```

It should be noted that a union can neither be a base class nor be derived from a base class. If there is essentially no difference between a struct and a class, then which type should we use? Essentially, it is one of convention. A **struct** is used to bundle together several related elements, while a **class** can do things and has responsibilities. An example of a struct is as follows:

```
struct Point     // A point in 3D space

{
   double m_x;
   double m_y;
   double m_z;
};
```

In the preceding code, we can see that it groups together three coordinates so that we can reason about a point in a 3D space. This structure can be passed as a coherent dataset to methods that need points, rather than three separate arguments per point. A class, on the other hand, models an object that can perform actions. Take a look at the following example:

```
class Matrix

{
public:
   Matrix& operator*(const Matrix& rhs)
      {
```

```
    // nitty gritty of the multiplication
  }
private:
  // Declaration of the 2D array to store matrix.
};
```

A rule of thumb is to use a class if there is at least one private member as this implies that the details of the implementation will be behind the public member functions.

## Visibility, Lifetime, and Access

We have talked about creating our own types and declaring variables and functions while mainly focusing on simple functions and a single file. We will now look at what happens when there are multiple source files (translation units) that contain classes and function definitions. Also, we'll check which variables and functions can be visible from the other parts of the source files, how long the variables live, and look at the difference between internal and external linkage. In *Chapter 1, Anatomy of Portable C++ Software,* we saw how the toolchain works to compile the source files and produce the object files and that the the linker puts it all together to form an executable program.

When a compiler processes a source file, it generates an object file that contains the translated C++ code and enough information for the linker to resolve any references from the compiled source file to another source file. In *Chapter 1, Anatomy of Portable C++ Software,* **CxxTemplate.cpp** called **sum()**, which is defined in the **SumFunc.cpp** file. When the compiler constructs an object file, it creates the following segments:

- **Code segment** (also known as text): This is the translation of the C++ functions into the target machine instructions.

- **Data segment**: This contains all the variables and data structures that are declared in the program, not local or allocated off the heap or stack, and are initialized.

- **BSS segment**: This contains all the variables and data structures that are declared in the program, not local or allocated off the heap or stack, and are not initialized (but will be initialized to zero).

- **Database of exported symbols**: A list of variables and functions that are in this object file and their location.

- **Database of referenced symbols**: A list of variables and functions this object file needs from outside itself and where they are used.

> **Note**
>
> BSS is used to name the uninitialized data segment and its name is historically derived from Block Started by Symbol.

The linker then collects all the code segments, data segments, and **BSS** segments together to form the program. It uses the information in the two databases (DB) to resolve all the referenced symbols to the exported symbols list and patch the code segments with this information so that they can operate correctly. Graphically, this is depicted as follows:

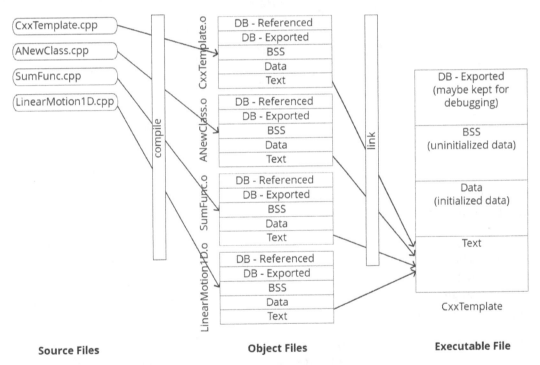

Figure 2B.10: Parts of the object files and the executable file

For the purposes of the discussion that follows, BSS and data segments will be referred to simply as data segment (the only difference being that BSS is not initialized). When a program is executed, it is loaded into memory and its memory looks a bit like the executable file layout – it contains the text segment, data segment, BSS segment, and free memory allocated by the host system, which contains what is known as the **stack** and the **heap**. The stack typically starts at the top of the memory and grows down, while the heap starts where BSS finishes and grows up, toward the stack:

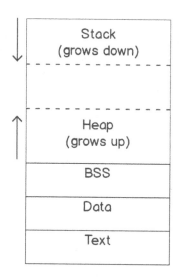

Figure 2B.11: CxxTemplate runtime memory map

The section of the program in which a variable or identifier is accessible is known as the **scope**. There are two broad categories of scope:

- **Local scope** (also known as **block scope**): This applies to anything declared within a block that is enclosed with curly braces (**{}**). The variable can be accessed inside the curly braces. Just like blocks can be nested, so can the scope of the variable. This typically includes local variables and function parameters, and these are generally stored in the stack.

- **Global / file scope**: This applies to variables declared outside a normal function or class, as well as to the normal functions. The variable can be accessed anywhere in the file and possibly from other files (global) if the linkage is correct. These variables are allocated memory by the linker in the data segment. The identifiers are placed into the global namespace, which is the default namespace.

## Namespaces

We can think of a namespace as a dictionary of names of variables, functions, and user-defined types. For small programs, it is ok to use the global namespace as there is very little chance of you creating multiple variables with the same name and getting name clashes. As programs get larger, and more third-party libraries are included, the chance of name clashes increases. Therefore, library writers will put their code into a namespace (that is hopefully unique). This allows the programmer to control access to the identifiers in the namespace. By using the standard library, we have already been using the std namespace. A namespace is declared like so:

```
namespace name_of_namespace {
    // put declarations in here
}
```

It is usual for name_of_namespace to be short, and namespaces can be nested.

> **Note**
>
> A good use of namespaces can be seen in the boost libraries here: https://www.boost.org/.

A variable has another attribute, that of **lifetime**. There are three fundamental lifetimes; two that are managed by the compiler and one that the programmer chooses:

- **Automatic lifetime**: Local variables are created when they are declared and are destroyed upon exiting the scope that they are in. These are managed by the stack.

- **Permanent lifetime**: Global variables and static local variables. The compiler causes global variables to be created when the program begins (before entering the main() function) and causes static local variables to be created when they are first accessed. In both cases, the variable is destroyed when the program exits. These variables are placed in the data segments by the linker.

- **Dynamic lifetime** : Variables are created and destroyed by request of the programmer (through the use of **new** and **delete**). These variables have their memory allocated from the heap.

The final attribute of a variable we will consider is **linkage**. Linkage indicates what the compiler and linker will do if they encounter variables and functions that have the same name (or identifier). For a function, its actually what is known as the mangled name – the compiler uses the name of the function, its return type, and its argument types to produce a mangled name. There are three types of linkage:

- **No linkage**: This means that the identifier only refers to itself and applies to local variables and locally defined user types (that is, inside a block).

- **Internal linkage**: This means that the identifier can be accessed anywhere in the file in which it is declared. This applies to static global variables, const global variables, static functions, and any variables or functions declared in an anonymous namespace within the file. An anonymous namespace is a namespace with no stated name.

- **External linkage**: This means that, with the right forward declarations, it can be accessed from within all files. This includes normal functions, non-static global variables, extern const global variables, and user-defined types.

While these are termed linkages, only the last one actually involves the linker. The other two are achieved by the compiler excluding information from the DB of exported identifiers.

## Templates – Generic Programming

As a computer scientist, or as a programming enthusiast, at some point in time, you probably had to write one (or more) sort algorithms. When discussing the algorithm, you were not particularly concerned about the type of data being sorted, just that the two objects of that type could be compared and that the domain is a totally ordered set (that is, if one object is compared with any other, you can determine which comes first). Different programming languages provide different solutions to this problem:

- **Python**: A dynamic language with built-in function sort and member functions on list. As a dynamic language, it does not need to concern itself with the type if it can call the comparison operator and a `swap` function.

- **C**: This has a function in its standard library called qsort that has the following signature:

```
void qsort (void* base, size_t num, size_t size,
                    int (*compare)(const void*,const void*));
```

This deals with different types as base is a **void pointer**. `size_t` size defines how big each object is, while the `compare()` function defines how to compare the two objects.

- **C++: `std::sort()`** is a function provided in its standard library, where one of its signatures is as follows:

  ```
  template< class RandomIt > void sort( RandomIt first, RandomIt last );
  ```

  In this case, the details of the type are captured in the iterator type called **RandomIt** and passed to the method when compiled.

In the next section, we will briefly define generic programming, show how C++ implements them through templates, highlight what the language already provides, and discuss how the compiler deducts the types so that they can be used for the template.

## What is Generic Programming?

When you developed a sort algorithm, you may have originally focused on just sorting plain numbers. But once that is established, you could then abstract that to any type, provided that the type exhibits certain attributes such as total ordered set (that is, the comparison operator, <, has meaning between all the elements in the domain we are sorting over). So, to express an algorithm in terms of generic programming, we define a placeholder in the algorithm for the type that needs to be manipulated by that algorithm.

**Generic programming** is the development of a type-agnostic general algorithm. The algorithm can be reused by passing types as arguments. In this way, algorithms are abstracted and allow the compiler to optimize based on types.

In other words, generic programming is an approach to programming where an algorithm is defined with types as parameters that are specified when the algorithm is instantiated. Many languages provide support for generic programming with different names. In C++, generic programming is supported through the language feature known as templates.

## Introducing C++ Templates

Templates are C++'s support for generic programming. Think of a template as a cookie cutter, and the type that we give it as a parameter as cookie dough (which can be chocolate brownie, ginger snap, or some other delicious flavor). When we apply the cookie cutter, we end up with instances of cookies that are in the same form but have different flavors. So, a template captures the definition of a generic function or class and when specified with types as arguments, the compiler goes to work to write the class or function for us as if the type was hand-coded by us. It has several advantages, such as the following:

- You only need to develop the class or algorithm once and evolve it.

- You can apply it to many types.

- You can hide complex details behind a simple interface and the compiler can apply optimizations to the generated code, based on the type.

So, how do we write a template? Let's start with a template that will allow us to clamp a value within a range from **lo** to **hi** and be able to use it on **int**, **float**, **double**, or any other built-in type:

```
template <class T>
T clamp(T val, T lo, T hi)
{
    return (val < lo) ? lo : (hi < val) ? hi : val;
}
```

Let's break this down:

- **Line 1**: **template <class T>** declares what follows to be a template and uses one type, which has a placeholder of **T** in the template.

- **Line 2**: Declares the prototype for this function when **T** is substituted. It declares that the function clamp takes three arguments of type **T** and returns a value of type **T**.

- **Line 4**: This is the beauty of templates – provided that the type that's passed in has a < operator, then we can perform a clamp on the three values so that **lo <= val <= hi**. This algorithm is valid for all the types that can be ordered.

Let's say we use it in the following program:

```
#include <iostream>

int main()
{
    std::cout << clamp(5, 3, 10) << "\n";
    std::cout << clamp(3, 5, 10) << "\n";
    std::cout << clamp(13, 3, 10) << "\n";
    std::cout << clamp(13.0, 3.0, 10.1) << "\n";
    std::cout << clamp<double>(13.0, 3, 10.2) << "\n";
    return 0;
}
```

We will get the following expected output:

```
$ ./a.out
5
5
10
10.1
10.2
```

Figure 2B.12: Clamp program output

In the last call to clamp, we have passed the template the double type between < and >. But we haven't followed the same for the other four calls. Why? It turns out that the compiler is getting smarter as it gets older. With every release of the standard, they improve what is known as **type deduction**. Because the compiler is able to deduce the type, we do not need to tell it what type to use. The reason for this is that the three arguments to the class without the template parameter have the same type – the first three are all int while the fourth one is double. But we had to tell the compiler which type to use for the final one because it has two doubles and an int as arguments, which resulted in a compilation error saying no function found. But then, it gave us information about why the template could not be used. This form, where you force the types, is known as **explicit template argument specification**.

## C++ Pre-Packaged Templates

The C++ Standard is comprised of two major parts:

- The language definition, that is, the keywords, syntax, lexical definitions, structures, and so on.

- The Standard Library, that is, all the pre-written general-purpose functions and classes to be provided by the compiler vendor. A subset of this library is implemented using templates and is known as the **Standard Template Library (STL)**.

The STL has origins in the generics provided in the Ada language that was developed by David Musser and Alexander Stepanov. Stepanov was a strong advocate for the use of generic programming as the basis for software development. In the 90s, he saw the opportunity to do this with the new language C++ to influence mainstream development, and proposed to the ISO C++ committee that the STL should be included as part of the language. The rest is history.

The STL is comprised of four categories of predefined generic algorithms and classes:

- **Containers**: General sequence (vector, list, deque) and associative containers (set, multiset, map)

- **Iterators**: A set of classes to traverse across containers and define the extent of the container (ranges expressed as **begin()** and **end()**). Note that one fundamental design choice in the STL is that **end()** points to a position one after the last item – mathematically, that is [**begin()**, **end()**).

- **Algorithms**: Over 100 different algorithms covering sorting, searching, set operations, and others.

- **Functions**: Support for functors (function objects where objects can be called like functions). One use is for predicates in template algorithms such as **find_if()**.

The clamp function template that we implemented previously is simplistic and while it would work for any type that supports the less than operator, it would not be very efficient – it could result in very large copies if the type has a large size. Since C++17, the STL includes a **std::clamp()** function that is declared more like this:

```
#include <cassert>


template<class T, class Compare>
const T& clamp( const T& v, const T& lo, const T& hi, Compare comp )
{
    return assert( !comp(hi, lo) ),
        comp(v, lo) ? lo : comp(hi, v) ? hi : v;
}


template<class T>
const T& clamp( const T& v, const T& lo, const T& hi )
{
    return clamp( v, lo, hi, std::less<>() );
}
```

As we can see, it uses references for the arguments and the return value. Changing the arguments to use references reduces what has to be passed on and returned on the stack. Also, note that the designers have worked to produce a more general version of the template so that we are not reliant on the < operator that exists for the type. However, we can define the ordering by passing comp.

From the preceding examples, we have seen that, like functions, templates can take multiple comma-separated parameters.

## Type Aliases – typedef and using

If you have used the **std::string** class, then you have been using an alias. There are a few template classes related to strings that need to implement the same functionality. But the type representing a character is different. For example, for **std::string**, the representation is **char**, while **std::wstring** uses **wchar_t**. There are several others for **char16_t** and **char32_t**. Any variation in the functionality will be managed through traits or template specialization.

Prior to C++11, this would have been aliased from the **std::basic_string** base class, as follows:

```
namespace std {

    typedef basic_string<char> string;

}
```

This does two main things:

- Reduces the amount of typing required to declare the variable. This is a simple case, but when you declare a unique pointer to a map of strings to object, it can get very long and you will make errors:

  ```
  typedef std::unique_ptr<std::map<std::string,myClass>> UptrMapStrToClass;
  ```

- Improves the readability as you now conceptually think of it as a string and do not need to worry about the details.

But C++11 introduced a better way – **alias declarations** – which utilizes the **using** keyword. The preceding code can be implemented like so:

```
namespace std {

    using string = basic_string<char>;

}
```

The preceding example is simple and the alias, either typedef or using, is not too hard to grok. But when the alias involves more complicated expressions, they too can be a little unreadable – particularly function pointers. Consider the following code:

```
typedef int (*FunctionPointer)(const std::string&, const Point&);
```

Now, consider the following code:

```
using FunctionPointer = int (*)(const std::string&, const Point&);
```

There is a reason for the new feature in C++11 where alias declaration may be incorporated easily into templates – they can be templatized. A **typedef** cannot be templatized and while it is possible to achieve the same outcome with **typedef**, the alias declaration (**using**) is the preferred method as it results in simpler and easier to understand template code.

## Exercise 2: Implementing Aliases

In this exercise, we will implement aliases using a typedef and see how the code becomes easier to read and efficient by using a reference. Follow these steps to implement this exercise:

1.  Open the **Lesson2B** project in Eclipse, and then in the Project Explorer, expand **Lesson2B**, then **Exercise02** and double-click on **Exercise2.cpp** to open the file for this exercise in the editor.

2.  Click on the **Launch Configuration** dropdown menu and select **New Launch Configuration....** Configure **L2BExercise2** to run with the name **Exercise2**. When that is complete, it will be the currently selected Launch Configuration.

3.  Click on the **Run** button. **Exercise 2** will run and produce something similar to the following output:

```
------ Exercise 2 ------
Array is : 2,4,6,1,3,5,
Complete.
```

Figure 2B.13: Exercise 2 output

4.  In the editor, before the declaration of the **printVector()** function, add the following line:

```
typedef std::vector<int> IntVector;
```

5.  Now, change all occurrences of **std::vector<int>** in the file with **IntVector**.

6.  Click on the **Run** button. The output should be the same as before.

7.  In the editor, change the line that you previously added to the following:

```
using IntVector = std::vector<int>;
```

8.  Click on the **Run** button. The output should be the same as before.

9.  In the editor, add the following line:

```
using IntVectorIter = std::vector<int>::iterator;
```

10. Now, change the one occurrence of `IntVector::iterator` to `IntVectorIter`.

11. Click on the **Run** button. The output should be the same as before.

In this exercise, there appears to be little difference between typedef and using alias. In either case, the use of a well-named alias makes code easier to read and understand. When more complicated aliases are involved, **using** produces an easier way to write an alias. Introduced in C++11, **using** is now the preferred method for defining an alias. It has other advantages over **typedef**, such as being able to use it inside templates.

## Templates – More than Generic Programming

Templates can also deliver much more than just generic programming (a cookie cutter with types). In the case of generic programming, the template operates as a blueprint that cannot be changed and delivers the compiled version of the template for the specified type or types.

Templates can be written to provide specialization of a function or algorithm based on the types involved. This is known as **template specialization** and is not generic programming in the sense we previously used it. It can only be called generic programming when it makes certain types behave as we would expect them to do in a given context. It cannot be called generic programming when the algorithm that's used for all types is modified.

Examine the following sample of specialization code:

```
#include <iostream>
#include <type_traits>


template <typename T, std::enable_if_t<sizeof(T) == 1, int> = 0>
void print(T val)
{
    printf("%c\n", val);
}


template <typename T, std::enable_if_t<sizeof(T) == sizeof(int), int> = 0>
void print(T val)
{
    printf("%d\n", val);
```

```
}

template <typename T, std::enable_if_t<sizeof(T) == sizeof(double), int> =
0>
void print(T val)
{
    printf("%f\n", val);
}

int main(int argc, char** argv)
{
    print('c');
    print(55);
    print(32.1F);
    print(77.3);
}
```

It defines a template that calls **printf()** with a different format string, based on the specialization of the template using **std::enable_if_t<>** and **sizeof()**. When we run it, the following output is generated:

```
c
55
-1073741824
77.300000
```

Figure 2B.14: Erroneous print template program output

## Substitution Failure Is Not An Error – SFINAE

The value printed for **32.1F** (**-1073741824**) does not bear any resemblance to the number. If we examine the code that was generated by the compiler for the following program, we will find that it has generated the code as if we wrote the following (and more):

```
template<typename int, int=0>
void print<int,0>(int val)
{
    printf("%d\n",val);
```

```
}
```

```
template<typename float, int=0>
void print<float,0>(float val)
{
    printf("%d\n", val);
}
```

Why does it generate this code? The preceding templates use a feature of the C++ compiler called **S**ubstitution **F**ailure **I**s **N**ot **A**n **E**rror, or **SFINAE**. Basically, during the substitution phase of a template, based on the types, if the compiler is unable to form valid code, then it just drops the definition and continues rather than producing an error. Let's try and fix the preceding code and get the right outcome for print. To do that, we will introduce the use of **std::enable_if_t<>** and access what are known as **type traits** to help us. Firstly, we will replace the last template with the following code:

```
#include <type_traits>

template <typename T, std::enable_if_t<std::is_floating_point_v<T>, int> = 0>
void print(T val)
{
    printf("%f\n", val);
}
```

This takes some explaining. Firstly, we consider the definition of **std::enable_if_t**, which is actually a type alias:

```
template<bool B, class T = void>
struct enable_if {};

template<class T>
struct enable_if<true, T> { typedef T type; };

template< bool B, class T = void >
using enable_if_t = typename enable_if<B,T>::type;
```

The first template for **enable_if** will result in the definition of an empty struct (or class). The second template for **enable_if** is a specialization for true as a first template argument that will result in the class with a typedef definition. The definition of **enable_if_t** is a helper template that removes the need for us to enter `::type` on the end of the template when we use it. So, how does this work? Consider the following code:

```
template <typename T, std::enable_if_t<condition, int> = 0>
void print(T val) { … }
```

If the condition that is evaluated at compile time results in **true**, then the **enable_if_t** template will result in a template that looks like this:

```
template <typename T, int = 0>
void print(T val) { … }
```

This is valid syntax and the function is added to the symbol table as a candidate function. If the condition that is calculated at compile time results in **false**, then the **enable_if_t** template will result in a template that looks like this:

```
template <typename T, = 0>
void print(T val) { … }
```

This is **malformed code** which is now discarded – SFINAE at work.

`std::is_floating_point_v<T>` is another helper class that accesses the `::value` member of the `std::is_floating_point<T>` template. Its name says it all – it will be true if T is a floating-point type (float, double, long double); otherwise, it will be false. If we make this change, then the compiler (GCC) generates the following error:

```
In function 'int main(int, char**)':
error: call of overloaded 'print(float)' is ambiguous
   46 |     print(32.1F);
```

Figure 2B.15: Compiler error for the modified print template program

The problem now is that we have two templates that can satisfy when the type is a float:

```
template <typename T, std::enable_if_t<sizeof(T) == sizeof(int), int> = 0>
void print(T val)
{
    printf("%d\n", val);
}
```

```
template <typename T, std::enable_if_t<std::is_floating_point_v<T>, int> = 0>

void print(T val)

{

    printf("%f\n", val);

}
```

It turns out that (usually) **sizeof(float) == sizeof(int)**, so we need to make another change. We'll replace the first condition with another type trait – **std::is_integral_v<>**:

```
template <typename T, std::enable_if_t<std::is_integral_v<T>, int> = 0>

void print(T val)

{

    printf("%d\n", val);

}
```

If we make this change, then the compiler (GCC) generates the following error:

```
In function 'int main(int, char**)':
error: call of overloaded 'print(char)' is ambiguous
   44 |      print('c');
```

Figure 2B.16: Second compiler error for the modified print template program

We fixed the floating-point ambiguity, but the problem here is that **std::is_integral_v(char)** returns true and again there are two functions that are generated by the templates for a type of char with the same prototype. It turns out that the conditions that's passed to **std::enable_if_t<>** obeys standard C++ logic expressions. So, to fix this problem, we will add an extra condition that will exclude chars:

```
template <typename T, std::enable_if_t<std::is_integral_v<T> && sizeof(T) != 1, int> = 0>

void print(T val)

{

    printf("%d\n", val);

}
```

If we compile the program now, it completes the compilation and links the program. If we run it, it now produces the following (expected) output:

```
c
55
32.099998
77.300000
```

Figure 2B.17: Corrected print template program output

## Floating-Point Representations

Shouldn't that **32.099998** be **32.1**? That is what was passed to the function. The problem with performing floating-point operations on a computer is that the representation automatically introduces an error. Real numbers form a continuous (infinite) domain. If you consider the numbers 1 and 2 in the real domain, then there is an infinite amount of real numbers between them. Unfortunately, a computer's representation of floating-point numbers quantizes the values and cannot represent all of the infinite number of numbers. The bigger the number of bits used to store the number, the better the representation of the value is on the real domain. So, long double is better than double is better than float. It really depends on your problem domain as to what is appropriate for storing the data. Back to **32.099998**. The computer stores the single precision numbers as the sum of powers of 2 and then shifts them by a power factor. Integral numbers are usually easy as they can be easily represented by the sum of **2^n** powers (n>=0). The fractional part, which in this case is 0.1, has to be expressed as the sum of **2^(-n) (n>0)**. We add more power-2 fractions to attempt to get the number closer to the target until we have used up the 24 bits that we have for precision in a single precision floating-point number.

> Note
>
> If you want to know more about how computers store floating-point numbers, research the IEEE 754 standard that defines it.

## Constexpr if Expressions

C++17 introduced the **constexpr if** expression to the language, which simplifies template writing greatly. We can rewrite the preceding three templates that use SFINAE as one simpler template:

```cpp
#include <iostream>
#include <type_traits>


template <typename T>
void print(T val)
{
    if constexpr(sizeof(T)==1) {
        printf("%c",val);
    }
    else if constexpr(std::is_integral_v<T>) {
        printf("%d",val);
    }
    else if constexpr(std::is_floating_point_v<T>) {
        printf("%f",val);
    }
    printf("\n");
}


int main(int argc, char** argv)
{
    print('c');
    print(55);
    print(32.1F);
    print(77.3);
}
```

For the call to **print(55)**, the compiler generates the function to call as follows:

```
template<>
void print<int>(int val)
{
    printf("%d",val);
    printf("\n");
}
```

What happened to the if/else if statements? What happens with a `constexpr if` expression is that the compiler contextually determines the value of the condition and converts it into a bool value (true/false). If the evaluated value is true, then the if condition and the else clause are discarded, leaving only the true clause to generate code. Likewise, if it is false, then the false clause is left to generate code. In other words, only the first constexpr if condition that evaluates to true will have the code for its clause generated, while the rest are discarded.

## Non-Type Template Arguments

So far, we have only seen template arguments that are types. It is also possible to pass an integral value as a template argument. This allows us to prevent array decay for a function. For example, consider a template function that calculates the **sum**:

```
template <class T>
T sum(T data[], int number)
{
    T total = 0;
    for(auto i=0U ; i<number ; i++)
    {
        total += data[i];
    }
    return total;
}
```

In this case, we need to pass the length of the array in the call:

```
float data[5] = {1.1, 2.2, 3.3, 4.4, 5.5};
auto total = sum(data, 5);
```

But wouldn't it be better if we could just call the following?

```
auto total = sum(data);
```

We can do it by making changes to the template, like in the following code:

```
template <class T, std::size_t size>
T sum(T (&data)[size])
{
  T total = 0;
  for(auto i=0U ; i< size; i++)
  {
    total += data[i];
  }
  return total;
}
```

Here, we changed the data to be a reference to an array of a certain size – a size that is passed to the template – and so the compiler figures it out. We no longer need the second argument to the function call. This simple example showed how to pass and use a non-type argument directly. We will explore this more in the *Template Type Deduction* section.

## Exercise 3: Implementing Stringify – specialization Versus constexpr

In this exercise, we will implement a stringify template by utilizing constexpr to produce an easier to read and simpler version of the code. Follow these steps to implement this exercise:

> **Note**
>
> The stringify specialization templates can be found at https://isocpp.org/wiki/faq/templates#template-specialization-example.

1. Open the **Lesson2B** project in Eclipse, and then in the **Project Explorer**, expand **Lesson2B**, then **Exercise03**, and double-click on **Exercise3.cpp** to open the file for this exercise in the editor.

2. Click on the **Launch Configuration** dropdown menu and select **New Launch Configuration....** Configure **L2BExercise3** to run with the name **Exercise3**.

3. Click on the **Run** button. **Exercise 3** will run and produce the following output:

```
------ Exercise 3 ------
stringify(true)              --> true
stringify(32)                --> 32
stringify(143.2109876F)  --> 143.211
stringify(1234.56789)     --> 1234.56789
Complete.
```

Figure 2B.18: Exercise 3 specialized template output

4. In **Exercise3.cpp**, comment out all of the template specializations for the stringify template while leaving the original general template.

5. Click on the **Run** button. The output will change to have the boolean printed as a number and the double printed to only two decimal places:

```
------ Exercise 3 ------
stringify(true)              --> 1
stringify(32)                --> 32
stringify(143.2109876F)  --> 143.211
stringify(1234.56789)     --> 1234.57
Complete.
```

Figure 2B.19: Exercise 3 general template only output

6. We will now "specialize" the template for the boolean type again. Add the **#include <type_traits>** directive with the other **#includes** and modify the template so that it reads as follows:

```cpp
template<typename T> std::string stringify(const T& x)
{
    std::ostringstream out;
    if constexpr (std::is_same_v<T, bool>)
    {
        out << std::boolalpha;
    }
    out << x;
    return out.str();
}
```

7. Click on the **Run** button. The output boolean stringify works as before:

```
------ Exercise 3 ------
stringify(true)            --> true
stringify(32)              --> 32
stringify(143.2109876F)  --> 143.211
stringify(1234.56789)      --> 1234.57
Complete.
```

**Figure 2B.20: stringify tailored for boolean**

8. We will now "specialize" the template for the floating-point types (**float**, **double**, **long double**) again. Modify the template so that it reads as follows:

```cpp
template<typename T> std::string stringify(const T& x)
{
    std::ostringstream out;
    if constexpr (std::is_same_v<T, bool>)
    {
        out << std::boolalpha;
    }
    else if constexpr (std::is_floating_point_v<T>)
    {
        const int sigdigits = std::numeric_limits<T>::digits10;
        out << std::setprecision(sigdigits);
    }
    out << x;
    return out.str();
}
```

9. Click on the **Run** button. The output is restored to the original:

```
------ Exercise 3 ------
stringify(true)            --> true
stringify(32)              --> 32
stringify(143.2109876F)  --> 143.211
stringify(1234.56789)      --> 1234.56789
Complete.
```

**Figure 2B.21: constexpr if version template output**

10. If you compare the original version with multiple templates to the final version, you will find that the final version is more like a normal function and is easier to read and maintain.

In the exercise, we learned how much simpler and compact our templates can be when using the new constexpr if construct in C++17.

## Function Overloading Revisited

When we first discussed function overloading, we only considered the scenarios where the name of the function came from the list of functions that we wrote by hand. Now, we need to update this. We can also write templated functions that can have the same name. Like we did previously, when the compiler meets the line **print(55)**, it needs to work out which of the previously defined functions to call. So, it performs the following process (grossly simplified):

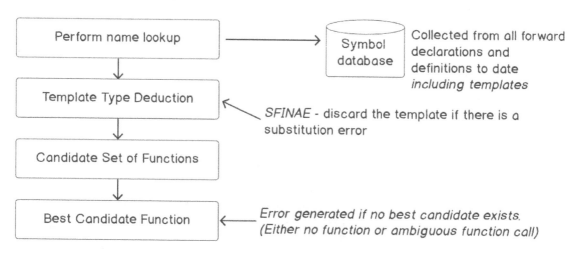

Figure 2B.22: Function overload resolution with templates (simplified)

## Template Type Deduction

When we first introduced templates, we touched on Template type deduction. Now, we are going to explore this further. We will start by considering the general declaration for a function template:

```
template<typename T>
void function(ParamType parameter);
```

The call for this might look like this:

```
function(expression);            // deduce T and ParamType from expression
```

When the compiler reaches this line, it must now deduce two types related to the template – **T** and **ParamType**. These are often different due to qualifiers and other attributes attached to the T in the ParamType (for example pointer, reference, const, and so on). The types are related but the deduction progresses differently, depending on the form of **expression** used.

## Displaying the Deduced Types

Before we look into the different forms, it might be useful if we could get the compiler to tell us the types that it has deduced. We have a few options here, including the IDE editors showing types, the compiler generating errors, and runtime support (which, due to the C++ standard, is not necessarily effective). We will use the compiler errors to help us explore some of the type deductions.

We can achieve a type displayer by declaring a template without a definition. Any attempt to instantiate the template will cause the compiler to generate an error message as there is no definition, along with the type information that it is trying to instantiate:

```
template<typename T>
struct TypeDisplay;
```

Let's attempt to compile the following program:

```
template<typename T>
class TypeDisplay;


int main()
{
    signed int x = 1;
    unsigned int y = 2;

    TypeDisplay<decltype(x)> x_type;
    TypeDisplay<decltype(y)> y_type;
    TypeDisplay<decltype(x+y)> x_y_type;

    return 0;
}
```

The compiler spits out the following errors:

```
$ g++ types.cpp -std=c++17 -o types.exe
types.cpp: In function 'int main()':
types.cpp:10:30: error: aggregate 'TypeDisplay<int> x_type' has incomplete type
and cannot be defined
   10 |      TypeDisplay<decltype(x)> x_type;
      |                               ^~~~~~
types.cpp:11:30: error: aggregate 'TypeDisplay<unsigned int> y_type' has
incomplete type and cannot be defined
   11 |      TypeDisplay<decltype(y)> y_type;
      |                               ^~~~~~
types.cpp:12:32: error: aggregate 'TypeDisplay<unsigned int> x_y_type' has
incomplete type and cannot be defined
   12 |      TypeDisplay<decltype(x+y)> x_y_type;
      |                                 ^~~~~~~~
```

Figure 2B.23: Compiler errors showing deduced types

Note that, in each case, the aggregate being named includes the type being deduced – for x, it is an int, for y, an unsigned int, and for x+y, an unsigned int. Also, note that the TypeDisplay template requires a type for its arguments and so the `decltype()` function is used to get the compiler to provide the type for the expression in brackets.

It is also possible to display the deduced type at runtime either using the built-in `typeid(T).name()` operator, which returns a std::string, or by using the boost library called type_index.

> **Note**
>
> For more information on this, visit the following link: https://www.boost.org/doc/libs/1_70_0/doc/html/boost_typeindex.html.

Because of the type deduction rules, the built-in operator will give you an indication of the type, but it will lose reference (**&**, and **&&**) and any constness information (const or volatile). If required at runtime, then consider `boost::type_index`, which will produce the same output for all the compilers.

## Template Type Deduction – the Details

Let's return to the generic template:

```
template<typename T>
void function(ParamType parameter);
```

Let's say that the call looks like this:

```
function(expression);          // deduce T and ParamType from expression
```

Type deduction proceeds differently depending on the form of ParamType used:

- **ParamType is a value (T)**: Pass-by-value function call
- **ParamType is a reference or pointer (T& or T*)**: Pass-by-reference function call
- **ParamType is a rvalue reference (T&&)**: Pass-by-reference function call or something else

### Case 1: ParamType is pass-by-value (T)

```
template<typename T>
void function(T parameter);
```

As a pass-by-value call, this means that the parameter will be a copy of whatever is passed in. Because this is a new instance of the object, the following rules are applied to the expression:

- If the expression's type is a reference, then ignore the reference part.
- If, after step 1, the remaining type is const and/or volatile, then ignore those as well.

What's left is T. Let's attempt to compile the following file code:

```
template<typename T>
class TypeDisplay;

template<typename T>
void function(T parameter)
{
    TypeDisplay<T> type;
}

void types()
{
    int x = 42;
    function(x);
}
```

The compiler produces the following error:

```
types.cpp: In instantiation of 'void function(T) [with T = int]':
types.cpp:13:15:   required from here
types.cpp:7:20: error: 'TypeDisplay<int> type' has incomplete type
    7 |      TypeDisplay<T> type;
```

Figure 2B.24: Compiler error showing a deduced type for the pass by type

So, the type is deduced to be **int**. Likewise, we get exactly the same error if we declare the following:

```
const int x = 42;

function(x);
```

The same will happen if we declare this version:

```
int x = 42;

const int& rx = x;

function(rx);
```

In all three cases, the deduced type is **int**, as per the rules stated previously.

## Case 2: ParamType is pass-by-reference (T&)

As a pass-by-reference call, this means that the parameter will be able to access the original storage location of the object. Because of this, the generated function has to honor the constness and volatileness we ignored before. The following rules are applied to type deduction:

- If the expression's type is a reference, then ignore the reference part.

- Pattern match what's left of the type of expression with ParamType to determine T.

Let's attempt to compile the following file:

```
template<typename T>
class TypeDisplay;


template<typename T>
void function(T& parameter)
{
    TypeDisplay<T> type;
```

```
}


void types()

{

    int x = 42;

    function(x);

}
```

The compiler will generate the following error:

```
types.cpp: In instantiation of 'void function(T&) [with T = int]':
types.cpp:13:15:    required from here
types.cpp:7:20: error: 'TypeDisplay<int> type' has incomplete type
    7 |      TypeDisplay<T> type;
```

Figure 2B.25: Compiler error showing the deduced type for pass by reference

From this, we can see that the compiler has T as an **int** from ParamType as **int&**. Changing x to be a const int provides no surprises as T is deduced to be **const int** from ParamType as **const int&**:

```
$ g++ -std=c++17 types.cpp   -o types.exe
types.cpp: In instantiation of 'void function(T&) [with T = const int]':
types.cpp:13:15:    required from here
types.cpp:7:20: error: 'TypeDisplay<const int> type' has incomplete type
    7 |      TypeDisplay<T> type;
```

Figure 2B.26: Compiler error showing the deduced type for pass by const reference

Likewise, introducing rx as a reference to a const int, as before, gives no surprises, as T is deduced to be **const int** from ParamType as **const int&**:

```
void types()

{

    const int x = 42;

    const int& rx = x;

    function(rx);

}
```

```
types.cpp: In instantiation of 'void function(T&) [with T = const int]':
types.cpp:14:16:    required from here
types.cpp:7:20: error: 'TypeDisplay<const int> type' has incomplete type
    7 |      TypeDisplay<T> type;
```

Figure 2B.27: Compiler error showing the deduced type when passing a const reference

If we change the declaration to include a const, then the compiler will honor the constness when it generates the function from the template:

```
template<typename T>

void function(const T& parameter)

{

    TypeDisplay<T> type;

}
```

This time, the compiler reports the following

- **int x**: T is int (as the constness will be honored), while the parameter's type is **const int&**.

- **const int x**: T is int (const is in the pattern, leaving int), while the parameter's type is **const int&**.

- **const int& rx**: T is int (reference is ignored, const is in the pattern, leaving int), while the parameter's type is **const int&**.

If we attempt to compile the following, what do we expect? Normally, an array decays to be a pointer:

```
int ary[15];

function(ary);
```

The compiler error is as follows:

```
types.cpp: In instantiation of 'void function(T&) [with T = int [15]]':
types.cpp:13:17:    required from here
types.cpp:7:20: error: 'TypeDisplay<int [15]> type' has incomplete type
    7 |        TypeDisplay<T> type;
```

Figure 2B.28: Compiler error showing the deduced type for the array argument when passed by reference

This time, the array is captured as a reference and the size is also included. So, if ary was declared as **ary[10]**, then a completely different function would result. Let's revert the template to the following:

```
template<typename T>

void function(T parameter)

{

    TypeDisplay<T> type;

}
```

If we attempt to compile the array call, then the error reports the following:

```
types.cpp: In instantiation of 'void function(T) [with T = int*]':
types.cpp:13:17:    required from here
types.cpp:7:20: error: 'TypeDisplay<int*> type' has incomplete type
    7 |      TypeDisplay<T> type;
```

Figure 2B.29: Compiler error showing the deduced type for the array argument
when passed by value

We can see that, in this case, the array has decayed as the usual behavior when passing an array to a function. We saw this behavior when talking about *Non-Type Template Arguments*.

**Case 3: ParamType is a rvalue reference (T&&)**

T&& is called a rvalue reference while T& is called a lvalue reference. C++ not only characterizes an expression by type but also by a property called the **value category**. These categories control expression evaluation in the compiler, including the rules for creating, copying, and moving temporary objects. There are five expression value categories defined in the C++17 standard that have the following relationships:

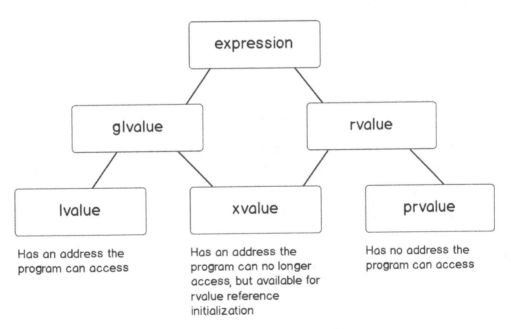

Figure 2B.30: C++ value categories

The definitions of each are as follows:

- An expression that determines the identity of an object is a `glvalue`.

- An expression whose evaluation initializes an object or the operand of an operator is a `prvalue`. Examples include a literal (except string literal) such as 3.1415, true or nullptr, the this pointer, post increment, and post decrement expressions.

- A glvalue object that has resources and can be reused (because its life is ending) is an `xvalue`. Examples include a function call whose return type is an rvalue reference to an object, such as `std::move()`.

- A glvalue that is not an xvalue is an `lvalue`. Examples include the name of a variable, a function or a data member, or a string literal.

- A prvalue or xvalue is an `rvalue`.

It does not matter if you do not fully understand these for the explanation that follows – just know that an expression that is considered to be an lvalue can have its address taken (using the address of operator, that is, "&"). The type deduction rules for the following require that you know what an lvalue is, as well as what it isn't:

```
template<typename T>
void function(T&& parameter)
{
    TypeDisplay<T> type;
}
```

The type deduction rules for this ParamType form are as follows:

- If the expression is an lvalue reference, then both T and ParamType are deduced to be an lvalue reference. This is the only scenario where the type is deduced to be a reference.

- If the expression is an rvalue reference, then the rules for Case 2 apply.

## SFINAE Expression and Trailing Return Types

C++11 introduced a feature called **trailing return types** to provide a mechanism for templates so that they can generalize the return type. A simple example is as follows:

```
template<class T>
auto mul(T a, T b) -> decltype(a * b)
{
    return a * b;
}
```

Here, **auto** is used to indicate that a trailing return type is defined. The trailing return type starts with the **->** pointer and in this case, the return type is the type that's returned by multiplying **a** and **b**. The compiler will process the content of the decltype and, if it is malformed, it will remove the definition from the function name's lookup, as per usual. This capability opens up many possibilities as the comma operator, ",", can be used inside **decltype** to check for certain attributes.

If we want to test that a class implements a method or contains a type then we can place this inside the decltype by converting it into a void (in case the comma operator has been overloaded) and then define an object of the real return type at the end of the comma operator. An example of this is shown in the following program:

```
#include <iostream>
#include <algorithm>
#include <utility>
#include <vector>
#include <set>


template<class C, class T>
auto contains(const C& c, const T& x)
            -> decltype((void)(std::declval<C>().find(std::declval<T>())),
    true)
{
    return end(c) != c.find(x);
}


int main(int argc, char**argv)
{
```

```
        std::cout << "\n\n------ SFINAE Exercise ------\n";


        std::set<int> mySet {1,2,3,4,5};
        std::cout << std::boolalpha;
        std::cout << "Set contains 5: " << contains(mySet,5) << "\n";
        std::cout << "Set contains 15: " << contains(mySet,15) << "\n";


        std::cout << "Complete.\n";
        return 0;
    }
```

When this program is compiled and executed, we obtain the following output:

```
------ SFINAE Exercise ------
Set contains 5: true
Set contains 15: false
Complete.
```

Figure 2B.31: Output from the SFINAE expression

The return type is given by the following code:

```
decltype( (void)(std::declval<C>().find(std::declval<T>())), true)
```

Let's break this down:

- The operand of **decltype** is a comma-separated list of expressions. This means that the compiler will construct but not evaluate the expressions and use the type of the right-most value to determine the return type for the function.

- **std::declval<T>()** allows us to convert the T type into a reference type that we can then use to access member functions without having to actually construct an object.

- As with all SFINAE-based operations, if any expression in the comma-separated list is invalid, then the function is discarded. If they are all valid, then it is added to the list of functions for lookup.

- The cast to void is to prevent any problems that may arise if the user overloads the comma operator.

- Basically, this is testing whether the **C** class has a member function called **find()** that takes **class T**, **class T&**, or **const class T&** as an argument.

This method will work for **std::set**, which has a **find()** method that takes one argument but will fail for other containers because they do not have a **find()** member method.

This approach works well if we are only dealing with one type. But if we have a function that needs to produce different implementations based on type, as we have seen before, the **if constexpr** approach is much cleaner and generally easier to understand. To use the **if constexpr** approach, we need to produce templates that will evaluate to **true** or **false** at compile time. The standard library provides helper classes for this: **std::true_type** and **std::false_type**. These two structures have a static constant member named value set to **true** and **false**, respectively. Using SFINAE and template overloads, we can create new detection classes that derive from either of these classes to give us the desired outcome:

```
template <class T, class A0>
auto test_find(long) -> std::false_type;


template <class T, class A0>
auto test_find(int)
-> decltype(void(std::declval<T>().find(std::declval<A0>())), std::true_
type{});


template <class T, class A0>
struct has_find : decltype(test_find<T,A0>(0)) {};
```

The first template for **test_find** creates the default behavior that will set the return type to **std::false_type**. Note that this has an argument type of **long**.

The second template for **test_find** creates a specialization that tests for a class that has a member function called **find()** and has a return type of **std::true_type**. Note that this has an argument type of **int**.

The **has_find<T,A0>** template works by deriving itself from the return types of the **test_find()** functions. If the T class does not have the **find()** method, then only the **std::false_type** version of **test_find()** is generated and so the **has_find<T,A0>::value** value will be false and can be used in **if constexpr()**.

The interesting part occurs if the T class has the `find()` method as both of the `test_find()` methods are generated. But the specialized version takes an argument of the `int` type while the default takes an argument of the `long` type. As we "call" the function with zero (0), it will match the specialized version and use it. The argument difference is important because you cannot have two functions with the same argument types and only differ by return type. If you want to check this behavior, then change the argument from 0 to 0L to force the long version.

## Class Templates

We have only dealt with function templates so far. But templates can also be used to provide blueprints for classes. The general structure of a templated class declaration is as follows:

```
template<class T>

class MyClass {

    // variables and methods that use T.

};
```

Whereas template functions allow us to produce generic algorithms, template classes allow us to produce generic data types and their associated behaviors.

When we introduced the Standard Template Library, we highlighted that it includes templates for containers – **vector**, **deque**, **stack**, and so on. These templates allow us to store and manage any data type that we want, but still behave as we would expect.

### Exercise 4: Writing a Class Template

Two of the most commonly used data structures in computing science are stack and queue. Both currently have implementations in the STL. But to get our feet wet with a templated class, we are going to write a stack template class that can be used for any type. Let's get started:

1. Open the **Lesson2B** project in Eclipse, and then in the **Project Explorer**, expand **Lesson2B**, then **Exercise04**, and double-click on **Exercise4.cpp** to open the file for this exercise in the editor.

2. Configure a new **Launch Configuration**, **L2BExercise4**, to run with the name **Exercise4**.

3. Also, configure a new C/C++ Unit Run Configuration, **L2BEx4Tests**, to run **L2BEx4tests**. Set the **Google Tests Runner**.

4. Click on the **Run** option for the test, which we have to run for the first time:

Figure 2B.32: Initial unit test for stacks

5. Open **Stack.hpp** in the editor. You will find the following code:

```
#pragma once
#include <vector>
#include <cstddef>

#define EXERCISE4_STEP       1

namespace acpp
{

template <typename T>
class Stack
{
public:

private:
    std::vector<T> m_stack;
};

} // namespace acpp
```

The first thing to note with a template definition is that it must be placed in a header file that can be included where we need to reuse it. Secondly, we have used a pragma directive (**#pragma once**) which tells the compiler that if it encounters this file again to be #included, it does not need to be. While not strictly part of the standard, nearly all modern C++ compilers support it. Finally, note that, for the purpose of this exercise, we have chosen to store the items in the STL vector.

6. In the editor, add the following declaration in the **public** section of the **Stack** class:

```
bool empty() const
{
  return m_stack.empty();
}
```

7. At the top of the file, change **EXERCISE4_STEP** to a value of **10**. Click on the **Run** button. The Exercise 4 tests should run and fail:

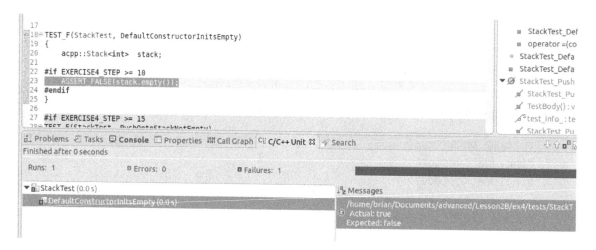

Figure 2B.33: Jumping to a Failing test

8. Click on the name of the failing test, that is, **DefaultConstructorInitsEmpty**. It will show the cause of the failure in the Messages section on the right. Double-click on the message. It will open the file with the failing test and jump to the offending line, as shown in the preceding screenshot. This test has an error. In the test, we are expecting the stack to be empty. However, we can see that `empty()` reports false.

9. Change `ASSERT_FALSE` to `ASSERT_TRUE` and rerun the test. This time, it passes because it is testing the right thing.

10. The next thing we will do is add some type aliases ready for use with the next few methods. In the editor, add the following lines just above the `empty()` method:

```
using value_type = T;
using reference = value_type&;
using const_reference = const value_type&;
using size_type = std::size_t;
```

11. Click on the **Run** button to rerun the tests. They should pass. When doing test-driven development, the mantra is to write a small test and see it fail, and then write just enough code to make it pass. In this case, we actually tested that we got the definition of the aliases correct because failing to compile is one form of test failure. We are now ready to add the push function.

12. In the editor, change **Stack.hpp** by adding the following code just below the **empty()** method:

```
void push(const value_type& value)
{
    m_stack.push_back(value);
}
```

13. At the top of the file, change **EXERCISE4_STEP** to a value of **15**. Click on the **Run** button. We now have two tests that run and pass. The new test, **PushOntoStackNotEmpty**, in **StackTests.cpp** proves that the push does something to make the stack no longer empty. We need to add more methods to make sure that it has done the expected.

14. In the editor, change **Stack.hpp** by adding the following code just below the **push()** method and change **EXERCISE4_STEP** to a value of **16**:

```
size_type size() const
{
    return m_stack.size();
}
```

15. Click on the **Run** button to run the tests. There should now have three passing tests.

16. In the editor, change **Stack.hpp** by adding the following code just below the **push()** method and change **EXERCISE4_STEP** to a value of **18**:

```
void pop()
{
    m_stack.pop_back();
}
```

17. Click on the **Run** button to run the tests. There should now be four passing tests.

18. In the editor, change **Stack.hpp** by adding the following code just below the **pop()** method and change **EXERCISE4_STEP** to a value of **20**:

```
reference top()
{
    m_stack.back();
}

const_reference top() const
{
    m_stack.back();
}
```

19. Click on the **Run** button to run the tests. There are now five passing tests and we have implemented a stack.

20. From the Launch Configuration dropdown, select **L2BExercise4** and click on the **Run** button. Exercise 4 will run and produce something similar to the following output:

```
------ Exercise 4 ------
Stack is empty
Pushing 0.0F onto stack
Stack is not empty
Pushing 3.14159F onto stack
Stack has 2 items
Top item is 3.14159
Complete.
```

Figure 2B.34: Exercise 4 output

Examine the code that is now in the **Stack.hpp** file. The approach of defining types inside the class is common throughout the STL (although they may use typedef because of their heritage). The `std::stack` template takes two arguments, with the second one defining the container to be used – vector could be the first. Examine the tests in **StackTests.cpp**. The tests should be named to indicate what they aim to test, and they should focus on doing that.

## Activity 1: Developing a Generic "contains" Template Function

The programming language Python has a membership operator called "in" that can be used on any sequence, that is, list, sequence, set, string, and so on. Even though C++ has over 100 algorithms, it does not have an equivalent method to achieve the same. C++ 20 introduced the `contains()` method on `std::set`, but that is not enough for us. We need to create a `contains()` template function that works with `std::set`, `std::string`, `std::vector`, and any other container that provides iterators. This is determined by the ability to call end() on it. We are aiming for best performance, so we will call the `find()` member method on any container that has one (it will be the most efficient) and otherwise fall back to using `std::end()` on the container. We also need to treat `std::string()` differently as its `find()` method returns a special value.

We could implement this using a general template and two specializations, but this activity is being used to get it working using the techniques of SFINAE and if constexpr. In addition, this template must only work on a class that supports `end(C)`. Follow these steps to implement this activity:

1. Load the prepared project from the **Lesson2B/Activity01** folder.

2. Define the helper template functions and class to detect the std:string case using the **npos** member.

3. Define the helper template functions and class to detect whether the class has a `find()` method.

4. Define the contains template function that uses constexpr to select between one of three implementations – string case, the has find method, or general case.

After implementing the preceding steps, the expected output should look as follows:

```
------ Activity 1 ------
Set contains 5: true
Set contains 15: false
Vector contains 5: true
Vector contains 15: false
String contains 'times': true
String contains 'Light': false
String contains 'm': true
String contains 'z': false

Complete.
```

**Figure 2B.35: Output from the successful implementation of contains**

**Note**

The solution for this activity can be found on page 653 .

## Summary

In this chapter, we learned about interfaces, inheritance, and polymorphism, which extended our skills of what we can do with our types. We had our first adventure into generic programming with C++ templates and touched on what the language gives us for free from the C++ Standard Library, which includes the STL. We explored a feature of C++ that just works, that is, template type deduction, which makes our life easier when using templates. We then went further with templates and learned how to control the parts of the template that are included by the compiler using SFINAE and if constexpr. These form the building blocks for our journey into C++. In the next chapter, we will revisit the stack and the heap, and understand what an exception is, what happens, and when it occurs. We'll also learn how to protect our programs from resource losses when exceptions occur.

# 3

# No Leaks Allowed - Exceptions and Resources

**Learning Objectives**

By the end of this chapter, you will be able to:

- Develop classes to manage resources

- Develop exception-robust code so that the resources do not leak through RAII

- Implement classes that can transfer resource ownership through move semantics

- Implement classes that control implicit conversion

In this chapter, you will learn how to use a class to manage resources, protect against leaks, and prevent copying a large amount of data.

# Introduction

In *Chapter 2A, No Ducks Allowed – Types, and Deduction*, we briefly touched on some concepts, such as smart pointers and move semantics. In this chapter, we'll be exploring them further. It turns out that these topics are very closely related to resource management and writing robust code (code that will run often and for long periods without problems).

To understand what happens, we are going to explore where variables get placed in memory, as well as when and what happens when they go out of scope.

We will look at what the compiler generates as assembler code for what we enter, and we will explore how all of this is affected when an exception occurs.

## Variable Scope and Lifetime

In *Chapter 2B, No Ducks Allowed – Templates, and Deduction*, we discussed variable scope and lifetimes. Let's quickly go through their different types:

**Scope:**

- **Local scope** (also known as **block scope**): This applies to anything that's declared within a block that is enclosed within curly braces (**{}**).

- **Global / file scope**: This applies to variables declared outside a normal function or a class, and also to the normal functions.

**Lifetime:**

- **Automatic lifetime**: Here, the local variables are created when they are declared, and destroyed when they exit the scope that they are in. These are managed by the stack.

- **Permanent lifetime**: Here, the global and static local variables have a permanent lifetime.

- **Dynamic lifetime**: Here, the variables are created and destroyed at the request of the programmer (using the `new` and `delete operators`). These variables have their memory allocated from the heap.

We are going to use the following program to get a clarity on the behavior of **local variables** – those that have an **automatic lifetime** and those that have a **dynamic lifetime**:

```
1: #include <iostream>
2:
3: struct Int
4: {
5:     Int(int value) : m_value(value)
6:     {
7:         std::cout << "Int(" << m_value << ") @" << this << " - intCon\n";
8:     };
9:     Int() : m_value(0)
10:     {
11:         std::cout << "Int(" << m_value << ") @" << this << " - DefCon\n";
12:     };
13:     ~Int()
14:     {
15:         std::cout << "~Int()  @" << this << "\n";
16:     };
17:     Int(const Int& rhs) : m_value(rhs.m_value)
18:     {
19:         std::cout << "Int(" << m_value << ") @" << this << " - CopyCon\n";
20:     };
21:     int m_value;
22: };
23:
24: Int add(Int a, Int b )
25: {
26:     return a.m_value+b.m_value;
27: }
28:
29: Int subtract(Int a, Int b)
30: {
31:     return a.m_value - b.m_value;
32: }
33:
34: void calculate()
35: {
36:     Int a{25};
37:     Int b{50};
38:
39:     {
40:         Int c = add(a, b);
41:         Int d = subtract(a, b);
42:     }
43:     Int* e = new Int(add(subtract(a, b), a));
44: }
45:
46: int main()
47: {
48:     calculate();
49: }
```

Figure 3.1: Test program for variable scope and lifetime

When we run the preceding program, the following output is generated:

```
user@linux:~$ ./lifetime
 1: Int(25) @0xffffcbc4 - intCon
 2: Int(50) @0xffffcbc0 - intCon
 3: Int(50) @0xffffcbc8 - CopyCon
 4: Int(25) @0xffffcbcc - CopyCon
 5: Int(75) @0xffffcbbc - intCon
 6: ~Int()   @0xffffcbcc
 7: ~Int()   @0xffffcbc8
 8: Int(50) @0xffffcbd0 - CopyCon
 9: Int(25) @0xffffcbd4 - CopyCon
10: Int(-25) @0xffffcbb8 - intCon
11: ~Int()   @0xffffcbd4
12: ~Int()   @0xffffcbd0
13: ~Int()   @0xffffcbb8
14: ~Int()   @0xffffcbbc
15: Int(50) @0xffffcbdc - CopyCon
16: Int(25) @0xffffcbe0 - CopyCon
17: Int(-25) @0xffffcbd8 - intCon
18: Int(25) @0xffffcbe4 - CopyCon
19: Int(0) @0x6000004d0 - intCon
20: ~Int()   @0xffffcbe4
21: ~Int()   @0xffffcbd8
22: ~Int()   @0xffffcbe0
23: ~Int()   @0xffffcbdc
24: ~Int()   @0xffffcbc0
25: ~Int()   @0xffffcbc4
user@linux:~$
```

Figure 3.2: Output from Lifetime test program

The hexadecimal numbers (0xNNNNNNNN) in the preceding output are the addresses of the Int objects that are being constructed or destructed. Our program starts by entering at **line 46** with the **main()** function. At this point, the program has already done a lot of initialization so that everything is readily available for us to use. The figures below that refer to two stacks – **PC Stack** and **Data Stack**.

These are the abstract concepts that help us explain what happens behind the scenes. The **PC Stack (Program Counter Stack)** is used to remember the values of the program counter (a register pointing to the next instruction that needs to be run), while the **Data Stack holds** the values or addresses that we are manipulating. Although these are two separate stacks, on the real CPU, it will most likely be implemented as one stack. Let's look at the following tables wherein we've used the abbreviation **0Ln** to refer to a line number from the output of the preceding program:

| Code line | What happens | PC Stack | Data Stack |
|---|---|---|---|
| Line 48 | Address of Line 49 is pushed to PC Stack and program jumps to calculate(). | Line 49 | – |
| Line 36 | The variable a is constructed with a value of 25 – OL1. | Line 49 | a = 25 |
| Line 37 | The variable b is constructed with a value of 50 – OL2. | Line 49 | a = 25<br>b = 50 |
| Line 40 | Copy of b copy constructed – OL3 and pushed to stack.<br><br>Copy of a copy constructed – OL4 and pushed to stack. | Line 49 | a = 25<br>b = 50<br>b = 50<br>a = 25 |
| Line 40 | Address of Line 40 is pushed to PC Stack and program jumps to add(). | Line 49<br>Line 40 | a = 25<br>b = 50<br>b = 50<br>a = 25 |
| Line 26 | Calculate the sum of a and b. Then, it constructs a new temporary Int with the result (OL5) and pushes it to the stack. | Line 49<br>Line 40 | a = 25<br>b = 50<br>b = 50<br>a = 25<br>temp = 75 |
| Line 26 | Pop PC from the PC Stack and returns it to the next instruction after the location we jumped from. | Line 49 | a = 25<br>b = 50<br>b = 50<br>a = 25<br>temp = 75 |

Figure 3.3: Detailed analysis of the test program's execution (part 1)

Below is the second part of the detailed analysis of the test program's execution:

| Code line | What happens | PC Stack | Data Stack |
|---|---|---|---|
| Line 48 | Initialize the c variable with the temporary value and clean up the copies of a and b (OL6–7) that were pushed to the stack. | Line 49 | a = 25<br>b = 50<br>c = 75 |
| Line 41 | Repeats these operations with subtract and the creation of d (OL8–12). | Line 49 | A = 25<br>B = 50<br>C = 75<br>D = 25 |
| Line 42 | Scope ends. Cleans up the c and d variables (OL13–14). | Line 49 | a = 25<br>b = 50 |
| Line 43 | Allocate enough memory for e Int (new) and then construct it from the calculated value. This is shown in the following diagram: 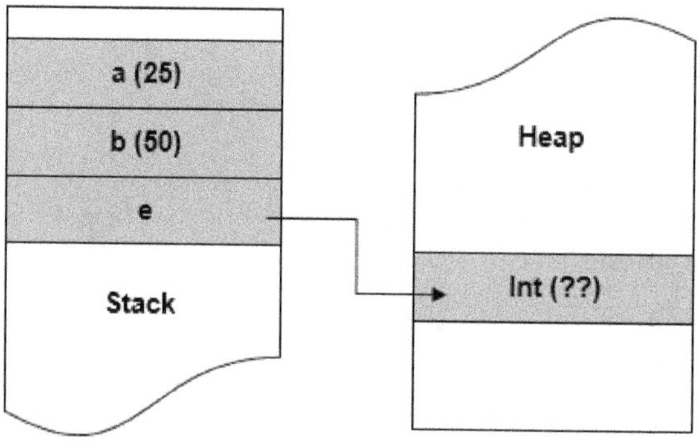 <br><br>a (25)<br>b (50)<br>e<br>Stack<br>Heap<br>Int (??) | Line 49 | a = 25<br>b = 50<br>e = pointer to int in heap |

Figure 3.4: Detailed analysis of the test program's execution (part 2)

Below is the third part of the detailed analysis of the test program's execution:

| Code line | What happens | PC Stack | Data Stack |
|---|---|---|---|
| Line 43 | Calculate: Push copies and a and b to stack (OL15–16), call add and get temporary (OL17), push a to the stack (OL18), and call subtract to get the result of 0 that was passed to constructor (OL19). Clean up the copies and temp (OL20–23). | Line 49 | a = 25<br><br>b = 50<br><br>e = pointer to Int (value = 0) |
| Line 44 | Scope ends. Clean up a, b, and e (OL24–25). This is shown in the following diagram:<br><br> | Line 49 | – |
| Line 44 | Pop PC from the PC Stack and return it to the next instruction after we jumped (Line 49). | – | – |
| Line 49 | Program exits. | | |

Figure 3.5: Detailed analysis of the test program's execution (part 3)

From this simple program, we learned some important facts:

- Copy constructors are called when we pass by value (as we did in this case).

- Returning a type causes only one constructor to be called (not two constructors – one to create the return object and one for the variable to store the returned data) – C++ calls this **copy elision** and it is now mandatory in the standard.

- On termination of scope (the closing curly bracket '**}**'), any variable that goes out of scope has its destructor called. If that is true, then why was the address **0x6000004d0** not shown with a destructor call (**~Int()**)? This leads us to the next fact.

- The destructor for a **raw pointer** only 'destroys' the pointer, not what it points at. This means that when we exited the **calculate()** method, we leaked some memory.

The last two facts are important in understanding and solving the problem of resource leaks when we forget to free the resources. We will look at resource management after we deal with exceptions in C++.

## Exceptions in C++

We have seen how C++ manages the local scope variables with automatic and dynamic lifetime. It calls the destructors of variables with an automatic lifetime when they go out of scope. We've also seen how raw pointers get destroyed when they go out of scope. As it does not clean up the dynamic lifetime variables, we lose them. This is a part of the story that builds us towards **Resource Acquisition Is Initialization** (**RAII**) later. But, first, we need to understand how exceptions change the flow of the program.

### The Need for Exceptions

In *Chapter 2A, No Ducks Allowed – Types and Deduction*, we were introduced to enumerations as a way of dealing with magic numbers for the **check_file()** function:

```
FileCheckStatus check_file(const char* name)
{
  FILE* fptr{fopen(name,"r")};

  if ( fptr == nullptr)
    return FileCheckStatus::NotFound;


  char buffer[30];
  auto numberRead = fread(buffer, 1, 30, fptr);
  fclose(fptr);
  if (numberRead != 30)
    return FileCheckStatus::IncorrectSize;
```

```
    if(is_valid(buffer))
        return FileCheckStatus::InvalidContents;


    return FileCheckStatus::Good;
}
```

The preceding function uses a technique known as **status** or **error codes** to report the outcome of the operation. This is the approach that's used for C-style programming, wherein errors related to the **POSIX API** and **Windows API** are handled.

> **Note**
>
> POSIX stands for **Potable Operating System Interface**. It is an IEEE standard for software compatibility between variants of Unix and other operating systems.

This means that, the caller of the method must check the return value and take the appropriate action for each error type. This approach works well when you can reason about the types of errors that the code will generate. This is not always true. For example, there may be a problem with the data that is fed to the program. This leads to an abnormal state in the program that cannot be handled. The part of the code that has the logic to deal with the error is removed from the section of code that detects the problem.

While it is possible to write code that deals with such a problem, it increases the complications of dealing with all error conditions, thereby making the program hard to read, hard to reason about what the function is supposed to do, and thus very hard to maintain.

For error handling, exceptions provide the following benefits over error codes:

- Error codes can be ignored – exceptions force the error to be dealt with (or the program terminates).

- Exceptions can flow up the stack to the best method to respond to the error. Error codes would require propagation out of each intermediate method.

- Exceptions separate the handling of errors from the main program flow, leading to easy readability and maintainability of the software.

- Exceptions separate the code that detects the error, from the code that handles the error.

Provided you follow the best practices and use exceptions for abnormal conditions, there is no (time) overhead in using exceptions. This is because a well-implemented compiler will deliver the C++ mantra – you do not pay for what you don't use. It may cost some memory and your code may be a little larger, but the running time should be unaffected.

C++ uses exceptions to deal with runtime anomalies. By using exceptions, we can detect an error, throw an exception, and the error propagates back to the location where it can be handled. Let's modify the previous program to introduce the **divide()** function and change the calculate() function to call it. We'll also add logging to the **main()** function so that we can explore how the exceptions behave:

```cpp
Int divide(Int a, Int b )
{
    return a.m_value/b.m_value;
}

void calculate()
{
    Int a{25};
    Int b{50};
    Int c{0};

    {
        auto result1 = divide(b, a);
        // auto result2 = divide(a, c);
    }
    auto sum = add(a,b);
}

int main()
{
    std::cout << "Enter main\n";
    calculate();
    std::cout << "Exit main\n";
}
```

Figure 3.6: Modified test program for investigating exceptions

When we compile and run the preceding program, the following output is generated:

```
+-------- Program Output --------+        +------------- Annotations -------------+
|                               |         |                                       |
user@linux:~$ ./except
Enter main
Int(25) @0xffffcbec - intCon              - calculate: Int a{25}
Int(50) @0xffffcbe8 - intCon              - calculate: Int b{50}
Int(0) @0xffffcbe4 - intCon               - calculate: Int c{0}
Int(25) @0xffffcbf0 - CopyCon             - copy a for call to divide()
Int(50) @0xffffcbf4 - CopyCon             - copy b for call to divide()
Int(2) @0xffffcbdc - intCon               - result of divide (50/25) to result1
~Int()  @0xffffcbf4                       - destroy copy of b for call to divide()
~Int()  @0xffffcbf0                       - destroy copy of a for call to divide()
~Int()  @0xffffcbdc                       - end of scope destroy result1
Int(50) @0xffffcbf8 - CopyCon             - copy b for call to add()
Int(25) @0xffffcbfc - CopyCon             - copy a for call to add()
Int(75) @0xffffcbe0 - intCon              - result of add(25,50) to sum
~Int()  @0xffffcbfc                       - destroy copy of a for call to add()
~Int()  @0xffffcbf8                       - destroy copy of b for call to add()
~Int()  @0xffffcbe0                       - end of calculate() scope destroy sum
~Int()  @0xffffcbe4                       - end of calculate() scope destroy c
~Int()  @0xffffcbe8                       - end of calculate() scope destroy b
~Int()  @0xffffcbec                       - end of calculate() scope destroy a
Exit main
user@linux:~$
```

Figure 3.7: Output from the test program

In the preceding code, you can see that the annotations are added to the right. Now, we remove the comment from the **result2** line in the program, recompile the program, and rerun it. The new output that's generated is shown as follows:

```
user@linux:~$ ./except
Enter main
Int(25) @0xffffcbe4 - intCon              - calculate: Int a{25}
Int(50) @0xffffcbe0 - intCon              - calculate: Int b{50}
Int(0) @0xffffcbdc - intCon               - calculate: Int c{0}
Int(25) @0xffffcbe8 - CopyCon             - copy a for call to divide()
Int(50) @0xffffcbec - CopyCon             - copy b for call to divide()
Int(2) @0xffffcbd4 - intCon               - result of divide (50/25) to result1
~Int()  @0xffffcbec                       - destroy copy of b for call to divide()
~Int()  @0xffffcbe8                       - destroy copy of a for call to divide()
Int(0) @0xffffcbf0 - CopyCon              - copy c for call to divide()
Int(25) @0xffffcbf4 - CopyCon             - copy a for call to divide()
Floating point exception (core dumped)
user@linux:~$
```

Figure 3.8: Output from the test program – result2

By comparing the outputs, we can see that the first eight lines of each are the same. The next two lines of the preceding output are added because the **divide()** function is called twice. The last line indicates that an exception was thrown and that the program was terminated.

The second call to the **divide()** function attempted to divide by zero – an abnormal operation. This leads to an exception. If an integer is divided by zero, then it leads to a floating-point exception. This has to do with the way exceptions are generated in a **POSIX** system – it uses something called a signal (we won't go into the details of signals here). When an integer is divided by zero, the **POSIX** system maps it to the signal called **SIGFPE** which was originally meant for **floating-point error** but is now the more generic **arithmetic error**.

> **Note**
>
> According to the C++ standard, if a zero appears as the divisor for either the '**/**' operator (divide) or the '**%**' operator (modulus), then the behavior is undefined. Most systems will choose to throw an exception.

So, we have learned one important fact from the preceding explanation: that an unhandled exception will terminate the program (internally, it calls **std::terminate()**). We will fix the **undefined behavior**, catch the exception, and see the changes in the output.

To fix the **undefined behavior**, we need to add **#include <stdexcept>** at the top of the file and modify the **divide()** function:

```
Int divide(Int a, Int b )
{
    if (b.m_value == 0)
        throw std::domain_error("divide by zero error!");
    return a.m_value/b.m_value;
}
```

When we re-compile and run the program, we get the following output:

```
user@linux:~$ ./except
Enter main
Int(25) @0xffffcbe4 - intCon
Int(50) @0xffffcbe0 - intCon
Int(0) @0xffffcbdc - intCon
Int(25) @0xffffcbe8 - CopyCon
Int(50) @0xffffcbec - CopyCon
Int(2) @0xffffcbd4 - intCon
~Int()   @0xffffcbec
~Int()   @0xffffcbe8
Int(0) @0xffffcbf0 - CopyCon
Int(25) @0xffffcbf4 - CopyCon
user@linux:~$
```

Figure 3.9: Output when we throw an exception

As we can see from the preceding output, not much has changed. It's just that we don't get a **floating-point exception** (core dumped) – the program still terminates but doesn't dump the core. We then added a **try/catch** block into the **main()** function to ensure that the exception was no longer unhandled.

```cpp
int main()
{
    std::cout << "Enter main\n";
    try
    {
        calculate();
    }
    catch(std::domain_error& e)
    {
        std::cout << e.what() << "\n";
    }
    std::cout << "Exit main\n";
}
```

Figure 3.10: Catching the Exception

Recompile the program and run it to get the following output:

```
user@linux:~$ ./except
Enter main
Int(25) @0xffffcbc4 - intCon       - calculate: Int a{25}
Int(50) @0xffffcbc0 - intCon       - calculate: Int b{50}
Int(0) @0xffffcbbc - intCon        - calculate: Int c{0}
Int(25) @0xffffcbc8 - CopyCon      - copy a for call to divide()
Int(50) @0xffffcbcc - CopyCon      - copy b for call to divide()
Int(2) @0xffffcbb4 - intCon        - result of divide (50/25) to result1
~Int()  @0xffffcbcc                - destroy copy of b for call to divide()
~Int()  @0xffffcbc8                - destroy copy of a for call to divide()
Int(0) @0xffffcbd0 - CopyCon       - copy c for call to divide()
Int(25) @0xffffcbd4 - CopyCon      - copy a for call to divide()
~Int()  @0xffffcbd4                - destroy copy of a for call to divide()
~Int()  @0xffffcbd0                - destroy copy of c for call to divide()
~Int()  @0xffffcbb4                - destroy result1
~Int()  @0xffffcbbc                - destroy c
~Int()  @0xffffcbc0                - destroy b
~Int()  @0xffffcbc4                - destroy a
divide by zero error!              - process exception in the catch statement
Exit main                          - terminate normally
user@linux:~$
```

Figure 3.11: Output from the program that catches the exception

In the preceding output, an exception is thrown on the second line that is annotated as "**copy a for call to divide**". Everything that is output after that is a result of the exception being handled.

Our code has transferred program control to the `catch()` statement in the `main()` function and has executed the destructors for all the variables that had been constructed on the stack (from the time the call was made in the `try` clause).

## Stack Unwinding

The process of destroying all local function variables, as guaranteed by the C++ language is known as **Stack Unwinding**. As the stack unwinds in the presence of an exception, C++ uses its well-defined rules to destroy all the objects in the scope.

When an exception occurs, the function call stack starts searching linearly from the current function back to the function that called it, to the one that called that, and so on, until an exception handler (expressed by a `catch` block) that matches the exception is found.

If an exception handler is found, then the stack unwinding occurs, destroying all the local variables for all the functions in the stack. The objects are destroyed in the reverse order that they were created. If no handler is found to deal with the thrown exception, then the program terminates (usually without warning the user).

## Exercise 1: Implementing exceptions in Fraction and Stack

In this exercise, we will return to two classes that we worked on in *Chapter 2A, No Ducks Allowed – Types and Deduction* and *Chapter 2B, No Ducks Allowed – Templates and Deduction* – **Fraction** and **Stack**, both of which can experience runtime anomalies. We are going to update their code so that they can raise exceptions whenever any problem is detected. Follow these steps to implement this exercise:

1. Open Eclipse and create a new project named **Lesson3** using the files found in the **Lesson3**   examples folder.

2. As this is a **CMake-based project**, change the current builder to be **CMake Build (portable)**.

3. Go to the **Project | Build All** menu to build all the exercises. By default, the console at the bottom of the screen will display the **CMake Console [Lesson3]**.

4. Configure a new **Launch Configuration**, **L3Exercise1** to run with the name **Exercise1**.

5. Also, configure a new C/C++ Unit Run Configuration, **L3Ex1Tests**, to run **L3Ex1tests**. Set the **Google Tests Runner**.

6. Click on the **Run** option for the existing **18** tests to run and pass.

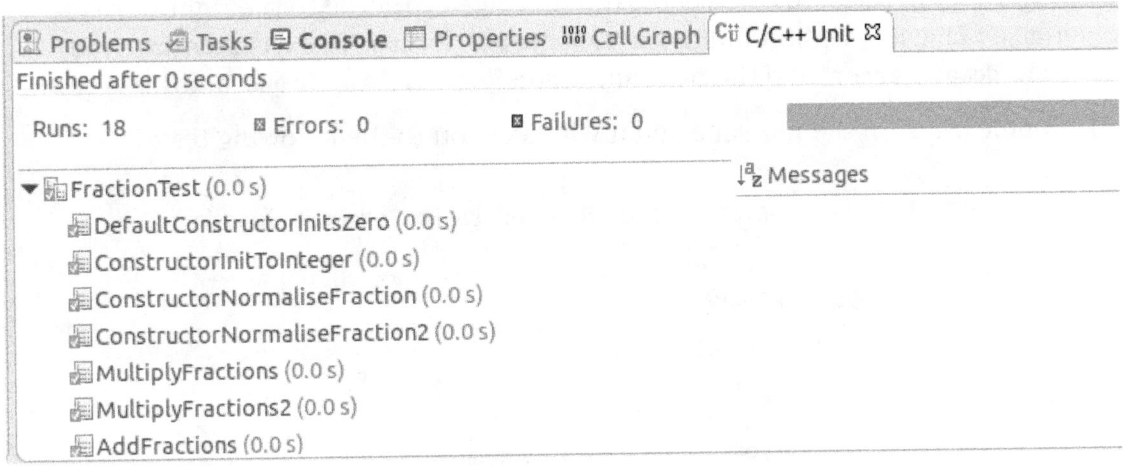

Figure 3.12: Existing tests all pass (Runs: 18)

7. Open **Fraction.hpp** in the editor and change the line at the top of the file to read like so:

```
#define EXERCISE1_STEP   14
```

8. Click on the **Run** button to re-run the tests – we have added one test that will attempt to create a **Fraction** with a zero denominator. The test expects that an exception has been thrown:

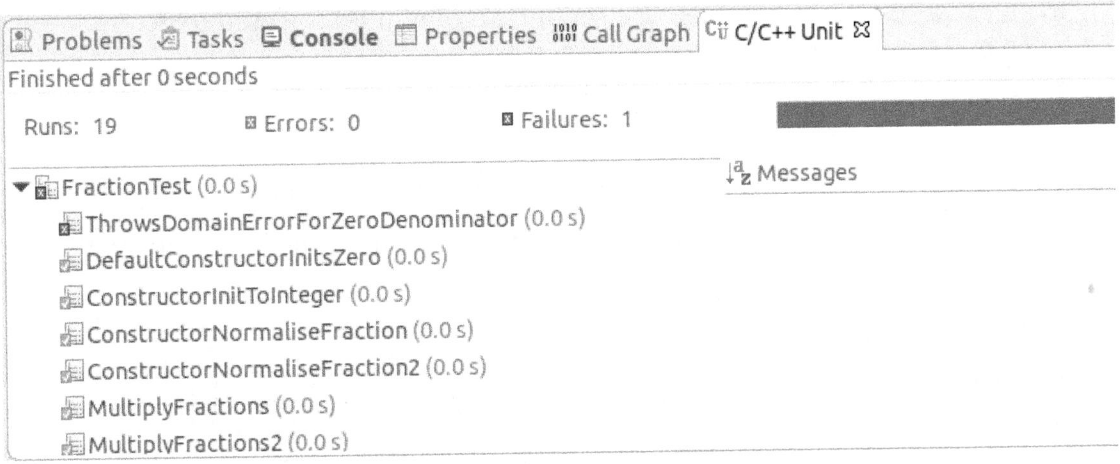

Figure 3.13: New failing test ThrowsDomainErrorForZeroDenominator

9. Click on the failing test name – the **Messages** window will now show the expected behavior and the actual behavior. You may need to scroll to the right to read it all. At the very right it indicates "**Expected … throws an exception of type std::domain_error**" and the next line states "**Actual: it throws nothing**".

10. Double-click on the message and it will take you to the following test:

```
20  TEST_F(FractionTest, ThrowsDomainErrorForZeroDenominator )
21  {
22      // ASSERT_THROW confirms the type of exception thrown
23      ASSERT_THROW(({
24          try
25          {
26              Fraction f1{1,0};
27          }
28          catch( const std::domain_error& e )
29          {
30              // and this tests that it has the correct message
31              EXPECT_STREQ( "Zero Denominator", e.what() );
32              throw;   // Re-throw for the EXPECT_THROW to check
33          }
34      }), std::domain_error );
35  }
```

Figure 3.14: The failing test

The **ASSERT_THROW()** macro requires two arguments. Since the **Fraction initializer** has a comma in it, it is necessary to wrap the whole first argument in an extra set of parentheses. The second argument is expected to get a **std::domain_error** from this constructor. The internal **try/catch** structure is present to confirm that the expected string is captured inside the exception object. If we do not want to check this, then we could simply write the test like so:

```
ASSERT_THROW(({Fraction f1{1,0}; }), std::domain_error);
```

11. Open the file **Fraction.cpp** in the editor. Insert the following line near the top of the file:

```
#include <stdexcept>
```

12. Modify the constructor to throw an exception if it's been created with a zero denominator:

```
Fraction::Fraction(int numerator, int denominator)
                        : m_numerator{numerator}, m_
denominator{denominator}
{
    if(m_denominator == 0)
    {
```

```
            throw std::domain_error("Zero Denominator");
        }
    }
```

13. Click on the **Run** button to re-run the tests. **19** tests now pass.

14. Open **Fraction.hpp** in the editor and change the line near the top of the file to read like so:

```
#define EXERCISE1_STEP   20
```

15. Click on the **Run** button to re-run the tests – the new test **ThrowsRunTimeErrorForZeroDenominator** fails.

16. Click on the failing test name – the **Messages** window will now show the expected behavior and the actual behavior. You may need to scroll to the right to read it all. At the very right it indicates "**Expected… throws an exception of type std::runtime_error**" and the next line states "**Actual: it throws a different type**".

17. Double-click on the message again to open the failing test:

```
39⊖ TEST_F(FractionTest, ThrowsRunTimeErrorForZeroDenominator )
40  {
41      // ASSERT_THROW confirms the type of exception thrown
42      ASSERT_THROW(({
43          try
44          {
45              Fraction f1{1,2};
46              Fraction f2{0,6};
47
48              f1 /= f2;
49          }
50          catch( const std::runtime_error& e )
51          {
52              // and this tests that it has the correct message
53              EXPECT_STREQ( "Fraction Divide By Zero", e.what() );
54              throw;  // Re-throw for the EXPECT_THROW to check
55          }
56      }), std::runtime_error );
57  }
```

Figure 3.15: Another failing test

This test is verifying that the division assignment operator will throw an exception for a divide by zero.

18. Open **Fraction.cpp** and locate the **operator/=()** function. You'll see that, inside this function, it actually uses the constructor for **Fraction**, so it will throw a **std::domain_error**.

19. Now modify **operator/=()** to detect this problem before the constructor is called so that it throws a **std::runtime_error** with the expected message.

20. Modify **Fraction.cpp** by adding a domain error that will detect the division operator:

```
Fraction& Fraction::operator/=(const Fraction& rhs)
{
    if (rhs.m_numerator == 0)
    {
        throw std::runtime_error("Fraction Divide By Zero");
    }
    Fraction tmp(m_numerator*rhs.m_denominator,
m_denominator*rhs.m_numerator);
    *this = tmp;
    return *this;
}
```

21. Click on the **Run** button to re-run the tests. All **20** tests pass.

22. Open **Stack.hpp** in the editor and change the line near the top of the file to read like so:

```
#define EXERCISE1_STEP   27
```

23. Click on the **Run** button to re-run the tests – we have added one test that will attempt to pop from an empty stack. In the **C/C++ Unit tab** window, click on the triangle next to **FractionTest** to collapse the lists of tests and show the **StackTest**:

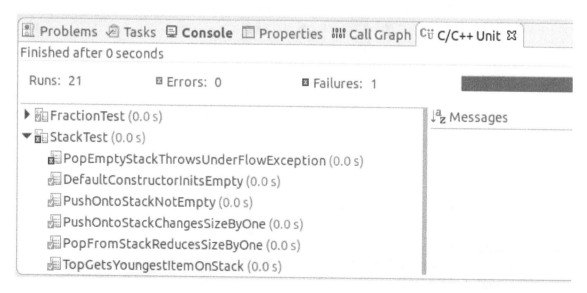

Figure 3.16: pop Stack test fails

24. Use the **C/C++ Unit** window to click through and locate the failing test. Determine the expected exception and then open **Stack.hpp**. Add **#include <stdexcept>** to the top of the file and then update the **pop()** function so that it looks like this:

```
void pop()
{
    if(empty())
        throw std::underflow_error("Pop from empty stack");
    m_stack.pop_back();
}
```

25. Click on the **Run** button to re-run the tests. **21** tests now pass.

26. Open **Stack.hpp** in the editor and change the line at the top of the file to read like so:

```
#define EXERCISE1_STEP   31
```

27. Click on the **Run** button to re-run the tests – the newly added test, **TopEmptyStackThrowsUnderFlowException**, fails.

28. Use the **C/C++ Unit** window to click through and locate the failing test. Determine the expected exception and then open **Stack.hpp**. Update the non-const **top()** method so that it looks as follows:

```
reference top()
{
    if(empty())
        throw std::underflow_error("Top from empty stack");
    return m_stack.back();
}
```

29. Click on the **Run** button to re-run the tests. **22** tests pass.

30. Open **Stack.hpp** in the editor and change the line at the top of the file to read like so:

```
#define EXERCISE1_STEP   35
```

31. Click on the **Run** button to re-run the tests – the newly added test, **TopEmptyConstStackThrowsUnderFlowException**, fails.

32. Use the **C/C++ Unit** window to click through and locate the failing test. Determine the expected exception and then open **Stack.hpp**. Update the const **top()** method so that it looks as follows:

```
const_reference top() const
{
```

```
        if(empty())
            throw std::underflow_error("Top from empty stack");
        return m_stack.back();
    }
```

33. Click on the **Run** button to re-run the tests. All **23** tests now pass.

In this exercise, we have added run time checking for pre-conditions that are part of the normal operation of using our **Fraction** and **Stack** classes. This code will only execute to throw an exception when one of the pre-conditions is violated, indicating that there's a problem with the data or how our program was executed.

## What Happens When an Exception is Thrown?

At some point, our program executes the following statement:

```
throw expression;
```

By executing this, we are signaling that an erroneous condition has occurred, and that we want it handled. The next thing that happens is a **temporary** object, known as the **exception object**, is constructed in an unspecified storage and copy-initialized from the expression (which may call the move constructor and may be subject to copy elision). The type of the exception object is statically determined from the expression with the const and volatile qualifiers removed. Array types decay to pointers, while function types are converted into a pointer of a function. If the type of expression is malformed or abstract, then a compiler error will occur.

After the construction of the exception object, the control, along with the exception object, is transferred to the exception handler. The exception handler that's chosen is the one that has the closest matching type to the exception object as the stack unwinds. The exception object exists until the last catch clause exits, unless it is rethrown. The type of the expression must have an accessible **copy constructor** and a **destructor**.

## Throw-by-Value or Throw-by-Pointer

Knowing that a temporary exception object is created, passed around, and then destroyed, what type should the throw expression use? A **value** or a **pointer**?

We haven't talked much about specifying the types in the catch statements yet. We will do that shortly. But for now, note that to catch a pointer type (which was thrown), the catch pattern also needs to be of a pointer type.

If a pointer to an object is thrown, then the throwing party must ensure that what the exception object will point at (as it will be a copy of a pointer) will be kept alive until the exception has been handled, even through the **stack unwinding**.

The pointer could be to a static variable, a global variable, or memory that's been allocated from the heap to ensure that the object being pointed to still exists when the exception is handled. Now, we have solved the problem of keeping the exception object alive. But when the handler has finished with it, what does the catcher do with it?

The catcher of the exception isn't aware about the creation of the exception object (**global**, **static**, or **heap**) and so it doesn't know whether it should delete the received pointer or not. Thus, throwing-by-pointer is not the recommended approach of throwing exceptions.

An object that is thrown will be copied to the created temporary exception object and handed off to the handler. When the exception has been handled, the temporary object will simply be destroyed, and the program will continue. There is no ambiguity as to what to do with it. Therefore, the best practice is to throw the **exception by value**.

## Standard Library Exceptions

The C++ Standard Library defines **std::exception** as the base class for all the Standard Library exceptions. The standard defines the following first-level hierarchy of **exceptions/errors** (the number in brackets indicates how many exceptions derive from that class):

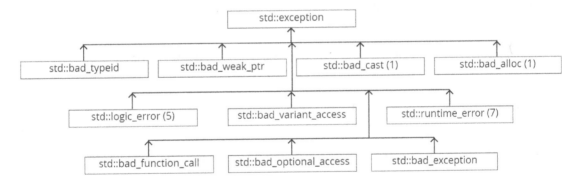

**Figure 3.17: Standard Library exception hierarchy (two levels)**

These exceptions are used through the C++ Standard Library including the STL. The best practice when creating your own exception class is deriving it from one of the standard exceptions. As we will see next, your special exception can be caught by a handler for one of the standard exceptions.

## Catching Exceptions

While discussing the need for exceptions, we introduced the idea of throwing the exceptions but did not really look at how C++ supports catching the exception. The process of exception handling starts with a section of code being wrapped in a **try** block to place it under **exception inspection**. The try block is followed by one or more catch blocks, which are the exception handlers. When an exceptional circumstance occurs while executing the code inside the try block, an exception is thrown, and control is transferred to the exception handlers. If no exceptions are thrown, then all the exception handlers are skipped, the code in the try block completes, and normal execution continues. Let's express these concepts in a code snippet:

```cpp
void SomeFunction()
{
  try {
    // code under exception inspection
  }
  catch(myexception e)        // first handler - catch by value
  {
    // some error handling steps
  }
  catch(std::exception* e)    // second handler - catch by pointer
  {
    // some other error handling steps
  }
  catch(std::runtime_error& e) // third handler - catch by reference
  {
    // some other error handling steps
  }
  catch(...)                  // default exception handler - catch any
exception
  {
    // some other error handling steps
  }
  // Normal programming continues from here
}
```

The preceding snippet shows the necessary keywords – **try**, and **catch** and introduces the three different types of catch pattern (excluding the default handler):

- **Catch exception by value**: This is a costly mechanism as the exception handler is processed like any other function. Catch-by-value means that a copy of the exception object must be created and then passed to the handler. The creation of the second copy slows down the exception handling process. This type can also suffer from object slicing where a subclass is thrown, and the catch clause is a super class. The catch clause will then only receive a copy of the super-class object that loses the attributes of the original exception object. Therefore, we should avoid catch-by-value exception handlers.

- **Catch exception by pointer**: As discussed when looking at throw-by-value, with throw-by-pointer, this style of exception handler can only catch exceptions thrown by the pointer. As we only want to throw by value, we should avoid catch-by-pointer exception handlers.

- **Catch expression by reference**: This is the recommended style of exception handler as it does not suffer from the issues related to catch-by-value and catch-by-pointer. As a reference is passed to the handler, no second copy of the exception object is made. Splicing does not occur because the reference still refers to the originally thrown exception object. And since the exception was thrown by value, the temporary exception object will be destroyed automatically when we are done with it.

> **Note**
>
> When dealing with exceptions, it is **throw-by-value** and **catch-by-reference**.

When there are multiple catch blocks, the exception object type is used to match the handlers in the order that they are specified. Once a handler is found to match, it is executed, and the remaining exception handlers are ignored. This is different to function resolution, where the compiler will find the best match to the arguments. Thus, the exception handlers (catch blocks) should be defined from the more specific to the more general. For example, the default handler (**catch(...)**) should always come last in the definition.

## Exercise 2: Implementing Exception Handlers

In this exercise, we will implement a hierarchy of exception handlers to manage how exceptions are processed. Follow these steps to implement this exercise:

1. Open the **Lesson3** project in Eclipse. Then in the **Project Explorer**, expand **Lesson3** then **Exercise02** and double click on **exceptions.cpp** to open the file for this exercise into the editor. This file contains the following code:

```
#include <exception>
#include <iostream>

void run_exceptions()
{
    try
    {
        throw std::domain_error("We got one!!!!");
    }
    catch(...)
    {
    std::cout << "Exception caught by default handler\n";
    }
    catch(const std::exception& e)
    {
        std::cout << "Exception '" << "' caught by std::exception
handler\n";
    }
    catch(const std::logic_error& e)
    {
    std::cout << "Exception '" << "' caught by std::logic_error
handler\n";
    }
    catch(const std::domain_error& e)
    {
        std::cout << "Exception '" << "' caught by std::domain_error
handler\n";
    }
}

int main()
{
    std::cout << "\n\n------ Exercise 2 ------\n";
    run_exceptions();
```

```
    std::cout << "Complete.\n";
    return 0;
}
```

> **Note**
>
> All the exception handlers have used the same name for the exception argument,
> that is, **e**. The scope for that variable is only the catch block that it is declared in.

2.  Click on the **Launch Configuration** drop down menu and select **New Launch Configuration....** Configure the **L3Exercise2** application from the **Search Project** menu to run it with the name **L3Exercise2**.

3.  When that is complete, it will be the currently selected **Launch Configuration**.

4.  Click on the **Run** button. Exercise 2 will run and produce the following output:

```
------ Exercise 2 ------
Exception caught by default handler
Complete.
```

Figure 3.18: Exercise 2 output – default handler caught the exception

5.  In the Console window, click on the **Display Selected Console** button, and select **CDT Global Build Console**. Scroll through the window. You will find (if the GCC compiler is being used) that there are five warning messages related to the order that we have placed our exception handlers in. (Actually, the first warning would normally be an error except that the **CMake** file sets the **-fpermissive** flag when it compiles this target.)

6.  In the editor, move the default exception handler, **catch(...)**, to just after the **std::domain_error** handler. Click on the **Run** button. Exercise 2 will run and produce the following output:

```
------ Exercise 2 ------
Exception 'We got one!!!!' caught by std::exception handler
Complete.
```

Figure 3.19: std::exception handler has been used

7.  In the editor, move the **std::exception** handler to just after the **std::domain_error** handler. Click on the **Run** button. This time, it will report that the **std::logic_error** handler was executed.

8. In the editor, move the `std:: logic_error` handler to just after the `std::domain_error` handler. Click on the **Run** button. This time, it will report that the `std::domain_error` handler was executed which is actually what we would expect.

9. Now change the **throw** line to be a `std::logic_error` exception. Click on the **Run** button. This time, it will report that `std::logic_error` handler was executed as expected.

10. Now change the **throw** line to be a `std::underflow_error` exception. Click on the **Run** button and this time it will report that the exception was caught by the `std::exception` handler as expected. `std::exception` is the base class for all Standard Library exceptions.

In this exercise, we implemented a series of exception handlers and observed how the order of exception handlers affects the way an exception is caught and how the exception hierarchy can be used.

## CMake Generator Expressions

When working with `CMake`, it is sometimes necessary to adjust the value of a variable. `CMake` is a build generator system that can generate build files for many build tools and compiler tool chains. Because of this flexibility, if you want to turn on some feature in the compiler, you only need to apply to it to one particular type. This is because the command-line options are different between vendors. For example, the command line option for the g++ compiler to enable C++17 support is **-std=c++17**, but for **msvc** it is **/std:c++17**. If you open the **CMakeLists.txt** file and locate **L3Exercise2 add_excutable**, then the following line will be after it:

```
target_compile_options(L3Exercise2 PRIVATE $<$<CXX_COMPILER_ID:GNU>:-
fpermissive>)
```

This uses the `$<CXX_COMPILER_ID:GNU>` variable query to check whether it is a GCC compiler. If yes, then it generates a 1 (true), otherwise 0 (false). It also uses the `$<condition:true_string>` condition expression to add **-fpermissive** to the compiler options for the **L3Exercise2** target, but only for the gcc compiler. These can be added for each compiler type as separate calls to **target_compile_options** or via one call.

> **Note**
>
> For more information on generator expressions, please take a look at the following link: https://cmake.org/cmake/help/v3.15/manual/cmake-generator-expressions.7.html.

## Exception Usage Guidelines

When using exceptions in your C++ code, remember the following points:

- Chant: **Throw by value and catch by reference**

- **Do not use exceptions for normal program flow**. If a function meets an abnormal condition and is not able meet its (functional) obligations, then and only then do you throw an exception. If the function can resolve the abnormal condition and fulfil its obligations, then it is not an exception. They are named exceptions for a reason and you will not incur any processing overhead if you do not use them.

- **Do not throw an exception from within a destructor**. Remember that because of stack unwinding, local variable destructors will be executed. If a destructor is called during the stack unwinding process and throws an exception, then the program will terminate.

- **Do not swallow exceptions**. Do not use the default catch handler and do nothing about the exception. The exception has been thrown to indicate that there is a problem and you should do something about it. Ignoring an exception can lead to a failure later that will be hard to troubleshoot. This is because any useful information is truly lost with the swallowed exception.

- **The exception object is copied from the throw**.

## Resource Management (in an Exceptional World)

So far, we have looked at local variable scope, and how `automatic` and `dynamic lifetime variables` are dealt with when the variable goes out of scope – automatic lifetime variables (those placed on the stack) are fully destructed while `dynamic lifetime variables` (those allocated to the heap by the programmer) are not destructed: we just lose any access to them. We have also seen that, when an exception is thrown, the nearest matching handler is found and all the local variables between the throw point and the handler will be destructed through the stack unwinding process.

We can use this knowledge to write robust resource management classes that will relieve us from the need to keep track of resources (dynamic lifetime variables, file handles, system handles, and so on) to ensure that they are released (back into the wild) when we are done with them. The technique that's utilized to manage resources, both under normal operating and under exceptions, is known as **Resource Acquisition is Initialization** (**RAII**).

## Resource Acquisition Is Initialization

RAII is another good example of a badly named concept (the other is **SFINAE**). **RAII**, or **Resource Acquisition is Initialization** describes the behavior of a class that's used to manage resources. It may be better if it were named **Destruction is Resource Release**, which really captures the essence of what the management class is attempting to do. We could infer from our previous discussions how to make this work, but it will be more instructive to show a separate example that will develop the resource management **File** class and show how RAII also improves the readability and our ability to reason about what a function does.

Consider the following code:

```
void do_something()
{
    FILE* out{};
    FILE* in = fopen("input.txt", "r");

    try
    {
        if (in != nullptr)
        {
            // UNSAFE - an exception here will create a resource leak
            out = fopen("output.txt", "w");

            if (out != nullptr)
            {
                // Do some work
                // UNSAFE - an exception here will create resource leaks
                fclose(out);
            }
            fclose(in);
        }
    }
    catch(std::exception& e)
    {
```

```
            // Respond to the exception
        }
    }
```

This code shows two potential problems with the management of resources:

- Most importantly, the occurrence of an exception between the opening and closing of a file results in the resource leaking. If this is a system resource, many of these can lead to system instability or application performance being adversely affected, since it starves for resources.

- In addition, the management of multiple resources within one method can lead to deeply nested clauses because of error handling. This is detrimental to the readability of the code and hence its understanding and maintainability. It is easy to forget to release a resource, especially when there are multiple exit points.

So, how can we manage the resource so that we have exception-safe and simpler code? This problem is not unique to C++ and different languages manage it differently. **Java**, **C#**, and **Python** use a garbage collection approach that sweeps through created objects and cleans them up when they are no longer referenced. But C++ does not have garbage collection, so what is the solution?

Consider the following class:

```cpp
class File {
public:
    File(const char* name, const char* access) {
        m_file = fopen(name, access);
        if (m_file == nullptr) {
            throw std::ios_base::failure("failed to open file");
        }
    }

    ~File() {
        fclose(m_file);
    }

    operator FILE*() {
        return m_file;
```

```
    }
private:
    FILE* m_file{};
};
```

This class implements the following characteristics:

- The constructor acquires the resource.
- If the resource is not acquired in the constructor, then an exception is thrown.
- When the class is destroyed, the resource is released.

If we use this class in the **do_something()** method, it then looks like this:

```
void do_something()
{
    try
    {

        File in("input.txt", "r");
        File out("output.txt", "w");

        // Do some work
    }
    catch(std::exception& e)
    {
        // Respond to the exception
    }
}
```

If an exception occurs while doing this, then C++ guarantees that all stack-based objects will have their destructors called (**stack unwinding**), thus ensuring that the files are closed. This solves the problem of resources leaking with the occurrence of an exception as the resources are now automatically cleaned up. In addition, this method is extremely easy to read so that we can understand the logic flow without having to worry about error handling.

This technique uses the lifetime of the **File** objects to acquire and release the resource, ensuring that the resources do not leak. The resource is acquired during the construction (initialization) of the management class and released during the destruction of the management class. It is this behavior of scope-bound resources that gives rise to the name **Resource Acquisition Is Initialization**.

The preceding example deals with managing file handles that are system resources. It applies to any resources that are required to be acquired before use, and then relinquished when finished. The RAII technique can be applied to a wide range of resources – open files, open pipes, allocated heap memory, open sockets, threads of execution, database connections, locking of mutexes/critical sections – basically any resource that is in short supply in the host system and needs to be managed.

### Exercise 3: Implementing RAII for Memory and File Handles

In this exercise, we will implement two different classes that will manage memory or files using the RAII technique. Follow these steps to implement this exercise:

1. Open the **Lesson3** project in Eclipse. Then in the **Project Explorer**, expand **Lesson3**, then **Exercise03**, and double click on **Exercise3.cpp** to open the file for this exercise into the editor.

2. Click on the **Launch Configuration** drop down menu and select **New Launch Configuration....** Configure the **L3Exercise3** application from the Search Project menu to run it with the name **L3Exercise3**.

3. Click on the **Run** button to run Exercise 3. This will produce the following output:

```
------ Exercise 3 ------
allocated 20 bytes @ 0x56364f043280
allocated 20 bytes @ 0x56364f0432a0
allocated 20 bytes @ 0x56364f0432c0
allocated 20 bytes @ 0x56364f0432e0
allocated 20 bytes @ 0x56364f043300
------ Complete. ------
Leaked Memory Pointers...
    0: 0x56364f043280
    1: 0x56364f0432a0
    2: 0x56364f0432c0
    3: 0x56364f0432e0
    4: 0x56364f043300
Leaked Files...
    0: HelloB1.txt
    1: HelloB2.txt
```

Figure 3.20: Leaky memory and files from Exercise3.cpp

The output shows that we allocated memory five times and that the addresses are returned by new. When executing from the **main()** function when the **monitor** is destructed, it dumps a report of memory that was allocated and released, as well as the files that were opened but never closed.

4. In the editor, type the following into the **Exercise3.cpp** file of the **File** class:

```
class File {
public:
    File(const char* name, const char* access) {
        m_file = fopen(name, access);
        if (m_file == nullptr) {
            throw std::ios_base::failure(""failed to open file"");
        }
    }

    ~File() {
        fclose(m_file);
    }

    operator FILE*() {
        return m_file;
    }
private:
    FILE* m_file{};
};
```

5. Click on the **Run** button to run Exercise 3 – it still leaks files and memory, but the code is correct.

6. Locate the **LeakFiles()** function and modify it so that it uses the new **File** class (like in the preceding code) to prevent file leaks:

```
void LeakFiles()
{
    File fh1{"HelloB1.txt", "w"};
    fprintf(fh1, "Hello B2\n");

    File fh2{"HelloB2.txt", "w"};
    fprintf(fh2, "Hello B1\n");
}
```

7. Click on the **Run** button to run Exercise 3. If you have modified **LeakFiles()** correctly, then the output will be as follows:

```
------ Exercise 3 ------
allocated 20 bytes @ 0x55a840b3a280
allocated 20 bytes @ 0x55a840b3a2a0
allocated 20 bytes @ 0x55a840b3a2c0
allocated 20 bytes @ 0x55a840b3a2e0
allocated 20 bytes @ 0x55a840b3a300
------ Complete. -------
Leaked Memory Pointers...
    0: 0x55a840b3a280
    1: 0x55a840b3a2a0
    2: 0x55a840b3a2c0
    3: 0x55a840b3a2e0
    4: 0x55a840b3a300
No Leaked Files
```

Figure 3.21: No file leaks

8. Now in **Exercise3.cpp**, add the following **CharPointer** class:

```cpp
class CharPointer
{
public:
    void allocate(size_t size)
    {
        m_memory = new char[size];
    }

    operator char*() { return m_memory;}

private:
    char* m_memory{};
};
```

9. Modify **LeakPointers()** to read like so:

```cpp
void LeakPointers()
{
    CharPointer memory[5];
    for (auto i{0} ; i<5 ; i++)
```

```
    {
        memory[i].allocate(20);
        std::cout << "allocated 20 bytes @ " << (void *)memory[i] << "\n";
    }
}
```

10. Click on the **Run** button to run Exercise 3 – it still has memory leaks, but the code is correct.

11. Now, add the following destructor to **CharPointer**. Note that the **delete** operator uses the array **[]** syntax:

```
~CharPointer()
{
    delete [] m_memory;
}
```

12. Click on the **Run** button again to run Exercise 3 – this time, you should see that the monitor reports no leaks:

```
------ Exercise 3 ------
allocated 20 bytes @ 0x55a47daca280
allocated 20 bytes @ 0x55a47daca2a0
allocated 20 bytes @ 0x55a47daca2c0
allocated 20 bytes @ 0x55a47daca2e0
allocated 20 bytes @ 0x55a47daca300
------ Complete. -------
No Leaked Memory
No Leaked Files
```

Figure 3.22: No leaks – memory or files

The implementation of **File** and **CharPointer** deliver on the **RAII** design approach, but there are other considerations when designing these. For example, do we want the copy constructor or copy assignment functions? In both cases, it could be a problem to just copy the resource from one object to another as this could result in two attempts to close a file handle or delete the memory. Typically, this would lead to undefined behavior. Next, we will re-visit the special member functions in light of implementing a resource management object such as **File** or **CharPointer**.

## Special Coding Techniques

The code for *Exercise 3, Implementing RAII for Memory and File Handles*, has been specially written so that we can monitor the usage of the memory and the file handles and report any leaks on exit. Visit the **monitor.h** and **monitor.cpp** files and examine the two techniques that were used to make the monitor possible:

- **Preprocessor macros**: This is the special use of a preprocessor macro to demonstrate the leaks and should not be used in production code, that is, replacing a function by text substitution.

  If you program to the Windows API, you may occasionally be caught with your method names clashing with the macros Microsoft uses for its API methods. For example, do not call any of your methods **SendMessage** if you include **windows.h**. If you do, then depending on whether you are building ASCII mode or Unicode mode, it will be substituted with **SendMessageA** or **SendMessageW** respectively.

- **Defining our own new handler**: This is an advanced technique and unless you write embedded code, it's unlikely you will need it.

## C++ doesn't Need finally

Other languages (**C#**, **Java**, and **Visual Basic.NET**) that support an exception throwing mechanism have a **try/catch/finally** paradigm where the code in the **finally** block is called on exit from the try block – either normally or by exception. C++ has no **finally** block because it has access to a better mechanism that ensures that we cannot forget to release a resource – RAII. Since the resource is represented by a local object, the local object's destructor will free the resource.

The added advantage of this design pattern is that if a lot of resources are being managed, then the **finally** block is proportionally large. RAII removes the need for finally and leads to code that is easier to maintain.

## RAII and the STL

The Standard Template Library (STL) utilizes RAII in many of its templates and classes. For example, the smart pointers that were introduced in C++11, that is **std::unique_ptr** and **std::shared_ptr**, help avoid many problems by ensuring that memory is deallocated when it has been finished with, or by ensuring that the memory is not deallocated if it is used elsewhere. Other examples in the STL include **std::string** (memory), **std::vector** (memory), and **std::fstream** (file handles).

## Who Owns This Object?

With the preceding implementations of **File** and **CharPointer**, we have tested Resource Management with RAII. Let's explore it further. Firstly, we will define a class that has more than just one resource:

```
class BufferedWriter
{
public:
```

```
BufferedWriter(const char* filename);
~BufferedWriter();


bool write(const char* data, size_t length);

private:
    const size_t BufferSize{4096};
    FILE* m_file{nullptr};
    size_t m_writePos{0};
    char* m_buffer{new char[BufferSize]};
};
```

The class is used for buffering the writing to the file.

> **Note**
>
> This is not usually necessary when using iostream derived classes as they already provide buffering.

Each call to the **write()** function will add data into the allocated buffer until it reaches the **BufferSize** at which point the data is actually written to the file and the buffer is reset.

But what if we wanted to assign this instance of **BufferedWriter** to another instance or copy it? What is the right behavior?

If we just let the default copy constructor/copy assignment do its their thing we get a member-wise copy of the items. This would mean that we have two instances of **BufferedWriter** that hold the same handle to the file and the pointer to the buffer. When the first instance of the object is destroyed, being the good programmers that we are, we will clean up the file by closing it and the memory by deleting it. The second instance now has a file handle that is defunct and a pointer to memory that we have told the operating system to recover for the next user. Any attempt to use these resources, including destroying them, will result in undefined behavior and mostly likely a program crash. The default copy constructor/copy-assignment operators execute what is known as a shallow copy – that is, it copies all the members as they are, bit by bit (but not what they refer to).

The two resources that we have can be treated differently. Firstly, there should only be one class that owns the **m_buffer**. There are two options in dealing with this:

- Prevent the copy of the class and hence the memory
- Perform a **deep copy** where the buffer in the second instance has been allocated by the constructor and the contents of the first buffer is copied

Secondly, there should only be one class that owns the file handle (**m_file**). There are two options in dealing with this:

- Prevent the copy of the class and hence the file handle
- Transfer the **ownership** from the original instance to the second instance and mark the original as invalid or empty (whatever that means)

It is easy enough to implement a deep copy, but how do we transfer ownership of a resource? To answer this question, we need to look at temporary objects and value categories again.

## Temporary Objects

A temporary object is created to store the intermediate results of an expression before the result is deposited into a variable (or just forgotten). An expression is any code that returns a value, including passing by value to a function, returning a value from a function, implicit conversion, literals, and binary operators. Temporary objects are **rvalue expressions** and they have memory, temporarily allocated for them as a location, to place the expression result. It is this creation of temporaries and copying data between them that caused some performance issues prior to C++11. To address this issue, C++11 introduced **rvalue references** to enable what is known as move semantics.

## Move Semantics

An **rvalue reference** (denoted by a double ampersand, '**&&**') is a reference that is only assigned an **rvalue** that will extend the rvalue's lifetime until the **rvalue reference** is done with it. So, **rvalues** can live beyond the expression that defined it. With **rvalue references**, we can now implement move semantics through the move constructor and move assignment operators. The purpose of move semantics is to steal resources from the referenced object and thus avoid the expensive copy operations. When the move is complete, the referenced object must be left in a stable state. In other words, the object that was moved from must be left in a state that will not cause any undefined behavior or a program crash when it is destroyed, nor should it affect the resources that were stolen from it.

C++11 also introduced a casting operator **std::move()**, that casts an **lvalue** to an **rvalue** so that the move constructor or move assignment operator gets called to 'move' the resources. The **std::move()** method does not actually move the data.

One unexpected thing to note is that, inside the move constructor and move assignment operator, the **rvalue** reference is actually an **lvalue**. This means that if you want to ensure move semantics happen within the method then you may need to use **std::move()** again on the member variables.

As C++11 introduced move semantics, it also updated the Standard Library to take advantage of this new capability. For example, **std::string** and **std::vector** have been updated to include move semantics. To get the benefits of move semantics; you just need to re-compile your code with the latest C++ compiler.

## Implementing a Smart Pointer

A smart pointer is a resource management class that holds a pointer to a resource and releases it when it goes out of scope. In this section, we will implement a smart pointer, observe its behavior as a copy supporting class, evolve it to support move semantics and finally remove its support for copy operations:

```
#include <iostream>


template<class T>
class smart_ptr
{
public:
  smart_ptr(T* ptr = nullptr) :m_ptr(ptr)
  {
  }


  ~smart_ptr()
  {
    delete m_ptr;
  }


  // Copy constructor --> Do deep copy
```

```
  smart_ptr(const smart_ptr& a)
  {
    m_ptr = new T;
    *m_ptr = *a.m_ptr;        // use operator=() to do deep copy
  }


  // Copy assignment --> Do deep copy
  smart_ptr& operator=(const smart_ptr& a)
  {
    // Self-assignment detection
    if (&a == this)
      return *this;


    // Release any resource we're holding
    delete m_ptr;


    // Copy the resource
    m_ptr = new T;
    *m_ptr = *a.m_ptr;


    return *this;
  }


  T& operator*() const { return *m_ptr; }
  T* operator->() const { return m_ptr; }
  bool is_null() const { return m_ptr == nullptr; }
private:
  T* m_ptr{nullptr};
};


class Resource
```

```cpp
{
public:
  Resource() { std::cout << "Resource acquired\n"; }
  ~Resource() { std::cout << "Resource released\n"; }
};


smart_ptr<Resource> createResource()
{
    smart_ptr<Resource> res(new Resource);                    // Step 1
    return res; // return value invokes the copy constructor    // Step 2
}


int main()
{
  smart_ptr<Resource> the_res;
  the_res = createResource(); // assignment invokes the copy assignment Step
3/4


  return 0; // Step 5
}
```

When we run this program, the following output generated:

```
$ ./smart_ptr.exe
Resource acquired
Resource acquired
Resource released
Resource released
$
```

Figure 3.23: Smart Pointer Program output

For such a simple program, there is a lot of acquiring and releasing of the resource. Let's pull this apart:

1. The local variable, res, inside **createResource()** is created and initialized on the heap (dynamic lifetime), causing the first "**Resource acquired**" message.

2.  It is possible for the compiler to create another temporary to return the value. However, the compiler has executed **copy elision** to remove the copy (that is, it is able to build the object directly onto a position in the stack allocated by the calling function). The compiler has **Return-Value-Optimization (RVO)** and **Named- Return-Value-Optimization (NRVO)** optimizations that it can apply and, under C++17 these have been made mandatory in certain circumstances.

3.  The temporary object is assigned to the **the_res** variable in the **main()** function by copy assignment. Since copy assignment is doing a deep copy, another copy of the resource is acquired.

4.  When the assignment completes, the temporary object goes out of scope and we get the first "Resource released" message.

5.  When the **main()** function returns, **the_res** goes out of scope, which releases the second Resource.

So, if the resource is large, we have a very inefficient method of creating the **the_res** local variable in **main()** as we are creating and copying around large chunks of memory because of the deep copy in the copy assignment. However, we know that when the temporary variable created by **createResource()** is no longer needed, then we are going to throw it away and release its resource. It would be more efficient in these scenarios to transfer (or move) the resource from the temporary to the other instance of the type. Move semantics makes it possible to rewrite our **smart_ptr** template to not do the deep copy but transfer the resource.

Let's add move semantics to our **smart_ptr** class:

```
// Move constructor --> transfer resource
smart_ptr(smart_ptr&& a) : m_ptr(a.m_ptr)
{
    a.m_ptr = nullptr;     // Put into safe state
}
// Move assignment --> transfer resource
smart_ptr& operator=(smart_ptr&& a)
{
    // Self-assignment detection
    if (&a == this)
        return *this;

    // Release any resource we're holding
```

```
    delete m_ptr;


    // Transfer the resource
    m_ptr = a.m_ptr;
    a.m_ptr = nullptr;    // Put into safe state
    return *this;
  }
}
```

After re-running our program, we get the following output:

```
$ ./smart_ptr.exe
Resource acquired
Resource released
$
```

Figure 3.24: Smart pointer program output using move semantics

Now, because move assignment is now available, the compiler uses it on this line:

```
the_res = createResource(); // assignment invokes the copy assignment Step
3/4
```

**Step 3** is now replaced with move assignment, meaning the deep copy has now been removed.

**Step 4** no longer frees the resource because the line with the comment "//" puts into a safe state – it no longer has a resource to free because its ownership was transferred.

Another point to note with the **move constructor** and **move assignment** is that where the arguments were const for their copy versions, they were **non-const** for their move versions. This is called the **transfer of ownership**, which means that we need to modify the parameter that is passed in.

An alternative implementation of the move constructor may look like the following:

```
// Move constructor --> transfer resource
smart_ptr(smart_ptr&& a)
{
  std::swap(this->m_ptr, a.m_ptr);
}
```

Essentially, we are swapping the resource, and the C++ STL has support for swap as a template with many specializations. This works because we used member initialization to set **m_ptr** to **nullptr**. So, we are swapping a **nullptr** with the value stored in **a**.

Now that we have fixed the unnecessary deep copy problem, we can actually remove the copy operations from **smart_ptr()** as the transfer of ownership is actually what we want. If we were to copy an instance of a non-temporary **smart_ptr** to another instance of a non-temporary instance of **smart_ptr**, then we would have two objects that would delete the resource when they go out of scope, and this is not the desired behavior. To remove the (deep) copy operations we change the definition of our member functions, as follows:

```
smart_ptr(const smart_ptr& a) = delete;

smart_ptr& operator=(const smart_ptr& a) = delete;
```

The postfix of **= delete** which we looked at in *Chapter 2A, No Ducks Allowed – Types and Deduction*, tells the compiler that an attempt to access a function with that prototype is now not valid code and causes an error.

## STL Smart Pointers

Instead of having to write our own **smart_ptr**, the STL provides classes that we can use to implement RAII on our objects. The original was **std::auto_ptr()**, which was deprecated in C++ 11 and removed in C++ 17. It was created before **rvalue** reference support and caused problems because it implemented move semantics using copy. C++ 11 introduced three new templates to manage lifetime and ownership of resources:

- **std::unique_ptr**: Owns and manages a **single object** via a pointer and destroys that object when **unique_ptr** goes out of scope. It has two versions: for single objects (created using **new**) and for array of objects (created using **new[]**). **unique_ptr** is as efficient as using the underlying pointer directly.

- **std::shared_ptr**: Retains shared ownership of an object through a pointer. It manages the resource through the use of a reference counter. Every copy of shared_ptr that's assigned to shared_ptr updates the reference count. When the reference count goes to zero, this means that there are no owners left and the resource is released/destroyed.

- **std::weak_ptr**: Provides an interface to the same resource as **shared_ptr**, but does not modify the counter. It can be checked to see if the resource still exists, but it will not prevent the resource from being destroyed. If you determine that the resource still exists, then it can be used to obtain a **shared_ptr** to the resource. One use case for it is a scenario where multiple **shared_ptrs** end in cyclic references. A cyclic reference would prevent the auto releasing of resources. **weak_ptr** is used to break the loop and allow the resources to be freed when they should be.

## std::unique_ptr

std::unique_ptr() was introduced in C++ 11 to replace std::auto_ptr() and gives us everything that **smart_ptr** does (and more). We can re-write our **smart_ptr** program as follows:

```
#include <iostream>

#include <memory>

class Resource

{

public:

   Resource() { std::cout << "Resource acquired\n"; }

   ~Resource() { std::cout << "Resource released\n"; }

};

std::unique_ptr<Resource> createResource()

{

   std::unique_ptr<Resource> res(new Resource);

   return res;

}

int main()

{

   std::unique_ptr<Resource> the_res;

   the_res = createResource(); // assignment invokes the copy assignment

   return 0;

}
```

We can go one step further than this, because C++ 14 introduced a helper method to ensure exception safety when dealing with **unique_ptrs**:

```
std::unique_ptr<Resource> createResource()

{

   return std::make_unique<Resource>();

}
```

Why is this necessary? Consider the following function call:

```
some_function(std::unique_ptr<T>(new T), std::unique_ptr<U>(new U));
```

The problem with this is that the compiler is free to order the sequence of operations in the argument list in any order it likes. It could call `new T`, then `new U`, then `std::unique_ptr<T>()`, and finally `std::unique_ptr<U>()`. The problem with this sequence is that if `new U` were to throw an exception, then the resource allocated by the call to `new T` has not been placed in a `unique_ptr` and will not be cleaned up automatically. The use of `std::make_unique<>()` guarantees the order of calls so that the construction of the resource and the construction of `unique_ptr` will occur together and not leak resources. The need for `make_unique` has been removed in C++17 where the rules around the order of evaluation in these circumstances have been tightened. However, it is still probably a good idea to use the `make_unique<T>()` approach as any future conversion to a shared_ptr will be easier.

The name `unique_ptr` makes the intent of the template clear, that is, it is the only owner of the object that it points to. This was not obvious from `auto_ptr`. Likewise, `shared_ptr` is clear in that it intends to share the resource. The `unique_ptr` template provides access to the following operators:

- **T* get()**: Returns the pointer to the hosted resource.

- **operator bool()**: Returns `true` if the instance manages a resource. (`get() != nullptr`).

- **T& operator*()**: A `lvalue` reference to the hosted resource. Same as `*get()`.

- **T* operator->()**: A pointer to the hosted resource. Same as `get()`.

- **T& operator[](size_t index)**: For `unique_ptr(new [])`, it provides access to the hosted array as if it were natively an array. Returns an `lvalue` reference so that the value can be set and get.

## std::shared_ptr

A shared pointer is used when you want to share the ownership of a resource. Why would you do this? Several scenarios would lend themselves well to the sharing of resources, such as in the case of a GUI program, where you would probably want to share the font objects, bitmap objects, and so on. The **GoF flyweight design pattern** would be another example.

`std::shared_ptr` provides all of the same facilities as `std::unique_ptr`, but with more overhead because it now has to track a reference count for the object. All of the operators described for `std::unique_ptr` are available for use on `std::shared_ptr`. One difference is that the recommended method to create a `std::shared_ptr` is to call `std::make_shared<>()`.

When writing libraries or factories, the author of the library will not always know how a user will want to use the objects that have been created, so the recommendation is to return **unique_ptr<T>** from your factory methods. The reason for this is that the user can easily convert a **std::unique_ptr** into a **std::shared_ptr** by assignment:

```
std::unique_ptr<MyClass> unique_obj = std::make_unique<MyClass>();

std::shared_ptr<MyClass> shared_obj = unique_obj;
```

This will transfer ownership and leave **unique_obj** empty.

> **Note**
>
> Once a resource has been made a shared resource, it cannot be reverted into a unique object.

## std::weak_ptr

A weak pointer is a variant of a shared pointer, but it doesn't hold a reference count to the resource. So, it does not prevent it from being released when the count goes to zero. Consider the following program structure, which may occur within a normal graphical user interface (GUI):

```cpp
#include <iostream>
#include <memory>
struct ScrollBar;
struct TextWindow;
struct Panel
{
    ~Panel() {
        std::cout << "--Panel destroyed\n";
    }
    void setScroll(const std::shared_ptr<ScrollBar> sb) {
        m_scrollbar = sb;
    }
    void setText(const std::shared_ptr<TextWindow> tw) {
        m_text = tw;
```

```cpp
    }
    std::weak_ptr<ScrollBar> m_scrollbar;
    std::shared_ptr<TextWindow> m_text;
};
struct ScrollBar
{
    ~ScrollBar() {
        std::cout << "--ScrollBar destroyed\n";
    }
    void setPanel(const std::shared_ptr<Panel> panel) {
        m_panel=panel;
    }
    std::shared_ptr<Panel> m_panel;
};
struct TextWindow
{
    ~TextWindow() {
        std::cout << "--TextWindow destroyed\n";
    }
    void setPanel(const std::shared_ptr<Panel> panel) {
        m_panel=panel;
    }
    std::shared_ptr<Panel> m_panel;
};
void run_app()
{
    std::shared_ptr<Panel> panel = std::make_shared<Panel>();
    std::shared_ptr<ScrollBar> scrollbar = std::make_shared<ScrollBar>();
    std::shared_ptr<TextWindow> textwindow = std::make_shared<TextWindow>();
    scrollbar->setPanel(panel);
    textwindow->setPanel(panel);
```

```
    panel->setScroll(scrollbar);
    panel->setText(textwindow);
}
int main()
{
    std::cout << "Starting app\n";
    run_app();
    std::cout << "Exited app\n";
    return 0;
}
```

When executed, it outputs the following:

```
$ ./weak_ptr.exe
Starting app
--ScrollBar destroyed
Exited app
$
```

Figure 3.25: Weak pointer program output

This shows that the panel and the **textwindow** were not destroyed when the app exited. This is because they both held a **shared_ptr** to each other and so the reference count for both would not go to zero and trigger the destruction. If we depict the structure diagrammatically, then we can see that it has a **shared_ptr** cycle:

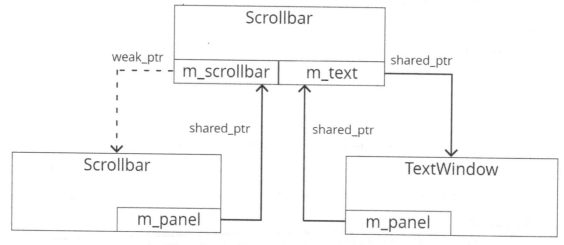

Figure 3.26: weak_ptr and shared_ptr cycles

## Smart Pointers and Calling Functions

Now that we can manage our resources, how do we use them? Do we pass around the smart pointers? When we have a smart pointer (**unique_ptr** or **shared_ptr**), we have four options when calling a function:

- Pass the smart pointer by value
- Pass the smart pointer by reference
- Pass the managed resource by pointer
- Pass the managed resource by reference

This is not an exhaustive list but are the main ones to consider. The answer to how we pass the smart pointer, or its resource, depends on our intent with the call to the function:

- Is the intend of the function to just use the resource?
- Does the function take ownership of the resource?
- Does the function replace the managed object?

If the function is just going to **use the resource**, then it does not even need to know that it is being handed a managed resource. It simply needs to use it and should be called using the resource by pointer, or resource by reference (or even resource by value):

```
do_something(Resource* resource);

do_something(Resource& resource);

do_something(Resource resource);
```

If you want to **pass the ownership** of the resource to the function, then the function should be called by smart pointer by value and called using **std::move()**:

```
do_something(std::unique_ptr<Resource> resource);

auto res = std::make_unique<Resource>();

do_something (std::move(res));
```

When **do_something()** returns, the **res** variable will be empty, and the resource is now owned by **do_something()**.

If you want to **replace the managed object** (a process known as **reseating**), then you pass the smart pointer by reference:

```
do_something(std::unique_ptr<Resource>& resource);
```

The following program puts all of this together to demonstrate each scenario and how to call the function:

```cpp
#include <iostream>
#include <memory>
#include <string>
#include <sstream>
class Resource
{
public:
    Resource() { std::cout << "+++Resource acquired ["<< m_id <<"]\n"; }
    ~Resource() { std::cout << "---Resource released ["<< m_id <<"]\n"; }
    std::string name() const {
        std::ostringstream ss;
        ss << "the resource [" << m_id <<"]";
        return ss.str();
    }
    int m_id{++m_count};
    static int m_count;
};
int Resource::m_count{0};
void use_resource(Resource& res)
{
    std::cout << "Enter use_resource\n";
    std::cout << "...using " << res.name() << "\n";
    std::cout << "Exit use_resource\n";
}
void take_ownership(std::unique_ptr<Resource> res)
{
    std::cout << "Enter take_ownership\n";
    if (res)
```

```cpp
        std::cout << "...taken " << res->name() << "\n";
    std::cout << "Exit take_ownership\n";
}
void reseat(std::unique_ptr<Resource>& res)
{
    std::cout << "Enter reseat\n";
    res.reset(new Resource);
    if (res)
        std::cout << "...reseated " << res->name() << "\n";
    std::cout << "Exit reseat\n";
}
int main()
{
  std::cout << "Starting...\n";
  auto res = std::make_unique<Resource>();
  // Use - pass resource by reference
  use_resource(*res);
  if (res)
    std::cout << "We HAVE the resource " << res->name() << "\n\n";
  else
    std::cout << "We have LOST the resource\n\n";
  // Pass ownership - pass smart pointer by value
  take_ownership(std::move(res));
  if (res)
    std::cout << "We HAVE the resource " << res->name() << "\n\n";
  else
    std::cout << "We have LOST the resource\n\n";
  // Replace (reseat) resource - pass smart pointer by reference
  reseat(res);
```

```
  if (res)
    std::cout << "We HAVE the resource " << res->name() << "\n\n";
  else
    std::cout << "We have LOST the resource\n\n";
  std::cout << "Exiting...\n";
  return 0;
}
```

When we run this program, we receive the following output:

```
$ ./pass_smart
Starting...
+++Resource acquired [1]
Enter use_resource
...using the resource [1]
Exit use_resource
We HAVE the resource the resource [1]

Enter take_ownership
...taken the resource [1]
Exit take_ownership
---Resource released [1]
We have LOST the resource

Enter reseat
+++Resource acquired [2]
...reseated the resource [2]
Exit reseat
We HAVE the resource the resource [2]

Exiting...
---Resource released [2]
$
```

Figure 3.27: Ownership passing Program output

**Note**

The *C++ Core Guidelines* has a whole section on *resource management,* smart pointers, and how to use them here: http://isocpp.github.io/CppCoreGuidelines/CppCoreGuidelines#S-resource. We have only touched on the most important that are aspects covered by the guidelines.

## Exercise 4: Implementing RAII with STL Smart Pointers

In this exercise, we will implement a sensor factory method that returns the sensor resource via a **unique_ptr**. We will implement a **unique_ptr** to hold an array, and then develop code that converts a **unique_ptr** into a shared pointer and then shares it some more. Follow these steps to implement this exercise:

1.  Open the **Lesson3** project in Eclipse. Then in the **Project Explorer**, expand **Lesson3**, then **Exercise04**, and double-click on **Exercise4.cpp** to open the file for this exercise into the editor.

2.  Click on the **Launch Configuration** drop-down menu and select **New Launch Configuration....** Configure the **L3Exercise4** application from the **Search Project** menu so that it runs with the name **L3Exercise4**.

3.  Click on the **Run** button to run Exercise 4. This will produce the following output:

```
------ Exercise 4 ------
+++Create Light Sensor
+++Create Pressure Sensor
+++Create Temperature Sensor
Light reading is 11
light sensor
    UniqP: Empty=false
---Destroy Temperature Sensor
---Destroy Pressure Sensor
---Destroy Light Sensor
------ Complete. -------
```

Figure 3.28: Exercise 4 output

4.  In the editor, examine the code, particularly the factory method, that is, **createSensor(type)**.

```cpp
std::unique_ptr<ISensor>
createSensor(SensorType type)
{
    std::unique_ptr<ISensor> sensor;

    if (type == SensorType::Light)
    {
        sensor.reset(new LightSensor);
    }
    else if (type == SensorType::Temperature)
    {
        sensor.reset(new TemperatureSensor);
```

```
        }
        else if (type == SensorType::Pressure)
        {
            sensor.reset(new PressureSensor);
        }
        return sensor;
}
```

This creates an empty unique pointer named sensor, and then resets the contained pointer with the desired sensor according to the passed in **type**.

5. Open Exercise4.cpp in the editor and change the line near the top of the file to read like so:

   ```
   #define EXERCISE4_STEP  5
   ```

6. Click on the **Run** button to compile the code, which will fail with the following error:

```
 Problems  Tasks  Console   Properties  Call Graph  C/C++ Unit  Search  Debug
CDT Build Console [Lesson3]
22:52:10 **** Incremental Build of configuration Debug for project Lesson3 ****
/usr/bin/make all
[ 20%] Built target L3Exercise3
[ 33%] Built target L3Exercise6
[ 46%] Built target L3Exercise2
[ 60%] Built target L3Exercise5
Scanning dependencies of target L3Exercise4
[ 66%] Building CXX object CMakeFiles/L3Exercise4.dir/Exercise04/Exercise4.cpp.o
/home/brian/Documents/advanced/Lesson3/Exercise04/Exercise4.cpp: In function 'void testSensors()':
/home/brian/Documents/advanced/Lesson3/Exercise04/Exercise4.cpp:71:25: error: conversion from 'std::unique_ptr<ISensor>' to non
    SensorSPtr light2 = light;
                        ^~~~~
make[2]: *** [CMakeFiles/L3Exercise4.dir/Exercise04/Exercise4.cpp.o] Error 1
CMakeFiles/L3Exercise4.dir/build.make:62: recipe for target 'CMakeFiles/L3Exercise4.dir/Exercise04/Exercise4.cpp.o' failed
CMakeFiles/Makefile2:220: recipe for target 'CMakeFiles/L3Exercise4.dir/all' failed
make[1]: *** [CMakeFiles/L3Exercise4.dir/all] Error 2
make: *** [all] Error 2
Makefile:94: recipe for target 'all' failed
"/usr/bin/make all" terminated with exit code 2. Build might be incomplete.

22:52:14 Build Failed. 4 errors, 0 warnings. (took 4s.109ms)
```

Figure 3.29: Compiler error for Step 5

The full error message is as follows:

```
error: conversion from 'std::unique_ptr<ISensor>' to non-scalar type
'SensorSPtr {aka std::shared_ptr<ISensor>}' requested
```

According to the error, we are attempting to assign a **unique_ptr** to a **shared_ptr** and that is not allowed.

7. Locate the line reporting the error and change it to read like so:

   ```
   SensorSPtr light2 = std::move(light);
   ```

8. Click on the **Run** button to compile and run the program. The output is as follows:

```
------ Exercise 4 ------
+++Create Light Sensor
+++Create Pressure Sensor
+++Create Temperature Sensor
Light reading is 11
light sensor
    UniqP: Empty=false
After move
    UniqP: Empty=true
Light2 reading is 11
Light 2
    SharedP: Empty=false, # owners=2
---Destroy Light Sensor
---Destroy Temperature Sensor
---Destroy Pressure Sensor
------ Complete. -------
```

Figure 3.30: Successful output for Exercise 4 (after EXERCISE4_STEP = 5)

The preceding output shows that we created three different sensors, that the light sensor pointer went from holding the resource until it was moved, and that the **Light 2** shared pointer has two owners. Wait! What? Two owners? But all we did was move the resource from `light` (a `unique_ptr`) to `light2` (a `shared_ptr`). The problem is actually the template method:

```
template<typename SP>
void printSharedPointer(SP sp, const char* message)
```

The first argument is passed by value, which means that a new copy of the **shared_ptr** will be created and passed to the method for printing.

9. Let's fix that now by changing the template to pass-by-reference. Click on the **Run** button to compile and run the program. The following output is generated:

```
------ Exercise 4 ------
+++Create Light Sensor
+++Create Pressure Sensor
+++Create Temperature Sensor
Light reading is 11
light sensor
    UniqP: Empty=false
After move
    UniqP: Empty=true
Light2 reading is 11
Light 2
    SharedP: Empty=false, # owners=1
---Destroy Light Sensor
---Destroy Temperature Sensor
---Destroy Pressure Sensor
------ Complete. -------
```

Figure 3.31: Corrected printSharedPointer output

10. Open **Exercise4.cpp** in the editor and change the line near the top of the file to read like so:

```
#define EXERCISE4_STEP   12
```

11. Click on the **Run** button to compile and run the program. The following output is generated:

```
------ Exercise 4 ------
+++Create Light Sensor
+++Create Pressure Sensor
+++Create Temperature Sensor
Light reading is 11
light sensor
    UniqP: Empty=false
After move
    UniqP: Empty=true
Light2 reading is 11
Light 2
    SharedP: Empty=false, # owners=1
+++Create Light Sensor ──────────── light = createSensor(SensorType::Light);
Second light ──────────── printUniquePointer(light, "Second light");
    UniqP: Empty=false          SensorSPtr light3(std::move(light));
Light 3                         printSharedPointer(light3, "Light 3");
    SharedP: Empty=false, # owners=1   light3 = light2;
---Destroy Light Sensor ──────────── 
Light 3                         printSharedPointer(light3, "Light 3");
    SharedP: Empty=false, # owners=2  }
---Destroy Light Sensor
---Destroy Temperature Sensor
---Destroy Pressure Sensor
------ Complete. -------
```

Figure 3.32: Annotated Step 12 output for Exercise 4

12. Compare the output with the code in the **testSensors()** method. We'll find that we can easily assign to an empty **unique_ptr (light)** and that we can assign from one **shared_ptr** to another (**light3 = light2**) without the need for **std::move()** in either case.

13. Open **Exercise4.cpp** in the editor and change the line near the top of the file to read like so:

```
#define EXERCISE4_STEP   15
```

14. Click on the **Run** button to compile and run the program. The output switches to the following:

```
------ Exercise 4 ------
11 12 13 14 15 16 17 18
21 22 23 24 25 26 27 28
31 32 33 34 35 36 37 38
41 42 43 44 45 46 47 48
51 52 53 54 55 56 57 58
61 62 63 64 65 66 67 68
71 72 73 74 75 76 77 78
81 82 83 84 85 86 87 88
------ Complete. -------
```

Figure 3.33: Managing arrays in unique_ptr

15. Open the editor and find the **testArrays()** method:

```
void testArrays()
{
    std::unique_ptr<int []> board = std::make_unique<int []>(8*8);

    for(int i=0  ; i<8 ; i++)
        for(int j=0 ; j<8 ; j++)
            board[i*8+j] = 10*(i+1)+j+1;

    for(int i=0  ; i<8 ; i++)
    {
        char sep{' '};
        for(int j=0 ; j<8 ; j++)
            std::cout << board[i*8+j] << sep;
        std::cout << "\n";
    }
}
```

There are several things to note in this snippet of code. Firstly, the type is declared as **int[]**. We have chosen **int** for this exercise, but it could be just about any type. Secondly, when **unique_ptr** (and **shared_ptr** since C++ 17) is used to manage an array, **operator[]** is defined. So, we simulate a two-dimensional array by calculating a one-dimensional index from the two-dimensional indices' **board[i*8+j]**.

16. Edit the first line of the method and declare the **auto** type:

```
auto board = std::make_unique<int []>(8*8);
```

17. Click on the **Run** button to compile and run the program – the output will be identical to the previous run. This is a case where auto is very helpful as you no longer need to type all the details into the type declaration, as well as the `make_unique()` call.

In this exercise, we implemented a factory function that served up manufactured sensors using `unique_ptr` to manage the lifetime of the sensor. We then implemented code to change it from a `unique_ptr` and share it to several objects. Finally, we developed a `unique_ptr` technique to manage a multi-dimensional array using a single-dimensional array.

## Rule of Zero/Five – A Different Perspective

When we introduced `BufferedWriter`, it had two resources being managed: memory and a file. We then discussed how the default compiler generated copy operations that are what are known as shallow copies. We talked about how we could manage the resources differently – stop the copy, perform a deep copy, or transfer ownership. What we decide to do in these circumstances is known as resource management policy. The policy that you choose, impacts how you execute the **Rule of Zero/Five**.

In terms of resource management, a class can manage no resources, manage a resource that can be copied but not moved, manage a resource that can be moved but not copied, or manage a resource that should be neither copied nor moved. The following classes show how these may be expressed:

```
struct NoResourceToManage
{
    // use compiler generated copy & move constructors and operators
};


struct CopyOnlyResource
{
    ~CopyOnlyResource()                                    {/* defined */ }
    CopyOnlyResource(const CopyOnlyResource& rhs)          {/* defined */ }
    CopyOnlyResource& operator=(const CopyOnlyResource& rhs) {/* defined */ }
    CopyOnlyResource(CopyOnlyResource&& rhs) = delete;
    CopyOnlyResource& operator=(CopyOnlyResource&& rhs) = delete;
```

```
};

struct MoveOnlyResource
{
    ~MoveOnlyResource()                                              {/* defined */ }
    MoveOnlyResource(const MoveOnlyResource& rhs)                     = delete;
    MoveOnlyResource& operator=(const MoveOnlyResource& rhs)   = delete;
    MoveOnlyResource(MoveOnlyResource&& rhs)                         {/* defined */ }
    MoveOnlyResource& operator=(MoveOnlyResource&& rhs)        {/* defined */ }
};


struct NoMoveOrCopyResource
{
    ~NoMoveOrCopyResource()                                          {/* defined */ }
    NoMoveOrCopyResource(const NoMoveOrCopyResource& rhs)                 =
delete;
    NoMoveOrCopyResource& operator=(const NoMoveOrCopyResource& rhs)  =
delete;
    NoMoveOrCopyResource(NoMoveOrCopyResource&& rhs)                      =
delete;
    NoMoveOrCopyResource& operator=(NoMoveOrCopyResource&& rhs)         =
delete;
};
```

Because of the complexity of managing resources in all contexts and under exceptions, the best practice is that if a class is responsible for managing a resource, then that class is only responsible for managing that resource.

## Activity 1: Implementing Graphics Processing with RAII and Move

In *Chapter 2A, No Ducks Allowed – Types and Deduction*, your team worked hard and got the implementation of **Point3d** and **Matrix3d**. Now, your company wants to market the library and it needs two major improvements before they can do that:

- The classes must be in a namespace for our company, that is, Advanced C Plus Plus Inc. So, the namespace for the graphics will be **accp::gfx**.

- The storage for the matrices in **Point3d** and **Matrix3d** is an intrinsic part of the class and so it is allocated from the stack and not the heap. As an evolution in the library matrix support, we need to allocate the memory from the heap. As we are working toward implementing larger matrices in a future release, we also want to introduce move semantics into our classes.

Follow these steps to achieve this:

1. Starting with our current version of the library (this can be found in the **Lesson3/ Activity01** folder), place all of our classes into the **acpp::gfx** namespace.

2. Fix all the failing tests because of the change. (Fail could mean a failure to compile, not just running the test.)

3. In **Matrix3d**, switch from declaring the matrix directly in the class to heap allocated memory for storage.

4. Fix the failing tests by implementing a deep copy implementation of the copy constructor and copy assignment operators. Make any other changes necessary to adjust to the new internal representations. Note that you should not need to modify any tests to get them to pass they only access the public interface which means we can change the internal structure without affecting the client.

5. Trigger another failure by forcing a move constructor to be called in **CreateTranslationMatrix()** by using **std::move** in the return statement. Introduce the required move operations in the **Matrix3d** class to get the tests to compile and pass.

6. Repeat steps 3 to 4 for **Point3d**.

After implementing the preceding steps, the expected output would look unchanged from the start:

```
------ Activity 1 ------
The point [ 1, 1, 1, 1 ]
...rotated around X by 90 degrees
...rotated around Y by 90 degrees
...rotated around Z by 90 degrees
moves to [ 1, 1, -1, 1 ]
...scaled by x=2, y = 3, z = 4
moves to [ 2, 3, -4, 1 ]
...translated by dx=-2, dy = 1, dz = -3
moves to [ 0, 4, -7, 1 ]

Complete.
```

Figure 3.34: Activity 1 output after successful conversion to use RAII

> **Note**
>
> The solution to this activity can be found on page: 657.

## When is a Function Called?

All the operations that are performed by a C++ program are essentially function calls (although the compiler may optimize these into inline sequences of operations). However, it may not be obvious that you are making a function call due to **syntactic sugar**. Syntactic sugar is the syntax within a programming language that makes it easier to read or express. For example, when you write **a = 2 + 5**, you are essentially calling **operator=(&a, operator+(2, 5))**. It is just that the language allows us to write the first form, but the second form allows us to overload operators and extend these capabilities to user-defined types.

The following mechanisms result in calls to a function:

- Explicit call to a function.

- All operators such as +, -, *, /, %, and so on along with new/delete.

- Declaration of variables – will result in a call to the constructors with arguments if the initialization values are present.

- User-defined literals – We have not dealt with these, but essentially, we define an overload for the **type operator "" name(argument)**. We can then write things such as 10_km, which make our code easier to understand as it carries semantic information.

- Casting from one value to another (**static_cast<>**, **const_cast<>**, **reinterpret_cast<>**, and **dynamic_cast<>**). Again, we have another operator overload which allows us to convert from one type into another.

- During function overload, it may be necessary to convert one type into another so that it matches the function prototype. It can do this by either calling a constructor with the right argument type to create a temporary or through a cast operator that's called implicitly.

Each and every one of these results in the compiler determine that a function must be called. Having determined that a function needs to be called, it must find the function that matches the name and arguments. This is what we'll be discussing in the next section.

## Which Function to Call

In *Chapter 2A, No Ducks Allowed – Types and Deduction*, we saw that function overload resolution was performed as follows:

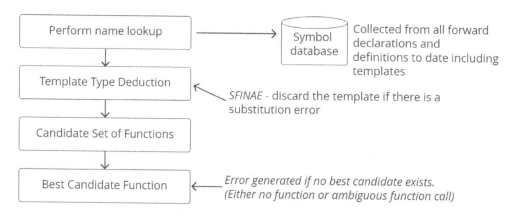

**Figure 3.35: Function overload resolution**

What we really did not dig into was the concept of name lookup. At some point the compiler will encounter the following call to the **func** function:

```
func(a, b);
```

When this happens, it must associate its name with the declaration that introduced it. This process is called **name lookup**. This name lookup is true for all the items in the program (variables, namespaces, classes, functions, function templates, and templates). For the program to compile, the name lookup process for variables, namespaces and classes must produce a single declaration. However, for functions and function templates the compiler may associate multiple declarations with the same name – mainly through function overloads which may be extended to consider additional functions due to **Argument-dependent Lookup** (**ADL**).

## Identifiers

As defined in the C++ standard, an **identifier** is a sequence of uppercase and lowercase Latin letters, digits, underscores, and most Unicode characters. A valid identifier must begin with a non-digit character and is arbitrarily long and case-sensitive. Every character is significant.

## Names

A **name** is used to refer to an entity or to a label. A name is of one of the following forms:

- An identifier
- An overloaded operator name in function notation (e.g. operator-, operator delete)
- A template name followed by its argument list (vector<int>)
- A user-defined conversion function name (operator float)
- A user-defined literal operator name (operator ""_ms)

Every entity and its name is introduced by a declaration while a name for a label is introduced by either a **goto** statement or by a labeled statement. A name can be used multiple times in one file (or translation unit) to refer to different entities depending on the scope. A name may also be used to refer to the same entity across multiple files (translation units), or different entities, depending upon the linkage. The compiler uses name lookup to associate a declaration that introduces a name with an unknown name in the program through **name lookup**.

## Name lookup

The name lookup process is one of two and is – selected based on the context:

- **Qualified name lookup**: The name appears to the right of the scope resolution operator, ::, or possibly after ::, followed by the **template** keyword. A qualified name may refer to a namespace member, class member or enumerator. The name to the left of the :: operator defines the scope to lookup the name from. If there is no name, then the global namespace is used.

- **Unqualified name lookup**: Everything else. In this case, name lookup examines the current scope and all enclosing scopes.

If the unqualified name is left of the function-call operator, '()' then it uses Argument-Dependent Lookup.

## Argument-Dependent Lookup

The set of rules for looking up unqualified function names is called **Argument-dependent lookup** (known as ADL), or **Koenig lookup** (named after Andrew Koenig, who defined it and is a longtime member of the C++ standards committee). Unqualified function names can appear as either a function-call expression or as part of an implicit function call to an overloaded operator.

ADL basically says that in addition to the scopes and namespaces considered during unqualified name lookup, the "associated namespaces" of all the arguments and template parameters are also considered. Consider the following code:

```
#include <iostream>
#include <string>


int main()
{
    std::string welcome{"Hello there"};
    std::cout << welcome;
    endl(std::cout);
}
```

When we compile this code and run it, the output is as expected:

```
$ ./adl.exe
Hello there
$
```

This is an unusual way to write the program. Typically, it would be written like so:

```
#include <iostream>
#include <string>


int main()
{
    std::string welcome{"Hello there"};
    std::cout << welcome << std::endl;
}
```

We are using the strange method of calling **endl()** to show ADL. But there are two ADL lookups occurring here.

The first function call that undergoes ADL is **std::cout << welcome**, which the compiler considers to be **operator<<(std::cout, welcome)**. The name operator, <<, is now looked up in the available scopes and the namespace of its arguments – **std**. This additional namespace resolves the name to the free method, that is, **std::operator<<(ostream& os, string& s)**, that's declared in the string header.

The second call is more obvious **endl(std::cout)**. Again, the compiler can access the std namespace to resolve this name lookup and finds the **std::endl** template in the header **ostream** (included in **iostream**).

Without ADL, the compiler has no way to find either of these functions, because they are free functions that are made known to us by the iostream and string packages. The magic of the insertion operator (<<) would be lost and it would be tedious for the programmer, if we were forced to write **std::operator<<(std::cout, welcome)**. It would be even worse if you consider chained insertions. Alternatively, you could write "**using namespace std;**". Neither of those options is ideal, and that is why we need ADL (Koenig lookup).

## Caveat Emptor

We have seen how ADL makes life easier for the programmer by including namespaces related to the function argument types. However, this lookup capability does not come without risk which, for the most part we can minimize. Consider the following sample code:

```cpp
#include <iostream>


namespace mylib
{
void is_substring(std::string superstring, std::string substring)
{
    std::cout << "mylib::is_substring()\n";
}


void contains(std::string superstring, const char* substring) {
    is_substring(superstring, substring);
}


}


int main() {
    mylib::contains("Really long reference", "included");
}
```

When we compile and run the preceding program, we get the expected output:

```
$ ./adl_caveat.exe
mylib::is_substring()
$
```

Figure 3.36: ADL Sample program output

The C++ standards committee then decides that it should introduce an **is_substring()** function that looks like this:

```
namespace std {
void is_substring(std::string superstring, const char* substring)
{
    std::cout << "std::is_substring()\n";
}
}
```

If we add this to the top of our file, compile it and re-run it, we now get the following output:

```
$ ./adl_caveat.exe
std::is_substring()
$
```

Figure 3.37: ADL issue program output

Thanks to ADL, the (next C++ standard) compiler has picked up a different implementation as a better fit for the unqualified function call of **is_substring()**. And because of implicit conversion of arguments it does not clash which would cause an ambiguity and a compiler error. It just silently adopts to the new method which could lead to subtle and hard to find bugs if the argument order is different. The compiler can only detect type and syntactic differences, not semantic ones.

> **Note**
>
> For the purposes of demonstrating how ADL works, we have added our function to the std namespace. Namespaces serve a purpose of separating concerns, and to add into someone else's namespace, in particular, the **Standard Library namespace (std)** is not good practice.

So, why caveat emptor (buyer beware)? If you use third-party libraries for your development (and that includes the C++ Standard Library), then when you upgrade the library, you need to ensure that changes to the interface are not going to cause you problems because of ADL.

## Exercise 5: Implementing Templates to Prevent ADL Issues

In this exercise, we will demonstrate a breaking change in C++17 STL that can potentially cause an issue in the wild. C++11 introduced templates for `std::begin(type)` and friends. As a developer, this is an appealing expression of the general interface and you may have written you own versions for size(type) and empty(type) already. Follow these steps to implement this exercise:

1. Open the **Lesson3** project in Eclipse. Then in the **Project Explorer**, expand **Lesson3**, then **Exercise05**, and double-click on **Exercise5.cpp** to open the file for this exercise into the editor.

2. Click on the **Launch Configuration** drop down menu and select **New Launch Configuration**.... Configure the **L3Exercise5** application from the Search Project menu so that it runs with the name **L3Exercise5**.

3. Click on the **Run** button to run Exercise 5. This will produce the following output:

```
------ Exercise 5 ------
Before adding numbers...
numbers.empty => true
empty(numbers) => true
size(numbers) => 0
After adding numbers...
numbers.empty => false
empty(numbers) => false
size(numbers) => 4
------ Complete. -------
```

Figure 3:38: Successful execution of Exercise 5

4. An examination of the code reveals two helper templates:

```
template<class T>
bool empty(const T& x)
{
    return x.empty();
}

template<class T>
int size(const T& x)
{
    return x.size();
}
```

5. Unlike all the other exercises, this exercise has been configured to build under C++ 14. Open the **CMakeLists.txt** file under **Lesson3** and locate the following line:

```
set_property(TARGET L3Exercise5 PROPERTY CXX_STANDARD 14)
```

6. Change **14** to a **17**.

7. Click on the **Run** button to compile the exercise which now fails:

```
 Problems  Tasks  Console ⌘  Properties  Call Graph  C/C++ Unit  Search  Debug
CDT Build Console [Lesson3]
22:56:22 **** Incremental Build of configuration Debug for project Lesson3 ****
/usr/bin/make all
[ 20%] Built target L3Exercise3
[ 33%] Built target L3Exercise6
[ 46%] Built target L3Exercise2
[ 53%] Building CXX object CMakeFiles/L3Exercise5.dir/Exercise05/Exercise5.cpp.o
/home/brian/Documents/advanced/Lesson3/Exercise05/Exercise5.cpp: In function 'int main()':
/home/brian/Documents/advanced/Lesson3/Exercise05/Exercise5.cpp:32:55: error: call of overloaded 'empty(std::vector<int>&)' is ambiguous
     std::cout << "empty(numbers) => " << empty(numbers) << "\n";
                                                       ^
/home/brian/Documents/advanced/Lesson3/Exercise05/Exercise5.cpp:13:6: note: candidate: bool empty(const T&) [with T = std::vector<int>]
 bool empty(const T& x)
      ^~~~
In file included from /usr/include/c++/7/string:51:0,
                 from /usr/include/c++/7/bits/locale_classes.h:40,
                 from /usr/include/c++/7/bits/ios_base.h:41,
                 from /usr/include/c++/7/ios:42,
                 from /usr/include/c++/7/ostream:38,
                 from /usr/include/c++/7/iostream:39,
                 from /home/brian/Documents/advanced/Lesson3/Exercise05/Exercise5.cpp:8:
```

Figure 3.39: Compilation fails under C++ 17 – ambiguous function call

8. Because the argument to the **empty()** and **size()** templates was a std::vector, the ADL pulled in the newly included STL versions of these templates and broke our code.

9. In the **Exercise5.cpp** file, locate the two occurrences of **empty()** and two occurrences of **size()** that are generating the errors and insert two colons, "**::**", before them (scope specifier).

10. Click on the **Run** button to compile and run the exercise. It now happily compiles and runs again because the calls to the **empty()** and **size()** function are now qualified. We could have equally specified **std::** scope instead.

In this exercise, we implemented two template functions in the global namespace that worked fine if we compiled the program under the C++ 14 standard. However, our implementation broke when we compiled under C++17 because the STL library changed and we had to change our implementation to ensure that the compiler located and used the templates that we wrote.

## Implicit Conversion

In determining the Candidate Set of Function in *Figure 3.36*, *Function overload resolution*, the compiler has to look at all of the available functions that have been found during the name lookup and determine whether the argument number and types match the call point. In determining whether the type matches, it will also examine all the available conversions to determine whether there is a mechanism to convert from the type T1 type (the type of the argument passed) to the T2 type (the type specified for the function parameter). If it can convert from T1 to T2 for all arguments, then it will add the function to the set of candidates.

This transformation from type T1 to type T2 is known as **implicit conversion** and occurs when some type, T1, is used in an expression or context that does not accept that type but accepts some other type, T2. This occurs in the following contexts:

- T1 is passed as an argument when calling a function declared with T2 as the parameter.

- T1 is used as an operand to an operator that expects T2.

- T1 is used to initialize a new object of T2 (including return statements).

- T1 is used in a `switch` statement (in which case, T2 is an int).

- T1 is used in an `if` statement or `do-while` or `while` loop (where T2 is bool).

If an unambiguous conversion sequence from T1 to 2 exists, then the program will compile. The conversions between built-in types are usually determined by the usual arithmetic conversions.

## Explicit – Preventing Implicit Conversion

Implicit conversion is a great feature that, make it possible for a programmer to express their intent, and it just works most of the time. However, the compiler's ability to convert one type into another without the programmer providing a hint, is not always desirable. Consider the following small program:

```
#include <iostream>


class Real
{
public:
```

```cpp
    Real(double value) : m_value{value} {}
    operator float() {return m_value;}

    float getValue() const {return m_value;}

private:
    double m_value {0.0};
};

void test(bool result)
{
    std::cout << std::boolalpha;
    std::cout << "Test => " << result << "\n";
}

int main()
{
    Real real{3.14159};

    test(real);

    if ( real )
    {
        std::cout << "true: " << real.getValue() << "\n";
    }
    else
    {
        std::cout << "false: " << real.getValue() << "\n";
    }
}
```

When we compile it and run the preceding program, we get the following output:

```
$ ./implicit.exe
Test => true
true: 3.14159
$
```

Figure 3.40: Implicit conversion sample program output

Well, it may be a little unexpected that this compiled and actually produced an output. The **real** variable is of the **Real** type which has a conversion operator to float – **operator float()**. The **test()** function takes a **bool** as an argument and the **if** condition must result in a **bool** as well. The compiler will convert any numeric type into a **boolean** type with a value of false if the value is zero or true if the value is not zero. But if this is not the behavior that we want we can prevent it by prefixing the declaration of the function with the explicit keyword. Let's say we change the line so that it reads like so:

```
explicit operator float() {return m_value;}
```

If we now attempt to compile it, we get two errors:

```
$ g++ -std=c++17 implicit.cpp -o implicit.exe
implicit.cpp: In function 'int main()':
implicit.cpp:29:10: error: cannot convert 'Real' to 'bool'
   29 |     test(real);
      |          ^~~~
      |          |
      |          Real
implicit.cpp:16:16: note:    initializing argument 1 of 'void test(bool)'
   16 | void test(bool result)
      |           ~~~~~^~~~~~
implicit.cpp:31:10: error: invalid user-defined conversion from 'Real' to 'bool' [
-fpermissive]
   31 |     if ( real )
      |          ^~~~
implicit.cpp:7:14: note: candidate is: 'Real::operator float()' <near match>
    7 |     explicit operator float() {return m_value;}
      |              ^~~~~~~~~
implicit.cpp:7:14: note:    return type 'float' of explicit conversion function can
not be converted to 'bool' with a qualification conversion
```

Figure 3.41: Compile errors because implicit conversion was removed.

Both are related to not being able to convert the Real type into a bool – first, at the call site to **test()** and then in the if condition.

Now, let's introduce a bool conversion operator to fix this problem.

```
operator bool() {return m_value == 0.0;}
```

We can now build the program again. We will receive the following output:

```
$ ./implicit.exe
Test => false
false: 3.14159
$
```

Figure 3.42: Introducing the bool operator replaces implicit conversion

The **boolean** value is now false, whereas it was true before. This is because the implicit conversion of the value that was returned by the float conversion was not zero and was then converted into true.

Since C++ 11, all constructors (except copy and move constructors) have been considered to be conversion constructors. This means that if they are not declared with explicit, then they are available for implicit conversion. Likewise, any casting operator that is not declared explicit is available for implicit conversion.

The **C++ Core Guidelines** has two rules related to implicit conversion:

- **C.46**: By default, declare single-argument constructors as explicit

- **C.164**: Avoid implicit conversion operators

## Contextual Conversion

If we now make one further change to our little program, we can get into what is known as contextual conversion. Let's make the bool operator explicit and attempt to compile the program:

```
explicit operator bool() {return m_value == 0.0;}
```

We will receive the following output:

```
$ g++ -std=c++17 implicit.cpp -o implicit.exe
implicit.cpp: In function 'int main()':
implicit.cpp:29:10: error: cannot convert 'Real' to 'bool'
   29 |     test(real);
      |          ^~~~
      |          |
      |          Real
implicit.cpp:16:16: note:   initializing argument 1 of 'void test(bool)'
   16 | void test(bool result)
      |           ~~~~~^~~~~~
```

Figure 3.43: Compile errors with explicit bool operator

This time we only have one error at the call site to **test()**, but not for the if condition. We can fix this error by using a C-style case (bool) or a C++ **static_cast<bool>(real)** (this is the preferred method). When we add the cast, the program compiles and runs once more.

So, if the bool cast is explicit, then why does the condition for the if expression not need a cast?

The C++ standard allows in certain contexts where the **bool** type is expected and the declaration for a bool conversion exists (whether marked explicit or not). If this happens, then an implicit conversion is allowed. This is known as **contextually converting into bool** and can occur in the following contexts:

- The condition (or controlling expression) of **if**, **while**, **for**

- The operands of the built-in logical operators: !(not), && (and) and || (or)

- The first operand of the ternary (or conditional) operator ?:.

## Exercise 6: Implicit and Explicit Conversions

In this exercise we will experiment with calling functions, implicit conversions, preventing them, and enabling them. Follow these steps to implement this exercise:

1. Open the **Lesson3** project in Eclipse. Then in the **Project Explorer**, expand **Lesson3** then **Exercise06** and double click on **Exercise6.cpp** to open the file for this exercise into the editor.

2. Click on the **Launch Configuration** drop down menu and select **New Launch Configuration....** Configure the **L3Exercise6** application from the **Search Project** menu so that it runs with the name **L3Exercise6**.

3. Click on the **Run** button to run Exercise 6. This will produce the following output:

```
------ Exercise 6 ------
Calculate for 1 volts
Calculate for 32 volts
use_float for 42
------ Complete. ------
```

Figure 3.44: Default output from Exercise 6

4. In the text editor, change the constructor of **Voltage** to be **explicit**:

```
struct Voltage
{
    explicit Voltage(float emf) : m_emf(emf)
    {
    }

    float m_emf;
};
```

5. Click on the **Run** button to recompile the code – now we get the following error:

```
 Problems   Tasks   Console    Properties   Call Graph   C/C++ Unit   Search   Debug
CDT Build Console [Lesson3]
23:02:44 **** Incremental Build of configuration Debug for project Lesson3 ****
/usr/bin/make all
[ 20%] Built target L3Exercise3
Scanning dependencies of target L3Exercise6
[ 26%] Building CXX object CMakeFiles/L3Exercise6.dir/Exercise06/Exercise6.cpp.o
/home/brian/Documents/advanced/Lesson3/Exercise06/Exercise6.cpp: In function 'int main()':
/home/brian/Documents/advanced/Lesson3/Exercise06/Exercise6.cpp:35:17: error: could not convert '32' from 'int' to 'Voltage'
     calculate(32);
                 ^
make[2]: *** [CMakeFiles/L3Exercise6.dir/Exercise06/Exercise6.cpp.o] Error 1
CMakeFiles/L3Exercise6.dir/build.make:62: recipe for target 'CMakeFiles/L3Exercise6.dir/Exercise06/Exercise6.cpp.o' failed
make[1]: *** [CMakeFiles/L3Exercise6.dir/all] Error 2
make: *** [all] Error 2
CMakeFiles/Makefile2:109: recipe for target 'CMakeFiles/L3Exercise6.dir/all' failed
Makefile:94: recipe for target 'all' failed
"/usr/bin/make all" terminated with exit code 2. Build might be incomplete.

23:02:46 Build Failed. 4 errors, 0 warnings. (took 2s.69ms)
```

Figure 3.45: Failed conversion of int to Voltage

6. Remove the explicit from the constructor and change the **calculate** function to take a reference:

```
void calculate(Voltage& v)
```

7. Click on the **Run** button to recompile the code – now, we get the following error:

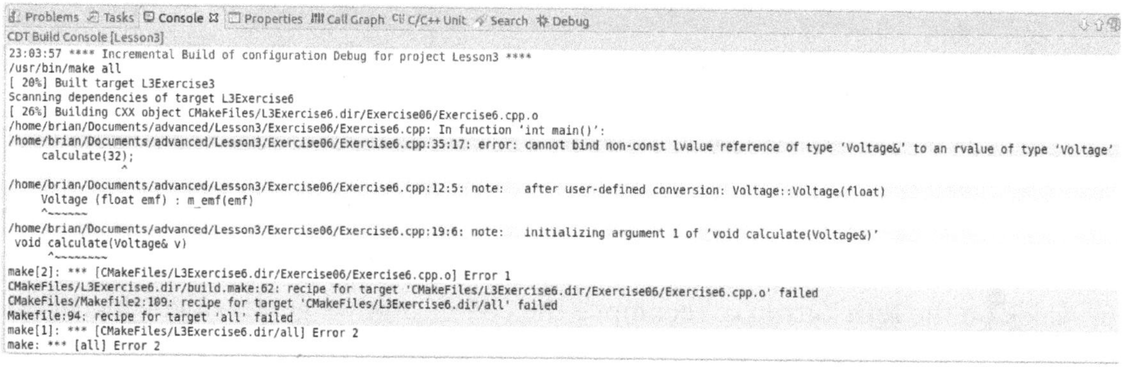

Figure 3.46: Failed conversion of int to Voltage&

The same line has the problem that we ran previously, but for a different reason. So, *implicit conversion only works with value types.*

8. Comment out the line generating the error, and then, after the call to **use_ float(42)**, add the following line:

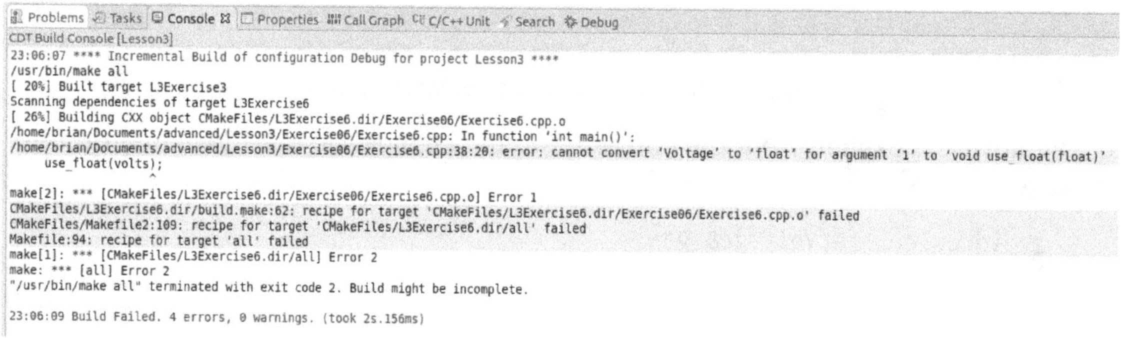

```
use_float(volts);
```

9. Click on the **Run** button to recompile the code – now we get the following error:

Figure 3.47: Failed conversion of Voltage to float

10. Now, add the following casting operator to the **Voltage** class:

```
operator float() const
{
    return m_emf;
}
```

11. Click on the **Run** button to recompile the code and run it:

```
------ Exercise 6 ------
Calculate for 1 volts
use_float for 42
use_float for 1
------ Complete. -------
```

**Figure 3.48: Successfully converted Voltage to float**

12. Now, place the **explicit** keyword in front of the cast that we just added and click on the **Run** button to recompile the code. Again, we get an error:

```
Problems  Tasks  Console ☒  Properties  Call Graph  C/C++ Unit  Search  Debug
CDT Build Console [Lesson3]
23:08:04 **** Incremental Build of configuration Debug for project Lesson3 ****
/usr/bin/make all
[ 20%] Built target L3Exercise3
Scanning dependencies of target L3Exercise6
[ 26%] Building CXX object CMakeFiles/L3Exercise6.dir/Exercise06/Exercise6.cpp.o
/home/brian/Documents/advanced/Lesson3/Exercise06/Exercise6.cpp: In function 'int main()':
/home/brian/Documents/advanced/Lesson3/Exercise06/Exercise6.cpp:44:20: error: cannot convert 'Voltage' to 'float' for argument '1' to 'void use_float(float)'
    use_float(volts);
                ^
make[2]: *** [CMakeFiles/L3Exercise6.dir/Exercise06/Exercise6.cpp.o] Error 1
CMakeFiles/L3Exercise6.dir/build.make:62: recipe for target 'CMakeFiles/L3Exercise6.dir/Exercise06/Exercise6.cpp.o' failed
CMakeFiles/Makefile2:109: recipe for target 'CMakeFiles/L3Exercise6.dir/all' failed
Makefile:94: recipe for target 'all' failed
make[1]: *** [CMakeFiles/L3Exercise6.dir/all] Error 2
make: *** [all] Error 2
"/usr/bin/make all" terminated with exit code 2. Build might be incomplete.

23:08:06 Build Failed. 4 errors, 0 warnings. (took 1s.780ms)
```

**Figure 3.49: Failure to convert Voltage to float**

13. By adding the explicit declaration to the cast, we are preventing the compiler from using the conversion operator. Change the line with the error to cast the volts variable to a float:

```
use_float(static_cast<float>(volts));
```

14. Click on the **Run** button to recompile the code and run it.

```
------ Exercise 6 ------
Calculate for 1 volts
use_float for 42
use_float for 1
------ Complete. -------
```

Figure 3.50: Conversion of Voltage into float with cast works again

In this exercise, we have seen that implicit conversions can occur between types (not references), and that we can control when they happen. Now we know how to control these conversions, we can strive to meet the guidelines previously quoted **C.46** and **C.164**.

## Activity 2: Implementing classes for Date Calculations

Your team is in charge of developing a library to help with calculations that are related to dates. In particular, we want to be able to determine the number of days between two dates and given a date, add (or subtract from it) a number of days to get a new date. This activity will develop two new types and enhance them to ensure that the programmer cannot accidentally have them interact with built-in types. Follow these steps to achieve this:

1. Design and implement a **Date** class that stores the **day**, **month**, and **year** as integers.

2. Add methods to access the internal day, month, and year values.

3. Define a type, **date_t** to represent the number of days since the **epoch date** of 1-Jan-1970.

4. Add a method to the **Date** class to convert this into **date_t**.

5. Add a method to set the **Date** class from a **date_t** value.

6. Create a **Days** class that stores the days value.

7. Add the **addition** operator to **Date** that takes **Days** as an argument.

8. Use **explicit** to prevent the addition of numbers.

9. Add the **subtraction** operator to return a **Days** value from the **difference** of two **Dates**.

After following these steps, you should receive the following output:

```
------ Activity 2 ------
There are 358 days between 1-Jan-2019 and 25-Dec-2019
There are 0.980172 years between 1-Jan-2019 and 25-Dec-2019

There are 364 days between 1-Jan-2019 and 31-Dec-2019
There are 0.996599 years between 1-Jan-2019 and 31-Dec-2019

There are 18255 days between 1-Jan-1970 and 25-Dec-2019
There are 49.9805 years between 1-Jan-1970 and 25-Dec-2019

There are 36525 days between 1-Jan-1970 and 1-Jan-2070
There are 100.002 years between 1-Jan-1970 and 1-Jan-2070

Complete.
```

**Figure 3.51: Output of a successful Date sample application**

**Note**

The solution for this activity can be found on page 664.

# Summary

In this chapter, we explored the lifetime of variables – both automatic and dynamic, where they are stored, and when they are destructed. We then used this information to develop **RAII** techniques that allow us to almost ignore resource management because the automatic variables will clean them up when they are destructed even in the presence of an exception. Then, we looked at throwing exceptions and catching them so that we can deal with abnormal conditions at the right level. From **RAII**, we went into a discussion on the ownership of resources and how **STL** smart pointers help us in this area. We discovered that just about everything is treated as a function call, thus allowing operator overloading and implicit conversions. We discovered the wonderful (or is it awful?) world of **argument-dependent lookup** (**ADL**) and how it can potentially trip us up in the future. We now have a good understanding of the fundamental features of C++. In the next chapter we will start to explore function objects and how they are realized and implemented using lambda functions. We will delve further into the offerings of STL and explore PIMPLs as we re-visit encapsulation.

# 4

# Separation of Concerns - Software Architecture, Functions, and Variadic Templates

**Learning Objectives**

By the end of this chapter, you will be able to:

- Develop classes using the PIMPL idiom to implement object-level encapsulation

- Implement a callback system using functors, std::function, and lambda expressions

- Implement lambdas using the right capture technique for the situation

- Develop variadic templates to implement C# style delegates for event handling.

This chapter will show you how to implement the PIMPL idiom, and how to develop a callback mechanism for your own programs.

# Introduction

In the previous chapter, we learned how to implement classes to properly manage resources even when the exceptions occurred using RAII. We also learned about ADL (**Argument Dependent Lookup**) and how it determines the function to be called. Finally, we talked about how the explicit keyword can be used to prevent automatic conversion between types by the compiler, known as implicit conversion

In this chapter, we will look into dependencies, both physical and logical, and see how they can affect build times adversely. We'll also learn how to separate the visible interface class from the implementation details to increase the speed of the build times. We will then learn to capture functions and contexts so that we can call them later using **functors**, **std::function** and **lambda expressions**. Finally, we will implement a variadic template to deliver an event-based callback mechanism.

## The Pointer to Implementation (PIMPL) Idiom

As projects implemented in C++ get larger and larger, there is the likelihood that the build times will grow at a faster rate than the number of files. This is because of the textual inclusion model used by the C++ build model. This is done so that the compiler can determine the size and layout of the class, causing a coupling between the **caller** and the **callee**, but allowing for optimization. Remember that everything must be defined before it can be used. A future feature called **Modules** promises to address this issue, but for now we need to understand the issue and the techniques used to address the problem.

## Logical and Physical Dependencies

When we wish to access a class from another class, we have a logical dependency. One class is logically dependent upon another class. If we consider the **Graphics** classes, **Point3d** and **Matrix3d** that we developed in *Chapter 2A, No Ducks Allowed – Types and Deduction* and *Chapter 3, The Distance between Can and Should – Objects, Pointers and Inheritance*, we have two logically independent classes **Matrix3d** and **Point3d**. However, because of how we implemented the multiplication operator between the two, we created a compile-time or **physical dependency**.

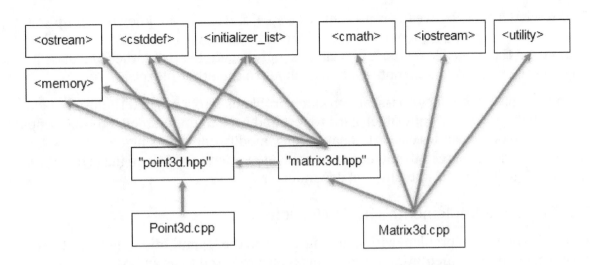

Figure 4.1: Physical Dependencies of Matrix3d and Point3d

As we can see with these relatively simple classes, the physical dependencies between the header files and the implementation files can quickly get complicated. It is this complexity that contributes to the build times of large projects because the number of physical (and logical) dependencies grows to thousands. We have shown only 13 dependencies in the preceding diagram as indicated by the arrows. But there are actually many more, as including a standard library header typically pulls in a hierarchy of include files. This means that if one header file is modified, then all files that are dependent upon it, either directly or indirectly, will need to be re-compiled to account for the change. This trigger for rebuilding also occurs if the change is to the private class members definition that users of the class cannot even access.

To help speed compile times, we have used the guard technique to prevent header files from being processed multiple times:

```
#if !defined(MY_HEADER_INCLUDED)

#define   MY_HEADER_INCLUDED

// definitions

#endif // !defined(MY_HEADER_INCLUDED)
```

And lately, most compilers now support the **#pragma once** directive which achieves the same result.

These relationships between entities (files, classes, and so on) are known as **coupling**. A file/class is **highly coupled** to another file/class if changes to the file/class result in changes to the other file/class. A file/class is **loosely coupled** to another file/class if changes to the file/class do not result in changes to the other file/class.

Highly coupled code (files/classes) introduce problems into a project. Highly coupled code is hard to change (inflexible), hard to test and hard to understand. Loosely coupled code on the other hand is easier to change (only modify one class), highly testable (only need the class being tested) and easier to read and understand. Coupling reflects, and is related to, the logical and physical dependencies.

## The Pointer to Implementation (PIMPL) Idiom

One solution to this problem with coupling is to use the "**Pimpl Idiom**" (which stands for **Pointer to Implementation Idiom**). This is also referred to as an opaque pointer, the compiler firewall idiom or even **Cheshire Cat technique**. Consider the **Qt library**, in particular, the **Qt Platform Abstraction** (**QPA**). It is an abstraction layer that hides the details of the Operating Systems and/or platforms that the Qt application is hosted on. One method to implement such a layer is to use the PIMPL idiom where the common interface is exposed to the application developer, but the implementation of how the functionality is delivered is hidden. Qt actually uses a variant of PIMPL known as d-pointer.

For example, one feature of a GUI is the use of a dialog that is a popup window that displays information or prompts for user input. It could be declared in **dialog.hpp** as follows:

> **Note**
>
> For more information about QT Platform Abstraction (QPA), visit the following link: https://doc.qt.io/qt-5/qpa.html#.

```
#pragma once


class Dialog
{
public:
    Dialog();
    ~Dialog();
```

```
    void create(const char* message);
    bool show();


private:
    struct DialogImpl;
    DialogImpl* m_pImpl;
};
```

The user has access to all the functions required to use a **Dialog** but has no knowledge of how it is implemented. Note that we have a declared **DialogImpl** but not defined it. In general, there is not much we can do with such a class as **DialogImpl**. But there is one thing that is allowed and that is to declare a pointer to it. This feature of C++ allows us to hide the implementation details in the implementation file. This means that in this simple case we do not have any include files for this declaration.

The implementation file **dialogImpl.cpp** may be implemented as:

```cpp
#include "dialog.hpp"
#include <iostream>
#include <string>


struct Dialog::DialogImpl
{
    void create(const char* message)
    {
        m_message = message;
        std::cout << "Creating the Dialog\n";
    }
    bool show()
    {
        std::cout << "Showing the message: '" << m_message << "'\n";
        return true;
    }


    std::string m_message;
```

```
};

Dialog::Dialog() : m_pImpl(new DialogImpl)
{
}

Dialog::~Dialog()
{
    delete m_pImpl;
}

void Dialog::create(const char* message)
{
    m_pImpl->create(message);
}

bool Dialog::show()
{
    return m_pImpl->show();
}
```

We note several things from this:

- We define the implementation class **DialogImpl** before we define the methods required for Dialog. This is necessary because **Dialog** will need to exercise the methods through **m_pImpl** which means that they need to be defined first.

- The **Dialog** constructor and destructor are responsible for the memory management.

- We include all the necessary header files required for the implementation, in the implementation file only. This reduces the coupling by minimizing the number of headers included in the **Dialog.hpp** file.

The program can be executed as follows:

```cpp
#include <iostream>
#include "dialog.hpp"

int main()
{
    std::cout << "\n\n------ Pimpl ------\n";
    Dialog dialog;

    dialog.create("Hello World");
    if (dialog.show())
    {
        std::cout << "Dialog displayed\n";
    }
    else
    {
        std::cout << "Dialog not displayed\n";
    }

    std::cout << "Complete.\n";
    return 0;
}
```

On execution, the above program produces the following output:

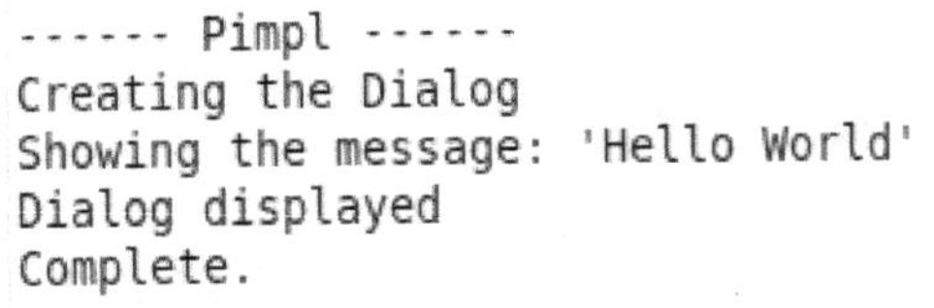

```
------ Pimpl ------
Creating the Dialog
Showing the message: 'Hello World'
Dialog displayed
Complete.
```

Figure 4.2: Sample Pimpl implementation output

## Advantages and Disadvantages of PIMPL

The biggest advantage in the use of PIMPL is that it breaks the compile-time dependencies between the clients of a class and its implementation. This allows for faster build times because PIMPL eliminates a large number of `#include` directives in the definition (header) file, instead pushing them to only be necessary in the implementation file.

It also decouples the implementation from the clients. We are now free to change the implementation of the PIMPL class and only that file needs recompilation. This prevents compilation cascades where changes to hidden members trigger the rebuilding of clients. This is called a compilation-firewall.

Some other advantages of the PIMPL idiom are as follows:

- **Data Hiding** – the internal details of implementation are truly isolated in the implementation class. If this is part of a library, then it can be used to prevent the disclosure of information, such as Intellectual property.

- **Binary Compatibility** – the binary interface of the class is now independent of the private fields. This means we can add fields to the implementation without affecting the client. It also means we could deploy the Implementation class in a shared library (**DLL**, or **.so** file) and be free to change it without affecting the client code.

Such advantages come at a cost. The disadvantages are as follows:

- **Maintenance Effort** – there is additional code in the visible class that forwards the calls to the Implementation class. This adds a level of indirection with a minor increase in complexity.

- **Memory Management** – the addition of a pointer for the implementation now requires us to manage the memory. It also requires additional storage to hold the pointer and, in a memory constrained system (For example: Internet of Things device) this may be critical.

## Implementing PIMPL with unique_ptr<>

Our current implementation of Dialog uses a raw pointer to hold the PIMPL implementation reference. In *Chapter 3, The Distance between Can and Should – Objects, Pointers and Inheritance*, we discussed ownership of objects and introduced smart pointers and RAII. The hidden object pointed to by the PIMPL pointer is a resource to be managed and should be executed using **RAII** and **std::unique_ptr**. As we shall see, there are some caveats for implementing **PIMPL** with **std::unique_ptr**.

Let's change our Dialog implementation to use smart pointers. Firstly, the header files changes to introduce the **#include <memory>** line and the destructor can be removed as the **unique_ptr** deletes the implementation class automatically.

```
#pragma once

#include <memory>


class Dialog
{
public:
    Dialog();
    void create(const char* message);
    bool show();


private:
    struct DialogImpl;
    std::unique_ptr<DialogImpl> m_pImpl;
};
```

Obviously, we remove the destructor from the implementation file, and we modify the constructor to use **std::make_unique**.

```
Dialog::Dialog() : m_pImpl(std::make_unique<DialogImpl>())
{
}
```

When re-compiling our new version, there are no problems with the **Dialog.hpp** and **DialogImpl.cpp** files, but our client **main.cpp** reports the following errors (with the gcc compiler), as you can see below:

```
/usr/bin/make all
Scanning dependencies of target Pimpl
[ 33%] Building CXX object CMakeFiles/Pimpl.dir/main.cpp.o
In file included from /usr/include/c++/7/memory:80:0,
                 from /home/brian/Documents/advanced/Lesson04/dialog.hpp:2,
                 from /home/brian/Documents/advanced/Lesson04/main.cpp:2:
/usr/include/c++/7/bits/unique_ptr.h: In instantiation of 'void std::default_delete<_Tp>::operator()(_Tp*) const [with _Tp
/usr/include/c++/7/bits/unique_ptr.h:268:17:   required from 'std::unique_ptr<_Tp, _Dp>::~unique_ptr() [with _Tp = Dialog::
/home/brian/Documents/advanced/Lesson04/dialog.hpp:4:7:   required from here
/usr/include/c++/7/bits/unique_ptr.h:76:22: error: invalid application of 'sizeof' to incomplete type 'Dialog::DialogImpl'
    static_assert(sizeof(_Tp)>0,
                  ^

make[2]: *** [CMakeFiles/Pimpl.dir/main.cpp.o] Error 1
CMakeFiles/Pimpl.dir/build.make:62: recipe for target 'CMakeFiles/Pimpl.dir/main.cpp.o' failed
CMakeFiles/Makefile2:72: recipe for target 'CMakeFiles/Pimpl.dir/all' failed
make[1]: *** [CMakeFiles/Pimpl.dir/all] Error 2
make: *** [all] Error 2
Makefile:94: recipe for target 'all' failed
"/usr/bin/make all" terminated with exit code 2. Build might be incomplete.

10:50:13 Build Failed. 4 errors, 0 warnings. (took 3s.507ms)
```

Figure 4.3: Failed compilation of Pimpl using unique_ptr

The first error reports **invalid application of 'sizeof' to incomplete type 'Dialog::DialogImpl'**. The problem is that in **main.cpp** file the compiler is trying to call the destructor of **Dialog** for us when **main()** function ends. As we discussed in *Chapter 2A, No Ducks Allowed – Types and Deduction* the compiler will generate a destructor for us (as we removed it). This generated destructor will call the destructor of **unique_ptr** which is the cause of the error. If we look at **line 76**, of **unique_ptr.h** file, we'll find the following implementation of the **operator()** function for the default **deleter** used by **unique_ptr** (the **deleter** is the function called by **unique_ptr** when it destroys the object it points to):

```
void

operator()(_Tp* __ptr) const

{

    static_assert(!is_void<_Tp>::value, "can't delete pointer to incomplete
type");

    static_assert(sizeof(_Tp)>0, "can't delete pointer to incomplete type");

    delete __ptr;

}
```

Our code is failing on the second **static_assert()** statement that terminates the compilation with an error. The problem is that the compiler is trying to generate the destructor for **std::unique_ptr<DialogImpl>** and **DialogImpl** is an incomplete type. So, to fix the problem, we control the generation of the destructor to be at a point where **DialogImpl** is a complete type.

To do this, we put the declaration of the destructor back into the class and add its implementation to the **DialogImpl.cpp** file.

```
Dialog::~Dialog()

{

}
```

When we compile and run our program, it produces exactly the same output as before. In fact, if we only need an empty destructor, we can replace the above code with the following code:

```
Dialog::~Dialog() = default;
```

If we compile and run our program, then following output will be produced:

```
------ Pimpl ------
Creating the Dialog
Showing the message: 'Hello World'
Dialog displayed
Complete.
```

Figure 4.4: Sample unique_ptr Pimpl implementation output

## unique_ptr<> PIMPL Special Functions

As PIMPL usually implies that the visible interface class owns the implementation class, the move-semantics are a natural fit. However, in the same way the compiler generated destructor implementation is correct, the compiler generated move constructor and move assignment operator will give the desired behavior, that is, perform a move on the member **unique_ptr**. The move operations both potentially need to perform a delete before assigning the transferred value, and so, suffer from the same problem as the destructor with incomplete types. The solution is the same as for the destructor – declare the method in the header file and implement when the type is complete – in the

implementation file. So, our header file looks like the following:

```
class Dialog

{

public:
```

```
    Dialog();
    ~Dialog();

    Dialog(Dialog&& rhs);
    Dialog& operator=(Dialog&& rhs);

    void create(const char* message);
    bool show();

private:
    struct DialogImpl;
    std::unique_ptr<DialogImpl> m_pImpl;
};
```

While the implementation looks like:

```
Dialog::Dialog() : m_pImpl(std::make_unique<DialogImpl>())
{
}


Dialog::~Dialog() = default;
Dialog::Dialog(Dialog&& rhs) = default;
Dialog& Dialog::operator=(Dialog&& rhs) = default;
```

Depending upon the data items that we are hiding in our implementation class, we may also desire copy functionality on our PIMPL classes. Using a `std::unique_ptr` inside the Dialog class prevents the automatic generation of a copy constructor and copy assignment operator, as the internal members do not support copy. Also, by defining the move member functions, as we saw in *Chapter 2A, No Ducks Allowed – Types and Deduction*, it also stops the compiler in generating the copy versions. In addition, if the compiler did generate copy semantics for us, it would only be a **shallow copy**. But due to the PIMPL implementation, we need a **deep copy**. So, we will need to write our own copy special member functions. Again, the definition goes in the header file and the implementation needs to be done where the type is complete, inside the **DialogImpl. cpp** file.

In the header file, we add the following declarations:

```
Dialog(const Dialog& rhs);
Dialog& operator=(const Dialog& rhs);
```

And the implementation would look like:

```
Dialog::Dialog(const Dialog& rhs) : m_pImpl(nullptr)
{
    if (this == &rhs)    // do nothing on copying self
    return;
    if (rhs.m_pImpl)     // rhs has something -> clone it
        m_pImpl = std::make_unique<DialogImpl>(*rhs.m_pImpl);
}


Dialog& Dialog::operator=(const Dialog& rhs)
{
    if (this == &rhs)    // do nothing on assigning to self
        return *this;
    if (!rhs.m_pImpl)    // rhs is empty -> delete ours
    {
        m_pImpl.reset();
    }
    else if (!m_pImpl)  // ours is empty -> clone rhs
    {
        m_pImpl = std::make_unique<DialogImpl>(*rhs.m_pImpl);
    }
    else // use copy of DialogImpl
    {
        *m_pImpl = *rhs.m_pImpl;
    }
}
```

Note the **if(this == &rhs)** clauses. These are there to prevent the object from copying itself unnecessarily. Also, note that we need to check if either **unique_ptr** is empty and process the copy accordingly.

> **Note**
>
> Before solving any practical in this chapter, download the GitHub repository https://github.com/TrainingByPackt/Advanced-CPlusPlus and import the folder of Lesson 4 in Eclipse, so that you can view the codes for each exercises, and activities.

## Exercise 1: Implementing a Kitchen with unique_ptr<>

In this exercise, we will hide the details of how the kitchen processes orders by implementing the **Pimpl idiom** with the **unique_ptr<>**. Follow the below steps to implement this exercise:

1.  Open the **Lesson4** project in Eclipse, and then in the **Project Explorer**, expand **Lesson4** then **Exercise01** and double click on **Exercise1.cpp** to open the file for this exercise into the editor.

2.  As this is a CMake based project, change the current builder to be CMake Build (portable).

3.  Click on the **Launch Configuration** drop down menu and select **New Launch Configuration....** Configure **L4Exercise1** to run with the name **Exercise1**.

4.  Click on the **Run** button. Exercise 1 will run and produce the following output:

```
------ Kitchen Exercise 1 ------
Chef 'TheChef' is serving you tonight
...Preparing Lamb Ragout
...Cooking Lamb Ragout
...Serving Lamb Ragout
Chef 'TheChef' is serving you tonight
---Serving Baked Alaska
Chef 'TheChef' is serving you tonight
#### sacre bleu: 'Turkey' ####
Chef 'TheChef' is serving you tonight
...Preparing Steak Diane
...Cooking Steak Diane
...Serving Steak Diane
Chef 'TheChef' is serving you tonight
---Serving Pavlova
Complete.
```

Figure 4.5: Exercise 1 Program output

5. Open **kitchen.hpp** in the editor, and you will find the following declaration:

```
class Kitchen
{
public:
    Kitchen(std::string chef);
    std::string processOrder(std::string order);

private:
    std::string searchForRecipe(std::string order);
    std::string searchForDessert(std::string order);
    std::string cookRecipe(std::string recipe);
    std::string serveDessert(std::string dessert);

    std::vector<Recipe>::iterator getRecipe(std::string recipe);
    std::vector<Dessert>::iterator getDessert(std::string recipe);

    std::string m_chef;
    std::vector<Recipe> m_recipes;


    std::vector<Dessert> m_desserts;

};
```

Everything in the private section is details about how the kitchen delivers the order to the customer. It has forced the inclusion of the header files **recipe.hpp** and **dessert.hpp** creating a coupling between these detail files and the clients of the `Kitchen`. We are going to move all the private members into an implementation class and hide the details.

6. In the **kitchen.hpp** file, add the `#include <memory>` directive to gain access to the `unique_ptr`. Add the declaration for the destructor `~Kitchen();` and then add the following two lines into the top of the private section:

```
struct Impl;
std::unique_ptr<Impl> m_impl;
```

7. Open the **kitchen.cpp** file and add the following after the `#include` directives:

```
struct Kitchen::Impl
{

};


Kitchen::~Kitchen() = default;
```

8. Click on the **Run** button to re-build the program. You'll see that the output is still the same as before.

9. Remove all the private members except the two new ones from the `Kitchen` class in **kitchen.hpp** and add them into the `Kitchen::Impl` declarations. The **kitchen. hpp** file has the following contents after removing the `#include <vector>`, `#include "recipe.hpp"` and `#include "dessert.hpp"`:

```
#pragma once
#include <string>
#include <memory>

class Kitchen
{
public:
    Kitchen(std::string chef);
    ~Kitchen();
    std::string processOrder(std::string order);

private:
    struct Impl;
    std::unique_ptr<Impl> m_impl;
};
```

10. In the **kitchen.cpp** file, change the Kitchen constructor to be the `Kitchen::Impl` constructor:

```
Kitchen::Impl::Impl(std::string chef) : m_chef{chef}
```

11. For the remainder of the original methods, change them to be scoped to `Kitchen::Impl` instead of `Kitchen::`. For example, `std::string Kitchen::processOrder(std::string order)` becomes `std::string Kitchen::Impl::processOrder(std::string order)`.

12. In **Kitchen::Impl**, add a constructor with a **std::string** argument and the **processOrder()** method. The **Kitchen::Impl** declaration should now look like the following:

```cpp
struct Kitchen::Impl
{
    Impl(std::string chef);
    std::string processOrder(std::string order);

    std::string searchForRecipe(std::string order);
    std::string searchForDessert(std::string order);
    std::string cookRecipe(std::string recipe);
    std::string serveDessert(std::string dessert);

    std::vector<Recipe>::iterator getRecipe(std::string recipe);
    std::vector<Dessert>::iterator getDessert(std::string recipe);

    std::string m_chef;
    std::vector<Recipe> m_recipes;
    std::vector<Dessert> m_desserts;
};
```

13. In **kitchen.cpp**, add the **#include <vector>**, **#include "recipe.hpp"** and **#include "dessert.hpp"** to the top of the file.

14. Click on the **Run** button to re-build the program, and this time it will fail with two undefined references – **Kitchen::Kitchen** and **Kitchen::processOrder**.

15. In **Kitchen.cpp**, after the **Kitchen::Impl** method definitions, add the following two methods:

```cpp
Kitchen::Kitchen(std::string chef) : m_impl(std::make_
unique<Kitchen::Impl>(chef))
{
}

std::string Kitchen::processOrder(std::string order)
{
    return m_impl->processOrder(order);
}
```

16. Click on the **Run** button to re-build the program. The program will run again to produce the original output.

```
------ Kitchen Exercise 1 ------
Chef 'TheChef' is serving you tonight
...Preparing Lamb Ragout
...Cooking Lamb Ragout
...Serving Lamb Ragout
Chef 'TheChef' is serving you tonight
---Serving Baked Alaska
Chef 'TheChef' is serving you tonight
#### sacre bleu: 'Turkey'
Chef 'TheChef' is serving you tonight
...Preparing Steak Diane
...Cooking Steak Diane
...Serving Steak Diane
Chef 'TheChef' is serving you tonight
---Serving Pavlova
Complete.
```

Figure 4.6: The Kitchen program output using Pimpl

In this exercise, we have taken a class that held many details in its private members and moved those details into a PIMPL class to hide the details and decouple the interface from the implementation using the techniques previously described.

## Function Objects and Lambda Expressions

One common pattern used in programming, particularly when implementing event-based processing, such as asynchronous input and output, is the use of the **callback**. A client registers that they want to be notified that an event has occurred (For example: data is available to read, or a data transmission is complete). This pattern is known as **Observer pattern** or **Subscriber Publisher pattern**. C++ supports a variety of techniques to provide the callback mechanism.

### Function Pointers

The first mechanism is the use of the **function pointers**. This is a legacy feature inherited from the C language. The following program shows an example of a function pointer:

```cpp
#include <iostream>


using FnPtr = void (*)(void);


void function1()
```

```
{
    std::cout << "function1 called\n";
}
int main()
{
    std::cout << "\n\n------ Function Pointers ------\n";
    FnPtr fn{function1};


    fn();


    std::cout << "Complete.\n";
    return 0;
}
```

This program when compiled and executed, produces the following output:

```
------ Function Pointers ------
function1 called
Complete.
```

Figure 4.7: Function Pointer Program output

Strictly speaking the code should be modified as follows:

```
FnPtr fn{&function1};


if(fn != nullptr)
    fn();
```

First, thing to note is that the address of (&) operator should be used to initialize the pointer. Secondly, we should check that the pointer is valid before calling it.

```
#include <iostream>


using FnPtr = void (*)(void);


struct foo
{
```

```
        void bar() { std::cout << "foo:bar called\n"; }
    };


    int main()
    {
        std::cout << "\n\n------ Function Pointers ------\n";
        foo object;


        FnPtr fn{&object.bar};


        fn();


        std::cout << "Complete.\n";
        return 0;
    }
```

When we attempt to compile this program, we get the following errors:

```
/usr/bin/make all
Scanning dependencies of target Pimpl
[ 33%] Building CXX object CMakeFiles/Pimpl.dir/main.cpp.o
/home/brian/Documents/advanced/Lesson04/main.cpp: In function 'int main()':
/home/brian/Documents/advanced/Lesson04/main.cpp:92:22: error: ISO C++ forbids taking the address of a bound member function to |form a pointer
     FnPtr fn{&object.bar};
              ^~~
/home/brian/Documents/advanced/Lesson04/main.cpp:92:25: error: cannot convert 'void (foo::*)()' to 'FnPtr {aka void (*)()}' in initialization
     FnPtr fn{&object.bar};
                         ^
CMakeFiles/Pimpl.dir/build.make:62: recipe for target 'CMakeFiles/Pimpl.dir/main.cpp.o' failed
make[2]: *** [CMakeFiles/Pimpl.dir/main.cpp.o] Error 1
make[1]: *** [CMakeFiles/Pimpl.dir/all] Error 2
make: *** [all] Error 2
CMakeFiles/Makefile2:72: recipe for target 'CMakeFiles/Pimpl.dir/all' failed
Makefile:94: recipe for target 'all' failed
"/usr/bin/make all" terminated with exit code 2. Build might be incomplete.
```

Figure 4.8: Errors compiling function pointer program

The text of the first error is **ISO C++ forbids taking the address of a bound member function to form a pointer to member function.  Say '&foo::bar'**. It tells us that we should use a different form to obtain the function address. The real error in this case is the second error message: **error: cannot convert 'void (foo::*)()' to 'FnPtr {aka void (*) ()}' in initialization**. The real problem is that non-static member functions take a hidden argument when they are called – the **this** pointer.

By changing the above program to the following:

```cpp
#include <iostream>

using FnPtr = void (*)(void);

struct foo
{
    static void bar() { std::cout << "foo:bar called\n"; }
};

int main()
{
    std::cout << "\n\n------ Function Pointers ------\n";

    FnPtr fn{&foo::bar};

    fn();

    std::cout << "Complete.\n";
    return 0;
}
```

It compiles and runs successfully:

```
------ Function Pointers ------
foo:bar called
Complete.
```

Figure 4.9: Function pointer program using static member function

The function pointer technique is often used when interfacing with C libraries that use callbacks and operating system notifications which also support callbacks. In these two cases, it would be normal for the callback to take an argument which is a **void** * to a user registered data blob pointer. The data blob pointer could be the **this** pointer of a class which is then dereferenced and the callback forwarded into a member function.

In other languages, such as Python and C#, it is a part of the language that capturing a function pointer will also capture the sufficient data to call that function (for example: **self** or **this**). C++ has the ability to make any object callable through the function call operator which we'll cover next.

## What is a Function Object?

C++ allows for the function call operator **operator()** to be overloaded. This leads to the ability to make any object **callable**. An object that can be callable is known as a **functor**. The **Scaler** class in the following program implements a **functor**.

```
struct Scaler
{
    Scaler(int scale) : m_scale{scale} {};

    int operator()(int value)
    {
        return m_scale * value;
    }

    int m_scale{1};
};

int main()
{
    std::cout << "\n\n------ Functors ------\n";
    Scaler timesTwo{2};
    Scaler timesFour{4};

    std::cout << "3 scaled by 2 = " << timesTwo(3) << "\n";
    std::cout << "3 scaled by 4 = " << timesFour(3) << "\n";


    std::cout << "Complete.\n";
```

```
        return 0;
}
```

There are two objects of type **Scaler** created and they are used as functions inside the lines generating output. The above program produces the following output:

```
------ Functors ------
3 scaled by 2 = 6
3 scaled by 4 = 12
Complete.
```

Figure 4.10: Functors program output

One advantage of **functors** over function pointers is that they can contain state, either as an object or across all instances. Another advantage is that they can be passed to STL algorithms that expect a function (for example **std::for_each**) or an operator (for example **std::transform**).

An example of such a use might look like following:

```
#include <iostream>
#include <vector>
#include <algorithm>

struct Scaler
{
    Scaler(int scale) : m_scale{scale} {};

    int operator()(int value)
    {
        return m_scale * value;
    }

    int m_scale{1};
};

void PrintVector(const char* prefix, std::vector<int>& values)
```

```cpp
{
    const char* sep = "";
    std::cout << prefix << " = [";
    for(auto n : values)
    {
        std::cout << sep << n;
        sep = ", ";
    }
    std::cout << "]\n";
}


int main()
{
    std::cout << "\n\n------ Functors with STL ------\n";
    std::vector<int> values{1,2,3,4,5};

    PrintVector("Before transform", values);
    std::transform(values.begin(), values.end(), values.begin(), Scaler(3));
    PrintVector("After transform", values);

    std::cout << "Complete.\n";
    return 0;
}
```

If we run this program, the output produced will look like the following:

```
------ Functors with STL ------
Before transform = [1, 2, 3, 4, 5]
After transform = [3, 6, 9, 12, 15]
Complete.
```

Figure 4.11: Program output showing Scaler transformed vectors

## Exercise 2: Implementing function objects

In this exercise, we will implement two different function objects that can work with the STL algorithm for_each.

1. Open the **Lesson4** project in Eclipse, and then in the **Project Explorer**, expand **Lesson4** then **Exercise02** and double click on **Exercise2.cpp** to open the file for this exercise into the editor.

2. As this is a CMake based project, change the current builder to be CMake Build (portable).

3. Click on the **Launch Configuration** drop down menu and select **New Launch Configuration....** Configure **L4Exercise2** to run with the name **Exercise2**.

4. Click on the **Run** button. Exercise 2 will run and produce the following output:

```
------ Exercise 2 ------
Average of [1, 2, 3, 4, 5, 6, 7, 8, 9, 10, ] = ??
Complete.
```

Figure 4.12: Exercise 2 Initial output

The first thing we will do is fix the formatting of the output by introducing a function object.

5. In the editor, before the definition of **main()** function add the following class definition:

```cpp
struct Printer
{
    void operator()(int n)
    {
        std::cout << m_sep << n;
        m_sep = ", ";
    }
    const char* m_sep = "";
};
```

6. Inside the **main()** method replace the following code

```cpp
std::cout << "Average of [";
for( auto n : values )
    std::cout << n << ", ";
std::cout << "] = ";
```

**with**

```
std::cout << "Average of [";
std::for_each(values.begin(), values.end(), Printer());
std::cout << "] = ";
```

7. Click on the **Run** button. The exercise will run and produce the following output:

```
------ Exercise 2 ------
Average of [1, 2, 3, 4, 5, 6, 7, 8, 9, 10] = ??
Complete.
```

Figure 4.13: Exercise 2 Improved output format

8. The internal state of the **Printer** class allows us to fix the formatting. Now, introduce an **aggregator** class that will allow us to calculate the **average**. Add the following class definition to the top of the file:

```
struct Averager
{
    void operator()(int n)
    {
        m_sum += n;
        m_count++;
    }

    float operator()() const
    {
        return static_cast<float>(m_sum)/(m_count==0?1:m_count);
    }

    int m_count{0};
    int m_sum{0};
};
```

9. Modifiy **main()** method to use the **Averager** class as follows:

```
int main(int argc, char**argv)
{
    std::cout << "\n------ Exercise 2 ------\n";
    std::vector<int> values {1,2,3,4,5,6,7,8,9,10};

    Averager averager = std::for_each(values.begin(), values.end(),
```

```
        Averager());

    std::cout << "Average of [";
    std::for_each(values.begin(), values.end(), Printer());
    std::cout << "] = ";
    std::cout << averager() << "\n";

    std::cout << "Complete.\n";
    return 0;
}
```

10. Click on the **Run** button. The exercise will run and produce the following output:

```
------ Exercise 2 ------
Average of [1, 2, 3, 4, 5, 6, 7, 8, 9, 10] = 5.5
Complete.
```

Figure 4.14: Exercise 2 output with average

Note that `std::for_each()` returns the instance of `Averager` passed into it. This instance is copied into the variable `averager` that then contains the data required to calculate the average. In this exercise, we implemented two function objects or **functor** classes: `Averager` and `Printer` that we could use as functions when passed to the STL algorithm `for_each`.

## std::function<> template

C++11 introduced a general polymorphic function wrapper template, `std::function<>`, that makes implementing callbacks and other function related capabilities easier. `std::function` holds a callable object known as the **target**. If it does not contain a target, then it is called **empty**. Calling an empty `std::function` will result in `std::bad_function_call` exception being thrown.

The function object can store, copy or invoke a target that is any of the following callable objects: functions, function objects (defines the **operator()**), a pointer to member function or a lambda expression. We will cover more about it in the topic *What is a Lambda Expression?*

When instantiating a **std::function** object, it is only necessary to provide the function signature and not the value to initialize it with, leading to an empty instance. The instantiation is done as follows:

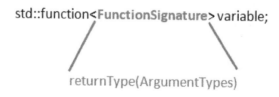

Figure 4.15: Structure of a std::function declaration

The arguments to the template, define the **function signature** of the target stored by **variable**. The signature starts with the return type (which may be void) and then places inside the parentheses the list of types that the function will be invoked with.

The use of free functions and **functors** with **std::function** is straight forward. Provided that the signature matches the parameters passed to the **std::function** template, we can simply equate the free function or **functor** to the instance.

```
void FreeFunc(int value);

struct Functor
{
    void operator()(int value);
};


std::function<void(int)> func;
Functor functor;


func = FreeFunc;                    // Set target as FreeFunc
func(32);                           // Call FreeFunc with argument 32


func = functor;                     // set target as functor
func(42);                           // Call Functor::operator() with
argument 42
```

However, if we want to use a method on an object instance then we need to use another STL helper template **std::bind()**. If we run the following program:

```
#include <iostream>
```

```cpp
#include <functional>

struct Binder
{
    void method(int a, int b)
    {
        std::cout << "Binder::method(" << a << ", " << b << ")\n";
    }
};

int main()
{
    std::cout << "\n\n------ Member Functions using bind ------\n";
    Binder binder;
    std::function<void(int,int)> func;

    auto func1 = std::bind(&Binder::method, &binder, 1, 2);
    auto func2 = std::bind(&Binder::method, &binder, std::placeholders::_1,
std::placeholders::_2);
    auto func3 = std::bind(&Binder::method, &binder, std::placeholders::_2,
std::placeholders::_1);

    func = func1;
    func(34,56);

    func = func2;
    func(34,56);

    func = func3;
    func(34,56);

    std::cout << "Complete.\n";
```

```
    return 0;
}
```

Then we get the following output:

```
------ Member Functions using bind ------
Binder::method(1, 2)
Binder::method(34, 56)
Binder::method(56, 34)
Complete.
```

**Figure 4.16: Program output using std::bind() and std::function**

Several points to note:

- The function `method()` is referenced using the class as a scope specifier;

- The address of the instance of `Binder` is passed as the second argument to `std::bind()` which makes it the first argument passed to `method()`. This is necessary as all non-static members have an implicit `this` pointer passed as the first argument.

- Using the `std::placeholders` definitions, we can bind arguments used when invoking the bound method and even change the order passed (as seen by `func3`).

C++11 introduced some syntactic sugar, known as lambda expressions, that make it easier to define anonymous functions that can also be used to bind methods and assign them to `std::function` instances expression. We'll cover more about it in the topic *What is a Lambda Expression?*

## Exercise 3: Implementing callbacks with std::function

In this exercise, we will implement function callbacks utilizing the `std::function<>` template. Follow the below steps to implement this exercise:

1. Open the **Lesson4** project in Eclipse, and then in the **Project Explorer**, expand **Lesson4** then **Exercise03** and double click on **Exercise3.cpp** to open the file for this exercise into the editor.

2. As this is a CMake based project, change the current builder to be CMake Build (portable).

3. Click on the **Launch Configuration** drop down menu and select **New Launch Configuration....** Configure **L4Exercise3** to run with the name **Exercise3**.

4. Click on the **Run** button. The exercise will run and produce the following output:

```
------ Exercise 3 ------
+++ Entering TestFunctionTemplate()
exception: bad_function_call
+++ Leaving TestFunctionTemplate()
Complete.
```

Figure 4.17: Exercise 3 output (Calling empty std::function)

5. The first thing we will do is prevent calling an empty **std::function**. Locate in the function **TestFunctionTemplate()** the line **func(42);** and replace it with the following code:

```
if (func)
{
    func(42);
}
else
{
    std::cout << "Not calling an empty func()\n";
}
```

6. Click on the **Run** button. The exercise will run and produce the following output:

```
------ Exercise 3 ------
+++ Entering TestFunctionTemplate()
Not calling an empty func()
+++ Leaving TestFunctionTemplate()
Complete.
```

Figure 4.18: Exercise 3 output (preventing call to empty std::function)

7. Add the **FreeFunction()** method to the file before the function **TestFunctionTemplate()**:

```
void FreeFunction(int n)
{

    std::cout << "FreeFunction(" << n << ")\n";

}
```

8. In **TestFunctionTemplate()** function, immediately before **if (func)** add the following line:

```
func = FreeFunction;
```

9. Click on the **Run** button. The exercise will run and produce the following output:

```
------ Exercise 3 ------
+++ Entering TestFunctionTemplate()
FreeFunction(42)
+++ Leaving TestFunctionTemplate()
Complete.
```

Figure 4.19: Exercise 3 output (FreeMethod)

10. Add the new class definition before **TestFunctionTemplate()** function:

```
struct FuncClass
{
    void member(int n)
    {
        std::cout << "FuncClass::member(" << n << ")\n";
    }
    void operator()(int n)
    {
        std::cout << "FuncClass object(" << n << ")\n";
    }
};
```

11. Replace the line **func = FreeFunction;** with the following code:

```
FuncClass funcClass;
func = funcClass;
```

12. Click on the **Run** button. The exercise will run and produce the following output:

```
------ Exercise 3 ------
+++ Entering TestFunctionTemplate()
FuncClass object(42)
+++ Leaving TestFunctionTemplate()
Complete.
```

4.20: Exercise 3 output (Object function call override)

13. Replace the line **func = funcClass;** with the following code:

```
func = std::bind(&FuncClass::member, &funcClass, std::placeholders::_1);
```

14. Click on the **Run** button. The exercise will run and produce the following output:

```
------ Exercise 3 ------
+++ Entering TestFunctionTemplate()
FuncClass::member(42)
+++ Leaving TestFunctionTemplate()
Complete.
```

Figure 4.21: Exercise 3 output (Member function)

15. Replace the line **func = std::bind(…);** with the following code:

```
func = [](int n) {std::cout << "lambda function(" << n << ")\n";};
```

16. Click on the **Run** button. The exercise will run and produce the following output:

```
------ Exercise 3 ------
+++ Entering TestFunctionTemplate()
lambda function(42)
+++ Leaving TestFunctionTemplate()
Complete.
```

Figure 4.22: Exercise 3 output (lambda function)

In this exercise, we implemented four different types of function callback using the **std::function** template – free method, class member function, class function call method and a lambda function (which we look at next).

## What is a Lambda Expression?

Since C++11, C++ has supported **anonymous functions**, also known as **lambda expressions**, or just **lambdas**. The two most common forms of lambda expression are:

[captures] (parameters) {function_body}         (1)

[captures] (parameters) -> ret_type {function_body}     (2)

Figure 4.23: Most common forms of lambda expressions

Under normal circumstances, the compiler is able to deduce the return type of the lambda based on the return statements within the **function_body** (as embodied by form (1) in the figure above). However, if the compiler cannot determine the return type, or if we wish to force a different type, then we can use form (2).

Everything after [captures] is the same as for a normal function definition, except that the name is missing. Lambdas are a convenient way of defining a short method (just a few lines) at the location it will be used. The lambda is often passed as an argument and will typically not be re-used. It should also be noted that a lambda can be assigned to a variable (usually declared with auto).

We can re-write the previous program where we used a **Scaler** class to use a lambda to achieve the same outcome:

```cpp
#include <iostream>
#include <vector>
#include <algorithm>


void PrintVector(const char* prefix, std::vector<int>& values)
{
    const char* sep = "";
    std::cout << prefix << " = [";
    for(auto n : values)
    {
        std::cout << sep << n;
        sep = ", ";
    }
    std::cout << "]\n";
}


int main()
{
    std::cout << "\n\n------ Lambdas with STL ------\n";
    std::vector<int> values{1,2,3,4,5};

    PrintVector("Before transform", values);
    std::transform(values.begin(), values.end(), values.begin(),
    [] (int n) {return 5*n;}
    );
```

```
    PrintVector("After transform", values);


    std::cout << "Complete.\n";

    return 0;

}
```

When this program runs the output shows that the vector has been scaled by 5:

```
------ Lambdas with STL ------
Before transform = [1, 2, 3, 4, 5]
After transform = [5, 10, 15, 20, 25]
Complete.
```

Figure 4.24: Transform using lambda for scaling

The lambda in this program is [] (int n) {return 5*n;} and has an empty capture clause []. The empty capture clause means that the lambda function does not access any variables from the surrounding scope. If there are no parameters passed to the lambda, then the parameters clause () is optional.

## Capturing data into Lambdas

The **capture clause**, or the **lambda introducer** (from the C++ specification), allows the anonymous function to capture data from the surrounding scope for later use. This combination of a function with a scope that resolves the functions variable is known as a **closure**. The scope in this case is a set of variable bindings specified in the capture clause. In the previous section, we said that lambdas are anonymous functions. With the addition of variable capture through closures, lambdas are more correctly identified as anonymous function objects. The compiler creates an anonymous class with an inline constructor to capture the variables and a function call operator operator().

A capture clause is a comma-separated list of zero or more captured variables. There is also the concept of default captures – either by reference or by value. So, the basic syntax for a capture is:

- [&] – captures all automatic storage duration variables in scope by reference

- [=] – captures all automatic storage duration variables in scope by value (make a copy)

- [&x, y] – captures x by reference and y by value

This is translated by the compiler into member variables that are initialized by the constructor of the anonymous **functor** class. In case of the default captures (**&** and **=**), they must come first and only the variables referenced in the body are captured. The default capture can be overridden by placing the specific variable into the capture clause after the default capture. For example, [&, x] will by default capture by reference everything except x which it will capture by value.

However, while the default captures are convenient, they are not the preferred method of capture. This is because it can lead to dangling references (capture by reference and the referenced variable no longer exists when accessed by the lambda) or dangling pointers (capture by value, especially this pointers). It is clearer to capture your variables explicitly, which has the added benefit of the compiler being able to warn you about unexpected effects (such as trying to capture global or static variables).

C++14 introduced the **init capture** to the capture clause allowing for safer code and some optimizations. An init capture declares a variable in the capture clause and initializes it for use inside the lambda. An example of this is:

```
int x = 5;
int y = 6;

auto fn = [z=x*x+y, x, y] ()
            {
                    std::cout << x << " * " << x << " + " << y << " = " << z <<
"\n";
            };
fn();
```

Here, **z** is declared and initialized in the capture clause so that it can be used in the lambda. If you want to use the x and y in the lambda, then they must be captured separately. As expected, when the lambda is called it produces the following output:

```
5 * 5 + 6 = 31
```

The init capture can also be used to capture movable objects into the lambda, or make copies of class members as follows:

```
struct LambdaCapture
{
    auto GetTheNameFunc ()
    {
```

```
    return [myName = myName] () { return myName.c_str(); };
  }


  std::string myName;
};
```

This captures the value of the member variable and happens to give it the same name for use inside the lambda.

By default, a lambda is a const function, meaning that it cannot change the value of a capture-by-value variable. Where it is desirable to modify the value, we need to use a third form of lambda expression shown below.

$$[captures]\ (parameters)\ specifiers\ \text{->}\ ret\_type\ \{function\_body\} \qquad (3)$$

Figure 4.25: Another form of lambda expression

In this case, **specifiers** is replaced by **mutable**, telling the compiler that we want to modify the captured values. If we don't add mutable, and we attempt to modify a captured value, then the compiler will produce an error.

## Exercise 4: Implementing Lambdas

In this exercise we will implement lambdas to perform a number of actions in the context of STL algorithms. Follow the below steps to implement this exercise:

1. Open the **Lesson4** project in Eclipse, and then in the **Project Explorer**, expand **Lesson4** then **Exercise04** and double click on **Exercise4.cpp** to open the file for this exercise into the editor.

2. As this is a CMake based project, change the current builder to be CMake Build (portable).

3. Click on the **Launch Configuration** drop down menu and select **New Launch Configuration....** Configure **L4Exercise4** to run with the name **Exercise4**.

4. Click on the **Run** button. The exercise will run and produce the following output:

```
------ Exercise 4 ------
Initial Vector = [46, 27, 26, 27, 32, 1, 18, 50, 21, 49]
Complete.
```

Figure 4.26: Initial output from Exercise 4

5. The program **Exercise4.cpp** contains two methods, `PrintVector()` and `main()`. `PrintVector()` is the same as the version we introduced in *What is a Function Object?*. Now modify it to use the `std::for_each()` library function and a lambda instead of the ranged-for loop. Update `PrintVector()` to be:

```cpp
void PrintVector(const char* prefix, std::vector<int>& values)
{
    const char* sep = "";
    std::cout << prefix << " = [";
    std::for_each(values.begin(), values.end(),
            [&sep] (int n)
            {
                std::cout << sep << n;
                sep = ", ";
            }
    );
    std::cout << "]\n";
}
```

6. Click on the **Run** button and we get the same output as before.

7. Examine the lambda, we have captured the local variable **sep** by reference. Remove the **&** from **sep** and click on the **Run** button. This time the compilation fails with the following error:

```
[ 11%] Building CXX object CMakeFiles/Exercise4.dir/Exercise04/Exercise4.cpp.o
/home/brian/Documents/advanced/Lesson4/Exercise04/Exercise4.cpp: In lambda function:
/home/brian/Documents/advanced/Lesson4/Exercise04/Exercise4.cpp:30:23: error: assignment of read-only variable 'sep'
         sep = ", ";
             ^~~~
make[2]: *** [CMakeFiles/Exercise4.dir/Exercise04/Exercise4.cpp.o] Error 1
CMakeFiles/Exercise4.dir/build.make:62: recipe for target 'CMakeFiles/Exercise4.dir/Exercise04/Exercise4.cpp.o' failed
```

Figure 4.27: Compilation failure due to modifying read-only variable

8. Change the lambda declaration to include the `mutable` specifier:

```cpp
[sep] (int n) mutable
{
    std::cout << sep << n;
    sep = ", ";
}
```

9. Click on the **Run** button and we get the same output as before.

10. But we can go one step further. Remove the declaration of **sep** from the function **PrintVector()** and change the lambda again to include an init capture. Write the following code to implement this:

```
[sep = ""] (int n) mutable
{
    std::cout << sep << n;
    sep = ", ";
}
```

11. Click on the **Run** button and we get the same output as before. If we re-format the function **PrintVector()** it now looks more compact as:

```
void PrintVector(const char* prefix, std::vector<int>& values)
{
    std::cout << prefix << " = [";
    std::for_each(values.begin(), values.end(), [sep = ""] (int n) mutable
                                { std::cout << sep << n; sep = ", ";} );
    std::cout << "]\n";
}
```

12. Add the following lines after the call to **PrintVector()** in **main()** method:

```
std::sort(values.begin(), values.end(), [](int a, int b) {return b<a;} );
PrintVector("After sort", values);
```

13. Click on the **Run** button and the output now adds the list of values sorted in descending order:

```
------ Exercise 4 ------
Initial Vector = [46, 27, 26, 27, 32, 1, 18, 50, 21, 49]
After sort = [50, 49, 46, 32, 27, 27, 26, 21, 18, 1]
Complete.
```

Figure 4.28: Program output for descending sort lambda

14. Change the lambda function body to be **{return a<b;}**. Click on the **Run** button and the output now shows the values sorted in ascending order:

```
------ Exercise 4 ------
Initial Vector = [46, 27, 26, 27, 32, 1, 18, 50, 21, 49]
After sort = [1, 18, 21, 26, 27, 27, 32, 46, 49, 50]
Complete.
```

Figure 4.29: Program output for ascending sort lambda

15. After the call to **PrintVector()** function, add the following lines of code:

```
int threshold{25};
auto pred = [threshold] (int a) { return a > threshold; };
auto count = std::count_if(values.begin(), values.end(), pred);
std::cout << "There are " << count << " values > " << threshold << "\n";
```

16. Click on the **Run** button and the output now reports the number of **values > 25**:

```
------ Exercise 4 ------
Initial Vector = [46, 27, 26, 27, 32, 1, 18, 50, 21, 49]
After sort = [1, 18, 21, 26, 27, 27, 32, 46, 49, 50]
There are 7 values > 25
Complete.
```

Figure 4.30: Output for count_if lambda stored in variable

17. Add the following lines after the ones above and click the **Run** button:

```
threshold = 40;
count = std::count_if(values.begin(), values.end(), pred);
std::cout << "There are " << count << " values > " << threshold << "\n";
```

Following output will be generated:

```
------ Exercise 4 ------
Initial Vector = [46, 27, 26, 27, 32, 1, 18, 50, 21, 49]
After sort = [1, 18, 21, 26, 27, 27, 32, 46, 49, 50]
There are 7 values > 25
There are 7 values > 40
Complete.
```

Figure 4.31: Erroneous output by re-using the pred lambda

18. The program wrongly reports that there are **seven (7) values > 40**; it should be **three (3)**. The problem is that when the lambda was created and stored in the variable **pred**, it captured the current value of threshold which was **25**. Change the line that defines **pred** to the following:

```
auto pred = [&threshold] (int a) { return a > threshold; };
```

19. Click on the **Run** button and the output now correctly reports the count:

```
------ Exercise 4 ------
Initial Vector = [46, 27, 26, 27, 32, 1, 18, 50, 21, 49]
After sort = [1, 18, 21, 26, 27, 27, 32, 46, 49, 50]
There are 7 values > 25
There are 3 values > 40
Complete.
```

Figure 4.32: Correct output re-using the pred lambda

In this exercise, we implemented several lambdas, using various features of the lambda expression syntax including init capture and mutable.

> Using lambdas
>
> While lambdas are a powerful feature of C++, they should be used appropriately. The goal is always to produce readable code. So, while a lambda might be short and to the point, sometimes it will be better for maintenance purposes to factor out the functionality into a well named method.

## Variadic Templates

In *Chapter 2B, No Ducks Allowed - Templates and Deduction*, we introduced generic programming and templates. Templates have been part of C++ before C++03. Prior to C++11, templates were limited to a fixed number of arguments. In some cases, where a variable number of arguments was required, it was necessary to write a template for each variant of argument numbers required. Alternatively, there were variadic functions like **printf()** that could take a variable number of arguments. The problem with variadic functions is that they are not type safe as access to the arguments was through type casts via the **va_arg** macro. C++11 changed all that with the introduction of variadic templates where a single template can take an arbitrary number of arguments. C++17 improved the writing of variadic templates by introducing the **constexpr** if construct that would allow the base case template to be merged with the "**recursive**" template.

The best approach is to implement a variadic template and explain how it works.

```cpp
#include <iostream>

#include <string>


template<typename T, typename... Args>

T summer(T first, Args... args) {
```

```cpp
    if constexpr(sizeof...(args) > 0)
        return first + summer(args...);
    else
        return first;
}


int main()
{
    std::cout << "\n\n------ Variadic Templates ------\n";

    auto sum = summer(1, 3, 5, 7, 9, 11);
    std::cout << "sum = " << sum << "\n";

    std::string s1{"ab"};
    std::string s2{"cd"};
    std::string s3{"ef"};
    std::string strsum = summer(s1, s2, s3);
    std::cout << "strsum = " << strsum << "\n";

    std::cout << "Complete.\n";
    return 0;
}
```

When we run this program, we get the following output:

```
------ Variadic Templates ------
sum = 36
strsum = abcdef
Complete.
```

Figure 4.33: Variadic Template Program Output

So, what are the parts of a variadic template? And how do we read one? Consider the template from the above program:

```cpp
template<typename T, typename... Args>
```

```
T summer(T first, Args... args) {
    if constexpr(sizeof...(args) > 0)
        return first + summer(args...);
    else
        return first;
}
```

In the above code:

- `typename... Args` declares `Args` as a `template parameter pack`.

- `Args... args` is a `function parameter pack`, that is a bag of parameters whose types are given by `Args`.

- `sizeof...(args)` returns the number of pack elements in `args`. It is a special form of pack expansion.

- `args...` expands the pack in the recursive call to `summer()`.

Alternatively, you can think of the template as effectively the equivalent of:

```
template<typename T, typename T1, typename T2, ..., typename Tn>
T summer(T first, T1 t1, T2, ..., Tn tn) {
    if constexpr(sizeof...( t1, t2, ..., tn) > 0)
        return first + summer(t1, t2, ..., tn);
    else
        return first;
}
```

When the compiler processes `summer(1, 3, 5, 7, 9, 11)` in the sample program, it performs the following:

- It deduces that `T` is int and `Args...` is our parameter pack with <int, int, int, int, int>.

- As there are more than zero args in the pack, the compiler generates `first + summer(args...)` with the ellipsis unpacking the template argument transforming `summer(args...)` into `summer(3,5,7,9,11)`.

- The compiler then generates the code for `summer(3,5,7,9,11)`. Again, resulting in `first + summer(args...)` being applied where `summer(5,7,9,11)`.

- This process is repeated until the compiler has to generate code for `summer(11)`. In this case, the else clause of the **constexpr** if statement is triggered which simply returns **first**.

As the types are determined by the arguments to the template, we are not restricted to the arguments having the same type. We have already met a couple of variadic templates in the STL – `std::function` and std::bind.

There is another type of variadic template, one which forwards its arguments onto another function or template. This kind of template does little on its own but provides a standard approach to things. One example is the `make_unique` template which could be implemented as:

```
template<typename T, typename... Args>
unique_ptr<T> make_unique(Args&&... args)
{
    return unique_ptr<T>(new T(std::forward<Args>(args)...));
}
```

`make_unique` has to call the new operator to allocate memory and then call the appropriate constructor for the type. The number of arguments required to call the constructor can vary greatly. This form of variadic template introduces some addition pack expansions:

- `Args&&...` means we have a list of forwarding references.

- `std::forward<Args>(args)...` which contains to parameter packs that are expanded together and must have the same number of elements – Args the template parameter pack and args the function parameter pack.

This pattern is used whenever we need to forward a function call to another function call in a variadic template.

## Activity 1: Implement a multicast event handler

Microsoft first introduced the **Microsoft Foundation Class (MFC)** in 1992 when C++ was in its infancy. This means that many of the design choices around the classes were restricted. For example, the handlers for events are typically routed through **OnEventXXX()** methods. These are usually configured using macros as part of a class derived from the MFC classes. Your team has been tasked with implementing multicast event handler more like delegates available in C# using templates that embody function objects and lead to variadic templates to achieve the variable argument lists.

In C#, you declare a delegate as follows:

```
delegate int Handler(int parameter);
```

This makes Handler a type that can be assigned a value which can be called. This is essentially what **std::function<>** delivers us in C++ except for the ability to multi-cast. Your team is asked to develop a template class **Delegate** that can perform the same way as the C# delegate.

- The delegate will take a **variable list of arguments** but only return **void**

- The **operator+=** will be used to add new callbacks to the delegate

- It will be called either using either syntax **delegate.Notify(…)** or **delegate(…)**

Follow these steps to develop the Delegate template:

1. Load the prepared project from the **Lesson4/Activity01** folder and configure the Current Builder for the project to be CMake Build (Portable).

2. Build the project, configure the launcher and run the unit tests (which fail the one dummy test). Recommend that the name used for the tests runner is **L4delegateTests**.

3. Implement a **Delegate** class that can wrap a single handler with all the required methods and supports a single int parameter for the callback.

4. Update the template class to support multi-casting.

5. Convert the **Delegate** class to a template that can take a single template argument that defines the argument type used by the callbacks.

6. Convert the **Delegate** template to a variadic template that can take zero or more arguments that define the types passed to the callbacks.

After following the above steps, the expected output looks like the following:

```
------ Activity 1 ------

------ Delegate - no args ------
Hello, World
------ Delegate - string argument ------
hello!-hello?-hello@-
------ Delegate - binary int argument ------
52 + 4 = 56
52 - 4 = 48
52 * 4 = 208
52 / 4 = 13

Complete.
```

Figure 4.34: Output from the successful implementation of Delegate

**Note**

The solution for this activity can be found on page 673.

## Summary

In this chapter, we implemented a data and method hiding design approach, PIMPL, that has the added benefit of reducing dependencies and reducing build times. We then implemented function objects directly as custom classes and then as lambda functions. We then expanded our template programming skills by diving into variadic templates culminating in a template which can be used for event callback processing. In the next chapter, we will learn how to use the features of C++ to develop programs with multiple thread and manage their co-operation through concurrency constructs.

# 5

# The Philosophers' Dinner – Threads and Concurrency

## Learning Objectives

By the end of this chapter, you will be able to:

- Create synchronous and asynchronous multithreaded applications
- Apply synchronization to handle data hazards and race conditions
- Develop efficient multithreaded code with C++ thread library primitives
- Create threads using move semantics for multithreading closures
- Implement thread communication with futures, promises, and async

In this chapter, we will clarify the difference between basic terms in multithreaded programming, learn how to write multi-threaded code, find out which resources are provided by the C++ Standard Library for data access synchronization, learn how to prevent our code from encountering race conditions and deadlocks.

# Introduction

In the previous chapter, we covered different types of dependencies and coupling in C++. We looked at how common API design patterns and idioms can be implemented in C++ and what data structures are provided by Standard Libraries, as well as their efficacy. We also learned how to work with functional objects, lambdas, and captures. This knowledge will help us learn how to write clear and efficient multithreaded programs.

The heading of this chapter contains the name of the most significant synchronization issue in concurrent programming – The Philosopher's Dinner. In a few words, this definition is as follows.

Three philosophers are sitting at a round dining table with bowls of sushi. Chopsticks are placed between each adjacent philosopher. Only one philosopher at a time can eat their sushi with two chopsticks. Perhaps each philosopher will take one chopstick and then wait until someone gives up another chopstick. Philosophers are an analogy for three working processes and chopsticks for shared resources. "Who will grab the two chopsticks first" symbolizes the **race condition**. When each philosopher holds a chopstick and waits until another chopstick is available, it leads to a **deadlock**. This analogy explains what problems occur during multithreading.

We will start our chapter with a brief introduction to the main multithreaded concepts. We will consider the difference between synchronous, asynchronous, and threaded execution. Using clear and simple examples, we will start with synchronization, data hazards, and race conditions. We will find out why they appear in our code and how we can manage them. The next part of this chapter is devoted to the C++ Standard Library for threaded execution. Using examples, we will learn how and when to use thread library primitives, and how does the **move semantic** interact with threads. We will also practice with **futures**, **promises**, and **async** to receive results from threads.

This chapter will be concluded with a challenging activity in which we'll create an Art Gallery simulator that works by simulating visitors and gallery staff. We will develop a multithreaded generator that will simultaneously create and remove visitors from the art gallery. Next, we will create a multithreaded class that is responsible for moving visitors through the gallery. They will interact with each other using synchronization techniques. Finally, we will create thread-safe storage, instances of which will be accessed from the different threads.

In the next section, we will clarify a nuanced distinction between the concepts of concurrent programming: **synchronous**, **asynchronous**, and **threaded** execution.

# Synchronous, Asynchronous, and Threaded Execution

There is a nuanced distinction between the concepts of concurrent programming: **synchronous**, **asynchronous**, and `threaded execution`. To clarify it, we will start from the very beginning, with the concept of concurrent and parallel programs.

## Concurrency

The idea of `concurrency` is more than one task being executed simultaneously. `Concurrency` doesn't specify how the simultaneity will be achieved. It only indicates that more than one task will be completed in a given period. Tasks can be **dependent**, `parallel`, **synchronous**, or **asynchronous**. The following diagram shows the concept of concurrent work:

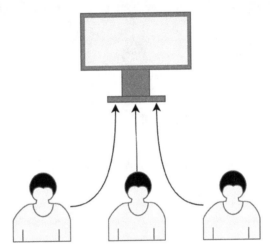

Figure 5.1: The abstraction of the concurrency - a few people working on the same computer

In the preceding diagram, three people are working at the same time on one computer. We aren't interested in the way they do that, it's doesn't matter for this level of the abstraction.

## Parallelism

**Parallelism** occurs when several tasks are performed simultaneously. The tasks work in parallel due to hardware capabilities. The best example of parallelism is a multi-core processor. For parallel execution, the tasks are divided into completely independent subtasks that are performed in different processors' cores. After that, the result of the execution can be combined. Look at the following diagram to understand the concept of parallelism:

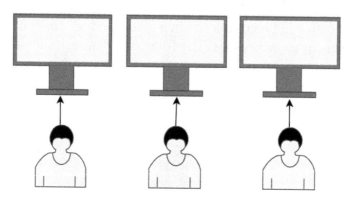

Figure 5.2: The abstraction of the parallelism - all of the tasks are executed by different people; they don't interact with each other

In the preceding diagram, there are three people working at the same time on their own computers – well, they're working in parallel.

> **Note**
>
> **Concurrency** and **parallelism** are not the same thing. **Parallelism** supplements concurrency. It tells us how tasks are performed: they are independent of each other and run in different computational units, that is, processors or cores.

Now, we will smoothly move toward a threaded execution concept. When we talk about threads, we mean the thread of execution. This is an abstraction of the operating system, which allows us to perform several tasks simultaneously. Remember that the entire program executes in a separate process. The operating system allocates the **address space**, **processor registers**, and some additional resources for the process. All of the worker threads are created within the process and share the same resources. Each process has at least one thread that executes the `main()` function. We can create a new thread for execution and assign a beginning function that will be the starting point of this thread.

> **Note**
>
> The address space and registers of the processor are called **Thread Context**. When the OS interrupts the thread's work, it must store the context of the current thread and load the context of the next one.

Let's consider the creation of a new thread in the following example. To create a new thread, we must include a **<thread>** header file. It contains classes and functions for managing threads. Actually, there are a few possible ways to create an **std::thread** object and thread of execution, as follows:

- Create an **std::thread** object without explicit initialization. Remember, the thread needs a start function to run its job. We didn't point out which function is the main one for this thread. This means that the thread of execution was not created. Let's look at the following code sample, where we create an empty **std::thread** object:

```
#include <thread>

int main()
{
   std::thread myThread;
   return 0;
}
```

- Create an **std::thread** object and pass a pointer to a function as a constructor argument. Now, the thread of execution will be created and will start its job from the function that we passed in the constructor. Let's look at the following code sample:

```cpp
#include <iostream>
#include <thread>

void printHello()
{
    std::cout << "hello" << std::endl;
}

int main()
{
    std::thread myThread(printHello);
    myThread.join();
    return 0;
}
```

Here, we created an **std::thread** object and initialized it with the function pointer. This is a simple function that returns **void** and doesn't take any parameters. Then, we tell the main thread to wait until the new thread finishes using the **join()** function. We always have to **join()** or **detach()** a thread until the end of the scope of the **std::thread** object. If we don't do that, our application will be terminated by the OS using an **std::terminate()** function that is called in the **std::thread** destructor. Instead of a function pointer, we can also pass any callable object, such as **lambda, std::function**, or a class with an overloaded **operator()**.

> **Note**
>
> The thread of execution can finish its job before the destruction of the **std::thread** object. It also can be destructed before the thread of execution finishes its job. Always **join()** or **detach()** an **std::thread** object before its destruction.

Now that we know about the main syntax for creating a thread, we can proceed to the next important concepts. Let's find out what synchronous, asynchronous, and multithreaded execution mean.

## Synchronous Execution

The term synchronous execution means that each subtask will be performed sequentially, one by one. In other words, this means that if we have a few tasks to execute, each of them can only start its work after the previous one has finished its work. This term does not specify a way to perform tasks, or whether they will be performed in a single or several threads. It only tells us about the execution order. Let's go back to the philosophers' dinner example. In a single-threaded world, the philosophers will eat one after the other.

The first philosopher takes two chopsticks and eats their sushi. Then, the second philosopher takes two chopsticks and eats their sushi. They take turns until all of them have finished their sushi. Take a look at the following diagram, which represents the synchronous execution of four tasks in a single thread:

Figure 5.3: Synchronous execution in a single thread

Here, each of the tasks waits for the previous task to finish. Tasks can also be performed synchronously in multiple threads. Consider the following diagram, which represents the synchronous execution of four tasks in multiple threads. Again, each of the tasks waits for the previous task to finish:

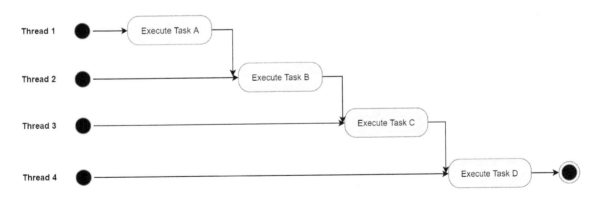

Figure 5.4: Synchronous execution in multiple threads

In this case, each task is launched in a separate thread, but only after the previous thread has completed its work. In a multithreaded world, the philosophers will still eat one after the other, but with a small difference. Now, each of them has their own chopsticks, but can only eat in a strict order.

> **Note**
>
> **Synchronous execution** means that the finishing time of each task is synchronized. The order of the execution of tasks is the main point here.

Let's consider synchronous execution on the following code sample. When we run tasks in a single thread, we just call the usual functions. For example, we implemented four functions that print a message to the terminal. We ran them in a synchronous, single-threaded way:

```cpp
#include <iostream>

void printHello1()
{
    std::cout << "Hello from printHello1()" << std::endl;
}

void printHello2()
{
    std::cout << "Hello from printHello2()" << std::endl;
}

void printHello3()
{
    std::cout << "Hello from printHello3()" << std::endl;
}

void printHello4()
{
    std::cout << "Hello from printHello4()" << std::endl;
```

```
}

int main()
{
    printHello1();
    printHello2();
    printHello3();
    printHello4();
    return 0;
}
```

Here, we call all the functions one by one, and every next function runs after the execution of the previous function. Now, let's run them in the different threads:

```
#include <iostream>
#include <thread>

void printHello1()
{
    std::cout << "Hello from printHello1()" << std::endl;
}

void printHello2()
{
    std::cout << "Hello from printHello2()" << std::endl;
}

void printHello3()
{
    std::cout << "Hello from printHello3()" << std::endl;
}

void printHello4()
{
```

```
        std::cout << "Hello from printHello4()" << std::endl;
}


int main()

{
        std::thread thread1(printHello1);
        thread1.join();
        std::thread thread2(printHello2);
        thread2.join();
        std::thread thread3(printHello3);
        thread3.join();
        std::thread thread4(printHello4);
        thread4.join();
        return 0;

}
```

In the preceding code sample, we created four threads and immediately joined them. Thus, every thread finishes its job before the one can be run. As you can see, nothing changes for the tasks – they are still executed in a strict order.

## Asynchronous Execution

This is where a few tasks can be executed simultaneously without blocking any thread execution. Usually, the main thread initiates an asynchronous operation and continues execution. After execution is finished, the results are sent to the main thread. Often, performing an asynchronous operation is not related to creating a separate thread for it. The task can be performed by someone else, such as another computing device, a remote web server, or an external device. Let's go back to the philosophers' dinner example.

In the case of **asynchronous execution**, all of the philosophers will have their own chopsticks and will eat independently from each other. When the sushi is ready and the waiter serves it, they all start to eat and can finish in their own time.

> **Note**
>
> In **asynchronous execution**, as all the tasks work independently of each other, it's not important to know the finish time of each task.

Take a look at the following diagram, which represents the asynchronous execution of four tasks in multiple threads:

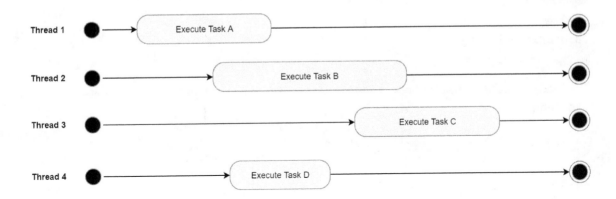

Figure 5.5: Asynchronous execution in multiple threads

Each of them was started and finished at a different time. Let's consider this asynchronous execution with a code sample. For example, we implemented four functions that print a message to the terminal. We ran them in different threads:

```cpp
#include <iostream>
#include <thread>
#include <chrono>


void printHello1()
{
    std::cout << "Hello from thread: " << std::this_thread::get_id() <<
std::endl;
}


void printHello2()
{
    std::cout << "Hello from thread: " << std::this_thread::get_id() <<
std::endl;
}


void printHello3()
{
```

```cpp
    std::cout << "Hello from thread: " << std::this_thread::get_id() <<
std::endl;
}


void printHello4()
{
    std::cout << "Hello from thread: " << std::this_thread::get_id() <<
std::endl;
}


int main()
{
    std::thread thread1(printHello1);
    std::thread thread2(printHello2);
    std::thread thread3(printHello3);
    std::thread thread4(printHello4);
    thread1.detach();
    thread2.detach();
    thread3.detach();
    thread4.detach();

    using namespace std::chrono_literals;
    std::this_thread::sleep_for(2s);
    return 0;
}
```

Let's see what happens here. We used four functions from the previous examples, but they were changed a little bit. We added the print of the thread's unique ID by using the **std::this_thread::get_id()** function. This function returns the **std::thread::id** object, which represents the unique ID of the thread. This class has overloaded operators for the output and comparison, so we can use it in a different manner. For example, we can check the thread ID and if it is the ID of the main thread, we can execute a special job. In our example, we can print the thread ID to the terminal. Next, we created four threads and detached them. This means that no thread will wait for the other to finish working. From this moment, they become **daemon threads**.

They will continue their job, but nobody knows about that. Then, we used the `std::this_thread::sleep_for(2s)` function to make the main thread wait for two seconds. We did that because when the main thread finishes its job, the application will stop, and we won't be able to view the output of the detached threads in the terminal. The following screenshot is an example of the output to the terminal:

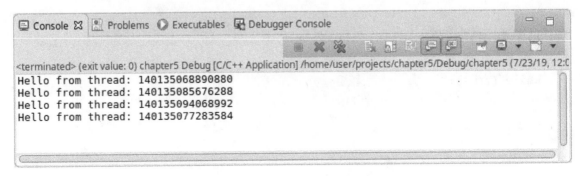

Figure 5.6: The result of an example execution

In your IDE, the output can change as the order of execution is undefined. A real-world example of asynchronous execution can be an internet browser wherein you can open multiple tabs. When a new tab is opened, the application starts a new thread and detaches them. Although the threads work independently, they can share some resources, such as a file handler, to write logs or do something else.

> **Note**
>
> `std::thread` has a member function called **get_id()** that returns the unique ID of the **std::thread** instance. If the **std::thread** instance wasn't initialized or was joined or detached, **get_id()** returns a default **std::thread::id** object. This means that no thread of execution is associated with the current **std::thread** instance.

Let's use some pseudocode to show an example where computations are done by another computational unit. For example, let's say we develop an application that performs calculations with currency exchange. The user inputs an amount in one currency, chooses another currency to exchange, and the application shows them the amount in that currency. The application, in the background, sends a request to a remote server that holds all the currency exchange rates.

The remote server calculates the amount of the given currency and sends the result back. Your application shows a progress bar at that time and allows the user to perform other operations. When it receives the results, it displays them on the window. Let's take a look at the following code:

```cpp
#include <thread>


void runMessageLoop()
{
    while (true)
    {
        if (message)
        {
            std::thread procRes(processResults, message);
            procRes.detach();
        }
    }
}


void processResults(Result res)
{
    display();
}


void sendRequest(Currency from, Currency to, double amount)
{
    send();
}


void displayProgress()
{
}
```

```cpp
void getUserInput()
{
    Currency from;
    Currency to;
    double amount;
    std::thread progress(displayProgress);
    progress.detach();
    std::thread request(sendRequest, from, to, amount);
    request.detach();
}

int main()
{
    std::thread messageLoop(runMessageLoop);
    messageLoop.detach();

    std::thread userInput(getUserInput);
    userInput.detach();

    return 0;
}
```

Let's see what happens here. In the **main()** function, we created a thread called **messageLoop** that executes the **runMessageLoop()** function. Some code that checks if there are any new results from the server can be placed in this function. If a new result is received, it creates a new thread, **procRes**, that will display the results in a window. We also created another thread, **userInput**, in the **main()** function that gets currencies and the amount from the user and creates a new thread, **request**, that will send a request to the remote server. After sending the request, it creates a new thread, **progress**, that will display a progress bar until the results are received. Since all the threads were detached, they were able to work independently. Sure, this is just pseudocode, but the main idea is clear – our application sends a request to the remote server, which performs calculations for our application.

Let's revise what we have learned about concurrency concepts using an example from daily life. Here is a background wherein you've to write an application and provide all the documentation and architectural concepts related to it:

- Single-threaded work: You write it yourself.

- Multi-threaded work: You invite your friends and write a project together. Somebody writes an architectural concept, somebody takes care of documentation work, and you focus on the coding part. All participants communicate with each other to clarify any questions and share documentation, such as questions about specifications.

- Parallel work: The tasks are divided. Someone writes the documentation for the project, someone designs the diagrams, someone writes the test cases, and you work independently. Participants don't communicate at all.

- Synchronized work: In this case, each of you are unable to understand what they are supposed to do. Thus, you all decide to work one after the other. When the architectural work is finished, the developer starts to write the code. Then, when the development work is finished, someone starts to write the documentation.

- Asynchronous work: In this case, you hire an outsource company to complete the project. While they are developing the project, you'll be engaged in some other task.

Now, let's apply our knowledge in practice and solve an exercise to see how all it works.

## Exercise 1: Creating Threads in a Different Way

In this exercise, we'll write a simple application that creates four threads; two of them will work in a synchronized way and two of them will work asynchronously. All of them will print some symbols to the terminal, so that we can see how the operating system switches thread execution.

> **Note**
>
> Add the pthread linker flag in your project settings to let the compiler know that you will use threading libraries. For Eclipse IDE you can do this following this path: **Project -> Properties -> C/C++ Build -> Settings -> G++ Linker -> Miscellaneous -> Linker flags enter '-pthread'**. This path is valid for `Eclipse Version: 3.8.1`, it may vary in different versions.

Perform the following steps to complete this exercise:

1. Include some headers for threading support, namely **<thread>**, streaming support, namely **<iostream>**, and functional objects support, namely **<functional>**:

```
#include <iostream>
#include <thread>
#include <functional>
```

2. Implement a free function, **printNumbers()**, that prints numbers from 0 to 100 in a **for** loop:

```
void printNumbers()
{
    for(int i = 0; i < 100; ++i)
    {
        std::cout << i << " ";
    }
    std::cout << std::endl;
}
```

3. Implement a callable object, that is, a **Printer** class with an overloaded **operator()** that prints a "*" symbol from 0 to 100000 in a **for** loop. For every **200** iterations, print a new line symbol for more readable output:

```
class Printer
{
    public:
    void operator()()
    {
        for(int i = 0; i < 100000; ++i)
        {
            if (!(i % 200))
            {
                std::cout << std::endl;
            }
            std::cout << "*";
        }
    }
};
```

4. Enter the **main()** function and then create a lambda object called **printRevers** that prints the numbers from 100 to 0 in a **for** loop:

```
int main()
{
    auto printRevers = []()
    {
        for(int i = 100; i >= 0; --i)
        {
            std::cout << i << " ";
        }
        std::cout << std::endl;
    };
    return 0;
}
```

5. Implement an **std::function** object called **printOther** that prints the "^" symbol from **0** to **100000** in a **for** loop. For every **200** iterations, print a new line symbol for more readable output:

```
std::function<void()> printOther = []()
{
    for(int i = 0; i < 100000; ++i)
    {
        if (!(i % 200))
        {
            std::cout << std::endl;
        }
        std::cout << "^";
    }
};
```

6. Create the first thread, **thr1**, and pass the **printNumbers** free function to its constructor. Join it:

```
std::thread thr1(printNumbers);
thr1.join();
```

7. Create a second thread, **thr2**, and pass the **printRevers** lambda object to its constructor. Join it:

```
std::thread thr2(printRevers);
thr2.join();
```

8. Create an instance of the **Printer** class called **print**. Create a third thread, **thr3**, and initialize it with the **print** object. Detach it using the **detach()** method:

```
Printer print;
std::thread thr3(print);
thr3.detach();
```

9. Create the last thread, **thr4**, and initialize it with the **printOther** object. Detach it:

```
std::thread thr4(printOther);
thr4.detach();
```

10. Add the **std::getchar()** function call before the exit of the **main()** function. This avoids closing the application. We'll have the possibility to see how detached threads work:

```
std::getchar();
```

11. Run this code in your editor. You will see that **thr1** starts execution and the program waits. After **thr1** has finished, **thr2** starts execution and the program waits. This is an example of synchronous execution. After **thr2** has finished its work, threads **thr3** and **thr4** start execution. They are detached, so the program can proceed with the execution. In the following output, you will see that the symbols are mixed. This happens because the operating system performs interruptions and the threads work at the same time.

Your output will be similar to the following:

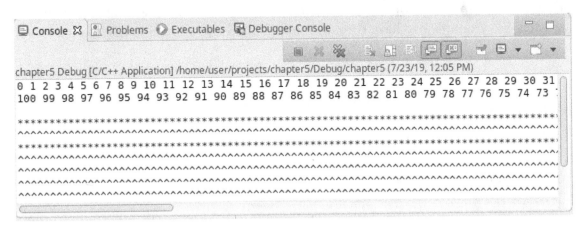

Figure 5.7: The result of the exercise's execution

In this exercise, we implemented four different ways we can initialize threads: with a free function, with a lambda object, with a callable object, and with an `std::function` object. There are a few more ways to initialize the thread, but we'll consider them in the next section. We've also reviewed how we can implement a synchronous program in multiple threads. We also tried to implement the asynchronous program and saw that threads really work at the same time and independently. In the next section, we'll learn about data hazards and race conditions and how we can avoid them by using synchronization techniques.

## Review Synchronization, Data Hazards, and Race Conditions

The key challenge of multithreaded programming is knowing how the threads work with **shared data**. Shared data, also known as resources, are not only variables, but also file descriptors and environment variables, and even Windows registries. For example, if the threads just read the data, then there are no problems and no synchronization is required. However, if at least one of the threads edits the data, **race conditions** could arise. Usually, the operations on the data are not atomic, that is, they require several steps. Even the simplest increment operation of a numeric variable is performed in the following three steps:

1. Read the value of the variable.

2. Increment it.

3. Write the new value.

Due to the OSes interruptions, the thread can be stopped before it completes the operation. For example, we have threads A and B and have a variable that is equal to 0.

Thread A starts the increment:

1. Reads the value of the variable (var = 0).

2. Increments it (tmp = 1).

3. Gets interrupted by the OS.

Thread B starts the increment:

1. Reads the value of the variable (var = 0).

2. Increments it (tmp = 1).

3. Writes the new value (var = 1).

4. Gets interrupted by the OS.

Thread A continues the increment:

1.   Writes the new value (var = 1).

Thus, we expect the variable to be equal to 2 after the completion of the work, but in fact, it is equal to 1. Have a look at the following diagram to get a better understanding of this example:

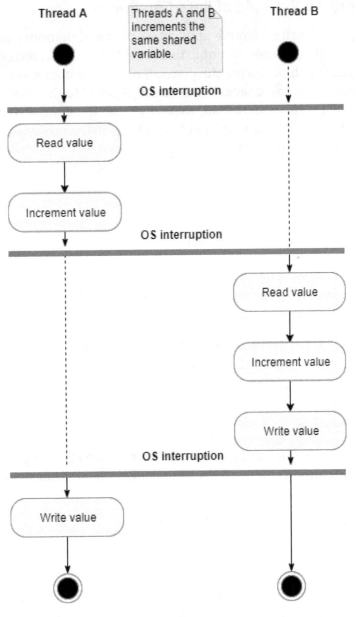

Figure 5.8: Two threads increment the same shared variable

Let's go back to the philosophers' dinner analogy. The original issue was that one philosopher had only one chopstick. If all of them are hungry, then they will hurry to grab two chopsticks. The first philosopher who grabs two chopsticks will be the first to eat, and the others must wait. They will race for the sticks.

Now, let's apply our knowledge to practice and write some code to see how the race conditions can appear in our code and can damage our data.

## Exercise 2: Writing an Example of Race Conditions

In this exercise, we will write a simple application that will demonstrate race conditions in action. We will create a classic example of a "check then act" race condition. We will create a thread, which performs the division of two numbers. We will pass these numbers by reference. After a check, if a dividend is equal to 0, we will set a small timeout. At this time in the main thread, we will set the dividend to 0. When the child thread wakes up, it will perform a division to 0. That will lead to an application crash. We will also add some logs to see the execution flow.

> **Note**
>
> By default, all the variables are copied when they are passed to the thread. To pass the variable as a reference, use the **std::ref()** function.

First, we implement the code without a race condition and ensure that it works as expected. Perform the following steps:

1. Include headers for threading support, namely **<thread>**, streaming support, namely **<iostream>**, and functional objects support, namely **<functional>**:

```
#include <iostream>
#include <chrono>
#include <thread>
```

2. Implement a **divide()** function, which performs a division of two integers. Pass the **divisor** and **dividend** variables by reference. Check whether a dividend is equal to 0. Then, add the logs:

```
void divide(int& divisor, int& dividend)
{
    if (0 != dividend)
    {
        std::cout << "Dividend = " << dividend << std::endl;
        std::cout << "Result: " << (divisor / dividend) << std::endl;
    }
```

```
        else
        {
            std::cout << "Error: dividend = 0" << std::endl;
        }
    }
```

3. Enter the **main()** function, create two integers called **divisor** and **dividend**, and initialize them with any non-zero values:

```
int main()
{
    int divisor = 15;
    int dividend = 5;
    return 0;
}
```

4. Create the **thr1** thread, pass the **divide** function, use **divisor** and **dividend** by reference, and then detach the thread:

```
std::thread thr1(divide, std::ref(divisor), std::ref(dividend));
thr1.detach();
std::getchar();
```

> **Note**
>
> In the **std::this_thread** namespace there is a function called **sleep_for** that blocks threads for a given period of time. As a parameter, it takes **std::chrono::duration** – a template class to represent a time interval.

5. Run this code in your editor. You will see that the **divide()** function works correctly in **thr1**. The output looks as follows:

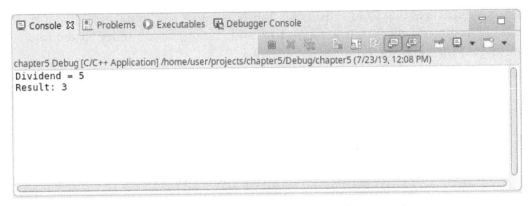

Figure 5.9: The result of the correct exercise execution

Now, we will continue and make changes that will demonstrate race conditions.

6.  Go back to the function and set the sleeping time in **2s** for the child thread after the **if** condition. Add the logs:

```
if (0 != dividend)
{
    std::cout << "Child thread goes sleep" << std::endl;
    using namespace std::chrono_literals;
    std::this_thread::sleep_for(2s);
    std::cout << "Child thread woke up" << std::endl;
    std::cout << "Dividend = " << dividend << std::endl;
    std::cout << (divisor / dividend) << std::endl;
}
```

7.  Go back to the **main()** function and set the sleeping time in **1s** for the main thread. After that, set the **dividend** variable to **0**. Add the logs:

```
std::cout << "Main thread goes sleep" << std::endl;
using namespace std::chrono_literals;
std::this_thread::sleep_for(1s);
std::cout << "Main thread woke up" << std::endl;
dividend = 0;
std::cout << "Main thread set dividend to 0" << std::endl;
```

> **Note**
>
> The **std::chrono_literals** namespace contains literals for time representations: `h` for **hours**, `min` for **minutes**, `s` for **seconds**, `ms` for **milliseconds**, `us` for **microseconds**, and `ns` for **nanoseconds**. To use them, you should just add them to the end of the number, for example, 1s, 1min, 1h, and so on.

8.  Add the **std::getchar()** function call before the exit of the **main()** function. This avoids us closing the application and we will have the possibility to see how detached threads work:

```
std::getchar();
```

9.  Run this code in your editor. You will see that the main thread goes to sleep for **1s**. Then, the child thread enters the **if** condition and goes to sleep for **2s**, which means that it validates a **dividend** and it is not equal to **0**. Then, the main thread wakes up and sets a **dividend** variable to 0. Then, the child thread wakes up and performs the division. But because the **dividend** is equal to **0** now, the application crashes. If you run this example in Debug mode, you will see a **SIGFPE exception** with a message: "Arithmetic exception". You will get the following output:

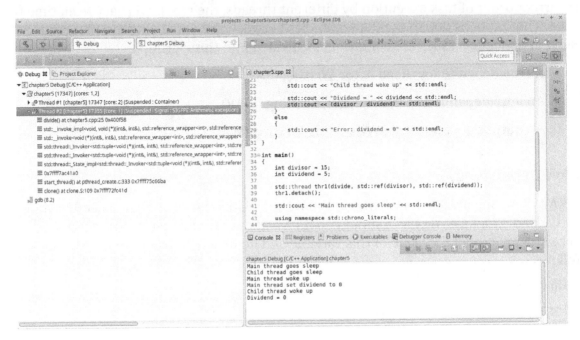

Figure 5.10: The result of the exercise's execution with race conditions

In this exercise, we considered "check then act" kinds of race conditions. We've set periods of sleep for threads to emulate the OS interruption, but in real-world programs, this situation may well happen but may not. It all depends on the OS and its scheduler. This makes it enormously difficult to debug and fix race conditions. To avoid race conditions in this example, we can act in a few ways:

*   Pass copies of variables to the threaded function instead of passing references.

*   Synchronize access to the shared variables between threads using Standard Library primitives.

*   Join child thread before the main thread changes a **dividend** value to 0.

Let's look at a few more ways to fix this race condition. All of them depend on a task that you try to implement. In the next section, we will consider synchronization primitives that are provided by the C++ Standard Library.

## Data Hazards

Previously, we considered the most harmless example, but sometimes, there are situations where the data is damaged, and this leads to undefined program behavior or abnormal termination. Such damage to data, as a result of race conditions or simply wrong design, are known as **data hazards**. In general, this term implies that the final result of a piece of work depends on the order of the thread's execution. If different threads work with shared data or global variables, it may happen that, due to an incorrect order of task execution by different threads, the result will vary from time to time. This happens due to the dependencies between the data being multi-threaded. Such dependency issues are conditionally divided into three groups:

* A **true dependency**: **Read After Writing** (RAW)
* An **anti-dependency**: **Write After Reading** (WAR)
* An **output dependency**: **Write After Writing** (WAW)

## RAW Dependency

A RAW dependency occurs when one thread calculates the value that is used by another thread. For example, **Thread A** should do its job and write the results to a variable. **Thread B** must read the value of this variable and do its job. In pseudocode, this looks as follows:

```
Thread A: a = doSomeStuff();
Thread B: b = a - doOtherStuff();
```

Difficulties will arise if **Thread B** executes first. It will lead to **Thread B** reads an invalid value. The order of the execution of threads should be strictly guaranteed. **Thread B** must read the value of the variable, but only after **Thread A** has written it. Otherwise,

it will lead to undefined behavior. The following diagram will help you clarify the RAW data dependency that leads to data hazards:

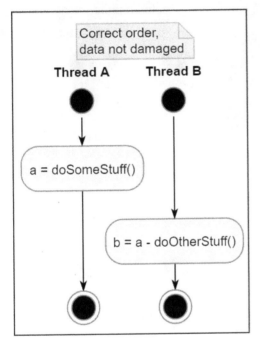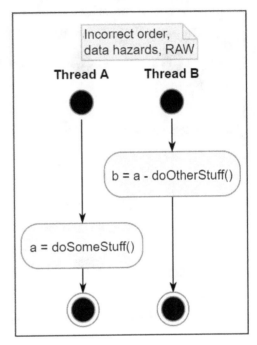

Figure 5.11: RAW data dependency between two threads

## WAR Dependency

A **WAR dependency** occurs when one thread changes the data that is used by another thread. For example, **Thread A** must read the value of a variable and do its job. After that, **Thread B** should do its job and write the results to a variable. In pseudocode, this looks as follows:

```
Thread A: b = a - doSomeStuff();
Thread B: a = doOtherStuff();
```

Difficulties will arise if **Thread B** executes first. It will lead to **Thread B** changing the value before **Thread A** reads it. The order of the execution of threads should be strictly guaranteed. **Thread B** should write the new value to a variable only after **Thread A** reads its value. The following diagram will help you clarify the RAW data dependency that leads to data hazards:

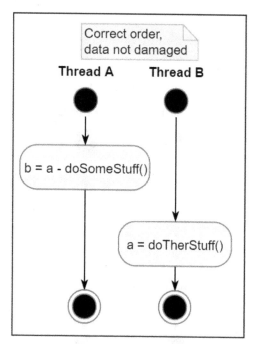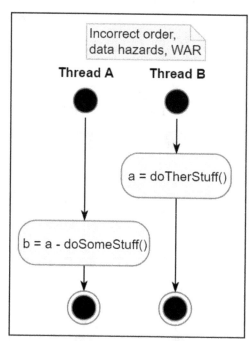

Figure 5.12: WAR data dependency between two threads

## WAW Dependency

A **WAW dependency** occurs when several threads change the value of the same variable, and some thread reads for its calculations. For example, **Thread A** executes its job and writes the results to a variable. **Thread B** reads the value of the variable and executes its job. **Thread C** executes its job and writes the results to the same variable. In pseudocode, this looks as follows:

```
Thread A: a = doSomeStuff();
Thread B: b = a - doOtherStuff();
Thread C: a = doNewStuff();
```

Difficulties will arise if **Thread C** executes before threads A and B. This leads to **Thread B** reads the value that it is not expected to be read. The order of the execution of threads should be strictly guaranteed. **Thread C** must write a new value to a variable, but only after **Thread A** has written its value and **Thread B** has read it. The following diagram will help you clarify the WAW data dependency that leads to data hazards:

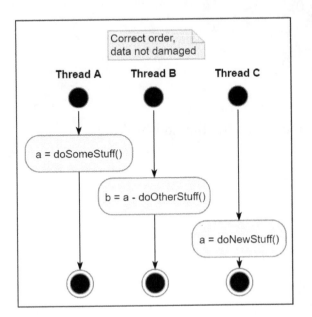 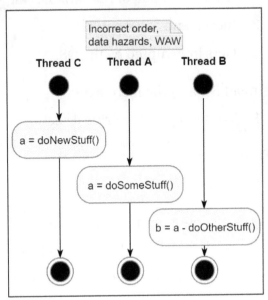

Figure 5.13: WAW data dependency between two threads

## Resource Synchronization

To prevent races and data hazards, there is a shared data locking mechanism where one of the streams intends to change or read these data. This mechanism is called **resource synchronization**. For synchronization, we need to allocate pieces of code that change or read shared resources. Such pieces of code are called `critical sections`. Synchronization consists of blocking critical sections when one of the threads enters it. Other threads that also intend to execute the code of this critical section will be blocked. When the thread executing the critical section leaves it, the lock is released. Then, the story will repeat with the next thread.

Consider the previous example with an increment, but now with synchronized access. Remember that we have threads A and B and have a variable that is equal to 0.

Thread A starts the increment:

1. Enters the critical section and locks it.

2. Reads the value of the variable (var = 0).

3. Increments it (tmp = 1).

4. Gets interrupted by the OS.

Thread B starts the increment:

1. Tries to enter the critical section; it's locked, so the thread is waiting.

Thread A continues the increment:

1. Writes the new value (var = 1).

Thread B continues the increment:

1. Enters the critical section and locks it.

2. Reads the value of the variable (var = 1).

3. Increments it (tmp = 2).

4. Writes the new value (var = 2).

After the completion of both threads, the variable contains the correct result. Thus, synchronization ensures that shared data will not be damaged. Have a look at the following diagram, to get a better understanding of this example:

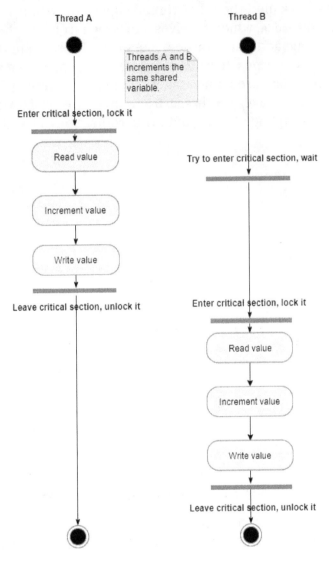

Figure 5.14: Two threads increment the same shared variable in a synchronized way

Highlighting critical sections and anticipating the possible consequences of non-synchronized access is a very difficult task. Because excessive synchronization negates the very essence of multithreaded work. If two or three threads work on one critical section rather quickly, however, there can be dozens of threads in the program where all of them will be blocked in the critical section. This will greatly slow down the program.

## Event Synchronization

There is another mechanism for synchronizing the work of threads – **event synchronization**. This means the synchronization of the work of the threads when one of them suspends its work until the other thread signals the occurrence of some event. For example, there's **Thread A**, which receives a message from another process. It writes the message to the queue and waits for new messages. There is another thread, **Thread B**, that processes these messages. It reads messages from the queue and performs some actions on them. When there are no messages, **Thread B** is sleeping. When **Thread A** receives a new message, it wakes up **Thread B** and processes it. The following diagram provides a clear understanding of the event synchronization of two threads:

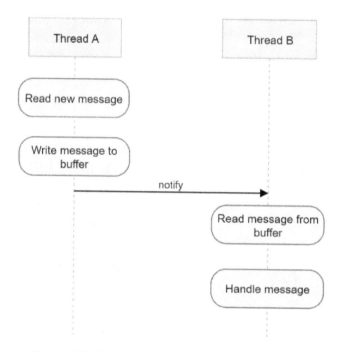

Figure 5.15: Event synchronization of two threads

However, even in synchronized code can appear another reason for a race conditions – a flawed interface of a class. To get an understanding of what this is, let's consider the following example:

```cpp
class Messages
{
    public:
    Messages(const int& size)
    : ArraySize(size)
    , currentIdx(0)
```

```
, msgArray(new std::string[ArraySize])
{}
void push(const std::string& msg)
{
    msgArray[currentIdx++] = msg;
}
std::string pop()
{
    auto msg = msgArray[currentIdx - 1];
    msgArray[currentIdx - 1] = "";
    --currentIdx;
    return msg;
}
bool full()
{
    return ArraySize == currentIdx;
}
bool empty()
{
    return 0 == currentIdx;
}


private:
const int ArraySize;
int currentIdx;
std::string * msgArray;
};
```

Here, we have a class called **Messages** that has a dynamically allocated array of strings. In the constructor, it takes the size of the array and creates an array of the given size. It has a function, **full()**, that returns **true** if the array is full and **false** otherwise. It also has an **empty()** function that returns true if the array is empty and false otherwise. It is the user's responsibility to check if the array is full before pushing a new value and checking if the array is empty, and before popping a new value from the array. This is an example of a poor interface of the class that leads to race conditions. Even if we protect the **push()** and **pop()** functions with locks, race conditions will not disappear. Let's look at the following example of using the **Messages** class:

```cpp
int main()
{
    Messages msgs(10);
    std::thread thr1([&msgs](){
    while(true)
    {
        if (!msgs.full())
        {
            msgs.push("Hello");
        }
        else
        {
            break;
        }
    }});
    std::thread thr2([&msgs](){
    while(true)
    {
        if (!msgs.empty())
        {
            std::cout << msgs.pop() << std::endl;
        }
        else
        {
            break;
```

```
        }
    }});
    thr1.detach();
    thr2.detach();
    using namespace std::chrono_literals;
    std::this_thread::sleep_for(2s);
    return 0;
}
```

Here, we created a **msgs** variable and then created the first thread, which pushes value to the **msgs**. Then, we created the second thread, which pops values from the array and detaches them. Even if we protect all the functions by using a locking mechanism, one of the threads can check the array's size and can be interrupted by the OS. At this time, another thread can change the array. When the first thread continues its work, it can try to push to the full array or pop from the empty array. So, synchronization is only effective in a pair with a good design.

## Deadlock

There is one more synchronization issue. Let's go back to the philosophers' dinner example. The original issue was that one philosopher has only one chopstick. So, they can eat their sushi one by one by sharing chopsticks with each other. Although it will take a long time for them to finish their sushi, all of them will be well-fed. But if each of them grabs a chopstick at the same time and doesn't want to share the second chopstick, they won't be able to eat their sushi as each of them will be waiting for the second chopstick forever. This leads to a **deadlock**. This happens when two threads are waiting for another thread to continue its job. One of the causes of deadlocks is when one thread joins another thread, but another thread joins the first thread. So, when both threads are joined to each other, none of them can continue their job. Let's consider the following example of a deadlock:

```
#include <thread>


std::thread* thr1;
std::thread* thr2;


void someStuff()
{
    thr1->join();
```

```
}

void someAnotherStuff()
{
    thr2->join();
}

int main()
{
    std::thread t1(someStuff);
    std::thread t2(someAnotherStuff);
    thr1 = &t1;
    thr2 = &t2;
    using namespace std::chrono_literals;
    std::this_thread::sleep_for(2s);
    return 0;
}
```

In the main function, we have two threads, **t1** and **t2**. We initialized the **t1** thread with the someStuff() function, which does some useful work. We also initialized the **t2** thread with the someAnotherStuff() function, which does some more useful work. We have global pointers to these threads and a join pointer to the **t1** thread in the function that's executed by **t2**. We also join a pointer to the **t2** thread into the function, which is executed by **t1**. By doing this, they joined each other. This causes a deadlock.

In the next section, we will consider C++ thread library primitives for synchronization and another cause of deadlocks.

## Move Semantics for Multithreading Closures

The std::thread class cannot be copied, but what if we want to store a few threads, or maybe 10 or 20? Sure, we can create the number of threads, and then we can join or detach them like so:

```
std::thread thr1(someFunc);
std::thread thr2(someFunc);
std::thread thr3(someFunc);
std::thread thr4(someFunc);
```

```
std::thread thr5(someFunc);
thr1.join();



thr2.join();
thr3.join();
thr4.join();
thr5.join();
```

But it's more convenient to store a bunch of threads in an **STL container**, for example, the vector of threads:

```
std::vector<std::thread> threads;
```

STL containers cannot be used with objects that don't support **copy semantic**. Thanks to the **move semantic**, we can store non-copiable objects that have a move constructor and move the assignment operator to the containers. Then, we can use a vector of threads with the **std::move()** function. To initialize the threads in the container, we can do something like the following:

```
for (int i = 0; i < 10; i++)
{
    auto t = std::thread([i]()
    {
        std::cout << "thread: " << i << "\n";
    });
    threads.push_back(std::move(t));
}
```

Then, we can join or detach all of them:

```
for (auto& thr: threads)
{
    if (thr.joinable())
    {
        thr.join();
    }
}
```

Move semantics can also be useful when we store an **std::thread** object as a class member. In this case, we should design our class carefully, delete the copy constructor and assignment operator, and implement a new move constructor and move assignment operator. Let's consider the following code example of such a class:

```cpp
class Handler
{
    std::thread  threadHandler;


public:
    Handler(const Handler&) = delete;
    Handler& operator=(const Handler&) = delete;


    Handler(Handler && obj)
    : threadHandler(std::move(obj.threadHandler))
    {}
    Handler & operator=(Handler && obj)
    {
        if (threadHandler.joinable())
        {
            threadHandler.join();
        }
        threadHandler = std::move(obj.threadHandler);
        return *this;
    }
    ~Handler()
    {
    if (threadHandler.joinable())
        {
            threadHandler.join();
        }
    }
};
```

In the move assignment operator, we first check if the thread is joinable. If so, we join it and only after that do we perform assignment operation.

> **Note**
>
> We should never assign one thread object to another without using **join()** or **detach()** on them. This will lead to an **std::terminate()** function call.

It's also possible to use the **std::move()** function to move objects into a thread function. It can be helpful for copying big objects, which is not advisable. Let's execute an exercise to ensure that the objects can be moved into thread functions.

## Exercise 3: Moving Objects to a Thread Function

In this exercise, we will write a simple application that demonstrates how **std::move()** works for **std::thread** classes. We will create a class that has both a copy constructor and a move constructor to see which one will be called when we move the object of this class into the **std::thread** function. Perform the following steps to complete this exercise:

1. Include headers for threading support, namely **<thread>**, and streaming support, namely **<iostream>**:

   ```
   #include <iostream>
   #include <thread>
   ```

2. Implement the **Handler** clas, which has the default constructor, destructor, copy constructor, assignment operator, move constructor, and move assignment operator. They will do nothing except print a log:

   ```
   class Handler
   {
   public:
       Handler()
       {
           std::cout << "Handler()" << std::endl;
       }
       Handler(const Handler&)
       {
           std::cout << "Handler(const Handler&)" << std::endl;
       }
       Handler& operator=(const Handler&)
       {
   ```

```
        std::cout << "Handler& operator=(const Handler&)" << std::endl;
        return *this;
    }
    Handler(Handler && obj)
    {
        std::cout << "Handler(Handler && obj)" << std::endl;
    }
    Handler & operator=(Handler && obj)
    {
        std::cout << "Handler & operator=(Handler && obj)" << std::endl;
        return *this;
    }
    ~Handler()
    {
        std::cout << "~Handler()" << std::endl;
    }
};
```

3. Implement the **doSomeJob()** function, which actually does nothing here and just prints a log message:

```
void doSomeJob(Handler&& h)
{
    std::cout << "I'm here" << std::endl;
}
```

4. Enter the **main()** function and create a **handler** variable of the **Handler** type. Create **thr1**, pass the **doSomeJob()** function, and move the handler variable:

```
Handler handler;
std::thread thr1(doSomeJob, std::move(handler));
```

5. Detach the **thr1** thread and add a small sleep for the main thread to avoid closing the application. We will be able to see the output from the detached thread:

```
thr1.detach();
using namespace std::chrono_literals;
std::this_thread::sleep_for(5s);
```

6. Run this code in your editor. In the terminal log, from the default constructor, you will see two logs from the move operator, one log from a destructor, a message from the **doSomeJob()** function, and, finally, two other log messages from the destructor. We can see that the move constructor is called twice.

You will get the following output:

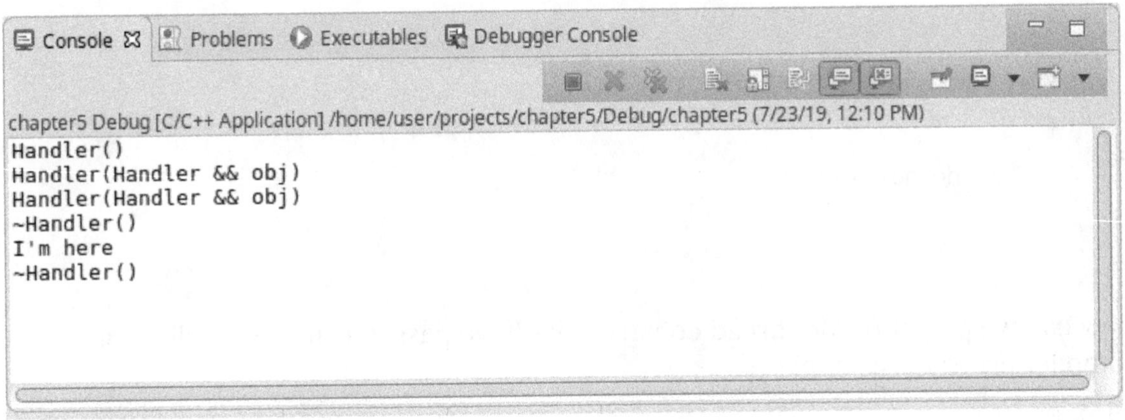

Figure 5.16: The result of the exercise's execution

As you can see, the **Handler** object was moved into the thread function. Despite that, all the parameters, that were passed without the **std::ref()** function, were copied to the thread's memory.

Let's consider one interesting issue. As you may remember, when we initialize **std::thread**, all of the constructor arguments are copied into thread memory, including a callable object – a lambda, a function, or an std::function. But what if our callable object doesn't support copy semantics? For example, we created a class that has only a move constructor and a move assignment operator:

```
class Converter
{
    public:

    Converter(Converter&&)
    {
    }

    Converter& operator=(Converter&&)
    {
        return *this;
    }

    Converter() = default;
```

```
    Converter(const Converter&) = delete;
    Converter& operator=(const Converter&) = delete;


    void operator()(const std::string&)
    {
        // do nothing
    }
};
```

How can we pass it to the thread constructor? If we pass it as it is, we will get a compiler error; for example:

```
int main()
{
    Converter convert;
    std::thread convertThread(convert, "convert me");
    convertThread.join();
    return 0;
}
```

You will get the following output:

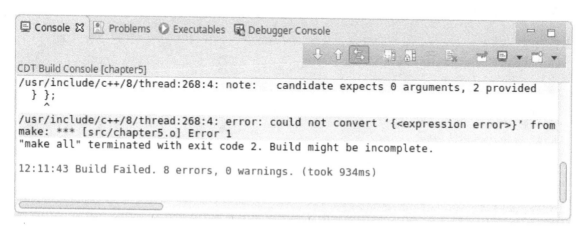

Figure 5.17: Example of a compilation error

There are lots of strange errors here. To fix this issue, we can use the **std::move()** function to move the callable:

```
std::thread convertThread(std::move(convert), "convert me");
```

Now, everything is ok – the code is compiled and does exactly what we want it to do.

Now, let's consider one more interesting example. For example, you have a lambda function that needs to capture a non-copiable object, for example, a **unique_ptr**:

```
auto unique = std::make_unique<Converter>();
```

Starting from C++ 14, we can use **std::move()** to capture movable objects. So, to capture a unique pointer, we can use the following code:

```
std::thread convertThread([ unique = std::move(unique) ] {
        unique->operator()("convert me");
});
```

As you can see, it's pretty useful to capture value in a lambda by using **std::move**. This can be also useful when we do not want to copy some objects because they might take a long time to copy.

Now, let's put our knowledge to practice and write an application example that demonstrates how we can use **std::move** with threads.

## Exercise 4: Creating and Working with an STL Container of Threads

In this exercise, we will write a simple application where we will use **std::move()** with threads. First of all, we will implement a class that is move constructible. This class will convert lowercase text into uppercase text. Then, we will create a vector of instances of this class. Next, we will create a vector of **std::thread** objects. Finally, we will initialize the threads with an object from the first vector.

Perform the following steps to complete this exercise:

1.  Include headers for threading support, namely **<thread>**, streaming support, namely **<iostream>**, and **<vector>**:

    ```
    #include <iostream>
    #include <thread>
    #include <vector>
    #include <string>
    ```

2. Implement the **Converter** class, which has the **m_bufferIn** private member of the **const std::vector<std::string>&** type. This is a reference to the original vector of strings in lowercase. It also has a user constructor, which takes the **bufferIn** variable. Then, we delete the copy constructor and assignment operators. Finally, we define the overloaded **operator()**, where we convert all lowercase symbols into uppercase. After conversion, we write the result to the result buffer:

```cpp
class Converter
{
    public:
    Converter(std::vector<std::string>& bufferIn)
        : m_bufferIn(bufferIn)
    {
    }

    Converter(Converter&& rhs)
        : m_bufferIn(std::move(rhs.m_bufferIn))
    {
    }

    Converter(const Converter&) = delete;
    Converter& operator=(const Converter&) = delete;
    Converter& operator=(Converter&&) = delete;

    void operator()(const int idx, std::vector<std::string>& result)
    {
        try
        {
            std::string::const_iterator end = m_bufferIn.at(idx).end();
            std::string bufferOut;

            for (std::string::const_iterator iter = m_bufferIn.at(idx).begin(); iter != end; iter++)
            {
                if (*iter >= 97 && *iter <= 122)
                {
                    bufferOut += static_cast<char>(static_cast<int>(*iter) - 32);
                }
                else
                {
                    bufferOut += *iter;
```

```
                }
            }
            result[idx] = bufferOut;
        }
        catch(...)
        {
            std::cout << "Invalid index" << std::endl;
        }
    }

private:
    const std::vector<std::string>& m_bufferIn;
};
```

3. Enter the **main()** function, create a constant value called **numberOfTasks**, and set it to **5**. Then, create a vector of a **Converter** object and reserve its size with **numberOfTasks**. Then, create a vector of **std::thread** objects and reserve its size with **numberOfTasks**:

```
const int numberOfTasks = 5;
std::vector<Converter> functions;
functions.reserve(numberOfTasks);
std::vector<std::thread> threads;
threads.reserve(numberOfTasks);
```

4. Create the vector of strings, **textArr**, and push five different big strings to be converted:

```
std::vector<std::string> textArr;
textArr.emplace_back("In the previous topics, we learned almost all that
we need to work with threads. But we still have something interesting
to consider - how to synchronize threads using future results. When
we considered condition variables we didn't cover the second type of
synchronization with future results. Now it's time to learn that.");
textArr.emplace_back("First of all, let's consider a real-life example.
Imagine, you just passed the exam at the university. You were asked to
wait some amount of time for results. So, you have time to coffee with
your mates, and every 10-15 mins you check are results available. Then,
when you finished all your other activities, you just come to the door of
the lecture room and wait for results.");
textArr.emplace_back("In this exercise, we will write a simple application
where we will use std::move() with threads. First of all, we will
implement a class that is move constructible. This class will convert
lowercase text into uppercase text. Then we will create a vector of
```

instances of this class. Next, we will create a vector of std::thread object. Finally, we will initialize threads with an object from the first vector");

textArr.emplace_back("Let's consider one interesting issue. As you remember when we initialize std::thread all constructor arguments are copied into thread memory, including a callable object - lambda, function, std::function. But what if our callable object doesn't support copy semantic? For example, we created a class that has only move constructor and a move assignment operator:");

textArr.emplace_back("Run this code in your editor. You will see in the terminal log from the default constructor, two logs from the move operator, then one log from a destructor, then message from the doSomeJob() function and, finally two other log messages from the destructor. We see that the move constructor is called twice. You will get the output like the following:");

5. Implement a **for** loop where we push **Converter** objects into the functions vector:

```
for (int i = 0; i < numberOfTasks; ++i)
{
    functions.push_back(Converter(textArr));
}
```

6. Create a result vector of strings and push five empty strings. Then, create a variable that will be an index of the array element:

```
std::vector<std::string> result;
for (int i = 0; i < numberOfTasks; ++i)
{
    result.push_back("");
}
int idx = 0;
```

7. Implement another **for** loop where we push **std::thread** objects into the threads vector:

```
for (auto iter = functions.begin(); iter != functions.end(); ++iter)
{
    std::thread tmp(std::move(*iter), idx, std::ref(result));
    threads.push_back(std::move(tmp));
    from = to;
    to += step;
}
```

8. Implement a third **for** loop where we detach **std::threads**:

```
for (auto iter = threads.begin(); iter != threads.end(); ++iter)
{
    (*iter).detach();
}
```

9. Add a small sleep for the main thread to avoid closing the application. Now, we can see how detached threads work:

```
using namespace std::chrono_literals;
std::this_thread::sleep_for(5s);
```

10. Finally print the result into the terminal:

```
for (const auto& str : result)
{
    std::cout << str;
}
```

11. Run this code in your editor. In the terminal, you can see that all strings are in uppercase, which means that all threads were moved and run successfully. You will get the following output:

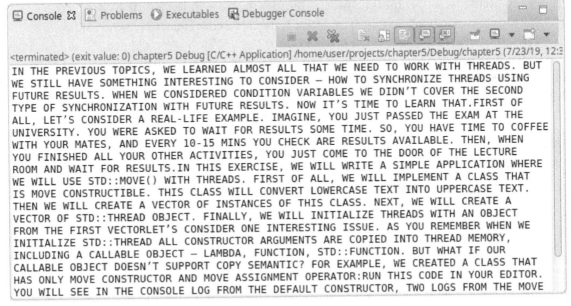

Figure 5.18: The result of the exercise's execution

In this exercise, we practiced how to create an STL container of move-only objects. We also considered how to pass non-copiable objects to a thread constructor. This knowledge will help us in the next section when we learn how to get the result from the thread.

## Futures, Promises, and Async

In the previous section, we learned almost all that we need to work with threads. But we still have something interesting to consider, that is, synchronizing threads using future results. When we considered condition variables, we didn't cover the second type of synchronization with future results. Now, it's time to learn about that.

Suppose there is a situation wherein we run some thread and continue with other work. When we need a result, we stop and check if it is ready. This situation describes the actual work with future results. In C++, we have a header file called **\<future\>** that contains two template classes which represent future results: **std::future\<\>** and **std::shared_future\<\>**. We use **std::future\<\>** when we need a single future result and use **std::shared_future\<\>** when we need multiple valid copies. We can compare them with **std::unique_ptr** and **std::shared_ptr**.

To work with future results, we need a special mechanism to run the task in the background and to receive the result later: the **std::async()** template function. It takes a callable as a parameter and the launch mode – deferred or async and, sure, parameters for the callable. The launch modes **std::launch::async** and **std::launch::deferred** indicate how to execute task. When we pass **std::launch::async**, we expect that function to be executed in a separate thread. When we pass **std::launch::deferred**, the function call will be deferred until we ask for the results. We can also pass both of them, for example, **std::launch::deferred|std::launch::async**. This means that the run mode will depend on the implementation.

Now, let's consider an example of usage **std::future** with **std::async**. We have a **toUppercase()** function, that converts the given string into uppercase:

```cpp
std::string toUppercase(const std::string& bufIn)
{
    std::string bufferOut;
    for (std::string::const_iterator iter = bufIn.begin(); iter != bufIn.
end(); iter++)
    {
        if (*iter >= 97 && *iter <= 122)
        {
            bufferOut += static_cast<char>(static_cast<int>(*iter) - 32);
```

```
        }
        else
        {
            bufferOut += *iter;
        }
    }
    return bufferOut;
}
```

Then, in the **main()** function, we create an **std::future** variable with a name **result** and initialize it using the **std::async()** return value. Then, we fetch the result by using the **get()** function of the result object:

```
#include <iostream>
#include <future>


int main()
{
    std::future<std::string> result = std::async(toUppercase, "please, make
it uppercase");
    std::cout << "Main thread isn't locked" << std::endl;
    std::cout << "Future result = " << result.get() << std::endl;
    return 0;
}
```

Actually, here, we created a future object:

```
std::future<std::string> result = std::async(toUppercase, "please, make it
uppercase");
```

As you can see, we didn't pass the launch mode to the **std::async()** function, which means that the default mode will be used: **std::launch::deferred | std::launch::async**. You can do this explicitly:

```
std::future<std::string> result = std::async(std::launch::async, toUppercase,
"please, make it uppercase");
```

Here, we are waiting for the results:

```
std::cout << "Future result = " << result.get() << std::endl;
```

If our task takes a long time, the thread will wait here until the end.

In general, we can use the **std::async()** function in the same way as we use the **std::thread** constructor. We can pass any callable object. All of the arguments are copied by default, and we can either move variables and callables or can pass them by reference.

The **std::future** object is not protected by race conditions. So, to access it from different threads and protect from damage, we should use mutexes. But if we need to share a future object, it's better to use **std::shared_future**. Shared future results are not thread-safe either. To avoid race conditions, we have to use mutexes or store the threads' own copy of **std::shared_future** in every thread.

> **Note**
>
> Race conditions for **std::future** objects are very tricky. When the thread calls **get()** function, the future object becomes invalid.

We can create a shared future by moving future to a constructor:

```
std::future<std::string> result = std::async(toUppercase, "please, make it
uppercase");

std::cout << "Main thread isn't locked" << std::endl;


std::shared_future<std::string> sharedResult(std::move(result));

std::cout << "Future result = " << sharedResult.get() << std::endl;


std::shared_future<std::string> anotherSharedResult(sharedResult);

std::cout << "Future result = " << anotherSharedResult.get() << std::endl;
```

As you can see, we created an **std::shared_future** variable from **std::future** and copied it. Both shared future objects are referring to the same result.

We can also create the shared future object using the **share()** member function of the **sdt::future** object:

```
std::future<std::string> result = std::async(toUppercase, "please, make it
uppercase");

std::cout << "Main thread isn't locked" << std::endl;


auto sharedResult = result.share();

std::cout << "Future result = " << sharedResult.get() << std::endl;
```

Pay attention that, in both cases, the **std::future** object becomes invalid.

Another way we can get a future result from a separate thread is by using the **std::packaged_task<>** template class. How do we work with them?

1.  We create a new **std::packaged_task** and declare the callable function signature:

    ```
    std::packaged_task<std::string(const std::string&)> task(toUppercase);
    ```

2.  Then, we store the future result in the **std::future** variable:

    ```
    auto futureResult = task.get_future();
    ```

3.  Next, we run this task in a separate thread or call it as a function:

    ```
    std::thread thr1(std::move(task), "please, make it uppercase");
    thr1.detach();
    ```

4.  Finally, we wait until the future results are ready:

    ```
    std::cout << "Future result = " << futureResult.get() << std::endl;
    ```

> **Note**
>
> **std::packaged_task** is non-copyable. So, to run it in the separate thread, use the **std::move()** function.

There is one more important thing to take note of. If you don't want any results from the thread and would prefer to wait until the thread finishes its work, you can use **std::future<void>**. Now, when you call **future.get()**, your current thread will wait at this point. Let's consider an example:

```cpp
#include <iostream>
#include <future>
void toUppercase(const std::string& bufIn)
{
    std::string bufferOut;
    for (std::string::const_iterator iter = bufIn.begin(); iter != bufIn.
end(); iter++)
    {
        if (*iter >= 97 && *iter <= 122)
        {
            bufferOut += static_cast<char>(static_cast<int>(*iter) - 32);
        }
        else
        {
            bufferOut += *iter;
        }
    }
    using namespace std::chrono_literals;
    std::this_thread::sleep_for(2s);
    std::cout << bufferOut << std::endl;
}

int main()
{
    std::packaged_task<void(const std::string&)> task(toUppercase);
    auto futureResult = task.get_future();
    std::thread thr1(std::move(task), "please, make it uppercase");
```

```
    thr1.detach();

    std::cout << "Main thread is not blocked here" << std::endl;

    futureResult.get();

    std::cout << "The packaged_task is done" << std::endl;

    return 0;

}
```

As you can see, by waiting for another thread, we are making use of several techniques such as condition variables, future results, and promises.

Now, let's move on to the next important feature in the Standard Library – the **std::promise<>** template class. With this class, we can set the value of the type that we want to receive and then get it using **std::future**. How do we work with them? For that, we need to implement a function that takes an **std::promise** parameter:

```
void toUppercase(const std::string& bufIn, std::promise<std::string> result)
```

When the work is done, we need to initialize a new value with **std::promise**:

```
result.set_value(bufferOut);
```

For creating **std::promise** in the place where we'll be using it, we need to write the following code:

```
std::promise<std::string> stringInUpper;
```

Once this is done, we must create **std::future** and get it from the promise:

```
std::future<std::string> futureRes = stringInUpper.get_future();
```

We need to run this function in the separate thread:

```
std::thread thr(toUppercase, "please, make it uppercase",
std::move(stringInUpper));

thr.detach();
```

Now, we need to wait until the future is set:

```
futureRes.wait();

std::cout << "Result = " << futureRes.get() << std::endl;
```

The complete example of getting the result using promises is as follows:

```cpp
#include <iostream>
#include <future>


void toUppercase(const std::string& bufIn, std::promise<std::string> result)
{
    std::string bufferOut;
    for (std::string::const_iterator iter = bufIn.begin(); iter != bufIn.
end(); iter++)
    {
        if (*iter >= 97 && *iter <= 122)
        {
            bufferOut += static_cast<char>(static_cast<int>(*iter) - 32);
        }
        else
        {
            bufferOut += *iter;
        }
    }


    result.set_value(bufferOut);
}


int main()
{
    std::promise<std::string> stringInUpper;
    std::future<std::string> futureRes = stringInUpper.get_future();
    std::thread thr(toUppercase, "please, make it uppercase",
std::move(stringInUpper));
```

```
    thr.detach();

    std::cout << "Main thread is not blocked here" << std::endl;

    futureRes.wait();


    std::cout << "Result = " << futureRes.get() << std::endl;

    return 0;

}
```

So, we covered almost everything that's required to write multithreaded applications, except one important thing – what would happen if an exception is thrown in the separate thread? For example, you pass a function in the thread and it throws an exception. In this case, **std::terminate()** will be called for this thread. Other threads will continue their job. Let's consider a simple example.

We have a **getException()** function that generates a message with a thread ID and throws **std::runtime_error**:

```
#include <sstream>

#include <exception>

#include <iostream>

#include <future>


std::string getException()

{

    std::stringstream ss;

    ss << "Exception from thread: ";

    ss << std::this_thread::get_id();

    throw std::runtime_error(ss.str());

}
```

We also have the **toUppercase()** function. Which converts the given string into uppercase and calls the **getException()** function, which throws an exception:

```
std::string toUppercase(const std::string& bufIn)

{

    std::string bufferOut;

    for (std::string::const_iterator iter = bufIn.begin(); iter != bufIn.
end(); iter++)
```

```
    {
        if (*iter >= 97 && *iter <= 122)
        {
            bufferOut += static_cast<char>(static_cast<int>(*iter) - 32);
        }
        else
        {
            bufferOut += *iter;
            getException();
        }
    }

    return bufferOut;
}
```

Here is the **main()** function, where we create a new thread, **thr**, in the **try-catch** block. We catch an exception and print the message to the terminal:

```
int main()
{
    try
    {
        std::thread thr(toUppercase, "please, make it uppercase");
        thr.join();
    }
    catch(const std::exception& ex)
    {
        std::cout << "Caught an exception: " << ex.what() << std::endl;
    }
    return 0;
}
```

If you run this code in your IDE, you will see the following output:

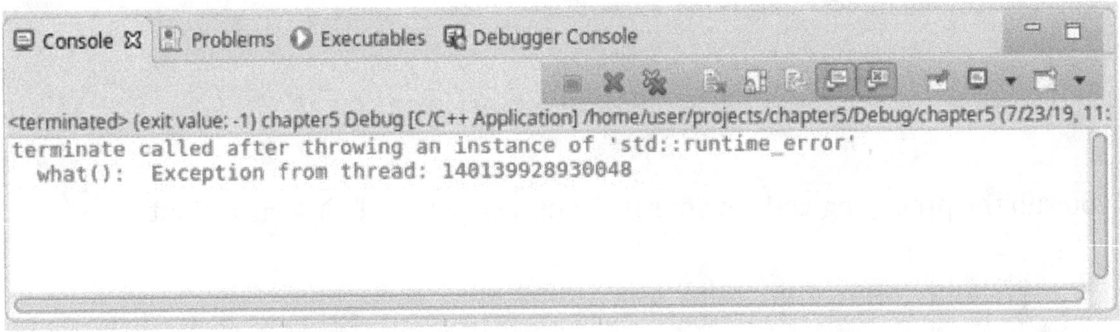

Figure 5.19: The result of an example's execution

We can see that `std::terminate()` was called after throwing an exception. When you have lots of threads in your program, it's very hard to find the right place where the thread was terminated. Fortunately, we have a few mechanisms for catching an exception from another thread. Let's consider them all.

The **std::async** function uses future results for transferring exceptions to the calling thread. It stores `std::exception_ptr` in the future result and sets the ready flag. Then, when you call `get()`, **std::future** checks if there any `std::exception_ptr` stored and rethrows the exception. All we need to do is place a `get()` call in the **try-catch** block. Let's consider an example. We will use two helper functions from the previous example, that is, `getException()` and `toUppercase()`. They will stay the same. In the `main()` function, we create an `std::future` object called **result** and run the `toUppercase()` function using the `std::async()` function. Then, we call the `get()` function of the result object in the **try-catch** block and catch an exception:

```
#include <iostream>
#include <future>


int main()
{
    std::future<std::string> result = std::async(toUppercase, "please, make
it uppercase");
    try
    {
        std::cout << "Future result = " << result.get() << std::endl;

    }
    catch(const std::exception& ex)
```

```
    {
        std::cout << "Caught an exception: " << ex.what() << std::endl;
    }
    return 0;
}
```

If you run the preceding code in your IDE, you will get the following output:

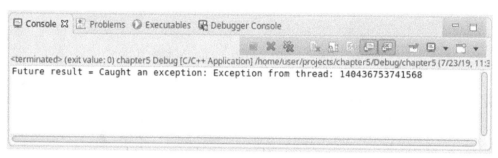

Figure 5.20: The result of the example's execution

As you can see, we caught an exception and now we can handle it in some way. The **std::packaged_task<>** class handles exceptions in the same way – it stores **std::exception_ptr** in the future result, sets the ready flag, and then **std::future** rethrows an exception in the **get()** call. Let's consider a small example. We will use two helper functions from the previous example - **getException()** and **toUppercase()**. They will stay the same. In the **main()** function, we create an **std::packaged_task** object called **task**. By using the type of our **toUppercase()** function, it returns an integer and takes two integers as parameters. We pass the **toUppercase()** function to the **task** object. Then, we create an **std::future** object called **result** and get the result from the task object using the **get_future()** function. Finally, we run the task object in the new thread, **thr**, and in the **try-catch** block call the **get()** function of the **result** variable:

```
#include <iostream>
#include <future>


int main()
{
    std::packaged_task<std::string(const std::string&)> task(toUppercase);
    auto result = task.get_future();
    std::thread thr(std::move(task), "please, make it uppercase");
    thr.detach();
```

```
    try
    {
        std::cout << "Future result = " << result.get() << std::endl;
    }
    catch(const std::exception& ex)
    {
        std::cout << "Caught an exception: " << ex.what() << std::endl;
    }
    return 0;
}
```

If you run this code in your IDE, you will get the following output:

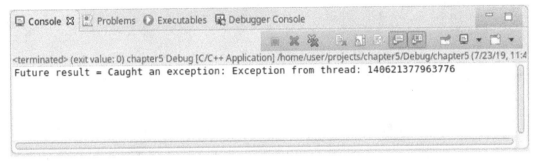

Figure 5.21: The result of this example's execution

The **std::promise<>** class handles exceptions in another way. It allows us to store an exception manually using the **set_exception()** or **set_exception_at_thread_exit()** function. To set an exception in **std::promise**, we have to catch it. If we do not catch an exception, an error will be set in the destructor of **std::promise** as **std::future_errc::broken_promise** in future result. When you call the **get()** function, an exception will be rethrown. Let's consider an example. We will use a helper function from the previous example – **getException()**. It's staying the same. However, we will change the **toUppercase()** function and add the third parameter, **std::promise**. Now, we will call the **getException()** function in the **try** block, catch an exception, and set it to the **std::promise** value:

```
void toUppercase(const std::string& bufIn, std::promise<std::string> result)
{
    std::string bufferOut;
    try
    {
```

```
        for (std::string::const_iterator iter = bufIn.begin(); iter !=
bufIn.end(); iter++)
        {
            if (*iter >= 97 && *iter <= 122)
            {
                    bufferOut += static_cast<char>(static_cast<int>(*iter) -
32);
            }
            else
            {
                bufferOut += *iter;
                getException();
            }
        }
    }
    catch(const std::exception& ex)
    {
        result.set_exception(std::make_exception_ptr(ex));
    }

    result.set_value(bufferOut);
}
```

> **Note**
>
> There are a few ways to set an exception to the promise. First of all, we can catch
> **std::exception** and convert it into **std::exception_ptr** using the **std::make_
> exception_ptr()** function. You can also use the **std::current_exception()**
> function, which returns the **std::exception_ptr** object.

In the **main()** function, we create a promise of the integer type called **upperResult**. We create a future result called **futureRes** and set it from the **upperResult** promise value. Next, we create a new thread, **thr**, pass the **toUppercase()** function to it, and move the **upperResult** promise. Then, we call the **wait()** function of the **futureRes** object, which makes the calling thread wait until the result becomes available. Then, in the **try-catch** block, we call the **get()** function of the **futureRes** object and it rethrows an exception:

```
#include <iostream>

#include <future>

int main()

{

    std::promise<std::string> upperResult;

    std::future<std::string> futureRes = upperResult.get_future();

    std::thread thr(toUppercase, "please, make it uppercase",
std::move(upperResult));

    thr.detach();

    futureRes.wait();


    try

    {

        std::cout << "Result = " << futureRes.get() << std::endl;

    }

    catch(...)

    {

        std::cout << "Caught an exception" << std::endl;

    }

    return 0;

}
```

> **Note**
>
> When we create an **std::promise<>** object, we promise that we will obligatorily set the value or the exception. If we do not do any that, the destructor of **std::promise** will throw an exception, that is, **std::future_error** - **std::future_errc::broken_promise**.

If you run this code in your IDE, you will get the following output:

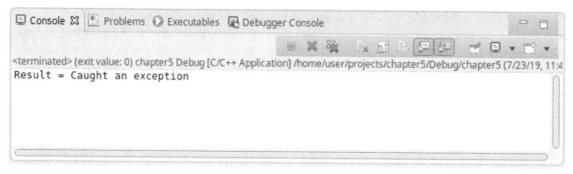

Figure 5.22: The result of this example's execution

That's all for handling exceptions in a multithreaded application. As you can see, it's very similar to what we do in a single thread. Now, let's put our knowledge to practice and write a simple application example that demonstrates how we can use different future results for synchronization.

## Exercise 5: Synchronization with Future Results

In this exercise, we will write a simple application to demonstrate how we can use future results to receive values from the separate threads. We will run the **ToUppercase()** callable object three times. We will execute the first task using the **std::async()** function, the second task using the **std::packaged_task<>** template class, and the last task using **std::thread** and **std::promise**.

Perform the following steps to complete this exercise:

1. Include the headers for threading support, namely **<thread>**, streaming support, namely **<iostream>**, and **<future>** for future results support:

   ```
   #include <iostream>
   #include <thread>
   #include <future>
   ```

2. Implement a **ToUppercase** class that will convert the given string into uppercase. It has two overloaded operators, **()**. The first **operator()** takes the string to be converted and returns the result value in uppercase. The second **operator()** takes the string to be converted and an **std::promise** and stores the return value in a promise:

   ```
   class ToUppercase
   {
       public:
       std::string operator()(const std::string& bufIn)
   ```

```cpp
    {
        std::string bufferOut;
        for (std::string::const_iterator iter = bufIn.begin(); iter !=
bufIn.end(); iter++)
        {
            if (*iter >= 97 && *iter <= 122)
            {
                bufferOut += static_cast<char>(static_cast<int>(*iter) -
32);
            }
            else
            {
                bufferOut += *iter;
            }
        }
        return bufferOut;
    }

    void operator()(const std::string& bufIn, std::promise<std::string>
result)
    {
        std::string bufferOut;
        for (std::string::const_iterator iter = bufIn.begin(); iter !=
bufIn.end(); iter++)
        {
            if (*iter >= 97 && *iter <= 122)
            {
                bufferOut += static_cast<char>(static_cast<int>(*iter) -
32);
            }
            else
            {
                bufferOut += *iter;
            }
        }
        result.set_value(bufferOut);
    }
};
```

3. Now, create a **ToUppercase** object, namely **ptConverter**, and create an
   **std::packaged_task**, namely **upperCaseResult1**, which takes the **ptConverter** object
   as a parameter. Create an **std::future** value and set it from **upperCaseResult1**. Run
   this task in a separate thread:

```
ToUppercase ptConverter;
std::packaged_task<std::string(const std::string&)>
upperCaseResult1(ptConverter);
std::future<std::string> futureUpperResult1= upperCaseResult1.get_
future();
std::thread thr1(std::move(ptConverter), "This is a string for the first
asynchronous task");
thr1.detach();
```

4. Now, create a second **ToUppercase** object, namely **fConverter**. Create an
   **std::future** object called **futureUpperResult2** and set it from **std::async()**:

```
ToUppercase fConverter;
std::future<std::string> futureUpperResult2 = std::async(fConverter, "This
is a string for the asynchronous task");
```

5. Now. create a third **ToUppercase** object. namely **pConverter**. Create an
   **std::promise** value called **promiseResult**. Then, create an **std::future** value called
   **futureUpperResult3** and set it from **promiseResult**. Now, run the **pConverter** task in
   the separate thread and pass **promiseResult** as an argument:

```
ToUppercase pConverter;
std::promise<std::string> promiseResult;
std::future<std::string> futureUpperResult3 = promiseResult.get_future();
std::thread thr2(pConverter, "This is a string for the task that returns a
promise", std::move(promiseResult));
thr2.detach();
```

6. Now, to receive the results from all the threads, wait for **futureUpperResult3** to be
   ready and then get all three results and print them:

```
futureUpperResult3.wait();
std::cout  << "Converted strings: "
          << futureUpperResult1.get() << std::endl
          << futureUpperResult2.get() << std::endl
          << futureUpperResult3.get() << std::endl;
```

7.  Run this code in your editor. You will see the converted strings from all three threads.

    You will get the following output:

**Figure 5.23: The result of this exercise's execution**

So, what have we done here? We split big calculations into smaller parts and ran them in separate threads. For long calculations, this will increase performance. In this exercise, we learned how to receive results from threads. In this section, we also learned how to pass an exception that was thrown in a separate thread to the calling thread. We also learned how to synchronize the work of a few threads by an event, not only with condition variables but also with future results.

## Activity 1: Creating a Simulator to Model the Work of the Art Gallery

In this activity, we are going to create a simulator to model the working of an Art Gallery. We have set a limit of visitors to the Gallery – only 50 people can be inside. To implement this simulation, we need to create a **Person** class that will represent people in the Art Gallery. Also, we need a **Persons** class, which is a thread-safe container for people. We also need a **Watchman** class that controls how many people are inside it. If the limit exceeds the Watchman, we put all the newcomers into a waiting list. Finally, we need a **Generator** class that has two threads – one for creating new visitors and another for notifying us that somebody has to leave the Gallery. Thus, we will cover working with threads, mutexes, condition variables, lock_guards, and unique_locks. This simulator will allow us to utilize the techniques that we've covered in this chapter. Thus, before attempting this activity, ensure that you have completed all the previous exercises in this chapter.

To implement this application, we need to describe our classes. We have the following classes:

| Class Name | Description |
| --- | --- |
| Person | The class that represents a visitor of the Art Gallery. |
| Persons | The thread-safe storage that keeps objects of the Person class. |
| PersonGenerator | The class that is responsible for creating new objects of the Person class at different intervals. This simulates new visitors to the Art Gallery. It is also responsible for simulating when people leave the Art Gallery. Due to this, it triggers the remove event at different intervals. |
| Watchman | The class that is responsible for controlling who enters the Art Gallery. With every new visitor, it checks the number of people in the Art Gallery, and if the number is less than 50, it puts a number Person into the list of people inside the Gallery. If this number is more than the limit, it puts the visitor in the waiting list. It also removes visitors from the list of people who are inside the Gallery by using the remove event, which is triggered by the PersonGenerator class. After every removal, it checks whether there are any visitors in the waiting list. If there are, it checks the number of people in the Art Gallery. If the number is less than 50, it will put a Person from the list of people into the Gallery. |

Figure 5.24: Description of the classes that are used in this activity

Let's create the class diagram before starting the implementation. All of the aforementioned classes with relationships are shown in the following diagram:

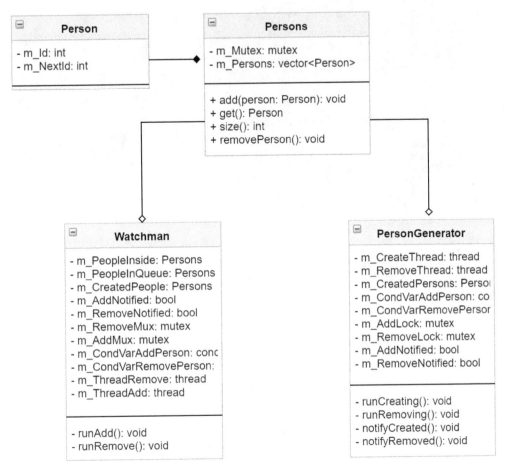

**Figure 5.25: The class diagram**

Follow these steps to implement this activity:

1. Define and implement the Person class, which does nothing except print logs.

2. Create some thread-safe storage for Persons that wraps the std::vector class.

3. Implement the PersonGenerator class, that, in an infinite loop in different threads, creates and removes visitors and notifies the Watchman class.

4. Create the Watchman class that, in an infinite loop in separate threads, moves visitors from the queue to another queue on notification from the PersonGenerator class.

5. Declare the corresponding objects in the main() function to simulate the Art Gallery and how it works.

After implementing these steps, you should get the following output, where you can see the logs from all the implemented classes. Ensure that the simulation flows as expected. The expected output should look similar to the following:

```
 1  //================================================================
 2  // Name        : Simulator.cpp
 3  // Author      : Olena Lizina
 4  // Description : The Art Gallery work simulator
 5  //================================================================
 6
 7  #include <iostream>
 8  #include <condition_variable>
 9
10  #include "Persons.hpp"
11  #include "Watchman.hpp"
12  #include "PersonGenerator.hpp"
13
14  int main()
15  {
16      {
```

```
Console ⊠    Problems  ⊙ Executables
<terminated> (exit value: -1) Simulator Debug [C/C++ Application] C:\Users\elena\Desktop\Chapter5\Activity\Simulator\|
Watchman | runAdd | welcome in our The Art Gallery
Watchman | runAdd | check people in queue
Watchman | runAdd | false awakening
PersonGenerator | runCreating | new person:
Person | Person | Hello! I'm 6
Watchman | runAdd | new person came
Watchman | runAdd | Sorry, we are full. Please wait
Watchman | runAdd | check people in queue
Watchman | runAdd | false awakening
PersonGenerator | runRemoving | somebody has left the gallery:
Persons | removePerson | removed
Watchman | runRemove | good buy
Watchman | runRemove | check people in queue
Watchman | runRemove | welcome in our The Art Gallery
Watchman | runRemove | false awakening
PersonGenerator | runCreating | new person:
Person | Person | Hello! I'm 7
Watchman | runAdd | new person came
Watchman | runAdd | Sorry, we are full. Please wait
Watchman | runAdd | check people in queue
Watchman | runAdd | false awakening
```

Figure 5.26: The result of the application's execution

### Note

The solution for this activity can be found on page 681.

# Summary

In this chapter, we learned about working with threads that are supported by the C++ Standard Library. This is fundamental if we want to write robust, fast, and clear multithreaded applications.

We started by looking at general concepts regarding concurrency – what parallel, concurrent, synchronous, asynchronous, and threaded execution is. Having a clear understanding of these concepts allowed us to understand the architectural design of the multithreaded application.

Next, we looked at the different issues that we faced while developing multithreaded applications, such as data hazards, race conditions, and deadlocks. Understanding these issues helped us build a clear synchronized architecture for our projects. We considered the synchronization concept on some real-life examples, which gave us a good understanding of the challenges that we may face while programming threaded applications.

Next, we tried to work with different Standard Library primitives for synchronization. We tried to figure out how to handle race conditions and implemented examples of synchronization by events and synchronization by data. Next, we considered how the move semantics apply to multithreading. We learned which classes from threading support libraries are non-copiable but movable. We also considered how the move semantics work in multithreaded closures. Finally, we learned how to receive results from separate threads and how to synchronize threads using futures, promises, and async.

We put all of these new skills into practice by building an Art Gallery simulator. We built a multithreaded application with one main thread and four child threads. We implemented communication between them by using condition variables. We protected them using shared data by mutexes. In all, we employed everything we learned about in this chapter.

In the next chapter, we're going to be taking a closer look at I/O operations and classes in C++. We will start by looking at the I/O support of the Standard Library. Then, we will move on to working with streams and asynchronous I/O operations. Next, we will learn about the interaction of threads and I/O. We will write an activity that will allow us to master our skills in I/O work in C++.

# 6

# Streams and I/O

**Learning Objectives**

By the end of this chapter, you will be able to:

- Write and read data to/from files or the console using the Standard I/O Library

- Format and parse data using the in-memory I/O interface

- Extend standard I/O streams for user-defined types

- Develop applications that use the I/O Standard Library from multiple threads

In this chapter, we'll develop flexible and maintainable applications using the I/O Standard Library, work with streams, learn how the I/O library can be used in multithreaded applications, and finally learn to format and parse data using the Standard Library.

# Introduction

In the previous chapter, we covered one of the most challenging topics – concurrency in C++. We looked at the main multithreaded concepts and differentiated between synchronous, asynchronous, and threaded execution in C++. We learned the key points about synchronization, data hazards, and race conditions. Finally, we looked at working with threads in modern C++. In this chapter, we will go deeper and learn how to handle I/O in multithreaded applications.

This chapter is dedicated to **streams** and **I/O** in C++. I/O is the general concept of input and output operations. The main purpose of this part of the Standard Library is to provide a clear interface regarding the input and output of data. But this is not the only goal. There are a lot of situations where I/O can help us in our applications. It's hard to imagine any application that doesn't write errors or exceptional situations into the log file with the purpose of sending it to the development team for analysis. In GUI applications, we always need to format the displayed information or parse the user input. In complex and large applications, we usually need to log internal data structures, and so on. In all these cases, we employ the I/O portion of the **Standard Library**.

We will start our chapter with a brief introduction to the Input/Output portion of the Standard Library. We will learn about the I/O and explore their main concepts and terms. Then, we will consider which types are supported by default and how we can extend streams to user-defined types. Next, we will study the structure of the I/O library and check the headers and classes available for our use. Finally, we will investigate how to work with streams, read and write to a file, create multithreaded applications with input and output operations, and format and parse text data.

This chapter will be concluded with a challenging and exciting activity in which we will improve our **Art Gallery Simulator** project from the previous chapter and create a robust, clear, multithreaded, and easy to use **Logger**. We will develop a class with a clear interface that can be accessed from any place in the project. Next, we will adapt it to work with several threads. Finally, we will integrate our robust logger into the Art Gallery Simulator project.

Let's start by looking at the I/O part of the C++ Standard Library and learn what opportunities are open to us with this set of tools.

## Reviewing the I/O Portion of the Standard Library

In computer science, I/O is the term that implies the communication between programs, devices, computers, and so on. In C++, we employ standard input and standard output terms to describe the I/O process. Standard input means the streams of data that are transferred into the program. To get this data, the program should perform the read operation. Standard output means the streams of data that are transferred from a program to an external device, such as a file, display, socket, printer, and so on. To output this data, the program should perform the write operation. Standard input and output streams are inherited from the main process and are common for all child threads. Take a look at the following diagram to get a better understanding of the considered terms:

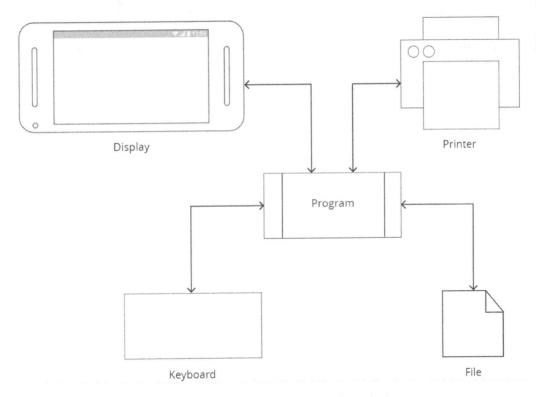

Figure 6.1: I/O communication between devices

In the C++ Standard Library, most of the I/O classes are generalized class templates. All of them are logically divided into two categories – abstractions and implementations. We are already familiar with the abstraction classes and know that we can use them for different purposes without recompiling the code. The same is true for the I/O library. Here, we have six abstract classes that are the basis of the I/O operations in C++. We will not deep dive into these interfaces. Usually, we use more high-level classes for our operations and appeal to them only if we need to implement our own derived class.

The **ios_base** abstract class is responsible for managing stream status flags, formatting flags, callbacks, and private storage. The **basic_streambuf** abstract class provides an interface for buffering input or output operations and provides access to the source of input, such as a file, socket, or sink of output, such as a string or vector. The **basic_ios** abstract class implements facilities for work with derived classes from the **basic_streambuf** interface. The **basic_ostream**, **basic_istream**, and **basic_iostream** abstract classes are wrappers for derived classes from the **basic_streambuf** interface and provide a high-level input/output interface, respectively. Let's briefly consider them and their relationships, which are shown in the following class diagram. You can see that all of them, except for **ios_base**, are template classes. Under the name of each class, you can find the file name where this class is defined:

> **Note**
>
> In the UML notation, we use the **<<interface>>** keyword to show that class is an abstract class.

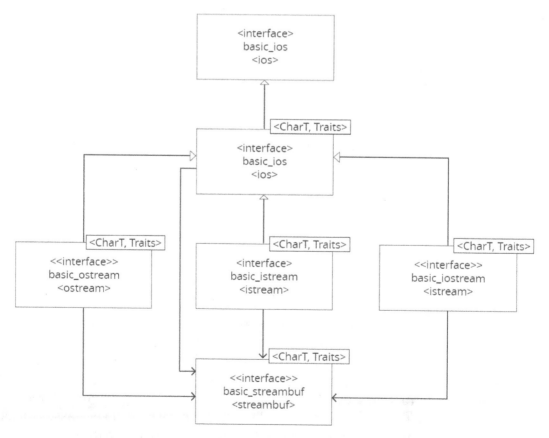

Figure 6.2: Class diagram of I/O abstract interfaces

Implementation classes are logically divided into the following categories: **File I/O**, **String I/O**, **Synchronized I/O**, **I/O manipulators**, and predefined standard stream objects. All of them are derived from the aforementioned abstract classes. Let's consider each of them in detail in the upcoming sections.

## Predefined Standard Stream Objects

We will start our acquaintance with the I/O Standard Library with the already familiar `std::cout` class from the `<iostream>` header file. We use it for outputting the data to the Terminal. You may also be aware about the `std::cin` class for reading user input – but not everyone knows that `std::cout` and `std::cin` are predefined standard stream objects that are used for formatting input and output to the Terminal. The `<iostream>` header file also contains `std::cerr` and `std::clog` stream objects, which are used for logging errors. As usual, there are also their analogs for wide characters with a prefix of "w": `wcout`, `wcin`, `wcerr`, and `wclog`. All of these objects are automatically created and initialized at system startup. Although it is safe to use these objects from multiple threads, the output can be mixed. Let's revise how to use them. Since they are only overloaded for built-in types, we should write our own overrides for user-defined types.

The `std::cout` stream object is often used with the `std::endl` manipulator. It inserts a newline character in the output sequence and flushes it. Here is an example of using them:

```
std::string name("Marilyn Monroe");
int age = 18;
std::cout << "Name: " << name << ", age: " << age << std::endl;
```

Originally, the `std::cin` object reads all input character sequence, symbol by symbol. But it has overloads for built-in types and can read values such as **numbers**, **strings**, **characters**, and so on. There is a little trick in reading strings; `std::cin` reads the string until the next whitespace or newline symbol. So, if you need it to read a string, you have to do it in a loop, read it word by word, or use the `std::getline()` function, which takes the `std::cin` object as the first parameter and the destination string as the second.

> **Note**
>
> The right shift operator, **>>**, of the `std::cin` stream object reads only one word from a line. Use `std::getline(std::cin, str)` to read the whole line.

Here is an example of using **std::cin** with different types:

```
std::string name;
std::string sex;
int age;


std::cout << "Enter your name: " << std::endl;
std::getline(std::cin, name);
std::cout << "Enter your age: " << std::endl;
std::cin >> age;
std::cout << "Enter your sex (male, female):" << std::endl;
std::cin >> sex;
std::cout << "Your name is " << name << ", your age is " << age << ", your
sex is " << sex << std::endl;
```

As you can see, here, we read the name using the **std::getline()** function because the user can input two or three words. We also read the age and then read the sex using the right shift operator, **>>**, because we need to read only a single word. We then print the read data to ensure that everything went well.

The **std::cerr** and **std::clog** stream objects differ in only one way – **std::cerr** immediately flushes the output sequence, while **std::clog** buffers it and flushes only when the buffer is full. When it comes to usage, they are very similar to **std::cout**. The only difference is that the messages from **std::cerr** and **std::clog** (in most of the IDEs) are red in color.

In the following screenshot, you can see the output from these stream objects:

```
 7  #include <iostream>
 8  #include <string>
 9
10  int main(int argc, char **argv)
11  {
12      if (true)
13      {
14          std::cerr << "Something bad happened" << std::endl;
15          std::clog << "Something bad happened" << std::endl;
16      }
17      return 0;
```

```
Problems    Tasks    Console 🔀    Properties
<terminated> (exit value: 0) Exercise 1 Debug [C/C++ Application] C:\Users\elena\Desktop\Chapter6\Deb
Something bad happened
Something bad happened
```

Figure 6.3: The output from the std::cerr and std::clog stream objects

Now, let's perform an exercise to consolidate everything we've learned.

## Exercise 1: Overriding the Left Shift Operator, <<, for User-Defined Types

In this exercise, we will write a very useful portion of code that you can use anywhere to output user-defined types. First of all, we will create a class with the name **Track** that represents a musical track. It will have the following private members: **name**, **singer**, **length**, and **date**. Then, we will override the left shift operator, <<, for this class. Next, we will create an instance of this class and output it using the **std::cout** stream object.

Perform the following steps to execute this exercise:

1. Include the required headers: **<iostream>** for output to a console and **<string>** for string support:

   ```
   #include <iostream>
   #include <string>
   ```

2. Declare the **Track** class and add the private section variables for keeping information about the **track**, that is, **m_Name**, **m_Singer**, **m_Date**, and **m_LengthInSeconds**. In the public section, add a constructor with parameters that initialize all the private variables. Also, add the **public** section getters for all class members:

   ```
   class Track
   {
   public:
       Track(const std::string& name,
             const std::string& singer,
             const std::string& date,
             const unsigned int& lengthInSeconds)
           : m_Name(name)
           , m_Singer(singer)
           , m_Date(date)
           , m_LengthInSeconds(lengthInSeconds)
       {
       }

           std::string getName() const { return m_Name; }
           std::string getSinger() const { return m_Singer; }
           std::string getDate() const { return m_Date; }
   ```

```
        unsigned int getLength() const { return m_LengthInSeconds; }

    private:
        std::string m_Name;
        std::string m_Singer;
        std::string m_Date;
        unsigned int m_LengthInSeconds;
    };
```

3. Now comes the most difficult part of the exercise: writing the overload function for the **Track** type. This is a **template** function that has two type parameters: **charT** and **Traits**:

```
template <typename charT, typename Traits>
```

4. We made this function inline to let the compiler know that we want it to perform optimization on this function. The return type of this function is a reference to a **std::basic_ostream<charT, Traits>** class. The name of this function is operator <<. This function takes two parameters: the first is the reference to the **std::basic_ostream<charT, Traits>** class and the second is a copy of the **Track** variable. The full function declaration is as follows:

```
template <typename charT, typename Traits>
inline std::basic_ostream<charT, Traits>&
operator<<(std::basic_ostream<charT, Traits>& os, Track trackItem);
```

5. Now, add the function definition. Use the **os** variable, just like we use the **std::cout** object, and format the output as you wish. Then, return the **os** variable from the function. The complete code of the overloaded operator, <<, is as follows:

```
template <typename charT, typename Traits>
inline std::basic_ostream<charT, Traits>&
operator<<(std::basic_ostream<charT, Traits>& os, Track trackItem)
{
    os << "Track information: ["
        << "Name: " << trackItem.getName()
        << ", Singer: " << trackItem.getSinger()
        << ", Date of creation: " << trackItem.getDate()
        << ", Length in seconds: " << trackItem.getLength()
        << "]";
    return os;
}
```

6.  Now, enter the **main** function and create and initialize the instance of the **Track** type with the name **track_001**. Finally, use **std::cout** to print the **track_001** value:

```
int main()
{
    Track track_001("Summer night city",
                    "ABBA",
                    "1979",
                    213);

    std::cout << track_001 << std::endl;

    return 0;
}
```

7.  Compile and execute the application. Run it. You will get the following output:

```
 Problems  Tasks  Console  Properties
<terminated> (exit value: 0) Exercise 1 Debug [C/C++ Application] C:\Users\elena\Desktop\Chapter6\Debug\Exercise 1.exe (02.09.19, 16:07)
Track information: [Name: Summer night city, Singer: ABBA, Date of creation: 1979, Length in seconds: 213]
```

**Figure 6.4: The result of executing Exercise 1**

Great job. Here, we considered using predefined standard stream objects and learned how to write our own overloaded shift operators for user-defined types. Let's move on and examine reading and writing to a file with the C++ Standard IO Library.

## File I/O Implementation Classes

File streams manage input and output to files. They provide an interface that implements the **Resource Acquisition Is Initialization** (**RAII**) – the file opens on a stream construction and closes automatically on its destruction. In the Standard Library, file streams are represented by the following classes: **basic_ifstream** for input operations, **basic_ofstream** for output operations, **basic_fstream** for both input and output operations, and **basic_filebuf** for the implementation of a raw file device. All of them are defined in the **<fstream>** header file. The Standard Library also provides typedefs for char and **wchar_t** types, that is, **ifstream**, **fstream**, and **ofstream**, and the same names with a "**w**" prefix for wide characters.

We can create a file stream in two ways. The first way is to do this in one line, that is, to open a file and connect a stream to a file by just passing the filename to a constructor:

```
std::ofstream outFile(filename);

std::ifstream outFile(filename);

std::fstream outFile(filename);
```

Another way is creating an object and then calling the **open()** function:

```
std::ofstream outFile;

outFile.open(filename);
```

> **Note**
>
> IO streams have bool variables: a **goodbit**, an **eofbit**, a **failbit**, and a **badbit**. They are used to check the state of the stream after each operation and indicate which error happened on the stream.

After the object's creation, we can check the stream status by checking the **failbit** or checking the stream associated with the open file. To check a **failbit**, call the **fail()** function on the **file** stream:

```
if (outFile.fail())
{
    std::cerr << filename << " file couldn't be opened"<< std::endl;
}
```

To check whether the stream is associated with the open file, call the **is_open()** function:

```
if (!outFile.is_open())
{
    std::cerr << filename << " file couldn't be opened"<< std::endl;
}
```

Input, output, and bidirectional file streams can also be opened in different modes by using flags. They are declared in the **ios_base** namespace. Besides the **ios_base::in** and **ios_base::out** flags, we also have the **ios_base::ate**, **ios_base::app**, **ios_base::trunc**, and **ios_base::binary** flags. The **ios_base::trunc** flag removes the content of the file. The **ios_base::app** flag always writes the output to the end of the file. Even if you decide to change the position in the file, you cannot do this. The **ios_base::ate** flag sets the position of the file descriptor to the end of the file but allows you to modify the position later. Finally, the **ios_base::binary** flag suppresses any formatting of the data so that it's read or wrote in "raw" format. Let's consider all the possible combinations of open modes.

By default, **std::ofstream** is opened in **ios_base::out** mode, **std::ifstream** is opened in **ios_base::in** mode, and **std::fstream** is opened in **ios_base::in|ios_base::out** mode. The **ios_base::out|ios_base::trunc** mode creates the file if it doesn't exist or removes all the content from the existing file. The **ios_base::out|ios_base::app** mode creates the file if it doesn't exist or opens the existing file and allows you to write only at the end of the file. Both of the aforementioned modes can be combined with the **ios_base::in** flag, so the file will be opened in read and write mode simultaneously.

Here is an example of how to open the file using the aforementioned modes:

```
std::ofstream outFile(filename, std::ios_base::out|std::ios_base::trunc);
```

You can also do the following:

```
std::ofstream outFile;

outFile.open(filename, std::ios_base::out|std::ios_base::trunc);
```

After we've opened the file stream in the required mode, we can start reading or writing to a file. The file streams allow us to change our position in the file. Let's consider how we can do this. To get the current file's position, we can call the **tellp()** function in **ios_base::out** mode and the **tellg()** function in **ios_base::in** mode. It can be used later so that we can return to this position if needed. We can also find the exact position in a file by using the **seekp()** function in **ios_base::out** mode and the **seekg()** function in **ios_base::in** mode. It takes two parameters: the number of characters to shift and from which file position it should count. There are allowed three types of positions to **seek**: **std::ios_base::beg**, that is, the beginning of file, **std::ios_base::end**, that is, the end of file, and **std::ios_base::cur**, that is, the current position. Here is an example of calling the **seekp()** function:

```
outFile.seekp(-5, std::ios_base::end);
```

As you can see, we ask to set the current file's position at the fifth character from the end of the file.

To write to the file, we can use the overloaded left shift operator, **<<**, for general formatted output, the **put()** function to write a single character, or the **write()** function to write a block of characters. Using the left shift operator is the most convenient way to write data to file as you can pass any built-in type as an argument:

```
outFile << "This is line No " << 1 << std::endl;
```

The **put()** and **write()** functions can only be used with character values.

To read from a file, we can use the overloaded right shift operator, **>>**, or use a set of functions for reading characters, such as **read()**, **get()**, and **getline()**. The right shift operator is overloaded for all built-in types and we can use it like this:

```
std::ifstream inFile(filename);

std::string str;

int num;

float floatNum;

// for data: "book 3 24.5"

inFile >> str >> num >> floatNum;
```

Finally, the file stream is closed when the execution leaves the scope of visibility, so we don't need to perform any additional actions to close the file.

> **Note**
>
> Be attentive while reading data from a file. The right shift operator, **>>**, only reads a string until a whitespace or newline character. To read the full string, you could use a loop or read each word in a separate variable, like we did in *Exercise 1, Overriding the Left Shift Operator ,<<, for User-Defined Types*.

Now, let's practice reading and writing data to a file using the C++ IO Standard Library.

## Exercise 2: Reading and Writing User-Defined Data Types to a File

In this exercise, we'll write a piece of code for a book shop. We need to store information about book prices in a file and then read that information from a file when needed. To implement this, we will create a class that represents a book with a name, author, year of publishing, and a price. Next, we will create an instance of this class and write it to a file. Later, we will read the information about the book from the file into the instance of the book class. Perform the following steps to complete this exercise:

1. Include the required headers: **<iostream>** for output to a console, **<string>** for string support, and **<fstream>** for I/O file library support:

   ```
   #include <fstream>
   #include <iostream>
   #include <string>
   ```

2. Implement the **Book** class, which represents the book in a book shop. In the private section, define four variables with self-explanatory names: **m_Name**, **m_Author**, **m_Year**, and **m_Price**. In the public section, define a constructor with parameters, which initializes all class members. Also, in the **public** section, define getters for all the class members:

   ```
   class Book
   {
   public:
           Book(const std::string& name,
                   const std::string& author,
                   const int year,
                   const float price)
           : m_Name(name)
           , m_Author(author)
           , m_Year(year)
           , m_Price(price) {}

           std::string getName() const { return m_Name; }
           std::string getAuthor() const { return m_Author; }
           int getYear() const { return m_Year; }
   ```

```
    float getPrice() const { return m_Price; }

private:
    std::string m_Name;
    std::string m_Author;
    int m_Year;
    float m_Price;
};
```

3. Enter the **main** function and declare the **pricesFile** variable, which holds the filename:

```
std::string pricesFile("prices.txt");
```

4. Next, create an instance of the **book** class and initialize it with **book name, author name, year**, and **price**:

```
Book book_001("Brave", "Olena Lizina", 2017, 33.57);
```

5. Write this class instance to a file. Create an instance of the **std::ofstream** class. Open our file with the **pricesFile** variable name. Check if the stream is successfully opened and print an error message if not:

```
std::ofstream outFile(pricesFile);
if (outFile.fail())
{
    std::cerr << "Failed to open file " << pricesFile << std::endl;
    return 1;
}
```

6. Then, write all the information about the **book_001** book to a file using getters with spaces between each item and a newline symbol at the end:

```
outFile << book_001.getName() << " "
        << book_001.getAuthor() << " "
        << book_001.getYear() << " "
        << book_001.getPrice() << std::endl;
```

7. Compile and execute the application. Now, go to the project folder and find where the '**prices.txt**' file is located. In the following screenshot, you can see the location of the created file in the project directory:

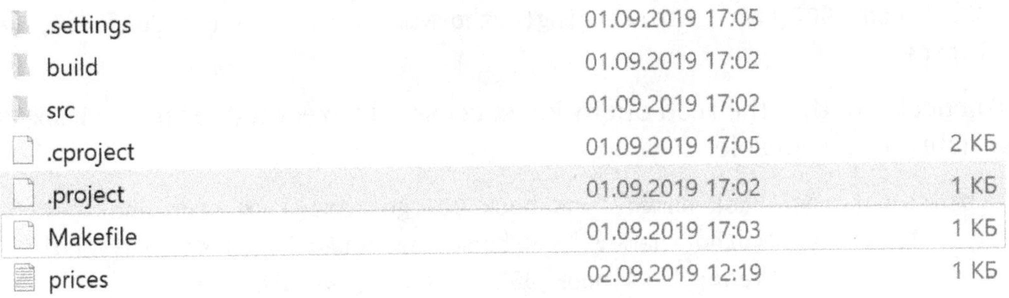

| | | |
|---|---|---|
| .settings | 01.09.2019 17:05 | |
| build | 01.09.2019 17:02 | |
| src | 01.09.2019 17:02 | |
| .cproject | 01.09.2019 17:05 | 2 КБ |
| .project | 01.09.2019 17:02 | 1 КБ |
| Makefile | 01.09.2019 17:03 | 1 КБ |
| prices | 02.09.2019 12:19 | 1 КБ |

**Figure 6.5: Location of the created file**

8. Open it in **Notepad**. In the following screenshot, you can see what the output to the file looks like:

```
prices.txt
1  Brave Olena Lizina 2017 33.57
2
```

**Figure 6.6: The result of the output of the user-defined type to the file**

9. Now, let's read this data to the variable. Create an instance of the **std::ifstream** class. Open the file called **pricesFile**. Check if the stream has been successfully opened and print an error message if not:

```
std::ifstream inFile(pricesFile);
if (inFile.fail())
{
    std::cerr << "Failed to open file " << pricesFile << std::endl;
    return 1;
}
```

10. Create the local variables that will be used for the input from a file, namely **name**, **authorName**, **authorSurname**, **year**, and **price**. Their names are self-explanatory:

```
std::string name;
std::string authorName;
std::string authorSurname;
int year;
float price;
```

11. Now, read the data from the file into variables in the order they are in the file:

```
inFile >> name >> authorName >> authorSurname >> year >> price;
```

12. Create a **Book** instance called **book_002** and initialize it with those read values:

```
Book book_002(name, std::string(authorName + " " + authorSurname), year,
price);
```

13. To check whether the read operation successfully executed, print the **book_002** variable to the console:

```
std::cout  << "Book name: " << book_002.getName() << std::endl
           << "Author name: " << book_002.getAuthor() << std::endl
           << "Year: " << book_002.getYear() << std::endl
           << "Price: " << book_002.getPrice() << std::endl;
```

14. Compile and execute the application again. In the console, you will see the following output:

```
 Problems   Tasks   Console     Properties
<terminated> (exit value: 0) Exercise 1 Debug [C/C++ Application] C:\Users\elena\Desktop\Chapter6\Debug\Exercise 1.exe (02.09.19, 13:17)
Book name: Brave
Author name: Olena Lizina
Year: 2017
Price: 33.57
```

**Figure 6.7: The result of executing Exercise 2**

As you can see, we wrote and read custom formatted data from a file without any difficulties. We created our own custom type, wrote it to the file using the **std::ofstream** class, and checked that everything was wrote successfully. Then, we read those data from a file to our custom variable using the **std::ifstream** class, output it to the console, and ensured that everything was read correctly. By doing this, we learned how to read and write data to a file using the I/O Standard Library. Now, let's move on and learn about the in-memory portion of the I/O library.

## String I/O Implementation

The I/O Standard Library allows input and output – not only to devices such as files but also to memory, in particular, to the **std::string** objects. In this case, the string can be a source for input operations as well as a sink for output operations. In the **<sstream>** header file, stream classes are declared that manage input and output to strings. They, like the file streams, also provides an interface that implements RAII – the string opens for reading or writing upon the stream's creation and closes on its destruction. They are represented in the Standard Library by the following classes: **basic_stringbuf**, which implements a raw string interface, **basic_istringstream** for input operations, **basic_ostringstream** for output operations, and **basic_stringstream** for both input and output operations. The Standard Library also provides typedefs for **char** and **wchar_t** types: **istringstream**, **ostringstream**, and **stringstream** and the same names with the "w" prefix for wide characters.

To create an object of the **std::istringstream** class, we should pass the initializer string as a constructor parameter or set it later using the **str()** function:

```
std::string track("ABBA 1967 Vule");

std::istringstream iss(track);
```

Alternatively, we can do the following:

```
std::string track("ABBA 1967 Vule");

std::istringstream iss;

iss.str(track);
```

Next, to read values from the stream, use the right shift operator, **>>**, which is overloaded for all built-in types:

```
std::string group;

std::string name;

int year;


iss >> group >> year >> name;
```

To create an object of the **std::ostringstream** class, we just declare a variable of its type:

```
std::ostringstream oss;
```

Next, to write data to the string, use the left shift operator, <<, which is overloaded for all built-in types:

```
std::string group("ABBA");

std::string name("Vule");

int year = 1967;


oss << group << std::endl
     << name << std::endl
     << year << std::endl;
```

To get the resulting string, use the **str()** function:

```
std::cout << oss.str();
```

The **std::stringstream** object works bidirectional, so it has both a default constructor and a constructor that takes the string. We can create the default **std::stringstream** object by declaring the variable of this type and then use it for reading and writing:

```
std::stringstream ss;

ss << "45";

int count;

ss >> count;
```

Also, we can create **std::stringstream** using the constructor with a string parameter. Then, we can use it for reading and writing as usual:

```
std::string employee("Alex Ismailow 26");

std::stringstream ss(employee);
```

Alternatively, we can create a default **std::stringstream** object and initialize it by setting a string using the **str()** function:

```
std::string employee("Charlz Buttler 26");

std::stringstream ss;

ss.str(employee);
```

Next, we can use the ss object for reading and writing:

```
std::string name;

std::string surname;

int age;


ss >> name >> surname >> age;
```

We can also apply open modes for these kinds of streams. Their functionality is similar to that of file streams but with a little difference. **ios_base::binary** is irrelevant in the case of working with string streams and **ios_base::trunc** is ignored. Thus, we can open any of the string streams in four modes: **ios_base::app**, **ios_base::ate**, and **ios_base::in/ios_base::out**.

Now, let's practice reading and writing data to a string using the C++ IO Standard Library.

### Exercise 3: Creating a Function for Replacement Words in a String

In this exercise, we will implement a function that parses the given string and replaces the given word by other words. To complete this exercise, we create a callable class that takes three parameters: the original string, the word to be replaced, and the word that will be used for replacing. As a result, the new string should be returned. Perform the following steps to complete this exercise:

1.  Include the required headers: **<iostream>** for the output to a Terminal and **<sstream>** for I/O string support:

    ```
    #include <sstream>
    #include <iostream>
    ```

2.  Implement the callable class with the name **Replacer**. It has only one function – an overloaded parentheses operator, (), that returns a string and takes three parameters: the original string, the word to be replaced, and the word to be used for replacing. The function declaration looks as follows:

    ```
    std::string operator()(const std::string& originalString,
                           const std::string& wordToBeReplaced,
                           const std::string& wordReplaceBy);
    ```

3.  Next, create the **istringstream** object, that is, **iss**, and set the **originalString** variable as the source of input:

    ```
    std::istringstream iss(originalString);
    ```

4. Create the **ostringstream** object, that is, **oss**, that will hold the converted string:

```
std::ostringstream oss;
```

5. Then, in the loop, while there is possible input, perform a read of the word to the word variable. Check if this word is equal to the **wordToBeReplaced** variable. If so, replace it with the **wordReplaceBy** variable and write to the **oss** stream. If they are unequal, write the original word to the **oss** stream. After each word, add a whitespace character since the **iss** stream truncates them. Finally, return the result. The complete class is as follows:

```cpp
class Replacer
{
public:
    std::string operator()(const std::string& originalString,
                           const std::string& wordToBeReplaced,
                           const std::string& wordReplaceBy)
    {
        std::istringstream iss(originalString);
        std::ostringstream oss;

        std::string word;
        while (iss >> word)
        {
            if (0 == word.compare(wordToBeReplaced))
            {
                oss << wordReplaceBy << " ";
            }
            else
            {
                oss << word << " ";
            }
        }

        return oss.str();
    }
};
```

6. Enter the **main** function. Create an instance of the **Replacer** class with a name of worker. Define the **foodList** variable and initialize it by the string that contains a list of food; some items should be repeated. Define the **changedList** string variable and initialize it by the return value of the **worker()** function. Use **std::cout** to display the result in the Terminal:

```
int main()
{
        Replacer worker;

        std::string foodList("coffee tomatoes coffee cucumbers sugar");
        std::string changedList(worker(foodList, "coffee", "chocolate"));

        std::cout << changedList;
        return 0;
}
```

7. Compile, build, and run the exercise. As a result, you will get the following output:

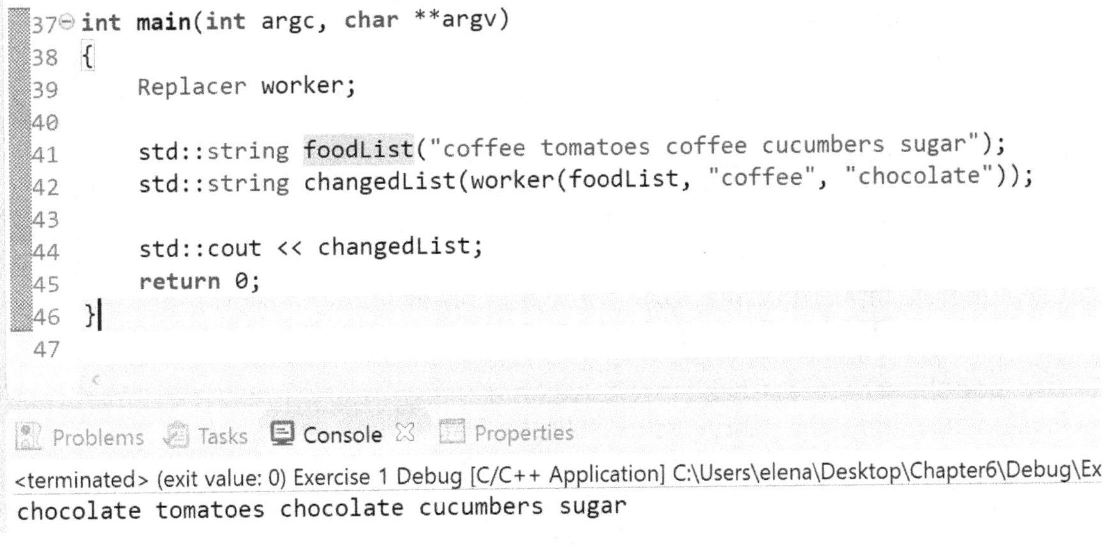

```
37⊖ int main(int argc, char **argv)
38  {
39         Replacer worker;
40
41         std::string foodList("coffee tomatoes coffee cucumbers sugar");
42         std::string changedList(worker(foodList, "coffee", "chocolate"));
43
44         std::cout << changedList;
45         return 0;
46  }
47
```

Problems   Tasks   Console ⊠   Properties

&lt;terminated&gt; (exit value: 0) Exercise 1 Debug [C/C++ Application] C:\Users\elena\Desktop\Chapter6\Debug\Ex
chocolate tomatoes chocolate cucumbers sugar

Figure 6.8: The result of executing Exercise 3

Well done! Here, we learned how to use string streams for formatting input and output. We created an application that easily replaces words in a sentence, strengthened our knowledge, and now we are ready to learn about I/O manipulators so that we can improve our skills regarding working with threads.

## I/O Manipulators

So far, we've learned about simple input and output using streams, but they are not sufficient in many cases. For more complex I/O data formatting, the Standard Library has a big set of I/O manipulators. They are functions that have been developed to work with shift operators, both left (<<) and right (>>), to control how streams behave. I/O manipulators are divided into two types – those that are invoked without arguments and those that needs arguments. Some of them work both for input and output. Let's briefly consider their meaning and usage.

## I/O Manipulators for Changing the Numeric Base of the Stream

In the **<ios>** header, there are declared functions for changing the numeric base of the stream: **std::dec**, **std::hex**, and **std::oct**. They are invoked without arguments and set the numeric base of the stream to decimal, hexadecimal, and octal, respectively. In the **<iomanip>** header, the **std::setbase** function is declared, which is invoked with the following arguments: 8, 10, and 16. They are interchangeable and work for both input and output operations.

In the **<ios>** header, there is also the **std::showbase** and **std::noshowbase** functions, which control displaying the numeric base of the stream. They only affect hexadecimal and octal integer output, except the zero value, and monetary input and output operations. Let's complete an exercise and learn how to use them in practice.

## Exercise 4: Displaying Entered Numbers in Different Numeric Bases

In this exercise, we will develop an application that, in the infinite loop, asks the user to enter an integer in one of the following numeric bases: decimal, hexadecimal, or octal. After reading the input, it displays this integer in other numeric representations. To perform this exercise, complete the following steps:

1. Include the **<iostream>** header for streaming support. Declare the enumeration called **BASE** and define three values: **DECIMAL**, **OCTAL**, and **HEXADECIMAL**:

```
#include <iostream>

enum BASE
{
        DECIMAL,
        OCTAL,
        HEXADECIMAL
};
```

2. Declare a function called **displayInBases** that takes two parameters – integer and base. Next, define the switch statement, which tests the received numeric base and displays the given integer in the other two numeric representations:

```cpp
void displayInBases(const int number, const BASE numberBase)
{
  switch(numberBase)
  {
  case DECIMAL:
    std::cout << "Your input in octal with base: "
          << std::showbase << std::oct << number
          << ", without base: "
          << std::noshowbase << std::oct << number << std::endl;
    std::cout << "Your input in hexadecimal with base: "
          << std::showbase << std::hex << number
          << ", without base: "
          << std::noshowbase << std::hex << number << std::endl;
    break;
  case OCTAL:
    std::cout << "Your input in hexadecimal with base: "
          << std::showbase << std::hex << number
          << ", without base: "
          << std::noshowbase << std::hex << number << std::endl;
    std::cout << "Your input in decimal with base: "
          << std::showbase << std::dec << number
          << ", without base: "
          << std::noshowbase << std::dec << number << std::endl;
    break;
  case HEXADECIMAL:
    std::cout << "Your input in octal with base: "
          << std::showbase << std::oct << number
          << ", without base: "
          << std::noshowbase << std::oct << number << std::endl;
    std::cout << "Your input in decimal with base: "
          << std::showbase << std::dec << number
          << ", without base: "
          << std::noshowbase << std::dec << number << std::endl;
    break;
  }
}
```

3. Enter the **main** function and define the integer variable that will be used for reading user input:

```
int integer;
```

4. Create an infinite while loop. Inside the loop, ask the user to enter a decimal value. Read the input as a decimal integer. Pass it to the **displayInBases** function. Next, ask the user to enter a hexadecimal value. Read the input as a hexadecimal integer. Pass it to the **displayInBases** function. Finally, ask the user to enter an octal value. Read the input as an octal integer. Pass it to the **displayInBases** function:

```
int main(int argc, char **argv)
{
  int integer;

  while(true)
  {
    std::cout << "Enter the decimal value: ";
    std::cin >> std::dec >> integer;
    displayInBases(integer, BASE::DECIMAL);

    std::cout << "Enter the hexadecimal value: ";
    std::cin >> std::hex >> integer;
    displayInBases(integer, BASE::HEXADECIMAL);

    std::cout << "Enter the octal value: ";
    std::cin >> std::oct >> integer;
    displayInBases(integer, BASE::OCTAL);
  }

  return 0;
}
```

5. Build and run the application. Follow the output and enter, for example, 12 in different numeric representations. The output should be as follows:

```
Problems    Tasks    Console ☒    Properties

Exercise 1 Debug [C/C++ Application] C:\Users\elena\Desktop\Chapter6\Debug\Exercise 1.exe (03.09.19, 17:08)
Enter the decimal value: 12
Your input in octal with base: 014, without base: 14
Your input in hexadecimal with base: 0xc, without base: c
Enter the hexadecimal value: 0xc
Your input in octal with base: 014, without base: 14
Your input in decimal with base: 12, without base: 12
Enter the octal value: 14
Your input in hexadecimal with base: 0xc, without base: c
Your input in decimal with base: 12, without base: 12
Enter the decimal value: |
```

Figure 6.9: The result of executing Exercise 4, part 1

6. Now, let's change **std::dec**, **std::oct**, and **std::hex** in the **std::setbase()** function to check whether the output will be the same. First, add the **<iomanip>** header for **std::setbase()** support. Next, in the main function in the loop, replace **std::dec** with **std::setbase(10)**, **std::hex** with **std::setbase(16)**, and **std::oct** with **std::setbase(8)**:

```cpp
int main(int argc, char **argv)
{
  int integer;

  while(true)
  {
    std::cout << "Enter the decimal value: ";
    std::cin >> std::setbase(10) >> integer;
    displayInBases(integer, BASE::DECIMAL);

    std::cout << "Enter the hexadecimal value: ";
    std::cin >> std::setbase(16) >> integer;
    displayInBases(integer, BASE::HEXADECIMAL);

    std::cout << "Enter the octal value: ";
    std::cin >> std::setbase(8) >> integer;
    displayInBases(integer, BASE::OCTAL);
  }

  return 0;
}
```

7. Again, build and run the application. Follow the output and enter the same integer (12) in different numeric representations. The output should be as follows:

```
 Problems    Tasks    Console    Properties
Exercise 1 Debug [C/C++ Application] C:\Users\elena\Desktop\Chapter6\Debug\Exercise 1.ex
Enter the decimal value: 12
Your input in octal with base: 014, without base: 14
Your input in hexadecimal with base: 0xc, without base: c
Enter the hexadecimal value: 0xc
Your input in octal with base: 014, without base: 14
Your input in decimal with base: 12, without base: 12
Enter the octal value: 14
Your input in hexadecimal with base: 0xc, without base: c
Your input in decimal with base: 12, without base: 12
Enter the decimal value:
```

Figure 6.10: The result of executing Exercise 4, part 2

Now, compare the results. As you can see, the output is identical. By doing this, we made sure that these functions are interchangeable.

## I/O Manipulators for Floating-Point Formatting

In the **<ios>** header, there are declared functions for changing floating-point digit formatting: **std::fixed**, **std::scientific**, **std::hexfloat**, and **std::defaultfloat**. They are invoked without arguments and set **floatfield** to fixed, scientific, fixed and scientific, and default values, respectively. There is also the **std:: showpoint** and **std::noshowpoint** functions, which control displaying floating-point digits. They only affect the output. The **std::noshowpoint** function only affects floating-point digits without the fractional part.

In the **<iomanip>** header, there is a declared **std:: setprecision** function that is invoked with a number that represents precision. When the digits to the right of the point are dropped, the result is rounded off. If the number is too big to be represented in the normal way, the precision specification is ignored, and the number is displayed in a more convenient way. You only need to set precision once and change it only when you need another precision. When you choose a data type to store a floating-point variable, you should notice some tricks. In C++, there are three data types that can represent floating-point values: float, double, and long double.

The float is usually 4 bytes, double is 8 bytes, and long double is 8, 12, or 16 bytes. So, the precision of each of those is limited. The float type can accommodate a maximum of 6-9 significant digits, the double type can accommodate a maximum of 15-18 significant digits, and the long double type can accommodate a maximum of 33-36 significant digits. Take a look at the following table if you wish to compare the difference between them:

| Type | Size in memory | Number of significant digits |
|---|---|---|
| float | 4 bytes | 6-9 |
| double | 8 bytes | 15-18 |
| long double | 8, 12, 16 bytes | 33-36 |

Figure 6.11: Comparison table of the floating-point types

Note

When you need precision for more than six significant digits, favor double, otherwise you will get unexpected results.

Let's complete an exercise and learn how to use them in practice.

### Exercise 5: Displaying Entered Floating-Point Numbers with Different Formatting

In this exercise, we will write an application that, in the infinite loop, asks the user to enter a floating-point number. After reading the input, it displays this number with different formatting types. To perform this exercise, complete the following steps:

1.  Include the **<iostream>** header for streaming support and **<iomanip>** for **std::setprecision** support:

    ```
    #include <iostream>
    #include <iomanip>
    ```

2. Next, declare a template **formattingPrint** function that has a template parameter called **FloatingPoint** and takes a parameter variable of this type. Next, store the previous precision in an auto variable by calling the **precision()** function in the **std::cout** object. Then, display the given number in different formats in the Terminal: with the point, without a point, and in the fixed, scientific, hexfloat, and defaultfloat formats. Next, in the for loop, from 0 to 22, display the given number with precision and the size of the loop counter. After the loop exits, set the precision back using the value we stored earlier:

```cpp
template< typename FloatingPoint >
void formattingPrint(const FloatingPoint number)
{
    auto precision = std::cout.precision();
    std::cout << "Default formatting with point: "
              << std::showpoint << number << std::endl
              << "Default formatting without point: "
              << std::noshowpoint << number << std::endl
              << "Fixed formatting: "
              << std::fixed << number << std::endl
              << "Scientific formatting: "
              << std::scientific << number << std::endl
              << "Hexfloat formatting: "
              << std::hexfloat << number << std::endl
              << "Defaultfloat formatting: "
              << std::defaultfloat << number << std::endl;

    for (int i = 0; i < 22; i++)
    {
        std::cout << "Precision: " << i
                  << ", number: " << std::setprecision(i)
                  << number << std::endl;
    }
    std::cout << std::setprecision(precision);
}
```

3. Enter the **main** function. Declare a **float** variable called **floatNum**, a double variable called **doubleNum**, and a long double variable called **longDoubleNum**. Then, in the infinite while loop, ask the user to input a floating-point number, read the input to **longDoubleNum**, and pass it to the **formattingPrint** function. Next, initialize **doubleNum** by using the **longDoubleNum** value and pass it to the **formattingPrint** function. Next, initialize **floatNum** by using the **longDoubleNum** value and pass it to the **formattingPrint** function:

```cpp
int main(int argc, char **argv)
{
    float floatNum;
    double doubleNum;
    long double longDoubleNum;

    while(true)
    {
        std::cout << "Enter the floating-point digit: ";
        std::cin >> std::setprecision(36) >> longDoubleNum;

        std::cout << "long double output" << std::endl;
        formattingPrint(longDoubleNum);

        doubleNum = longDoubleNum;

        std::cout << "double output" << std::endl;
        formattingPrint(doubleNum);

        floatNum = longDoubleNum;

        std::cout << "float output" << std::endl;
        formattingPrint(floatNum);
    }

    return 0;
}
```

4. Build and run the application. Follow the output and enter the floating-point value with **22** significant digits, for example, **0.2222222222222222222222**. We will get a long output. Now, we need to split it for analysis. Here is a screenshot of part of the long double value's output:

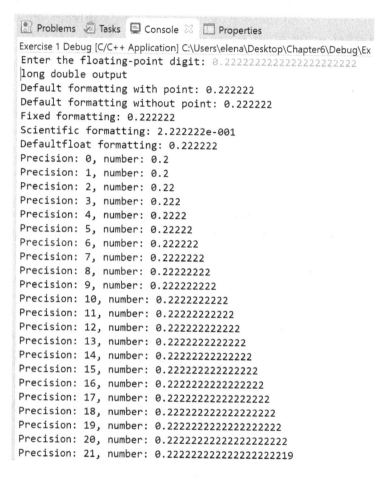

Figure 6.12: The result of executing Exercise 5, part 1

We can see that, with the default, the fixed and **defaultfloat** formations only output six significant digits. With scientific formatting, the output of the value looks as expected. When we call **setprecision(0)** or **setprecision(1)**, we expect that no one digit will be outputted after the point. But with numbers less than 1 setprecision, this will leave one digit after the point. By doing this, we will see the correct output until 21 precision. This means that on our system, the maximum precision for a long double is 20 significant digits. Now, let's analyze the output for the double value:

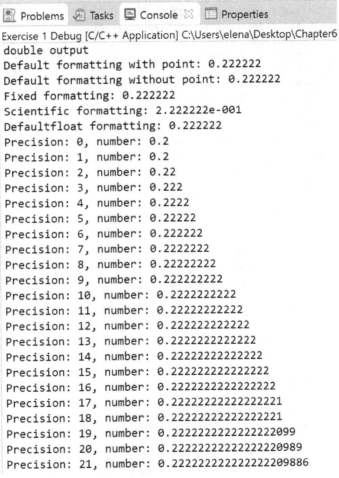

Figure 6.13: The result of executing Exercise 5, part 2

Here, we can see the same results for formatting, but different for precision. The inaccurate output starts from precision 17. This means that, on our system, the maximum precision for double is 16 significant digits. Now, let's analyze the output for float value:

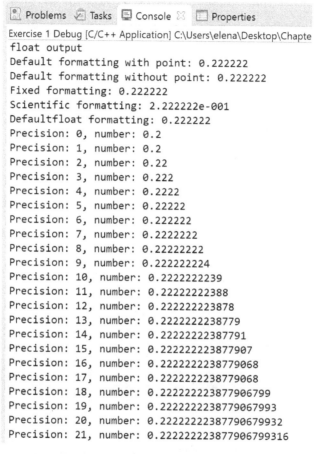

**Figure 6.14: The result of executing Exercise 5, part 3**

Here, we can see the same results for formatting, but different ones for precision. The inaccurate output starts from precision 8. This means that, on our system, the maximum precision for the float is 8 significant digits. The results on different systems should be different. An analysis of them will help you choose the correct data type for your applications.

> **Note**
>
> Never use the float data type for representing money or exchange rates; you may get the wrong result.

## I/O Manipulators for Boolean Formatting

In the **<ios>** header, there are declared functions for changing boolean formatting: **std::boolalpha** and **std::noboolalpha**. They are invoked without arguments and allow us to display boolean values in textual or digital ways, respectively. They are used for both input and output operations. Let's consider an example of using these I/O manipulators for output operations. We will display the Boolean both as text and as a digit:

```
std::cout << "Default formatting of bool variables: "
        << "true: " << true
        << ", false: " << false << std::endl;


std::cout << "Formatting of bool variables with boolalpha flag is set: "
        << std::boolalpha
        << "true: " << true
        << ", false: " << false << std::endl;


std::cout << "Formatting of bool variables with noboolalpha flag is set: "
        << std::noboolalpha
        << "true: " << true
        << ", false: " << false << std::endl;
```

After compiling and running this example, you will get the following output:

```
Default formatting of bool variables: true: 1, false: 0
Formatting of bool variables with boolalpha flag is set: true: true, false:
false
Formatting of bool variables with noboolalpha flag is set: true: 1, false: 0
```

As you can see, the default formatting of bool variables is performed with the `std::noboolalpha` flag. To use these functions in input operations, we need to have a source string that contains true/false words or 0/1 symbols. The `std::boolalpha` and `std::noboolalpha` function calls in the input operation are as follows:

```
bool trueValue, falseValue;


std::istringstream iss("false true");

iss >> std::boolalpha >> falseValue >> trueValue;

std::istringstream iss("0 1");

iss >> std::noboolalpha >> falseValue >> trueValue;
```

If you then output these variables, you will see that they were initialized correctly by reading boolean values.

## I/O Manipulators for Field Width and Fill Control

In the Standard Library, there are also functions for manipulating by the width of the outputted field, which characters should be used in the case when the width is more than the output data, and in which place these filling characters should be inserted. These functions will be useful when you want to align your output to the left or right position or when you want to replace spaces with some other symbols. For example, let's say you need to print prices in two columns. If you use standard formatting, you will get the following output:

```
2.33 3.45

2.2 4.55

3.67 3.02
```

This doesn't look very good and it's hard to read. If we apply the formatting, the output will be as follows:

```
2.33    3.45

2.2     4.55

3.67    3.02
```

This looks better. Again, you may want to check which characters are being used to fill in empty spaces and which are actually spaces that you inserted between digits. Let's set the filling character to "*", for example. You will get the following output:

```
2.33* 3.45*

2.2** 4.55*

3.67* 3.02*
```

Now, you can see that the blank space is filled with stars. Now that we've considered where it can be useful to format width and fill with output, let's consider how we can do that with I/O manipulators. The **std::setw** and **std::setfill** functions are declared in the **<iomanip>** header. **std::setw** takes an integer value as a parameter and sets the width of the stream to exact n characters. There are a few cases where the width will be set to 0. They are as follows:

- When the shift operator is called with **std::string** or **char**
- When the **std::put_money()** function is called
- When the **std::quoted()** function is called

In the **<ios>** header, there are declared functions for changing the place where filling characters should be inserted: **std::internal**, **std::left**, and **std::right**. They are only used for output operations and only affect integer, floating-point, and monetary values.

Now, let's consider an example of using all of them together. Let's output positive, negative, floating-point, and hexadecimal values with a  width of 10 and replace the filling character with "#":

```cpp
std::cout << "Internal fill: " << std::endl
         << std::setfill('#')
         << std::internal
         << std::setw(10) << -2.38 << std::endl
         << std::setw(10) << 2.38 << std::endl
         << std::setw(10) << std::hex << std::showbase << 0x4b << std::endl;


std::cout << "Left fill: " << std::endl
         << std::left
         << std::setw(10) << -2.38 << std::endl
         << std::setw(10) << 2.38 << std::endl
```

```
            << std::setw(10) << std::hex << std::showbase << 0x4b << std::endl;


    std::cout << "Right fill: " << std::endl
            << std::right
            << std::setw(10) << -2.38 << std::endl
            << std::setw(10) << 2.38 << std::endl
            << std::setw(10) << std::hex << std::showbase << 0x4b << std::endl;
```

After building and running this example, you will get the following output:

```
Internal fill:
-#####2.38
######2.38
0x######4b


Left fill:
-2.38#####
2.38######
0x4b######


Right fill:
#####-2.38
######2.38
######0x4b
```

## I/O Manipulators for Other Numeric Formatting

If you need to output a positive numeric value with a "+" sign, you can use another I/O manipulator from the **<ios>** header – the **std::showpos** function. The opposite of meaning manipulator also exists – the **std::noshowpos** function. They both have an effect on the output. Their use is very easy. Let's consider the following example:

```
std::cout << "Default formatting: " << 13 << " " << 0 << std::endl;
std::cout << "showpos flag is set: " << std::showpos << 13 << " " << 0 <<
std::endl;
std::cout << "noshowpos flag is set: " << std::noshowpos << 13 << " " << 0 <<
std::endl;
```

Here, we made the output with default formatting, then with the **std::showpos** flag, and finally with the **std::noshowpos** flag. If you build and run this small example, you will see that, by default, the **std::noshowpos** flag is set. Look at the result of execution:

```
Default formatting: 13 0

showpos flag is set: +13 +0

noshowpos flag is set: 13 0
```

You will also want to output uppercase characters for floating-point or hexadecimal digits so that you can use functions from the **<ios>** header: **std::uppercase** and **std::nouppercase**. They only work on the output. Let's consider a small example:

```
std::cout << "12345.0 in uppercase with precision 4: "
          << std::setprecision(4) << std::uppercase << 12345.0 << std::endl;

std::cout << "12345.0 in no uppercase with precision 4: "
          << std::setprecision(4) << std::nouppercase << 12345.0 <<
std::endl;


std::cout << "0x2a in uppercase: "
          << std::hex << std::showbase << std::uppercase << 0x2a <<
std::endl;

std::cout << "0x2a in nouppercase: "
          << std::hex << std::showbase << std::nouppercase << 0x2a <<
std::endl;
```

Here, we output floating-point and hexadecimal digits with and without the **std::uppercase** flag. By default, the **std::nouppercase** flag is set. Look at the result of execution:

```
12345.0 in uppercase with precision 4: 1.234E+004

12345.0 in no uppercase with precision 4: 1.234e+004

0x2a in uppercase: 0X2A

0x2a in nouppercase: 0x2a
```

## I/O Manipulators for Whitespace Processing

In the Standard Library, there are functions for processing whitespaces. The **std::ws** function from the **<istream>** header only works with input streams and discards leading whitespaces. The **std::skipws** and **std::noskipws** functions from the **<ios>** header are used to control reading and writing leading whitespaces. They work for both input and output streams. When the **std::skipws** flag is set, the stream ignores whitespaces in front of the input of the character sequence. By default, the **std::skipws** flag is set. Let's consider an example of using these I/O manipulators. First, we will read the input with default formatting and output what we have read. Next, we will clear our strings and read data with the **std::noskipws** flag:

```
std::string name;
std::string surname;


std::istringstream("Peppy Ping") >> name >> surname;
std::cout << "Your name: " << name << ", your surname: " << surname <<
std::endl;


name.clear();
surname.clear();


std::istringstream("Peppy Ping") >> std::noskipws >> name >> surname;
std::cout << "Your name: " << name << ", your surname: " << surname <<
std::endl;
```

After building and running this example, we will get the following output:

```
Your name: Peppy, your surname: Ping
Your name: Peppy, your surname:
```

As you can see from the preceding output, if we set the **std::noskipws** flag, we will read whitespaces as well.

In the **<iomanip>** header, an unusual manipulator for this header has been declared: **std::quoted**. When this function is applied to the input, it wraps a given string in quotes with escaping characters. If the input string already contains escaped quotes, it reads them as well. In order to understand this, let's consider a small example. We will initialize a source string with some text without quotes and another string will initialize with text with escaped quotes. Next, we will read them by using **std::ostringstream** without a flag is set and provide the output via **std::cout**. Take a look at the following example:

```cpp
std::string str1("String without quotes");
std::string str2("String with quotes \"right here\"");

std::ostringstream ss;
ss << str1;
std::cout << "[" << ss.str() << "]" << std::endl;
ss.str("");

ss << str2;
std::cout << "[" << ss.str() << "]" << std::endl;
```

As a result, we will get the following output:

```
[String without quotes]
[String with quotes "right here"]
```

Now, let's do the same output but with **std::quoted** call:

```cpp
std::string str1("String without quotes");
std::string str2("String with quotes \"right here\"");

std::ostringstream ss;
ss << std::quoted(str1);
std::cout << "[" << ss.str() << "]" << std::endl;
ss.str("");

ss << std::quoted(str2);
std::cout << "[" << ss.str() << "]" << std::endl;
```

Now, we will have a different result:

```
["String without quotes"]
["String with quotes \"right here\""]
```

Did you notice that the first string is wrapped by quotes and that the substring "right here" from the second string is stored with escape characters?

Now, you know how to wrap any string in the quotes. You can even write your own wrapper to decrease the number of lines when you use **std::quoted()**. For example, we moved the work with the stream to a separate function:

```
std::string quote(const std::string& str)

{

        std::ostringstream oss;

        oss << std::quoted(str);

        return oss.str();

}
```

Then, we do the following when we need we call our wrapper:

```
std::string str1("String without quotes");

std::string str2("String with quotes \"right here\"");


std::coot << "[" << quote(str1) << "]" << std::endl;

std::cout << "[" << quote(str2) << "]" << std::endl;
```

Now, it looks much better. The first topic has come to an end, so let's revise what we have just learned. In practice, we learned about the usage of predefined stream objects, I/O operations with files with inner memory, I/O formatting, and the I/O of user-defined types. Now that we have a complete understanding of how to work with the I/O library in C++, we will consider what to do when the standard stream is not enough.

## Making Additional Streams

When the provided interface of streams is not enough for resolving your task, you may want to create an additional stream that will reuse one of the existing interfaces. You may need to output or provide input from a specific external device, or you may need to add the Id of the thread that invoked the I/O operation. There are a few ways to do that. You may create a new class that will aggregate one of the existing streams as a private member. It will implement all the needed functions, such as shift operators, through already existing stream functions. Another way to do this is to inherit one of the existing classes and override all the virtual functions in a way you need them.

First of all, you have to choose the appropriate class to be used. Your choice should depend on which modification you want to add. Choose `std::basic_istream`, `std::basic_ostream`, and `std::basic_iostream` if you need to modify input or output operations. Choose `std::ios_base` if you want to modify the state information, control information, private storage, and so on. Choose `std::basic_ios` if you want to modify something related to the stream buffer. After you choose the correct base class, inherit one of the aforementioned classes to create an additional stream.

There's one more thing you have to know – how to initialize correctly standard streams. In terms of the initialization of a file or string stream and basic stream classes, there are some big differences. Let's review them. To initialize the object of class that is derived from the file stream class, you need to pass the file name. To initialize the object of the class that is derived from the string stream class, you need to call the default constructor. Both of them have their own stream buffers, so they don't need additional manipulation on initialization. To initialize the object of the class that is derived from the basic stream class, you need to pass a pointer to a stream buffer. You can create a variable of the buffer or you may use the buffer of the predefined stream objects, such as `std::cout` or `std::cerr`.

Let's review these two methods of creating additional streams in detail.

## How to Make an Additional Stream – Composition

Composition means that you declare some of the standard stream objects in the private section of your class as a class member. When you choose an appropriate standard stream class, go to its header and notice which constructor it has. Then, you need to correctly initialize this member in the constructor of your class. To use your class as a stream object, you need to implement basic functions such as the shift operator, `str()`, and so on. As you may remember, every stream class has overloaded shift operators for built-in types. They also have overloaded shift operators for predefined functions such as `std::endl`. You need to be able to use your class as a real stream object. Instead of declaring all 18 overloaded shift operators, we just need to create one template. Also, to allow for the use of predefined manipulators, we must declare a shift operator that takes a pointer to a function.

This doesn't look very hard, so let's try to implement such a "wrapper" for the `std::ostream` object.

## Exercise 6: Composing the Standard Stream Object in the User-Defined Class

In this exercise, we will create own stream object that wraps the **std::ostream** object and adds additional features. We will create a class called **extendedOstream** that will output data to the Terminal and insert the following data in front of each piece of output: date and time and thread ID. To complete this exercise, perform the following steps:

1. Include the required headers: **<iostream>** for **std::endl** support, **<sstream>** for **std::ostream** support, **<thread>** for **std::this_thread::get_id()** support, **<chrono>** for **std::chrono::system_clock::now()**, and **<ctime>** for converting timestamps into readable representations:

> **Note**
>
> Don't forget to add the **pthread** linker flag to the Eclipse project settings for threading support: **Project** -> **Properties** -> **C/C++ Build** -> **Settings** -> **G++ Linker** -> **Miscellaneous** -> **Linker flags** enter '-pthread'. This path is valid for Eclipse Version: 3.8.1; it may vary for different versions.

```
#include <iostream>
#include <sstream>
#include <thread>
#include <chrono>
#include <ctime>
```

2. Next, declare the **extendedOstream** class. Declare the **std::ostream** variable called **m_oss** and the bool variable called **writeAdditionalInfo**. This bool variable will be used to indicate whether extended data should be printed or not:

```
class extendedOstream
{
private:
        std::ostream& m_oss;
        bool writeAdditionalInfo;
};
```

3. Next, in the public section, define a default constructor and initialize **m_oss** with `std::cout` to redirect output to the Terminal. Initialize **writeAdditionalInfo** with **true**:

```
extendedOstream()
      : m_oss(std::cout)
      , writeAdditionalInfo(true)
{
}
```

4. Define a template overloaded left shift operator, **<<**, that returns a reference to **extendedOstream** and takes a template parameter called value. Then, if **writeAdditionalInfo** is **true**, output the time, thread ID, and the given value, and then set **writeAdditionalInfo** to **false**. If **writeAdditionalInfo** is **false**, output only the given value. This function will be used for the output of all built-in types:

```
template<typename T>
extendedOstream& operator<<(const T& value)
{
      if (writeAdditionalInfo)
      {
            std::string time = fTime();
            auto id = threadId();
            m_oss << time << id << value;
            writeAdditionalInfo = false;
      }
      else
      {
            m_oss << value;
      }
      return *this;
}
```

5. Define another overloaded left shift operator that takes a pointer to the function as a parameter and returns the reference to **std::ostream**. In the function body, set **writeAdditionalInfo** to **true**, call the given function, and pass **m_oss** as an argument. This overloaded operator will be used for predefined functions such as **std::endl**:

```
extendedOstream&
operator<<(std::ostream& (*pfn)(std::ostream&))
{
    writeAdditionalInfo = true;
    pfn(m_oss);
    return *this;
}
```

6. In the private section, define the **fTime** function, which returns std::string. It gets a system time. Format it into a readable representation and return it:

```
std::string fTime()
{
    auto now = std::chrono::system_clock::now();
    std::time_t time = std::chrono::system_clock::to_time_t(now);
    std::ostringstream oss;
    std::string strTime(std::ctime(&time));
    strTime.pop_back();
    oss << "[" << strTime << "]";
    return oss.str();
}
```

7. In the private section, define the **threadId()** function, which returns a string. Get the **id** of the current thread, format it, and return it:

```
std::string threadId()
{
    auto id = std::this_thread::get_id();
    std::ostringstream oss;
    oss << "[" << std::dec << id << "]";
    return oss.str();
}
```

8.  Enter the **main** function. To test how our stream object works, create an object of the **extendedOstream** type called **oss**. Output different data, for example, integer, float, hexadecimal, and bool:

```
extendedOstream oss;
oss << "Integer: " << 156 << std::endl;
oss << "Float: " << 156.12 << std::endl;
oss << "Hexadecimal: " << std::hex << std::showbase
    << std::uppercase << 0x2a << std::endl;
oss << "Bool: " << std::boolalpha << false << std::endl;
```

9.  Then, create a thread, initialize it with a lambda function, and put the same output inside the lambda. Don't forget to join the thread:

```
std::thread thr1([]()
    {
        extendedOstream oss;
        oss << "Integer: " << 156 << std::endl;
        oss << "Float: " << 156.12 << std::endl;
        oss << "Hexadecimal: " << std::hex << std::showbase
            << std::uppercase << 0x2a << std::endl;
        oss << "Bool: " << std::boolalpha << false << std::endl;
    });
thr1.join();
```

10. Now, build and run the application. You will get the following output:

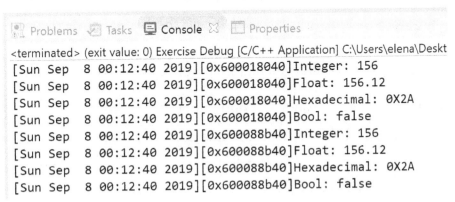

Figure 6.15: The result of executing Exercise 6

Consider each line of the output. You can see the next format of the output: "[date and time][thread ID]output data". Ensure that the thread ID differs from thread to thread. Then, the data was output in the expected format. So, as you can see, it's not too hard to implement your own I/O stream object using the composition of the standard stream.

## How to Make an Additional Stream – Inheritance

Inheritance means that you create your own stream class and inherit it from one of the standard stream objects that has a virtual destructor. Your class must be a template class and have template parameters, just like in the parent class. To use all your inherited functions with the object of your class, the inheritance should be public. In the constructor, you should initialize the parent class, depending on the class type – with the file name, with the stream buffer, or by default. Next, you should override those basic functions that you would change according to your requirements.

The most common case where we need to inherit standard stream classes is when we want to implement I/O operations for a new device, such as a socket or printer. All of the defined standard stream classes are responsible for formatting input and output and have overloads for strings, files, and the Terminal. Only the `std::basic_streambuf` class is responsible for work with devices, so we need to inherit this class, write our own implementation, and set it as a stream buffer for standard classes. The core functionality of **streambuf** classes is to transport characters. It can use buffers to store characters between flushing or can flush immediately after each call. These concepts are called buffered and unbuffered characters transport.

The buffered characters transport for output operations works as follows:

1. Characters are buffered into the internal buffer by the **sputc()** function call.

2. When the buffer is full, **sputc()** invokes the protected virtual member, that is, **overflow()**.

3. The **overflow()** function transfers all buffer content to the external device.

4. When the **pubsync()** function is called, it calls the protected virtual member known as **sync()**.

5. The **sync()** function transfers all buffer content to the external device.

The unbuffered characters transport for output operations works slightly differently:

1. Characters are passed to the **sputc()** function.

2. The **sputc()** function immediately calls the protected virtual member known as **overflow()**.

3. The **overflow()** function transfers all buffer content to the external device.

So, for buffered and unbuffered characters transport for output operations, we should override the **overflow()** and sync() functions, which do the actual work.

The buffered characters transport for input operations works as follows:

1. The **sgetc()** function reads the character from the internal buffer.

2. The **sgetc()** function invokes the **sungetc()** function, which makes the consumed character available again.

3. If the internal buffer is empty, the **sgetc()** function invokes the **underflow()** function.

4. The **underflow()** function reads characters from the external device to the internal buffer.

The **sgetc()** and **underflow()** functions always return the same character. To read different characters each time, we have another pair of functions: **sbumpc()** and **uflow()**. The algorithm of reading characters with them is the same:

1. The **sbumpc()** function reads the character from the internal buffer.

2. The **sbumpc()** function invokes the **sputbackc()** function, which makes the next character available for input.

3. If the internal buffer is empty, the **sbumpc()** function invokes the **uflow()** function.

4. The **uflow()** function reads characters from the external device to the internal buffer.

The unbuffered characters transport for input operations works as follows:

1. The **sgetc()** function invokes a protected virtual member known as **underflow()**.

2. The **underflow()** function reads characters from the external device to the internal buffer.

3. The **sbumpc()** function invokes a protected virtual member known as **uflow()**.

4. The **uflow()** function reads characters from the external device to the internal buffer.

In the case of any errors, the protected virtual member known as **pbackfail()** is invoked, which handles error situations. So, as you can see, to override the **std::basic_streambuf** class, we need to override the virtual members that work with external devices. For the input **streambuf**, we should override the **underflow()**, **uflow()**, and **pbackfail()** members. For the output **streambuf**, we should override the **overflow()** and **sync()** members.

Let's consider all of these steps in more detail.

## Exercise 7: Inheriting the Standard Stream Object

In this exercise, we will create a class called **extended_streambuf** that inherits from
**std::basic_streambuf**. We will use a buffer of the **std::cout** stream object and override
the overflow() function so that we can write data to an external device (**stdout**). Next,
we will write an **extended_ostream** class that inherits from the **std::basic_ostream** class
and set a stream buffer to **extended_streambuf**. Finally, we will make minor changes to
our wrapper class and use **extended_ostream** as a private stream member. To complete
this exercise, perform the following steps:

1.  Include the required headers: **<iostream>** for **std::endl** support, **<sstream>**
    for **std::ostream** and **std::basic_streambuf** support, **<thread>** for **std::this_
    thread::get_id()** support, **<chrono>** for **std::chrono::system_clock::now()**, and
    **<ctime>** for converting timestamps into a readable state.

2.  Create a template class called **extended_streambuf** that inherits from the
    **std::basic_streambuf** class. Override a public member called **overflow()** that
    writes a character to the output stream and returns the EOF or the written
    character:

    ```
    template< class CharT, class Traits = std::char_traits<CharT> >
    class extended_streambuf : public std::basic_streambuf< CharT, Traits >
    {
    public:
        int overflow( int c = EOF ) override
        {
            if (!Traits::eq_int_type(c, EOF))
            {
                return fputc(c, stdout);
            }
            return Traits::not_eof(c);
        }
    };
    ```

3.  Next, create a template class called **extended_ostream** that is derived from the **std::basic_ostream** class. In the private section, define a member of the **extended_streambuf** class, namely buffer. Initialize the **std::basic_ostream** parent class with a buffer member. Next, in the constructor body, invoke the **init()** function from the parent class with buffer as an argument. Also, overload the **rdbuf()** function, which returns a pointer to the buffer variable:

```
template< class CharT, class Traits = std::char_traits<CharT> >
class extended_ostream : public std::basic_ostream< CharT, Traits >
{
public:
    extended_ostream()
        : std::basic_ostream< CharT, Traits >::basic_ostream(&buffer)
        , buffer()
    {
        this->init(&buffer);
    }

    extended_streambuf< CharT, Traits >* rdbuf () const
    {
        return (extended_streambuf< CharT, Traits >*)&buffer;
    }

private:
    extended_streambuf< CharT, Traits > buffer;
};
```

4.  Rename an **extendedOstream** class to the logger to avoid misunderstandings with similar names. Leave the existing interface as is but replace the **std::ostream&** member with our own stream, that is, **object - extended_ostream**. The complete class looks as follows:

```
class logger
{
public:
    logger()
        : m_log()
        , writeAdditionalInfo(true)
    {
    }

    template<typename T>
    logger& operator<<(const T& value)
```

```
    {
        if (writeAdditionalInfo)
        {
            std::string time = fTime();
            auto id = threadId();
            m_log << time << id << value;
            writeAdditionalInfo = false;
        }
        else
        {
            m_log << value;
        }
        return *this;
    }

    logger&
    operator<<(std::ostream& (*pfn)(std::ostream&))
    {
        writeAdditionalInfo = true;
        pfn(m_log);
        return *this;
    }

private:
    std::string fTime()
    {
        auto now = std::chrono::system_clock::now();
        std::time_t time = std::chrono::system_clock::to_time_t(now);
        std::ostringstream log;
        std::string strTime(std::ctime(&time));
        strTime.pop_back();
        log << "[" << strTime << "]";
        return log.str();
    }

    std::string threadId()
    {
        auto id = std::this_thread::get_id();
        std::ostringstream log;
```

```
        log << "[" << std::dec << id << "]";
        return log.str();
    }

    private:
        extended_ostream<char> m_log;
        bool writeAdditionalInfo;
};
```

5. Enter the **main** function and change the **extendedOstream** object to the **logger** object. Leave the rest of the code as is. Now, build and run the exercise. You will see the output that was given in the previous exercise but in this case, we used our own stream buffer, our own stream object, and a wrapper class that adds additional information to the output. Look at the result of the execution that's shown in the following screenshot and compare it with the previous result. Make sure they are similar. If they are, that means we did a good job and our inherited classes work as expected:

Figure 6.16: The result of executing Exercise 7

In this topic, we have done a lot and learned how to create additional streams in different ways. We considered all the appropriate classes for inheritance and which class is better to use for different needs. We also learned how to inherit from basic streambuf classes to implement work with external devices. Now, we will learn how to use I/O streams in an asynchronous way.

## Leveraging Asynchronous I/O

There are a lot of cases where I/O operations can take a lot of time, for example, creating a backup file, searching a huge database, reading large files, and so on. You can use threads to execute I/O operations without blocking the application's execution. But for some applications, it's not a suitable way to handle long I/O, for example, when there can are thousands of I/O operations per second. In those cases, C++ developers use asynchronous I/O. It saves thread resources and ensure that the thread of the execution cannot be blocked. Let's consider what synchronous and asynchronous I/O is.

As you may recall from Chapter 5, The Philosophers' Dinner – Threads and Concurrency, synchronous operation means that some thread invokes the operation and waits for it to complete. It may be a single-threaded or multi-threaded application. The main point is that the thread is waiting for the I/O operation to complete.

The asynchronous execution takes place when an operation does not block the execution of the working thread. The thread that performs the asynchronous I/O operation sends an asynchronous request and continues with another task. When the operation has finished, the initial thread will be notified about the finish and it can handle the results as necessary.

From this, it looks like asynchronous I/O is much better than synchronous, but it depends on the situation. If you need to perform lots of fast I/O operations, it would be more suitable to follow the synchronous way due to the overhead of processing kernel I/O requests and signals. Thus, you need to consider all possible scenarios while developing an architecture for your application.

The Standard Library doesn't support asynchronous I/O operations. So, to leverage asynchronous I/O, we need to consider alternative libraries or write our own implementations. First, let's consider platform-dependent implementations. Then, we will look at cross-platform libraries.

## Asynchronous I/O on Windows Platforms

Windows supports I/O operations for a variety of devices: files, directories, drives, ports, pipes, sockets, terminals, and so on. In general, we use the same interface for I/O for all of these devices, but some settings differ from device to device. Let's consider an I/O operation on a file in Windows.

So, in Windows, we need to open a device and get a Handler for it. Different devices open in different ways. To open a file, directory, drive, or port, we use the `CreateFile` function from the `<Windows.h>` header. To open a pipe, we use the `CreateNamedPipe` function. To open a socket, we use the socket() and accept() functions. To open a terminal, we use the `CreateConsoleScreenBuffer` and `GetStdHandle` functions. All of them return a device handler that is used in all the functions for work with that device.

The `CreateFile` function takes seven parameters that manage the work with the opened device. The function declaration looks as follows:

```
HANDLE CreateFile( PCTSTR pszName,
                   DWORD  dwDesiredAccess,
                   DWORD  dwShareMode,
                   PSECURITY_ATTRIBUTES psa,
                   DWORD  dwCreationDisposition,
                   DWORD  dwFlagsAndAttributes,
                   HANDLE hFileTemplate);
```

The first parameter is **pszName** – the path to the file. The second parameter calls **dwDesiredAccess** and manages access to the device. It can take one of the following values:

```
0 // only for configuration changing

GENERIC_READ // only reading

GENERIC_WRITE // only for writing

GENERIC_READ | GENERIC_WRITE // both for reading and writing
```

The third parameter, **dwShareMode**, manages how the OS should handle all the new `CreateFile` invocations when the file is already open. It can take one of the following values:

```
0 // only one application can open device simultaneously

FILE_SHARE_READ // allows reading by multiple applications simultaneously

FILE_SHARE_WRITE // allows writing by multiple applications simultaneously

FILE_SHARE_READ | FILE_SHARE_WRITE // allows both reading and writing by
multiple applications simultaneously

FILE_SHARE_DELETE // allows moving or deleting by multiple applications
simultaneously
```

The fourth parameter, **psa**, is usually set to **NULL**. The fifth parameter, **dwCreationDisposition**, manages whether the file be opened or created. It can take one of the following values:

```
CREATE_NEW // creates new file or fails if it is existing

CREATE_ALWAYS // creates new file or overrides existing

OPEN_EXISTING // opens file or fails if it is not exists

OPEN_ALWAYS // opens or creates file

TRUNCATE_EXISTING // opens existing file and truncates it or fails if it is
not exists
```

The sixth parameter, **dwFlagsAndAttributes**, manages the cache or work with the file. It can take one of the following values for managing caching:

```
FILE_FLAG_NO_BUFFERING // do not use cache

FILE_FLAG_SEQUENTIAL_SCAN // tells the OS that you will read the file
sequentially

FILE_FLAG_RANDOM_ACCESS // tells the OS that you will not read the file in
sequentially

FILE_FLAG_WR1TE_THROUGH // write without cache but read with
```

It can take one of the following values for managing work with files:

```
FILE_FLAG_DELETE_ON_CLOSE // delete file after closing (for temporary files)

FILE_FLAG_BACKUP_SEMANTICS // used for backup and recovery programs

FILE_FLAG_POSIX_SEMANTICS // used to set case sensitive when creating or
opening a file

FILE_FLAG_OPEN_REPARSE_POINT // allows to open, read, write, and close files
differently

FILE_FLAG_OPEN_NO_RECALL // prevents the system from recovering the contents
of the file from archive media

FILE_FLAG_OVERLAPPED // allows to work with the device asynchronously
```

It can take one of the following values for file attributes:

```
FILE_ATTRIBUTE_ARCHIVE // file should be deleted

FILE_ATTRIBUTE_ENCRYPTED // file is encrypted

FILE_ATTRIBUTE_HIDDEN // file is hidden

FILE_ATTRIBUTE_NORMAL // other attributes are not set

FILE_ATTRIBUTE_NOT_CONTENT_ INDEXED // file is being processed by the
indexing service
```

```
FILE_ATTRIBUTE_OFFLINE // file is transferred to archive media
FILE_ATTRIBUTE_READONLY // only read access
FILE_ATTRIBUTE_SYSTEM // system file
FILE_ATTRIBUTE_TEMPORARY // temporary file
```

The last parameter, **hFileTemplate**, takes a handler to the open file or **NULL** as parameters. If the file handler is passed, the **CreateFile** function ignores all the attributes and flags and the use the attributes and flags of the open file.

That's all regarding **CreateFile** parameters. If it cannot open a device, it returns **INVALID_HANDLE_VALUE**. The following example demonstrates how to open a file for reading:

```cpp
#include <iostream>
#include <Windows.h>


int main()
{
    HANDLE hFile = CreateFile(TEXT("Test.txt"), GENERIC_READ,
                        FILE_SHARE_READ | FILE_SHARE_WRITE,
                        NULL, OPEN_ALWAYS, FILE_ATTRIBUTE_NORMAL,
NULL);

    if (INVALID_HANDLE_VALUE == hFile)
        std::cout << "Failed to open file for reading" << std::endl;
    else
        std::cout << "Successfully opened file for reading" << std::endl;

    CloseHandle(hFile);

    return 0;
}
```

Next, to perform an input operation, we use the **ReadFile** function. It takes the file descriptor as the first parameter, the source buffer as the second parameter, the maximum number of bytes to read as the third parameter, the number of reading bytes as the fourth parameter, and the **NULL** value for synchronous execution or the pointer to a valid and unique OVERLAPPED structure as the last parameter. If the operation succeeds, the **ReadFile** returns true, or false otherwise. The following example demonstrates how to input from the previously opened file for reading:

```
BYTE pb[20];
DWORD dwNumBytes;
ReadFile(hFile, pb, 20, &dwNumBytes, NULL);
```

To perform the output operation, we use the **WriteFile** function. It has the same declaration as **ReadFile**, but the third parameter sets the number of bytes to write and the fifth parameter is a number of written bytes. The following example demonstrates how to output to a previously opened file for writing:

```
BYTE pb[20] = "Some information\0";
DWORD dwNumBytes;
WriteFile(hFile, pb, 20, &dwNumBytes, NULL);
```

To write cached data to a device, use the **FlushFileBuffer** function. It takes a single parameter – the file descriptor. Let's move to the asynchronous I/O. To let the OS know that you plan to work with the device asynchronously, you need to open it with the **FILE_FLAG_OVERLAPPED** flag. Now, opening the file for writing or reading looks as follows:

```
#include <iostream>
#include <Windows.h>


int main()
{
    HANDLE hFile = CreateFile(TEXT("Test.txt"), GENERIC_READ,
                             FILE_SHARE_READ | FILE_SHARE_WRITE,
                             NULL, OPEN_ALWAYS, FILE_FLAG_OVERLAPPED,
NULL);


    if (INVALID_HANDLE_VALUE == hFile)
        std::cout << "Failed to open file for reading" << std::endl;
    else
```

```
        std::cout << "Successfully opened file for reading" << std::endl;


        CloseHandle(hFile);


        return 0;
}
```

We use the same operations to perform reading or writing to files, that is, **ReadFile** and **WriteFile**, with the only difference that the number of reads or wrote bytes are set to NULL and we must pass a valid and unique **OVERLAPPED** object. Let's consider what the structure of the OVERLAPPED object is:

```
typedef struct _OVERLAPPED {
DWORD  Internal; // for error code
DWORD  InternalHigh; // for number of read bytes
DWORD  Offset;
DWORD  OffsetHigh;
HANDLE hEvent; // handle to an event
} OVERLAPPED, *LPOVERLAPPED;
```

The Internal member is set to **STATUS_PENDING**, which means that the operation hasn't started yet. The number of read or wrote bytes will be written into the **InternalHigh** member. **Offset** and **OffsetHigh** are ignored in asynchronous operations. The **hEvent** member is used for receiving events about the completion of the asynchronous operation.

> **Note**
>
> The order of the I/O operations is not guaranteed, so you cannot rely on this. If you plan to write to a file at one place, and read from a file at another place, you cannot rely on the order.

There is one unusual thing in working with **ReadFile** and **WriteFile** in asynchronous mode. They return a non-zero value if the I/O request was performed synchronously. If they return **FALSE**, you need to invoke the **GetLastError** function to check why **FALSE** was returned. If the error code is **ERROR_IO_PENDING**, this means that the I/O request was successfully handled, is in a pending state, and will be performed later.

The last thing that you should remember is that you can't move or remove the **OVERLAPPED** object or buffer with data until the I/O operation finishes. For each I/O operation, you should create a new OVERLAPPED object.

Finally, let's consider the ways in which the system notifies us about completing the I/O operation. There are a few such mechanisms: releasing the device, releasing the event, producing an alert, and using I/O ports.

**The "bad" approach**: The **WriteFile** and **ReadFile** functions set a device to the "occupied" state. When the I/O operation is finished, the driver sets a device to the "free" state. We can check if the finished I/O operation is invoking the **WaitForSingleObject** or **WaitForMultipleObject** functions. The following example demonstrates this approach:

```
#include <Windows.h>

#include <WinError.h>

int main()

{

    HANDLE hFile = CreateFile(TEXT("Test.txt"), GENERIC_READ,

                                    FILE_SHARE_READ | FILE_SHARE_WRITE,
NULL,

                                    OPEN_ALWAYS, FILE_FLAG_OVERLAPPED,
NULL);


    BYTE bBuffer[100];

    OVERLAPPED o = { 0 };

    BOOL bResult = ReadFile(hFile, bBuffer, 100, NULL, &o);

    DWORD dwError = GetLastError();


    if (bResult && (dwError == ERROR_IO_PENDING))

    {

        WaitForSingleObject(hFile, INFINITE);
```

```
            bResult = TRUE;

    }


    CloseHandle(hFile);


    return 0;

}
```

This is the easiest way to check if the I/O operation has finished. But this approach makes the calling thread wait on the **WaitForSingleObject** call, so it becomes a synchronous call. Moreover, you can initiate a few I/O operations for this device, but you cannot be sure that the thread will wake up on the needed release of the device.

**A little bit better, but not the best approach**: Do you remember the last member of the overlapped structure? You create an event by invoking the **CreateEvent** function and set it to the **OVERLAPPED** object. Then, when the I/O operation has finished, the system releases this event by calling the **SetEvent** function. Next, when the calling thread needs to get the result of an executing I/O operation, you invoke **WaitForSingleObject** and pass the descriptors for this event. The following example demonstrates this approach:

```
#include <Windows.h>
#include <synchapi.h>


int main()
{
    HANDLE hFile = CreateFile(TEXT("Test.txt"), GENERIC_READ,
                              FILE_SHARE_READ | FILE_SHARE_WRITE,
                              NULL, OPEN_ALWAYS, FILE_FLAG_OVERLAPPED,
NULL);

    BYTE bInBuffer[10];
    OVERLAPPED o = { 0 };
    o.hEvent = CreateEvent(NULL,TRUE,FALSE,"IOEvent");
    ReadFile(hFile, bInBuffer, 10, NULL, &o);

    ///// do some work
```

```
    HANDLE hEvent = o.hEvent;

    WaitForSingleObject(hEvent, INFINITE);


    CloseHandle(hFile);


    return 0;

}
```

It's a pretty easy approach if you wish to notify the calling thread about the end of the I/O operation. But this is not the ideal way to do this because when there are a lot of these operations, you need to create an event object for each of them.

**One more approach that's not the best**: The alertable I/O works in the following way. We call **ReadFileEx** and **WriteFileEx** to the input/output. They are similar to the standard **ReadFile** and **WriteFile**, but we don't pass the variable that stores the number of read or wrote characters and we pass an address of the callback function. This callback function is called a completion routine and has the following declaration:

```
VOID WINAPI

CompletionRoutine(DWORD dwError,

                DWORD dwNumBytes,

                OVERLAPPED* po);
```

**ReadFileEx** and **WriteFileEx** pass the address of the callback function to the device driver. When the operation has finished on the device, the driver adds the address of the callback function to the APC queue and the pointer to the OVERLAPPED structure. Then, the OS invokes this function and passes the number of read or wrote bytes, error code, and pointer to the OVERLAPPED structure.

The main cons of this approach are writing callback functions and using a lot of global variables because callback functions have a small amount of information in the context. Another reason not to use this approach is that only the calling thread can receive the notification regarding completion.

Now that we've gone over the bad, let's look at the best approach for handling I/O results – I/O ports. The I/O completion ports are developed to be used with thread pools. To create such a port, we use `CreateIoCompletionPort`. The declaration of this function looks as follows:

```
HANDLE

CreateIoCompletionPort(HANDLE hFile,

                       HANDLE hExistingCompletionPort,

                       ULONG_PTR CompletionKey,

                       DWORD dwNumberOfConcurrentThreads);
```

This function creates an I/O completion port and associates the device with this port. To complete this action, we need to call it twice. To create the new completion port, we invoke the `CreateIoCompletionPort` function and pass `INVALID_HANDLE_VALUE` as the first parameter, NULL as a second parameter, 0 as a third parameter, and pass the number of the threads for this port. Passing 0 as the fourth parameter will set the number of threads equal to the number of processors.

> **Note**
>
> For the I/O completion port, it is recommended to use the number of threads that is equal to the number of processors, multiplied twice.

Next, we need to associate this port with the input/output device. So, we invoke the `CreateIoCompletionPort` function for the second time and pass a descriptor of the device, a descriptor of the created completion port, the constant that will indicate reading or writing to the device, and 0 as the number of threads. Then, when we need to get the result of completion, we call `GetQueuedCompletionStatus` from our port descriptor. If the operation completes, the function returns a result immediately. If it doesn't, then the thread waits to complete. The following example demonstrates this approach:

```
#include <Windows.h>

#include <synchapi.h>


int main()

{

    HANDLE hFile = CreateFile(TEXT("Test.txt"), GENERIC_READ,

                              FILE_SHARE_READ | FILE_SHARE_WRITE,
```

```
                                        NULL, OPEN_ALWAYS, FILE_FLAG_OVERLAPPED,
    NULL);


        HANDLE m_hIOcp = CreateIoCompletionPort(INVALID_HANDLE_VALUE, NULL, 0,
    0);

        CreateIoCompletionPort(hFile, m_hIOcp, 1, 0);


        BYTE bInBuffer[10];

        OVERLAPPED o = { 0 };

        ReadFile(hFile, bInBuffer, 10, NULL, &o);


        DWORD dwNumBytes;

        ULONG_PTR completionKey;

        GetQueuedCompletionStatus(m_hIOcp, &dwNumBytes, &completionKey,
    (OVERLAPPED**) &o, INFINITE);


        CloseHandle(hFile);


        return 0;

    }
```

## Asynchronous I/O on Linux Platforms

The asynchronous I/O on Linux supports input and output to different devices such as sockets, pipes, and TTYs, except files. Yes, this is pretty strange, but Linux developers decided that I/O operations with files are fast enough.

To open an I/O device, we use the open() function. It has the following declaration:

```
int open (const char *filename, int flags[, mode_t mode])
```

The first parameter is a filename, while the second parameter is a bitmask that controls how the file should be opened. If the system cannot open the device, open() returns a value of –1. In the case of success, it returns a device descriptor. The possible flags for open mode are **O_RDONLY**, **O_WRONLY**, and **O_RDWR**.

To perform input/output operations, we use the **POSIX** interface called **aio**. They have a defined set of functions such as **aio_read**, **aio_write**, **aio_fsync**, and so on. They are used to initiate the asynchronous operations. To get the result of execution, we can use signal notification or the instantiation of a thread. Alternatively, we can choose not to be notified at all. All of them are declared in the **<aio.h>** header.

Almost all of these take the **aiocb** structure (asynchronous IO control block) as a parameter. It controls the IO operations. The declaration of this structure looks as follows:

```
struct aiocb
{
    int aio_fildes;
    off_t aio_offset;
    volatile void *aio_buf;
    size_t aio_nbytes;
    int aio_reqprio;
    struct sigevent aio_sigevent;
    int aio_lio_opcode;
};
```

The **aio_fildes** member is a descriptor to the opened device, while the **aio_offset** member is an offset in the device where read or write operations should be done. The **aio_buf** member is a pointer to the buffer to read or write from. The **aio_nbytes** member is the size of the buffer. The **aio_reqprio** member is the priority of the execution of this IO operation. The **aio_sigevent** member is a structure that points out how the calling thread should be notified about the finish. The **aio_lio_opcode** member is a type of I/O operation. The following example demonstrates how to initialize the **aiocb** structure:

```
std::string fileContent;
constexpr int BUF_SIZE = 20;
fileContent.resize(BUF_SIZE, 0);


aiocb aiocbObj;
aiocbObj.aio_fildes = open("test.txt", O_RDONLY);
if (aiocbObj.aio_fildes == -1)
{
```

```
    std::cerr << "Failed to open file" << std::endl;
    return -1;
}
```

```
aiocbObj.aio_buf = const_cast<char*>(fileContent.c_str());
aiocbObj.aio_nbytes = BUF_SIZE;
aiocbObj.aio_reqprio = 0;
aiocbObj.aio_offset = 0;
aiocbObj.aio_sigevent.sigev_notify = SIGEV_SIGNAL;
aiocbObj.aio_sigevent.sigev_signo = SIGUSR1;
aiocbObj.aio_sigevent.sigev_value.sival_ptr = &aiocbObj;
```

Here, we created a buffer for reading file content, namely **fileContent**. Then, we created an **aiocb** structure called **aiocbObj**. Next, we opened a file for reading and checked if this operation was successful. Then, we set the pointer to a buffer and a buffer size. The buffer size tells the driver how many bytes should be read or wrote. Next, we pointed out that we will read from the beginning of the file by setting the offset to 0. Then, we set the notification type in **SIGEV_SIGNAL**, which means we would like to get a signal notification about the finish operation. Then, we set the signal number, which should trigger the notification about the finish. In our case, it's **SIGUSR1** – the user-defined signal. Next, we set the pointer to the **aiocb** structure to the signal handler.

After the creation and correct initialization of an **aiocb** structure, we can perform input or output operations. Let's complete an exercise to understand how to use async I/O on Linux platforms.

## Exercise 8: Asynchronously Reading from a File in Linux

In this exercise, we will develop an application that reads data from a file in an asynchronous way and outputs the read data to the console. When the read operation is performed, the driver notifies the application using the triggering signal. To do this exercise, perform the following steps:

1.  Include all the required headers: **<aio.h>** for asynchronous reading and writing support, **<signal.h>** for signal support, **<fcntl.h>** for operations with files, **<unistd.h>** for symbolic constants support, **<iostream>** for output to the Terminal, **<chrono>** for time options, and **<thread>** for threading support:

    ```
    #include <aio.h>
    #include <signal.h>
    #include <fcntl.h>
    ```

```
#include <unistd.h>
#include <iostream>
#include <chrono>
#include <thread>
```

2. Create a bool variable called **isDone** that will indicate when the operation has been completed:

```
bool isDone{};
```

3. Define the function that will be our signal handler, that is, **aioSigHandler**. It will be called when the async operation is done. Signal handlers should have the following signature:

```
void name(int number, siginfo_t* si, void* additional)
```

4. The first parameter is a signal number, the second parameter is a structure that contains information about why the signal was generated, and the last parameter is additional information. It can be cast to a pointer of the **ucontext_t** structure so that we can receive the thread context that was interrupted by this signal. In **aioSigHandler**, check whether the signal regarding the async I/O operation is constant using **SI_ASYNCIO**. If so, output a message. Next, set **isDone** to **true**:

```
void
aioSigHandler(int no, siginfo_t* si, void*)
{
    std::cout << "Signo: " << no << std::endl;
    if (si->si_code == SI_ASYNCIO)
    {
        std::cout << "I/O completion signal received" << std::endl;
    }
    isDone = true;
}
```

5. Define another helping function called **initSigAct**. It will initialize the **sigaction** structure. This structure defines which signal will be sent on the I/O operation's finish and which handler should be called. Here, we chose **SIGUSR1** – a user-defined signal. In **sa_flags**, set that we want this signal to be delivered on action restart or information received:

```
bool
initSigAct(struct sigaction& item)
{
    item.sa_flags = SA_RESTART | SA_SIGINFO;
    item.sa_sigaction = aioSigHandler;
```

```
if (-1 == sigaction(SIGUSR1, &item, NULL))
{
        std::cerr << "sigaction usr1 failed" << std::endl;
        return false;
}
std::cout << "Successfully set up a async IO handler to SIGUSR1
action" << std::endl;
        return true;
}
```

6. Define the helping function called **fillAiocb**, which fills in the **aiocb** structure with the given parameters. It will take the reference to the aiocb structure, the file descriptor, the pointer to a buffer, and the buffer's size as parameters. Set **sigev_signo** in **SIGUSR1**, which we initialized previously:

```
void
fillAiocb(aiocb& item, const int& fileDescriptor,
        char* buffer, const int& bufSize)
{
        item.aio_fildes = fileDescriptor;
        item.aio_buf = static_cast<void*>(buffer);
        item.aio_nbytes = bufSize;
        item.aio_reqprio = 0;
        item.aio_offset = 0;
        item.aio_sigevent.sigev_notify = SIGEV_SIGNAL;
        item.aio_sigevent.sigev_signo = SIGUSR1;
        item.aio_sigevent.sigev_value.sival_ptr = &item;
}
```

7. Enter the **main** function. Define the variable called **buf_size**, which holds the buffer size. Create a buffer of that size:

```
constexpr int bufSize = 100;
char* buffer = new char(bufSize);

if (!buffer)
{
        std::cerr << "Failed to allocate buffer" << std::endl;
        return -1;
}
```

8. Create a variable called **fileName** that holds a file called "**Test.txt**". Then, open this file with read-only access:

```cpp
const std::string fileName("Test.txt");
int descriptor = open(fileName.c_str(), O_RDONLY);
if (-1 == descriptor)
{
    std::cerr << "Failed to opene file for reading" << std::endl;
    return -1;
}
std::cout << "Successfully opened file for reading" << std::endl;
```

9. Create a **sigaction** structure and initialize it using the **initSigAct** function:

```cpp
struct sigaction sa;
if (!initSigAct(sa))
{
    std::cerr << "failed registering signal" << std::endl;
    return -1;
}
```

10. Create an **aiocb** structure and initialize it using the **fillAiocb** function:

```cpp
aiocb aiocbObj;
fillAiocb(aiocbObj, descriptor, buffer, bufSize);
```

11. Perform a **read** operation using the **aio_read** function:

```cpp
if (-1 == aio_read(&aiocbObj))
{
    std::cerr << "aio_read failed" << std::endl;
}
```

12. Next, in the loop, evaluate the **isDone** variable. If it is false, make the thread sleep for **3ms**. By doing this, we will wait for the I/O operation to finish:

```cpp
while (!isDone)
{
    using namespace std::chrono_literals;
    std::this_thread::sleep_for(3ms);
}
std::cout << "Successfully finished read operation. Buffer: " << std::endl
          << buffer;
```

13. Before running this exercise, create a **Test.txt** file in the project directory and write different symbols. For example, our file contains the following data:

```
a1a"1 a1\a1 a1     a1
a1a"1 a1\a1 a1     a1
a1a"1 a1\a1 a1     a1
a1a"1 a1\a1 a1     a1
a1a"1 a1\a1 a1     a1
a1a"1 a1\a1 a1     a1
a1a"1 a1\a1 a1     a1
a1a"1 a1\a1 a1     a1
a1a"1 a1\a1 a1     a1
a1a"1 a1\a1 a1     a1
a1a"1 a1\a1 a1     a1
a1a"1 a1\a1 a1     a1
a1a"1 a1\a1 a1     a1
a1a"1 a1\a1 a1     a1
```

Here, there's alphabetical characters, numerical characters, special symbols, spaces, tabulation characters, and newline characters.

14. Now, build and run this exercise in your IDE. Your output will be similar to the following:

```
Problems   Tasks   Console   Properties   Include Browser
<terminated> (exit value: -1 073 741 819) Exercise Debug [C/C++ Application]
Successfully opened file for reading
Successfully set up a async IO handler to SIGUSR1 action
Signo: 30
I/O completion signal received
Successfully finished read operation. Buffer:
a1a"1 a1\a1 a1   a1
a1a"1 a1\a1 a1   a1
a1a"1 a1\a1 a1   a1
a1a"1 a1\a1 a1   a1
a1a"1 a1\a1 a1   a1
```

Figure 6.17: The result of executing Exercise 8

You can see that the file was successfully opened for reading and that we successfully set the **SIGUSR1** signal and handler for it. Then, we received signal number 30, that is, the **SI_ASYNCIO** signal. Finally, we can output what we have read and compare it with the file content. By doing this, we can ensure that all the data was read correctly.

That's all for async I/O in Linux systems.

> **Note**
>
> You can find more information about asynchronous IO in Linux by going to Linux's man pages: http://man7.org/linux/man-pages/man7/aio.7.html.

Now, let's learn about what we can use for cross-platform applications.

## Asynchronous Cross-Platform I/O Libraries

We've already considered the platform-specific decision for asynchronous I/O. Now, to write a cross-platform application, you can use these platform-specific approaches and use them with preprocessor directives; for example:

```
#ifdef WIN

#include <WinAIO.hpp>

#else

#include <LinAIO.hpp>

#endif
```

In both the headers, you can declare the same interface for platform-specific implementations. You can also implement your own AIO library, which will use some state machines or queue in the separate thread. Also, you can use some of the free libraries that implement the necessary features. The most popular library is **Boost.Asio**. It provides a lot of interfaces for asynchronous work, such as the following:

- Concurrency without threads

- Threads

- Buffers

- Streams

- Coroutines

- TCP, UDP, and ICMP

- Sockets

- SSL

- Timers

- Serial ports

Let's briefly consider its interface for I/O operations. We can use the interface of the **Asio** library for synchronous and asynchronous operations. All of the I/O operations start from the **io_service** class, which provides core I/O functionality. It is declared in the **<boost/asio/io_service.hpp>** header file. The synchronous I/O invokes the **run()** function of the **io_service** object for a single operation that blocks the calling thread until the job is done. The asynchronous I/O uses the **run()**, **run_one()**, **poll()**, and **poll_one()** functions. The **run()** function runs the event loop to process request handlers. The **run_one()** function does the same, but the event loop should process only one handler. The **poll()** function runs the event loop to execute all the ready handlers. **poll_one()** does the same but only for one handler. The following example demonstrates the usage of all these functions:

```
boost::asio::io_service io_service1;
io_service1.run();


boost::asio::io_service io_service2;
io_service2.run_one();


boost::asio::io_service io_service3;
io_service3.poll();


boost::asio::io_service io_service4;
io_service4.poll_one();
```

It's possible to run the event handler before the actual I/O operations are called. Use the working class with the **io_service** class to implement this feature in your code. The work class guarantees that the run function will not return until you've decided that there will not be any future I/O operations. For example, you can make the working class a member of another class and remove it from the destructor. So, during the lifetime of your class, **io_service** will be running:

```
boost::asio::io_service io_service1;
boost::asio::io_service::work work(io_service1);
io_service1.run();


boost::asio::io_service io_service2;
boost::asio::io_service::work work(io_service2);
io_service2.poll();
```

Next, to perform any I/O operations, we need the exact the I/O device, for example, file, socket, and so on. There are many classes that implement work with different I/O devices, for example, **boost::asio::ip::tcp::socket** from the **<boost/asio/ip/tcp.hpp>** header. Next, to read and write to the socket, we make use of **boost::asio::async_read** and **boost::asio::async_write**. They take a socket, **boost::asio::buffer**, and the callback function as parameters. When the async operation is performed, the callback function is invoked. We can pass a lambda function as a callback function or bind an existing function using the boost::bind function. **boost::bind** creates a callable object. The following example demonstrates how to write to a socket using **Boost::Asio**:

```cpp
boost::asio::io_service ioService;

tcp::socket socket;


int length = 15;

char* msg = new char(length);

msg = "Hello, world!";


auto postHandler = [=]()

{

    auto writeHandler = [=](boost::system::error_code ec, std::size_t
length)

    {

        if (ec)

        {

            socket_.close();

        }

        else

        {
```

```
                    // wrote length characters
            }
        };
        boost::asio::async_write(socket, boost::asio::buffer(msg, length),
    writeHandler);
    };


    ioService.post(postHandler);
```

Here, we used lambda functions as callbacks for async I/O operations.

> **Note**
>
> The **Boost.Asio** is well-documented at https://www.boost.org/doc/libs/1_63_0/
> doc/html/boost_asio.html. There are lots of examples with different IO devices
> and different approaches. You can refer to this documentation if you decide to use
> **Boost.Asio** in your projects.

Here, we've considered different ways we can implement asynchronous I/O operations. Depending on your requirements, environment, and allowed utilities, you can choose the appropriate way to implement asynchronous I/O in your applications. Remember that if you choose to perform many fast I/O operations, it's better to do them in a synchronous way as it doesn't take up a lot of system resources. Now that we know how to leverage asynchronous I/O, let's learn how to use I/O in multithreaded applications.

## Interaction of Threads and I/O

The I/O Standard Library is not thread-safe. In the documentation of the Standard Library, we can find an explanation that states that the concurrent access to the stream or stream buffer can lead to a data race and, as a result, an undefined behavior. To avoid this, we should synchronize access to the streams and buffers using the techniques that we learned about in *Chapter 5, The Philosophers' Dinner – Threads and Concurrency.*

Let's talk a little bit about the **std::cin** and **std::cout** objects. Each call to them is thread-safe, but let's consider the following example:

```
std::cout << "Counter: " << counter << std::endl;
```

In this line, we see that **std::cout** is called once, but each call to the shift operator is actually a different call to the **std::cout** object. So, we can rewrite this line as follows:

```
std::cout << "Counter: ";

std::cout << counter;

std::cout << std::endl;
```

This code does exactly the same as the previous single line, that is, if you call this single line from the different threads, your output will be mixed and unclear. You can modify it to make it really thread-safe like so:

```
std::stringsream ss;

ss << "Counter: " << counter << std::endl;

std::cout << ss.str();
```

So, if you output to the Terminal using the second method, your output will be clear and thread-safe. This behavior can vary, depending on the compiler or std library version. You also have to know that **std::cout** and **std::cin** are synchronized among them. This means that invoking **std::cout** always flushes the **std::cin** stream and the invocation of **std::cin** always flushes the **std::cout** stream.

The best approach is to wrap all I/O operations in a guard class that will control access to the stream using mutexes. If you need to output to the Terminal from multiple threads using **std::cout**, you can implement a very simple class that does nothing but lock the mutex and invoke **std::cout**. Let's complete an exercise and create such class.

## Exercise 9: Developing a Thread-Safe Wrapper for std::cout

In this exercise, we will develop a simple **std::cout** wrapper that produces a thread-safe output. We will write a small test function to check how it works. Let's start and perform the following steps:

1.  Include all the required headers:

```
#include <iostream> // for std::cout
#include <thread>   // for std::thread
#include <mutex>    // for std::mutex
#include <sstream>  // for std::ostringstream
```

Now, let's think about our wrapper. We can create a variable of this class somewhere and pass it to each created thread. However, this is a bad decision because in complex applications, this will take a lot of effort. We can also do this as a singleton so that we have access to it from everywhere. Next, we have to think about the content of our class. Actually, we can use the classes that we created in *Exercise 7, Inheriting the Standard Stream Object*. In that exercise, we overloaded `std::basic_streambuf` and `std::basic_ostream` and set `std::cout` as the output device. We can add a mutex to the overloaded function and use it as is. Note that we don't need any additional logic – just the output data using `std::cout`. To do this, we can create a simpler class. If we did not set the output device, applying the left shift operator will not take effect and will store the data to be outputted in the internal buffer. Great! Now, we need to think about how to get this buffer to output using `std::cout`.

2.  Implement a function such as **write()** that will lock a mutex and output to `std::cout` from the internal buffer. The usage of this function will look as follows:

    ```
    mtcout cout;
    cout << msg << std::endl;
    cout.write();
    ```

3.  We have one function that will always be called automatically, and we can put the code of the write function into it. It's a destructor. In this case, we combine the creation and destruction into a single line. The usage of such an object will look as follows:

    ```
    mtcout{} << msg << std::endl;
    ```

4.  Now, let's define our **mtcout** (multithreaded cout) class. It has a public default constructor. In the private section, it has a static mutex variable. As you may recall, the static variable is shared among all the instances of the class. In the destructor, we lock the mutex and output using cout. Add a prefix to the output – the ID of the current thread and a space character:

    ```
    class mtcout : public std::ostringstream
    {
    public:
        mtcout() = default;
        ~mtcout()
        {
    ```

```
        std::lock_guard<std::mutex> lock(m_mux);
            std::cout << std::this_thread::get_id() << " " << this->str();
    }
private:
        static std::mutex m_mux;
};
```

5. Next, declare the **mutex** variable outside the class. We are doing this because we must declare a static variable in any source file:

```
std::mutex mtcout::m_mux;
```

6. Enter the main function. Create a lambda called **func**. It will test our **mtcout** class. It takes string as a parameter and outputs this string in the loop from **0** to **1000** using **mtcout**. Add the same output using **std::cout** and comment it out. Compare the output in both cases:

```
auto func = [](const std::string msg)
{
        using namespace std::chrono_literals;
        for (int i = 0; i < 1000; ++i)
        {
                mtcout{} << msg << std::endl;
//              std::cout << std::this_thread::get_id() << " " << msg <<
std::endl;
        }
};
```

7. Create four threads and pass a lambda function as a parameter. Pass different strings to each thread. Finally, join all four threads:

```
std::thread thr1(func, "111111111");
std::thread thr2(func, "222222222");
std::thread thr3(func, "333333333");
std::thread thr4(func, "444444444");

thr1.join();
thr2.join();
thr3.join();
thr4.join();
```

8. Build and run the exercise for the first time. You will get the following output:

Figure 6.18: The result of executing Exercise 9, part 1

Here, we can see that each of threads outputs its own message. This message has not been interrupted and the output looks clear.

9. Now, uncomment the output with **std::cout** in the lambda and comment out the output using **mtcout**.

10. Again, build and run the application. Now, you will get a "dirty", mixed output, like the following:

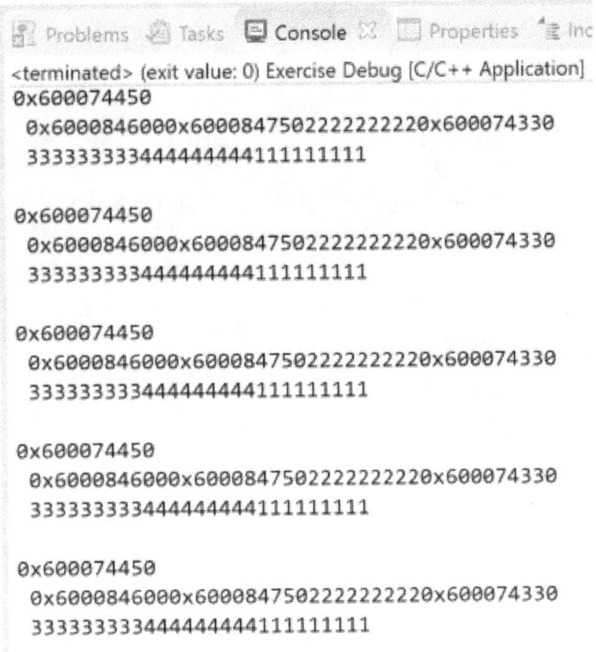

Figure 6.19: The result of executing Exercise 9, part 2

You can see this mixed output because we don't output a single string; instead, we invoke **std::cout** four times:

```
std::cout << std::this_thread::get_id();

std::cout << " ";

std::cout << msg;

std::cout << std::endl;
```

Sure, we can format the string before outputting it, but it is more convenient to use the mtcout class and not have to worry about formatting. You can create similar wrappers for any stream so that you can perform I/O operations safely. You can change the output and add any additional information, such as the ID of the current thread, time, or whatever you need. Employ the things we learned about in *Chapter 5, The Philosophers' Dinner – Threads and Concurrency*, to synchronize the I/O operations, extend streams and make the output more useful for your needs.

## Using Macros

In the activity for this chapter, we will use macro definitions to simplify and beautify our code, so let's do a refresher on how to use them. Macro definitions are preprocessor directives. The syntax of the macro definition is as follows:

```
#define [name] [expression]
```

Here, [name] is any meaningful name and[expression] is any small function or value.

When the preprocessor faces the macro name, it replaces it with the expression. For example, let's say you have the following macro:

```
#define MAX_NUMBER 15
```

Then, you use it in a few places in your code:

```
if (val < MAX_NUMBER)
```

```
while (val < MAX_NUMBER)
```

When the preprocessor finishes its work, the code will be as follows:

```
if (val < 15)
```

```
while (val < 15)
```

The preprocessor does the same work for functions. For example, let's say you have a macro for getting the maximum number:

```
#define max(a, b) a < b ? b : a
```

Then, you use it in a few places in your code:

```
int res = max (5, 3);
```

```
std::cout << (max (a, b));
```

When the preprocessor finishes its work, the code will be as follows:

```
int res = 5 < 3 ? 3 : 5;
```

```
std::cout << (a < b ? b : a);
```

As an expression, you can use any valid expression, such as a function call, inline function, value, and so on. If you need to write the expression in more than one line, use the back-slash operator, "\". For example, the max definition we can write in two lines is as follows:

```
#define max(a, b) \
a < b ? b : a
```

> **Note**
>
> The macro definitions came from the C language. It's better to use const variables or inline functions instead. However, there are still cases when it's more convenient to use macro definitions, for example, in loggers when you wish to define different logging levels.

Now. we know everything we need to complete the activity. So, let's sum up what we have learned in this chapter and let's improve the project that we wrote in *Chapter 5, The Philosophers' Dinner – Threads and Concurrency.* We'll be developing a thread-safe logger and integrating it into our project.

## Activity 1: The Logging System for The Art Gallery Simulator

In this activity, we are going to develop a logger that will output formatted logs to the Terminal. We will output logs in the following format:

```
[dateTtime][threadId][logLevel][file:line][function] | message
```

We will implement macro definitions for different logging levels that will be used instead of straightforward calls. This logger will be thread-safe, and we will invoke it from different threads simultaneously. Finally, we will integrate it into the project – The Art Gallery Simulator. We will run the simulation and observe pretty-printed logs. We will create an additional stream, use streams with concurrency, and format the output. We will implement almost everything that we have learned about in this chapter. We will also employ a synchronization technique from the previous chapter.

Thus, before attempting this activity, ensure that you have completed all the previous exercises in this chapter.

Before we implement this application, let's describe our classes. We have the following newly created classes:

| Class Name | Description |
|---|---|
| LoggerUtils | The class that provides an interface for output formatting. |
| StreamLogger | The thread-safe logger that outputs data to the terminal. |

Figure 6.20: Descriptions of the classes that should be implemented

We also have the following classes already implemented in The Art Gallery Simulator project:

| Class Name | Description |
|---|---|
| Person | The class that represents a visitor to the Art Gallery. |
| Persons | The thread-safe storage which keeps objects of the Person class. |
| PersonGenerator | The class is responsible for creating new objects of the Person class at different intervals. This simulates new visitors to the Art Gallery. It is also responsible for the simulation of the situation when people leave the Art Gallery. For this purpose, it triggers remove events at different intervals. |
| Watchman | The class that is responsible for controlling entrance to the Art Gallery. With every new visitor, it checks the number of people in the Art Gallery and if the number is less than 50, it puts a new Person into the list of persons inside the Gallery. If this number is more than the limit, it puts the visitor into the waiting list. It also removes visitors from the list of Persons that are inside the Gallery by using the remove event, which is triggered by the PersonGenerator class. After every removal, it checks whether there are any visitors on the waiting list. If so, it checks the number of people in the Art Gallery and if the number is less than 50, it puts a Person into the lists of persons inside the Gallery. |

Figure 6.21: The table of already implemented classes in The Art Gallery Simulator project

Let's add our new classes to the class diagram before we start the implementation. All of the described classes with relationships are composed in the following diagram:

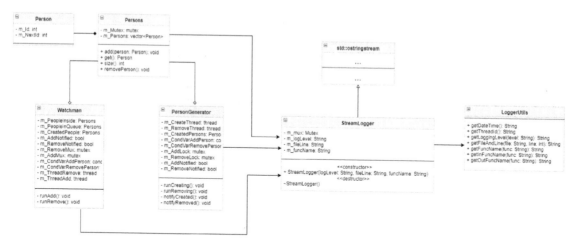

Figure 6.22: The class diagram

To receive the output in the desired format, the **LoggerUtils** class should have the following **static** functions:

| Function | Description |
|---|---|
| getDateTime | Gets the current system data and time and converts it into the following format: [dd.mm.yyThh:mm:s] |
| getThreadId | Gets the current thread id and converts it into the following format: [hex] |
| getLoggingLevel | Converts the giving logging level into the following format: [logging level] |
| getFileAndLine | Converts the given file and line strings into the following format: [file:line: ] |
| getFuncName | Converts the given function name into the following format: [name() --- ] |
| getInFuncName | Converts the given function name into the following format: [name() --> ] |
| getOutFuncName | Converts the given function name into the following format: [name() <-- ] |

Figure 6.23: Descriptions of the LoggerUtils member functions

Follow these steps to complete this activity:

1. Define and implement the **LoggerUtils** class, which provides an interface for output formatting. It contains static variables that format given data into the required representation.

2. Define and implement the **StreamLogger** class, which provides a thread-safe interface for output to the Terminal. It should format the output like so:

   ```
   [dateTtime][threadId][logLevel][file:line: ][function] | message
   ```

3. In a separate header file, declare the macro definitions for different logging levels that return a temporary object of the **StreamLogger** class.

4. Integrate the implemented logger into the classes from the Art Gallery simulator.

5. Replace all invocations of **std::cout** with the appropriate macro definition calls.

After implementing the aforementioned steps, you should get some output on the Terminal regarding the logs from all the implemented classes. Take a look and ensure that the logs are outputted in the desired format. The expected output should as follows:

Figure 6.24: The result of the application's execution

> **Note**
>
> The solution for this activity can be found on page 696.

## Summary

In this chapter, we learned about I/O operations in C++. We considered the I/O Standard Library, which provides an interface for synchronous I/O operations. Also, we considered platform-dependent native tools for asynchronous I/O, and the **Boost.Asio** library for cross-platform asynchronous I/O operations. We also learned how to use I/O streams in multithreaded applications.

We started by looking at the basic features that the Standard Library provides for I/O operations. We learned about predefined stream objects such as **std::cin** and **std::cout**. In practice, we learned how to work with standard streams and override shift operators for easy read and write custom data types.

Next, we practiced how to create additional streams. We inherited from the basic stream class, implemented our own stream buffer class, and practiced their usage in the exercises. We learned about the most appropriate stream classes for inheritance and considered their pros and cons.

Then, we considered the approaches of asynchronous I/O operations on different operating systems. We briefly considered using the cross-platform I/O library known as **Boost.Asio**, which provides an interface for both synchronous and asynchronous operations.

Finally, we learned about how to perform I/O operations in multithreaded applications. We put all of these new skills into practice by building a multithreaded logger. We created a logger abstraction and employed it in the Art Gallery simulator. As a result, we created an easy, clear, and robust logging system that allows us to easily debug the application using logs. In all, we employed everything we learned about in this chapter.

In the next chapter, we're going to be taking a closer look at testing and debugging applications. We will start by learning about assertions and safety netting. Then, we will practice writing unit tests and mocks for interfaces. After, we will practice debugging applications in the IDE: we will use breakpoints, watchpoints, and data visualization. Finally, we will write an activity that will master our skills of testing code.

# Everybody Falls, It's How You Get Back Up – Testing and Debugging

**Learning Objectives**

By the end of this chapter, you will be able to:

- Describe different types of assertions
- Implement compile-time and runtime assertions
- Implement exception handling
- Describe and implement unit testing and mock testing
- Debug C++ code using breakpoints and watchpoints
- Inspect data variables and C++ objects in the debugger

In this chapter, you'll learn how to add assertions appropriately, add unit test cases so that code behaves as per the requirements, and learn about debugging techniques so that you can find bugs in the code and trace the root cause of them.

# Introduction

During the **Software Development Life Cycle** (**SDLC**), once the requirement gathering phase is complete, then generally comes the Design and Architecture phase, wherein the high-level flow of the project is defined and broken down into smaller components of modules. When there are many team members in a project, it is necessary that each team member is clearly assigned a specific part of the module and that they are aware of their requirements. This way, they can independently write their part of the code in an isolated environment and make sure it works fine. Once their part of the work is complete, they can integrate their module with the other developer's modules and make sure the overall project is executing as per the requirements.

This concept can be applied to small projects too, where the developer is completely working on a requirement, breaking it down into smaller components, developing components in an isolated environment, making sure it executes as per the plan, integrating all the small modules to complete the project, and finally testing it to ensure that the overall project is working fine.

There is a good amount of testing required when the whole project is integrated and executed. There may be a separate team (known as **Quality Assurance**, that is, **QA**) dedicated to performing this task. Rather than finding issues at the project level, it is a good strategy to test the code at each isolated stage. This testing needs to be performed by the developer who's responsible for that module. This type of testing is known as unit testing. Here, a developer can simulate the environment that's needed to run that module and make sure they test a specific part of functionality written in a module. For example, let's assume that, in a big project, there is a small module whose functionality is to parse the configuration file and get the parameters that are needed to set up the environment. If part of the code that parses the file takes an `IP address` as a `string`, then the developer needs to ensure it is in the format `XXX.XXX.XXX.XXX`, where `X` is a digit from `0-9`. The length of the string must be of limited size.

Here, the developer can create a test program that executes their part of the code: parsing the file, extracting the `IP address` as a string, and testing if it is in the correct format. Similarly, if the configuration has other parameters to be parsed and they need to be in a specific format such as `userid / password`, file location for the log or mount point, and so on, then all these will be part of the unit testing for that module. In this chapter, we'll explain techniques such as `assertions`, `safety nesting` (`exception handling`), `unit testing`, `mocking`, `breakpoints`, `watchpoints`, and `data visualization` to pinpoint the source of errors and limit their growth. In the next section, we'll explore the assertion technique.

## Assertions

Using testing condition for the aforementioned scenario will help the project develop in a better way as the flaws will be caught at a base level rather than at the later QA level. There may be scenarios wherein even after writing the unit test cases and successful execution of the code, issues may be found sch as the application crashing, the program exiting unexpectedly, or the behavior is not as expected. To overcome such scenarios, generally, a developer uses a debug mode binary to recreate the problem. **Asserts** are used to ensure that the conditions are checked, otherwise the program's execution is terminated.

This way, the problem can be traced fast. Also, in **Debug Mode**, the developer can traverse the actual execution of the program line by line and check if the flow of code is as expected or if the variables are set as expected and accessed correctly. Sometimes, accessing pointer variables causes unexpected behaviors if they are not pointing to a valid memory location.

When writing code, we can check if the necessary condition is satisfied. If not, then the programmer may not want to execute the code further. This can be easily done using an assertion. An **assertion** is a macro where the specific condition is checked and if it doesn't meet the criteria, abort is called (program execution is stopped) and an error message is printed as a **standard error**. This is generally a **runtime assertion**. There can also be an assertion done at compile time. We will talk about this later. In the next section, we'll solve an exercise wherein we'll be writing and testing our first assertion.

## Exercise 1: Writing and Testing Our First Assertion

In this exercise, we'll write a function to parse an **IP address** and check if it's valid. As part of our requirements, the **IP address** will be passed as a string literal in the **XXX. XXX.XXX.XXX** format. In this format, **X** represents a digit from **0-9**. So, as part of testing to check whether the **string** being parsed is correct or not, we need to ensure that the **string** is **not null** and has a **length** that's less than **16**. Follow these steps to implement this exercise:

1. Create a new file named **AssertSample.cpp**.

2. Open the file and write the following code to include the header files:

```
#include<iostream>
#include<cassert>
#include<cstring>

using std::cout;
using std::endl;
```

In the preceding code, `#include<cassert>` shows that we need to include the
`cassert` file where assert is defined.

3. Create a function named `checkValidIp()` that will take the **IP address** as input and
   return a **true** value if the **IP address** meets our requirements. Write the following
   code to define the function:

```
bool checkValidIp(const char * ip){
    assert(ip != NULL);
    assert(strlen(ip) < 16);
    cout << "strlen: " << strlen(ip) << endl;
    return true;
}
```

Here, `assert(ip != NULL)` shows that the assert macro is used to check condition
if the "**ip**" variable that was passed is not **NULL**. If it's **NULL**, then it will abort with
an error message. Also, `assert(strlen(ip) < 16)` shows that the assert is used to
check if "**ip**" is **16** character or less. If not, then it aborts with **error message**.

4. Now, create a **main** function that passes a different string literal to our
   `checkValidIp()` function and makes sure it can be tested appropriately. Write the
   following code for the **main** function:

```
int main(){
    const char * ip;
    ip = NULL;
    bool check = checkValidIp(ip);
    cout << " IP address is validated as :" << (check ? "true" : "false")
<< endl;
    return 0;
}
```

In the preceding code, we've deliberately passed **NULL** to the **ip** variable to make
sure **assert** is called.

5. Open the **Command Prompt** and go to the location where the **AssertSample.cpp** file is
   stored. Compile it with the **g++** compiler by typing the following command:

```
g++ AssertSample.cpp
```

With this command, the **a.out** binary file is generated.

6.  Run the **a.out** binary file by typing the following command in the compiler:

    ```
    ./a.out
    ```

    You will see the following output:

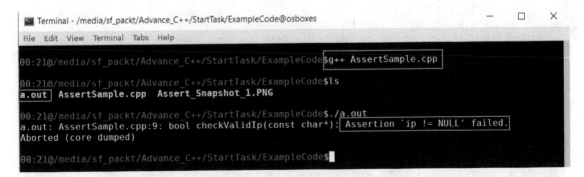

**Figure 7.1: Running the Assertion binary on the Command Prompt**

In the preceding screenshot, you can see three pieces of code circled in red. The first highlighted portion shows the compilation of the **.cpp** file. The second highlighted portion shows the **a.out** binary that that was generated by the preceding compilation. The third highlighted part shows assertion throwing an error for the **NULL** value being passed. It indicates the line number and function name where the assertion is called.

7.  Now, inside the **main** function, we will pass **ip** with a length greater than **16** and check if the **assert** is called here too. Write the following code to implement this:

    ```
    ip = "111.111.111.11111";
    ```

    Again, open the compiler, compile the **.cpp** file, and run the binary file that's generated. The following output will be displayed in the compiler:

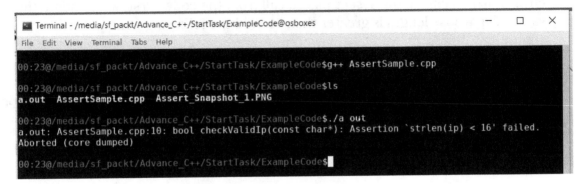

**Figure 7.2: Running the Assertion binary on the Command Prompt**

In the preceding screenshot, the assertion throws an error as the **ip** length that was passed is greater than **16**.

8. Now, to satisfy the **assert** condition so that the binary runs fine, we need to update the value of **ip** inside the **main** function. Write the following code to do this:

```
ip = "111.111.111.111";
```

Again, open the compiler, compile the **.cpp** file, and run the binary file that was generated. The following output is displayed in the compiler:

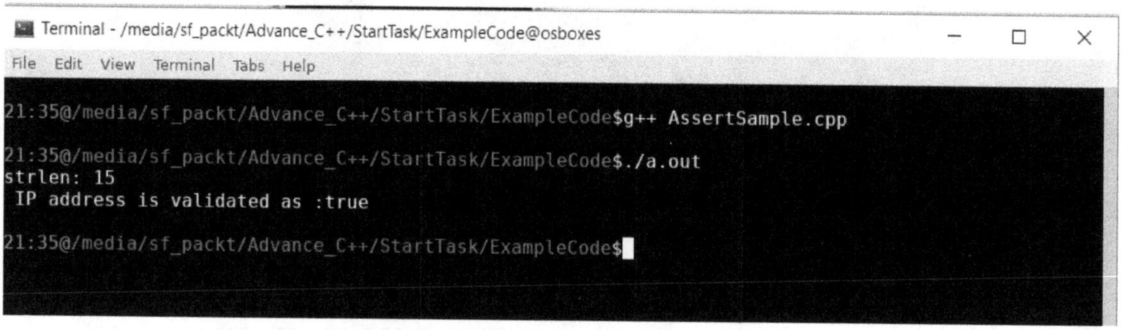

Figure 7.3: Running the Assertion binary on the Command Prompt

> **Note**
>
> As we're just dealing with **assert** here, we haven't added any extra functionality to our **checkValidIP()** function. However, we'll use the same example in the *Exception Handling* and *Unit Testing* sections wherein we'll add more functionality to our function.

9. If we don't want the executable to abort due to assert in production or the release environment, remove the **assert** macro call from the code. First, we'll update the value of **ip** whose length is greater than **16**. Add the following code to the file:

```
ip = "111.111.111.11111";
```

10. Now, during compilation, pass the **-DNDEBUG** macro. This will make sure that the assert is not called in the binary. Write the following command to compile our **.cpp** file in the Terminal:

```
g++ -DNDEBUG AssertSample.cpp
```

After this, when we execute the binary file, the following output is generated:

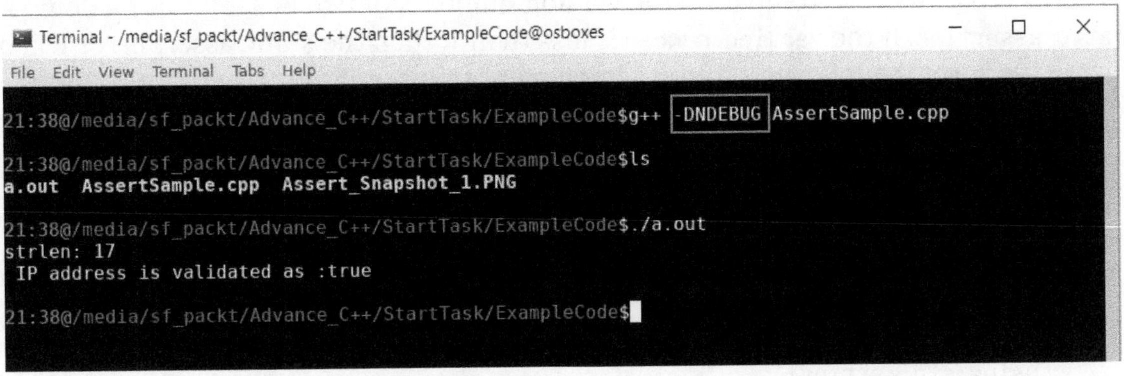

Figure 7.4: Running the Assertion binary on the Command Prompt

In the preceding screenshot, since **assert** is not called, it will show the string length as **17** and the **true** value as the IP address will be validated. In this exercise, we saw that the assertion was called when the binary was executed. We can also have an assertion during the compilation of the code. This was introduced in C++ 11. It is called a **static assertion** and we'll explore it in the next section.

## Static Assertions

Sometimes, we can do condition checks at compilation time to avoid any future errors. For example, in a project, we may use a third-party library that has some data structure declared in it. This structure information, such as its **size** and **member variables**, are known to us from its header file. Using this information, we can allocate or deallocate memory correctly, as well as work on its member variable. This structure property may change in a third-party library with a different version. However, if our project code is still using the structure of the earlier version, then it will create a problem when we use it. We may get an error at a later stage when running the binary. We can catch this error at compile time itself using **static assertion**. We can make a comparison of static data such as the version number of libraries, thus making sure our code will not have to face any problems. In the next section, we'll solve an exercise based on this.

## Exercise 2: Testing Static Assertions

In this exercise, we'll be comparing the version numbers of two header files by doing a **static assertion**. If the **version number** is less than **1**, then the static assert error will be thrown. Perform the following steps to implement this exercise:

1.  Create a header file named **PersonLibrary_ver1.h** and add the following code:

    ```
    #ifndef __PERSON_H__
    #define __PERSON_H__

    #include<string>

    using std::string;

    #define PERSON_LIB_VERSION 1

    struct person{
        string name;
        int age;
        string address;
    };

    #endif
    ```

    In the preceding code, the struct person is defined and consists of the following attributes: **name**, **age**, and **address**. It also has the version number **1**.

2.  Create another header file named **PersonLibrary_ver2.h** and add the following code:

    ```
    #ifndef __PERSON_H__
    #define __PERSON_H__

    #include<string>

    using std::string;

    #define PERSON_LIB_VERSION 2

    struct person{
        string name;
    ```

```
    int age;
    string address;
    string Mobile_No;
};

#endif
```

In the preceding code, the **struct person** is defined and consists of the following attributes: **name**, **age**, **address**, and **Mobile_No**. It also has the **version number 2**. Now, **version 1** is the old version and **version 2** is the new one. The following is a screenshot of the two header files side by side:

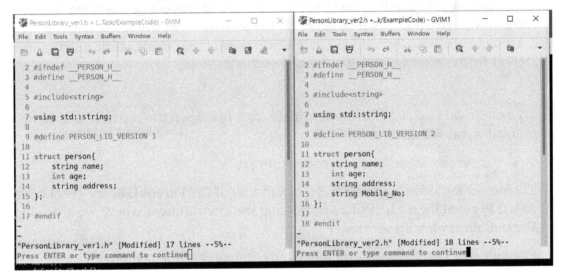

Figure 7.5: Library file with a different version

3. Create a file named **StaticAssertionSample.cpp** and add the following code:

```
#include<iostream>
#include"PersonLibrary.h"

void doSanityCheck(){
    static_assert(PERSON_LIB_VERSION > 1 , "PERSON LIBRARY VERSION not
greater than 1");
    // Do any more sanity check before starting app ...
}

int main(){
    doSanityCheck();
    return 0;
}
```

In the preceding code, we're doing a sanity check for our project before we build and execute it. We have created a function named **doSanityCheck()** that performs a version check for the library. It is done using static assertion and it is performed at compile time. The second line of the code shows that the **PersonLibrary.h** file is included. Inside the **doSanityCheck()** function, the **static_assert()** function checks if this version of the library is greater than 1.

> **Note**
>
> If your project needs a struct of person defined in **version 2** or higher of the library to execute it correctly, we need files that match **version 2**, that is, **PERSON_LIB_VERSION** should be set to **2** at least. If a developer gets **version 1** of the library and tries to create a binary for the project, it may create a problem in execution. To avoid this scenario, in the main code of the project, we do a sanity check for the project before it builds and executes.

4. To include **version 1** of the library in our **.cpp** file, open the terminal and write the following command:

   ```
   ln -s PersonLibrary_ver1.h PersonLibrary.h
   ```

   The preceding command will create a soft link of the **PersonLibrary_ver1.h** file called **PersonLibrary.h**. It's like simulating the environment where we are using **PersonLibrary.h** with **version 1**.

5. Compile our **.cpp** file using the following command in the terminal:

   ```
   g++ StaticAssertionSample.cpp
   ```

   Here is the output generated in the terminal:

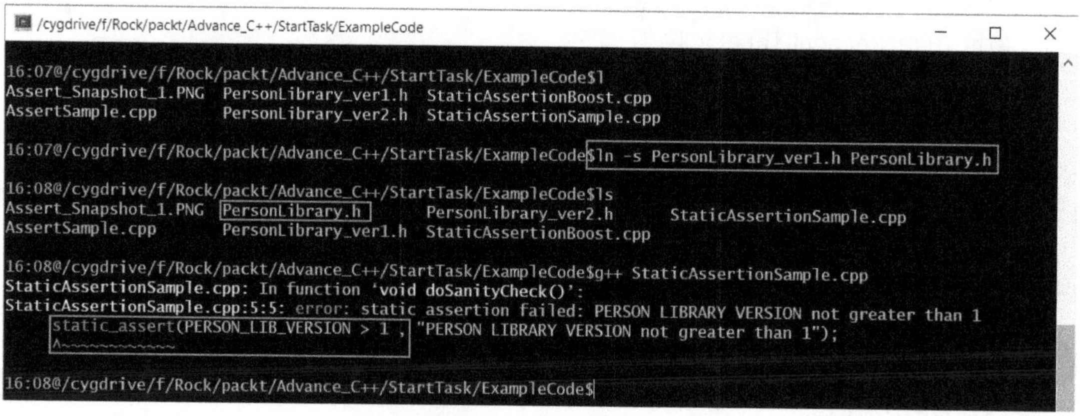

Figure 7.6: Seeing a static error

In the preceding screenshot, three regions are circled in red. The first one gives the command to create a soft link. The second command shows the **PersonLibrary.h** file we created. The third region shows the **static_assert** error that was thrown since the version of the library is not matching.

6. Now, to compile the program correctly, remove the soft link of **ProgramLibrary** and create a new one pointing to **version2** and compile it again. This time, it will compile fine. Type the following commands into the terminal to remove a soft link:

```
rm PersonLibrary.h
ln -s PersonLibrary_ver2.h PersonLibrary.h
g++ StaticAssertionSample.cpp
```

The following is a screenshot of the same:

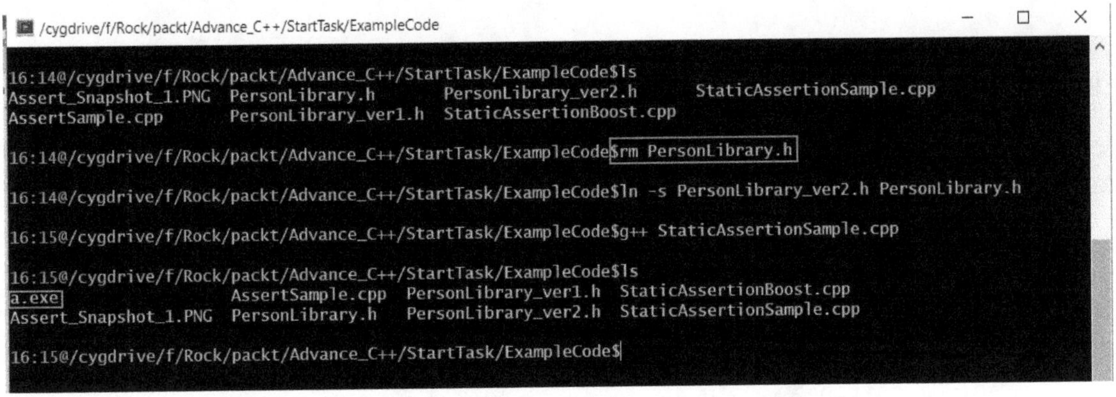

Figure 7.7: Static assertion compilation file

As you can see, a region marked in red shows that the correct version of **PersonLibrary** is used and compilation goes ahead with no problem. After the compilation, a binary file called "**a.exe**" is created. In this exercise, we performed static assertion by comparing the version numbers of two header files. In the next section, we'll explore the concept of exception handling.

## Understanding Exception Handling

As we saw earlier in the debug mode binary, we can use runtime assert to abort the program when a certain condition is not satisfied. But in a release mode binary or production environment, when the client is using this product, it will not be a good idea to abort the program abruptly. It would be better to handle such error conditions and proceed with the next part of the execution of the binary.

The worst case occurs when the binary needs to exit. It'll do so gracefully by adding the correct log messages and cleaning all the allocated memory for this process. For such a scenario, exception handling is used. Here, when an error condition is hit, execution is transferred to a special block of code. The exception consists of three sections, which are as follows:

- **try block**: Here, we check if the criteria match the necessary condition.

- **throw block**: It throws an exception if the criteria do not match.

- **catch block**: It catches the exception and performs the necessary execution for that error condition.

In the next section, we'll solve an exercise wherein we'll perform exception handling on our code.

## Exercise 3: Performing Exception Handling

In this exercise, we'll be performing exception handling on our **AssertSample.cpp** code. We'll replace the assert condition with our exception. Perform the following steps to implement this exercise:

1. Create a file named **ExceptionSample.cpp**.

2. Add the following codes to add header files:

   ```
   #include<iostream>
   #include<cstring>

   using std::cout;
   using std::endl;
   ```

3. Create a **checkValidIp()** function wherein we have a try-catch block. If the condition present in the try block is not satisfied, an exception will be thrown and the message in the catch block will be printed. Add the following code to accomplish this:

   ```
   bool checkValidIp(const char * ip){
       try{
           if(ip == NULL)
               throw ("ip is NULL");

           if(strlen(ip) > 15)
               throw int(strlen(ip));
       }
       catch(const char * str){
   ```

```
            cout << "Error in checkValidIp :"<< str << endl;
            return false;
    }
    catch(int len){
            cout << "Error in checkValidIp, ip len:" << len <<" greater than
    15 characters, condition fail" << endl;
            return false;
    }

        cout << "strlen: " << strlen(ip) << endl;
        return true;
    }
```

In the preceding code, you can see the try block where the condition is checked. Inside the try block, if **ip** is **NULL**, then it will throw an exception of the (**const char \***) type. In the next condition, if **ip** is **greater than 15**, then it will throw an exception with the int parameter type. This throw is caught by a correct catch with matching parameters (**int** or **const char \***). Both exceptions return **false** with some error message. Alternatively, in the **catch** block, you can perform extra steps if any cleaning is needed or use the default values for variables that were used for comparison in the exception.

> **Note**
>
> There is a default exception; for example, if there's a nested function that throws an error with a different parameter, it can be caught as a higher-level function with a parameter such as catch(...). Again, in the generic catch, you can create a default behavior for exception handling.

4. Create the **main()** function and write the following code inside it:

```
    int main(){
        const char * ip;
        ip = NULL;
        if (checkValidIp(ip))
            cout << "IP address is correctly validated" << endl;
        else {
```

```
            /// work on error condition
            // if needed exit program gracefully.
            return -1;
        }
        return 0;
    }
```

5. Open the terminal, compile our file, and run the binary. You will see the following output:

Figure 7.8: Example execute code with exception handling

The preceding example throws an exception for **ip** being **NULL** and exits gracefully.

6. Now, modify the value of **ip** in the **main** function by providing more than **15** characters. Write the following code to do this:

```
ip = "111.111.111.11111";
```

7. Open the terminal, compile our file, and run the binary. You will see the following output:

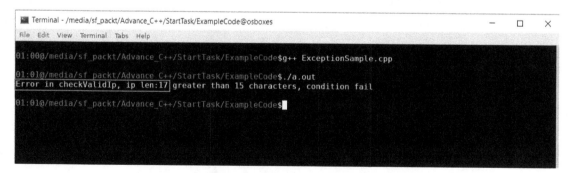

Figure 7.9: Another example of exception handling

It throws an error with a **length mismatch** for the **ip string**.

8.  Again, modify the value of `ip` in the `main` function by providing less than **15** characters. Write the following code to do this:

    ```
    ip = "111.111.111.111";
    ```

9.  Open the terminal, compile our file, and run the binary. You will see the following output:

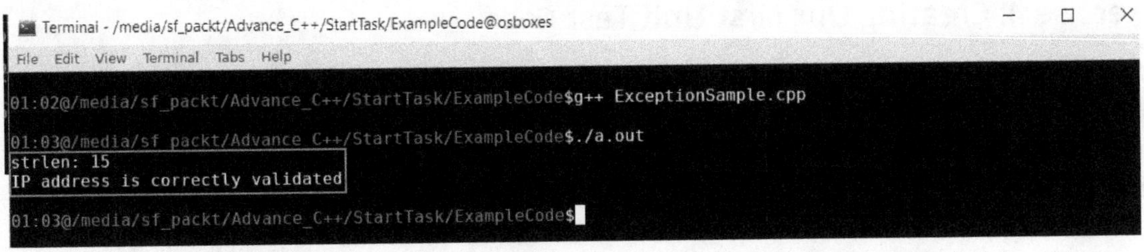

Figure 7.10: The binary runs fine without throwing an exception

As you can see from the preceding screenshot, the binary file executes properly without any exceptions. Now that you've understood how to handle exceptions, in the next section, we'll explore the concepts of **unit testing** and **mock testing**.

## Unit Testing and Mock Testing

When a developer starts writing code, they need to ensure it is tested correctly at the unit level. It may happen that the boundary conditions are missed, and the code may break when it runs on the client's site. To avoid this situation, generally, it is a good idea to do **unit testing** for the code. **Unit testing** is testing that's performed at the unit level or the base level of the code where a developer can test their code in an isolated environment, assuming the required setup has been fulfilled to run a feature of the code. Generally, it is good practice to break down modules into small functions and test each function separately.

For example, suppose part of the functionality is to read the configuration file and get the environment set up with the parameters from the configuration file. We can create a dedicated function to write this functionality. So, to test this function, we can create a set of unit test cases that will check various combinations that may fail or behave incorrectly. Once these test cases have been identified, the developer can write code to cover the functionality and make sure it passes all the unit test cases. This is good practice as part of development where you keep on adding test cases first and add code accordingly, and then run all the test cases for that function and make sure they behave appropriately.

There are a good number of tools available for writing and integrating unit test cases for a project. A few of them are **cppunit**, **Google Test**, **Microsoft Unit Testing Framework**, and **catch**. For our example's purpose, we'll work on the `Google Test framework`. It is freely available and can be integrated with the project. It uses the **xUnit test framework** and has a collection of asserts that can be used to test the condition for test cases. In the next section, we'll solve an exercise wherein we'll be creating our first unit test case.

## Exercise 4: Creating Our First Unit Test Case

In this exercise, we'll work on the same scenario we discussed in the previous section wherein the developer is tasked with writing a function to parse the `configuration file`. Different valid parameters are passed in the configuration file, for example, `product executable name`, `version number`, `database connectivity information`, `IP address` to connect to the server, and so on. Assume that the developer will break down all this functionality of parsing the file and setting and testing the parameters for individual properties in a separate function. In our case, we assume that the developer is writing functionality where they have parsed the `IP address` as a `string` and wants to deduce if the `string` is the valid `IP address`. For now, the criteria to match the `IP address` to be valid needs to satisfy the following conditions:

- The `string` should not be null.

- The `string` should contain no more than **16** characters

- The `string` should be in the **XXX.XXX.XXX.XXX** format, where **X** must be a digit from **0-9**.

Perform the following steps to implement this exercise:

1. Create the **CheckIp.h** header file and write the following code inside it:

```
#ifndef  _CHECK_IP_H_
#define _CHECK_IP_H_
include <iostream>
include <cstring>
using namespace std;
bool checkValidIp(const char *);
#endif
```

In the preceding code, we wrote a function named **checkValidIp()** to check if the **IP address** is valid. Again, just to understand the **Google unit test**, we will write minimal code to understand the feature.

2. Create a **CheckIp.cpp** file and write the following code, wherein we'll check if **ip** is **not NULL** and that the length is less than **16**:

```cpp
#include "CheckIp.h"
#include<string>
#include<sstream>
bool checkValidIp(const char * ip){
    if(ip == NULL){
        cout << "Error : IP passes is NULL " << endl;
        return false;
    }
    if(strlen(ip) > 15){
        cout << "Error: IP size is greater than 15" << endl;
        return false;
    }
    cout << "strlen: " << strlen(ip) << endl;
    return true;
}
```

In the preceding code, if both conditions fail, the function returns **false**.

3. Call the **checkValidIp()** function to create a new file named **MainIp.cpp**. This file, in general, will contain the main flow of the project but for our exercise's purpose, we are just calling our **checkValidIP()** function. Add the following code inside it:

```cpp
#include"CheckIp.h"

int main(){
    const char * ip;
    //ip = "111.111.111.111";
    ip = "111.111.111.11111";

    if (checkValidIp(ip))
        cout << "IP address is correctly validated" << endl;
    else {
        /// work on error condition
        // if needed exit program gracefully.
        cout << " Got error in valid ip " << endl;
        return -1;
    }
    return 0;
}
```

4. To create test code, we'll create our first **.cpp** file, that is, **TestCases.cpp**. This will contain test cases for our **checkValidIp** function. Write the following code inside it:

```
#include"CheckIp.h"
#include<gtest/gtest.h>
using namespace std;
const char * testIp;
TEST(CheckIp, testNull){
    testIp=NULL;
    ASSERT_FALSE(checkValidIp(testIp));
}
TEST(CheckIp, BadLength){
    testIp = "232.13.1231.1321.123";
    ASSERT_FALSE(checkValidIp(testIp));
}
```

In the second line of the preceding code, we're including the **gtest.h** file. We're also calling test cases using the **TEST** function, which takes two parameters: the first is the **testsuite** name and the second is the **testcase** name. For our case, we have created **TestSuite CheckIp**. In the **TEST** block, you will see that we have the **Google test** define an **assert** called **ASSERT_FALSE** that will check if the condition is **false**. If it's not, it will fail the test case and show the same in the results.

> **Note**
>
> Generally, for a **Google test** case and test suite, you can group them in a common namespace and call the **RUN_ALL_TESTS** macro, which runs all the test cases attached to test binary. For each test case, it calls the **SetUp** function to initialize (like constructor in class), then it calls the actual test case, and finally, it calls the **TearDown** function (like destructor in class). It is not necessary to write the **SetUp** and **TearDown** functions unless you have to initialize something for the test cases.

5. Now, to run the test cases, we will create the main **.cpp** file for the test cases and call the **RUN_ALL_TESTS** macro. Alternatively, we can create an executable by linking the **Google Test library** that invokes **RUN_ALL_TESTS**. For our case, we will do the latter. Open the terminal and run the following command to create a test run binary:

```
g++ -c CheckIp.cpp
```

This will include the object file of **CheckIp.cpp** since the **CheckValidIp** function is defined in it.

6. Now, type the following command to add the necessary libraries that will be linked for creating a binary:

```
g++ CheckIp.o TestCases.cpp -lgtest -lgtest_main -pthread -o TestRun
```

7. Now, run the binary with the following command:

```
./TestRun
```

This shows two test cases that were passed for the **CheckIp testsuite**. The first test case, **CheckIp.testNull**, is called and it passes. The second testcase, **CheckIp. BadLength**, is called and it passes too. This result is visible in the following screenshot:

```
03:04@/media/sf_packt/Advance_C++/StartTask/ExampleCode/gtest$g++ -c CheckIp.cpp

03:04@/media/sf_packt/Advance_C++/StartTask/ExampleCode/gtest$g++ CheckIp.o TestCases.cpp -lgtest -lgtest_main -pthread -o
 TestRun

03:05@/media/sf_packt/Advance_C++/StartTask/ExampleCode/gtest$l
CheckIp.cpp  CheckIp.h  CheckIp.o  MainIp.cpp  TestCases.cpp  TestMain.cpp  Test.make  TestRun

03:05@/media/sf_packt/Advance_C++/StartTask/ExampleCode/gtest$./TestRun
Running main() from src/gtest_main.cc
[==========] Running 2 tests from 1 test suite.
[----------] Global test environment set-up.
[----------] 2 tests from CheckIp
[ RUN      ] CheckIp.testNull
ERROR : IP passed is NULL
[       OK ] CheckIp.testNull (0 ms)
[ RUN      ] CheckIp.BadLength
ERROR : IP size is greater than 15
[       OK ] CheckIp.BadLength (0 ms)
[----------] 2 tests from CheckIp (0 ms total)

[----------] Global test environment tear-down
[==========] 2 tests from 1 test suite ran. (0 ms total)
[  PASSED  ] 2 tests.

03:05@/media/sf_packt/Advance_C++/StartTask/ExampleCode/gtest$
```

Figure 7.11: Compiling and executing test cases

Note

In **Google Test**, we can also use other asserts, but for our test cases, we are fine with **ASSERT_FALSE** since we are only checking the false condition for the IP address that we pass.

8. Now, we will add more test cases to make our code robust. This is generally good practice for writing code. First, create the test cases and make sure the code runs fine for new test cases and old test cases along with the correct functionality of the code. To add more test cases, add the following code to the **TestCases.cpp** file:

```cpp
TEST(CheckIp, WrongTokenCount){
    testIp = "22.13111.11";
    ASSERT_FALSE(checkValidIp(testIp));
}
TEST(CheckIp, WrongTokenEmpty){
    testIp = "22.131..11";
    ASSERT_FALSE(checkValidIp(testIp));
}
TEST(CheckIp, WrongTokenStart){
    testIp = ".2.1.31.11";
    ASSERT_FALSE(checkValidIp(testIp));
}
TEST(CheckIp, WrongTokenEnd){
    testIp = "2.13.11.1.";
    ASSERT_FALSE(checkValidIp(testIp));
}
TEST(CheckIp, SpaceToken){
    testIp = "2.13.11. 1";
    ASSERT_FALSE(checkValidIp(testIp));
}
TEST(CheckIp, NonDigit){
    testIp = "2.13.b1.A1";
    ASSERT_FALSE(checkValidIp(testIp));
}
TEST(CheckIp, NonValidDigit){
    testIp = "2.13.521.61";
    ASSERT_FALSE(checkValidIp(testIp));
}
TEST(CheckIp, CorrectIp){
    testIp = "232.13.123.1";
    ASSERT_FALSE(checkValidIp(testIp));
}
```

In the preceding code, the first and second cases should fail with incorrect tokens. The third case should fail if the **IP** starts with "." The fourth case should fail if the **IP** ends with "." The fifth case should fail if **IP** has space in-between. The sixth case should fail if the **IP** contains any non-digit characters. The seventh case should fail if **IP** has a token value less than **0** and greater than **255**. The last case should fail if **IP** has wrong token counts.

9. Now, add the following code inside the **CheckValidIp()** function of the **CheckIp. cpp** file. This code is required to handle new test cases:

```cpp
if(ip[strlen(ip)-1] == '.'){
    cout<<"ERROR : Incorrect token at end"<<endl;
    return false;
}
isstringstream istrstr(ip);
vector<string> tokens;
string token;
regex expression("[^0-9]");
smatch m;
while(getline(istrstr, token, '.')){
    if(token.empty()){
        cout<<"ERROR : Got empty token"<<endl;
        return false;
    }
    if(token.find(' ') != string::npos){
        cout<<"ERROR : Space character in token"<<endl;
        return false;
    }
    if(regex_search(token,m,expression)){
        cout<<"ERROR : NonDigit character in token"<<endl;
        return false;
    }
    int val = atoi(token.c_str());
    if(val<0 || val>255){
        cout<<"ERROR : Invalid digit in token"<<endl;
        return false;
    }
    tokens.push_back(token);
}
if(tokens.size()!=4){
```

```
        cout<<"ERROR : Incorrect IP tokens used"<<endl;
        return false;
    }
    cout<<"strlen: "<<strlen(ip)<<endl;
    return true;
    }
```

10. Open the terminal and write the following command to run the binary file:

```
./TestRun
```

All the test cases have been executed, as shown in the following screenshot:

```
03:30@/media/sf_packt/Advance_C++/StartTask/ExampleCode/gtest$./TestRun
Running main() from src/gtest_main.cc
[==========] Running 10 tests from 1 test suite.
[----------] Global test environment set-up.
[----------] 10 tests from CheckIp
[ RUN      ] CheckIp.testNull
ERROR : IP passed is NULL
[       OK ] CheckIp.testNull (0 ms)
[ RUN      ] CheckIp.BadLength
ERROR : IP size is greater than 15
[       OK ] CheckIp.BadLength (0 ms)
[ RUN      ] CheckIp.WrongTokenCount
ERROR : Invalid Digit in token
[       OK ] CheckIp.WrongTokenCount (3 ms)
[ RUN      ] CheckIp.WrongTokenEmpty
ERROR : Got empty token
[       OK ] CheckIp.WrongTokenEmpty (1 ms)
[ RUN      ] CheckIp.WrongTokenStart
ERROR : Got empty token
[       OK ] CheckIp.WrongTokenStart (0 ms)
[ RUN      ] CheckIp.WrongTokenEnd
ERROR : Incorrect token at end
[       OK ] CheckIp.WrongTokenEnd (0 ms)
[ RUN      ] CheckIp.SpaceToken
ERROR : Space character in token
[       OK ] CheckIp.SpaceToken (0 ms)
[ RUN      ] CheckIp.NonDigit
ERROR : NonDigit character in token
[       OK ] CheckIp.NonDigit (1 ms)
[ RUN      ] CheckIp.NonValidDigit
ERROR : Invalid Digit in token
[       OK ] CheckIp.NonValidDigit (0 ms)
[ RUN      ] CheckIp.CorrectIp
strlen: 12
[       OK ] CheckIp.CorrectIp (1 ms)
[----------] 10 tests from CheckIp (6 ms total)

[----------] Global test environment tear-down
[==========] 10 tests from 1 test suite ran. (6 ms total)
[  PASSED  ] 10 tests.
```

Figure 7.12: Output of test cases run

The preceding screenshot shows that there are **10** test cases in the **CheckIp** test suite and that all the test cases ran fine. In the next section, we'll learn about unit testing using mock objects.

## Unit Testing Using Mock Objects

When a developer works on unit testing, there may be scenarios wherein certain interfaces are called after concrete actions have taken place. For example, as we discussed in the preceding scenarios, let's assume that the project is designed in such a way that, before its execution, it takes all the configuration information from the database. It queries the database to get specific parameters, for example, the web server's **IP address**, **user**, and **password**. It then tries to connect to a web server (maybe there is another module that handles network-related tasks) or starts acting on the items that are needed for an actual project. Previously, we worked on testing the validity of the IP address. Now, we'll go a step further. Let's assume that the IP address is fetched from the database and that we have a utility class that handles connecting to **DB** and querying **IP addresses**.

Now, to test the IP address' validity, we need to assume the database connectivity has been set up. This means that the application can query the database correctly and get the results of the query, one of which is an **IP address**. Only then can we test the IP address' validity. Now, in order to perform such testing, we must assume that all the necessary activities have been completed and that we've got an **IP address** to test. Here comes the mock object, which behaves like the real object. It provides the facility for unit testing so that the application is under the impression that the IP address has already been fetched from the database, but in reality, we have imitated it. To create a mock object, we need to inherit it from the class that it needs to imitate. In the next section, we'll walk through an exercise to get a better understanding of the mock object.

## Exercise 5: Creating Mock Objects

In this exercise, we'll create mock objects by assuming that all the interfaces are working as expected. Using these objects, we'll test a few functionalities such as validating the **IP address**, checking DB connectivity, and checking whether the **username** and **password** are in correct format. Once all the tests have passed, we'll confirm the application and make it ready for **QA**. Perform the following steps to implement this exercise:

1.  Create a header file named **Misc.h** and include the necessary libraries:

    ```
    #include<iostream>
    #include<string>
    #include<sstream>
    #include<vector>
    #include<iterator>
    #include<regex>
    using namespace std;
    ```

2.  Create a class named **ConnectDatabase** that will connect to the database and return the result of the query. Within the class, declare the **Dbname**, user, and passwd variables. Also, declare a constructor and two virtual functions. Out of these two virtual functions, the first one must be a destructor, and the second one must be the **getResult()** function, which returns the query result from the database. Add the following code to implement this:

    ```
    class ConnectDatabase{
        string DBname;
        string user;
        string passwd;

    public:
        ConnectDatabase() {}
        ConnectDatabase(string _dbname, string _uname, string _passwd) :
            DBname(_dbname), user(_uname), passwd(_passwd) { }

        virtual ~ConnectDatabase() {}
        virtual string getResult(string query);
    };
    ```

3.  Create another class named **WebServerConnect**. Declare three **string** variables inside the **class**, namely **Webserver**, **uname**, and **passwd**. Create constructor and two virtual functions. Out of these two virtual functions, the first one must be a destructor, and the second one must be the **getRequest()** function. Add the following code to implement this:

```
class WebServerConnect{
        string Webserver;
        string uname;
        string passwd;

        public :
        WebServerConnect(string _sname, string _uname, string _passwd) :
                Webserver(_sname), uname(_uname), passwd(_passwd) { }

                virtual ~WebServerConnect() {}
                virtual string getRequest(string req);
};
```

> **Note**
>
> **Virtual functions** are required since we are going to create a **Mock class** from the preceding class and call these functions.

4.  Create a class named **App**. Create the constructors, and destructors and call all the functions. Add the following code to implement this:

```
class App {
        ConnectDatabase *DB;
        WebServerConnect *WB;

        public :
                App():DB(NULL), WB(NULL) {}
                ~App() {
                        if ( DB )  delete DB;
                        if ( WB )  delete WB;
                }
                bool checkValidIp(string ip);
                string getDBResult(string query);
                string getWebResult(string query);
```

```
        void connectDB(string, string, string);
        void connectDB(ConnectDatabase *db);
        void connectWeb(string, string, string);
        void run();
};
```

In the preceding code, the app will first query the database and get the **IP address**. It then connects to the web server with the necessary information and query it to get the required information.

5. Create a class named **MockMisc.h** and add the following code:

```
#include"Misc.h"
#include<gtest/gtest.h>
#include<gmock/gmock.h>

class MockDB : public ConnectDatabase {
    public :
        MockDB() {}
        virtual ~MockDB(){}

        MOCK_METHOD1(getResult, string( string) );
};
```

In the preceding code, you can see that we have included the **gmock** header file, which is needed to create a mock class. Also, the **MockDB** class is inherited from the **ConnectDatabase** class. The **MOCK_METHOD1(getResult, string(string));** line states that we are going to mock the **getResult** interface. So, during unit testing, we can call the **getResult** function directly with the desired result without creating the **ConnectDatabase** class and running a real query to the database. One important point that needs to be noted here is that the function we need to mock must be defined with the **MOCK_METHOD[N] macro**, where N is the number of parameters the interface will take. In our case, the **getResult** interface takes one parameter. Thus, it is mocked with the **MOCK_METHOD1** macro.

6. Create a file named **Misc.cpp** and add the following code:

```
#include"Misc.h"
#include <unistd.h>

string ConnectDatabase::getResult(string query){
    // dummy func, need to implement..
    // assuming query sent to DB is success and
    // will return some dummy string
    return string("DB returned success");
```

```
}

string WebServerConnect::getRequest(string req){
    // dummy func, need to implement..
    // assume no req string is sent to webserver. .
    // its returns the result returned from server.
    return string("Webserver returned success");
}

void App::connectDB(string dbname, string user, string passwd){
    if ( DB )
        delete DB;
    DB = new ConnectDatabase(dbname, user, passwd);
}

void App::connectDB(ConnectDatabase *db){
    if ( DB )
        delete DB;
    DB = db;
}

void App::connectWeb(string webname, string user, string passwd){
    if ( WB )
        delete WB;
    WB = new WebServerConnect(webname, user, passwd);
}

string App::getDBResult(string query){
    return DB->getResult(query);
}

string App::getWebResult(string query) {
    return WB->getRequest(query);
}

void App::run(){
    if ( (DB == NULL) || (WB == NULL) )
        return ;
    while( true ){
        // read some request to be run on web and get result. ..
        cout << getWebResult("dummy request to webserver") << endl;;
        sleep(5);
```

```cpp
        }
    }

bool App::checkValidIp(string ip){
    if(ip.empty()){
        cout << "ERROR : IP passed is NULL " << endl;
        return false;
    }

    if(ip.size() > 15){
        cout << "ERROR : IP size is greater than 15" <<endl;
        return false;
    }

    //check if last character in ip is not '.' as that is not captured in
tokenizing
    if (ip[ip.size()-1] == '.'){
        cout <<"ERROR : Incorrect token at end" << endl;
        return false;
    }

    istringstream istrstr(ip);
    vector<string> tokens;
    string token;
    regex expression("[^0-9]");
    smatch m;
    while( getline(istrstr, token, '.') ){
        if ( token.empty() ){
            cout << "ERROR : Got empty token " << endl;
            return false;
        }
        if ( token.find(' ') != string::npos){
            cout << "ERROR : Space character in token " << endl;
            return false;
        }
        if ( regex_search(token, m, expression) ){
            cout << "ERROR : NonDigit character in token " << endl;
            return false;
        }
        int val = atoi(token.c_str());
        if ( val < 0 || val > 255 ){
            cout << "ERROR : Invalid Digit in token " << endl;
```

```
            return false;
        }
        tokens.push_back(token);
    }
    if ( tokens.size() != 4 ){
cout << " ERROR : Incorect IP tokens used" << endl;
return false;
    }
        cout << "strlen: " << ip.size() << endl;
        return true;

}
```

In the preceding code, we have created a minimal interface and dummy parameters to make it run so that we can understand the actual functionality. We've developed basic functionalities for the **getResult()** and **getRequest()** functions, where the DB query and **WebServer** query return a default string. Here, the **App::run()** function assumes that both DB connectivity and web server connectivity has been executed and now it can execute web queries at regular intervals. At the end of each query, it will return the "**Webserver returned success**" string by default.

7. Now, create a file named **RunApp.cpp** and write the following code inside the main function:

```
#include"Misc.h"

int main(){

    App app;
    app.connectDB("dbname","dbuser", "dbpasswd");
    string ip = app.getDBResult("dummy");
    // DB query to get Webserver IP
    // Similarly some miscellaneous activities to get configuratio
information
    // Like querying DB to get correct username/passwd to connect to
WebServer..

    // After getting IP from DB, check if the IP is valid..
    //app.checkValidIp(ip);

    // Now conect to webserver with parameters extracted from DB.
    app.connectWeb("webname","user", "passwd");
```

```
    // Now run the App, like sending some request to webserver,
    // getting result and doing activity with received data.
    app.run();

    return 0;
}
```

As you can see in the preceding code, the App class instance is created. Using this instance, we connect to the database with the help of dummy parameters, namely **dbname**, **dbuser**, and **dbpasswd**. Then, we query to the database to get the IP address and other config parameters. We've commented the **app.checkValidIp(ip)** line as we're assuming that the IP address that we've fetched from the DB needs to be validated. Also, this function needs to be unit tested. Using the **connectWeb()** function, we can connect to the web server by passing dummy parameters such as **webname**, **user**, and **passwd**. Finally, we call the **run()** function, which will run in iteration, thereby querying the web server and giving the default output.

8. Save all the files and open the terminal. In order to get the basic functionality required to execute the project, we'll build the binary file and execute it to see the result. Run the following command in the terminal:

   ```
   g++ Misc.cpp RunApp.cpp -o RunApp
   ```

   The preceding code will create binary file called **RunApp** in the current folder.

9. Now, write the following command to run the executable:

   ```
   ./RunApp
   ```

   The preceding command generates the following output in the Terminal:

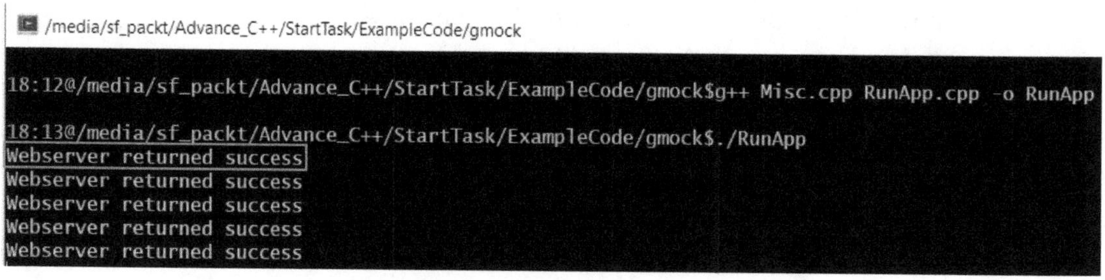

Figure 7.13: Running the app

As you can see in the preceding screenshot, the binary displays the output "**Webserver returned success**" in a timely fashion. So far, our application is running fine as it is assuming that all the interfaces are working as expected. But we still have to test a few functionalities such as validating the **IP address**, **DB connectivity**, checking whether the **username** and **password** are in the correct format if any, and more before making it ready for **QA**.

10. Using the same infrastructure, start unit testing each functionality. For our exercise, we'll assume that the **DB connectivity** has already been done and has been queried to get the **IP address**. After that, we can start unit testing the validity of the **IP address**. So, in our test case, the Database class needs to be mocked and the **getDBResult** function must return the **IP address**. This **IP address** will be passed to the **checkValidIP** function later, wherein we'll test it. To implement this, create a class named **TestApp.cpp** wherein we'll be calling the **checkValidIP** function:

```cpp
#include"MockMisc.h"

using ::testing::_;
using ::testing::Return;

class TestApp : public ::testing::Test {
    protected :
        App testApp;
        MockDB *mdb;

        void SetUp(){
            mdb = new MockDB();
            testApp.connectDB(mdb);
        }

        void TearDown(){
        }
};

TEST_F(TestApp, NullIP){
    EXPECT_CALL(*mdb, getResult(_)).
                WillOnce(Return(""));

    ASSERT_FALSE(testApp.checkValidIp(testApp.getDBResult("")));
}

TEST_F(TestApp, SpaceTokenIP){
```

```
            EXPECT_CALL(*mdb, getResult(_)).
                      WillOnce(Return("13. 21.31.68"));

         ASSERT_FALSE(testApp.checkValidIp(testApp.getDBResult("")));
    }


    TEST_F(TestApp, NonValidDigitIP){
         EXPECT_CALL(*mdb, getResult(_)).
                      WillOnce(Return("13.521.31.68"));

         ASSERT_FALSE(testApp.checkValidIp(testApp.getDBResult("")));
    }


    TEST_F(TestApp, CorrectIP){
         EXPECT_CALL(*mdb, getResult(_)).
                      WillOnce(Return("212.121.21.45"));

         ASSERT_TRUE(testApp.checkValidIp(testApp.getDBResult("")));
    }
```

Here, we have used the testing and **testing::Return** namespaces to call mock
class interfaces and return the user-defined values that are meant for test cases.
Within the **TEST_F** function, we used the **EXPECT_CALL** function, wherein we pass the
instance of a mock object as the first parameter and pass the **getResult()** function
as the second parameter. The **WillOnce(Return(""))** line states that the interface
needs to be called once and will return  "" and an empty string. This is the value
that needs to be passed to the **checkValidIP** function to test for the empty
string. This is checked with the **ASSERT_FALSE** macro. Similarly, other test cases
can be created using the mocked object of DB and passing the IP address to the
**checkValidIP** function. To create various test cases, the **TestApp** class is inherited
from the **testing::Test** class, which contains the App instance and Mocked object
of Database. Within the **TestApp** class, we have defined two functions, namely
**SetUp()** and **TearDown()**. Inside the **SetUp()** function, we created a **MockDB** instance
and tagged it to the testApp instance. Since nothing needs to be done for the
**TearDown()** function, we've kept it empty. Its destructor is called in the destructor
of the **App** class. Also, we passed two parameters inside the **TEST_F** function. The
first parameter is the Test class while the second parameter is the test case's
name.

11. Save all the files and open the terminal. Run the following command:

```
g++ Misc.cpp TestApp.cpp -lgtest -lgmock -lgtest_main -pthread -o TestApp
```

In the preceding command, we have also linked the **gmock library**. Now, type the following command to run the test cases:

```
./TestApp
```

The preceding command generates the following output:

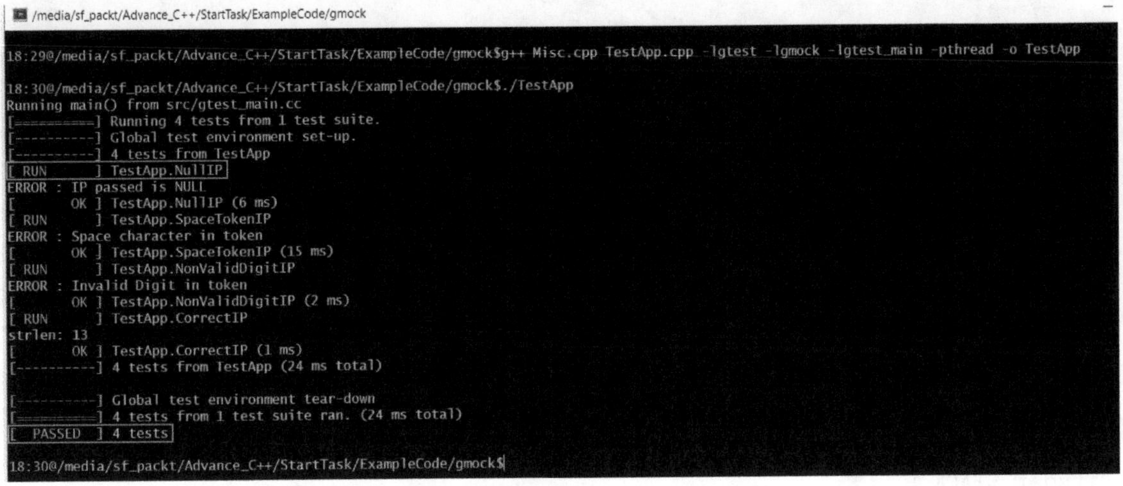

Figure 7.14: Running the Gmock test

From the preceding command, we can see that all the test cases executed and passed successfully. In the next section, we'll discuss **breakpoints**, **watchpoints**, and **data visualization**.

## Breakpoints, Watchpoints, and Data Visualization

In the previous section, we discussed that unit testing needs to be done before a developer checks code into the repository branch and can be seen by other team members so that they can integrate it with other modules. Although unit testing is done well and the developer checks the code in, there may be a chance that whenever the code is integrated and the QA team starts testing, they may find a bug in the code. Generally, in such a scenario, an error may be thrown in a module that was caused due to changes in the other module. It may become difficult for the team to crack down on the real reason for such issues. In such cases, **debugging** comes into the picture. It tells us exactly how the code is behaving, and the developer can get granular information of the code's execution. A developer can see what parameters the function is getting and what value it is returning. It can tell exactly what value is assigned to a variable or a pointer or what the content in memory is. This becomes very helpful for the developer to identify in which part of the code the issue is. In the next section, we'll implement a stack and perform a few operations on it.

## Working with the Stack Data Structure

Consider a scenario wherein a developer has been asked to develop his/her own stack structure that can take in any parameter. Here, the requirement is that the stack structure must follow the **Last In First Out** (**LIFO**) principle, where elements are placed on top of each other and when they're removed from the stack, the last element should be removed first. It should have the following functions:

- **push()** to place a new element on top of the stack
- **top()** to display the top element of the stack, if any
- **pop()** to remove the last inserted element from the stack
- **is_empty()** to check if the stack is empty
- **size()** to display the number of elements present in the stack
- **clean()** to empty the stack if it has any elements in it

The following lines of code show how to include the necessary libraries within the **Stack.h** header file:

```
#ifndef STACK_H__
#define STACK_H__
#include<iostream>
using namespace std;
```

As we already know, the stack consists of various operations. To define each of these functions, we'll write the following code:

```
template<typename T>
struct Node{
    T element;
    Node<T> *next;
};
template<typename T>
class Stack{
    Node<T> *head;
    int sz;

    public :
```

```
        Stack():head(nullptr), sz(0){}
        ~Stack();

        bool is_empty();
        int size();
        T top();
        void pop();
        void push(T);
        void clean();
};
template<typename T>
Stack<T>::~Stack(){
    if ( head ) clean();
}
template<typename T>
void Stack<T>::clean(){
    Node<T> *tmp;
    while( head ){
        tmp = head;
        head = head -> next;
        delete tmp;
        sz--;
    }
}
template<typename T>
int Stack<T>::size(){
    return sz;
}
template<typename T>
bool Stack<T>::is_empty(){
        return (head == nullptr) ? true : false;
}
```

```cpp
template<typename T>
T Stack<T>::top(){
    if ( head == nullptr){
        // throw error ...
        throw(string("Cannot see top of empty stack"));
    }else {
        return head -> element;
    }
}
template<typename T>
void Stack<T>::pop(){
    if ( head == nullptr ){
        // throw error
        throw(string("Cannot pop empty stack"));
    }else {
        Node<T> *tmp = head ;
        head = head -> next;
        delete tmp;
        sz--;
    }
}
template<typename T>
void Stack<T>::push(T val){
    Node<T> *tmp = new Node<T>();
    tmp -> element = val;
    tmp -> next = head;
    head = tmp;
    sz++;
}
// Miscellaneous functions for stack..

template<typename T>
```

```
void displayStackStats(Stack<T> &st){
    cout << endl << "-----------------------------" << endl;
    cout << "Showing Stack basic Stats ...  " << endl;
    cout << "Stack is empty : " << (st.is_empty() ? "true" : "false") <<
endl;
    cout << "Stack size :" << st.size() << endl;
    cout << "-------------------------------" << endl << endl;

}


#endif
```

So far, we've seen how to implement a stack using a **Single Linked List**. Every time **push** is called in Stack, a new element of a given value will be created and attached to the beginning of the stack. We call this a head member variable and is where the head will point to the next element in the stack and so on. When **pop** is called, the head will be removed from the stack and will point to the next element of the stack.

Let's write the implementation of the previously created Stack in the **Main.cpp** file. The main function has a try block that creates a Stack of integers, as well as a Stack of characters. A few push and pop are done for both, and in-between, the top of the Stack is called to display the latest element. For a stack of integers, there are three pushes involved in the beginning: **22**, **426**, and **57**. When the `displayStackStats()` function is called, it should state the size of the stack to be **3**. Then, we pop out **57** from the stack and the top element must display **426**. We'll do the same operation for the stack of **char**. Here is the complete implementation of the stack:

```
#include"Stack.h"

int main(){
    try {
        Stack<int> si;
        displayStackStats<int>(si);
        si.push(22);
        si.push(426);
        cout << "Top of stack contains " << si.top() << endl;
        si.push(57);
        displayStackStats<int>(si);
```

```cpp
            cout << "Top of stack contains " << si.top() << endl;

            si.pop();
            cout << "Top of stack contains " << si.top() << endl;

            si.pop();
            displayStackStats<int>(si);

            Stack<char> sc;
            sc.push('d');
            sc.push('l');
            displayStackStats<char>(sc);
            cout << "Top of char stack contains:" << sc.top() << endl;
        }
        catch(string str){
            cout << "Error : " << str << endl;
        }
        catch(...){
            cout << "Error : Unexpected exception caught " << endl;
        }
        return 0;
    }
```

When we compile the **Main.cpp** file by writing the following command, the Main executable will be created in debug mode (since the **-g** option is being used). Thus, you can debug the binary if needed:

```
g++ -g Main.cpp -o Main
```

We'll write the following command to execute the binary:

```
./Main
```

The preceding command generates the following output:

```
15:34@/media/sf_packt/Advance_C++/StartTask/ExampleCode/debugging$g++ -g Main.cpp -o Main

15:34@/media/sf_packt/Advance_C++/StartTask/ExampleCode/debugging$./Main

------------------------------
Showing Stack basic Stats ...
Stack is empty : true
Stack size :0
------------------------------

Top of stack contains 426

------------------------------
Showing Stack basic Stats ...
Stack is empty : false
Stack size :3
------------------------------

Top of stack contains 0
Top of stack contains 549216960

------------------------------
Showing Stack basic Stats ...
Stack is empty : false
Stack size :1
------------------------------


------------------------------
Showing Stack basic Stats ...
Stack is empty : false
Stack size :2
------------------------------

Top of char stack contains:█
double free or corruption (fasttop)
Aborted (core dumped)

15:36@/media/sf_packt/Advance_C++/StartTask/ExampleCode/debugging$
```

Figure 7.15: Main function using the Stack class

In the preceding output, the red ink in the second call to the statistics function shows the correct information of showing three elements in a stack of int. However, the red ink calls to the top of the int stack show random or garbage values. If the program is run again, it will show some other random numbers and not the expected values of **57** and **426**. Similarly, for the stack of char, the section highlighted in the red ink, that is, top of **char**, shows a garbage value instead of the expected value, that is, "l". Later, the execution shows the error of double free or corruption, which means free was called to the same memory location again. Finally, the executable gave core dump. The program didn't execute as expected and it may not be clear from the display where the actual error lies. To debug **Main**, we'll write the following command:

```
gdb ./Main
```

The preceding command generates the following output:

```
01:46@/media/sf_packt/Advance_C++/StartTask/ExampleCode/debugging$gdb ./Main
GNU gdb (Ubuntu 8.2-0ubuntu1) 8.2
Copyright (C) 2018 Free Software Foundation, Inc.
License GPLv3+: GNU GPL version 3 or later <http://gnu.org/licenses/gpl.html>
This is free software: you are free to change and redistribute it.
There is NO WARRANTY, to the extent permitted by law.
Type "show copying" and "show warranty" for details.
This GDB was configured as "x86_64-linux-gnu".
Type "show configuration" for configuration details.
For bug reporting instructions, please see:
<http://www.gnu.org/software/gdb/bugs/>.
Find the GDB manual and other documentation resources online at:
    <http://www.gnu.org/software/gdb/documentation/>.

For help, type "help".
Type "apropos word" to search for commands related to "word"...
Reading symbols from ./Main...done.
(gdb) b main
Breakpoint 1 at 0x1280: file Main.cpp, line 3.
(gdb) r
Starting program: /media/sf_packt/Advance_C++/StartTask/ExampleCode/debugging/Main

Breakpoint 1, main () at Main.cpp:3
3          int main(){
(gdb) n
5               Stack<int> si;
(gdb)
6               displayStackStats<int>(si);
(gdb) watch si
Hardware watchpoint 2: si
(gdb) n

---------------------------------
Showing Stack basic Stats ...
Stack is empty : true
Stack size :0
---------------------------------

7               si.push(22);
(gdb)

Hardware watchpoint 2: si

Old value = {head = 0x0, sz = 0}
New value = {head = 0x55555556b280, sz = 0}
Stack<int>::push (this=0x7fffffffe2c0, val=22) at Stack.h:75
75          sz++;
(gdb)
```

Figure 7.16: Debugger display – I

In the preceding screenshot, the marks highlighted in blue show how the debugger is used and what it displays. The first mark shows the debugger being called using the **gdb** command. After entering the **gdb** command, the user goes to the command mode of the debugger. Here is some brief information about the commands being used in the command mode:

- **b main**: This tells the debugger to break at the main function call.
- **r**: It is the short form that's used to run the executable. It can be run by passing parameters too.
- **n**: It is a short form for the next command, which tells us to execute the next statement.
- **watch si**: This watches the **si** variable when it is called in the code and its value is changed. The debugger will display the content of the code where this variable is being used.
- **s**: It is a short form for the "`step in`" command.

The next statement that will be executed is `si.push(22)`. Since **si** has been updated, the watchpoint invokes and displays the old value of **si** and a new value of **si** wherein it shows that the old value of **si** was head with NULL and **sz** was 0. After `si.push`, the head is updated with the new value and its execution comes to line 75 of the **Stack.h** file, which is where the **sz** variable is incremented. If the *Enter* key is pressed again, it will execute it.

Note that the execution has automatically moved from the main function to the **Stack::push** function. The following is a screenshot of the continued commands on the debugger:

```
Hardware watchpoint 2: si

Old value = {head = 0x55555556b280, sz = 0}
New value = {head = 0x55555556b280, sz = 1}
Stack<int>::push (this=0x7fffffffe2c0, val=22) at Stack.h:76
76      }
(gdb)
main () at Main.cpp:8
8               si.push(426);
(gdb) s
Stack<int>::push (this=0x7fffffffe2c0, val=426) at Stack.h:71
71          Node<T> *tmp = new Node<T>();
(gdb) n
72          tmp -> element = val;
(gdb)
73          tmp -> next = head;
(gdb)
74          head = tmp;
(gdb)

Hardware watchpoint 2: si

Old value = {head = 0x55555556b280, sz = 1}
New value = {head = 0x55555556b2a0, sz = 1}
Stack<int>::push (this=0x7fffffffe2c0, val=426) at Stack.h:75
75          sz++;
(gdb)

Hardware watchpoint 2: si

Old value = {head = 0x55555556b2a0, sz = 1}
New value = {head = 0x55555556b2a0, sz = 2}
Stack<int>::push (this=0x7fffffffe2c0, val=426) at Stack.h:76
76      }
(gdb) n
main () at Main.cpp:9
9               cout << "Top of stack contains " << si.top() << endl;
(gdb)
Top of stack contains 426
10              si.push(57);
(gdb) n

Hardware watchpoint 2: si

Old value = {head = 0x55555556b2a0, sz = 2}
New value = {head = 0x55555556b2c0, sz = 2}
Stack<int>::push (this=0x7fffffffe2c0, val=57) at Stack.h:75
75          sz++;
(gdb)
```

Figure 7.17: Debugger display – II

The next command shows that **sz** has been updated with a new value of **1**. After pressing *Enter*, the execution of code moves back from **Stack::push** on the **line 76** back to the main function at line 8. This is highlighted in the following screenshot. It shows that the execution stopped at the **si.push(426)** call. Once we step in, **Stack::push** will be called. The execution moves to **line 71** of the **Stack.h** program, as shown in the red ink. Once execution comes to **line 74**, as shown in the red ink, the watch is called which displays that **si** was updated with the new value. You can see that after the completion of the **Stack::push** function, the flow went back to the Main code. The following is a screenshot of the steps that were executed in the debugger:

```
11                    displayStackStats<int>(si);
(gdb)

-----------------------------------
Showing Stack basic Stats ...
Stack is empty : false
Stack size :3
-----------------------------------

12                    cout << "Top of stack contains " << si.top() << endl;
(gdb)
Top of stack contains 0
14                    si.pop();
(gdb)

Hardware watchpoint 2: si

Old value = {head = 0x55555556b2c0, sz = 3}
New value = {head = 0x55555556b2a0, sz = 3}
Stack<int>::pop (this=0x7fffffffe2c0) at Stack.h:64
64                    delete tmp;
(gdb)
65                        sz--;
(gdb)

Hardware watchpoint 2: si

Old value = {head = 0x55555556b2a0, sz = 3}
New value = {head = 0x55555556b2a0, sz = 2}
Stack<int>::pop (this=0x7fffffffe2c0) at Stack.h:67
67            }
(gdb)
main () at Main.cpp:15
15                    cout << "Top of stack contains " << si.top() << endl;
(gdb)
Top of stack contains 1431745216
17                    si.pop();
(gdb)

Hardware watchpoint 2: si

Old value = {head = 0x55555556b2a0, sz = 2}
New value = {head = 0x55555556b280, sz = 2}
Stack<int>::pop (this=0x7fffffffe2c0) at Stack.h:64
64                    delete tmp;
```

Figure 7.18: Debugger display – III

After pressing *Enter*, you will see that **displayStackStats** is called at **line** 11. In the **Main.cpp** program, the next command displays the top element of the Stack, which is being called on **line** 12. However, the display shows the value as **0** instead of the expected value of **57**. This is an error that we are still unable to figure out – why was the value changed? However, it is clear that the value may have changed somewhere in the preceding calls to the main function. So, this may not make us interested in continuing with the debugging ahead of us. However, we need to proceed and debug from the beginning again.

The following screenshot shows the commands that will be used to debug the code:

```
(gdb) r
The program being debugged has been started already.
Start it from the beginning? (y or n) y
Starting program: /media/sf_packt/Advance_C++/StartTask/ExampleCode/debugging/Main

Breakpoint 1, main () at Main.cpp:3
3          int main(){
(gdb) n
5               Stack<int> si;
(gdb)
6               displayStackStats<int>(si);
(gdb)

-----------------------------------
Showing Stack basic Stats ...
Stack is empty : true
Stack size :0
-----------------------------------

7               si.push(22);
(gdb) display *si.head
1: *si.head = <error: Cannot access memory at address 0x0>
(gdb) n
8               si.push(426);
1: *si.head = {element = 22, next = 0x0}
(gdb) n
9               cout << "Top of stack contains " << si.top() << endl;
1: *si.head = {element = 426, next = 0x55555556b280}
(gdb)
Top of stack contains 426
10              si.push(57);
1: *si.head = {element = 426, next = 0x55555556b280}
(gdb)
11              displayStackStats<int>(si);
1: *si.head = {element = 57, next = 0x55555556b2a0}
(gdb)

-----------------------------------
Showing Stack basic Stats ...
Stack is empty : false
Stack size :3
-----------------------------------

12              cout << "Top of stack contains " << si.top() << endl;
1: *si.head = {element = 0, next = 0x55555556b2a0}
(gdb)
```

Figure 7.19: Debugger display – IV

To rerun the program from the start, we must press $r$, and for confirmation and continuation, we need to press $y$, which means we rerun the program from the start. It will ask for confirmation; press y to continue. All of these commands are highlighted in blue in the preceding screenshot. During execution at line 7, we need to run the 'display *si.head' command, which will continuously display the contents of the si.head memory location after every statement that's executed. As shown in the red ink, after 22 is pushed onto the stack, the head is updated with the correct values. Similarly, for values 426 and 57, when inserted into the stack using push, the call to head is updated correctly.

Later, when `displayStackStats` is called, it shows the correct `size` of **3**. But when the top command is called, there is the wrong value shown in the head. This is highlighted in red ink. Now, the code for the top command doesn't alter the value of head, so it is clear that an error occurred in the previous statement of execution, that is, at `displayStackStats`.

So, we have narrowed down the code where there may be an issue. We can run the debugger to point `displayStackStats` and move inside `displayStackStats` to find the reasons that caused the values to be altered inside the Stack. The following is a screenshot of the same wherein the user needs to start the debugger from the beginning:

```
(gdb)
11              displayStackStats<int>(si);
1: *si.head = {element = 57, next = 0x55555556b2a0}
(gdb) s
displayStackStats<int> (st=...) at Stack.h:93
93          cout << endl << "--------------------------------" << endl;
(gdb) n

--------------------------------
94          cout << "Showing Stack basic Stats ... " << endl;
(gdb) s
Showing Stack basic Stats ...
95          cout << "Stack is empty : " << (st.is_empty() ? "true" : "false") << endl;
(gdb)
Stack<int>::is_empty (this=0x7fffffffe2e0) at Stack.h:43
43              return (head == nullptr) ? true : false;
(gdb)
44      }
(gdb)
displayStackStats<int> (st=...) at Stack.h:95
95          cout << "Stack is empty : " << (st.is_empty() ? "true" : "false") << endl;
(gdb)
Stack is empty : false
96          cout << "Stack size :" << st.size() << endl;
(gdb)
Stack<int>::size (this=0x7fffffffe2e0) at Stack.h:38
38              return sz;
(gdb)
39      }
(gdb)
Stack size :3
displayStackStats<int> (st=...) at Stack.h:97
97          cout << "--------------------------------" << endl << endl;
(gdb)
--------------------------------

98      }
(gdb)
Stack<int>::~Stack (this=0x7fffffffe2e0, __in_chrg=<optimized out>) at Stack.h:33
33              if ( head ) clean();
(gdb)
Stack<int>::clean (this=0x7fffffffe2e0) at Stack.h:81
81          while( head ){
(gdb)
82              tmp = head;
(gdb)
83              head = head -> next;
(gdb)
84              delete tmp;
```

Figure 7.20: Debugger display – IV

After restarting the debugger from the beginning and coming to the execution point at line 11 where **displayStackStats** is called, we need to step in. The flow is to go to the start of the **displayStackStats** function. Also, we need to execute the next statement. Since the initial checks in the function are clear, they don't alter the value of the head and we can press *Enter* to execute the next steps. When we suspect that the next steps can alter the value of the variable that we're looking for, we need to step in. This is done in the preceding snapshot, highlighted in red. The latter execution comes to **line 97**, that is, the last line for the **displayStackStats** function.

After typing in s, the execution moves to the destructor stack and calls the clean function at line 81. This clean command deletes the **tmp** variable, which has the same value as that of the head. The function empties the stack, which was not expected to run. It was only the **displayStackStats** function that was supposed to be called and executed to finally return to the main function. But the destructor may be called due to the local variable in the function that goes out of scope after the function is completed. Here, the local variable was the variable that was declared as a parameter to the **displayStackStats** function at **line 92**. So, a local copy of the **si** variable from the main function was created when the **displayStackStats** function was called. This variable called the destructor of Stack when it went out of scope. Now, the pointers from the **si** variable have been copied to the temporary variable and deleted the pointer at the end by mistake. This was not intended by the developer. Thus, at the end of the execution of the code, a double free error was stated. The **si** variable must call the Stack destructor when it goes out of scope as it will try to free the same memory again. To resolve this issue, it is clear that the **displayStackStats** function must be called with the passing parameter as a reference. For that, we must update the code of the **displayStackStats** function in the **Stack.h** file:

```
template<typename T>
void displayStackStats(Stack<T> &st){
    cout << endl << "------------------------------" << endl;
    cout << "Showing Stack basic Stats ...  " << endl;
    cout << "Stack is empty : " << (st.is_empty() ? "true" : "false") <<
endl;
    cout << "Stack size :" << st.size() << endl;
    cout << "------------------------------" << endl << endl;
}
```

Now, when we save and compile the **Main.cpp** file, the binary will be generated:

```
./Main
```

The preceding command generates the following output in the Terminal:

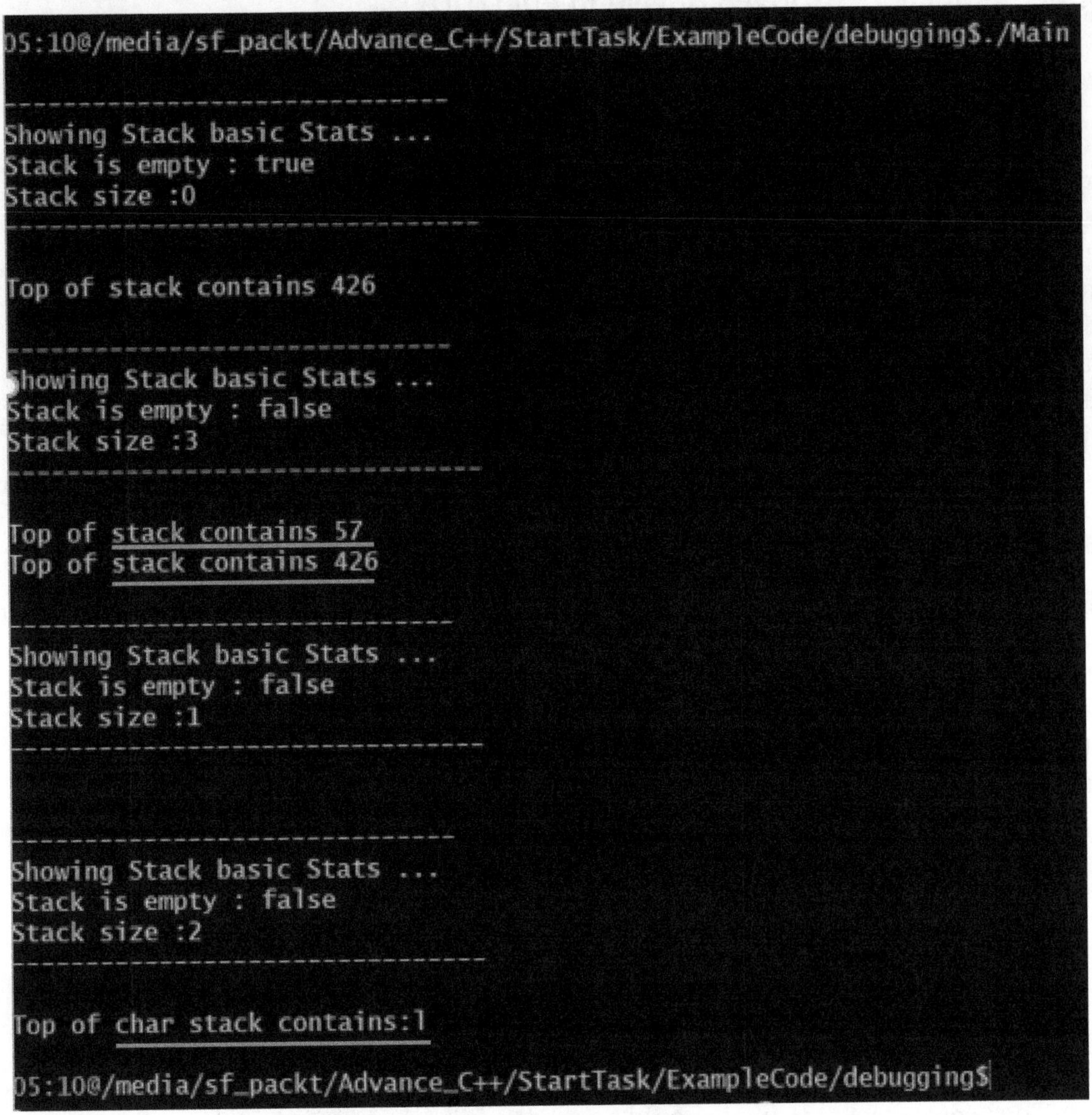

```
05:10@/media/sf_packt/Advance_C++/StartTask/ExampleCode/debugging$./Main

-------------------------------------
Showing Stack basic Stats ...
Stack is empty : true
Stack size :0
-------------------------------------

Top of stack contains 426

-------------------------------------
Showing Stack basic Stats ...
Stack is empty : false
Stack size :3
-------------------------------------

Top of stack contains 57
Top of stack contains 426

-------------------------------------
Showing Stack basic Stats ...
Stack is empty : false
Stack size :1
-------------------------------------


-------------------------------------
Showing Stack basic Stats ...
Stack is empty : false
Stack size :2
-------------------------------------

Top of char stack contains:1
05:10@/media/sf_packt/Advance_C++/StartTask/ExampleCode/debugging$
```

Figure 7.21: Debugger display – IV

From the preceding screenshot, we can see that the expected values of **57** and **426** are shown at the top of the stack. The **displayStackStats** function also displays the correct information for int and the char Stack. Finally, we located the error using the debugger and fixed it. In the next section, we'll solve an activity wherein we'll be developing functions for parsing files and writing test cases to check the accuracy of the functions.

## Activity 1: Checking the Accuracy of the Functions Using Test Cases and Understanding Test-Driven Development (TDD)

In this activity, we'll be developing functions so that we can parse files and then write test cases to check the correctness of the functions we've developed.

An IT team in a big retail organization wants to keep track of product sales by storing Product details and Customer details in its database as part of its reconciliation. On a periodic basis, the sales department will provide this data to the IT team in a simple text format. As the developer, you need to ensure that the basic sanity checking of data is done and that all the records are parsed correctly before the company stores records in the database. The sales department will provide two text files that hold Customer information and Currency information for all the sales transactions. You need to write parsing functions to process these files. The two files are **RecordFile.txt** and **CurrencyConversion.txt**. The **RecordFile.txt** file contains details of the customer, the products they have purchased, and the total price in regional currency and foreign currency. The **CurrencyConversion.txt** file contains two fields, namely `Currency` and `ConversionRatio`.

All the necessary information for the environment's setup for this project is kept in the Configuration file. This will also hold filenames, along with other parameters (such as `DB`, `RESTAPI`, and so on) and variable values in a file called **parse.conf**. It will contain two fields per line separated by the "=" delimiter. The first line will be a header that states "CONFIGURATION_FILE". For the Record file, the variable name is `recordFile` and similarly for the Currency file, the variable name is `currencyFile`.

The following are the test conditions we'll be writing to check the accuracy of the function that's used to parse the **CurrencyConversion.txt** file:

- The first line should be the header line and its first field should contain the "`Currency`" string.

- The `Currency` field should be made up of three characters. For example: "`USD`", "`GBP`" is valid.

- The `ConversionRatio` field should be made of floating-point numbers. For example, `1.2`, `0.06` is valid.

- There should be exactly two fields for each line.

- The delimiter that's used for the record is "|".

The following are test conditions we'll be writing to check the accuracy of the function that's used to parse the **RecordFile.txt** file:

- The first line should contain the header line and its first field should contain the "**Customer Id**" string.

- The **Customer Id**, **Order Id**, **Product Id**, and **Quantity** should all be integer values. For example, **12312, 4531134** is valid.

- **TotalPrice (Regional Currency)** and **TotalPrice (USD)** should be floating-point values. For example, **2433.34, 3434.11** is valid.

- The **RegionalCurrency** field should have its value present in the **CurrencyConversion.txt** file or **std::map**.

- There should be exactly nine fields in each line, as defined in the **HEADER** information of the file.

- The delimiter for the record is "|".

Follow these steps to implement this activity:

1. Parse the **parse.conf** configuration file, which includes the environment variables for the project to run.

2. Set the **recordFile** and **currencyFile** variables correctly from Step 1.

3. Using these variables we retrieved from the Config file, parse the Currency file with all conditions met. If the condition is not met, return the appropriate error message.

4. Parse the Record file with all the conditions we've met. If not, then return an error message.

5. Create a header file named **CommonHeader.h** and declare all the utility functions, that is, **isAllNumbers()**, **isDigit()**, **parseLine()**, **checkFile()**, **parseConfig()**, **parseCurrencyParameters()**, **fillCurrencyMap()**, **parseRecordFile()**, **checkRecord()**, **displayCurrencyMap()**, and **displayRecords()**.

6. Create a file named **Util.cpp** and define all the utility functions.

7. Create a file named **ParseFiles.cpp** and call the **parseConfig()**, **fillCurrencyMap()**, and **parseRecordFile()** function.

8. Compile and execute the **Util.cpp** and **ParseFiles.cpp** files.

9. Create a file named **ParseFileTestCases.cpp** and write test cases for the functions, that is, **trim()**, **isAllNumbers()**, **isDigit()**, **parseCurrencyParameters()**, **checkFile()**, **parseConfig()**, **fillCurrencyMap()**, and **parseRecordFile()**.

10. Compile and execute the **Util.cpp** and **ParseFileTestCases.cpp** files.

The following is the flow diagram for parsing different files and displaying information:

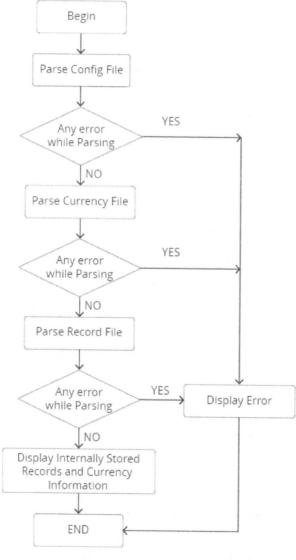

Figure 7.22: Flow diagram

From above flowchart we have rough idea of executing the flow. To have a clear understanding before writing the code, let's look at the finer details. It'll help define test cases for each execution block.

For parsing Config File block, we can break down steps into the following:

1. Check if config file exists and has read permission.

2. Check if it has appropriate header.

3. Parse whole file line by line.

4. For each line, parse fields with '=' as delimiter.

5. If there are 2 fields from above step , process to see if it is **Currency file** or **Record file** variables and store appropriately.

6. If there are no 2 fields from step 4 go to next line.

7. After completely parsing file, check if both variables from above step are not empty.

8. If empty, return with error.

For parsing **Currency File** block, we can break down steps into the following:

1. Read variable for **CurrencyFile** and see if the file exists and has read permission.

2. Check if it has appropriate header.

3. Parse whole file line by line, with '|' as delimiter.

4. If there are exactly 2 fields found for each line, consider first as **Currency field** and second as **conversion field**.

5. If there are no 2 fields found from step 3, return with appropriate error message.

6. From step 4, do all checks for **Currency field** (it should be of 3 characters) and **Conversion Field** ( should be digit).

7. If passed from step 6, store the **currency/conversion** value as pair on map with key as **Currency** and value as digit.

8. If not passed from step 6, return error stating for that **currency**.

9. After complete parsing of the **Currency** file, there will be map created that will have conversion values for all the currencies.

For parsing **Record File** block, we can break down steps into the following:

1. Read variable for **RecordFile** and see if the file exists and has read permission.

2. Check if it has appropriate header.

3. Parse whole file line by line, with '|' as delimiter.

4.  If there no 9 fields found from above step return with appropriate error message.

5.  If there are 9 fields found, do corresponding checks for all fields listed in start of activity.

6.  If step 5 does not pass, return with appropriate error message.

7.  If step 5 is passed, store the record in vector of records.

8.  After completely parsing Record file, all the records will be stored in vector of records.

While creating flow for parsing all the three files, we see few steps repeating for all 3 files such as:

Checking if file exists and is readable

Checking if file has a correct header information

Parsing the records with delimiter

Checking if field is **Digit** is common in **Currency** and **Record file**

Checking if field is **Numeric** is common in **Currency** and **Record file**

The above points will help in refactoring the code. Also, there will be one common function for parsing the fields with delimiter, that is **trim function**. So, when we parse records with delimiter we can get value with space or tab at begin or end and that may not be needed , so we need to trim it once when parse the record.

Now we know we have above steps that are common we can write individual function for them. To start with TDD, we first understand requirement for function and start writing unit test cases first to test these functionalities. Then we write function such that it will pass the unit test cases. If few test cases fail we iterate the steps of updating function and executing test cases, until all of them pass.

For our example, above we can write **trim** function,

Now we know in trim function we need to remove first and last extra spaces/tab. For example, if string contains " AA " , the trim should return "AA" remove all the spaces.

The trim function can return new string with expected value or it can update the same string which was passed to it.

So now we can write signature of the trim function : **string trim ( string &) ;**

We can write the following test cases for it:

- With only extra characters (" "), returns empty string ().
- With only empty characters in beginning(" AA") return string with end characters ("AA")
- With only empty characters at end("AA ") , should return string with begin characters("AA")
- With characters in middle (" AA ") return string with characters ("AA")
- With empty space in middle ("AA BB") , return the same string ("AA BB")
- All steps 3,4,5 with single character. Should return string with single character.

To create test cases , please check file **ParseFileTestCases.cpp**, test cases for `trim` function are written in test suite `trim`. Now write **Util.cpp** file (All miscellaneous functions are written in **Util.cpp**). Write `trim` function with signature shown above in file. Execute test cases of `trim` function and check if it passes. It doesn't change the function appropriately and test it again. Repeat till all test cases pass.

Now we are confident to use `trim` function in the project. Repeat similar steps for the rest of the common functions (`isDigit`, `isNumeric`, `parseHeader` and so on). Please refer the **Util.cpp** file and **ParseFiletestCases.cpp** for the same and test all the common functions.

After completing common functions, we can write parse each file function separately. Main thing to understand and learn here is how to break down module to small functions. Find small repetitive tasks and create small functions for each so it is refactored. Understand the detail functionality of these small functions and create appropriate unit test cases.

Complete single function and thoroughly test it, if it fails, then update the function till it passes all test cases. Similarly, complete other functions. Then write and execute test cases for bigger functions, that should be relatively easy since we are calling small functions tested above in these bigger functions.

After implementing the preceding steps, we'll get the following output:

```
00:35@/media/sf_packt/Advance_C++/StartTask/Activity/unitTesting$./ParseFileTestCases
Running main() from src/gtest_main.cc
[==========] Running 32 tests from 8 test suites.
[----------] Global test environment set-up.
[----------] 8 tests from trim
[ RUN      ] trim.empty
[       OK ] trim.empty (1 ms)
[ RUN      ] trim.start_space
[       OK ] trim.start_space (0 ms)
[ RUN      ] trim.end_space
[       OK ] trim.end_space (0 ms)
[ RUN      ] trim.string_middle
[       OK ] trim.string_middle (0 ms)
[ RUN      ] trim.space_middle
[       OK ] trim.space_middle (0 ms)
[ RUN      ] trim.single_char_start
[       OK ] trim.single_char_start (0 ms)
[ RUN      ] trim.single_char_end
[       OK ] trim.single_char_end (0 ms)
[ RUN      ] trim.single_char_middle
[       OK ] trim.single_char_middle (0 ms)
[----------] 8 tests from trim (1 ms total)

[----------] 5 tests from isNumber
[ RUN      ] isNumber.alphabets_present
[       OK ] isNumber.alphabets_present (0 ms)
[ RUN      ] isNumber.special_character_present
[       OK ] isNumber.special_character_present (0 ms)
[ RUN      ] isNumber.correct_number
[       OK ] isNumber.correct_number (0 ms)
[ RUN      ] isNumber.decimal_begin
[       OK ] isNumber.decimal_begin (0 ms)
[ RUN      ] isNumber.decimal_end
[       OK ] isNumber.decimal_end (0 ms)
[----------] 5 tests from isNumber (0 ms total)

[----------] 3 tests from isDigit
[ RUN      ] isDigit.alphabet_present
[       OK ] isDigit.alphabet_present (1 ms)
[ RUN      ] isDigit.decimal_present
[       OK ] isDigit.decimal_present (0 ms)
[ RUN      ] isDigit.correct_digit
[       OK ] isDigit.correct_digit (0 ms)
[----------] 3 tests from isDigit (1 ms total)

[----------] 2 tests from CurrencyParameters
[ RUN      ] CurrencyParameters.extra_currency_chararcters
[       OK ] CurrencyParameters.extra_currency_chararcters (0 ms)
[ RUN      ] CurrencyParameters.correct_parameters
[       OK ] CurrencyParameters.correct_parameters (0 ms)
[----------] 2 tests from CurrencyParameters (0 ms total)
```

Figure 7.23: All tests running properly

Below is the screenshot of the next steps:

```
[       OK ] CurrencyParameters.correct_parameters (0 ms)
[----------] 2 tests from CurrencyParameters (0 ms total)

[----------] 5 tests from checkFile
[ RUN      ] checkFile.no_file_present
[       OK ] checkFile.no_file_present (0 ms)
[ RUN      ] checkFile.empty_file
[       OK ] checkFile.empty_file (1 ms)
[ RUN      ] checkFile.no_header
[       OK ] checkFile.no_header (0 ms)
[ RUN      ] checkFile.incorrect_header
[       OK ] checkFile.incorrect_header (1 ms)
[ RUN      ] checkFile.correct_file
[       OK ] checkFile.correct_file (0 ms)
[----------] 5 tests from checkFile (2 ms total)

[----------] 3 tests from parseConfig
[ RUN      ] parseConfig.missing_currency_file
ERROR : currencyfile or recordfile not set correctly.
[       OK ] parseConfig.missing_currency_file (1 ms)
[ RUN      ] parseConfig.missing_record_file
ERROR : currencyfile or recordfile not set correctly.
[       OK ] parseConfig.missing_record_file (0 ms)
[ RUN      ] parseConfig.correct_config_file
[       OK ] parseConfig.correct_config_file (1 ms)
[----------] 3 tests from parseConfig (2 ms total)

[----------] 3 tests from fillCurrencyMap
[ RUN      ] fillCurrencyMap.wrong_delimiter
ERROR: Processing Currency Conversion , got incorrect parameters for Currency: USD , 1.00
[       OK ] fillCurrencyMap.wrong_delimiter (1 ms)
[ RUN      ] fillCurrencyMap.extra_column
ERROR: Processing Currency Conversion , got incorrect parameters for Currency: GBP
[       OK ] fillCurrencyMap.extra_column (0 ms)
[ RUN      ] fillCurrencyMap.correct_file
[       OK ] fillCurrencyMap.correct_file (1 ms)
[----------] 3 tests from fillCurrencyMap (2 ms total)

[----------] 3 tests from parseRecordFile
[ RUN      ] parseRecordFile.wrong_delimiter
ERROR: Processing Record, for Customer Id: 2312,Albert , Springs, 435351, 452536 , 11 , 13243.25 , USD , 12343.25
[       OK ] parseRecordFile.wrong_delimiter (0 ms)
[ RUN      ] parseRecordFile.extra_column
ERROR: Processing Record, for Customer Id: 2312
[       OK ] parseRecordFile.extra_column (1 ms)
[ RUN      ] parseRecordFile.correct_file
[       OK ] parseRecordFile.correct_file (1 ms)
[----------] 3 tests from parseRecordFile (2 ms total)

[----------] Global test environment tear-down
[==========] 32 tests from 8 test suites ran. (10 ms total)
[  PASSED  ] 32 tests.
```

Figure 7.24: All tests running properly

Note

The solution to this activity can be found on page 706.

## Summary

In this chapter, we looked at various ways in which errors that are thrown by executables can be grabbed at compile time and runtime using asserts. We also learned about static assertion. We understood how exceptions are generated and how to handle them in the code. We also saw how unit testing can act as a savior to developers as they'll be able to identify any issues in the code at the beginning. We utilized mock objects for the classes that needed to be used in the test cases. We then learned about the debugger, breakpoints, watchpoints, and visualizing the data. We were able to locate the issues in the code using the debugger and fix them. We also solved an activity wherein we wrote the necessary test cases to check the accuracy of the functions that were used for parsing the files.

In the next chapter, we'll learn how to optimize our code. We'll review how the processors execute the code and access the memory. We'll also learn how to determine the excess time that will be taken by the software to execute. Finally, we'll learn about memory alignment and cache access.

# 8

# Need for Speed – Performance and Optimization

**Learning Objectives**

By the end of this chapter, you will be able to:

- Time your code performance manually
- Use source code instrumentation to measure code execution time
- Use the perf tool to analyze program performance
- Use the godbolt compiler explorer tool to analyze machine code generated by a compiler
- Use compiler flags to generate better code
- Apply code idioms that result in performance
- Write cache-friendly code
- Apply algorithm-level optimizations to real-world problems

In this chapter, we will explore concepts that will allow us to write fast code in general and several practical techniques that apply to C++ in particular.

## Introduction

In today's world of extremely large and complicated software systems, **stability** and **maintainability** are usually considered the major goals for most software projects, whereas optimization has not been widely seen as a worthwhile goal since the 2000s. This is because of the rapid acceleration of hardware technology that overtook software demands on a regular schedule.

For many years, it seemed like the hardware improvements would continue to keep up with the performance demands of software, but applications continued to grow larger and more complex. Low-level native-compiled languages such as C and C++ dropped in popularity compared to less performant but easier to use interpreted languages such as **Python** or **Ruby**.

By the late 2000s, though, the trend of CPU transistor count (and performance) doubling every 18 months (a consequence of **Moore's Law**) had stopped, and performance improvements had flattened out. The expectation of 5 to 10 GHz processors being widely available by the 2010s never materialized due to limitations of physics and manufacturing costs. However, the rapid adoption of mobile devices and the rise of high-performance computing applications for data science and machine learning, suddenly resurrected the demand for fast and efficient code. Performance per watt has become the new metric to aim for as large data centers consume enormous amounts of power. For example, Google servers in the US used more power than the entire nation of the UK in 2017.

So far in this book, we've learned how the C++ language has evolved in terms of ease of use, without sacrificing any performance potential over a traditional language such as C. This means we can write fast code in C++ without necessarily sacrificing readability or stability. In the next section, we will learn about the concept of performance measurement.

## Performance Measurement

The most important aspect of optimization is the **measurement of code execution time**. Unless we measure our application's performance with a wide range of input datasets, we will have no clue as to which part takes the most time and, our optimization efforts will be shot in the dark, with no guarantee of a result. There are several approaches for measurement, and some of them are listed here:

- Runtime instrumentation or profiling
- Source code instrumentation

- Manual execution timing
- Studying generated assembly code
- Manual estimation by studying the code and algorithms used

The preceding list is ordered in terms of how accurate the measurement is (with the most accurate one first). However, each of these methods has different advantages. The choice of which approach to adopt depends on the goals and scope of the optimization effort. In an all-out effort to get the fastest possible implementation, all of these may be required. We will examine each of these approaches in the following sections.

## Manual Estimation

The biggest possible improvement in performance occurs when we replace an algorithm with a superior one. For example, consider the two versions of a trivial function that sums the integers from **1** to **n**:

```
int sum1(int n)
{
   int ret = 0;
   for(int i = 1; i <= n; ++i)
   {
      ret += i;
   }
   return ret;
}
int sum2(int n)
{
   return (n * (n + 1)) / 2;
}
```

The first function, **sum1**, uses a simple loop to calculate the sum and has a runtime complexity that is proportional to **n**, whereas the second function, **sum2**, uses the algebraic summation formula and takes constant time independent of **n**. In this quite contrived example, we have optimized a function simply by using the basic knowledge of algebra.

There are many well-known algorithms for every conceivable operation that have been proven to be the most optimal. The best way to make our code run as fast as possible is by using algorithms.

It is essential to have a vocabulary of algorithms. We do not need to be an algorithm expert, but we need to at least be aware of the existence of efficient algorithms in various domains, even if we are not capable of implementing them from scratch. A slightly deeper knowledge of algorithms will help us find parts of our program that perform similar, if not exactly the same, computations as well-known algorithms. Certain code features such as nested loops or linear scanning of data are often obvious candidates for improvement, provided we can verify that these constructs are within hotspots in the code. A **hotspot** is a section of code that runs very often and affects performance significantly. The C++ standard library includes a lot of basic algorithms that can be used as building blocks to improve the efficiency of many common operations.

## Studying Generated Assembly Code

**Assembly language** is a human readable representation of the binary machine code that actually executes on the processor. For any serious programmer of a compiled language such as C++, a basic understanding of assembly language is a great asset.

Studying the generated assembly code for a program can give us some good insights into how the compiler works and estimates of code efficiency. There are many cases where this is the only approach possible to determine efficiency bottlenecks.

Apart from this, a basic knowledge of assembly language is essential to be able to debug C++ code since some of the most difficult bugs to catch are those related to the low-level generated code.

A very powerful and popular online tool that's used for analyzing compiler-generated code is the **Compiler Explorer** that we will be using in this chapter.

> **Note**
>
> The `Godbolt compiler explorer` can be found at https://godbolt.org.

The following is a screenshot of the Godbolt compiler explorer:

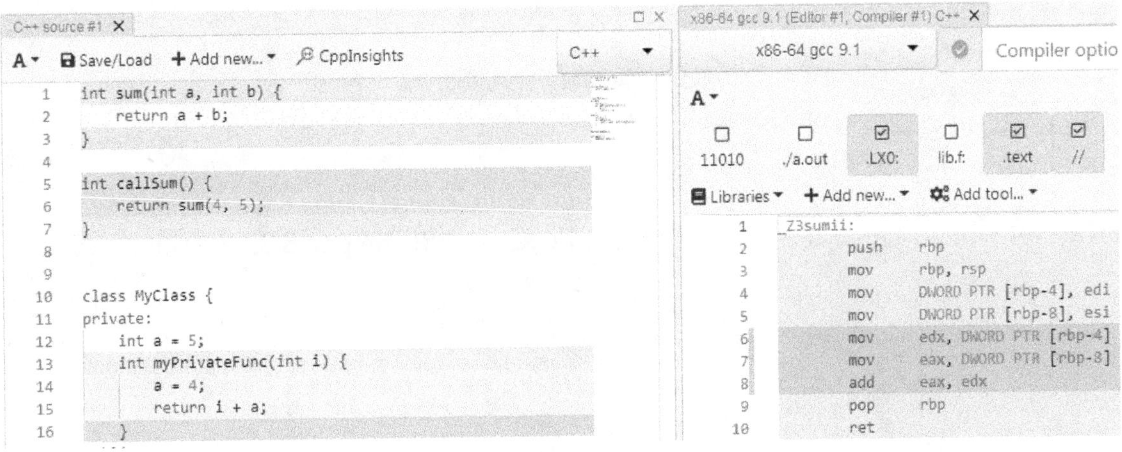

Figure 8.1: Godbolt compiler explorer

As you can see, the Godbolt compiler explorer consists of two panes. The one on the left is where we type the code in, while the one on the right displays the generated assembly code. The left-hand pane has a dropdown so that we can choose the desired language. For our purposes, we will use the C++ language with the gcc compiler.

The right-hand pane has options that we can use to choose a compiler version. Almost all the versions of popular compilers such as **gcc**, **clang**, and **cl (Microsoft C++)** are present, including the ones for non-X86 architectures such as ARM.

> **Note**
>
> We will refer to the Intel processor architecture as **x86** for simplicity, even though the correct definition is **x86/64**. We will skip mentioning the "64" since almost all processors being manufactured today are **64-bit**. Even though **x86** was invented by Intel, now all PC processor manufacturers are licensed to use it.

In order to get familiar with the basics of the **Compiler Explorer tool** and understand the **x86** assembly code at a basic level, let's examine the assembly code generated by a compiler for a simple function that sums up the integers from **1** to **N**. Here is the sum function that needs to be written in the left-hand pane of the Compiler Explorer:

```
int sum(int n)
{
    int ret = 0;
    for(int i = 1; i <= n; ++i)
```

```
    {
        ret += i;
    }


    return ret;
}
```

In the right-hand pane, the compiler must be set to **x86-64 gcc 8.3**, like this:

Figure 8.2: C++ compiler

Once this is done, the left-hand pane's code is automatically recompiled and the assembly code is generated and displayed on the right-hand pane. Here, the output is color-coded to show which lines of assembly code is generated from which lines of C++ code. The following screenshot shows the assembly code that was generated:

```
1  sum(int):
2          push    rbp
3          mov     rbp, rsp
4          mov     DWORD PTR [rbp-20], edi
5          mov     DWORD PTR [rbp-4], 0
6          mov     DWORD PTR [rbp-8], 1
7  .L3:
8          mov     eax, DWORD PTR [rbp-8]
9          cmp     eax, DWORD PTR [rbp-20]
10         jg      .L2
11         mov     eax, DWORD PTR [rbp-8]
12         add     DWORD PTR [rbp-4], eax
13         add     DWORD PTR [rbp-8], 1
14         jmp     .L3
15 .L2:
16         mov     eax, DWORD PTR [rbp-4]
17         pop     rbp
18         ret
```

Figure 8.3: Assembly result

Let's analyze the preceding assembly code briefly. Each instruction in the assembly language consists of an **opcode** and one or more **operands**, which can be registers, constant values, or memory addresses. A **register** is a very fast storage location in the CPU. In the x86 architecture, there are eight main registers, namely **RAX**, **RBX**, **RCX**, **RDX**, **RSI**, **RDI**, **RSP**, and **RBP**. The Intel x86/x64 architecture uses a curious pattern of register naming:

- **RAX** is a general-purpose 64-bit integer register.

- **EAX** refers to the bottom 32 bits of **RAX**.

- **AX** refers to the bottom 16 bits of **EAX**.

- **AL** and **AH** refer to the bottom and top 8 bits of **AX**, respectively.

The same convention applies to other general-purpose registers such as **RBX**, **RCX**, and **RDX**. The **RSI**, **RDI**, and **RBP** registers have 16-bit and 32-bit versions but not the 8-bit sub-registers. The opcode of an instruction can be of several types including arithmetic, logical, bitwise, comparison or jump operations. It is common to refer to an opcode as an instruction. For example, "**mov instruction**" means an instruction whose **opcode** is **mov**. Here is the snapshot of the assembly code for our **sum** function:

```
1  sum(int):
2          push    rbp
3          mov     rbp, rsp
4          mov     DWORD PTR [rbp-20], edi
5          mov     DWORD PTR [rbp-4], 0
6          mov     DWORD PTR [rbp-8], 1
```

Figure 8.4: Assembly code of the sum function

In the preceding screenshot, the first few lines are called a **function prologue**, that is, the instructions that are used to set up the **stack frame** and local variables. A stack frame represents the localized data in a function that includes the arguments and the local variables. When the function returns, the stack frame is discarded. The **mov** instruction initializes a register or memory location with a constant value. The syntax of the assembly code here is called **Intel syntax**. The convention with this syntax is that the destination operand is always the first one. For example, the MOV RAX, RBX assembly code means move the value in the **RBX** register to the **RAX** register.

> **Note**
>
> Assembly language is usually not case-sensitive, so **EAX** and **eax** mean the same thing.

The **DWORD PTR [rbp-8]** expression in assembly is equivalent to the **(\*(DWORD\*)(rbp - 8))** C expression. In other words, the memory address **rbp-8** is accessed as a 4 byte DWORD (a double word of memory – 32 bits). The square brackets in assembly code represent dereferencing, much like the * operator in C/C++. The **rbp** register is the base pointer that always contains the address of the base of the currently executing functions stack. It is not essential to know how exactly this stack frame works but remember that since the stack starts at a higher address and moves down, function arguments and local variables have addresses as negative offsets from **rbp**. If you see some negative offset from **rbp**, it refers to a local variable or argument.

In the preceding screenshot, the first **mov** instruction puts the value from the **edi** register onto the stack—in this case, it represents the **n** argument that was passed in. The last two **mov** instructions initialize the **ret** variable and the **i** loop variable in our code to **0** and **1**, respectively.

Now, examine the snapshot of the assembly code that follows the prologue and initialization – this is our **for()** loop:

```
.L3:
        mov     eax, DWORD PTR [rbp-8]
        cmp     eax, DWORD PTR [rbp-20]
        jg      .L2
```

Figure 8.5: Assembly code of the for loop

In the preceding screenshot, the lines that have a string followed by a colon are called **labels**. They're very similar to labels in programming languages such as **BASIC**, **C/C++**, or **Pascal** and are used as targets of **jump** instructions (the assembly language equivalent of **goto** statements).

Instructions starting with J on x86 assembly are all jump instructions, such as **JMP, JG, JGE, JL, JLE, JE, JNE**, and so on. Jump instructions are conditional or unconditional gotos. In the preceding screenshot, the **mov** instruction loads the value of the **i** variable from memory to the **eax** register. Then, it is compared against the **n** value in memory with the **cmp** instruction.

> **Note**
>
> The **JG** instruction here means **jump if greater**.

If the comparison was greater, then the execution jumps to the **.L2** label (which is outside the loop). If not, the execution continues with the next instruction, like so:

```
mov     eax, DWORD PTR [rbp-8]
add     DWORD PTR [rbp-4], eax
add     DWORD PTR [rbp-8], 1
jmp     .L3
```

Figure 8.6: Assembly code of the next instruction

Here, the value of **i** is reloaded again into **eax**, which seems unnecessary. But remember that this assembly code is not optimized, so the compiler has generated code that would be suboptimal and may include unnecessary work. Then, the value in **eax** is added to **ret**, after which 1 is added to **i**. Finally, the execution jumps back to the **.L3** label. These instructions between the **.L2** and **.L3** labels form the code that executes the **for** loop and sums up the sequence of integers up to **n**, like so:

```
.L2:
        mov     eax, DWORD PTR [rbp-4]
        pop     rbp
        ret
```

Figure 8.7: Assembly code of the for loop

This is called the **function epilog**. First, the value to be returned, **ret**, is moved into the **eax** register – this is typically the register where the return value of a function is stored. Then, the stack frame is reset and finally **ret** returns from the **sum()** function.

> **Note**
>
> The "ret" in the above assembly listing is the mnemonic for the RETURN instruction and should not be confused with the "ret" variable in our C++ code example.

It is not a simple job to figure out what a sequence of assembly instructions does, but a general idea of the mapping between the source code and instructions can be gained by observing the following points:

- Constant values in code can be directly recognized in the assembly.

- Arithmetic operations such as **add**, **sub**, **imul**, **idiv**, and many others can be recognized.

- Conditional jumps map to loops and conditionals.

- Function calls can be directly read (the function name appears in the assembly code).

Now, let's observe the effect of the code if we add a compiler flag for optimization in the compiler options field at the top-right:

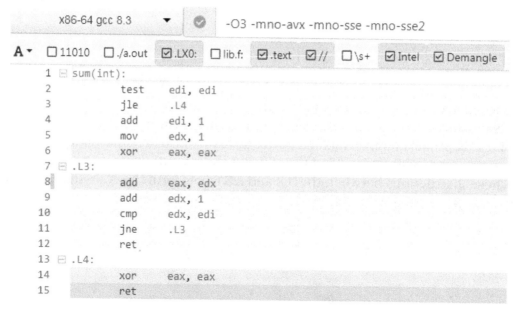

Figure 8.8: Adding a compiler flag for optimization

In the preceding screenshot, **O3** stands for **maximum optimization**. The other flags, such as **-mno-avx**, **-mno-sse**, and **-mno-sse2**, are used to prevent the compiler from generating **vector instructions** that are not relevant to the current example. We can see that the compiler is no longer accessing memory and only working with registers. Notice the line **xor eax, eax**, which has an effect of storing **0** in **eax**—this is more efficient than loading a constant **0** from memory into the register. Since memory takes several clock cycles to access (anywhere from **5** to **100** clock cycles), using registers alone will itself produce a massive speedup.

When the compiler in the dropdown is changed to **x86-64 clang 8.0.0**, the assembly code is changed, which can be seen in the following screenshot:

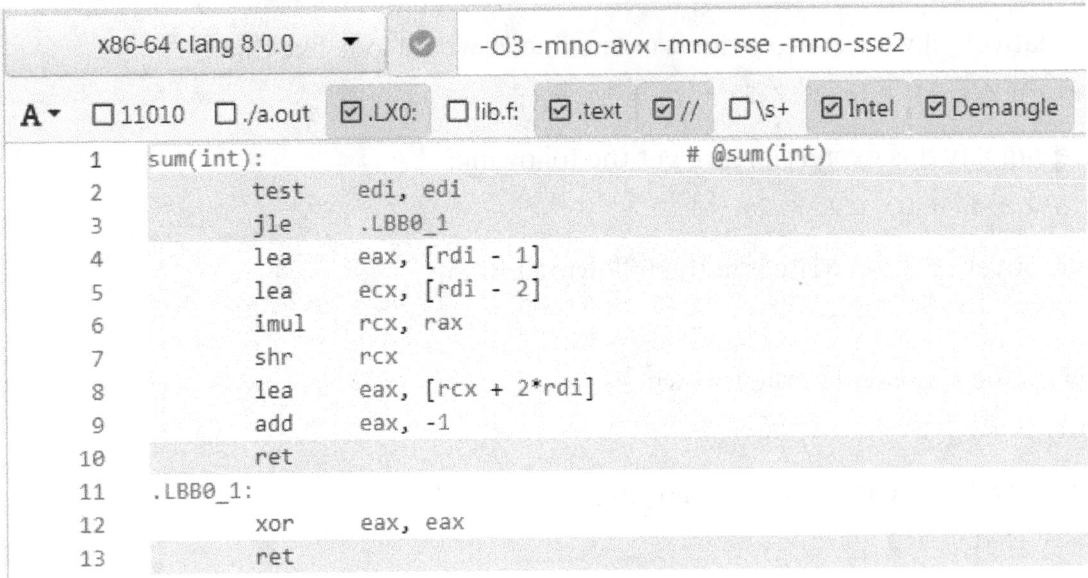

```
x86-64 clang 8.0.0    ▼    ✓    -O3 -mno-avx -mno-sse -mno-sse2

A▾  ☐11010  ☐./a.out  ☑.LX0:  ☐lib.f:  ☑.text  ☑//  ☐\s+  ☑Intel  ☑Demangle
 1    sum(int):                                # @sum(int)
 2            test    edi, edi
 3            jle     .LBB0_1
 4            lea     eax, [rdi - 1]
 5            lea     ecx, [rdi - 2]
 6            imul    rcx, rax
 7            shr     rcx
 8            lea     eax, [rcx + 2*rdi]
 9            add     eax, -1
10            ret
11    .LBB0_1:
12            xor     eax, eax
13            ret
```

Figure 8.9: Assembly code with the new compiler

In the preceding assembly listing, observe that there is no instruction starting with **J** (for jump). Thus, there is no looping construct at all! Let's examine how the compiler is calculating the sum of **1** to **n**. If the value of **n** is <= **0**, then it jumps to the **.LBB0_1** label where it exits, returning **0**. Let's analyze the following instructions:

```
lea     eax, [rdi - 1]
lea     ecx, [rdi - 2]
imul    rcx, rax
shr     rcx
lea     eax, [rcx + 2*rdi]
add     eax, -1
ret
```

Figure 8.10: Assembly code with the new compiler

The following code is the C equivalent of the previous instructions. Remember that **n** is in the **EDI** register (and hence also in the RDI register, since they overlap):

```
eax = n - 1;
ecx = n - 2;
rcx *= rax;
rcx >>= 1;
```

```
eax = rcx + 2 * n;
eax--;
return eax;
```

Alternatively, if we were to write it in one line, it would look like this:

```
return ((n-1) * (n-2) / 2) + (n * 2) - 1;
```

If we simplify this expression, we get the following:

```
((n^2 - 3n + 2) / 2) + 2n - 1
```

Alternatively, we can write it in the following format:

```
((n^2 - 3n + 2) + 4n - 2) / 2
```

This can be simplified to the following:

```
(n^2 + n) / 2
```

Alternatively, we can write the following:

```
(n * (n+1)) / 2
```

This is the closed form equation for the summation of numbers **1** to **n** inclusive, and the fastest way to compute it. The compiler was extremely clever—rather than just looking at our code line by line, it reasoned that the effect of our loop was to calculate the sum, and it figured out the algebra on its own. It did not figure out the simplest possible expression, but an equivalent one that took a few extra operations. Nevertheless, taking out the loop makes this function very much optimal.

If we modify the initial or final values of the **i** variable in the **for** loop to create a different summation, the compiler is still able to perform the necessary algebraic manipulation to derive a closed form solution needing no loops.

This is just one example of how compilers have become extremely efficient and appear almost intelligent. However, we must understand that this particular optimization of summations has been specifically programmed into the **clang** compiler. It does not mean that the compiler can do this kind of trick for any possible loop computation – that would actually require the compiler to have general artificial intelligence, as well as all the mathematical knowledge in the world.

Let's explore another example of compiler optimization via generated assembly code. Look at the following code:

```
#include <vector>


int three()
```

```
{
    const std::vector<int> v = {1, 2};
    return v[0] + v[1];
}
```

In the compiler options, if we select the **x86-64 clang 8.0.0** compiler and add **-O3 -stdlib=libc++**, the following assembly code is generated:

Figure 8.11: Assembly code generated with the new compiler

As you can see in the preceding screenshot, the compiler decided correctly that the vector was not relevant to the function and removed all the baggage. It also did the addition at compile time and directly used the result, **3**, as a constant. The main things to take forward from this section are as follows:

- Compilers can be extremely clever when optimizing code, given the right options.

- Studying generated assembly code is very useful to get a high-level estimate of execution complexity.

- A basic understanding of how machine code works is valuable for any C++ programmer.

In the next section, we'll learn about manual execution timing.

## Manual Execution Timing

This is the easiest way to quickly time small programs. We can use a command-line tool to measure the time taken for a program to execute. On Windows 7 and above, the following PowerShell command can be used:

```
powershell -Command "Measure-Command {<your program and arguments here>}"
```

On **Linux**, **MacOS**, and other **UNIX-like** systems, the **time** command can be used:

```
time <your program and arguments here>
```

In the next section, we'll implement a small program and examine some caveats about timing a program's execution in general.

## Exercise 1: Timing a Program's Execution

In this exercise, we will write a program that performs a summation of an array. The idea here is to time the summation function. This method is useful when we wish to test a function written in isolation. Thus, the test program's only purpose is to execute one single function. Since the calculation is very simple, we will need to run the function thousands of times in order to get a measurable execution time. In this case, we'll just call the **sumVector()** function from the **main()** function, passing an **std::vector** of random integers.

> **Note**
>
> A program that's meant to test a single function is sometimes referred to as a **driver program** (not to be confused with a device driver).

Perform the following steps to complete this exercise:

1. Create a file named **Snippet1.cpp**.

2. Define a function named **sumVector** that sums up each element in a loop:

```cpp
int sumVector(std::vector<int> &v)
{
    int ret = 0;
    for(int i: v)
    {
        ret += i;
    }

    return ret;
}
```

3. Define the **main** function. Use the C++11 random number generation facilities to initialize a vector of **10,000** elements and then call the **sumVector** function **1,000** times. Write the following code to implement this:

```cpp
#include <random>
#include <iostream>

int main()
{
    // Initialize a random number generator
    std::random_device dev;
    std::mt19937 rng(dev());
    // Create a distribution range from 0 to 1000
    std::uniform_int_distribution<std::mt19937::result_type> dist(0,1000);

    // Fill 10000 numbers in a vector
    std::vector<int> v;
    v.reserve(10000);
    for(int i = 0; i < 10000; ++i)
    {
        v.push_back(dist(rng));
    }
    // Call out function 1000 times, accumulating to a total sum
    double total = 0.0;
    for(int i = 0; i < 1000; ++i)
    {
        total += sumVector(v);
    }
    std::cout << "Total: " << total << std::endl;
}
```

4. Compile, run, and time this program on a Linux Terminal using the following commands:

```
$ g++ Snippet1.cpp
$ time ./a.out
```

The output of the previous command is as follows:

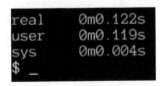

**Figure 8.12: Output of timing the Snippet1.cpp code**

As you can see from the preceding output, for this system, the program executed in **0.122** seconds (note that the results will vary, depending on your system's configuration). If we run this timing command repeatedly, we may get slight variations in the results as the program will be loaded in the memory after the first run and will be marginally faster. It is best to run and time the program about **5** times and get an average value. We are usually not interested in the absolute value of the time taken, but rather how the value improves as we optimize our code.

5. Use the following commands to explore the effect of using compiler optimization flags:

```
$ g++ -O3 Snippet1.cpp
$ time ./a.out
```

The output is as follows:

Figure 8.13: Output of timing the Snippet1.cpp code compiled with -O3

From the preceding output, it seems that the program has become about **60** times faster, which seems quite unbelievable.

6. Change the code to execute the loop **100,000** times rather than **1,000** times:

```
// Call out function 100000 times
for(int i = 0; i < 100000; ++i)
{
    total += sumVector(v);
}
```

7. Recompile and time again using the following commands:

```
$ g++ -O3 Snippet1.cpp
$ time ./a.out
```

The output after executing previous command is as follows:

```
real    0m0.002s
user    0m0.002s
sys     0m0.000s
```

Figure 8.14: Output of timing the Snippet1.cpp code with 10,000 iterations

From the preceding output, it still seems to take the exact same time. This seems impossibe, but actually what happens is that since we never caused any side effect in our program, such as printing the sum, the compiler is free to replace our code with an empty program. Functionally, according to the C++ standard, this program and an empty program are identical because there are no side effects of running it.

8. Open the Compiler Explorer and paste in the entire code. Set the compiler options to **-03** and observe the generated code:

```cpp
1   #include <random>
2   #include <iostream>
3
4   int sumVector(std::vector<int> &v)
5   {
6       int ret = 0;
7       for(int i: v)
8       {
9           ret += 1;
10      }
11
12      return ret;
13  }
14
15  int main()
16  {
17      // Initialize a random number generator
18      std::random_device dev;
19      std::mt19937 rng(dev());
20
21      // Create a distribution range from 0 to 1000
22      std::uniform_int_distribution<std::mt19937::result_type> dist(0,1000);
23
24      // Fill 10000 numbers in a vector
25      std::vector<int> v;
26      v.reserve(10000);
27      for(int i = 0; i < 10000; ++i)
28      {
29          v.push_back(dist(rng));
30      }
31
32      // Call out function 1000 times, accumulating to a total sum
33      double total = 0.0;
34      for(int i = 0; i < 100000; ++i)
35      {
36          total += sumVector(v);
37      }
38  }
```

Figure 8.15: Snippet1.cpp code in Compiler Explorer

As you can see from the preceding screenshot, the lines within the **for** loop are not color-coded and no assembly code was generated for them.

9. Change the code to make sure that the sum must be performed by printing a value that depends on the computation with the following line:

```cpp
std::cout<<"Total:"<<total<<std::endl;
```

10. Here, we are just summing the result of `sumVector()` to a dummy double value many time and printing it. After you make the changes in the code, open the Terminal and write the following commands:

```
$ g++ -O3 Snippet1.cpp
$ time ./a.out
```

The output of the previous commands is as follows:

```
Total: 4.99092e+11

real    0m0.120s
user    0m0.119s
sys     0m0.000s
```

Figure 8.16: Output of timing the Snippet1.cpp code with a side effect of printing the value

In the preceding output, we can see that the program actually performed the computation instead of just running as an empty program. Printing the total to **cout** is a side effect that causes the compiler not to elide the code. Causing a side effect (such as printing a result) that depends on the code's execution is one way to prevent the compiler optimizer from removing code. In the next section, we'll learn how to time programs without side effects.

## Timing Programs without Side Effects

As seen in the previous exercise, we needed to create a side effect (using **cout**) in our program so that the compiler did not ignore all the code we wrote. Another technique to make the compiler believe that a piece of code has a side effect is to assign its result to a **volatile** variable. The volatile qualifier tells the compiler: "This variable must always be read from memory and written to memory, and not from a register." The main purpose of a volatile variable is to access device memory, and such device memory access must follow the rule mentioned above. Effectively, volatile variables are considered by the compiler as if they could change from effects outside of the current program, and thus will never be optimized. We will use this technique in the upcoming sections.

There are more advanced ways to bypass this problem, that is, by specifying special assembly code directives to the compiler rather than using side effects. But they are outside the scope of this introductory material. For the examples that follow, we'll always add code that ensures that a function's result is used in a side effect or is assigned to a volatile variable. In future sections, we'll learn how to examine the compiler generated assembly code and detect instances when the compiler elides code for optimization purposes.

## Source Code Instrumentation

**Instrumentation** is a term that refers to the process of adding extra code to a program, without changing its behavior, and capturing the information as it executes. This may include performance timing (and possibly other measurements such as memory allocation, or disk usage patterns). In the case of source code instrumentation, we manually add code to time the execution of our program and log that data when the program ends, for analysis. The advantage of this approach is its portability and avoidance of any external tools. It also allows us to selectively add the timing to any part of the code we choose.

## Exercise 2: Writing a Code Timer Class

In this exercise, we'll create an `RAII` class that allows us to measure the execution time of individual blocks of code. We will use this as the primary timing mechanism for the code in the exercises that follow. It is not as sophisticated as other methods of performance measurement but is much easier to use and serves most purposes. The basic requirement of our class is as follows:

- We need to be able to record the cumulative time taken by a block of code.

- We need to be able to record the number of times it is invoked.

Perform the following steps to complete this exercise:

1. Create a file named **Snippet2.cpp**.

2. Include the following headers:

```cpp
#include <map>
#include <string>
#include <chrono>
#include <iostream>
#include <cstdint>

using std::map;
using std::string;
using std::cerr;
using std::endl;
```

3. Define the `Timer` class and the class member functions by writing the following code:

```
class Timer
{
    static map<string, int64_t> ms_Counts;
    static map<string, int64_t> ms_Times;
    const string &m_sName;
    std::chrono::time_point<std::chrono::high_resolution_clock> m_tmStart;
```

As you can see from the preceding code, the class members consist of a name, a starting timestamp, and two **static maps**. Every instance of this class is meant to time a certain block of code. The block can be a function scope or any other block delimited by curly braces. The usage pattern is to define an instance of the `Timer` class at the top of the block while passing in a name (can be a function name or some other convenient label). When instantiated, the current timestamp is recorded, and when the block exits, the destructor of this class records the cumulative time elapsed for this block, as well as the count of the number of times this block executed. The times and counts are stored in the static maps `ms_Times` and `ms_Counts`, respectively.

4. Define the constructor of the `Timer` class by writing the following code:

```
public:
    // When constructed, save the name and current clock time
    Timer(const string &sName): m_sName(sName)
    {
        m_tmStart = std::chrono::high_resolution_clock::now();
    }
```

5. Define the destructor of the `Timer` class by writing the following code:

```
    // When destroyed, add the time elapsed and also increment the count
    // under this name
    ~Timer()
    {
        auto tmNow = std::chrono::high_resolution_clock::now();
        auto msElapsed = std::chrono::duration_
cast<std::chrono::milliseconds>(tmNow - m_tmStart);
        ms_Counts[m_sName]++;
        ms_Times[m_sName] += msElapsed.count();
    }
```

In the preceding code, the elapsed time is calculated in milliseconds. Then, we add that to the cumulative elapsed time for this block name and increment the count of how many times this block was executed.

6. Define a **static** function named **dump()** that prints out the summary of the timed results:

```
// Print out the stats for each measured block/function
static void dump()
{
  cerr << "Name\t\t\tCount\t\t\tTime(ms)\t\tAverage(ms)\n";
  cerr << "-----------------------------------------------------------
----------------------\n";
  for(const auto& it: ms_Times)
  {
    auto iCount = ms_Counts[it.first];
    cerr << it.first << "\t\t\t" << iCount << "\t\t\t" << it.second <<
"\t\t\t" << it.second / iCount << "\n";
  }
}
};
```

In the preceding code, the name, execution count, total time, and average time is printed in a tabular form. We use multiple tabs between the field names and field values to make them line up vertically on a console. This function can be modified as we wish. For example, we can modify this code to dump the output as a CSV file, so that it can be imported into a spreadsheet for further analysis.

7. Finally, define the **static** members to complete the class:

```
// Define static members
map<string, int64_t> Timer::ms_Counts;
map<string, int64_t> Timer::ms_Times;
const int64_t N = 1'000'000'000;
```

8. Now that we have defined the **Timer** class, define two simple functions that we will time as an example. One will add and the other will multiply. Since these operations are trivial, we will loop **1 billion times** so that we can have some measurable result.

> **Note**
>
> C++ 14 and above let us use the single-quote symbol within integer constants for readability; for example, we can write **1'000'000** rather than **1000000**.

Write the functions for addition and multiplication. Both functions simply add and multiply the integers 1 to N, respectively:

```
unsigned int testMul()
{
  Timer t("Mul");

  unsigned int x = 1;
  for(int i = 0; i < N; ++i)
  {
    x *= i;
  }

  return x;
}

unsigned int testAdd()
{
  Timer t("Add");

  unsigned int x = 1;
  for(int i = 0; i < N; ++i)
  {
    x += i;
  }

  return x;
}
```

In the preceding code, we used **unsigned int** for the variable that we repeatedly **add/multiply**. We used an unsigned type so that overflow during arithmetic does not result in undefined behavior. Had we used a signed type, the program would have undefined behavior and not be guaranteed to work in any way. Secondly, we return the calculated value from the **testAdd()** and **testMul()** functions so that we can ensure that the compiler does not remove the code (because of the lack of side effects). In order to time each of these functions, we need to simply declare an instance of a **Timer** class with a suitable label at the start of the function. The timing is started as soon as the **Timer** object is instantiated and stopped when that object goes out of scope.

9. Write the **main** function, where we will simply call both test functions **10** times each:

```
int main()
{
    volatile unsigned int dummy;
    for(int i = 0; i < 10; ++i)
        dummy = testAdd();
    for(int i = 0; i < 10; ++i)
        dummy = testMul();
    Timer::dump();
}
```

As you can see in the preceding code, we're calling each function **10** times so that we can demonstrate the **Timer** class timing multiple runs of a function. Assigning the result of the functions to a volatile variable forces the compiler to assume that there is a global side effect. Hence, it will not elide the code in our test functions. Before exiting, we call the **Timer::dump** static function to display the results.

10. Save the program and open a terminal. Compile and run the program with different optimization levels – on the **gcc** and **clang** compilers, this is specified by the **-ON** compiler flag, where **N** is a number from **1** to **3**. Add the **-01** compiler flag first:

```
$ g++ -01 Snippet2.cpp && ./a.out
```

This code generates the following output:

| Name | Count | Time(ms) | Average(ms) |
|------|-------|----------|-------------|
| Test Add | 10 | 6314 | 631 |
| Test Mul | 10 | 9399 | 939 |

Figure 8.17: Snippet2.cpp code performance when compiled with the -O1 option

11. Now, add the **-02** compiler flag in the terminal and execute the program:

```
$ g++ -02 Snippet2.cpp && ./a.out
```

This generates the following output:

| Name | Count | Time(ms) | Average(ms) |
|------|-------|----------|-------------|
| Test Add | 10 | 3167 | 316 |
| Test Mul | 10 | 9315 | 931 |

Figure 8.18: Snippet2.cpp code performance when compiled with the -O2 option

12. Add the **-03** compiler flag in the terminal and execute the program:

```
$ g++ -03 Snippet2.cpp && ./a.out
```

This generates the following output:

| Name | Count | Time(ms) | Average(ms) |
|------|-------|----------|-------------|
| Test Add | 10 | 1566 | 156 |
| Test Mul | 10 | 6194 | 619 |

Figure 8.19: Snippet2.cpp code performance when compiled with the -O3 option

Notice that the **testMul** function became faster only at **O3**, but the **testAdd** function got faster at **O2** and much faster at **O3**. We can verify this by running the program multiple times and averaging the times. There are no obvious reasons why some functions speed up while others do not. We would have to exhaustively check the generated code to understand why. It is not guaranteed that this will happen on all the systems with different compilers or even compiler versions. The main point to take home is that we can never assume performance but have to always measure it, and always re-measure if we believe any change we made affects the performance.

13. To make it easier to use our **Timer** class for timing individual functions, we can write a macro. C++ 11 and above support a special compiler built-in macro called **__func__** that always contains the currently executing function's name as a **const char***. Use this to define a macro so that we don't need to specify a label for our **Timer** instances, as follows:

```
#define TIME_IT Timer t(__func__)
```

14. Add the **TIME_IT** macro to the start of the two functions, changing the existing line that creates a Timer object:

```
unsigned int testMul()
{
    TIME_IT;
unsigned int testAdd()
{
    TIME_IT;
```

15. Save the program and open the terminal. Compile and run it again by using the following command:

```
$ g++ -O3 Snippet2.cpp && ./a.out
```

The output of the previous command is as follows:

| Name | Count | Time(ms) | Average(ms) |
|------|-------|----------|-------------|
| testAdd | 10 | 1566 | 156 |
| testMul | 10 | 6182 | 618 |

Figure 8.20: Snippet2.cpp code output when using a macro for timing

In the preceding output, notice that the actual function name is printed now. Another advantage of using this macro is that we can add this to all potentially time-consuming functions by default, and disable it for production builds by simply changing the definition to a no-op, which will cause the timing code to never run - avoiding the need to edit the code extensively. We will use this same Timer class for timing code in forthcoming exercises.

## Runtime Profiling

**Profiling** is a non-intrusive method of measuring the performance of the functions in a program. Profilers work by sampling a program's current execution address at frequent intervals (hundreds of times in a second) and making a log of which functions happened to be executing at the time. This is a statistical sampling approach that has reasonable accuracy. Sometimes, though, the results can be confusing as a program may spend a lot of time on functions that are a part of the operating system kernel. The most popular runtime profiling tool on Linux is **perf**. In the next section, we'll make use of perf to profile our program.

### Exercise 3: Using perf to Profile Programs

**perf** can be installed on **Ubuntu** as follows:

```
apt-get install linux-tools-common linux-tools-generic
```

To get familiar with the basics of using **perf**, we'll profile and analyze the program from the previous exercise with the help of the **perf** tool. Perform the following steps to complete this exercise:

1.  Open the **Snippet2.cpp** file we created in the previous exercise, and remove the **TIME_IT** macros from the two functions.

2.  Open the terminal, recompile the code again with the **-03** flag, and then create a profile data sample with **perf** as follows:

    ```
    $ g++ -03 Snippet2.cpp
    $ perf record ./a.out
    ```

    The output of the previous command is as follows:

```
Name                       Count                    Time(ms)            Average(ms)
-------------------------------------------------------------------------------------
Test Add                     10                        811                    81
Test Mul                     10                       6321                   632
[ perf record: Woken up 5 times to write data ]
[ perf record: Captured and wrote 1.073 MB perf.data (28086 samples) ]
```

Figure 8.21: Using the perf command to analyze the code in Snippet2.cpp

This creates a file called **perf.data** which can be analyzed or visualized.

3. Now, use the following command to visualize the recorded data:

```
$ perf report
```

A console-based GUI will show the following data after executing the previous command:

```
Samples: 28K of event 'cycles:u', Event count (approx.): 22762680478
Overhead  Command  Shared Object          Symbol
  88.66%  a.out    a.out                  [.] testMul
  11.32%  a.out    a.out                  [.] testAdd
   0.01%  a.out    [unknown]              [k] 0xffffffff85000b07
   0.01%  a.out    ld-2.29.so             [.] _dl_lookup_symbol_x
   0.00%  a.out    libstdc++.so.6.0.25    [.] std::locale::_Impl::_M_init_extra
   0.00%  a.out    ld-2.29.so             [.] get_common_indices.constprop.0
   0.00%  a.out    ld-2.29.so             [.] _dl_start
```

Figure 8.22: Using the perf command to analyze the code in Snippet2.cpp

You can move the cursor up and down to select a function and press *Enter* to get a list of options.

4. Highlight **testMul**, press *Enter*, and choose **Annotate testMul** in the resulting list. A list of assembly code is shown, with annotations describing the percentage of execution time for each line of code, as follows:

```
      │ 5e:   xor    %eax,%eax
      │       mov    $0x1,%r12d
      │       nop
 9.05 │ 70:   imul   %eax,%r12d
 0.86 │       add    $0x1,%eax
      │       cmp    $0x3b9aca00,%eax
 0.09 │     ↑ jne    70
      │     → callq  std::chrono::_V2::system_clock::now@plt
```

Figure 8.23: Viewing the timing statistics using the perf command for the Snippet2.cpp code

Notice that the **Integer Multiply (IMUL)** instruction (integer multiply) took over **99%** of the time to execute. Traditionally, integer multiplications are always expensive on the **x86** architecture and this continues to be true, even in the latest generation of CPUs. This annotation view displays arrows next to each jump or branching instruction which, when highlighted, shows what comparison instruction it is associated with and what address it jumps to with line drawings. You can navigate to the previous view by pressing the left arrow key and exit the program using the *q* key.

Up until now, we've looked at several methods that are used to assess the performance of our programs. This is the most critical stage of optimization since it tells us where we need to direct our efforts. In the upcoming sections, we will explore various techniques that will help us optimize our code.

## Optimization Strategies

Optimization of code can be done in several ways, such as the following:

- Compiler-based optimization
- Source code micro-optimization
- Cache-friendly code
- Algorithmic optimization

Here, each technique has its pros and cons. We will examine each of these methods in detail in the upcoming sections. Roughly speaking, these are ordered in terms of effort required and also potential gains in performance. We'll look at compiler-based optimization in the next section.

### Compiler-Based Optimization

Passing the correct options to the compiler can net many performance benefits. A real-world example of this is the Clear Linux **distro** (Linux distribution) that was created by Intel. This distro has been compiled to extract the maximum performance from all the code and outperforms most other Linux distributions by 30% on most benchmarks, which is a very significant speedup. On the `gcc` and `clang` family of compilers, the most basic option for optimization is `-O<N>`, where `N` is one of the numbers 1, 2, or 3. `-O3` enables almost every optimization in the compiler, but there are several others not enabled by that flag that can make a difference.

### Loop Unrolling

**Loop unrolling** is a technique that can be used by compilers to reduce the number of branches that are executed. Every time a branch is executed, there is a certain performance overhead. This can be reduced by repeating the loop body multiple times, and reducing the number of times the loop is executed. Loop unrolling can be done at the source level by the programmer, but modern compilers do a very good job automatically.

Even though modern processors mitigate the overhead of branching by means of **branch prediction** and **speculative execution** circuits, loop unrolling still produces performance benefits. Loop unrolling optimizations can be enabled on the **gcc** and **clang** family of compilers with the **-funroll-loops** command-line flag. In the next section, we'll test the performance of a program with and without loop unrolling enabled.

## Exercise 4: Using Loop Unrolling Optimizations

In this exercise, we'll write a simple program that uses nested loops and test its performance with and without loop unrolling enabled. We'll understand the way compilers implement the automatic unrolling of loops.

Perform these steps to complete this exercise:

1.  Create a file named **Snippet3.cpp**.

2.  Write a program that takes the first **10,000** numbers and prints out how many of these are factors of each other (the full code can be found in **Snippet3.cpp**):

```cpp
# include <iostream>
int main()
{
  int ret = 0;
  for(size_t i = 1; i < 10000; ++i)
  {
    for(size_t j = 1; j < 10000; ++j)
    {
      if(i % j == 0)
      {
        ++ret;
      }
    }
  }

  std::cout << "Result: " << ret << std::endl;
}
```

3.  Save the program and open the terminal. Compile the program with the **-03** flag first and time it using the following command:

```
$ g++ -03 Snippet3.cpp
$ time ./a.out
```

The output of the previous command is as follows:

```
Result: 93643

real     0m0.792s
user     0m0.788s
sys      0m0.003s
```

Figure 8.24: Output of the code in Snippet3.cpp

4.  Now, compile the same code with the loop unrolling enabled and time it again:

```
$ g++ -O3 -funroll-loops Snippet3.cpp
$ time ./a.out
```

The output of the previous command is as follows:

```
Result: 93643

real     0m0.684s
user     0m0.684s
sys      0m0.000s
```

Figure 8.25: Output of the code in Snippet3.cpp compiled with the loop unrolling option

5.  Open the **Godbolt compiler explorer** and paste the preceding complete code into the left-side.

6.  On the right-hand side, select **x86-64 gcc 8.3** from the compiler options and write the **-O3** flag in the options. Assembly code will be generated. For the for loop, you'll see the following output:

```
.L3:
        xor     edx, edx
        mov     rax, rsi
        div     rcx
        cmp     rdx, 1
        adc     ebx, 0
        add     rcx, 1
        cmp     rcx, 10000
        jne     .L3
        add     rsi, 1
        cmp     rsi, 10000
        jne     .L4
```

Figure 8.26: Assembly code of the for loop

From the preceding screenshot, you can clearly see RCX being compared to 10,000 with the CMP instruction, followed by a conditional jump, JNE (Jump if Not Equal). Just after this code, the outer loop comparison is seen, with RSI being compared to 10,000, followed by another conditional jump to the L4 label. Overall, the inner conditional branch and jump executes 100,000,000 times.

7. Now, add the following options: -O3 -funroll-loops. Assembly code will be generated. In this code, you'll notice this code pattern repeating eight times (except for the LEA instruction, whose offset value changes):

```
xor     edx, edx
div     rdi
mov     rax, rcx
lea     rdi, [rsi+6]
cmp     rdx, 1
adc     ebx, 0
```

Figure 8.27: Assembly code of the for loop

The compiler decided to unroll the body of the loop eight times, reducing the number of conditional jump instructions executed by a factor of 87.5% (about 8,300,000 times). This alone caused the execution time to improve by 10%, which is a very significant speedup. In this exercise we have seen the benefits of loop unrolling - next, we'll learn about profile guided optimization.

## Profile Guided Optimization

**Profile Guided Optimization** (PGO) is a feature that most compilers support. When a program is compiled with PGO enabled, the compiler adds instrumentation code to the program. Running this PGO-enabled executable creates a log file that contains information about the execution statistics of the program. The term **profiling** refers to the process of running a program to gather performance metrics. Typically, this profiling stage should be run with a real-world dataset so that an accurate log is produced. After this profiling run, the program is recompiled with a special compiler flag. This flag enables the compiler to perform special optimizations based on the statistical execution data that was recorded. Significant performance gains can be achieved with this approach. Let's solve an exercise based on profile guided optimization to get a better understanding of this.

## Exercise 5: Using Profile Guided Optimization

In this exercise, we will use profile guided optimization on the code from the previous exercise. We'll understand how to use profile guided optimization with the **gcc** compiler.

Perform these steps to complete this exercise:

1.  Open the terminal and compile the code from the previous exercise with profiling enabled. Include any other optimization flags that we need (in this case, **-O3**). Write the following code to implement this:

    ```
    $ g++ -O3 -fprofile-generate Snippet3.cpp
    ```

2.  Now, run the profiled version of the code by writing the following command:

    ```
    $ ./a.out
    ```

    The program runs normally and prints the result, and no other output is seen - but it generates a file containing data that will help the compiler in the following step. Note that with profiling enabled, the program executes several times slower than it would normally. This is something to keep in mind with large programs. After executing the previous command, a file called **Snippet3.gcda** will be generated, which contains profile data. When doing this with large, complex applications, it is important to run the program with the datasets and workflows that it will most commonly encounter in the production environment. By choosing the data correctly here, the eventual performance gain will be higher.

3.  Recompile with the PGO optimization flags, that is, **-fprofile-use** and **-fprofile-correction**, as illustrated in the following code:

    ```
    $ g++ -O3 -fprofile-use -fprofile-correction Snippet3.cpp
    ```

    Note that other than the profile-related compiler options, the other options must be exactly the same as the ones in the previous compilation step.

4.  Now, if we time the executable, we will see a large performance improvement:

    ```
    $ time ./a.out
    ```

    The output of the previous command is as follows:

```
Result: 93643

real      0m0.257s
user      0m0.257s
sys       0m0.000s
```

Figure 8.28: Timing results of the code in Snippet3.cpp with PGO optimization

In this exercise, we have seen the performance benefits gained by using profile guided optimizations provided by the compiler. For this code, the improvement in performance was about **2.7x** - on larger programs, this can be even higher.

## Parallelization

Most CPUs today have multiple cores, and even mobile phones have quad core processors. We can exploit this parallel processing power very simply with compiler flags that instruct it to generate parallelized code. One mechanism of parallelizing code is to use the **OpenMP** extensions of the C/C++ language. However, this means changing the source code and having detailed knowledge of how to use those extensions. The other simpler option is a feature specific to the **gcc** compiler – it provides an extended standard library that implements most algorithms to run as parallel ones.

> **Note**
>
> This automatic parallelization is only available for STL algorithms on gcc and is not part of the C++ standard. The C++ 17 standard proposes extensions to the standard library for parallel versions of most algorithms but is not supported by all compilers yet. Also, in order to take advantage of this feature, the code would have to be rewritten extensively.

## Exercise 6: Using Compiler Parallelization

In this exercise, we will use the **gcc** parallel extensions feature to accelerate standard library functions. Our aim is to understand how to use **gcc** parallel extensions.

Perform these steps to complete this exercise:

1. Create a file named **Snippet4.cpp**.

2. Write a simple program to sum up an initialized array with **std::accumulate**. Add the following code to implement this:

```
#include <vector>
#include <string>
#include <iostream>
#include <algorithm>
#include <numeric>

#include <cstdint>

using std::cerr;
```

```
using std::endl;
int main()
{
  // Fill 100,000,000 1s in a vector
  std::vector<int> v( 100'000'000, 1);
  // Call accumulate 100 times, accumulating to a total sum
  uint64_t total = 0;
  for(int i = 0; i < 100; ++i)
  {
    total += std::accumulate(v.begin(), v.end(), 0);
  }
  std::cout << "Total: " << total << std::endl;
}
```

3. Save the program and open the terminal. Compile the program normally and time the execution using the following commands:

```
$ g++ -O3 Snippet4.cpp
$ time ./a.out
```

The output of the previous command is as follows:

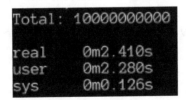

Figure 8.29: Output of the code in Snippet4.cpp

4. Now, compile the code with the parallelization options, that is, **-O3 -fopenmp** and **-D_GLIBCXX_PARALLEL**:

```
$ g++ -O3 -fopenmp -D_GLIBCXX_PARALLEL Snippet4.cpp
$ time ./a.out
```

The output is as follows:

```
Total: 10000000000

real    0m1.856s
user    0m13.007s
sys     0m0.163s
```

Figure 8.30: Output of the code in Snippet4.cpp compiled with parallelization options

In the previous output, the **user** field shows the cumulative CPU time and the **real** field shows the wall time. The ratio seen between the two is about **7x**. This ratio will vary, depending on how many CPU cores the system has (in this particular case, there were eight cores). For this system, the ratio could reach 8x if the compiler was able to perform **100%** parallelization. Note that even though eight cores were used, the actual improvement in execution time was only about **1.3x**. This is probably because the allocation and initialization of the vector takes up most of the time. This is a case of **Ahmdal's law**, which says that the serial parts of program dominate execution time when the parallelizable parts are made parallel. Despite this, we got a **1.3x** speedup in our code, which is a very good optimization result.

So far, we have covered some of the more impactful compiler optimization features available in modern compilers. Apart from these, there are several other optimization flags, but they may not produce very large improvements in performance. Two particular optimization flags that apply to large projects with many different source files is **Link time optimization** or **Link time code generation**. These are worth enabling for large projects. In the next section, we'll look into source code micro optimizations.

## Source Code Micro Optimizations

These are techniques that involve using certain idioms and patterns in the source code that are usually faster than their equivalents. In earlier times, these kinds of micro-optimizations were very fruitful, because compilers were not very clever. But today, compiler technology is very much advanced, and the effect of these micro-optimizations are not so marked. In spite of this, it is a very good habit to use these because they will make the code faster even if compiled without optimization. Even in development builds, code that is faster saves time when testing and debugging. We'll look at the std::vector container in the next section:

## Using the std::vector Container Efficiently

**std::vector** is one of the most simple and useful containers in the standard library. It has no overhead over normal C style arrays, but has the ability to grow, as well as optional bounds checking. You should almost always use **std::vector** when the number of elements is not known at compile time.

A common idiom that's used with **std::vector** is to call **push_back** on it in a loop – as it grows, the vector reallocates a new buffer, which is larger than the existing one by a certain factor (the exact value of this growth factor depends on the standard library implementation). In theory, this reallocation has minimal costs because it occurs infrequently, but in practice, the operation of resizing in a vector involves copying the elements of its buffer to a newly allocated larger buffer, which can be very expensive.

We can avoid these multiple allocations and copies by using the **reserve()** method. When we know how many elements a vector will contain, calling the **reserve()** method to pre-allocate the storage makes quite a difference. Let's implement an exercise in the next section to optimize vector growth.

## Exercise 7: Optimizing Vector Growth

In this exercise, we will time the effect of the **push_back** method in a loop, with and without calling the reserve method. First, we will extract the **Timer** class we used in the previous sections into a separate header and implementation file – this will allow us to use it as common code for all the succeeding code snippets. Perform these steps to complete this exercise:

1.  Create a header file named **Timer.h**.

2.  Include the necessary header files:

    ```
    #include <map>
    #include <string>
    #include <chrono>
    #include <cstdint>
    ```

3.  Create a class named **Timer**. Within the **Timer** class, declare four variables, namely **ms_Counts**, **ms_Times**, **m_tmStart**, and **m_sName**. Declare a constructor, destructor, and the **dump()** method. Add the following code to implement this:

    ```
    class Timer
    {
       static std::map<std::string, int64_t> ms_Counts;
       static std::map<std::string, int64_t> ms_Times;
       std::string m_sName;
       std::chrono::time_point<std::chrono::high_resolution_clock> m_tmStart;
       public:
          // When constructed, save the name and current clock time
          Timer(std::string sName);
          // When destroyed, add the time elapsed and also increment the count
    under this name
          ~Timer();
          // Print out the stats for each measured block/function
          static void dump();
    };
    ```

4. Define a helper macro named **TIME_IT** to time functions by writing the following code:

```
// Helper macro to time functions
#define TIME_IT Timer t(__func__)
```

5. Once the header file has been created, create a new file named **Timer.cpp** and include the **Timer.h** file in it. Also, write the actual implementation for the constructors, destructors, and the **dump()** method inside the **Timer.cpp** file. Write the following code to implement this:

```
#include <string>
#include <iostream>
#include <cstdint>
#include "Timer.h"

using std::map;
using std::string;
using std::cerr;
using std::endl;


// When constructed, save the name and current clock time
Timer::Timer(string sName): m_sName(sName)
{
    m_tmStart = std::chrono::high_resolution_clock::now();
}
// When destroyed, add the time elapsed and also increment the count under
this name
Timer::~Timer()
{
    auto tmNow = std::chrono::high_resolution_clock::now();
    auto msElapsed = std::chrono::duration_
cast<std::chrono::milliseconds>(tmNow - m_tmStart);
    ms_Counts[m_sName]++;
    ms_Times[m_sName] += msElapsed.count();
}
// Print out the stats for each measured block/function
void Timer::dump()
{
    cerr << "Name\t\t\tCount\t\t\tTime(ms)\t\tAverage(ms)\n";
    cerr << "------------------------------------------------------------------
----------------------\n";
    for(const auto& it: ms_Times)
```

```
    {
        auto iCount = ms_Counts[it.first];
        cerr << it.first << "\t\t\t" << iCount << "\t\t\t" << it.second <<
    "\t\t\t" << it.second / iCount << "\n";
    }
}
// Define static members
map<string, int64_t> Timer::ms_Counts;
map<string, int64_t> Timer::ms_Times;
```

6. Now, create a new file named **Snippet5.cpp** and write two functions that simply fill a vector with the first **1,000,000** integers using the **push_back()** method. The second function calls the **reserve()** method beforehand, but the first one does not. Write the following code to implement this:

```cpp
#include <vector>
#include <string>
#include <iostream>
#include "Timer.h"

using std::vector;
using std::cerr;
using std::endl;

const int N = 1000000;

void withoutReserve(vector<int> &v)
{
    TIME_IT;
    for(int i = 0; i < N; ++i)
    {
        v.push_back(i);
    }
}
void withReserve(vector<int> &v)
{
    TIME_IT;
    v.reserve(N);
    for(int i = 0; i < N; ++i)
    {
        v.push_back(i);
    }
}
```

7. Now, write the **main** function. Note the use of redundant braces to ensure that the **v1** and **v2** vectors are destroyed after every iteration of the loop:

```
int main()
{
  {
    vector<int> v1;
    for(int i = 0; i < 100; ++i)
    {
      withoutReserve(v1);
    }
  }
  {
    vector<int> v2;
    for(int i = 0; i < 100; ++i)
    {
      withReserve(v2);
    }
  }
  Timer::dump();
}
```

The reason we pass the vector by reference is to prevent the compiler from optimizing out the entire code in the two functions. If we passed the vectors by value, the functions would have no visible side effects and the compiler may just elide the functions totally.

8. Save the program and open the terminal. Compile the **Timer.cpp** and **Snippet5.cpp** files and run them as follows:

```
$ g++ -O3 Snippet5.cpp Timer.cpp
$ ./a.out
```

The output is as follows:

| Name | Count | Time(ms) | Average(ms) |
|------|-------|----------|-------------|
| withReserve | 100 | 580 | 5 |
| withoutReserve | 100 | 604 | 6 |

Figure 8.31: Output of the code in Snippet5.cpp showing the effect of vector::reserve()

As we can see, the effect of calling **reserve()** has resulted in an improvement of about 4% in execution time. In a larger program that has run for a long time, the system memory often becomes very fragmented. In such cases, the improvement by pre-allocating memory with **reserve()** could be much better. In general, it is usually faster to reserve memory beforehand, rather than doing it incrementally on the fly. Even the Java Virtual Machine, for performance reasons, uses this technique of allocating a huge chunk of memory upfront when starting up.

## Short-Circuit Logical Operators

The **&&** and **||** logical operators are **short-circuited**, which means that the following:

- If the left-hand side of the **||** operator is **true**, the right-hand side is not evaluated.

- If the left-hand side of the **&&** operator is **false**, the right-hand side is not evaluated.

By keeping the more unlikely (or less expensive) expression on the left-hand side, we can reduce the amount of work that needs to be done. In the next section, we'll solve an exercise and learn how to write logical expressions optimally.

## Exercise 8: Optimizing Logical Operators

In this exercise, we will examine the impact of ordering conditional expressions when used with logical operators. Perform these steps to complete this exercise:

1. Create a new file named **Snippet6.cpp**.

2. Include the necessary libraries and the Timer.h file that we created in the previous exercise by writing the following code:

```cpp
#include <vector>
#include <string>
#include <iostream>
#include <random>

#include "Timer.h"

using std::vector;
using std::cerr;
using std::endl;
```

3. Define a function named **sum1()** that computes the sum of the integers between **0** and **N**. Each number is summed only if it meets either or of two specific criteria. The first condition is that the number must be less than **N/2**. The second condition is that the number, when divided by 3, must return 2 as a remainder. Here, we set **N** to **100,000,000** so we have some measurable time taken by the code. Write the following code to implement this:

```
const uint64_t N = 100000000;

uint64_t sum1()
{
   TIME_IT;
   uint64_t ret = 0;
   for(uint64_t b=0; b < N; ++b)
   {
      if(b % 3 == 2 || b < N/2)
      {
         ret += b;
      }
   }

   return ret;
}
```

4. Now, define another function named **sum2()**. It must contain the same logic that we wrote for the previous function, **sum1()**. The only change here is that we reverse the order of the conditional expression of the **if** statement. Write the following code to implement this:

```
uint64_t sum2()
{
   TIME_IT;
   uint64_t ret = 0;
   for(uint64_t b=0; b < N; ++b)
   {
      if(b < N/2 || b % 3 == 2)
      {
         ret += b;
      }
   }

   return ret;
}
```

Note that in the **sum2** function, the **b < N/2** condition will evaluate to true half of the time. Thus, the second condition, that is, **b % 3 == 2**, is only evaluated for half of the iterations. If we assume for simplicity that both conditionals take 1 unit of time, the total time taken for **sum2()** would be **N/2 + (2 * N/2) = N * 3/2**. In the case of the **sum1()** function, the condition on the left-hand side will evaluate to **true** only 33% of the time, and the remaining 66% of the time, both conditions will be evaluated. Thus, the estimated time taken would be **N/3 + (2 * N * 2/3) = N * 5/3**. We expect that the ratio between the times for the **sum1** and **sum2** function would be **5/3** to **3/2** – that is, **sum1** is **11%** slower.

5.  Add the following code in the main function:

```
int main()
{
  volatile uint64_t dummy = 0;
  for(int i = 0; i < 100; ++i)
  {
    dummy = sum1();
  }
  for(int i = 0; i < 100; ++i)
  {
    dummy = sum2();
  }
  Timer::dump();
}
```

6.  Save the file and open the terminal. Compile and time the preceding program, as well as the **Timer.cpp** file, by writing the following commands:

```
$ g++ -O3 Snippet6.cpp Timer.cpp
$ ./a.out
```

The output is as follows:

| Name | Count | Time(ms) | Average(ms) |
|------|-------|----------|-------------|
| sum1 | 100 | 10995 | 109 |
| sum2 | 100 | 7918 | 79 |

Figure 8.32: Output of the code in Snippet6.cpp showing the effect of optimizing boolean conditions

As you can see from the preceding output, we ended up with about **38%** improvement in speed, which is much more than expected. Why would this happen? The answer is that the **%** operator performs an integer division, which is much more expensive than a comparison, but the compiler will not generate a division instruction for the **N/2** expression because it is a constant value.

The `sum1()` function code executes the modulus operation for every iteration of the loop and the overall execution time is dominated by the division. To summarize this, we must always consider short-circuit logical operators and calculate how each side of the expression is, and how many times it exectures in order to choose the optimal order in which they should appear in the expression. This is equivalent of doing an expected value calculation of probability theory. In the next section, we'll learn about branch prediction.

## Branch Prediction

Modern processors use a pipelined architecture, which is similar to a factory assembly line, where an instruction flows along a pipeline and is processed by various workers simultaneously. After each clock cycle, the instruction moves along the pipeline to the next stage. This means that although each instruction may take many cycles to go from start to finish, the overall throughput is one instruction completed per cycle.

The drawback here is that, if there is a conditional branch instruction, the CPU has no idea which set of instructions are to be loaded after that (since there are two possible alternatives). This condition is called a **pipeline stall**, and the processor must wait until the condition of the branch has been evaluated completely, wasting precious cycles.

To mitigate this, modern processors use something called **branch prediction** – they try to predict which way the branch goes. As the branch is encountered a greater number of times, it gets more confident as to which way the branch is likely to take.

Despite this, the CPU is not omniscient, so if it starts loading the instructions of one predicted branch, and later the conditional branch turned out to go the other way, the entire pipeline after the branch has to be cleared and the actual branch needs to be loaded from scratch. All the work done on the "`assembly line`" downstream of the branch instruction has to be discarded and any changes need to be reversed.

This is a major bottleneck for performance, and it can be avoided – the simplest way is to make sure a branch always goes one way as much as possible – like a loop.

## Exercise 9: Optimization for Branch Prediction

In this exercise, we will explore and demonstrate the effect of CPU branch prediction on performance. To explore this, we'll write two functions in a program – both perform the same computation using two nested loops which iterate `100` and `100,000,000` times, respectively. The difference between the two functions is that, in the first function, the outer loop is the bigger one, whereas in the second function, the outer loop is the smaller one.

For the first function, the outer loop fails branch prediction only once when it exits, but the inner loop fails branch prediction **100,000,000** times – each time it exits. For the second one, once again, the outer loop fails branch prediction only once when it exits, but the inner loop fails branch prediction only 100 times – each time it exits. The factor of **1,000,000** between these branch prediction failure counts will result in the first function being slower than the second. Perform these steps to complete this exercise:

1. Create a file named **Snippet7.cpp** and include the necessary libraries:

```
#include <vector>
#include <string>
#include <iostream>
#include <random>
#include "Timer.h"

using std::vector;
using std::cerr;
using std::endl;
```

2. Define a function named **sum1()** with a nested loop. The outer **for** loop should cycle **N** times, whereas the inner for loop should iterate **100** times. Set the value of **N** to **100000000**. Write the following code to implement this:

```
const uint64_t N = 100000000;
uint64_t sum1()
{
  TIME_IT;
  uint64_t ret = 0;
  for(int i = 0; i < N; ++i)
  {
    for(int j = 0; j < 100; ++j)
    {
      ret += i ^ j;
    }
  }
  return ret;
}
```

If we assume that the processor predicts branches in loops (statistically, the branch instruction at the end of the loop is more likely to jump to the start of the loop than not), then it will end up mispredicting every time j reaches **100** – in other words, **N** times.

3. Define a new function, **sum2()**, with a nested loop. The only change here is that we must set the inner loop count to **N** and the outer loop count to **100**. Add the following code to implement this:

```
uint64_t sum2()
{
  TIME_IT;
  uint64_t ret = 0;
  for(int i = 0; i < 100; ++i)
  {
    for(int j = 0; j < N; ++j)
    {
      ret += i ^ j;
    }
  }
  return ret;
}
```

Now, our reasoning is that the branch misprediction happens only **100** times.

4. Add the following code in the main function:

```
int main()
{
  volatile uint64_t dummy;
  dummy = sum1();
  dummy = sum2();
  Timer::dump();
}
```

5. Save the file and open the terminal. Compile the preceding program, along with the **Timer.cpp** file, and time them using the following commands. Remember that you need to have the Timer.cpp and Timer.h files you created earlier in the same directory:

```
$ g++ -O3 Snippet7.cpp Timer.cpp
$ ./a.out
```

The output of executing the previous command is as follows:

| Name | Count | Time(ms) | Average(ms) |
|------|-------|----------|-------------|
| sum1 | 1 | 2442 | 2442 |
| sum2 | 1 | 2377 | 2377 |

Figure 8.33: Output of the code in Snippet7.cpp showing the effect of branch prediction optimization

As you can see from the preceding output, there is a small but certainly significant speedup of about **2%** that can be attributed to the processor being able to predict branches better for the sum2 function. In the next section, we'll explore more optimization techniques.

## Further Optimizations

Several other techniques exist that can be implemented as you code; some of them are not guaranteed to produce better code, but it takes very little effort to change your coding habits to do these reflexively. They cost nothing but may result in gains. A few of these techniques are as follows:

- Pass parameters that are not primitive types by **const** reference when possible. Even though **move constructors** can make copying inexpensive, they still involve more overhead than using a **const** reference.

- Use pre-increment (**++i**) or pre-decrement (**--i**) operators rather than the postfix versions. This usually has no utility for simple types such as integers but may do so for complex types with a custom increment operator. Getting into a habit of writing **++i** rather than **i++** is good practice unless post-increment is actually the desired behavior. Apart from performance benefits, such code declares the intent more clearly by using the right operator.

- Declare variables as late as possible – it is common in C to declare every variable at the top of a function, but in C++, since variables can have non-trivial constructors, it makes sense to only declare them in the actual block where they are used.

- In terms of **loop hoisting**, if there is any code or calculation in a loop that does not change with the loop iteration, it makes sense to move it outside the loop. This includes creating objects in a loop body. Often, it is more efficient to declare them once, outside the loop. Modern compilers do this automatically, but it doesn't take extra effort to do this yourself.

- Use **const** wherever possible. It does not change the meaning of the code, but it lets the compiler make stronger assumptions about your code that may lead to better optimization. Apart from this, using **const** makes code more readable and reasonable.

- Integer division, modulus, and multiplication (especially by numbers that are not powers of 2) are some of the slowest operations possible on X86 hardware. If you need to perform such operations in a loop, perhaps you can do some algebraic manipulation to get rid of them.

As we mentioned, several such optimizations may be done by the compiler itself, but doing them as a habit makes the code fast even in debug mode, which is a big advantage when debugging. We have examined a few techniques for micro-optimizing code already – the level of code change required to do these is relatively minor, and some of these can produce major improvements in efficiency. If you want to write faster code in general, you should aim to integrate these techniques as a default coding style over time. In the next section, we'll learn about cache-friendly code.

## Cache Friendly Code

Computer science was developed in the mid-20th century, when computers hardly existed, but nevertheless, by the 1980s, most of the useful data structures and algorithms had been discovered and refined. Algorithmic complexity analysis is a topic that anyone who learns computer science encounters – and there are well-accepted textbook definitions of the complexity of data structure operations. However, after 50 years since these things were analyzed, computers have evolved in a way that is quite different from what could have been envisaged. For example, a common "fact" is that the list data structures are faster for insertion operations than arrays. This seems like common sense because inserting an element into an array involves moving all the items after that point to new locations, whereas inserting into a list is merely a few pointer manipulations. We will test this hypothesis in the following exercise.

### Exercise 10: Exploring the Effect of Caches on Data Structures

In this exercise, we will examine the impact of the cache on arrays and lists in the C++ standard library. Perform these steps to complete this exercise:

1. Create a file named **Snippet8.cpp**.

2. Include the necessary libraries, along with the **Timer.h** header file. Write the following code to implement this:

```cpp
#include <vector>
#include <list>
#include <algorithm>
#include <string>
#include <iostream>
#include <random>
#include "Timer.h"

using std::vector;
using std::list;
using std::cerr;
using std::endl;
```

3. Create a constant integer variable, **N**, and set its value to **100000**:

```
const int N = 100000;
```

4. Initialize a random number generator and create a distribution range from **0** to **1000**. Add the following code to achieve this:

```
std::random_device dev;
std::mt19937 rng(dev());
std::uniform_int_distribution<std::mt19937::result_type> dist(0,N);
```

5. Create a method named **insertRandom()** and insert elements from **0** to **N** into a container at random positions. Add the following code to implement this:

```
template<class C> void insertRandom(C &l)
{
  // insert one element to initialize
  l.insert(l.end(), 0);
  for(int i = 0; i < N; ++i)
  {
    int pos = dist(rng) % l.size();
    auto it = l.begin();
    advance(it, pos);
    l.insert(it, i);
  }
}
```

6. Create a method named **insertStart()** and insert elements from **0** to **N** into a container at the start. Add the following code to implement this:

```
template<class C> void insertStart(C &l)
{
  for(int i = 0; i < N; ++i)
  {
    l.insert(l.begin(), i);
  }
}
```

7. Create a method named **insertEnd()** and insert elements from **0** to **N** into a container at the end. Add the following code to implement this:

```
template<class C> void insertEnd(C &l)
{
  for(int i = 0; i < N; ++i)
  {
    l.insert(l.end(), i);
  }
}
```

8. Write the following code in the **main** method:

```
int main()
{
  std::list<int> l;
  std::vector<int> v;
  // list
  {
    Timer t("list random");
    insertRandom(l);
  }

  {
    Timer t("list end");
    insertEnd(l);
  }
  {
    Timer t("list start");
    insertStart(l);
  }
  // vector
  {
    Timer t("vect random");
    insertRandom(v);
  }

  {
    Timer t("vect end");
    insertEnd(v);
  }
  {
    Timer t("vect start");
```

```
            insertStart(v);
        }
        cerr << endl << l.size() << endl << v.size() << endl;
        Timer::dump();
    }
```

9.  Save the file and open the terminal. Compile the preceding program, along with the **Timer.cpp** file, by writing the following commands:

    ```
    $ g++ -O3 Snippet8.cpp Timer.cpp
    $ ./a.out
    ```

The preceding command generates the following output:

```
300001
300001
Name                     Count                    Time(ms)                 Average(ms)

list end                 1                        3                        3
list random              1                        30597                    30597
list start               1                        3                        3
vect end                 1                        0                        0
vect random              1                        229                      229
vect start               1                        2870                     2870
```

Figure 8.34: Output of the code in Snippet8.cpp contrasting the timing
of std::list and std::vector insertion

As you can see from the preceding output, the code measures the time taken to insert **100000** integers at the start, end, and random locations for **std::vector** and **std::list**. The vector clearly wins by a factor of 100 or more for the random case, and even the worst case for the vector is 10x faster than the random case for the list.

Why does this happen? The answer lies in the way modern computer architecture has evolved. CPU clock speeds have increased from about **1 Mhz** in the early 80s to **5 GHz** as of mid-2019 – a speedup of **5,000x** in clock frequency – and while the earliest CPUs used multiple cycles per instruction, modern ones execute several instructions per cycle on a single core (due to advanced techniques such as pipelining, which we described earlier).

For example, the **IDIV** instruction on the original **Intel 8088** took over 100 clock cycles to complete, whereas on modern processors, it can be completed in less than 5 cycles. On the other hand, RAM bandwidth (the time taken to read or write a byte of memory) has increased very slowly.

Historically, processors have increased in speed by a factor of about **16,000x** between 1980 and 2010. At the same time, the speed increase in RAM has been an order of magnitude smaller – less than 100x. Thus, it is possible that single access to RAM by an instruction causes the CPU to wait for a huge number of clock cycles. This would be an unacceptable degradation of performance, and there have been a lot of technologies to mitigate this issue. Before we explore this, let's measure the impact of memory access in the next exercise.

## Exercise 11: Measuring the Impact of Memory Access

In this exercise, we will examine the performance impact of randomly accessing memory. Perform these steps to complete this exercise:

1.  Create a new file named **Snippet9.cpp**.

2.  Include the necessary libraries, along with the **Timer.h** header file. Create two constant integer variables, **SIZE** and **N**, and set their values to **100000000**. Also, create a random number generator and a distribution range from **0** to **N-1**. Write the following code to implement this:

```cpp
#include <vector>
#include <list>
#include <algorithm>
#include <string>
#include <iostream>
#include <random>
#include "Timer.h"

using std::vector;
using std::list;
using std::cerr;
using std::endl;

const int SIZE = 100'000'000;
const int N = 100'000'000;

std::random_device dev;
std::mt19937 rng(dev());

std::uniform_int_distribution<std::mt19937::result_type> dist(0,SIZE-1);
```

3. Create the **getPRIndex()** function, which returns a pseudo random index between **0** and **SIZE-1**, where **SIZE** is the number of elements in the array. Write the following code to implement this:

> **Note**
>
> We will discuss why we use a random number later.

```
uint64_t getPRIndex(uint64_t i)
{
    return (15485863 * i) % SIZE;
}
```

4. Write a function named **sum1()** that accesses a large array of data randomly and sums those elements:

```
uint64_t sum1(vector<int> &v)
{
    TIME_IT;
    uint64_t sum = 0;
    for(int i = 0; i < N; ++i)
    {
        sum += v[getPRIndex(i)];
    }
    return sum;
}
```

5. Write a function named **sum2()** that sums random numbers without any memory access:

```
uint64_t sum2()
{
    TIME_IT;
    uint64_t sum = 0;
    for(int i = 0; i < N; ++i)
    {
        sum += getPRIndex(i);
    }
    return sum;
}
```

6. In the main function, initialize the vector so that v[i] == i, thus, the only difference between sum1() and sum2() is that sum1() accesses memory and sum2() only performs computations. As usual, we use volatile to prevent the compiler from removing all the code, since it has no side effects. Write the following code in the main() function:

```cpp
int main()
{
    // Allocate SIZE integers
    std::vector<int> v(SIZE, 0);
    // Fill 0 to SIZE-1 values into the vector
    for(int i = 0; i < v.size(); ++i)
    {
        v[i] = i;
    }
    volatile uint64_t asum1 = sum1(v);
    volatile uint64_t asum2 = sum2();
    Timer::dump();
}
```

7. Save the program and open the terminal. Compile and run the program by writing the following commands:

```
$ g++ -O3 Snippet9.cpp Timer.cpp
$ ./a.out
```

The preceding code generates the following output:

| Name | Count | Time(ms) | Average(ms) |
|------|-------|----------|-------------|
| sum1 | 1 | 1283 | 1283 |
| sum2 | 1 | 88 | 88 |

Figure 8.35: Output of the code in Snippet9.cpp contrasting the timing of computation versus random memory access

From the preceding output, we can clearly see a factor of about **14x** difference in performance.

8. Create a new file named **Snippet10.cpp** and add the same code that was present in **Snippet9.cpp**. Add a new function named sum3() that accesses memory linearly instead of randomly. Also, edit the main function. The updated code is as follows:

```cpp
uint64_t sum3(vector<int> &v)
{
    TIME_IT;
    uint64_t sum = 0;
```

```
        for(int i = 0; i < N; ++i)
        {
          sum += v[i];
        }
        return sum;
    }
    int main()
    {
        // Allocate SIZE integers
        std::vector<int> v(SIZE, 0);

        // Fill 0 to SIZE-1 values into the vector
        for(int i = 0; i < v.size(); ++i)
        {
          v[i] = i;
        }
        volatile uint64_t asum1 = sum1(v);
        volatile uint64_t asum2 = sum2();
        volatile uint64_t asum3 = sum3(v);
        Timer::dump();
    }
```

9. Save the file and open the Terminal. Compile and run the program:

```
$ g++ -O3 Snippet10.cpp Timer.cpp
$ ./a.out
```

The preceding commands generate the following output:

| Name | Count | Time(ms) | Average(ms) |
|------|-------|----------|-------------|
| sum1 | 1 | 1225 | 1225 |
| sum2 | 1 | 87 | 87 |
| sum3 | 1 | 32 | 32 |

Figure 8.36: Output of the code in Snippet10.cpp contrasting the timing
of computation versus random and linear memory access

In the preceding output, notice that the memory access is now more than **35** times faster than before, and **2.5** times faster than the calculation in **sum2()**. We used the random access pattern in **sum1()** to demonstrate the contrast between linear and random memory access. What makes linear memory access so much faster than random access? The answer lies in two mechanisms in modern processors that are used to mitigate the effects of slow memory – **caching** and **prefetch** – both of which we will discuss in the following sections.

## Caching

Modern processors have multiple layers of cache memory between the processor registers and the RAM. These caches are labeled L1, L2, L3, L4, and so on, where L1 is closest to the processor and L4 is the furthest. Every cache layer is faster (and usually smaller) than the level below it. Here is an example of the cache/memory sizes and latencies for a `Haswell` family processor:

- L1: 32 KB, 4 cycles
- L2: 256 KB, 12 cycles
- L3: 6 MB, 20 cycles
- L4: 128 MB, 58 cycles
- RAM: many GB, 115 cycles

A simple model of how caches work to help performance is as follows: when a memory address is accessed, it is looked up in the L1 cache – if found, it is retrieved from there. If not, it is looked up in the L2 cache, if not found, then the L3 cache and so on – if it wasn't found in any of the caches, it is fetched from memory. When fetched from memory, it is stored in each of the caches for faster access later. This method in itself would be fairly useless because it would only improve performance if we accessed the same memory address again and again.

The second aspect, called **prefetching**, is the mechanism that can make caches really pay off.

## Prefetching

Prefetching is a process where, when memory access is performed, nearby data is also fetched into caches, even though it was not accessed directly. The first aspect of prefetching is related to memory bus granularity – it can be thought of as "What is the minimum amount of data that the RAM subsystem can send to the processor?". In most modern processors, this is 64 bits – in other words, whether you ask for a single byte or a 64-bit value from memory, the entire `machine word` of 64 bits that includes that address is read from RAM. This data is stored in each layer of cache for faster access later. Obviously, this would immediately improve memory performance – say we read a byte of memory at address `0x1000`; we also get the 7 other bytes after that address into the caches. If we then access the byte at address `0x1001`, it comes from the cache, avoiding expensive RAM access.

The second aspect of prefetch takes this one step further – when the contents of the RAM at an address is read, the processor reads not only that memory word, but much more. On the x86 family of processors, this is between 32 and 128 bytes. This is called the **cache line** size – the processor always writes and reads memory in chunks of that size. When the CPU hardware detects that memory is being accessed in a linear fashion, it prefetches memory into one cache line, based on its prediction of what addresses are likely to be accessed subsequently.

CPUs are very clever in detecting regular access patterns both forwards and backwards, and will prefetch efficiently. You can also provide hints to the processor using special instructions to make it prefetch data according to the programmer's direction. These instructions are provided as intrinsic functions on most compilers in order to avoid the use of inline assembly language. When a memory address is read or written that is not in a cache, it is termed a **cache miss**, and is a very expensive event and to be avoided at all costs. The CPU hardware tries its best to mitigate cache misses, but the programmer can analyze and modify the data access patterns to reduce cache misses maximally. The description of caching here is a simplified model for instructional purposes – in reality, CPUs have L1 caches for instructions as well as data, multiple cache lines, and very complex mechanisms to make sure that multiple processors can keep their separate caches in synchronization.

> **Note**
>
> A comprehensive description of cache implementations (and lots of other information about memory subsystems) can be found in this famous online article: https://lwn.net/Articles/250967/.

## Effects of Caching on Algorithms

Having learned about caches, we can now reason why our first example of vector versus list showed surprising results – from a computer science perspective, the following is true:

**For a list**:

- Iterating to the Nth position is order N complexity.

- Inserting or deleting an element is an order 1 complexity.

**For an array (or vector)**:

- Iterating to the Nth position is order 1 complexity.

- Inserting or deleting an element at location N has complexity proportional to (S - N), where S is the size of the array.

However, for modern architectures, the cost of a memory access is extremely high, but the cost of accessing an adjacent address subsequently is almost 0 because it would already be in the cache. This means that the iteration upon elements in a `std::list` that are located non-sequentially in memory are likely to always cause a cache miss, causing slow performance. On the other hand, since the elements of an array or `std::vector` are always adjacent, caching and prefetching would reduce the overall cost of copying (S-N) elements to a new location by a very large margin. Hence, the traditional analysis of the two data structures that declares that lists work better for random insertions, while technically correct, is not practically true, especially given the clearly sophisticated caching behavior of modern CPU hardware. When our programs are *data bound*, the analysis of algorithm complexity has to be augmented by understanding of what is known as **data locality**.

Data locality can be defined simply as the average distance from the memory address that was just accessed to the one that was accessed previously. In other words, making memory access across addresses that are far from each other is a severe slowdown, since data from closer addresses are likely to have been prefetched into the caches. When data is already present in the cache(s), it is termed "hot"; otherwise, it is termed "cold". Code that takes advantage of the cache is termed **cache friendly**. Cache-unfriendly code, on the other hand would cause the cache lines to be wastefully reloaded (termed **cache invalidation**). In the remainder of this section, we will look at strategies regarding how to write cache-friendly code.

## Optimizing for Cache-Friendliness

In the old days, optimization of code involved trying to minimize the number of machine instructions in code, using more efficient instructions, and even reordering instructions to allow pipelines to remain full. As of this day and age, compilers perform all the aforementioned optimization to a level that most programmers would be unable to – especially considering that compilers can do it across entire programs of hundreds of millions of instructions. What remains firmly the responsibility of the programmer even now is the ability to optimize data access patterns to take advantage of caching.

The task is very simple – make sure that memory is accessed close to the memory that was accessed before – but the methodology to achieve this can require lots of effort.

> **Note**
>
> The famous game programmer and code optimization guru Terje Mathisen, in the 90s, is claimed to have said: "All programming is an exercise in caching." Today, in 2019, this statement applies more than ever in this sub-domain of trying to write fast code.

There are some basic rules of thumb for increasing cache-friendliness:

- The stack is always "hot", and so we should use local variables as much as possible.

- Dynamically allocated objects rarely have data locality with each other – avoid them or use a preallocated pool of objects so they are in sequential in memory.

- Pointer-based data structures such as trees – and especially lists – consist of multiple nodes allocated on the heap, and are very cache unfriendly.

- Runtime dispatch of virtual functions in OO code invalidates the instruction cache – avoid a dynamic dispatch in performance-critical code.

In the next section, we'll explore the cost of heap allocations.

## Exercise 12: Exploring the Cost of Heap Allocations

In this exercise, we will examine the performance impact of dynamically allocated memory and examine how heap memory affects the code's performance. Perform these steps to complete this exercise:

1. Create a file named **Snippet11.cpp**.

2. Add the following code to include the necessary libraries:

```cpp
#include <string>
#include <iostream>
#include <random>
#include "Timer.h"

using std::string;
using std::cerr;
using std::endl;
```

3. Declare a constant variable, N, and a character array called fruits. Assign values to them:

```
const int N = 10'000'000;
const char* fruits[] =
    {"apple", "banana", "cherry", "durian", "guava", "jackfruit", "kumquat",
    "mango", "orange", "pear"};
```

4. Create a function named **fun1()** that just loops over each string in fruits, copies it to a string, and sums the characters of that string:

```
uint64_t fun1()
{
    TIME_IT;
    uint64_t sum = 0;
    string s1;
    for(uint64_t i = 0; i < N; ++i)
    {
        s1 = fruits[i % 10];
        for(int k = 0; k < s1.size(); ++k) sum += s1[k];
    }
    return sum;
}
```

5. Create another function named **sum2()** that uses a locally declared character array instead of a string and a loop to copy:

```
uint64_t fun2()
{
    TIME_IT;
    uint64_t sum = 0;
    char s1[32];

    for(uint64_t i = 0; i < N; ++i)
    {
        char *ps1 = s1;
        const char *p1 = fruits[i % 10];
        do { *ps1++ = *p1; } while(*p1++);
        for(ps1 = s1; *ps1; ++ps1) sum += *ps1;
    }
    return sum;
}
```

6. Write the following code inside the **main()** function:

```cpp
int main()
{
    for(int i = 0; i < 10; ++i)
    {
        volatile uint64_t asum1 = fun1();
        volatile uint64_t asum2 = fun2();
    }
    Timer::dump();
}
```

7. Save the file and open the terminal. Compile and run the program:

```
$ g++ -O3 Snippet11.cpp Timer.cpp
$ ./a.out
```

The preceding commands generate the following output:

| Name | Count | Time(ms) | Average(ms) |
|------|-------|----------|-------------|
| fun1 | 10 | 1291 | 129 |
| fun2 | 10 | 649 | 64 |

Figure 8.37: Output of the code in Snippet11.cpp showing the effect of heap allocation on the timing

From the preceding output, notice that **fun2()** is almost twice as fast as **fun1()**.

8. Now, use the **perf** command to profile:

```
$ perf record ./a.out
```

The preceding command generates the following output:

| Name | Count | Time(ms) | Average(ms) |
|------|-------|----------|-------------|
| fun1 | 10 | 1315 | 131 |
| fun2 | 10 | 672 | 67 |

```
[ perf record: Woken up 2 times to write data ]
[ perf record: Captured and wrote 0.301 MB perf.data (7855 samples) ]
```

Figure 8.38: Output of the perf command profiling the code in Snippet11.cpp

9. Now, we can check the performance report with the following code:

```
$ perf report
```

We receive the following output:

```
Samples: 7K of event 'cycles:u', Event count (approx.): 6310020083
Overhead  Command  Shared Object        Symbol
 34.08%  a.out    a.out                [.] fun2
 26.95%  a.out    a.out                [.] fun1
 22.30%  a.out    libstdc++.so.6.0.26  [.] std::__cxx11::basic_string<char, std::c
  8.71%  a.out    libc-2.29.so         [.] __strlen_avx2
  4.71%  a.out    libc-2.29.so         [.] __memmove_avx_unaligned_erms
```

Figure 8.39: Output of the perf command's timing report for the code in Snippet11.cpp

In the preceding output, notice that about **33%** of the execution time was taken by the `std::string` constructor, `strlen()`, and `memmove()`. All of these are associated with the `std::string` that was used in `fun1()`. The heap allocation in particular is the slowest operation.

## Struct of Arrays Pattern

In many programs, we often use an array of objects of the same type – these could represent records from a database, entities in a game, and so on. A common pattern is to iterate through a large array of structures and perform an operation on some fields. Even though the structs are sequential in memory, if we access only a few of fields, a larger size structure will make caching less effective.

The processor may prefetch several structs into cache, but the program only accesses a fraction of that cached data. Since it is not using every field of each struct, most of the cached data is discarded. To avoid this, another kind of data layout can be used – instead of using an **array of structs (AoS)** pattern, we use a **struct of arrays (SoA)** pattern. In the next section, we'll solve an exercise wherein we'll examine the performance benefit of using the SoA pattern versus the AoS pattern.

## Exercise 13: Using the Struct of Arrays Pattern

In this exercise, we will examine the performance benefits of using the SoA versus AoS pattern. Perform these steps to complete this exercise:

1. Create a file named **Snippet12.cpp**.

2. Include the necessary libraries, along with the `Timer.h` header file. Initialize a random number generator and also create a distribution range from 1 to N-1. Create a constant integer variable, N, and initialize it with a value of 100,000,000. Add the following code to implement this:

```
#include <vector>
#include <list>
#include <algorithm>
#include <string>
```

```
#include <iostream>
#include <random>
#include "Timer.h"

using std::vector;
using std::list;
using std::cerr;
using std::endl;

const int N = 100'000'000;

std::random_device dev;
std::mt19937 rng(dev());

std::uniform_int_distribution<std::mt19937::result_type> dist(1,N-1);
```

3. Write two different ways to represent data -- anarray of structs and a struct of arrays. Use six fields of **uint64_t** so that we can emulate a large-sized structure that would be more representative of a real- world program:

```
struct Data1
{
   uint64_t field1;
   uint64_t field2;
   uint64_t field3;
   uint64_t field4;
   uint64_t field5;
   uint64_t field6;
};
struct Data2
{
   vector<uint64_t> field1;
   vector<uint64_t> field2;
   vector<uint64_t> field3;
   vector<uint64_t> field4;
   vector<uint64_t> field5;
   vector<uint64_t> field6;
};
```

```
struct Sum
{
  uint64_t field1;
  uint64_t field2;
  uint64_t field3;
  Sum(): field1(), field2(), field3() {}
};
```

4. Define two functions, namely **sumAOS** and **sumSOA**, that sum the values in `field1`, `field2`, and `field3` for the two preceding data structures. Write the following code to implement this:

```
Sum sumAOS(vector<Data1> &aos)
{
  TIME_IT;
  Sum ret;
  for(int i = 0; i < N; ++i)
  {
    ret.field1 += aos[i].field1;
    ret.field2 += aos[i].field2;
    ret.field3 += aos[i].field3;
  }
  return ret;
}
Sum sumSOA(Data2 &soa)
{
  TIME_IT;
  Sum ret;
  for(int i = 0; i < N; ++i)
  {
    ret.field1 += soa.field1[i];
    ret.field2 += soa.field2[i];
    ret.field3 += soa.field3[i];
  }
  return ret;
}
```

5. Write the following code inside the **main** function:

```
int main()
{
    vector<Data1> arrOfStruct;
    Data2 structOfArr;

    // Reserve space
    structOfArr.field1.reserve(N);
    structOfArr.field2.reserve(N);
    structOfArr.field3.reserve(N);
    arrOfStruct.reserve(N);
    // Fill random values
    for(int i = 0; i < N; ++i)
    {
      Data1 temp;
      temp.field1 = dist(rng);
      temp.field2  = dist(rng);
      temp.field3 = dist(rng);
      arrOfStruct.push_back(temp);
      structOfArr.field1.push_back(temp.field1);
      structOfArr.field2.push_back(temp.field2);
      structOfArr.field3.push_back(temp.field3);
    }
    Sum s1 = sumAOS(arrOfStruct);
    Sum s2 = sumSOA(structOfArr);
    Timer::dump();
}
```

6. Save the program and open the Terminal. Run the program to time it by adding the following commands:

```
$ g++ -O3 Snippet12.cpp Timer.cpp
$ ./a.out
```

The preceding code generates the following output:

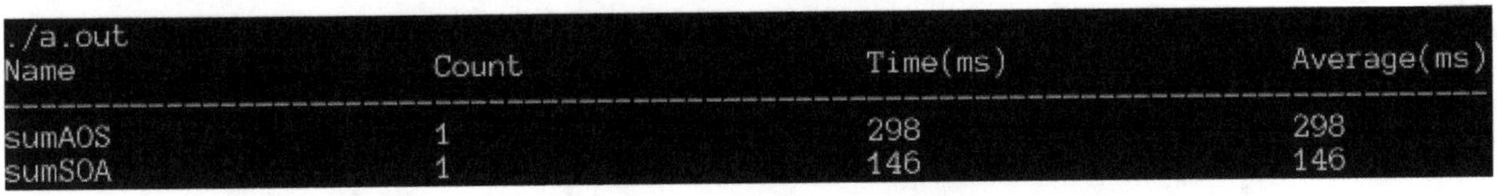

| ./a.out<br>Name | Count | Time(ms) | Average(ms) |
| --- | --- | --- | --- |
| sumAOS | 1 | 298 | 298 |
| sumSOA | 1 | 146 | 146 |

Figure 8.40: Output of the code in Snippet12.cpp contrasting the timing
of the AOS and SOA patterns

The struct of arrays approach is twice as fast as the array of structs approach. Considering that the addresses of the vectors in the struct would be quite far apart, we may wonder why the caching behavior is better in the SoA case. The reason is because of how caches are designed – rather than treating a cache as a single monolithic block, it is divided into multiple lines, as we discussed earlier. When a memory address is accessed, the 32- or 64-bit address is converted into a "tag" of a few bits and the cache line associated with that tag is used. Memory addresses that are very close together will get the same tag and reach the same cache line. If a highly differing address is accessed, it reaches a different cache line. The effect of this line-based cache design on our test program is that it is as if we have separate independent caches for each vector.

The preceding explanation for cache lines is a very much simplified one, but the basic concept of cache lines applies. Code readability may seem slightly worse for this structure of array pattern, but considering the increase in performance, it is well worth it. This particular optimization becomes more effective as the size of the structure grows larger. Also, remember that padding structures can inflate their size by a big factor if the fields are of various sizes. We have explored the performance effects of memory latency and learned a few ways to help the processor's caches be effective. When writing a program that is performance-critical, we should keep caching effects in mind. Sometimes, it makes sense to start out with a more cache-friendly architecture in the first place. As always, we should always measure the performance of code before we attempt to make radical changes in data structures. Optimization should be focused on the most time-consuming areas of a program and not every part of it.

## Algorithmic Optimizations

The simplest form of algorithmic optimization is to look for libraries that perform your task – the most popular libraries are highly optimized and well-written. For example, the **Boost** library provides many useful libraries that can come in handy in many projects, such as **Boost.Geometry**, **Boost.Graph**, **Boost.Interval**, and **Boost. Multiprecision**, to mention a few. It is far easier and wiser to use a professionally written library than to attempt to create them yourself. For example, **Boost.Graph** implements a dozen algorithms to process topological graphs, and each of them is highly optimized.

Many computations can be reduced to a series of standard algorithms composed together – if done correctly, these can result in extremely efficient code – and often even be parallelized to take advantage of multiple cores or SIMD by the compiler. For the rest of this section, we will take one single program and attempt to optimize it in various ways – this will be a word count program with the following specifications:

- To isolate the time taken by disk I/O, we will read the entire file to memory before processing.

- Unicode support will be ignored, and we will assume English text in ASCII.

- We will use a large public domain literary text available online as test data.

## Exercise 14: Optimizing a Word Count Program

In this lengthy exercise, we'll optimize a program using various optimization techniques. We'll perform the incremental optimization of the practical program. The test data that we will be using consists of the book named "A Tale of Two Cities", which has been appended together 512 times.

> **Note**
>
> The dataset that's used in this exercise is available here: https://github.com/ TrainingByPackt/Advanced-CPlusPlus/blob/master/Lesson8/Exercise14/data.7z. You will need to extract this 7zip archive and copy the resulting file, called data.txt, into the folder where you work with this exercise.

Perform these steps to complete this exercise:

1. Write the basic boilerplate code that reads the file (the full code can be found in **SnippetWC.cpp**). This will be a common driver for all the versions of the word count that we write:

```cpp
int wordCount(const string &s);
int main(int argc, char **argv)
{
  if(argc > 1)
  {
    TIME_IT;
    string sContent;
    ostringstream buf;
    ifstream ifs(argv[1]);
    {
```

```
            Timer t("Read file");
            buf << ifs.rdbuf();
            sContent = buf.str();
            sContent.push_back(' ');
        }
        cerr << wordCount(sContent) << endl;
    }
    Timer::dump();
}
```

We will use a dummy block to separate the timing of the code that reads the file and also time **main()** itself to get the overall execution time.

Note that **push_back** adds a space at the end – this makes sure that the data ends with a whitespace, simplifying the algorithms we use.

2.  Write a basic word count function. The logic is very simple – for every character in the string, if the character is not whitespace and the following one is, then it is the end of a word and should be counted. Since our boilerplate code has added a space at the end, any final word will be counted. This function is defined in **Snippet13.cpp**:

```
int wordCount(const std::string &s)
{
    int count = 0;
    for(int i = 0, j = 1; i < s.size() - 1; ++i, ++j)
    {
        if(!isspace(s[i]) && isspace(s[j]))
        {
            ++count;
        }
    }
    return count;
}
```

3.  Let's compile, run, and get an idea of the performance. We will verify that it is working right by comparing the result of our code with the results provided by the standard **wc** program:

```
$ g++ -O3 Snippet13.cpp SnippetWC.cpp Timer.cpp
$ ./a.out data.txt
```

We receive the following output:

```
71108096
Name                        Count              Time(ms)          Average(ms)
-----------------------------------------------------------------------------
File read                   1                      1035                 1035
Word count                  1                      2557                 2557
|Total Time|                1                      3631                 3631
```

Figure 8.41: Output of the code in Snippet13.cpp with a baseline wordcount implementation

Let's time the wc program:

```
$ time wc -w data.txt
```

We receive the following output:

```
71108096 data.txt

real    0m2.367s
user    0m2.268s
sys     0m0.097s
```

Figure 8.42: Output of timing the wc program

The *wc* program displays the same word count, that is, **71108096**, so we know our code is correct. Our code took about **3.6 seconds**, including reading the file, which is much slower than wc.

4.  Our first strategy to optimize is to see if there is a better way to implement **isspace()**. Instead of a function, we can use a lookup table that can tell if a character is a space or not (the code for this can be found in **Snippet14.cpp**):

```cpp
int wordCount(const std::string &s)
{
  // Create a lookup table
  bool isSpace[256];
  for(int i = 0; i < 256; ++i)
  {
    isSpace[i] = isspace((unsigned char)i);
  }
  int count = 0;
  int len = s.size() - 1;
  for(int i = 0, j = 1; i < len; ++i, ++j)
  {
    count += !isSpace[s[i]] & isSpace[s[j]];
  }
  return count;
}
```

Remember that boolean variables in C/C++ take on integer values 0 or 1, and so we can directly write the following:

```
!isSpace[s[i]] & isSpace[s[j]]
```

This means we don't have to write this:

```
(!isSpace[s[i]] && isSpace[s[j]]) ? 1 : 0
```

Using booleans directly as numbers can sometimes result in faster code because we avoid the conditional logic operators && and ||, which may result in a branch instruction.

5.  Compile and test the performance now:

```
$ g++ -O3 Snippet14.cpp SnippetWC.cpp Timer.cpp
$ ./a.out data.txt
```

We receive the following output:

```
71108096
Name                          Count              Time(ms)               Average(ms)
------------------------------------------------------------------------------------
File read                     1                      1034                      1034
Word count                    1                       317                       317
|Total Time|                  1                      1389                      1389
```

Figure 8.43: Output of the code in Snippet14.cpp

We have achieved a speedup of 8x for the word counting code, with the simple principle of using a lookup table. Can we do even better than this? Yes – we can take the lookup table concept further – for every pair of characters, there are four possibilities, which should result in a corresponding action:

[Space Space]: No action, [Non-Space Space]: Add 1 to count, [Space  Non-Space]: No action, [Non-Space, Non-Space]: No action

So, we can manufacture a table of **65536** entries (**256 \* 256**) to cover all possible pairs of characters.

6.  Write the following code to create the table:

```
// Create a lookup table for every pair of chars
bool table[65536];
for(int i = 0; i < 256; ++i)
{
    for(int j = 0; j < 256; ++j)
    {
```

```
        int idx = j + i * 256;
        table[idx] = !isspace(j) && isspace(i);
    }
}
```

The loop to count the words becomes the following (the full code can be found in **Snippet15.cpp**):

```
int count = 0;
for(int i = 0; i < s.size() - 1; ++i)
{
    // grab the 2 bytes at s[i] as a 16 bit value
    unsigned short idx;
    memcpy(&idx, &s[i], 2);
    count += table[idx];
}
```

We read each character of the string as a single 16-bit value. Directly casting a pointer from char* to another type and dereferencing it is undefined behavior – the correct way to do this is to use **memcpy()**. The compiler is smart enough to use the CPU memory access instructions rather than actually call **memcpy()** for 2 bytes. We have ended up with the loop containing no conditional statement, which should make it much faster. Remember that X86 architecture is *little-endian* – so a 16-bit value read from a character array will have the first character as its LSB and the second as the MSB.

7. Now, time the code we wrote:

```
$ g++ -O3 Snippet15.cpp SnippetWC.cpp Timer.cpp
$ ./a.out data.txt
```

| 71108096 | | | |
| Name | Count | Time(ms) | Average(ms) |
| --- | --- | --- | --- |
| File read | 1 | 1033 | 1033 |
| Word count | 1 | 175 | 175 |
| Total Time | 1 | 1249 | 1249 |

Figure 8.44: Output of the code in Snippet15.cpp

This larger lookup table resulted in a 1.8x speed improvement for **wordCount()**. Let's step back and look at this from another angle so that we can use existing the standard library effectively. The advantages of this are two-fold – firstly, the code is less prone to errors, and secondly, we could take advantage of the parallelization available with some compilers.

Let's rewrite the version of the program that uses the lookup table for `isspace` using the standard algorithms. If we look at the main loop that counts the words, we are taking 2 characters, and depending on some logic, we are accumulating 1 or 0 into the **count** variable. This is a common pattern seen in a lot of code:

```
X OP (a[0] OP2 b[0]) OP (a[1] OP2 b[1]) OP (a[2] OP2 b[2]) ... OP (a[N]
OP2 b[N])
```

Here, **a** and **b** are arrays of size **N**, **X** is an initial value, and **OP** and **OP2** are operators. There is a standard algorithm that encapsulates this pattern called **std::inner_ product** – it takes two sequences, applies an operator (OP2) between each pair of elements, and applies another operator (OP) across these, starting with an initial value X.

8. We can write the function as follows (the full code can be found in **Snippet16.cpp**):

```cpp
int wordCount(const std::string &s)
{
  // Create a lookup table for every char
  bool table[256];
  for(int i = 0; i < 256; ++i)
  {
    table[i] = isspace((unsigned char)i) ? 1 : 0;
  }

  auto isWordEnd = [&](char a, char b)
  {
    return !table[a] & table[b];
  };

  return std::inner_product(s.begin(), s.end()-1, s.begin()+1, 0,
  std::plus<int>(), isWordEnd);
}
```

This **inner_product()** call applies the **isWordEnd()** lambda on every **s[n]** and **s[n+1]** and applies the standard addition function between the results of these. In effect, we are adding 1 to the total when **s[n]** and **s[n+1]** are on a word ending.

---

> **Note**
>
> Even though this looks like a number of nested function calls, the compiler inlines everything and there is no overhead.

9. Compile and time the execution of this version:

```
$ g++ -O3 Snippet16.cpp SnippetWC.cpp Timer.cpp
$ ./a.out data.txt
```

We receive the following output:

71108096
Name                    Count                   Time(ms)            Average(ms)
-----------------------------------------------------------------------------
File read                 1                        1082                  1082
Word count                1                         268                   268
|Total Time|              1                        1389                  1389

Figure 8.45: Output of the code in Snippet16.cpp

Surprisingly, the code is slightly faster than our initial looped version in **Snippet14.cpp**.

10. Can we adapt the same code to use the large lookup table? Indeed, we can – the new function looks like this (the full code can be found in **Snippet17.cpp**):

```
int wordCount(const std::string &s)
{
  // Create a lookup table for every pair of chars
  bool table[65536];
  for(int i = 0; i < 256; ++i)
  {
    for(int j = 0; j < 256; ++j)
    {
      int idx = j + i * 256;
      table[idx] = !isspace(j) && isspace(i);
    }
  }
  auto isWordEnd = [&](char a, char b)
  {
    unsigned idx = (unsigned)a | (((unsigned)b) << 8);
    return table[idx];
  };
  return std::inner_product(s.begin(), s.end()-1, s.begin()+1, 0,
  std::plus<int>(), isWordEnd);
}
```

The only thing that changes from the previous loop-based code is that instead of using `memcpy()` to convert two consecutive bytes into a word, we use a bitwise **OR** operator to combine them.

11. Compile and time the code:

```
$ g++ -O3 Snippet17.cpp SnippetWC.cpp Timer.cpp
$ ./a.out data.txt
```

We receive the following output:

```
71108096
Name                        Count              Time(ms)          Average(ms)
File read                     1                   1016               1016
Word count                    1                    251                251
|Total Time|                  1                   1308               1308
```

Figure 8.46: Output of the code in Snippet17.cpp

This code is not quite as fast as the loop0based version we had in **Snippet15. cpp**. The reason for this is that, in the looped version, we were reading 2 bytes combined as a **short** to get the index, which requires no computation, but here, we read 2 bytes into a **short** with a bitwise operation.

12. Now that we have the code where the bulk of the work is done by a standard library function, we can now get automatic parallelization for free – compile and test as follows:

```
$ g++ -O3 -fopenmp -D_GLIBCXX_PARALLEL Snippet17.cpp SnippetWC.cpp Timer.
cpp
$ ./a.out data.txt
```

We receive the following output:

```
71108096
Name                        Count              Time(ms)          Average(ms)
File read                     1                   1032               1032
Word count                    1                     89                 89
|Total Time|                  1                   1166               1166
```

Figure 8.47: Output of the code in Snippet17.cpp with the parallelized standard library

Clearly, it cannot be completely parallelized, so we only get about 2.5x improvement in terms of speed, but we got it without having to do anything to the code. Could we have made the loop-based code parallelizable in the same way? In theory, yes – we could manually use **OpenMP** directives to achieve this; however, it would require changes to the code and a knowledge of how to use OpenMP. What about the version in **Snippet16.cpp**?

```
$ g++ -O3 -fopenmp -D_GLIBCXX_PARALLEL Snippet16.cpp SnippetWC.cpp Timer.
cpp
$ ./a.out data.txt
```

We receive the following output:

```
71108096
Name                        Count               Time(ms)            Average(ms)
File read                     1                    1035                  1035
Word count                    1                     97                    97
|Total Time|                  1                    1177                  1177
```

Similar improvements can be seen for this version too. Are we finished or can this be even faster? **Michael Abrash**, a famous game programmer, coined the acronym **TANSTATFC** – it stands for "There ain't no such thing as the fastest code". What he meant is that, given enough effort, it was always possible to make code faster. This seems impossible, but time and again, people have found faster and faster ways of performing a computation – our code is no exception and we can still go a bit further. One of the tradeoffs we can make for optimization is to make the code less general – we already put some constraints on our code – for example, that we only handle **ASCII** English text. By adding some more constraints on the input data, we can do even better. Let's assume that there are no non-printable characters in the file. This is a reasonable assumption for our input data. If we assume this, then we can simplify the condition for detecting spaces – since all the whitespace characters are greater than or equal to ASCII 32, we can avoid the lookup table itself.

13. Let's implement the code based on our previous idea (the full code can be found in **Snippet18.cpp**):

```cpp
int wordCount(const std::string &s)
{
  auto isWordEnd = [&](char a, char b)
  {
    return a > 32 & b < 33;
  };
  return std::inner_product(s.begin(), s.end()-1, s.begin()+1, 0,
std::plus<int>(), isWordEnd);
}
```

14. Compile and run the program:

```
$ g++ -O3 Snippet18.cpp SnippetWC.cpp Timer.cpp
$ ./a.out data.txt
```

We receive the following output:

```
71108096
Name                             Count                 Time(ms)               Average(ms)
File read                          1                      1042                     1042
Word count                         1                        55                       55
|Total Time|                       1                      1140                     1140
```

Figure 8.49: Output of the code in Snippet18.cpp with simplified logic for detecting spaces

This version is twice as fast as the one that was parallelized, and it is just a few lines of code.

Will using parallelization improve it even more?

```
$ g++ -O3 -fopenmp -D_GLIBCXX_PARALLEL Snippet18.cpp SnippetWC.cpp Timer.
cpp
$ ./a.out data.txt
```

We receive the following output:

```
71108096
Name                             Count                 Time(ms)               Average(ms)
File read                          1                      1039                     1039
Word count                         1                       111                      111
|Total Time|                       1                      1196                     1196
```

Figure 8.50: Output of the code in Snippet18.cpp with the parallelized standard library

Unfortunately, this is not the case – it is actually slower. The overhead of managing multiple threads and thread contention is sometimes more expensive than the benefits of multithreaded code. At this point, we can see that the file-read code is taking up most of the time – can we do anything about this?

15. Let's change the **main()** function to time the individual parts of it (the full code can be found in **SnippetWC2.cpp**):

```
{
    Timer t("File read");
    buf << ifs.rdbuf();
}
{
    Timer t("String copy");
    sContent = buf.str();
}
{
    Timer t("String push");
    sContent.push_back(' ');
}
```

```
int wc;
{
  Timer t("Word count");
  wc = wordCount(sContent);
}
```

16. Compile and run the preceding code:

```
$ g++ -O3 Snippet18.cpp SnippetWC2.cpp Timer.cpp
$ ./a.out data.txt
```

We receive the following output:

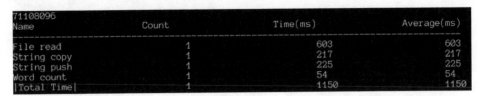

| Name | Count | Time(ms) | Average(ms) |
|---|---|---|---|
| File read | 1 | 603 | 603 |
| String copy | 1 | 217 | 217 |
| String push | 1 | 225 | 225 |
| Word count | 1 | 54 | 54 |
| \|Total Time\| | 1 | 1150 | 1150 |

Figure 8.51: Output of the code in Snippet18.cpp with all operations timed

The majority of the time is taken by **push_back()** and copying the string. Since the string is exactly the size of the file, **push_back()** ends up allocating a new buffer for the string and copying the contents. How can we eliminate this **push_back()** call? We appended a space to the end to be able to consistently count the last word, if any, since our algorithm counts the ends of words. There are three ways to avoid this: count the start of a word, rather than the end; count the last word, if any, separately; and use the **c_str()** function so that we have a **NUL** character at the end. Let's try each of these in turn now.

17. First, write the main function without **push_back** (the full code can be found in **SnippetWC3.cpp**):

```
{
  Timer t("File read");
  buf << ifs.rdbuf();
}
{
  Timer t("String copy");
  sContent = buf.str();
}
int wc;
{
  Timer t("Word count");
  wc = wordCount(sContent);
}
```

18. Change the code in wordCount() by renaming **isWordEnd()** to **isWordStart()** and invert the logic. Consider a word as starting, if the current character is a space and the succeeding one is not. Also, count one extra word if the string starts with a non-space (the full code can be found in **Snippet19.cpp**):

```
int wordCount(const std::string &s)
{
    auto isWordStart = [&](char a, char b)
    {
        return a < 33 & b > 32;
    };
    // Count the first word if any
    int count = s[0] > 32;
    // count the remaining
    return std::inner_product(s.begin(), s.end()-1, s.begin()+1, count,
std::plus<int>(), isWordStart);
}
```

19. Now, write the second alternative – to count the last word, if any. The code is almost same as the **Snippet18.cpp** version, except we check for the last word (the full code can be found in **Snippet20.cpp**):

```
int count = std::inner_product(s.begin(), s.end()-1, s.begin()+1, 0,
std::plus<int>(), isWordEnd);

// count the last word if any
if(s.back() > 32)
{
    ++count;
}

return count;
```

20. Write the third version that uses **c_str()** – all we need to do is change the parameters for **inner_product()** (the full code can be found in **Snippet21.cpp**)

```
int wordCount(const std::string &s)
{
    auto isWordEnd = [&](char a, char b)
    {
        return a > 32 & b < 33;
    };
    const char *p = s.c_str();
```

```
    return std::inner_product(p, p + s.size(), p+1, 0, std::plus<int>(),
  isWordEnd);
  }
```

Since `c_str()` has a **NUL** at the end, it works as before.

21. Compile and time all three versions:

```
$ g++ -O3 Snippet19.cpp SnippetWC3.cpp Timer.cpp
$ ./a.out data.txt
```

We receive the following output:

```
71108096
Name                    Count                   Time(ms)              Average(ms)
----------------------------------------------------------------------------------
File read                 1                        596                     596
String copy               1                        212                     212
Word count                1                        53                      53
|Total Time|              1                        904                     904
```

Figure 8.52: Output of the code in Snippet19.cpp, which counts the beginnings of words rather than the ends

Now enter the following command:

```
$ g++ -O3 Snippet20.cpp SnippetWC3.cpp Timer.cpp
$ ./a.out data.txt
```

We receive the following output:

```
71108096
Name                    Count                   Time(ms)              Average(ms)
----------------------------------------------------------------------------------
File read                 1                        595                     595
String copy               1                        213                     213
Word count                1                        53                      53
|Total Time|              1                        903                     903
```

Figure 8.53: Output of the code in Snippet20.cpp

Now enter the following command:

```
$ g++ -O3 Snippet21.cpp SnippetWC3.cpp Timer.cpp
$ ./a.out data.txt
```

We receive the following output:

```
71108096
Name                      Count              Time(ms)           Average(ms)
File read                   1                   601                   601
String copy                 1                   216                   216
Word count                  1                    54                    54
|Total Time|                1                   912                   912
```

Figure 8.54: Output of the code in Snippet21.cpp

All three run in approximately the same time – the minor difference of a few milliseconds can be ignored.

22. Now, we can tackle the time taken for string copying – instead of using **std::stringstream**, we will directly read the file into a string buffer (the full code can be found in **SnippetWC4.cpp**):

```cpp
string sContent;
{
  Timer t("String Alloc");
  // Seek to end and reserve memory
  ifs.seekg(0, std::ios::end);
  sContent.resize(ifs.tellg());
}
{
  Timer t("File read");
  // Seek back to start and read data
  ifs.seekg(0, std::ios::beg);
  ifs.read(&sContent[0], sContent.size());
}
int wc;
{
  Timer t("Word count");
  wc = wordCount(sContent);
}
```

23. Compile and run this version:

```
$ g++ -O3 Snippet21.cpp SnippetWC4.cpp Timer.cpp
```

We receive the following output:

```
71108096
Name                    Count                 Time(ms)              Average(ms)
--------------------------------------------------------------------------------
File read                 1                      78                      78
String Alloc              1                     177                     177
Word count                1                      57                      57
|Total Time|              1                     333                     333
```

Figure 8.55: Output of the code with changed file load code in SnippetWC4.cpp

We have now reduced the time taken by our file read code from about 1,000 ms to 250 ms – a 4x improvement. The word count code started at about **2,500ms** and reduced to about 60 ms – a 40x improvement. The total performance improvement for the entire program is 3.6x. We can still ask if this is the limit – indeed, TANSTATFC still applies and there are a few more things that can be done: instead of reading data into a **std::string**, use **memory-mapped I/O** to get a buffer that directly points to the file. This could possibly be faster than allocation and reading – it will require changing the word count code to accept a **const char\*** and a length, or an **std::string_view**. Use a different, faster allocator to allocate memory. Compile for the native CPU using the **-march=native** flag. However, it seems unlikely that we will be able to get very large performance gains from this, since these optimizations have nothing to do with the word counting algorithm itself. Another final attempt could be to forego the C++ constructs and write inline SIMD code using **compiler intrinsics** (these are the functions that the compiler translates directly into single assembly instructions). The knowledge that's required to do this is beyond the scope of this introductory material.

24. Nevertheless, for the curious student, an **AVX2** (256-bit SIMD) version of **wordCount()** is provided (Snippet23.cpp). This version needs the input string to have a length that is a multiple of 32 and a space at the end. This means that the main function has to be rewritten (SnippetWC5.cpp):

```
$ g++ -O3 -march=native Snippet22.cpp SnippetWC5.cpp Timer.cpp
$ ./a.out data.txt
```

We receive the following output:

```
71108096
Name                    Count                 Time(ms)              Average(ms)
--------------------------------------------------------------------------------
File read                 1                      78                      78
String Alloc              1                     181                     181
Word count                1                      40                      40
|Total Time|              1                     321                     321
```

Figure 8.56: Output of the code in Snippet22.cpp that uses SIMD intrinsics

Note that we need to use the **-march=native** flag so that the compiler uses the AVX SIMD instruction set. If the processor does not support it, a compile error will result. If this executable is compiled for an AVX target, and run on a system where the processor does not support those instructions, the program crashes with an "Illegal instruction" exception. There seems to be a very small improvement, but not significant – the effort and learning curve required to optimize with the assembler or SIMD is usually too high to be justified unless your application or industry has those demands. The SIMD version processes 32 bytes at a time – yet there is practically no performance improvement. In fact, if you check the generated assembly code for the regular C++ implementation in the other snippets with the compiler explorer, you will see that the compiler itself has used SIMD – this just goes to show how far compilers go in terms of making your code fast.

Another point to note is that our file read and memory allocation is taking up most of the time now – leaving aside memory allocation, we can conclude that our code has become **I/O bound** as opposed to **CPU bound**. This means that no matter how fast we write the code, it will be limited by how fast the data can be fetched. We started with a very simple implementation of a word count algorithm, increased its complexity and speed, and finally were able to go back to a very simple implementation that ended up being the fastest. The overall speed improvement for the algorithm was a factor of 40x. We used a number of approaches that ranged from just rearranging code a bit, to reimagining the problem in different ways, to performing micro-optimizations. No single approach can work all the time, and optimization remains a creative endeavor that needs imagination and skill and often, lateral thinking. As compilers get smarter and smarter, it gets harder and harder to outdo them – yet, the programmer is the only one who actually understands the code's intent, and there is always scope to make the code faster.

## Activity 1: Optimizing a Spell Check Algorithm

In this activity, we will attempt to optimize a program step by step. This activity is about a simple spell checker that takes a dictionary and a text file and prints out a list of the words in the text that are not present in the dictionary. A basic skeleton program is provided in **Speller.cpp**, along with an example dictionary and text file as **dict.txt** and **data.txt**, respectively. A file called out.txt is provided, which contains the desired output of the program (a list of the indices of misspelled words). The text files are present in the **7zip archive**, that is, **activity1.7z**.

The dictionary is taken from the Linux word list that is provided with many Linux distributions. The text file is like the one we used in the previous exercise – it is the same large file we used in the word count exercise, with all punctuation removed and converted into lower case.

Note that the dictionary is only an example, so do not assume that all valid words exist in it – many of the words in the output could well be correctly spelled words. The skeleton code reads the dictionary and text files and calls the spell check code (which you will write) on it. After that, it compares the resultant output with the contents of **out.txt** and prints whether the program worked as expected. The function that does the spell check returns a vector of indices of the words that were not in the dictionary. Since we are focusing on only the spellcheck algorithm, only that code is timed. The time taken for reading the files and comparing the output is not taken into consideration. You will develop successively faster versions of this program – reference implementations are provided in the reference folder as **Speller1.cpp**, **Speller2.cpp**, and so on.

At each step, you will be only given hints as to what to change to make it faster – only the code in the `getMisspelt()` function is to be modified, and not any other code. The student is free to implement the code however they wish, as long as it produces the correct results and the code within `main()` is not changed.

> **Note**
>
> Optimization is a creative and non-deterministic process – it is not guaranteed nor always possible for the student to come up with the same code as the reference implementations. It should not be a surprise if the code that you write does not perform as well as the reference implementations. In fact, it may even be possible that your code is faster than the reference.

Perform the following steps to implement this activity:

Make a copy of Speller.cpp called Speller1.cpp and implement the code for the `getMisspelt()` function.Use `std::set` and its `count()` method to implement this.

1. Write the next version of the program as Speller2.cpp, and then compile it and time it as before. Try using `std::unordered_set` rather than `std::set`. You should get about a 2x speedup with this implementation.

In the final version, **Speller3.cpp**, use a **Bloom filter** data structure to implement the spell check algorithm. Experiment with different numbers of hash functions and sizes for the bloom filter to see what works best.

2. For each of the preceding steps, compile the program and run it as follows (change the input file name as required):

```
$ g++ -O3 Speller1.cpp Timer.cpp
$ ./a.out
```

> **Note**
>
> You should not expect the timings to be exactly as shown here, but if you implement the code correctly, the relative improvement in speed should be close to what we see here.

After executing the preceding commands for each step, the following outputs will be generated. The outputs will show the timing for your code and an initial message if your output is correct. The following is the output for Step 1:

| Output is correct | | | |
| Name | Count | Time(ms) | Average(ms) |
| --- | --- | --- | --- |
| Spell check | 1 | 5883 | 5883 |

Figure 8.57: Example output of the code for Step 1

The following is the output for Step 2:

| Output is correct | | | |
| Name | Count | Time(ms) | Average(ms) |
| --- | --- | --- | --- |
| Spell check | 1 | 2240 | 2240 |

Figure 8.58: Example output of the code for Step 2

The following is the output for Step 3:

| Output is correct | | | |
| Name | Count | Time(ms) | Average(ms) |
| --- | --- | --- | --- |
| Spell check | 1 | 2193 | 2193 |

Figure 8.59: Example output of the code for Step 3

> **Note**
>
> The solution for this activity can be found on page 725.

# Summary

We have covered a lot of complex material in this chapter. Optimizing code is a difficult but necessary skill for any modern C++ developer. The demands of machine learning, hyper-realistic games, big data analysis, and energy-efficient computing make this a very vital area to learn about for any C++ professional. We have learned that the process of performance optimization is divided into two stages.

Firstly, optimization starts with a proper performance measurement strategy, with test conditions mirroring real-world data and usage patterns. We have learned how to measure performance by various methods – studying assembler code, manual timing, source code instrumentation, and using runtime profilers. Once we have accurate measurements, we can actually understand which portions of our programs are actually slow and focus our efforts there to get the maximum improvements.The second stage involves actually modifying the program – we learned about several strategies, starting with using the best compiler options for our code, using parallelization features, and also using profile data to help the compiler, followed by some simple code transformations that produce small but useful performance gains without major code changes. We then learned about how to improve performance by structuring our loops and conditionals in a way that makes the code more friendly to branch prediction.

Then, we learned about the dramatic and significant effects of caching on performance and looked at some techniques, such as the SOA pattern, to make our code take advantage of the caches in modern CPUs. Finally, we put all these things together for a real-world example of a word count program and simple spell checker to practice what we learned hands-on. There are a lot of other advanced techniques and theory that need to be studied over and above the material in this chapter, but what we have covered here should give any student a solid foundation for future learning.

By the end of these chapters, you have explored a number of topics related to using advanced C++. In the first few chapters, you have learned how to write portable software, use the type system to your advantage with templates, and learned to use pointers and inheritance effectively. Then you have explored the C++ standard library, including streams and concurrency, which are essential tools for building large real world applications. In the final sections, you learned how to test and debug your programs, and optimize your code to run efficiently. Among the widely used programming languages C++ is perhaps the most complex, as well as being the most expressive. This book is only a beginning, and would have given you a solid platform to continue your further learning.

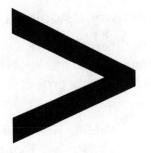

# Appendix

**About**

This section is included to assist the students to perform the activities in the book. It includes detailed steps that are to be performed by the students to achieve the objectives of the activities.

# Chapter 1 - Anatomy of Portable C++ Software

## Activity 1: Adding a New Source-Header File Pair to the Project

In this activity, we will create a new source-header file pair that contains a new function named **sum**. It takes two parameters and returns their sum. This file pair will be added to the existing project. Follow these steps to implement this activity:

1.  First, open the Eclipse IDE with the existing project that we created in *Exercise 3, Adding New Source Files to CMake and Eclipse CDT*. Right-click on the **src** folder in the **Project Explorer** pane.

    > **Note**
    >
    > We can either create the .**cpp** and .**h** files separately or use the new class wizard and later remove the class code. Using the new class wizard is handy since it also creates useful boilerplate code.

2.  Select **New | Class** from the pop-up menu. Type **SumFunc** and click on the **Finish** button.

3.  Next, edit the **SumFunc.h** file to look like the following code:

    ```
    #ifndef SRC_SUMFUNC_H_
    #define SRC_SUMFUNC_H_

    int sum(int a, int b);

    #endif /* SRC_SUMFUNC_H_ */
    ```

    Note that we will actually delete the class and provide a single function instead. We could have created these two files separately. However, the **add class** function creates them both and adds some boilerplate code that we will make use of. Here, our file starts and ends with an **include** guard, which is a common strategy to prevent the double-inclusion problem. We have the forward declaration of our function, which lets other files call the function after including this header file.

4. Next, edit the **SumFunc.cpp** file as illustrated here:

```cpp
#include "SumFunc.h"
#include <iostream>

int sum(int a, int b) {
   return a + b;
}
```

In this file, we include header files and provide the body of our function, which adds and returns two given integers.

5. Edit the **CMakeFiles.txt** file so that its **add_executable** section reflects the following code:

```cmake
add_executable(CxxTemplate
   src/CxxTemplate.cpp
   src/ANewClass.cpp
   src/SumFunc.cpp
)
```

Here, we added the **src/SumFunc.cpp** file to the list of executable source files so that it is linked into the executable.

6. Make the following changes in **CxxTemplate.cpp**:

```cpp
#include "CxxTemplate.h"
#include "ANewClass.h"
#include "SumFunc.h" //add this line

. . .

CxxApplication::CxxApplication( int argc, char *argv[] ) {
   std::cout << "Hello CMake." << std::endl;
   ANewClass anew;
   anew.run();
   std::cout << sum(3, 4) << std::endl; // add this line
}
```

> **Note**
>
> The complete code of this file can be found here: https://github.com/TrainingBy-Packt/Advanced-CPlusPlus/blob/master/Lesson1/Activity01/src/CxxTemplate.cpp.

Here, we added a line in which we call the **sum** function with **3** and **4** and print the result to the console.

7. Build and run the project (**Project | Build All | Run | Run**). The output you see should be as follows:

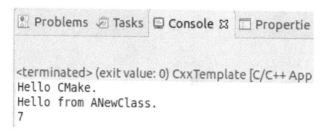

Figure 1.57: The output

With this activity, you practiced adding a new source-header file pair to your project. These file pairs are a very common pattern in C++ development. They can host global functions such as the ones we had in this activity. More commonly, they host classes and their definitions. Throughout your development effort, you will be adding many more source-header file pairs to your application. Therefore, it is important to get used to adding them and not dragging your feet, which would result in large monolithic files that are difficult to maintain and test.

## Activity 2: Adding a New Class and Its Test

In this activity, we will add a new class that simulates **1D** linear motion. The class will have double fields for **position** and **velocity**. It will also have a **advanceTimeBy()** method, which receives a double **dt** parameter, which modifies **position** based on the value of **velocity**. Use **EXPECT_DOUBLE_EQ** instead of **EXPECT_EQ** for double values. In this activity, we will add a new class and its test to the project. Follow these steps to perform this activity:

1. Open the Eclipse IDE with our existing project. To create a new class, right-click the **src** folder in the **Project Explorer** pane and select **New | Class**. Type **LinearMotion1D** as the name and create the class.

2. Open the **LinearMotion1D.h** file that we created in the previous step. Add the **position** and **velocity double** fields into it. Also, add the forward reference to the **advanceTimeBy** method, which takes a **double dt** variable as a parameter. The constructors and destructors were already in the class. The following is the end result of these changes in **LinearMotion1D.h**:

```
#ifndef SRC_LINEARMOTION1D_H_
#define SRC_LINEARMOTION1D_H_

class LinearMotion1D {
public:
  double position;
  double velocity;
  void advanceTimeBy(double dt);
  LinearMotion1D();
  virtual ~LinearMotion1D();
};


#endif /* SRC_LINEARMOTION1D_H_ */
```

3. Now open **LinearMotion1D.cpp** and add the implementation for the **advanceTimeBy** method. Our **velocity** is a field in our class and the time difference is a parameter to this method. A change in **position** is equal to the **velocity** multiplied by the time change, so we calculate the result and add it to the **position** variable. We also use the existing constructor code to initialize **position** and **velocity** to 0. The following is the end result of these changes in **LinearMotion1D.cpp**:

```
#include "LinearMotion1D.h"

void LinearMotion1D::advanceTimeBy(double dt) {
  position += velocity * dt;
}

LinearMotion1D::LinearMotion1D() {
  position = 0;
  velocity = 0;
}

LinearMotion1D::~LinearMotion1D() {
}
```

4. Create a test for this class. Right-click the **tests** folder and select **New | Source File**. Type `LinearMotion1DTest.cpp` as the name and create it.

5. Now open `LinearMotion1DTest.cpp`. Create two tests for motions in two different directions, left and right. For each of them, create a `LinearMotion1D` object, initialize its position and velocity, and call `advanceTimeBy` to actually have the motion happen. Then, check whether it moved to the same location that we expected. The following is the end result of these changes in `LinearMotion1DTest.cpp`:

```
#include "gtest/gtest.h"
#include "../src/LinearMotion1D.h"

namespace {

class LinearMotion1DTest: public ::testing::Test {};

TEST_F(LinearMotion1DTest, CanMoveRight) {
  LinearMotion1D l;
  l.position = 10;
  l.velocity = 2;
  l.advanceTimeBy(3);
  EXPECT_DOUBLE_EQ(16, l.position);
}

TEST_F(LinearMotion1DTest, CanMoveLeft) {
  LinearMotion1D l;
  l.position = 10;
  l.velocity = -2;
  l.advanceTimeBy(3);
  EXPECT_DOUBLE_EQ(4, l.position);
}

}
```

6. Now modify our CMake configuration files so that these source files that we generated are also used. For the **LinearMotion1D** class, add its **.cpp** file as an executable so that it is compiled and linked together with the other source files. Here is what the **add_executable** section of **CMakeLists.txt** becomes:

```
add_executable(CxxTemplate
    src/CxxTemplate.cpp
    src/ANewClass.cpp
    src/SumFunc.cpp
    src/LinearMotion1D.cpp # added
)
```

7. For the tests that we just created, edit **tests/CMakeLists.txt**. There, we need to add both the test source file, **LinearMotion1DTest.cpp**, and the source file of the class that it uses, **LinearMotion1D.cpp**. Since they are in different directories, access them as **../src/LinearMotion1D.cpp**. Here is what the **add_executable** section of **tests/CMakeLists.txt** becomes:

```
add_executable(tests
    CanTest.cpp
    SumFuncTest.cpp
    ../src/SumFunc.cpp
    LinearMotion1DTest.cpp # added
    ../src/LinearMotion1D.cpp # added
)
```

8. Build the project and run the tests. We will see that all the tests are successful:

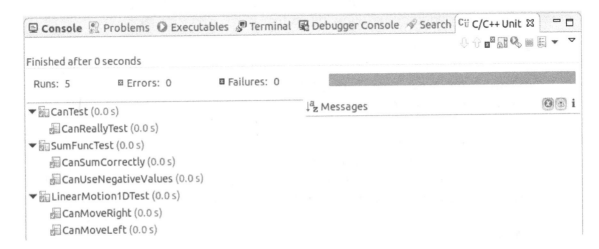

Figure 1.58: All tests are successful

With this activity, you performed the task of adding a new class and its test to the project. You created a class that simulates one-dimensional motion and you wrote unit tests to ensure that it is working properly.

## Activity 3: Making Code More Readable

In this activity, you will practice improving the quality of a given code. Follow these steps to implement this activity:

1. Open Eclipse CDT and create a class in a source-header file pair in Eclipse. To do this, right-click the **src** folder in **Project Explorer**. Select **New | Class** from the pop-up menu.

2. Type **SpeedCalculator** as the header filename and click **Finish**. It will create two files: **SpeedCalculator.h** and **SpeedCalculator.cpp**. We provided the code for both files above. Add the code that was provided for each file.

3. Now we need to add the class to the CMake project. Open the **CMakeLists.txt** file in the root of your project (outside the **src** folder) and make the following change in the file:

```
    src/LinearMotion1D.cpp
    src/SpeedCalculator.cpp # add this line
)
```

4. Now select **File | Save All** to save all the files and build the project by selecting **Project | Build All**. Make sure there are no errors.

5. Create an instance of the **SpeedCalculator** class in our **main()** function and call its **run()** method. Open **CxxTemplate.cpp** and include our new class, then edit the **main** function by adding the following code:

```cpp
#include "SpeedCalculator.h"

int main( int argc, char *argv[] ) {
    cxxt::CxxApplication app( argc, argv );

    // add these three lines
    SpeedCalculator speedCalculator;
    speedCalculator.initializeData(10);
    speedCalculator.calculateAndPrintSpeedData();

    return 0;
}
```

6. To fix the style, simply use **Source | Format** and choose to format the entire file. Luckily, the variable names do not have any problems.

7. Simplify the code to make it more understandable. The loop in `calculateAndPrint-SpeedData` is doing a couple of things at the same time. It's calculating the speed, finding the minimum and maximum values of it, checking whether we crossed a threshold, and storing the speed. If the speed was a transient value, taking it apart would mean storing it somewhere to loop on it one more time. However, since we are storing it in the speeds array anyway, we can loop one more time on it for clarity of code. Here is the updated version of the loop:

```cpp
for (int i = 0; i < numEntries; ++i) {
    double dt = timesInSeconds[i + 1] - timesInSeconds[i];
    assert(dt > 0);
    double speed = (positions[i + 1] - positions[i]) / dt;
    speeds[i] = speed;
}

for (int i = 0; i < numEntries; ++i) {
    double speed = speeds[i];
    if (maxSpeed < speed) {
        maxSpeed = speed;
    }

    if (minSpeed > speed) {
        minSpeed = speed;
    }
}

for (int i = 0; i < numEntries; ++i) {
    double speed = speeds[i];
    double dt = timesInSeconds[i + 1] - timesInSeconds[i];

    if (speed > speedLimit) {
        limitCrossDuration += dt;
    }
}
```

This is somewhat a matter of taste, but making the big **for** loop lighter helps with the readability. In addition, it separates the tasks and removes the possibility of them interacting with each other during a loop iteration. The first loop creates and saves the speed values. The second loop finds the minimum and maximum speed values. The third loop determines how long the speed limit was crossed for. Note that this is a slightly less efficient implementation; however, it clearly separates the actions taken and we do not have to mentally separate the discrete actions in the long iteration of a loop.

8. Run the preceding code and observe the problem at runtime. While the code is better in terms of style now, it suffers from several mistakes, some of which will create runtime errors. First, when we run the application, we see the following output in Eclipse:

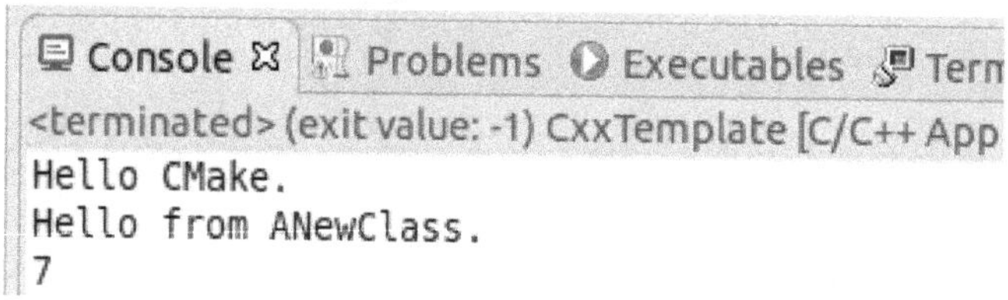

Figure 1.59: Program output in Eclipse CDT

Note **exit value: -1** at the top. When this is not **0**, it means there was a problem with our code.

9. Execute the program manually in the console. Here's the output we get:

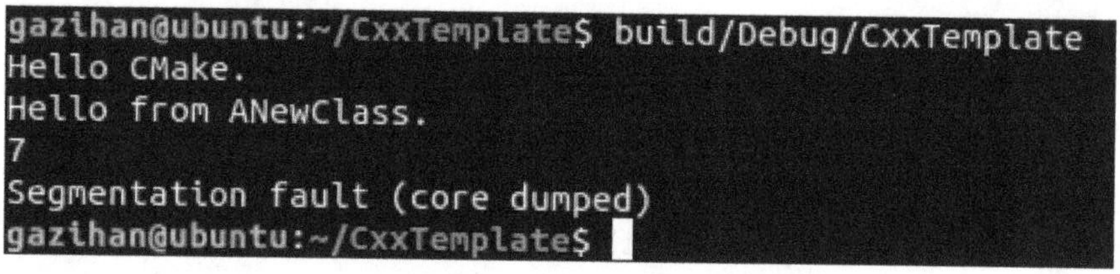

Figure 1.60: Program output in the terminal with the error

Unfortunately, we do not get the segmentation fault error output in Eclipse, therefore you have to check the exit value in the Eclipse console view. To find the problem, we will use the debugger in the next step.

10. Press the debug toolbar button in Eclipse to start the application in debug mode. Press the resume button to continue execution. It will stop at line 40 of **SpeedCalculator.cpp**, right when an error is about to happen. If you hover over **speeds**, you realize that it is an invalid memory reference:

```
36      for (int i = 0; i < numEntries; ++i) {
37          double dt = timesInSeconds[i + 1] - timesInSe
38          assert(dt > 0);
39          double speed = (positions[i + 1] - positions[
40          speeds[i] = speed;
41      }
42
43      for
44
45
46
47
48
49
```

| Expression | Type |
| --- | --- |
| ▼ ⇒ speeds | double * |
| (x)= *speeds | double |

```
Failed to execute MI command:
-data-evaluate-expression *(speeds)
Error message from debugger back end:
Cannot access memory at address 0xa55756cc0
```

Console ⊠

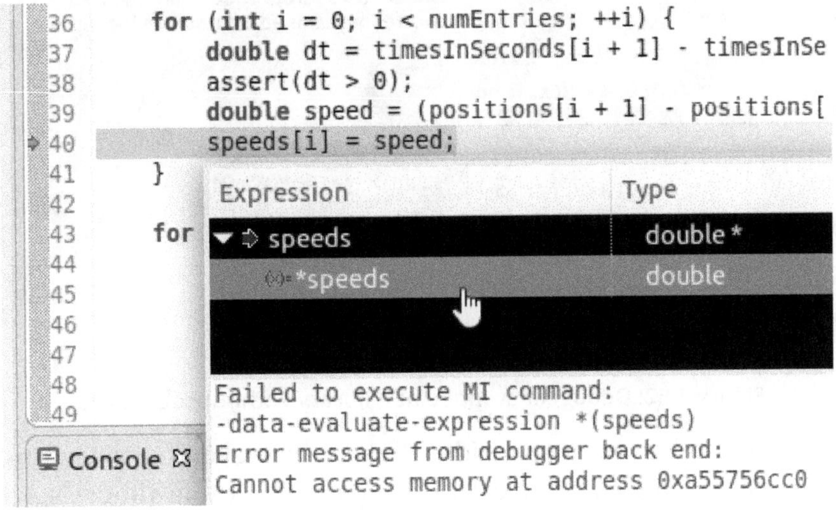

Figure 1.61: Invalid memory reference

11. Upon further examination, we realize that we never initialized the **speeds** pointer to anything. Allocate memory for it in our speed calculator function:

```
void SpeedCalculator::calculateAndPrintSpeedData() {
    speeds = new double[numEntries]; // add this line
    double maxSpeed = 0;
```

12. Run it again. We get the following output:

```
Hello CMake.
Hello from ANewClass.
7
CxxTemplate: SpeedCalculator.cpp:38: void
SpeedCalculator::calculateAndPrintSpeedData(): Assertion `dt > 0' failed.
```

Note that this was an assertion that the code had to make sure that the calculated **dt** was always larger than zero. This is something that we are sure of, and we would like it to help us catch errors during development. Assert statements are ignored in the production builds, so you can place them liberally in your code as safeguards to catch errors during development. Especially since C++ lacks many safety checks compared to higher-level languages, placing **assert** statements in potentially unsafe code helps catch errors.

13. Let's investigate why our **dt** ended up not larger than zero. For this, we fire up the debugger again. It stops at this strange place:

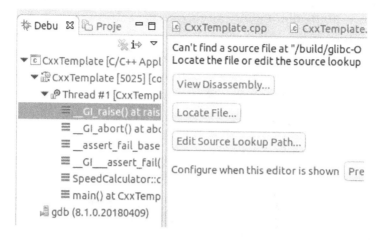

Figure 1.62: Debugger stopped at a library without source code

14. The actual error is raised deep inside a library. However, our own functions are still on the stack and we can investigate their state at that time. Click on **Speed-Calculator** above **main** in the tree to the left:

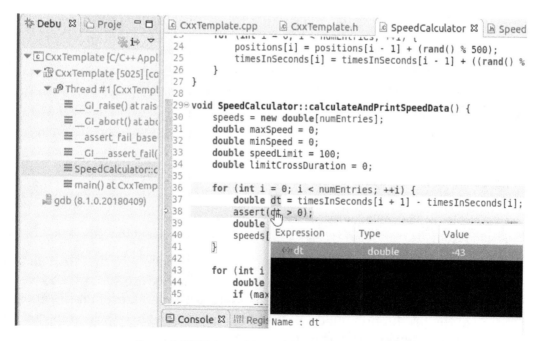

Figure 1.63: Value of dt as the program is running

It seems our **dt** becomes **-43** here (the exact value is not important). Looking at the **Variables** view, we realize that **i** is **9**, which is the last element of our input array:

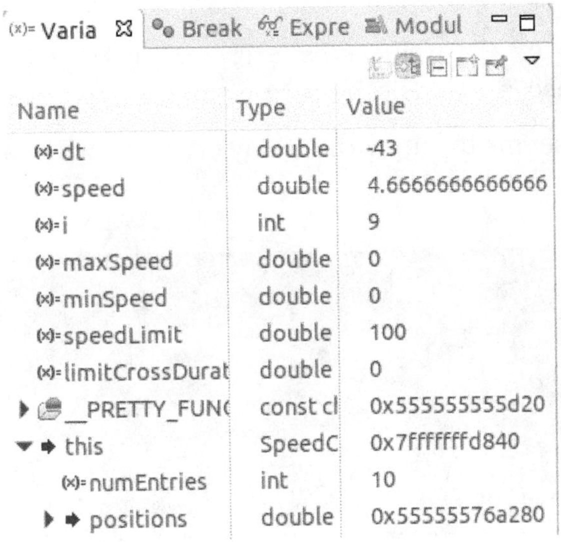

| Name | Type | Value |
|---|---|---|
| (x)= dt | double | -43 |
| (x)= speed | double | 4.6666666666666 |
| (x)= i | int | 9 |
| (x)= maxSpeed | double | 0 |
| (x)= minSpeed | double | 0 |
| (x)= speedLimit | double | 100 |
| (x)= limitCrossDurat | double | 0 |
| ▶ 🗐 _PRETTY_FUN( | const cl | 0x555555555d20 |
| ▼ ➡ this | SpeedC | 0x7fffffffd840 |
| (x)= numEntries | int | 10 |
| ▶ ➡ positions | double | 0x55555576a280 |

Figure 1.64: Values of variables

This feels like a boundary problem. Looking closely at the code, we realize that we are using **timesInSeconds[10]**, which is the non-existent eleventh element of the array. Thinking further, we realize that we can only have 9 position-pair subtractions, thus 9 speeds, when we have 10 positions. This is a very common and hard-to-catch mistake as C++ does not enforce you to stay within the array.

15. Rework our whole code for this problem:

```
void SpeedCalculator::calculateAndPrintSpeedData() {
  speeds = new double[numEntries - 1];
  double maxSpeed = 0;

  ...

  for (int i = 0; i < numEntries - 1; ++i) {
    double dt = timesInSeconds[i + 1] - timesInSeconds[i];

  ...

  for (int i = 0; i < numEntries - 1; ++i) {
```

```
            double speed = speeds[i];

    . . . .

        for (int i = 0; i < numEntries - 1; ++i) {
            double speed = speeds[i];
```

Finally, our code seems to run without any errors as we can see in the following output:

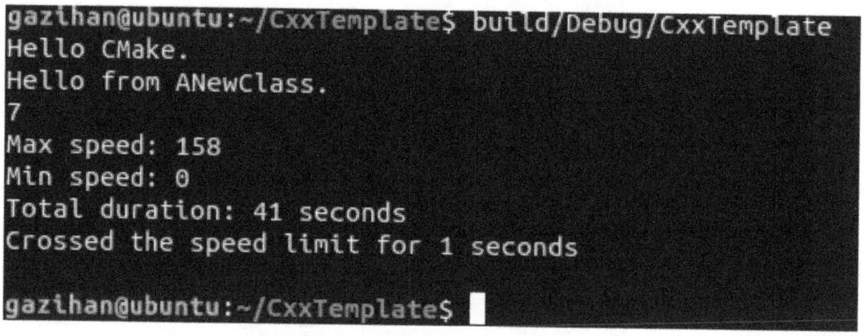

Figure 1.65: Program output

16. However, there is a curious point here: **Min speed** is always **0**, no matter how many times you run it. To investigate, let's put a breakpoint at the following line:

Figure 1.66: Placing a breakpoint

17. When we debug our code, we see that it never stops here. This is obviously wrong. Upon further investigation, we realize that `minSpeed` is initially 0, and every other speed value is larger than that. We should initialize it to either something very large, or we need to get the very first element as the minimum value. Here, we choose the second approach:

```
    for (int i = 0; i < numEntries - 1; ++i) {
        double speed = speeds[i];
        if (i == 0 || maxSpeed < speed) { // changed
            maxSpeed = speed;
        }
```

```
  if (i == 0 || minSpeed > speed) { // changed
    minSpeed = speed;
  }
}
```

While **maxSpeed** did not need this, it's good to be consistent. Now when we run the code, we see that we do not get **0** as our minimum speed anymore:

```
gazihan@ubuntu:~/CxxTemplate$ build/Debug/CxxTemplate
Hello CMake.
Hello from ANewClass.
7
Max speed: 467
Min speed: 25.5
Total duration: 43 seconds
Crossed the speed limit for 6 seconds

gazihan@ubuntu:~/CxxTemplate$
```

Figure 1.67: Program output

18. Our code seems to be running fine. However, there is another mistake that we have made. When we debug our code, we see that our first elements are not zero:

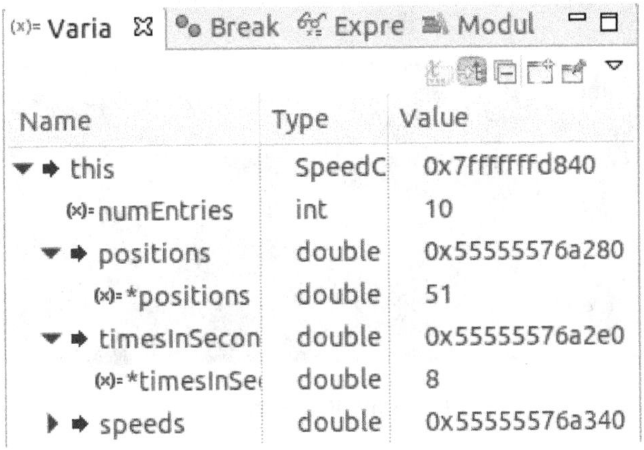

| Name | Type | Value |
|------|------|-------|
| ▼ ➧ this | SpeedC | 0x7fffffffd840 |
| (x)= numEntries | int | 10 |
| ▼ ➧ positions | double | 0x55555576a280 |
| (x)= *positions | double | 51 |
| ▼ ➧ timesInSecon | double | 0x55555576a2e0 |
| (x)= *timesInSe | double | 8 |
| ▶ ➧ speeds | double | 0x55555576a340 |

Figure 1.68: Values of variables

19. The pointer dereferenced the first element in the array. We had initialized elements to zero here, but they do not seem to be zero. Here is the updated code:

```
// add these two lines:
timesInSeconds[0] = 0.0;
positions[0] = 0.0;
for (int i = 0; i < numEntries; ++i) {
  positions[i] = positions[i - 1] + (rand() % 500);
  timesInSeconds[i] = timesInSeconds[i - 1] + ((rand() % 10) + 1);
}
```

When we investigate, we realize that we start the loop at zero and overwrite the first items. Furthermore, we try to access **positions[0 - 1]**, which is a mistake and another example of C++ not enforcing array boundaries. When we let the loop start from 1, all these problems are gone:

```
timesInSeconds[0] = 0.0;
positions[0] = 0.0;
for (int i = 1; i < numEntries; ++i) {
  positions[i] = positions[i - 1] + (rand() % 500);
  timesInSeconds[i] = timesInSeconds[i - 1] + ((rand() % 10) + 1);
}
```

Here is the output generated with the updated code:

```
gazihan@ubuntu:~/CxxTemplate$ build/Debug/CxxTemplate
Hello CMake.
Hello from ANewClass.
7
Max speed: 258
Min speed: 7.33333
Total duration: 46 seconds
Crossed the speed limit for 7 seconds

gazihan@ubuntu:~/CxxTemplate$
```

Figure 1.69: Program output

Just by looking at this code, we cannot tell the difference. It's all random values that do not look very different than before. Such bugs are very hard to find and can cause random behavior, leaving us with hard-to-track errors. Things that you can do to avoid such errors include being extra careful when dereferencing pointers, especially in loops; separating code into functions and writing unit tests for them; and using **assert** statements liberally to enforce things that the compiler or the runtime does not.

# Chapter 2A - No Ducks Allowed – Types and Deduction

## Activity 1: Graphics Processing

In this activity, we will implement two classes (**Point3d** and **Matrix3d**), along with the multiplication operators so that we can translate, scale, and rotate points. We will also implement some helper methods that create the necessary matrices for the transformations. Follow these steps to implement this activity:

1. Load the prepared project from the **Lesson2A/Activity01** folder and configure the Current Builder for the project to be **CMake Build (Portable)**. Build and configure the launcher and run the unit tests (which fail). Recommend that the name that's used for the test runner is **L2AA1graphicstests**.

> **CMake Configuration**
>
> Follow *step 9* of *Exercise 1, Declaring Variables and Exploring Sizes,* to configure the project as a CMake project.

2. Add a test for the **Point3d** class to verify that the default constructor creates an **origin point [0, 0, 0, 1]**.

3. Open the **point3dTests.cpp** file and add the following line at the top.

4. Replace the failing existing test with the following test:

```
TEST_F(Point3dTest, DefaultConstructorIsOrigin)
{
    Point3d pt;
    float expected[4] = {0,0,0,1};

    for(size_t i=0 ; i < 4 ; i++)
    {
        ASSERT_NEAR(expected[i], pt(i), Epsilon) << "cell [" << i << "]";
    }
}
```

This test requires us to write an access operator.

5. Replace the current class definition in **point3d.hpp** file with the following code:

```
include <cstddef>

class Point3d
{
public:
    static constexpr size_t NumberRows{4};

    float operator()(const int index) const
    {
        return m_data[index];
    }

private:

    float m_data[NumberRows];
};
```

The test now builds and runs but fails.

6. Add the declaration for the default constructor to the **Point3d** declaration:

```
Point3d();
```

7. Add the implementation to the **point3d.cpp** file:

```
Point3d::Point3d()
{
    for(auto& item : m_data)
    {
        item = 0;
    }
    m_data[NumberRows-1] = 1;
}
```

The test now builds, runs, and passes.

8. Add the next test:

```
TEST_F(Point3dTest, InitListConstructor3)
{
    Point3d pt {5.2, 3.5, 6.7};
    float expected[4] = {5.2,3.5,6.7,1};

    for(size_t i=0 ; i < 4 ; i++)
```

```
    {
        ASSERT_NEAR(expected[i], pt(i), Epsilon) << "cell [" << i << "]";
    }
}
```

This test fails to compile. Therefore, we need to implement another constructor – the one that takes **std::initializer_list<>** as an argument.

9.  Add the following include to the header file:

```
#include <initializer_list>
```

10. Add the following constructor declaration to the Point3d class in the header file:

```
Point3d(std::initializer_list<float> list);
```

11.  Add the following code to the implementation file. This code ignores error handling, which will be added in *Lesson 3, The Distance Between Can and Should – Objects, Pointers, and Inheritance*:

```
Point3d::Point3d(std::initializer_list<float> list)
{
    m_data[NumberRows-1] = 1;
    int i{0};
    for(auto it1 = list.begin();
        i<NumberRows && it1 != list.end();
        ++it1, ++i)
    {
        m_data[i] = *it1;
    }
}
```

The tests should now build, run, and pass.

12. Add the following test:

```
TEST_F(Point3dTest, InitListConstructor4)
{
    Point3d pt {5.2, 3.5, 6.7, 2.0};
    float expected[4] = {5.2,3.5,6.7,2.0};
    for(size_t i=0 ; i < 4 ; i++)
    {
        ASSERT_NEAR(expected[i], pt(i), Epsilon) << "cell [" << i << "]";
    }
}
```

The tests should still build, run, and pass.

13. It is now time to refactor the test cases by moving the verification loop into a templated function in the **Point3dTest** class. Add the following template inside this class:

```
template<size_t size>
void VerifyPoint(Point3d& pt, float (&expected)[size])
{

    for(size_t i=0 ; i< size ; i++)
    {
        ASSERT_NEAR(expected[i], pt(i), Epsilon) << "cell [" << i << "]";
    }
}
```

14. This now means that the last test can be rewritten as follows:

```
TEST_F(Point3dTest, InitListConstructor4)
{
    Point3d pt {5.2, 3.5, 6.7, 2.0};
    float expected[4] = {5.2,3.5,6.7,2.0};

    VerifyPoint(pt, expected);
}
```

It is just as important to keep your tests readable in the same way as your production code.

15. Next, add support for the equality and inequality operators through the following tests:

```
TEST_F(Point3dTest, EqualityOperatorEqual)
{
    Point3d pt1 {1,3,5};
    Point3d pt2 {1,3,5};

    ASSERT_EQ(pt1, pt2);
}

TEST_F(Point3dTest, EqualityOperatorNotEqual)
{
    Point3d pt1 {1,2,3};
    Point3d pt2 {1,2,4};

    ASSERT_NE(pt1, pt2);
}
```

16. To implement these, add the following declarations/definition in the header file:

```
bool operator==(const Point3d& rhs) const;
bool operator!=(const Point3d& rhs) const
{
    return !operator==(rhs);
}
```

17. Now, add the equality implementation in the .cpp file:

```
bool Point3d::operator==(const Point3d& rhs) const
{
    for(int i=0 ; i<NumberRows ; i++)
    {
        if (m_data[i] != rhs.m_data[i])
        {
            return false;
        }
    }
    return true;
}
```

18. When we first added **Point3d**, we implemented a constant accessor. Add the following test, where we need a non-constant accessor so that we can assign it to the member:

```
TEST_F(Point3dTest, AccessOperator)
{
    Point3d pt1;
    Point3d pt2 {1,3,5};

    pt1(0) = 1;
    pt1(1) = 3;
    pt1(2) = 5;
    ASSERT_EQ(pt1, pt2);
}
```

19. To get this test to build, add the following accessor to the header:

```
float& operator()(const int index)
{
    return m_data[index];
}
```

Note that it returns a reference. Thus, we can assign it to a member value.

20. To finish off **Point3d**, add lines to the class declaration for the default copy constructor and copy assignment:

```
Point3d(const Point3d&) = default;
Point3d& operator=(const Point3d&) = default;
```

21. Now, add the **Matrix3d** classes. First, create two empty files, **matrix3d.hpp** and **matrix3d.cpp**, in the top-level folder of the current project and then add an empty file in the tests folder called **matrix3dTests.cpp**.

22. Open the CmakeLists.txt file in the top folder and add **matrix3d.cpp** to the following line:

```
add_executable(graphics point3d.cpp main.cpp matrix3d.cpp)
```

23. Open the **CMakeLists.txt** file in the **tests** folder, add ../**matrix3d.cpp** to the definition of **SRC_FILES**, and add **matrix3dTests.cpp** to the definition of **TEST_FILES**:

```
SET(SRC_FILES
    ../matrix3d.cpp
    ../point3d.cpp)


SET(TEST_FILES
    matrix3dTests.cpp
    point3dTests.cpp)
```

The existing **point3d** tests should still build, run, and pass if you made those changes correctly.

24. Add the following test plumbing to **matrix3dTests.cpp**:

```
#include "gtest/gtest.h"
#include "../matrix3d.hpp"


class Matrix3dTest : public ::testing::Test
{
public:
};


TEST_F(Matrix3dTest, DummyTest)
{
    ASSERT_TRUE(false);
}
```

25. Build and run the tests. The test that we just added should fail.

26. Replace DummyTest with the following test in **matrix3dTests.cpp**:

```
TEST_F(Matrix3dTest, DefaultConstructorIsIdentity)
{
    Matrix3d mat;

    for( int row{0} ; row<4 ; row++)
        for( int col{0} ; col<4 ; col++)
        {
            int expected = (row==col) ? 1 : 0;
            ASSERT_FLOAT_EQ(expected, mat(row,col)) << "cell[" << row <<
"][" << col << "]";
        }
}
```

Building the tests will now fail because we have not defined the **Matrix3d** class. We will do this now in **matrix3d.hpp**.

27. Add the following definition to **matrix3d.hpp**:

```
class Matrix3d
{
public:
    float operator()(const int row, const int column) const
    {
        return m_data[row][column];
    }

private:
    float m_data[4][4];

};
```

The tests will now build but still fail because we haven't created a default constructor that creates an identity matrix.

28. Add the declaration of the default constructor to the header file in the public section of **Matrix3d**:

```
Matrix3d();
```

29. Add this definition to **matrix3d.cpp**:

```
#include "matrix3d.hpp"

Matrix3d::Matrix3d()
{
    for (int i{0} ; i< 4 ; i++)
        for (int j{0} ; j< 4 ; j++)
            m_data[i][j] = (i==j);
}
```

The tests now build and pass.

30. Refactor the code slightly to make it more readable. Modify the header to read like so:

```
#include <cstddef>    // Required for size_t definition

class Matrix3d
{
public:
    static constexpr size_t NumberRows{4};
    static constexpr size_t NumberColumns{4};

    Matrix3d();

    float operator()(const int row, const int column) const
    {
    return m_data[row][column];
    }

private:
    float m_data[NumberRows][NumberColumns];
};
```

31. Update the **matrix3d.cpp** file to use the constants:

```
Matrix3d::Matrix3d()
{
    for (int i{0} ; i< NumberRows ; i++)
        for (int j{0} ; j< NumberColumns ; j++)
            m_data[i][j] = (i==j);
}
```

32. Rebuild the tests and make sure that they still pass.

33. Now, we need to add the initializer list constructor. To do that, add the following test:

```
TEST_F(Matrix3dTest, InitListConstructor)
{
    Matrix3d mat{ {1,2,3,4}, {5,6,7,8},{9,10,11,12}, {13,14,15,16}};

    int expected{1};
    for( int row{0} ; row<4 ; row++)
        for( int col{0} ; col<4 ; col++, expected++)
        {
            ASSERT_FLOAT_EQ(expected, mat(row,col)) << "cell[" << row <<
"][" << col << "]";
        }
}
```

34. Add the include file for the initializer list support and declare the constructor in **matrix3d.hpp**:

```
#include <initializer_list>

class Matrix3d
{
public:
    Matrix3d(std::initializer_list<std::initializer_list<float>> list);
```

35. Finally, add the implementation of the constructor to the .cpp file:

```
Matrix3d::Matrix3d(std::initializer_list<std::initializer_list<float>>
list)
{
    int i{0};
    for(auto it1 = list.begin(); i<NumberRows ; ++it1, ++i)
    {
        int j{0};
        for(auto it2 = it1->begin(); j<NumberColumns ; ++it2, ++j)
            m_data[i][j] = *it2;
    }
}
```

36. To improve the readability of our tests, add a helper method to the test framework. In the **Matrix3dTest** class, declare the following:

```
static constexpr float Epsilon{1e-12};
void VerifyMatrixResult(Matrix3d& expected, Matrix3d& actual);
```

37. Add the definition of the helper method:

```
void Matrix3dTest::VerifyMatrixResult(Matrix3d& expected, Matrix3d&
actual)
{
    for( int row{0} ; row<4 ; row++)
        for( int col{0} ; col<4 ; col++)
        {
        ASSERT_NEAR(expected(row,col), actual(row,col), Epsilon)
<< "cell[" << row << "][" << col << "]";
        }
}
```

38. Write a test to multiply two matrices and get a new matrix (expected will be calculated by hand):

```
TEST_F(Matrix3dTest, MultiplyTwoMatricesGiveExpectedResult)
{
    Matrix3d mat1{ {5,6,7,8}, {9,10,11,12}, {13,14,15,16}, {17,18,19,20}};
    Matrix3d mat2{ {1,2,3,4}, {5,6,7,8},    {9,10,11,12}, {13,14,15,16}};
    Matrix3d expected{ {202,228,254,280},
                       {314,356,398,440},
                       {426,484,542,600},
                       {538,612,686,760}};


    Matrix3d result = mat1 * mat2;
    VerifyMatrixResult(expected, result);
}
```

39. In the header file, define **operator*=**:

```
Matrix3d& operator*=(const Matrix3d& rhs);
```

Then, implement the inline version of **operator*** (outside the class declaration):

```
inline Matrix3d operator*(const Matrix3d& lhs, const Matrix3d& rhs)
{
    Matrix3d temp(lhs);
    temp *= rhs;
```

```
        return temp;
    }
```

40. And the implementation to the **matrix3d.cpp** file:

```
Matrix3d& Matrix3d::operator*=(const Matrix3d& rhs)
{
    Matrix3d temp;

    for(int i=0 ; i<NumberRows ; i++)
        for(int j=0 ; j<NumberColumns ; j++)
        {
            temp.m_data[i][j] = 0;
            for (int k=0 ; k<NumberRows ; k++)
                temp.m_data[i][j] += m_data[i][k] * rhs.m_data[k][j];
        }

    *this = temp;
    return *this;
}
```

41. Build and run the tests – again, they should pass.

42. Introduce a second helper function to the test class by declaring it in the **Matrix-3dTest** class:

```
void VerifyMatrixIsIdentity(Matrix3d& mat);
```

Then, declare it so that we can use it:

```
void Matrix3dTest::VerifyMatrixIsIdentity(Matrix3d& mat)
{
for( int row{0} ; row<4 ; row++)
    for( int col{0} ; col<4 ; col++)
    {
        int expected = (row==col) ? 1 : 0;
        ASSERT_FLOAT_EQ(expected, mat(row,col))
                        << "cell[" << row << "][" << col << "]";
    }
}
```

43. Update the one test to use it:

```
TEST_F(Matrix3dTest, DefaultConstructorIsIdentity)
{
    Matrix3d mat;
```

```
        VerifyMatrixIsIdentity(mat);
    }
```

44. Write one sanity check test:

```
    TEST_F(Matrix3dTest, IdentityTimesIdentityIsIdentity)
    {
        Matrix3d mat;

        Matrix3d result = mat * mat;
        VerifyMatrixIsIdentity(result);
    }
```

45. Build and run the tests – they should still pass.

46. Now, we need to be able to multiply points and matrices. Add the following test:

```
    TEST_F(Matrix3dTest, MultiplyMatrixWithPoint)
    {
        Matrix3d mat { {1,2,3,4}, {5,6,7,8},    {9,10,11,12},   {13,14,15,16}};
        Point3d pt {15, 25, 35, 45};
        Point3d expected{350, 830, 1310, 1790};

        Point3d pt2 = mat * pt;

        ASSERT_EQ(expected, pt2);
    }
```

47. In **matrix3d.hpp**, add the include directive for point3d.hpp and add the following declaration after the **Matrix3d** class declaration:

```
    Point3d operator*(const Matrix3d& lhs, const Point3d& rhs);
```

48. Add the definition of the operator to the **matrix3d.cpp** file:

```
    Point3d operator*(const Matrix3d& lhs, const Point3d& rhs)
    {
        Point3d pt;
        for(int row{0} ; row<Matrix3d::NumberRows ; row++)
        {
            float sum{0};
            for(int col{0} ; col<Matrix3d::NumberColumns ; col++)
            {
                sum += lhs(row, col) * rhs(col);
            }
```

```
            pt(row) = sum;
        }
        return pt;
    }
```

49. Build and run the tests. They should all be passing again.

50. At the top of **matrix3dtests.cpp**, add the include file:

```
    #include <cmath>
```

51. Start adding the transformation matrix factory methods. Using the following tests, we will develop the various factory methods (the tests should be added one at a time):

```
TEST_F(Matrix3dTest, CreateTranslateIsCorrect)
{
    Matrix3d mat = createTranslationMatrix(-0.5, 2.5, 10.0);
    Matrix3d expected {{1.0, 0.0, 0.0, -0.5},
                       {0.0, 1.0, 0.0, 2.5},
                       {0.0, 0.0, 1.0, 10.0},
                       {0.0, 0.0, 0.0, 1.0}
    };
    VerifyMatrixResult(expected, mat);
}


TEST_F(Matrix3dTest, CreateScaleIsCorrect)
{
    Matrix3d mat = createScaleMatrix(3.0, 2.5, 11.0);
    Matrix3d expected {{3.0, 0.0,  0.0, 0.0},
                       {0.0, 2.5,  0.0, 0.0},
                       {0.0, 0.0, 11.0, 0.0},
                       {0.0, 0.0,  0.0, 1.0}
    };
    VerifyMatrixResult(expected, mat);
}



TEST_F(Matrix3dTest, CreateRotateX90IsCorrect)
{
    Matrix3d mat = createRotationMatrixAboutX(90.0F);

    Matrix3d expected {{1.0, 0.0,  0.0, 0.0},
                       {0.0, 0.0, -1.0, 0.0},
```

```
                                 {0.0, 1.0,  0.0, 0.0},
                                 {0.0, 0.0,  0.0, 1.0}
        };
        VerifyMatrixResult(expected, mat);
    }


    TEST_F(Matrix3dTest, CreateRotateX60IsCorrect)
    {
        Matrix3d mat = createRotationMatrixAboutX(60.0F);
        float sqrt3_2 = static_cast<float>(std::sqrt(3.0)/2.0);

        Matrix3d expected {{1.0, 0.0,      0.0,      0.0},
                           {0.0, 0.5,      -sqrt3_2, 0.0},
                           {0.0, sqrt3_2,  0.5,      0.0},
                           {0.0, 0.0,      0.0,      1.0}
        };
        VerifyMatrixResult(expected, mat);
    }


    TEST_F(Matrix3dTest, CreateRotateY90IsCorrect)
    {
        Matrix3d mat = createRotationMatrixAboutY(90.0F);

        Matrix3d expected {{0.0, 0.0,  1.0, 0.0},
                           {0.0, 1.0,  0.0, 0.0},
                           {-1.0, 0.0, 0.0, 0.0},
                           {0.0, 0.0,  0.0, 1.0}
        };
        VerifyMatrixResult(expected, mat);
    }


    TEST_F(Matrix3dTest, CreateRotateY60IsCorrect)
    {
        Matrix3d mat = createRotationMatrixAboutY(60.0F);
        float sqrt3_2 = static_cast<float>(std::sqrt(3.0)/2.0);

        Matrix3d expected {{0.5,      0.0,  sqrt3_2, 0.0},
                           {0.0,      1.0,  0.0,     0.0},
                           {-sqrt3_2, 0.0,  0.5,     0.0},
                           {0.0,      0.0,  0.0,     1.0}
        };
        VerifyMatrixResult(expected, mat);
```

```
}

TEST_F(Matrix3dTest, CreateRotateZ90IsCorrect)
{
    Matrix3d mat = createRotationMatrixAboutZ(90.0F);

    Matrix3d expected {{0.0, -1.0,  0.0, 0.0},
                       {1.0, 0.0,  0.0, 0.0},
                       {0.0, 0.0,  1.0, 0.0},
                       {0.0, 0.0,  0.0, 1.0}
    };
    VerifyMatrixResult(expected, mat);
}

TEST_F(Matrix3dTest, CreateRotateZ60IsCorrect)
{
    Matrix3d mat = createRotationMatrixAboutZ(60.0F);
    float sqrt3_2 = static_cast<float>(std::sqrt(3.0)/2.0);

    Matrix3d expected {{0.5,     -sqrt3_2,  0.0, 0.0},
                       {sqrt3_2,      0.5,  0.0, 0.0},
                       {0.0,         0.0,  1.0, 0.0},
                       {0.0,         0.0,  0.0, 1.0}
    };
    VerifyMatrixResult(expected, mat);
}
```

52. Add the following declarations to the matrix3d header file:

```
Matrix3d createTranslationMatrix(float dx, float dy, float dz);
Matrix3d createScaleMatrix(float sx, float sy, float sz);
Matrix3d createRotationMatrixAboutX(float degrees);
Matrix3d createRotationMatrixAboutY(float degrees);
Matrix3d createRotationMatrixAboutZ(float degrees);
```

53. At the top of the matrix3d implementation file, add **#include <cmath>**.

54. Finally, add the following implementations to the **matrix3d** implementation file:

```
Matrix3d createTranslationMatrix(float dx, float dy, float dz)
{
    Matrix3d matrix;
    matrix(0, 3) = dx;
    matrix(1, 3) = dy;
```

```
        matrix(2, 3) = dz;
        return matrix;
    }


    Matrix3d createScaleMatrix(float sx, float sy, float sz)
    {
        Matrix3d matrix;
        matrix(0, 0) = sx;
        matrix(1, 1) = sy;
        matrix(2, 2) = sz;
        return matrix;


    }


    Matrix3d createRotationMatrixAboutX(float degrees)
    {
        Matrix3d matrix;
        double pi{4.0F*atan(1.0F)};
        double radians = degrees / 180.0 * pi;

        float cos_theta = static_cast<float>(cos(radians));
        float sin_theta = static_cast<float>(sin(radians));

        matrix(1, 1) =  cos_theta;
        matrix(2, 2) =  cos_theta;
        matrix(1, 2) = -sin_theta;
        matrix(2, 1) =  sin_theta;

        return matrix;
    }

    Matrix3d createRotationMatrixAboutY(float degrees)
    {
        Matrix3d matrix;
        double pi{4.0F*atan(1.0F)};
        double radians = degrees / 180.0 * pi;

        float cos_theta = static_cast<float>(cos(radians));
        float sin_theta = static_cast<float>(sin(radians));

        matrix(0, 0) =  cos_theta;
        matrix(2, 2) =  cos_theta;
```

```
    matrix(0, 2) =  sin_theta;
    matrix(2, 0) = -sin_theta;

    return matrix;
}

Matrix3d createRotationMatrixAboutZ(float degrees)
{
    Matrix3d matrix;
    double pi{4.0F*atan(1.0F)};
    double radians = degrees / 180.0 * pi;
    float cos_theta = static_cast<float>(cos(radians));
    float sin_theta = static_cast<float>(sin(radians));

    matrix(0, 0) =  cos_theta;
    matrix(1, 1) =  cos_theta;
    matrix(0, 1) = -sin_theta;
    matrix(1, 0) =  sin_theta;

    return matrix;
}
```

55. To get this to compile and pass the test, we need to add one more accessor to the declaration of **matrix3d**:

```
float& operator()(const int row, const int column)
{
    return m_data[row][column];
}
```

56. Build and run all the tests again to show that they all pass.

57. In **point3d.hpp**, add the include for **<ostream>** and add the following friend declaration to the Point3d class at the end:

```
friend std::ostream& operator<<(std::ostream& , const Point3d& );
```

58. Write the inline implementation of the operator after the class:

```
inline std::ostream&
operator<<(std::ostream& os, const Point3d& pt)
{
    const char* sep = "[ ";
    for(auto value : pt.m_data)
    {
```

```
            os << sep   << value;
            sep = ", ";
        }
        os << " ]";
        return os;
    }
```

59. Open the **main.cpp** file and remove the comment delimiters, //, from the line:

```
//#define ACTIVITY1
```

60. Build and run the application called `graphics` – you will need to create a new Run Configuration. If your implementations of `Point3d` and `Matrix3d` are correct, then the program will display the following output:

```
------ Activity 1 ------
The point [ 1, 1, 1, 1 ]
...rotated around X by 90 degrees
...rotated around Y by 90 degrees
...rotated around Z by 90 degrees
moves to [ 1, 1, -1, 1 ]
...scaled by x=2, y = 3, z = 4
moves to [ 2, 3, -4, 1 ]
...translated by dx=-2, dy = 1, dz = -3
moves to [ 0, 4, -7, 1 ]

Complete.
```

Figure 2A.53: Successfully running the activity program

In this activity, we implemented two classes that form the basis of all the operations that are required to implement 3D graphics rendering. We used operator overloading to achieve this so that Matrix3d and Point3d can be used as if they were native types. This can be easily extended to deal with vectors of points, which is required if we wish to manipulate whole objects.

# Chapter – 2B - No Ducks Allowed – Templates and Deduction

## Activity 1: Developing a Generic "contains" Template Function

In this activity, we will implement several helper classes that will be used to detect the **std::string** class case and the **std::set** case and then use them to tailor the contains function to the particular container. Follow these steps to implement this activity:

1. Load the prepared project from the **Lesson2B/Activity01** folder. Build and configure the launcher and run the unit tests (which fail the one dummy test). We recommend that the name that's used for the tests runner is **L2BA1 tests**.

2. Open the **containsTests.cpp** file and replace the existing test with the following:

```
TEST_F(containsTest, DetectNpos)
{
    ASSERT_TRUE(has_npos_v<std::string>);
    ASSERT_FALSE(has_npos_v<std::set<int>>);
    ASSERT_FALSE(has_npos_v<std::vector<int>>);
}
```

This test requires us to write a set of helper templates to detect if the container class supports a static member variable called npos.

3. Add the following code to the **contains.hpp** file:

```
template <class T>
auto test_npos(int) -> decltype((void)T::npos, std::true_type{});

template <class T>
auto test_npos(long) -> std::false_type;

template <class T>
struct has_npos : decltype(test_npos<T>(0)) {};

template< class T >
inline constexpr bool has_npos_v = has_npos<T>::value;
```

The tests now run and pass.

4. Add the following tests to the **containsTest.cpp** file:

```
TEST_F(containsTest, DetectFind)
{
    ASSERT_TRUE((has_find_v<std::string, char>));
    ASSERT_TRUE((has_find_v<std::set<int>, int>));
```

```
        ASSERT_FALSE((has_find_v<std::vector<int>, int>));
}
```

This test requires us to write a set of helper templates to detect if the container class has a **find()** method that takes one argument.

5. Add the following code to the **contains.hpp** file:

```
template <class T, class A0>
auto test_find(int) ->
        decltype(void(std::declval<T>().find(std::declval<A0>())),
                                                std::true_type{});

template <class T, class A0>
auto test_find(long) -> std::false_type;

template <class T, class A0>
struct has_find : decltype(test_find<T,A0>(0)) {};

template< class T, class A0 >
inline constexpr bool has_find_v = has_find<T, A0>::value;
```

The tests now run and pass.

6. Add the implementation for the generic container; in this case, the vector. Write the following tests in the **containsTest.cpp** file:

```
TEST_F(containsTest, VectorContains)
{
    std::vector<int> container {1,2,3,4,5};

    ASSERT_TRUE(contains(container, 5));
    ASSERT_FALSE(contains(container, 15));
}
```

7. Add the basic implementation of **contains** to the **contains.hpp** file:

```
template<class C, class T>
auto contains(const C& c, const T& key) -> decltype(std::end(c), true)
{
        return std::end(c) != std::find(begin(c), end(c), key);
}
```

The tests now run and pass.

8. The next step is to add the tests for the **set** special case to **containsTest.cpp**:

```
TEST_F(containsTest, SetContains)
{
    std::set<int> container {1,2,3,4,5};

    ASSERT_TRUE(contains(container, 5));
    ASSERT_FALSE(contains(container, 15));
}
```

9. The implementation of **contains** is updated to test for the built-in **set::find()** method:

```
template<class C, class T>
auto contains(const C& c, const T& key) -> decltype(std::end(c), true)
{
    if constexpr(has_find_v<C, T>)
    {
        return std::end(c) != c.find(key);
    }
    else
    {
        return std::end(c) != std::find(begin(c), end(c), key);
    }
}
```

The tests now run and pass.

10. Add the tests for the **string** special case to the **containsTest.cpp** file:

```
TEST_F(containsTest, StringContains)
{
    std::string container{"This is the message"};

    ASSERT_TRUE(contains(container, "the"));
    ASSERT_TRUE(contains(container, 'm'));
    ASSERT_FALSE(contains(container, "massage"));
    ASSERT_FALSE(contains(container, 'z'));
}
```

11. Add the following implementation of **contains** to test for the presence of **npos** and tailor the use of the **find()** method:

```
template<class C, class T>
auto contains(const C& c, const T& key) -> decltype(std::end(c), true)
{
```

```
if constexpr(has_npos_v<C>)
{
    return C::npos != c.find(key);
}
else
if constexpr(has_find_v<C, T>)
{
    return std::end(c) != c.find(key);
}
else
{
    return std::end(c) != std::find(begin(c), end(c), key);
}
}
```

The tests now run and pass.

12. Build and run the application called **contains**. Create a new Run Configuration. If your implementation of the contains template is correct, then the program will display the following output:

```
------ Activity 1 ------
Set contains 5: true
Set contains 15: false
Vector contains 5: true
Vector contains 15: false
String contains 'times': true
String contains 'Light': false
String contains 'm': true
String contains 'z': false

Complete.
```

**Figure 2B.36: Output from the successful implementation of contains**

In this activity, we used various templating techniques in conjunction with SFINAE to select the appropriate implementation of a **contains()** function based upon the capability of the containing class. We could have achieved the same result using a generic template function and some specialized templates, but we took the path less travelled and flexed our newly found template skills.

# Chapter 3 - The Distance between Can and Should – Objects, Pointers and Inheritance

## Activity 1: Implementing Graphics Processing with RAII and Move

In this activity, we will develop our previous `Matrix3d` and `Point3d` classes to use a `unique_ptr<>` to manage the memory associated with the data structures that are required to implement these graphics classes. Let's get started:

1. Load the prepared project from the **Lesson3/Activity01** folder and configure the Current Builder for the project to be **CMake Build (Portable)**. Build and configure the launcher and run the unit tests. We recommend that the name that's used for the tests runner is **L3A1graphicstests**.

2. Open **point3d.hpp** and add the lines marked with a comment to the file:

   ```
   // ... lines omitted
   #include <initializer_list>
   #include <ostream>

   namespace acpp::gfx { // Add this line

   class Point3d
   {
   // ... lines omitted

   };

   } // Add this line
   ```

   Note that the closing brace that's added to the end of the file does NOT have a closing semi-colon. The nested namespace syntax **acpp::gfx**, is a new feature of C++17. Previously, it would have required the explicit use of the **namespace** keyword twice. Also, beware that, in trying to be helpful, your friendly neighborhood IDE may insert the closing brace just after the line that you put the namespace declaration.

3. Repeat the same treatment for **matrix3d.hpp**, **matrix3d.cpp**, and **point3d.cpp** – ensure that the include files are not included in the scope of the namespace.

4. In the respective files (**main.cpp, matrix3dTests.cpp**, and **point3dTests.cpp**), just after completing the #include directives, insert the following line:

   ```
   using namespace acpp::gfx;
   ```

5. Now, run all the tests. All **18** existing tests should pass again. We have successfully put our classes into a namespace.

6. Now we will move onto converting the `Matrix3d` class to use heap allocated memory. In the **matrix3d.hpp** file, add an **#include <memory>** line to give us access to the **unique_ptr<>** template.

7. Next, change the type of the declaration for **m_data**:

```
std::unique_ptr<float[]> m_data;
```

8. From this point forward, we will use the compiler and its errors to give us hints as to what needs fixing. Attempting to build the tests now reveals that we have a problem with the following two methods in the header file

```
float operator()(const int row, const int column) const
{
    return m_data[row][column];
}
float& operator()(const int row, const int column)
{
    return m_data[row][column];
}
```

The problem here is that **unique_ptr** holds a pointer to a single dimension array and not a two- dimensional array. So, we need to convert the row and column into a single index.

9. Add a new method called **get_index()** to get the one-dimensional index from the row and column and update the preceding functions to use it:

```
float operator()(const int row, const int column) const
{
    return m_data[get_index(row,column)];
}
float& operator()(const int row, const int column)
{
    return m_data[get_index(row,column)];
}
private:
size_t get_index(const int row, const int column) const
{
    return row * NumberColumns + column;
}
```

10. After recompiling, the next error from the compiler refers to the following inline function:

```
inline Matrix3d operator*(const Matrix3d& lhs, const Matrix3d& rhs)
{
    Matrix3d temp(lhs);    // <=== compiler error - ill formed copy
constructor
    temp *= rhs;
    return temp;
}
```

11. Whereas before, the default copy constructor was sufficient for our purposes, it just did a shallow copy of all the elements of the array and that was correct. We now have indirection to the data we need to copy and so we need to implement a deep copy constructor and copy assignment. We will also need to address the existing constructors. For now, just add the constructor declarations to the class (adjacent to the other constructors):

```
Matrix3d(const Matrix3d& rhs);
Matrix3d& operator=(const Matrix3d& rhs);
```

Attempting to build the tests will now show that we have resolved all the issues in the header file, and that we can move onto the implementation file.

12. Modify the two constructors to initialize **unique_ptr** as follows:

```
Matrix3d::Matrix3d() : m_data{new float[NumberRows*NumberColumns]}
{
    for (int i{0} ; i< NumberRows ; i++)
        for (int j{0} ; j< NumberColumns ; j++)
            m_data[i][j] = (i==j);
}

Matrix3d::Matrix3d(std::initializer_list<std::initializer_list<float>>
list)
        : m_data{new float[NumberRows*NumberColumns]}
{
    int i{0};
    for(auto it1 = list.begin(); i<NumberRows ; ++it1, ++i)
    {
        int j{0};
        for(auto it2 = it1->begin(); j<NumberColumns ; ++it2, ++j)
            m_data[i][j] = *it2;
    }
}
```

13. We now need to address the single-dimensional array look-up. We need to change the statements of the **m_data[i][j]** type with **m_data[get_index(i,j)]**. Change the default constructor to read like so:

```
Matrix3d::Matrix3d() : m_data{new float[NumberRows*NumberColumns]}
{
    for (int i{0} ; i< NumberRows ; i++)
        for (int j{0} ; j< NumberColumns ; j++)
            m_data[get_index(i, j)] = (i==j);          // <= change here
}
```

14. Change the initializer list constructor to be the following:

```
Matrix3d::Matrix3d(std::initializer_list<std::initializer_list<float>>
list)
        : m_data{new float[NumberRows*NumberColumns]}
{
    int i{0};
    for(auto it1 = list.begin(); i<NumberRows ; ++it1, ++i)
    {
        int j{0};
        for(auto it2 = it1->begin(); j<NumberColumns ; ++it2, ++j)
            m_data[get_index(i, j)] = *it2;          // <= change here
    }
}
```

15. Change the multiplication operator, being careful with the indices:

```
Matrix3d& Matrix3d::operator*=(const Matrix3d& rhs)
{
    Matrix3d temp;

    for(int i=0 ; i<NumberRows ; i++)
        for(int j=0 ; j<NumberColumns ; j++)
        {
            temp.m_data[get_index(i, j)] = 0;          // <= change here
            for (int k=0 ; k<NumberRows ; k++)
                temp.m_data[get_index(i, j)] += m_data[get_index(i, k)]
                                    * rhs.m_data[get_index(k, j)];
                                    // <= change here
        }
    *this = temp;
    return *this;
}
```

16. With these changes in place, we have fixed all the compiler errors, but now we have a linker error to deal with – the copy constructor that we only declared back in step 11.

17. In the **matrix3d.cpp** file add the following definitions:

```
Matrix3d::Matrix3d(const Matrix3d& rhs) :
    m_data{new float[NumberRows*NumberColumns]}
{
    *this = rhs;
}

Matrix3d& Matrix3d::operator=(const Matrix3d& rhs)
{
    for(int i=0 ; i< NumberRows*NumberColumns ; i++)
        m_data[i] = rhs.m_data[i];
    return *this;
}
```

18. The tests will now build and all of them will pass. The next step is to force a move constructor. Locate the **createTranslationMatrix()** method in **matrix3d.cpp** and change the return statement as follows:

```
return std::move(matrix);
```

19. In **matrix3d.hpp** declare the **move** constructor.

```
Matrix3d(Matrix3d&& rhs);
```

20. Rebuild the tests. Now, we get an error related to the move constructor not being present.

21. Add the implementation of the constructor into **matrix3d.cpp** and rebuild the tests.

```
Matrix3d::Matrix3d(Matrix3d&& rhs)
{
    //std::cerr << "Matrix3d::Matrix3d(Matrix3d&& rhs)\n";
    std::swap(m_data, rhs.m_data);
}
```

22. Rebuild and run the tests. They all pass again.

23. Just to confirm that the move constructor is being called, add **#include <iostream>** to **matrix3d.cpp**, remove the comment from the output line in the move constructor. and re-run the test. It will report an error after the tests have completed because we sent it to the standard error channel (**cerr**). After the check, make the line a comment again.

> **Note**
>
> Just a quick note about the move constructor – we did not explicitly initialize **m_data** like we did for the other constructors. This means that it will be initialized as empty and then swapped with the parameter that is passed in, which is a temporary and so it is acceptable for it to not hold an array after the transaction – it removes one allocation and deallocation of memory.

24. Now let's convert the **Point3d** class so that it can use heap allocated memory. In the **point3d.hpp** file, add an **#include <memory>** line so that we have access to the **unique_ptr<>** template.

25. Next, change the type of the declaration for **m_data** to be like so:

```
std::unique_ptr<float[]> m_data;
```

26. The compiler now tells us that we have a problem with the insertion operator (<<) in **point3d.hpp** because we can't use a ranged-for on **unique_ptr**: Replace the implementation with the following:

```
inline std::ostream&
operator<<(std::ostream& os, const Point3d& pt)
{
    const char* sep = "[ ";
    for(int i{0} ; i < Point3d::NumberRows ; i++)
    {
        os << sep << pt.m_data[i];
        sep = ", ";
    }
    os << " ]";
    return os;
}
```

27. Open **point3d.cpp** and modify the default constructors to initialize the `unique_ptr` and change the initialization loop since a ranged for cannot be used on the `unique_ptr`:

```
Point3d::Point3d() : m_data{new float[NumberRows]}
{
    for(int i{0} ; i < NumberRows-1 ; i++) {
        m_data[i] = 0;
    }
    m_data[NumberRows-1] = 1;
}
```

28. Modify the other constructor by initializing the `unique_ptr`:

```
Point3d::Point3d(std::initializer_list<float> list)
            : m_data{new float[NumberRows]}
```

29. Now all the tests run and pass, like they did previously.

30. Now, if we run the original application, **L3graphics**, then the output will be identical to the original, but the implementation uses RAII to allocate and manage the memory that's used for the matrices and points.

```
------ Activity 1 ------
The point [ 1, 1, 1, 1 ]
...rotated around X by 90 degrees
...rotated around Y by 90 degrees
...rotated around Z by 90 degrees
moves to [ 1, 1, -1, 1 ]
...scaled by x=2, y = 3, z = 4
moves to [ 2, 3, -4, 1 ]
...translated by dx=-2, dy = 1, dz = -3
moves to [ 0, 4, -7, 1 ]

Complete.
```

Figure 3.52: Activity 1 output after successful conversion to use RAII

# Activity 2: Implementing classes for Date Calculations

In this activity, we will implement two classes, **Date** and **Days** that will make it very easy for us to work with dates and the time differences between them. Let's get started:

1. Load the prepared project from the **Lesson3/Activity02** folder and configure the Current Builder for the project to be **CMake Build (Portable)**. Build and configure the launcher and run the unit tests. We recommend that the name that's used for the tests runner is **L3A2datetests**. The project has dummy files and one failing test.

2. Open the **date.hpp** file in the editor and add the following lines inside the basic **Date** class to allow access to the stored values:

```
int Day()   const {return m_day;}
int Month() const {return m_month;}
int Year()  const {return m_year;}
```

3. Open the **dateTests.cpp** file and add the following code to the **DateTest** class:

```
void VerifyDate(const Date& dt, int yearExp, int monthExp, int dayExp)
const
{
    ASSERT_EQ(dayExp, dt.Day());
    ASSERT_EQ(monthExp, dt.Month());
    ASSERT_EQ(yearExp, dt.Year());
}
```

Normally, you would refactor this test as the tests develop, but we will pull it out up front.

4. Replace **ASSERT_FALSE()** in the existing test with the following test:

```
Date dt;
VerifyDate(dt, 1970, 1, 1);
```

5. Rebuild and run the tests – they should now all pass.

6. Add the following test:

```
TEST_F(DateTest, Constructor1970Jan2)
{
    Date dt(2, 1, 1970);
    VerifyDate(dt, 1970, 1, 2);
}
```

7.  To make this test we need to add the following two constructors to the **Date** class:

```
Date() = default;
Date(int day, int month, int year) :
        m_year{year}, m_month{month}, m_day{day}
{
}
```

8.  We now need to introduce the functions to convert to/from the **date_t** type. Add the following alias to the **date.hpp** file inside our namespace:

```
using date_t=int64_t;
```

9.  To the **Date** class, add the declaration of the following method:

```
date_t ToDateT() const;
```

10. Then, add the following test:

```
TEST_F(DateTest, ToDateTDefaultIsZero)
{
    Date dt;
    ASSERT_EQ(0, dt.ToDateT());
}
```

11. As we are doing (**TDD**), we add the minimal implementation of the method to pass the test.

```
date_t Date::ToDateT() const
{
    return 0;
}
```

12. Now, we add the next test:

```
TEST_F(DateTest, ToDateT1970Jan2Is1)
{
    Date dt(2, 1, 1970);
    ASSERT_EQ(1, dt.ToDateT());
}
```

13. We continue to add one more test and then another, all the time refining the algorithm in **ToDateT()** firstly to deal with dates in **1970**, then **1-Jan-1971**, and then a date in **1973**, which means we span one leap year, and so on. The full set of tests that are used to develop the **ToDateT()** method are as follows:

```
TEST_F(DateTest, ToDateT1970Dec31Is364)
{
```

```
        Date dt(31, 12, 1970);
        ASSERT_EQ(364, dt.ToDateT());
    }
    TEST_F(DateTest, ToDateT1971Jan1Is365)
    {
        Date dt(1, 1, 1971);
        ASSERT_EQ(365, dt.ToDateT());
    }
    TEST_F(DateTest, ToDateT1973Jan1Is1096)
    {
        Date dt(1, 1, 1973);
        ASSERT_EQ(365*3+1, dt.ToDateT());
    }
    TEST_F(DateTest, ToDateT2019Aug28Is18136)
    {
        Date dt(28, 8, 2019);
        ASSERT_EQ(18136, dt.ToDateT());
    }
```

14. To pass all of these tests, we add the following items to the declaration of the **Date** class:

```
public:
    static constexpr int EpochYear = 1970;
    static constexpr int DaysPerCommonYear = 365;
    static constexpr int YearsBetweenLeapYears = 4;
private:
    int GetDayOfYear(int day, int month, int year) const;
    bool IsLeapYear(int year) const;
    int CalcNumberLeapYearsFromEpoch(int year) const;
```

15. The implementation of **ToDateT()** and the supporting methods in **date.cpp** is as follows:

```
namespace {
int daysBeforeMonth[2][12] =
{
    { 0, 31, 59, 90, 120, 151, 181, 212, 243, 273, 204, 334}, // Common
Year
    { 0, 31, 50, 91, 121, 152, 182, 213, 244, 274, 205, 335}  // Leap Year
};
}
namespace acpp::date
{
```

```
int Date::CalcNumberLeapYearsFromEpoch(int year) const
{
    return (year-1)/YearsBetweenLeapYears
                            - (EpochYear-1)/YearsBetweenLeapYears;

}
int Date::GetDayOfYear(int day, int month, int year) const
{
    return daysBeforeMonth[IsLeapYear(year)][month-1] + day;
}
bool Date::IsLeapYear(int year) const
{
    return (year%4)==0;   // Not full story, but good enough to 2100
}
date_t Date::ToDateT() const
{
    date_t value = GetDayOfYear(m_day, m_month, m_year) - 1;
    value += (m_year-EpochYear) * DaysPerCommonYear;
    date_t numberLeapYears = CalcNumberLeapYearsFromEpoch(m_year);
    value += numberLeapYears;
    return value;

}
}
```

16. Now that **ToDateT()** is working, we turn to its inverse, that is, **FromDateT()**. Again, we build up the tests one at a time to develop the algorithm over a range of dates. The following tests were used:

```
TEST_F(DateTest, FromDateT0Is1Jan1970)
{
    Date dt;
    dt.FromDateT(0);
    ASSERT_EQ(0, dt.ToDateT());
    VerifyDate(dt, 1970, 1, 1);
}
TEST_F(DateTest, FromDateT1Is2Jan1970)
{
    Date dt;
    dt.FromDateT(1);
    ASSERT_EQ(1, dt.ToDateT());
    VerifyDate(dt, 1970, 1, 2);
}
TEST_F(DateTest, FromDateT364Is31Dec1970)
{
```

```
        Date dt;
        dt.FromDateT(364);
        ASSERT_EQ(364, dt.ToDateT());
        VerifyDate(dt, 1970, 12, 31);
    }
    TEST_F(DateTest, FromDateT365Is1Jan1971)
    {
        Date dt;
        dt.FromDateT(365);
        ASSERT_EQ(365, dt.ToDateT());
        VerifyDate(dt, 1971, 1, 1);
    }
    TEST_F(DateTest, FromDateT1096Is1Jan1973)
    {
        Date dt;
        dt.FromDateT(1096);
        ASSERT_EQ(1096, dt.ToDateT());
        VerifyDate(dt, 1973, 1, 1);
    }
    TEST_F(DateTest, FromDateT18136Is28Aug2019)
    {
        Date dt;
        dt.FromDateT(18136);
        ASSERT_EQ(18136, dt.ToDateT());
        VerifyDate(dt, 2019, 8, 28);
    }
```

17. Add the following declarations to the header file:

```
public:
    void FromDateT(date_t date);
private:
    int CalcMonthDayOfYearIsIn(int dayOfYear, bool IsLeapYear) const;
```

18. Use the following implementation since the preceding tests are added one at a time:

```
void Date::FromDateT(date_t date)
{
    int number_years = date / DaysPerCommonYear;
    date = date - number_years * DaysPerCommonYear;
    m_year = EpochYear + number_years;
    date_t numberLeapYears = CalcNumberLeapYearsFromEpoch(m_year);
    date -= numberLeapYears;
```

```
        m_month = CalcMonthDayOfYearIsIn(date, IsLeapYear(m_year));
        date -= daysBeforeMonth[IsLeapYear(m_year)][m_month-1];
        m_day = date + 1;
    }
    int Date::CalcMonthDayOfYearIsIn(int dayOfYear, bool isLeapYear) const
    {
        for(int i = 1 ; i < 12; i++)
        {
        if ( daysBeforeMonth[isLeapYear][i] > dayOfYear)
                return i;
        }
        return 12;

    }
```

19. Now that we have the supporting routines ready, we can implement the real feature of the **Date** class difference between two dates and determine the new date by adding a number of days. Both of these operations need a new type (class) **Days**.

20. Add the following implementation of **Days** to the header (above **Date**):

```
    class Days
    {
    public:
        Days() = default;
        Days(int days) : m_days{days}      {    }
        operator int() const
        {
            return m_days;
        }

    private:
        int m_days{0};
    };
```

21. The first operator will be an addition of **Days** to **Date**. Add the following method declaration (inside the public section of the **Date** class) :

```
    Date& operator+=(const Days& day);
```

22. Then, add the inline implementation (outside the **Date** class) to the header file:

```
    inline Date operator+(const Date& lhs, const Days& rhs )
    {
        Date tmp(lhs);
```

```
        tmp += rhs;
        return tmp;
    }
```

23. Write the following tests to verify the **sum** operation:

```
TEST_F(DateTest, AddZeroDays)
{
    Date dt(28, 8, 2019);
    Days days;
    dt += days;
    VerifyDate(dt, 2019, 8, 28);
}
TEST_F(DateTest, AddFourDays)
{
    Date dt(28, 8, 2019);
    Days days(4);
    dt += days;
    VerifyDate(dt, 2019, 9, 1);
}
```

24. The actual implementation of the **sum** operation is simply based on the two support methods

```
Date& Date::operator+=(const Days& day)
{
    FromDateT(ToDateT()+day);
    return *this;
}
```

25. Add the following test:

```
TEST_F(DateTest, AddFourDaysAsInt)
{
    Date dt(28, 8, 2019);
    dt += 4;
    VerifyDate(dt, 2019, 9, 1);
}
```

26. When we run the tests, they all build and this test passes. But this is not the desired outcome. We do not want them to be able to add naked integers to our dates. (A future version may add months and years, so what does adding an integer mean?). To make this fail by causing the build to fail, we change the Days constructor to be **explicit**:

```
explicit Days(int days) : m_days{days}    {    }
```

27. Now the build fails, so we need to fix the test by changing the addition line to cast to **Days** as follows:

```
dt += static_cast<Days>(4);
```

All tests should pass again.

28. The final functionality we want is the difference between two dates. Here are the tests that were used to verify the implementation:

```
TEST_F(DateTest, DateDifferences27days)
{
    Date dt1(28, 8, 2019);
    Date dt2(1, 8, 2019);

    Days days = dt1 - dt2;
    ASSERT_EQ(27, (int)days);
}

TEST_F(DateTest, DateDifferences365days)
{
    Date dt1(28, 8, 2019);
    Date dt2(28, 8, 2018);

    Days days = dt1 - dt2;
    ASSERT_EQ(365, (int)days);
}
```

29. Add the following declaration of the function to the public section of the **Date** class in the header file:

```
Days operator-(const Date& rhs) const;
```

30. Add the following code after the Date class in the header file:

```
inline Days Date::operator-(const Date& rhs) const
{
    return Days(ToDateT() - rhs.ToDateT());
}
```

Because we made the **Days** constructor explicit, we must call it in the return statement. With all these changes in place, all the tests should pass.

31. Configure **L3A2date** as a **datetools** binary and open main.cpp in the editor. Remove the comment from the definition of **ACTIVITY2**:

    #define ACTIVITY2

32. Build and then run the sample application. This will produce the following output:

```
------ Activity 2 ------
There are 358 days between 1-Jan-2019 and 25-Dec-2019
There are 0.980172 years between 1-Jan-2019 and 25-Dec-2019

There are 364 days between 1-Jan-2019 and 31-Dec-2019
There are 0.996599 years between 1-Jan-2019 and 31-Dec-2019

There are 18255 days between 1-Jan-1970 and 25-Dec-2019
There are 49.9805 years between 1-Jan-1970 and 25-Dec-2019

There are 36525 days between 1-Jan-1970 and 1-Jan-2070
There are 100.002 years between 1-Jan-1970 and 1-Jan-2070

Complete.
```

Figure 3.53: Output of successful Date sample application

We have implemented all of the requirements of the Date and Days classes and delivered them all with unit tests. The unit tests allowed us to implement incremental functionality to build up the two complicated algorithms, **ToDateT** and **FromDateT** which form the underlying support for the functionality that we wanted to deliver.

# Chapter 4 - Separation of Concerns - Software Architecture, Functions, Variadic Templates

## Activity 1: Implement a multicast event handler

1. Load the prepared project from the **Lesson4/Activity01** folder and configure the Current Builder for the project to be CMake Build (Portable). Build the project, configure the launcher and run the unit tests (which fail the one dummy test). Recommend that the name used for the tests runner is *L4delegateTests*.

2. In **delegateTests.cpp**, replace the failing dummy test with the following test:

```
TEST_F(DelegateTest, BasicDelegate)
{
    Delegate delegate;

    ASSERT_NO_THROW(delegate.Notify(42));
}
```

3. This now fails to build, so we need to add a new method to **Delegate**. As this will evolve into a template, we will do all of this development in the header file. In **delegate.hpp**, and the following definition:

```
class Delegate
{
public:
    Delegate() = default;

    void Notify(int value) const
    {

    }
};
```

The test now runs and passes.

4. Add the following line to the existing test:

```
ASSERT_NO_THROW(delegate(22));
```

5. Again, the build fails, so we update the **Delegate** definition as follows (we could have had Notify call **operator()**, but this is easier to read):

```
void operator()(int value)
{
    Notify(value);
}
```

The test again runs and passes.

6. Before we add the next test, we are going to add some infrastructure to help us develop our tests. The easiest thing to do with handlers is have them write to **std::cout**, and to be able to verify that they were called, we need to capture the output. To do this, re-route the standard output stream to a different buffer by changing the **DelegateTest** class as follows:

```
class DelegateTest : public ::testing::Test
{
public:
    void SetUp() override;
    void TearDown() override;

    std::stringstream m_buffer;

    // Save cout's buffer here
    std::streambuf *m_savedBuf{};
};

void DelegateTest::SetUp()
{
    // Save the cout buffer
    m_savedBuf = std::cout.rdbuf();
    // Redirect cout to our buffer
    std::cout.rdbuf(m_buffer.rdbuf());
}

void DelegateTest::TearDown()
{
    // Restore cout buffer to original
    std::cout.rdbuf(m_savedBuf);
}
```

7. Also add the include statements for **<iostream>**, **<sstream>** and **<string>** to the top of the file.

8. With this support framework in place, add the following test:

```
TEST_F(DelegateTest, SingleCallback)
{
    Delegate delegate;

    delegate += [] (int value) { std::cout << "value = " << value; };
    delegate.Notify(42);
    std::string result = m_buffer.str();
    ASSERT_STREQ("value = 42", result.c_str());
}
```

9. To make the tests build and run again, add the following code in the **delegate.h** class:

```
Delegate& operator+=(const std::function<void(int)>& delegate)
{
    m_delegate = delegate;
    return *this;
}
```

Along with the following code:

```
private:
        std::function<void(int)> m_delegate;
```

The tests now build, but our new test fails.

10. Update the **Notify()** method to be:

```
void Notify(int value) const
{
    m_delegate(value);
}
```

11. The tests now build and our new test passes, but the original test now fails. The call to the delegate is throwing an exception, so we need to check that the delegate is not empty before calling it. Write the following code to do this:

```
void Notify(int value) const
{
    if(m_delegate)
        m_delegate(value);
}
```

All the tests now run and pass.

12. We now need to add multicast support to the **Delegate** class. Add the new test:

```
TEST_F(DelegateTest, DualCallbacks)
{
    Delegate delegate;

    delegate += [] (int value) { std::cout << "1: = " << value << "\n"; };
    delegate += [] (int value) { std::cout << "2: = " << value << "\n"; };
    delegate.Notify(12);
    std::string result = m_buffer.str();
    ASSERT_STREQ("1: = 12\n2: = 12\n", result.c_str());
}
```

13. Of course, this test now fails because the **operator+=()** only assigns to the member variable. We need to add a list to store our delegates. We choose vector so we can add to the end of the list as we want to call the delegates in the order that they are added. Add **#include <vector>** to the top of **delegate.hpp** and update Delegate replace **m_delegate** with **m_delegates** vector of the callbacks:

```
class Delegate
{
public:
    Delegate() = default;

    Delegate& operator+=(const std::function<void(int)>& delegate)
    {
        m_delegates.push_back(delegate);
        return *this;
    }

    void Notify(int value) const
    {
        for(auto& delegate : m_delegates)
        {
            delegate(value);
        }
    }

    void operator()(int value)
    {
        Notify(value);
    }
private:
```

```
        std::vector<std::function<void(int)>> m_delegates;
    };
```

The tests all run and pass again.

14. We now have the basic multicast **delegate** class implemented. We now need to convert it to a template- based class. Update the existing tests, by changing all of the declarations of **Delegate** to **Delegate<int>** in the three tests.

15. Now update the Delegate class by adding **template<class Arg>** before the class to convert it to a template, and substituting the four occurrences of **int** with **Arg**:

```
template<class Arg>
class Delegate
{
public:
    Delegate() = default;

    Delegate& operator+=(const std::function<void(Arg)>& delegate)
    {
        m_delegates.push_back(delegate);
        return *this;
    }

    void Notify(Arg value) const
    {
        for(auto& delegate : m_delegates)
        {
            delegate(value);
        }
    }

    void operator()(Arg value)
    {
        Notify(value);
    }
private:
    std::vector<std::function<void(Arg)>> m_delegates;
};
```

16. All the tests now run and pass as previously, so it stills works for **int** arguments for the handlers.

17. Add the following test and re-run the tests to confirm that the template conversion is correct:

```
TEST_F(DelegateTest, DualCallbacksString)
{
    Delegate<std::string&> delegate;

    delegate += [] (std::string value) { std::cout << "1: = " << value <<
"\n"; };
    delegate += [] (std::string value) { std::cout << "2: = " << value <<
"\n"; };
    std::string hi{"hi"};
    delegate.Notify(hi);
    std::string result = m_buffer.str();
    ASSERT_STREQ("1: = hi\n2: = hi\n", result.c_str());
}
```

18. Now it operates as a template that takes one argument. We need to convert it into a variadic template that takes zero or more arguments. Using the information from the last topic, update the template to the following:

```
template<typename... ArgTypes>
class Delegate
{
public:
    Delegate() = default;

    Delegate& operator+=(const std::function<void(ArgTypes...)>& delegate)
    {
        m_delegates.push_back(delegate);
        return *this;
    }

    void Notify(ArgTypes&&... args) const
    {
        for(auto& delegate : m_delegates)
        {
            delegate(std::forward<ArgTypes>(args)...);
        }
    }

    void operator()(ArgTypes&&... args)
    {
```

```cpp
            Notify(std::forward<ArgTypes>(args)...);
    }
    private:
        std::vector<std::function<void(ArgTypes...)>> m_delegates;
};
```

The tests should still run and pass.

19. Add two more tests – zero argument test, and a mutliple argument test:

```cpp
    TEST_F(DelegateTest, DualCallbacksNoArgs)
    {
        Delegate delegate;

        delegate += [] () { std::cout << "CB1\n"; };
        delegate += [] () { std::cout << "CB2\n"; };
        delegate.Notify();
        std::string result = m_buffer.str();
        ASSERT_STREQ("CB1\nCB2\n", result.c_str());
    }


    TEST_F(DelegateTest, DualCallbacksStringAndInt)
    {
        Delegate<std::string&, int> delegate;

        delegate += [] (std::string& value, int i) {
                std::cout << "1: = " << value << "," << i << "\n"; };
        delegate += [] (std::string& value, int i) {
            std::cout << "2: = " << value << "," << i << "\n"; };
        std::string hi{"hi"};
        delegate.Notify(hi, 52);
        std::string result = m_buffer.str();
        ASSERT_STREQ("1: = hi,52\n2: = hi,52\n", result.c_str());
    }
```

All the tests run and pass showing that we have now implemented the desired **Delegate** class.

20. Now, change the Run configuration to execute the program **L4delegate**. Open the **main.cpp** file in the editor and change the definition at the top of the file to the following and run the program:

```
#define ACTIVITY_STEP 27
```

We get the following output:

```
------ Activity 1 ------

------ Delegate - no args ------
Hello, World
------ Delegate - string argument ------
hello!-hello?-hello@-
------ Delegate - binary int argument ------
52 + 4 = 56
52 - 4 = 48
52 * 4 = 208
52 / 4 = 13

Complete.
```

Figure 4.35: Output from the successful implementation of Delegate

In this activity, we started by implementing a class that provides the basic single delegate functionality and then added multicast capability. With that implemented, and unit tests in place, we were quickly able to convert to a template with one argument and then to a variadic template version. Depending on the functionality that you are developing, the approach of the specific implementation transitioning to a general form and then to an even more general form is the correct one. Development of variadic templates is not always obvious.

# Chapter 5 - The Philosophers' Dinner – Threads and Concurrency

## Activity 1: Creating a Simulator to Model the Work of the Art Gallery

The Art Gallery work simulator is an application that simulates how the visitors and the watchman behave. There is a quantity limit for visitors, that is, only 50 people can be inside the gallery simultaneously. Visitors constantly come to the gallery. The watchman checks if the limit of visitors has been exceeded. If so, it asks new visitors to wait and puts them on a waiting list. If not, it allows them to enter the gallery. Visitors can leave the gallery at any time. If somebody leaves the gallery, the watchman lets somebody from the waiting list enter the gallery.

Follow these steps to implement this activity:

1. Create a file that will contain all the constants that we need for this project – **Common.hpp**.

2. Add the include guards and the first variable, **CountPeopleInside**, which represents that the limit for visitors is 50 people:

```
#ifndef COMMON_HPP
#define COMMON_HPP
constexpr size_t CountPeopleInside = 5;
#endif // COMMON_HPP
```

3. Now, create a header and the source files for the **Person** class, that is, **Person.hpp** and **Person.cpp**. Also, add the include guards. Define the **Person** class and delete the copy constructor and copy assignment operator; we will only use the user-defined default constructor, move constructor, and move assignment operator and default destructor. Add a private variable called **m_Id**; we will use it for logging. Also, add a private static variable called **m_NextId**; it will be used for generating unique IDs:

```
#ifndef PERSON_HPP
#define PERSON_HPP

class Person
{
public:
    Person();
    Person& operator=(Person&);
    Person(Person&&);
    ~Person() = default;

    Person(const Person&) = delete;
```

```
    Person& operator=(const Person&) = delete;

private:
    int m_Id;
    static int m_NextId;
};
```

```
#endif // PERSON_HPP
```

4. In the source file, define our static variable, **m_NextId**. Then, in the constructor, initialize the **m_Id** variable with the value of **m_NextId**. Print the log in the constructor. Implement the move copy constructor and the move assignment operator. Now, implement thread-safe storage for our **Person** objects. Create the required header and source files, that is, **Persons.hpp** and **Persons.cpp**. Also, add the include guards. Include "**Person.hpp**" and the **<mutex>** and **<vector>** headers. Define the **Persons** class with a user-defined default constructor and default destructor. Declare the **add()** function for adding the Person and **get()** for getting the Person and removing it from the list. Define the **size()** function to get the count of Person elements, as well as **removePerson()**, which removes any person from the storage. In the private section, declare a variable of the mutex type, namely **m_Mutex**, and the vector to store Persons, namely **m_Persons**:

```
#ifndef PERSONS_HPP
#define PERSONS_HPP

#include "Person.hpp"
#include <mutex>
#include <vector>

class Persons
{
public:
    Persons();
    ~Persons() = default;

    void add(Person&& person);
    Person get();

    size_t size() const;
    void removePerson();

private:
    std::mutex m_Mutex;
```

```
    std::vector<Person> m_Persons;
};
```

```
#endif // PERSONS_HPP
```

5. In the source file, declare the user-defined constructor where we reserve the size of the vector to be 50 elements (to avoid resizing during growth):

```
Persons::Persons()
{
    m_Persons.reserve(CountPeopleInside);
}
```

6. Declare the **add()** function, which takes an rvalue parameter of the **Person** type, locks the mutex, and adds **Person** to the vector using the **std::move()** function:

```
void Persons::add(Person&& person)
{
    std::lock_guard<std::mutex> m_lock(m_Mutex);
    m_Persons.emplace_back(std::move(person));
}
```

7. Declare the **get()** function, which locks the mutex and returns the last element and then removes it from the vector. If the vector is empty, it will throw an exception:

```
Person Persons::get()
{
    std::lock_guard<std::mutex> m_lock(m_Mutex);
    if (m_Persons.empty())
    {
        throw "Empty Persons storage";
    }

    Person result = std::move(m_Persons.back());
    m_Persons.pop_back();
    return result;
}
```

8. Declare the **size()** function, which returns the size of the vector:

```
size_t Persons::size() const
{
    return m_Persons.size();
}
```

9. Finally, declare the **removePerson()** function, which locks the mutex and removes the last item from the vector:

```
void Persons::removePerson()
{
    std::lock_guard<std::mutex> m_lock(m_Mutex);
    m_Persons.pop_back();
    std::cout << "Persons | removePerson | removed" << std::endl;
}
```

10. Now, implement the PersonGenerator class, which is responsible for creating and removing Person items. Create the respective header and source files, that is, **PersonGenerator.hpp** and **PersonGenerator.cpp**. Also, add the include guards. Include the "**Person.hpp**", **<thread>**, and **<condition_variable>** headers. Define the **PersonGenerator** class. In the private section, define two **std::thread** variables, namely **m_CreateThread** and **m_RemoveThread**. In one thread, we will create new **Person** objects and will notify the user about removing **Person** objects in the other thread asynchronously. Define a reference to a shared variable of the **Persons** type, namely **m_CreatedPersons**. We will place every new person in it. **m_CreatedPersons** will be shared between several threads. Define two references to **std::condition_variable**, namely **m_CondVarAddPerson** and **m_CondVarRemovePerson**. They will be used for communication between threads. Define two references to the **std::mutex** variables, namely **m_AddLock** and **m_RemoveLock**. They will be used for receiving access to condition variables. Finally, define two references to a **bool** value, namely **m_AddNotified** and **m_RemoveNotified**. They will be used for checking whether the notification is true or false. Also, in the private section, define two functions that will be start functions for our threads – **runCreating()** and **runRemoving()**. Next, define two functions that will trigger condition variables, namely **notifyCreated()** and **notifyRemoved()**. In the public section, define a constructor that takes all the references that we defined in the private section as a parameter. Finally, define a destructor. This will ensure that the other default generated functions are deleted:

```
#ifndef PERSON_GENERATOR_HPP
#define PERSON_GENERATOR_HPP

#include "Persons.hpp"
#include <condition_variable>
#include <thread>

class PersonGenerator
{
public:
    PersonGenerator(Persons& persons,
```

```cpp
        std::condition_variable& add_person,
        std::condition_variable& remove_person,
        std::mutex& add_lock,
        std::mutex& remove_lock,
        bool& addNotified,
        bool& removeNotified);

    ~PersonGenerator();

    PersonGenerator(const PersonGenerator&) = delete;
    PersonGenerator(PersonGenerator&&) = delete;
    PersonGenerator& operator=(const PersonGenerator&) = delete;
    PersonGenerator& operator=(PersonGenerator&&) = delete;

private:
    void runCreating();
    void runRemoving();

    void notifyCreated();
    void notifyRemoved();

private:
    std::thread m_CreateThread;
    std::thread m_RemoveThread;

    Persons& m_CreatedPersons;

    // to notify about creating new person
    std::condition_variable& m_CondVarAddPerson;
    std::mutex& m_AddLock;
    bool& m_AddNotified;

    // to notify that person needs to be removed
    std::condition_variable& m_CondVarRemovePerson;
    std::mutex& m_RemoveLock;
    bool& m_RemoveNotified;
};

#endif // PERSON_GENERATOR_HPP
```

11. Now, move on to the source file. Include the **<stdlib.h>** file so that we can access the **srand()** and **rand()** functions, which are used for random number generation. Include the **<time.h>** header so that we can access the **time()** function, as well as the **std::chrono** namespace. They are used for when we work with time. Include the **<ratio>** file, which used for typedefs so that we can work with the time library:

```cpp
#include "PersonGenerator.hpp"
#include <iostream>
#include <stdlib.h>      /* srand, rand */
#include <time.h>        /* time, chrono */
#include <ratio>         /* std::milli */
```

12. Declare the constructor and initialize all the parameters except the threads in the initializer list. Initialize the threads with the appropriate functions in the constructor body:

```cpp
PersonGenerator::PersonGenerator(Persons& persons,
                    std::condition_variable& add_person,
                    std::condition_variable& remove_person,
                    std::mutex& add_lock,
                    std::mutex& remove_lock,
                    bool& addNotified,
                    bool& removeNotified)
    : m_CreatedPersons(persons)
    , m_CondVarAddPerson(add_person)
    , m_AddLock(add_lock)
    , m_AddNotified(addNotified)
    , m_CondVarRemovePerson(remove_person)
    , m_RemoveLock(remove_lock)
    , m_RemoveNotified(removeNotified)
{
    m_CreateThread = std::thread(&PersonGenerator::runCreating, this);
    m_RemoveThread = std::thread(&PersonGenerator::runRemoving, this);
}
```

13. Declare a destructor and check if the threads are joinable. Join them if not:

```cpp
PersonGenerator::~PersonGenerator()
{
    if (m_CreateThread.joinable())
    {
        m_CreateThread.join();
    }
    if (m_RemoveThread.joinable())
```

```
    {
        m_RemoveThread.join();
    }
}
```

14. Declare the **runCreating()** function, which is the start function for the **m_CreateTh-read** thread. In this function, in an infinite loop, we will generate a random number from 1 to 10 and make the current thread sleep for this time. After this, create a Person value, add it to the shared container, and notify other threads about it:

```
void PersonGenerator::runCreating()
{
    using namespace std::chrono_literals;
    srand (time(NULL));
    while(true)
    {
        std::chrono::duration<int, std::milli> duration((rand() % 10 +
1)*1000);
        std::this_thread::sleep_for(duration);
        std::cout << "PersonGenerator | runCreating | new person:" <<
std::endl;
        m_CreatedPersons.add(std::move(Person()));
        notifyCreated();
    }
}
```

15. Declare the **runRemoving()** function, which is the start function for the **m_RemoveTh-read** thread. In this function, in an infinite loop, we will generate a random number from 20 to 30 and make the current thread sleep for this time. After this, notify the other threads that some of the visitors should be removed:

```
void PersonGenerator::runRemoving()
{
    using namespace std::chrono_literals;
    srand (time(NULL));
    while(true)
    {
        std::chrono::duration<int, std::milli> duration((rand() % 10 +
20)*1000);
        std::this_thread::sleep_for(duration);
        std::cout << "PersonGenerator | runRemoving | somebody has left
the gallery:" << std::endl;
```

```
        notifyRemoved();
    }
}
```

16. Declare the **notifyCreated()** and **notifyRemoved()** functions. In their bodies, lock the appropriate mutex, set the appropriate bool variable to true, and call the **notify_all()** functions on the appropriate condition variables:

```
void PersonGenerator::notifyCreated()
{
    std::unique_lock<std::mutex> lock(m_AddLock);
    m_AddNotified = true;
    m_CondVarAddPerson.notify_all();
}
void PersonGenerator::notifyRemoved()
{
    std::unique_lock<std::mutex> lock(m_RemoveLock);
    m_RemoveNotified = true;
    m_CondVarRemovePerson.notify_all();
}
```

17. Finally, we need to create the files for our last class, Watchman, namely **Watchman.hpp** and **Watchman.cpp**. As usual, add the include guards. Include the "**Persons.hpp**", **<thread>**, **<mutex>**, and **<condition_variable>** headers. Define the **Watchman** class. In the private section, define two **std::thread** variables, namely **m_ThreadAdd** and **m_ThreadRemove**. In one of the threads, we will move new **Person** objects to the appropriate queue and will remove **Person** objects in the other thread asynchronously. Define the references to the shared **Persons** variables, namely **m_CreatedPeople**, **m_PeopleInside**, and **m_PeopleInQueue**. We will take every new person from the **m_CreatedPeople** list and move them to the **m_PeopleInside** list if the limit is not exceeded. We will move them to the **m_PeopleInQueue** list otherwise. They will be shared between several threads. Define two references to **std::condition_variable**, namely **m_CondVarAddPerson** and **m_CondVarRemovePerson**. They will be used for communication between threads. Define two references to the **std::mutex** variables, namely **m_AddMux** and **m_RemoveMux**. They will be used for receiving access to condition variables. Finally, define two references to a **bool** value, namely **m_AddNotified** and **m_RemoveNotified**. They will be used for checking if the notification is true or false. Also, in the private section, define two functions that will be start functions for our threads – **runAdd()** and **runRemove()**. In the public section, define a constructor that takes all the references that we defined in the private section as parameters. Now, define a destructor. Make sure that all the other default generated functions are deleted:

```cpp
#ifndef WATCHMAN_HPP
#define WATCHMAN_HPP
#include <mutex>
#include <thread>
#include <condition_variable>
#include "Persons.hpp"
class Watchman
{
public:
    Watchman(std::condition_variable&,
             std::condition_variable&,
             std::mutex&,
             std::mutex&,
             bool&,
             bool&,
             Persons&,
             Persons&,
             Persons&);
    ~Watchman();
    Watchman(const Watchman&) = delete;
    Watchman(Watchman&&) = delete;
    Watchman& operator=(const Watchman&) = delete;
    Watchman& operator=(Watchman&&) = delete;
private:
    void runAdd();
    void runRemove();
private:
    std::thread m_ThreadAdd;
    std::thread m_ThreadRemove;
    std::condition_variable& m_CondVarRemovePerson;
    std::condition_variable& m_CondVarAddPerson;
    std::mutex& m_AddMux;
    std::mutex& m_RemoveMux;
    bool& m_AddNotified;
    bool& m_RemoveNotified;
    Persons& m_PeopleInside;
    Persons& m_PeopleInQueue;
    Persons& m_CreatedPeople;
};
#endif // WATCHMAN_HPP
```

18. Now, move on to the source file. Include the "`Common.hpp`" header so that we can access the `m_CountPeopleInside` variable and the other necessary headers:

```
#include "Watchman.hpp"
#include "Common.hpp"
#include <iostream>
```

19. Declare the constructor and initialize all the parameters except for the threads in the initializer list. Initialize the threads with the appropriate functions in the constructor's body:

```
Watchman::Watchman(std::condition_variable& addPerson,
            std::condition_variable& removePerson,
            std::mutex& addMux,
            std::mutex& removeMux,
            bool& addNotified,
            bool& removeNotified,
            Persons& peopleInside,
            Persons& peopleInQueue,
            Persons& createdPeople)
    : m_CondVarRemovePerson(removePerson)
    , m_CondVarAddPerson(addPerson)
    , m_AddMux(addMux)
    , m_RemoveMux(removeMux)
    , m_AddNotified(addNotified)
    , m_RemoveNotified(removeNotified)
    , m_PeopleInside(peopleInside)
    , m_PeopleInQueue(peopleInQueue)
    , m_CreatedPeople(createdPeople)
{
    m_ThreadAdd = std::thread(&Watchman::runAdd, this);
    m_ThreadRemove = std::thread(&Watchman::runRemove, this);
}
```

20. Declare a destructor and check if the threads are joinable. Join them if not:

```
Watchman::~Watchman()
{
    if (m_ThreadAdd.joinable())
    {
        m_ThreadAdd.join();
    }
    if (m_ThreadRemove.joinable())
    {
```

```
        m_ThreadRemove.join();
    }
}
```

21. Declare the **runAdd()** function. Here, we create an infinite loop. In the loop, we are waiting for a condition variable. When the condition variable notifies, we take people from the **m_CreatedPeople** list and move them to the appropriate list, that is, **m_PeopleInside**, or **m_PeopleInQueue** if the limit has been exceeded. Then, we check if there are any people in the **m_PeopleInQueue** list and if **m_PeopleInside** is not full, we move them into this list:

```cpp
void Watchman::runAdd()
{
    while (true)
    {
        std::unique_lock<std::mutex> locker(m_AddMux);
        while(!m_AddNotified)
        {
            std::cerr << "Watchman | runAdd | false awakening" <<
std::endl;
            m_CondVarAddPerson.wait(locker);
        }
        std::cout << "Watchman | runAdd | new person came" << std::endl;
        m_AddNotified = false;
        while (m_CreatedPeople.size() > 0)
        {
            try
            {
                auto person = m_CreatedPeople.get();
                if (m_PeopleInside.size() < CountPeopleInside)
                {
                    std::cout << "Watchman | runAdd | welcome in our The
Art Gallery" << std::endl;
                    m_PeopleInside.add(std::move(person));
                }
                else
                {
                    std::cout << "Watchman | runAdd | Sorry, we are full.
Please wait" << std::endl;
                    m_PeopleInQueue.add(std::move(person));
                }
            }
            catch(const std::string& e)
```

```
                    {
                         std::cout << e << std::endl;
                    }
              }
           std::cout << "Watchman | runAdd | check people in queue" <<
     std::endl;
           if (m_PeopleInQueue.size() > 0)
           {
              while (m_PeopleInside.size() < CountPeopleInside)
              {
                  try
                  {
                      auto person = m_PeopleInQueue.get();
                      std::cout << "Watchman | runAdd | welcome in our The
     Art Gallery" << std::endl;
                      m_PeopleInside.add(std::move(person));
                  }
                  catch(const std::string& e)
                  {
                      std::cout << e << std::endl;
                  }
              }
           }
        }
     }
```

22. Next, declare the **runRemove()** function, where we will remove visitors from **m_PeopleInside**. Here, also in the infinite loop, we are waiting for the **m_CondVarRemovePerson** condition variable. When it notifies the thread, we remove people from the list of visitors. Next, we will check if there's anybody in the **m_PeopleInQueue** list and if the limit is not exceeded, we add them to **m_PeopleInside**:

```
void Watchman::runRemove()
{
    while (true)
    {
        std::unique_lock<std::mutex> locker(m_RemoveMux);
        while(!m_RemoveNotified)
        {
            std::cerr << "Watchman | runRemove | false awakening" <<
    std::endl;
            m_CondVarRemovePerson.wait(locker);
        }
```

```
        m_RemoveNotified = false;
        if (m_PeopleInside.size() > 0)
        {
            m_PeopleInside.removePerson();
            std::cout << "Watchman | runRemove | good buy" << std::endl;
        }
        else
        {
            std::cout << "Watchman | runRemove | there is nobody in The
Art Gallery" << std::endl;
        }
        std::cout << "Watchman | runRemove | check people in queue" <<
std::endl;
        if (m_PeopleInQueue.size() > 0)
        {
            while (m_PeopleInside.size() < CountPeopleInside)
            {
                try
                {
                    auto person = m_PeopleInQueue.get();
                    std::cout << "Watchman | runRemove | welcome in our
The Art Gallery" << std::endl;
                    m_PeopleInside.add(std::move(person));
                }
                catch(const std::string& e)
                {
                    std::cout << e << std::endl;
                }
            }
        }
    }
}
```

23. Finally, move to the **main()** function. First, create all the shared variables that we used in the **Watchman** and **PersonGenerator** classes. Next, create the **Watchman** and **PersonGenerator** variables and pass those shared variables to the constructors. At the end of the main function read the character to avoid closing the application:

```
int main()
{
    {
        std::condition_variable g_CondVarRemovePerson;
        std::condition_variable g_CondVarAddPerson;
```

```cpp
        std::mutex g_AddMux;
        std::mutex g_RemoveMux;
        bool g_AddNotified = false;;
        bool g_RemoveNotified = false;
        Persons g_PeopleInside;
        Persons g_PeopleInQueue;
        Persons g_CreatedPersons;
        PersonGenerator generator(g_CreatedPersons, g_CondVarAddPerson,
g_CondVarRemovePerson,
                    g_AddMux, g_RemoveMux, g_AddNotified, g_
RemoveNotified);
        Watchman watchman(g_CondVarAddPerson,
                g_CondVarRemovePerson,
                g_AddMux,
                g_RemoveMux,
                g_AddNotified,
                g_RemoveNotified,
                g_PeopleInside,
                g_PeopleInQueue,
                g_CreatedPersons);
    }

    char a;
    std::cin >> a;
    return 0;
}
```

24. Compile and run the application. In the terminal, you will see logs from different threads about creating and moving people from one list to another. Your output will be similar to the following screenshot:

```
//============================================================================
// Name        : Simulator.cpp
// Author      : Olena Lizina
// Description : The Art Gallery work simulator
//============================================================================

#include <iostream>
#include <condition_variable>

#include "Persons.hpp"
#include "Watchman.hpp"
#include "PersonGenerator.hpp"

int main()
{
    {
```

```
Console  Problems  Executables
<terminated> (exit value: -1) Simulator Debug [C/C++ Application] C:\Users\elena\Desktop\Chapter5\Activity\Simulator\
Watchman | runAdd | welcome in our The Art Gallery
Watchman | runAdd | check people in queue
Watchman | runAdd | false awakening
PersonGenerator | runCreating | new person:
Person | Person | Hello! I'm 6
Watchman | runAdd | new person came
Watchman | runAdd | Sorry, we are full. Please wait
Watchman | runAdd | check people in queue
Watchman | runAdd | false awakening
PersonGenerator | runRemoving | somebody has left the gallery:
Persons | removePerson | removed
Watchman | runRemove | good buy
Watchman | runRemove | check people in queue
Watchman | runRemove | welcome in our The Art Gallery
Watchman | runRemove | false awakening
PersonGenerator | runCreating | new person:
Person | Person | Hello! I'm 7
Watchman | runAdd | new person came
Watchman | runAdd | Sorry, we are full. Please wait
Watchman | runAdd | check people in queue
Watchman | runAdd | false awakening
```

**Figure 5.27: The result of the application's execution**

As you can see, all the threads communicate with each other in a very easy and clean way. We protected our shared data by using mutexes so that we can avoid race conditions. Here, we used an exception to warn about the empty lists and caught them in the thread's functions so that our threads handle exceptions on their own. We also checked if the thread is joinable before joining it in the destructor. This allowed us to avoid the unexpected termination of the program. Thus, this small project demonstrates our skills when it comes to working with threads.

# Chapter 6 – Streams and I/O

## Activity 1 The Logging System for The Art Gallery Simulator

The thread-safe logger allows us to output data to the Terminal simultaneously. We implement this logger by inheriting from the **std::ostringstream** class and using a mutex for synchronization. We will implement a class that provides an interface for the formatted output and our logger will use it to extend the basic output. We define macro definitions for different logging levels to provide an interface that will be easy and clear to use. Follow these steps to complete this activity:

1. Open the project from Lesson6.

2. Create a new directory called logger inside the **src/** directory. You will get the following hierarchy:

| | |
|---|---|
| logger | 15.09.2019 0:39 |
| Common | 31.08.2019 13:29 |
| Person | 15.09.2019 0:35 |
| Person | 31.08.2019 14:15 |
| PersonGenerator | 15.09.2019 0:35 |
| PersonGenerator | 31.08.2019 15:44 |
| Persons | 15.09.2019 0:34 |
| Persons | 31.08.2019 14:30 |
| Simulator | 15.09.2019 0:35 |
| Watchman | 15.09.2019 0:34 |
| Watchman | 31.08.2019 15:43 |

Figure 6.25: The hierarchy of the project

3. Create a header and source file called **LoggerUtils**. In **LoggerUtils.hpp**, add include guards. Include the <string> header to add support for working with strings. Define a namespace called logger and then define a nesting namespace called **utils**. In the **utils** namespace, declare the **LoggerUtils** class.

4. In the public section, declare the following static functions: **getDateTime**, **getThreadId**, **getLoggingLevel**, **getFileAndLine**, **getFuncName**, **getInFuncName**, and **getOutFuncName**. Your class should look as follows:

```
#ifndef LOGGERUTILS_HPP_
#define LOGGERUTILS_HPP_

#include <string>
```

```
namespace logger
{
namespace utils
{
class LoggerUtils
{
public:
    static std::string getDateTime();
    static std::string getThreadId();
    static std::string getLoggingLevel(const std::string& level);
    static std::string getFileAndLine(const std::string& file, const int&
line);
    static std::string getFuncName(const std::string& func);
    static std::string getInFuncName(const std::string& func);
    static std::string getOutFuncName(const std::string& func);
};
} // namespace utils
} // namespace logger

#endif /* LOGGERUTILS_HPP_ */
```

5. In **LoggerUtils.cpp**, add the required includes: the "**LoggerUtils.hpp**" header, **<sstream>** for **std::stringstream** support, and **<ctime>** for date and time support:

```
#include "LoggerUtils.hpp"
#include <sstream>
#include <ctime>
#include <thread>
```

6. Enter the **logger** and **utils** namespaces. Write the required function definitions. In the **getDateTime()** function, get the local time using the **localtime()** function. Format it into a string using the **strftime()** function. Convert it into the desired format using **std::stringstream**:

```
std::string LoggerUtils::getDateTime()
{
    time_t rawtime;
    struct tm * timeinfo;
    char buffer[80];

    time (&rawtime);
    timeinfo = localtime(&rawtime);
```

```
        strftime(buffer,sizeof(buffer),"%d-%m-%YT%H:%M:%S",timeinfo);
        std::stringstream ss;
        ss << "[";
        ss << buffer;
        ss << "]";
        return ss.str();
    }
```

7. In the **getThreadId()** function, get the current thread ID and convert it into the desired format using **std::stringstream**:

```
    std::string LoggerUtils::getThreadId()
    {
        std::stringstream ss;
        ss << "[";
        ss << std::this_thread::get_id();
        ss << "]";
        return ss.str();
    }
```

8. In the **getLoggingLevel()** function, convert the given string into the desired format using **std::stringstream**:

```
    std::string LoggerUtils::getLoggingLevel(const std::string& level)
    {
        std::stringstream ss;
        ss << "[";
        ss << level;
        ss << "]";
        return ss.str();
    }
```

9. In the **getFileAndLine()** function, convert the given file and line into the desired format using **std::stringstream**:

```
    std::string LoggerUtils::getFileAndLine(const std::string& file, const int&
    line)
    {
        std::stringstream ss;
        ss << " ";
        ss << file;
        ss << ":";
```

```
        ss << line;
        ss << ":";
        return ss.str();

    }
```

10. In the **getFuncName()** function, convert the function name into the desired format using **std::stringstream**:

```
std::string LoggerUtils::getFuncName(const std::string& func)
{
    std::stringstream ss;
    ss << " --- ";
    ss << func;
    ss << "()";
    return ss.str();

}
```

11. In the **getInFuncName()** function convert the function name to the desired format using **std::stringstream**.

```
std::string LoggerUtils::getInFuncName(const std::string& func)
{
    std::stringstream ss;
    ss << " --> ";
    ss << func;
    ss << "()";
    return ss.str();

}
```

12. In the **getOutFuncName()** function, convert the function name into the desired format using **std::stringstream**:

```
std::string LoggerUtils::getOutFuncName(const std::string& func)
{
    std::stringstream ss;
    ss << " <-- ";
    ss << func;
    ss << "()";
    return ss.str();

}
```

13. Create a header file called **LoggerMacroses.hpp**. Add include guards. Create macro definitions for each **LoggerUtils** function: **DATETIME** for the **getDateTime()** function, **THREAD_ID** for the **getThreadId()** function, **LOG_LEVEL** for the **getLoggingLevel()** function, **FILE_LINE** for the **getFileAndLine()** function, **FUNC_NAME** for the **getFunc-Name()** function, **FUNC_ENTRY_NAME** for the **getInFuncName()** function, and **FUNC_EXIT_NAME** for the **getOutFuncName()** function. As a result, the header file should look as follows:

```
#ifndef LOGGERMACROSES_HPP_
#define LOGGERMACROSES_HPP_
#define DATETIME \
    logger::utils::LoggerUtils::getDateTime()
#define THREAD_ID \
    logger::utils::LoggerUtils::getThreadId()
#define LOG_LEVEL( level ) \
    logger::utils::LoggerUtils::getLoggingLevel(level)
#define FILE_LINE \
    logger::utils::LoggerUtils::getFileAndLine(__FILE__, __LINE__)
#define FUNC_NAME \
    logger::utils::LoggerUtils::getFuncName(__FUNCTION__)
#define FUNC_ENTRY_NAME \
    logger::utils::LoggerUtils::getInFuncName(__FUNCTION__)
#define FUNC_EXIT_NAME \
    logger::utils::LoggerUtils::getOutFuncName(__FUNCTION__)
#endif /* LOGGERMACROSES_HPP_ */
```

14. Create a header and source file called **StreamLogger**. In **StreamLogger.hpp**, add the required include guards. Include the **LoggerMacroses.hpp** and **LoggerUtils.hpp** header files. Then, include the **<sstream>** header for **std::ostringstream** support, the **<thread>** header for **std::thread** support, and the **<mutex>** header for **std::mu-tex** support:

```
#include "LoggerMacroses.hpp"
#include "LoggerUtils.hpp"
#include <sstream>
#include <thread>
#include <mutex>
```

15. Enter the **namespace** logger. Declare the **StreamLogger** class, which inherits from the **std::ostringstream** class. This inheritance allows us to use an overloaded left shift operator, <<, for logging. We don't set the output device, so the output will not be performed – just stored in the internal buffer. In the private section, declare a static **std::mutex** variable called **m_mux**. Declare constant strings so that you can store the logging level, file and line, and function name. In the public section, declare a constructor that takes the logging level, file and line, and function name as parameters. Declare a class destructor. The class declaration should look like as follows:

```
namespace logger
{
class StreamLogger : public std::ostringstream
{
public:
    StreamLogger(const std::string logLevel,
                 const std::string fileLine,
                 const std::string funcName);
    ~StreamLogger();
private:
    static std::mutex m_mux;
    const std::string m_logLevel;
    const std::string m_fileLine;
    const std::string m_funcName;
};
} // namespace logger
```

16. In **StreamLogger.cpp**, include the **StreamLogger.hpp** and **<iostream>** headers for **std::cout** support. Enter the **logger** namespace. Define the constructor and initialize all the members in the initializer list. Then, define the destructor and enter its scope. Lock the **m_mux** mutex. If the internal buffer is empty, output only the date and time, thread ID, logging level, file and line, and the function name. As a result, we will get the line in the following format: **[dateTtime][threadId] [logLevel][file:line: ][name() --- ]**. If the internal buffer contains any data, output the same string with the buffer at the end. As a result, we will get the line in the following format: **[dateTtime][threadId][logLevel][file:line: ][name() --- ] | message**. The complete source file should look as follows:

```
#include "StreamLogger.hpp"
#include <iostream>

std::mutex logger::StreamLogger::m_mux;
```

```
namespace logger
{
StreamLogger::StreamLogger(const std::string logLevel,
                const std::string fileLine,
                const std::string funcName)
        : m_logLevel(logLevel)
        , m_fileLine(fileLine)
        , m_funcName(funcName)
{}


StreamLogger::~StreamLogger()
{
    std::lock_guard<std::mutex> lock(m_mux);
    if (this->str().empty())
    {
        std::cout << DATETIME << THREAD_ID << m_logLevel << m_fileLine <<
m_funcName << std::endl;
    }
    else
    {
        std::cout << DATETIME << THREAD_ID << m_logLevel << m_fileLine <<
m_funcName << " | " << this->str() << std::endl;
    }
}
}
```

17. Create a header file called **Logger.hpp** and add the required include guards. Include the **StreamLogger.hpp** and **LoggerMacroses.hpp** headers. Next, create the macro definitions for the different logging levels: **LOG_TRACE()**, **LOG_DEBUG()**, **LOG_WARN()**, **LOG_TRACE()**, **LOG_INFO()**, **LOG_ERROR()**, **LOG_TRACE_ENTRY()**, and **LOG_TRACE_EXIT()**. The complete header file should look as follows:

```
#ifndef LOGGER_HPP_
#define LOGGER_HPP_

#include "StreamLogger.hpp"
#include "LoggerMacroses.hpp"

#define LOG_TRACE() logger::StreamLogger{LOG_LEVEL("Trace"), FILE_LINE,
FUNC_NAME}
#define LOG_DEBUG() logger::StreamLogger{LOG_LEVEL("Debug"), FILE_LINE,
FUNC_NAME}
#define LOG_WARN() logger::StreamLogger{LOG_LEVEL("Warning"), FILE_LINE,
```

```
FUNC_NAME}
#define LOG_TRACE() logger::StreamLogger{LOG_LEVEL("Trace"), FILE_LINE,
FUNC_NAME}
#define LOG_INFO() logger::StreamLogger{LOG_LEVEL("Info"), FILE_LINE, FUNC_
NAME}
#define LOG_ERROR() logger::StreamLogger{LOG_LEVEL("Error"), FILE_LINE,
FUNC_NAME}
#define LOG_TRACE_ENTRY() logger::StreamLogger{LOG_LEVEL("Error"), FILE_
LINE, FUNC_ENTRY_NAME}
#define LOG_TRACE_EXIT() logger::StreamLogger{LOG_LEVEL("Error"), FILE_
LINE, FUNC_EXIT_NAME}

#endif /* LOGGER_HPP_ */
```

18. Replace all the **std::cout** calls with the appropriate macro definition call. Include the **logger/Logger.hpp** header in the **Watchman.cpp** source file. In the **runAdd()** function, replace all instances of **std::cout** with macro definitions for different logging levels. The **runAdd()** function should look as follows:

```
void Watchman::runAdd()
{
    while (true)
    {
        std::unique_lock<std::mutex> locker(m_AddMux);
        while(!m_AddNotified)
        {
            LOG_DEBUG() << "Spurious awakening";
            m_CondVarAddPerson.wait(locker);
        }

        LOG_INFO() << "New person came";
        m_AddNotified = false;
        while (m_CreatedPeople.size() > 0)
        {
            try
            {
                auto person = m_CreatedPeople.get();
                if (m_PeopleInside.size() < CountPeopleInside)
                {
                    LOG_INFO() << "Welcome in the our Art Gallery";
                    m_PeopleInside.add(std::move(person));
                }
                else
```

```
                    {
                            LOG_INFO() << "Sorry, we are full. Please wait";
                            m_PeopleInQueue.add(std::move(person));
                    }
            }
            catch(const std::string& e)
            {
                    LOG_ERROR() << e;
            }
        }

        LOG_TRACE() << "Check people in queue";
        if (m_PeopleInQueue.size() > 0)
        {
            while (m_PeopleInside.size() < CountPeopleInside)
            {
                    try
                    {
                            auto person = m_PeopleInQueue.get();
                            LOG_INFO() << "Welcome in the our Art Gallery";
                            m_PeopleInside.add(std::move(person));
                    }
                    catch(const std::string& e)
                    {
                            LOG_ERROR() << e;
                    }
            }
        }
    }
}
```

19. Notice how we use our new logger. We invoke the macro definition with parentheses and use the left shift operator:

```
LOG_ERROR() << e;
Or
LOG_INFO() << "Welcome in the our Art Gallery";
```

20. Do the same replacement for the rest of code.

21. Build and run the application. In the Terminal, you will see that log messages appear from the different threads with different logging levels and with useful information. After some time has passed, you will get some output similar to the following:

```
 Problems   Tasks   Console   Properties   Include Browser
Simulator Debug [C/C++ Application] C:\Users\elena\Desktop\Chapter6\Activity\Simulator\Debug\Simulator.exe (15.09.19, 11:31)
[15-09-2019T11:31:13][0x6000743e0][Trace] ../src/PersonGenerator.cpp:41: --> runCreating()
[15-09-2019T11:31:13][0x6000744e0][Trace] ../src/PersonGenerator.cpp:57: --> runRemoving()
[15-09-2019T11:31:13][0x600078f10][Debug] ../src/Watchman.cpp:48: --- runAdd() | Spurious awakening
[15-09-2019T11:31:13][0x600079150][Warning] ../src/Watchman.cpp:103: --- runRemove() | Spurious awakening
[15-09-2019T11:31:23][0x6000743e0][Info] ../src/PersonGenerator.cpp:48: --- runCreating() | New person:
[15-09-2019T11:31:23][0x6000743e0][Trace] ../src/Person.cpp:10: --- Person() | Hello! I'm 0
[15-09-2019T11:31:23][0x6000743e0][Debug] ../src/Persons.cpp:15: --- add() | Count of persons: 1
[15-09-2019T11:31:23][0x600078f10][Info] ../src/Watchman.cpp:52: --- runAdd() | New person came
[15-09-2019T11:31:23][0x600078f10][Info] ../src/Watchman.cpp:61: --- runAdd() | Welcome in the our Art Gallery
[15-09-2019T11:31:23][0x600078f10][Debug] ../src/Persons.cpp:15: --- add() | Count of persons: 1
[15-09-2019T11:31:23][0x600078f10][Trace] ../src/Watchman.cpp:76: --- runAdd() | Check people in queue
[15-09-2019T11:31:23][0x600078f10][Debug] ../src/Watchman.cpp:48: --- runAdd() | Spurious awakening
[15-09-2019T11:31:32][0x6000743e0][Info] ../src/PersonGenerator.cpp:48: --- runCreating() | New person:
[15-09-2019T11:31:32][0x6000743e0][Trace] ../src/Person.cpp:10: --- Person() | Hello! I'm 1
[15-09-2019T11:31:32][0x6000743e0][Debug] ../src/Persons.cpp:15: --- add() | Count of persons: 1
[15-09-2019T11:31:32][0x600078f10][Info] ../src/Watchman.cpp:52: --- runAdd() | New person came
[15-09-2019T11:31:32][0x600078f10][Info] ../src/Watchman.cpp:61: --- runAdd() | Welcome in the our Art Gallery
[15-09-2019T11:31:32][0x600078f10][Debug] ../src/Persons.cpp:15: --- add() | Count of persons: 2
[15-09-2019T11:31:32][0x600078f10][Trace] ../src/Watchman.cpp:76: --- runAdd() | Check people in queue
[15-09-2019T11:31:32][0x600078f10][Debug] ../src/Watchman.cpp:48: --- runAdd() | Spurious awakening
```

**Figure 6.26: The execution result of the activity project**

As you can see, it's really easy to read and understand logs. You can easily change the **StreamLogger** class to write logs to the file on the filesystem if your needs differ. You can add any other information that you may need to debug your application using logs, such as output function parameters. You can also override the left shift operator for your custom types to output debug information easily.

In this project, we employed many things that we have learned about during this chapter. We created an additional stream for thread-safe output, we formatted the output to the desired representation, we employed **std::stringstream** to perform formatting data, and we used macro definitions for convenient logger usage. Thus, this project demonstrates our skills in working with concurrent I/O.

# Chapter 7 - Everybody Falls, It's How You Get Back Up – Testing and Debugging

## Activity 1: Checking the Accuracy of the Functions Using Test Cases and Understanding Test-Driven Development (TDD)

For this activity, we'll develop the functions to parse the **RecordFile.txt** and **CurrencyConversion.txt** files and write test cases to check the accuracy of the functions. Follow these steps to implement this activity:

1. Create a configuration file named **parse.conf** and write the configurations.

2. Note that only two variables are of interest here, that is, `currencyFile` and `recordFile`. The rest are meant for other environment variables:

```
CONFIGURATION_FILE
currencyFile = ./CurrencyConversion.txt
recordFile = ./RecordFile.txt
DatabaseServer = 192.123.41.112
UserId = sqluser
Password = sqluser
RestApiServer = 101.21.231.11
LogFilePath = /var/project/logs
```

3. Create a header file named `CommonHeader.h` and declare all the utility functions, that is, `isAllNumbers()`, `isDigit()`, `parseLine()`, `checkFile()`, `parseConfig()`, `parseCurrencyParameters()`, `fillCurrencyMap()`, `parseRecordFile()`, `checkRecord()`, `displayCurrencyMap()`, and `displayRecords()`.

```cpp
#ifndef __COMMON_HEADER__H
#define __COMMON_HEADER__H
#include<iostream>
#include<cstring>
#include<fstream>
#include<vector>
#include<string>
#include<map>
#include<sstream>
#include<iterator>
#include<algorithm>
#include<iomanip>

using namespace std;
```

```cpp
// Forward declaration of global variables.
extern string configFile;
extern string recordFile;
extern string currencyFile;
extern map<string, float> currencyMap;
struct record;
extern vector<record>      vecRecord;

//Structure to hold Record Data .
struct record{
    int     customerId;
    string  firstName;
    string  lastName;
    int     orderId;
    int     productId;
    int     quantity;
    float   totalPriceRegional;
    string  currency;
    float   totalPriceUsd;

    record(vector<string> & in){
        customerId      = atoi(in[0].c_str());
        firstName       = in[1];
        lastName        = in[2];
        orderId         = atoi(in[3].c_str());
        productId       = atoi(in[4].c_str());
        quantity        = atoi(in[5].c_str());
        totalPriceRegional = static_cast<float>(atof(in[6].c_str()));
        currency        = in[7];
        totalPriceUsd   = static_cast<float>(atof(in[8].c_str()));
    }
};


// Declaration of Utility Functions..
string trim (string &);
bool isAllNumbers(const string &);
bool isDigit(const string &);
void parseLine(ifstream &, vector<string> &, char);
bool checkFile(ifstream &, string &, string, char, string &);
bool parseConfig();
bool parseCurrencyParameters( vector<string> &);
```

```
bool fillCurrencyMap();
bool parseRecordFile();
bool checkRecord(vector<string> &);
void displayCurrencyMap();
ostream& operator<<(ostream &, const record &);
void displayRecords();
#endif
```

4. Create a file named **Util.cpp** and define all the utility functions. Write the following code to define the **trim()** function:

```cpp
#include<CommonHeader.h>


// Utility function to remove spaces and tabs from start of string and end
of string..
string trim (string &str) { // remove space and tab from string.
    string res("");
    if ((str.find(' ') != string::npos) || (str.find(' ') != string::npos)){
// if space or tab found..
        size_t begin, end;
        if ((begin = str.find_first_not_of(" \t")) != string::npos){ // if
string is not empty..
            end = str.find_last_not_of(" \t");
            if ( end >= begin )
                res = str.substr(begin, end - begin + 1);
        }
    }else{
        res = str; // No space or tab found..
    }
    str = res;
    return res;
}
```

5. Write the following code to define the **isAllNumbers()**, **isDigit()**, and **parseLine()** functions:

```cpp
// Utility function to check if string contains only digits ( 0-9) and
only single '.'
// eg . 1121.23 , .113, 121. are valid, but 231.14.143 is not valid.
bool isAllNumbers(const string &str){ // make sure, it only contains digit
and only single '.' if any
    return ( all_of(str.begin(), str.end(), [](char c) { return (
isdigit(c) || (c == '.')); })
            && (count(str.begin(), str.end(), '.') <= 1) );
```

```
}

//Utility function to check if string contains only digits (0-9)..
bool isDigit(const string &str){
    return ( all_of(str.begin(), str.end(), [](char c) { return
isdigit(c); }));
}

// Utility function, where single line of file <infile> is parsed using
delimiter.
// And store the tokens in vector of string.
void parseLine(ifstream &infile, vector<string> & vec, char delimiter){
    string line, token;

    getline(infile, line);
    istringstream ss(line);
    vec.clear();
    while(getline(ss, token, delimiter)) // break line using delimiter
        vec.push_back(token);   // store tokens in vector of string
}
```

6. Write the following code to define the **parseCurrencyParameters()** and **check-Record()** functions:

```
// Utility function to check if vector string of 2 strings contain correct
// currency and conversion ratio. currency should be 3 characters,
conversion ratio
// should be in decimal number format.
bool parseCurrencyParameters( vector<string> & vec){
    trim(vec[0]);   trim(vec[1]);
    return ( (!vec[0].empty()) && (vec[0].size() == 3) && (!vec[1].
empty()) && (isAllNumbers(vec[1])) );
}

// Utility function, to check if vector of string has correct format for
records parsed from Record File.
// CustomerId, OrderId, ProductId, Quantity should be in integer format
// TotalPrice Regional and USD should be in decimal number format
// Currecny should be present in map.
bool checkRecord(vector<string> &split){
    // Trim all string in vector
    for (auto &s : split)
        trim(s);
```

```
    if ( !(isDigit(split[0]) && isDigit(split[3]) && isDigit(split[4]) &&
isDigit(split[5])) ){
        cerr << "ERROR: Record with customer id:" << split[0] << " doesnt
have right DIGIT parameter" << endl;
        return false;
    }

    if ( !(isAllNumbers(split[6]) && isAllNumbers(split[8])) ){
        cerr << "ERROR: Record with customer id:" << split[0] << " doesnt
have right NUMBER parameter" << endl;
        return false;
    }

    if ( currencyMap.find(split[7]) == currencyMap.end() ){
        cerr << "ERROR: Record with customer id :" << split[0] << " has
currency :" << split[7] << " not present in map" << endl;
        return false;
    }

    return true;
}
```

7. Write the following code to define the **checkFile()** function:

```
// Function to test initial conditions of file..
// Check if file is present and has correct header information.
bool checkFile(ifstream &inFile, string &fileName, string parameter, char
delimiter, string &error){
    bool flag = true;
    inFile.open(fileName);
    if ( inFile.fail() ){
        error = "Failed opening " + fileName + " file, with error: " +
strerror(errno);
        flag = false;
    }
    if (flag){
        vector<string> split;
        // Parse first line as header and make sure it contains parameter
as first token.
        parseLine(inFile, split, delimiter);
        if (split.empty()){
            error = fileName + " is empty";
```

```
                    flag = false;
                } else if ( split[0].find(parameter) == string::npos ){
                    error = "In " + fileName + " file, first line doesnt contain
header ";
                    flag = false;
                }
            }
        return flag;
    }
}
```

8. Write the following code to define **parseConfig()** function:

```
// Function to parse Config file. Each line will have '<name> = <value>
format
// Store CurrencyConversion file and Record File parameters correctly.
bool parseConfig() {
    ifstream coffle;
    string error;
    if (!checkFile(confFile, configFile, "CONFIGURATION_FILE", '=', error))
{
        cerr << "ERROR: " << error << endl;
        return false;
    }

    bool flag = true;
    vector<string> split;
    while (confFile.good()){
        parseLine(confFile, split, '=');
        if ( split.size() == 2 ){
            string name = trim(split[0]);
            string value = trim(split[1]);

            if ( name == "currencyFile" )
                currencyFile = value;
            else if ( name == "recordFile")
                recordFile = value;
        }
    }

    if ( currencyFile.empty() || recordFile.empty() ){
        cerr << "ERROR : currencyfile or recordfile not set correctly." <<
endl;
        flag = false;
```

```
        }

        return flag;
    }
```

9.  Write the following code to define the **fillCurrencyMap()** function:

```
// Function to parse CurrencyConversion file and store values in Map.
bool fillCurrencyMap() {
    ifstream currFile;
    string error;
    if (!checkFile(currFile, currencyFile, "Currency", '|', error)){
        cerr << "ERROR: " << error << endl;
        return false;
    }

    bool flag = true;
    vector<string> split;
    while (currFile.good()){
        parseLine(currFile, split, '|');

        if (split.size() == 2){
            if (parseCurrencyParameters(split)){
                currencyMap[split[0]] = static_cast<float>(atof(split[1].c_
str())); // make sure currency is valid.
            } else {
                cerr << "ERROR: Processing Currency Conversion file for
Currency: "<< split[0] << endl;
                flag = false;
                break;
            }
        } else if (!split.empty()){
            cerr << "ERROR: Processing Currency Conversion , got incorrect
parameters for Currency: " << split[0] << endl;
            flag = false;
            break;
        }
    }

    return flag;
}
```

10. Write the following code to define the **parseRecordFile()** function:

```
// Function to parse Record File ..
bool parseRecordFile(){
    ifstream recFile;
    string error;
    if (!checkFile(recFile, recordFile, "Customer Id", '|', error)){
        cerr << "ERROR: " << error << endl;
        return false;
    }

    bool flag = true;
    vector<string> split;
    while(recFile.good()){
        parseLine(recFile, split, '|');
        if (split.size() == 9){
            if (checkRecord(split)){
                vecRecord.push_back(split); //Construct struct record and
save it in vector...
            }else{
                cerr << "ERROR : Parsing Record, for Customer Id: " <<
split[0] << endl;
                flag = false;
                break;
            }
        } else if (!split.empty()){
            cerr << "ERROR: Processing Record, for Customer Id: " <<
split[0] << endl;
            flag = false;
            break;
        }
    }

    return flag;
}
```

11. Write the following code to define the **displayCurrencyMap()** function:

```
void displayCurrencyMap(){

    cout << "Currency MAP :" << endl;
    for (auto p : currencyMap)
        cout << p.first <<"  :  " << p.second << endl;
```

```
        cout << endl;
    }

    ostream& operator<<(ostream& os, const record &rec){
        os << rec.customerId <<"|" << rec.firstName << "|" << rec.lastName <<
    "|"
            << rec.orderId << "|" << rec.productId << "|" << rec.quantity <<
    "|"
            << fixed << setprecision(2) << rec.totalPriceRegional << "|" << rec.
    currency << "|"
            << fixed << setprecision(2) << rec.totalPriceUsd << endl;
        return os;
    }
```

12. Write the following code to define the **displayRecords()** function:

```
    void displayRecords(){
        cout << " Displaying records with '|' delimiter" << endl;
        for (auto rec : vecRecord){
            cout << rec;
        }
        cout << endl;
    }
```

13. Create a file named **ParseFiles.cpp** and call the **parseConfig()**, **fillCurrencyMap()**, and **parseRecordFile()** functions:

```
    #include <CommonHeader.h>
    // Global variables ...
    string configFile = "./parse.conf";
    string recordFile;
    string currencyFile;
    map<string, float>  currencyMap;
    vector<record>      vecRecord;
    int main(){
        // Read Config file to set global configuration variables.
        if (!parseConfig()){
            cerr << "Error parsing Config File " << endl;
            return false;
        }
        // Read Currency file and fill map
        if (!fillCurrencyMap()){
            cerr << "Error setting CurrencyConversion Map " << endl;
            return false;
```

```
    }
    if (!parseRecordFile()){
        cerr << "Error parsing Records File " << endl;
        return false;
    }
        displayCurrencyMap();
    displayRecords();
    return 0;
}
```

14. Open the compiler. Compile and execute the **Util.cpp** and **ParseFiles.cpp** files by writing the following command:

```
g++ -c -g -I. -Wall Util.cpp
g++ -g -I. -Wall Util.o ParseFiles.cpp -o ParseFiles
```

The binary files for both will be generated.

In the following screenshot, you will see that both commands are stored in the build.sh script and executed. After running this script, you will see that the latest **Util.o** and **ParseFiles** files have been generated:

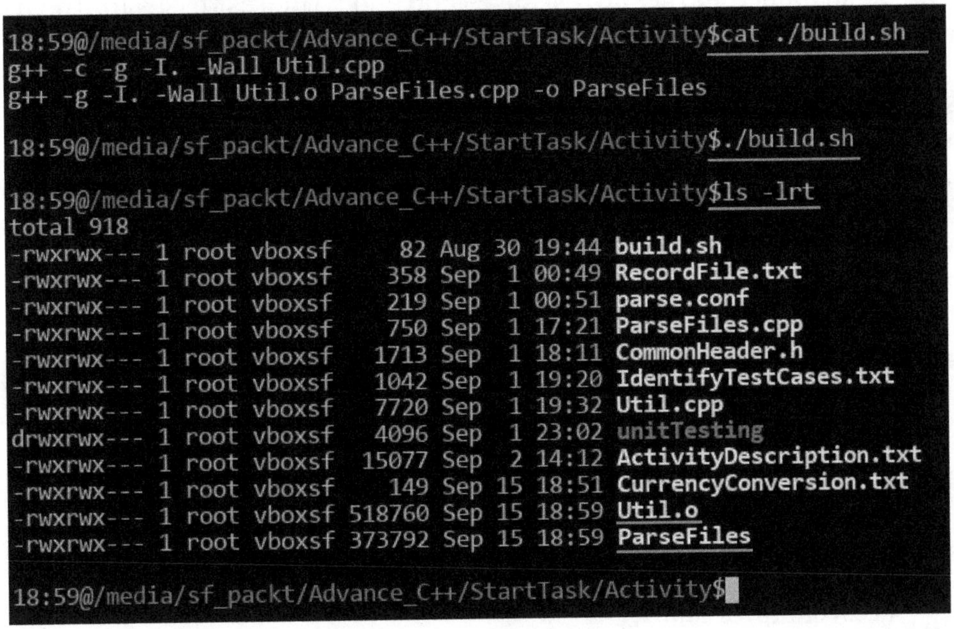

Figure 7.25: New files generated

15. After running the **ParseFiles** executable, we'll receive the following output:

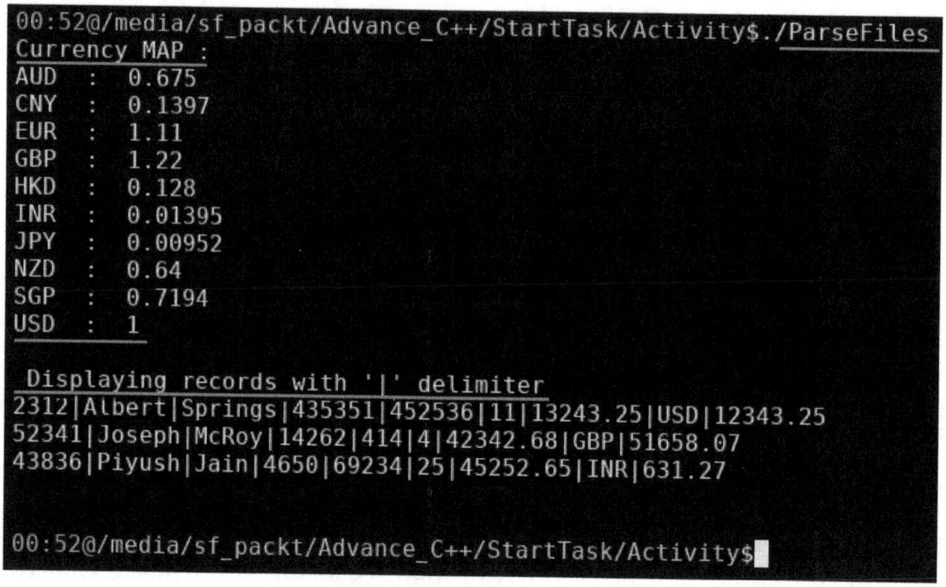

```
00:52@/media/sf_packt/Advance_C++/StartTask/Activity$./ParseFiles
Currency MAP :
AUD   :   0.675
CNY   :   0.1397
EUR   :   1.11
GBP   :   1.22
HKD   :   0.128
INR   :   0.01395
JPY   :   0.00952
NZD   :   0.64
SGP   :   0.7194
USD   :   1

 Displaying records with '|' delimiter
2312|Albert|Springs|435351|452536|11|13243.25|USD|12343.25
52341|Joseph|McRoy|14262|414|4|42342.68|GBP|51658.07
43836|Piyush|Jain|4650|69234|25|45252.65|INR|631.27

00:52@/media/sf_packt/Advance_C++/StartTask/Activity$
```

Figure 7.26: New files generated

16. Create a file named **ParseFileTestCases.cpp** and write test cases for the utility functions. Write the following test cases for the **trim** function:

```cpp
#include<gtest/gtest.h>
#include"../CommonHeader.h"

using namespace std;

// Global variables ...
string configFile = "./parse.conf";
string recordFile;
string currencyFile;
map<string, float>  currencyMap;
vector<record>      vecRecord;

void setDefault(){
    configFile = "./parse.conf";
    recordFile.clear();
    currencyFile.clear();
    currencyMap.clear();
    vecRecord.clear();
}
```

```
// Test Cases for trim function ...
TEST(trim, empty){
    string str="     ";
    EXPECT_EQ(trim(str), string());
}


TEST(trim, start_space){
    string str = "    adas";
    EXPECT_EQ(trim(str), string("adas"));
}


TEST(trim, end_space){
    string str = "trip       ";
    EXPECT_EQ(trim(str), string("trip"));
}


TEST(trim, string_middle){
    string str = "  hdgf   ";
    EXPECT_EQ(trim(str), string("hdgf"));
}


TEST(trim, single_char_start){
    string str = "c  ";
    EXPECT_EQ(trim(str), string("c"));
}


TEST(trim, single_char_end){
    string str = "   c";
    EXPECT_EQ(trim(str), string("c"));
}


TEST(trim, single_char_middle){
    string str = "     c  ";
    EXPECT_EQ(trim(str), string("c"));
}
```

17. Write the following test cases for the **isAllNumbers** function:

```
// Test Cases for isAllNumbers function..
TEST(isNumber, alphabets_present){
    string str = "11.qwe13";
    ASSERT_FALSE(isAllNumbers(str));
}
```

```
TEST(isNumber, special_character_present){
    string str = "34.^%3";
    ASSERT_FALSE(isAllNumbers(str));
}
TEST(isNumber, correct_number){
    string str = "54.765";
    ASSERT_TRUE(isAllNumbers(str));
}
TEST(isNumber, decimal_begin){
    string str = ".624";
    ASSERT_TRUE(isAllNumbers(str));
}
TEST(isNumber, decimal_end){
    string str = "53.";
    ASSERT_TRUE(isAllNumbers(str));
}
```

18. Write the following test cases for the **isDigit** function:

```
// Test Cases for isDigit funtion...
TEST(isDigit, alphabet_present){
    string str = "527A";
    ASSERT_FALSE(isDigit(str));
}

TEST(isDigit, decimal_present){
    string str = "21.55";
    ASSERT_FALSE(isDigit(str));
}

TEST(isDigit, correct_digit){
    string str = "9769";
    ASSERT_TRUE(isDigit(str));
}
```

19. Write the following test cases for the **parseCurrencyParameters** function:

```
// Test Cases for parseCurrencyParameters function
TEST(CurrencyParameters, extra_currency_chararcters){
    vector<string> vec {"ASAA","34.22"};
    ASSERT_FALSE(parseCurrencyParameters(vec));
}
```

```
TEST(CurrencyParameters, correct_parameters){
    vector<string> vec {"INR","1.44"};
    ASSERT_TRUE(parseCurrencyParameters(vec));
}
```

20. Write the following test cases for the **checkFile** function:

```
//Test Cases for checkFile function...
TEST(checkFile, no_file_present){
    string fileName = "./NoFile";
    ifstream infile;
    string parameter("nothing");
    char delimit =';';
    string err;
    ASSERT_FALSE(checkFile(infile, fileName, parameter, delimit, err));
}
TEST(checkFile, empty_file){
    string fileName = "./emptyFile";
    ifstream infile;
    string parameter("nothing");
    char delimit =';';
    string err;
    ASSERT_FALSE(checkFile(infile, fileName, parameter, delimit, err));
}
TEST(checkFile, no_header){
    string fileName = "./noHeaderFile";
    ifstream infile;
    string parameter("header");
    char delimit ='|';
    string err;
    ASSERT_FALSE(checkFile(infile, fileName, parameter, delimit, err));
}
TEST(checkFile, incorrect_header){
    string fileName = "./correctHeaderFile";
    ifstream infile;
    string parameter("header");
    char delimit ='|';
    string err;
    ASSERT_FALSE(checkFile(infile, fileName, parameter, delimit, err));
}
TEST(checkFile, correct_file){
    string fileName = "./correctHeaderFile";
    ifstream infile;
```

```
        string parameter("Currency");
        char delimit ='|';
        string err;
        ASSERT_TRUE(checkFile(infile, fileName, parameter, delimit, err));
    }
```

> **Note**
>
> The **NoFile, emptyFile, noHeaderFile**, and **correctHeaderFile** files that were
> used as input parameters in the preceding functions can be found here: https://
> github.com/TrainingByPackt/Advanced-CPlusPlus/tree/master/Lesson7/Activity01.

21. Write the following test cases for the **parseConfig** function:

```
    //Test Cases for parseConfig function...
    TEST(parseConfig, missing_currency_file){
        setDefault();
        configFile = "./parseMissingCurrency.conf";
        ASSERT_FALSE(parseConfig());
    }

    TEST(parseConfig, missing_record_file){
        setDefault();
        configFile = "./parseMissingRecord.conf";
        ASSERT_FALSE(parseConfig());
    }

    TEST(parseConfig, correct_config_file){
        setDefault();
        configFile = "./parse.conf";
        ASSERT_TRUE(parseConfig());
    }
```

> **Note**
>
> The **parseMissingCurrency.conf, parseMissingRecord.conf**, and **parse.
> conf** files that were used as input parameters in the preceding functions can be
> found here: https://github.com/TrainingByPackt/Advanced-CPlusPlus/tree/master/
> Lesson7/Activity01.

22. Write the following test cases for the **fillCurrencyMap** function:

```
//Test Cases for fillCurrencyMap function...
TEST(fillCurrencyMap, wrong_delimiter){
    currencyFile = "./CurrencyWrongDelimiter.txt";
    ASSERT_FALSE(fillCurrencyMap());
}

TEST(fillCurrencyMap, extra_column){
    currencyFile = "./CurrencyExtraColumn.txt";
    ASSERT_FALSE(fillCurrencyMap());
}

TEST(fillCurrencyMap, correct_file){
    currencyFile = "./CurrencyConversion.txt";
    ASSERT_TRUE(fillCurrencyMap());
}
```

> **Note**
>
> The **CurrencyWrongDelimiter.txt**, **CurrencyExtraColumn.txt**, and **CurrencyConversion.txt** files that were used as input parameters in the preceding functions can be found here: https://github.com/TrainingByPackt/Advanced-CPlus-Plus/tree/master/Lesson7/Activity01.

23. Write the following test cases for the parseRecordFile function:

```
//Test Cases for parseRecordFile function...
TEST(parseRecordFile, wrong_delimiter){
    recordFile = "./RecordWrongDelimiter.txt";
    ASSERT_FALSE(parseRecordFile());
}

TEST(parseRecordFile, extra_column){
    recordFile = "./RecordExtraColumn.txt";
    ASSERT_FALSE(parseRecordFile());
}

TEST(parseRecordFile, correct_file){
```

```
        recordFile = "./RecordFile.txt";
        ASSERT_TRUE(parseRecordFile());
    }
```

The **RecordWrongDelimiter.txt**, **RecordExtraColumn.txt**, and **RecordFile.txt** files that were used as input parameters in the preceding functions can be found here: https://github.com/TrainingByPackt/Advanced-CPlusPlus/tree/master/Lesson7/Activity01.

24. Open the compiler. Compile and execute the `Util.cpp` and `ParseFileTestCases.cpp` files by writing the following commands:

```
g++ -c -g -Wall ../Util.cpp -I../
g++ -c -g -Wall ParseFileTestCases.cpp
g++ -g -Wall Util.o ParseFileTestCases.o -lgtest -lgtest_main -pthread -o
ParseFileTestCases
```

The following is a screenshot of this. You will see all the commands stored in **Test.make** script file. Once executed, it will create the binary program that was meant for unit testing called **ParseFileTestCases**. You will also notice that a directory has been created in Project called **unitTesting**. In this directory, all the unit testing-related code is written, and a binary file is created. Also, the dependent library of the project, **Util.o**, is also created by compiling the project in the **Util.cpp** file:

Figure 7.27: Executing all commands present in the script file

25. Type the following command to run all the test cases:

```
./ParseFileTestCases
```

The output on the screen will display the total tests running, that is, 31 from 8 test suites. It will also display the statistics of individual test suites, along with pass/fail results:

```
19:08@/media/sf_packt/Advance_C++/StartTask/Activity/unitTesting$./ParseFileTestCases
Running main() from src/gtest_main.cc
[==========] Running 31 tests from 8 test suites.
[----------] Global test environment set-up.
[----------] 7 tests from trim
[ RUN      ] trim.empty
[       OK ] trim.empty (0 ms)
[ RUN      ] trim.start_space
[       OK ] trim.start_space (0 ms)
[ RUN      ] trim.end_space
[       OK ] trim.end_space (0 ms)
[ RUN      ] trim.string_middle
[       OK ] trim.string_middle (0 ms)
[ RUN      ] trim.single_char_start
[       OK ] trim.single_char_start (0 ms)
[ RUN      ] trim.single_char_end
[       OK ] trim.single_char_end (0 ms)
[ RUN      ] trim.single_char_middle
[       OK ] trim.single_char_middle (0 ms)
[----------] 7 tests from trim (0 ms total)

[----------] 5 tests from isNumber
[ RUN      ] isNumber.alphabets_present
[       OK ] isNumber.alphabets_present (0 ms)
[ RUN      ] isNumber.special_character_present
[       OK ] isNumber.special_character_present (0 ms)
[ RUN      ] isNumber.correct_number
[       OK ] isNumber.correct_number (0 ms)
[ RUN      ] isNumber.decimal_begin
[       OK ] isNumber.decimal_begin (0 ms)
[ RUN      ] isNumber.decimal_end
[       OK ] isNumber.decimal_end (0 ms)
[----------] 5 tests from isNumber (1 ms total)

[----------] 3 tests from isDigit
[ RUN      ] isDigit.alphabet_present
[       OK ] isDigit.alphabet_present (0 ms)
[ RUN      ] isDigit.decimal_present
[       OK ] isDigit.decimal_present (0 ms)
[ RUN      ] isDigit.correct_digit
[       OK ] isDigit.correct_digit (0 ms)
[----------] 3 tests from isDigit (0 ms total)

[----------] 2 tests from CurrencyParameters
[ RUN      ] CurrencyParameters.extra_currency_chararcters
[       OK ] CurrencyParameters.extra_currency_chararcters (0 ms)
[ RUN      ] CurrencyParameters.correct_parameters
[       OK ] CurrencyParameters.correct_parameters (0 ms)
[----------] 2 tests from CurrencyParameters (0 ms total)

[----------] 5 tests from checkFile
[ RUN      ] checkFile.no_file_present
[       OK ] checkFile.no_file_present (0 ms)
[ RUN      ] checkFile.empty_file
[       OK ] checkFile.empty_file (1 ms)
[ RUN      ] checkFile.no_header
[       OK ] checkFile.no_header (1 ms)
```

Figure 7.28: All tests running properly

Below is the screenshot of the next tests:

```
[----------] 5 tests from checkFile
[ RUN      ] checkFile.no_file_present
[       OK ] checkFile.no_file_present (0 ms)
[ RUN      ] checkFile.empty_file
[       OK ] checkFile.empty_file (1 ms)
[ RUN      ] checkFile.no_header
[       OK ] checkFile.no_header (1 ms)
[ RUN      ] checkFile.incorrect_header
[       OK ] checkFile.incorrect_header (0 ms)
[ RUN      ] checkFile.correct_file
[       OK ] checkFile.correct_file (1 ms)
[----------] 5 tests from checkFile (3 ms total)

[----------] 3 tests from parseConfig
[ RUN      ] parseConfig.missing_currency_file
ERROR : currencyfile or recordfile not set correctly.
[       OK ] parseConfig.missing_currency_file (0 ms)
[ RUN      ] parseConfig.missing_record_file
ERROR : currencyfile or recordfile not set correctly.
[       OK ] parseConfig.missing_record_file (1 ms)
[ RUN      ] parseConfig.correct_config_file
[       OK ] parseConfig.correct_config_file (1 ms)
[----------] 3 tests from parseConfig (2 ms total)

[----------] 3 tests from fillCurrencyMap
[ RUN      ] fillCurrencyMap.wrong_delimiter
ERROR: Processing Currency Coversion , got incorrect parameters for Currency: USD , 1.00
[       OK ] fillCurrencyMap.wrong_delimiter (0 ms)
[ RUN      ] fillCurrencyMap.extra_column
ERROR: Processing Currency Coversion , got incorrect parameters for Currency: GBP
[       OK ] fillCurrencyMap.extra_column (1 ms)
[ RUN      ] fillCurrencyMap.correct_file
[       OK ] fillCurrencyMap.correct_file (0 ms)
[----------] 3 tests from fillCurrencyMap (1 ms total)

[----------] 3 tests from parseRecordFile
[ RUN      ] parseRecordFile.wrong_delimiter
ERROR: Processing Record, for Customer Id: 2312,Albert , Springs, 435351, 452536 , 11 , 13243.25 , USD , 12343.25
[       OK ] parseRecordFile.wrong_delimiter (1 ms)
[ RUN      ] parseRecordFile.extra_column
ERROR: Processing Record, for Customer Id: 2312
[       OK ] parseRecordFile.extra_column (0 ms)
[ RUN      ] parseRecordFile.correct_file
[       OK ] parseRecordFile.correct_file (0 ms)
[----------] 3 tests from parseRecordFile (2 ms total)

[----------] Global test environment tear-down
[==========] 31 tests from 8 test suites ran. (9 ms total)
[  PASSED  ] 31 tests.
```

Figure 7.29: All tests running properly

Finally, we checked the accuracy of the functions that we developed by parsing two files with the help of our test cases. This will ensure that our project will be running fine when it's integrated with different functions/modules that have test cases.

# Chapter 8 - Need for Speed – Performance and Optimization

## Activity 1: Optimizing a Spell Check Algorithm

In this activity, we'll be developing a simple spell check demonstration and try to make it faster incrementally. You can use the skeleton file, **Speller.cpp**, as a starting point. Perform the following steps to implement this activity:

1. For the first implementation of the spell check (the full code can be found in **Speller1.cpp**) – create a dictionary set in the **getMisspelt()** function:

   ```
   set<string> setDict(vecDict.begin(), vecDict.end());
   ```

2. Loop over the text words and check for words not in the dictionary with the **set::count()** method. Add the misspelled words to the result vector:

   ```
   vector<int> ret;
   for(int i = 0; i < vecText.size(); ++i)
   {
     const string &s = vecText[i];
     if(!setDict.count(s))
     {
       ret.push_back(i);
     }
   };
   ```

3. Open the terminal. Compile the program and run it as follows:

   ```
   $ g++ -O3 Speller1.cpp Timer.cpp
   $ ./a.out
   ```

   The following output will be generated:

| Output is correct<br>Name | Count | Time(ms) | Average(ms) |
|---|---|---|---|
| Spell check | 1 | 5883 | 5883 |

Figure 8.60: Example output of the solution for Step 1

4. Open the **Speller2.cpp** file and add the **unordered_set** header file to the program:

   ```
   #include <unordered_set>
   ```

5. Next, change the set type that's used for the dictionary to **unordered_set**:

   ```
   unordered_set<string> setDict(vecDict.begin(), vecDict.end());
   ```

6. Open the Terminal. Compile the program and run it as follows:

```
$ g++ -O3 Speller2.cpp Timer.cpp
$ ./a.out
```

The following output will be generated:

| Output is correct |  |  |  |
|---|---|---|---|
| Name | Count | Time(ms) | Average(ms) |
| Spell check | 1 | 2240 | 2240 |

Figure 8.61: Example output of the solution for Step 2

7. For the third and final version, that is, **Speller3.cpp**, we will use a bloom filter. Start by defining a hash function based on the **BKDR** function. Add the following code to implement this:

```
const size_t SIZE = 16777215;
template<size_t SEED> size_t hasher(const string &s)
{
  size_t h = 0;
  size_t len = s.size();
  for(size_t i = 0; i < len; i++)
  {
    h = h * SEED + s[i];
  }
  return h & SIZE;
}
```

Here, we used an integer template parameter so that we can create any number of different hash functions with the same code. Notice the use of the **16777215** constant, which is equal to **2^24 - 1**. This lets us use the fast bitwise-and operator instead of the modulus operator to keep the hashed integer less than **SIZE**. If you want to change the size, keep it as one less than a power of two.

8. Next, let's declare a vector<bool> for a bloom filter in **getMisspelt()** and populate it with the words in the dictionary. Use three hash functions. The BKDR hash can be seeded with values such as **131**, **3131**, **31313**, and so on. Add the following code to implement this:

```
vector<bool> m_Bloom;
m_Bloom.resize(SIZE);
for(auto i = vecDict.begin(); i != vecDict.end(); ++i)
{
  m_Bloom[hasher<131>(*i)] = true;
  m_Bloom[hasher<3131>(*i)] = true;
```

```
      m_Bloom[hasher<31313>(*i)] = true;
   }
```

9.  Write the following code to create a loop that checks the words:

```
for(int i = 0; i < vecText.size(); ++i)
{
   const string &s = vecText[i];
   bool hasNoBloom =
            !m_Bloom[hasher<131>(s)]
      &&    !m_Bloom[hasher<3131>(s)]
      &&    !m_Bloom[hasher<31313>(s)];

   if(hasNoBloom)
   {
      ret.push_back(i);
   }
   else if(!setDict.count(s))
   {
      ret.push_back(i);
   }
}
```

The bloom filter is checked first and if it finds the word in the dictionary, we have to verify it, like we did previously.

10. Open the terminal. Compile the program and run it as follows:

```
$ g++ -O3 Speller3.cpp Timer.cpp
$ ./a.out
```

The following output will be generated:

| Output is correct Name | Count | Time(ms) | Average(ms) |
|---|---|---|---|
| Spell check | 1 | 2193 | 2193 |

Figure 8.62: Example output of the solution for Step 3

In the preceding activity, we attempted to solve a real-world problem and make it more efficient. Let's consider some points for each of the implementations in the three steps, as follows:

- For the first version, the most obvious solution with a `std::set` is used – however, the performance is likely to be low because the set data structure is based on a binary tree, which has `O(log N)` complexity for finding an element.

- For the second version, we can gain a large performance improvement simply by switching to `std::unordered_set`, which uses a hash table as the underlying data structure. If the hash function is good, the performance will be close to `O(1)`.

- The third version, based on the **Bloom filter** data structure, requires some consideration.-
  The primary performance benefit of a bloom filter is because it is a compact data structure that does not actually store the actual elements in it, thereby providing very good cache performance.

From an implementation perspective, the following guidelines apply:

- `vector<bool>` can be used as the backing store as it is an efficient way to store and retrieve bits.

- The false positive percentage of the bloom filter should be minimal – anything more than 5% will not be efficient.

- There are many string hashing algorithms – the **BKDR** hash algorithm is used in the reference implementation. A comprehensive of string hash algorithms with implementation can be found here: http://www.partow.net/programming/hash-functions/index.html.

- The number of hash functions and the size for the bloom filter that's used are very critical to get the performance benefits.

- The nature of the dataset should be taken into account when deciding what parameters the bloom filter should use – consider that, in this example, there are very few words that are misspelled, and the majority of them are in the dictionary.

There are some questions worth probing, given the results we received:

- Why is the improvement in performance so meager with the Bloom Filter?

- What is the effect of using a larger or smaller capacity Bloom filter?

- What happens when fewer or more hash functions are used?

- Under what conditions would this version be much faster than the one in **Speller2.cpp**?

Here are the answers to these questions:

- Why is the improvement in performance so meager with the Bloom Filter?

  `std::unordered_set` performs one hash operation and perhaps a couple of memory accesses before reaching the value that's stored. The Bloom filter we use performs three hash operations and three memory accesses. So, in essence, the work that's done by the bloom filter is more than the hash table. Since there are only 31,870 words in our dictionary, the cache benefits of the Bloom filter are lost. This is another case where the traditional analysis of data structures does not correspond to real-life results because of caching.

- What is the effect of using a larger or smaller capacity Bloom filter?

  When a larger capacity is used, the number of hash collisions reduce, along with false positives, but the caching behavior worsens. Conversely, when a smaller capacity is used, the hash collisions and the false positives increase, but the caching behavior improves.

- What happens when fewer or more hash functions are used?

  The more hash functions are used, the fewer the false positives, and vice versa.

- Under what conditions would this version be much faster than the one in Speller2. cpp?

  Bloom filters work best when the cost of testing a few bits is less than the cost of accessing the value in the hash table. This only becomes true when the Bloom filter bits fit completely within the cache and the dictionary does not.

# Index

**About**

All major keywords used in this book are captured alphabetically in this section. Each one is accompanied by the page number of where they appear.

# A

ability: 22, 73, 190, 220,
    262, 294, 317, 568, 590
absolute: 28-29,
    60-61, 550
abstract: 108, 140-141,
    146, 148, 157, 197,
    212, 393-395
accelerate: 566
acceptable: 90
access: 14, 90-92, 102, 110,
    114-115, 123, 132-133,
    141-142, 146, 151-152,
    155, 165, 178, 184, 219,
    221, 224, 227, 235, 237,
    252, 257, 270, 274-275,
    277, 287, 307, 313, 321,
    345, 350-351, 370,
    394, 443-445, 457,
    462-464, 532, 544, 552,
    584-590, 594, 603
accounting: 16
accumulate: 566-567
accuracy: 523-525,
    532, 559
activity: 16-17, 26, 30-31,
    66, 68, 76, 134-135, 137,
    147, 190-191, 252-253,
    270-271, 317-318, 322,
    385-389, 392, 468-470,
    473-474, 506, 523-525,
    528, 531-532, 614-616
address: 91-92, 120-122,
    182, 200, 229, 274,
    291-292, 302, 325, 450,
    478-480, 483-485, 489,
    492-493, 495, 499-500,
    502, 506-508, 542,
    559-560, 588-590, 598
adversely: 221, 274
advocate: 159

aggregate: 72, 176, 430
aggregator: 298
algorithm: 49-50, 60,
    65, 156-158, 163, 183,
    295, 297, 299, 306,
    437, 537-538, 566,
    580, 584, 590, 594,
    604, 609, 613-615
aliases: 161-163, 188
allocate: 74-75, 92-93, 110,
    225-226, 252, 316, 349,
    456, 483, 586-587, 613
amount: 56, 107, 161, 168,
    193, 333-335, 365,
    450, 478, 573, 588
analyze: 40, 134,
    421-422, 535, 541,
    545, 559-560, 589
anatomy: 1, 76-77, 152
applied: 113, 177-178,
    223, 316, 428, 478
apt-get: 559
article: 589
assert: 67, 160, 188, 208,
    282-283, 480-488,
    494-496, 507-508
assertion: 478-479,
    481-484, 486-487, 532
assignment: 74-75, 84-85,
    111-115, 117, 122, 124,
    209, 226, 228-234,
    236, 238, 252, 283-284,
    357-359, 361, 364, 366
associate: 73-74,
    107, 255, 451
asterisk: 91
atomic: 340
attach: 100
augment: 135

# B

background: 333, 336, 368
back-slash: 469
backup: 442, 444
backwards: 589
bandwidth: 583
beautify: 468
benchmarks: 561
billion: 555
binaries: 79
binary: 3, 57, 147, 229,
    280, 401, 409, 479-483,
    486-488, 490-491,
    494-495, 498, 506-507,
    514, 522, 538
bindings: 307
bitmap: 237
bitmask: 452
bitwise: 541, 605-606
blocked: 349, 351,
    373, 375, 442
boolean: 59, 172-173,
    264-265, 423-424,
    575, 602
bottleneck: 576
bottom: 24, 46, 48, 77,
    127, 147, 206, 541
boundaries: 75
boundary: 491
bounds: 568
braces: 57, 62, 154,
    194, 554, 572
bracket: 200
branch: 509, 561-562,
    564, 576-578, 602, 617
breakpoint: 52-53
breaks: 280
button: 10-11, 13, 25,
    48-49, 51, 53, 55, 77,
    80, 82-86, 89-90, 95,
    97-99, 104-107, 118-120,
    123-124, 128-130,
    148, 150, 162-163,

CPSIA information can be obtained
at www.ICGtesting.com
Printed in the USA
FFHW010906271119
56119858-62226FF